Landscape Plants for Subtropical Climates

D1712606

DISCARD

Landscape Plants
for Subtropical Climates

Bijan Dehgan

University Press of Florida
Gainesville/Tallahassee/Tampa/Boca Raton
Pensacola/Orlando/Miami/Jacksonville

03 02 01 00 99 98   6 5 4 3 2 1

Library of Congress Cataloging-in-Publication Data
Dehgan, Bijan.
Landscape plants for subtropical climates / Bijan Dehgan.
p. cm.
ISBN 0-8130-1627-4 (hardcover: alk. paper).—ISBN 0-8130-1628-2 (pbk.: alk. paper)
1. Landscape plants—Tropics. 2. Tropical plants. I. Title.
SB407.3.T73D45   1998   98-24892
635.9'523—dc21

The University Press of Florida is the scholarly publishing agency for the State University System of Florida, comprising Florida A&M University, Florida Atlantic University, Florida International University, Florida State University, University of Central Florida, University of Florida, University of North Florida, University of South Florida, and University of West Florida.

University Press of Florida
15 Northwest 15th Street
Gainesville, FL 32611
http://nersp.nerdc.ufl.edu/~upf

Contents

Ferns

Gymnosperms

Angiosperms - Monocots

Angiosperms - Dicots

Preface

One of the most pleasurable and satisfying ventures for a lover of plants is to be able to identify them, know them, grow them, and talk about them with others. Many outstanding plant identification manuals and an extraordinary number of plant and flower books have been written to provide information on characteristics and growth requirements of landscape plants. However, because the southeastern United States has uniform summer climate but markedly different winter temperatures between the colder northern and the consistently warmer southern portions, information on the southern subtropical plants is usually scant. This is perfectly understandable since more than 90 percent of the population are not familiar with a vast majority of the plants grown in warm temperate and subtropical regions. Florida, with its variety of climates and habitats, includes a diversity of vegetational and climatic types, ranging from the humid temperate northern Panhandle to the tropical Keys and the Caribbean islands. Accordingly, an enormously large and diverse number of plants are used in the landscape.

In his 1929 book *Gardening in the Lower South*, Professor Harold Hume noted: *"The possibilities of southern ornamental gardening have scarcely been touched. There remain three great but almost undeveloped fields of endeavor. These are (1) the working out of the South's own typical style of garden treatment; (2) the introduction, testing and use of exotic plant material, new or uncommon; and (3) the bringing into garden use of the vast extent of excellent native plants that make up the natural gardens and landscapes of the whole region. Never will the South come into the fullness of its own garden development until all these requisites are accomplished. Here is a task to fire the soul of a plant lover, worthy of the hand of a master garden-maker."*

Professor Hume would have been pleasantly surprised and equally overwhelmed by the enormous strides made in all three "fields of endeavor." To imply that all known cultivated plants are covered in this manual would be a gross exaggeration. About one-fifth of the approximately 5000 indigenous Florida and southeastern species and perhaps thousands of exotic ornamental and tropical fruit crops, hybrids, and cultivars that have been introduced since 1929 are now in cultivation. A mere glance at the number of palm, orchid, and cactus genera listed in this manual provides a yardstick for the total number of cultivated plant taxa. The genera listed under each family description are those actually reported from cultivation, though only the most common of these have been discussed here. To address all cultivated plants of warm temperate and subtropical regions would be a monumental task.

This plant identification manual is a culmination of the contributions by several past and present faculty, staff, and graduate students in the Department of Environmental Horticulture at the University of Florida. It has been in use by students for about 18 years. Originally it consisted of two volumes, which corresponded to each of the two plant identification courses (temperate and tropical) taught in the department. Although initially these were made available exclusively for student use, their serviceability became apparent when several community colleges and extension programs, including those of the garden clubs and master gardeners, requested copies for their use. Each semester, when copies were placed on the University Bookstore shelves, many were sold to individuals who were not enrolled in these courses.

Over the years additional descriptions were included as new plants gained popularity, until it was determined that such a book was needed for public as well as classroom use. Where possible, additional species and cultivars are listed, often, for reasons mentioned above, with a few or no remarks. This manual is intended as a textbook/laboratory manual primarily for urban and ornamental plant identification courses. Inclusion of less commonly used plants would be not only impractical but cumbersome. Nevertheless, enumeration of related genera, species, and taxa of lower ranks in cultivation should provide the foundation for further research and additional information about individual or groups of taxa mentioned.

The plants in this book are arranged according to the generally accepted taxonomic hierarchy of major groups. To simplify its use, however, within each of the major plant groups (ferns, gymnosperms, monocotyledons, and dicotyledons), families, genera, and species are organized alphabetically. When in doubt as to the exact placement of a given plant, check the cross-referenced index of common and scientific names at the end of the book.

A comprehensive glossary of the descriptive terms has been included to facilitate recognition of the features addressed in the text. A brief discussion of the nomenclatural rules pertaining to the taxonomic hierarchies also is included.

We owe special thanks to Phyllis Stambaugh for the herculean task of typing, retyping, and organizing much of the manual. We are indebted to Nancy Dehgan, whose patience and painstaking search and revision of names and their spellings constitute a service to all users of this manual. Inaccurate names have a strange tendency to become perpetuated through frequent usage. Despite her diligence, no book of this nature is ever completely free of lapses and one should also expect many disagreements, particularly with reference to some recent name changes. We wish to thank Charles Johnson, Edwin Duke, Ed Gilman, and Linda Schneider for their input and contributions. We also thank Terril Nell, whose encouragement and insistence proved to be the driving force in a complete revision and publication of this manual.

Primary Contributors

William E. Barrick   Executive Vice President and Director of Callaway Gardens, Georgia

Greg L. Davis   Assistant Professor, University of Nebraska

Bijan Dehgan   Professor, Department of Environmental Horticulture, University of Florida, Gainesville

Steven Farnsworth   Former graduate student, currently owner and operator of Farnsworth Nursery in Florida

Timothy L. Nance   Former graduate student, currently a private horticultural consultant in Naples, Florida

Barbara Poole   Former Graduate Student

Bart Schutzman   Computer Programmer/Analyst, Department of Environmental Horticulture, University of Florida, Gainesville

Linda Schneider   Former Student Assistant

Illustrators

As there have been several contributors to the texts, there have been as many or more illustrators, including, in alphabetical order, Ian M. Breheny, Amy Brown, Linda Chandler, Merald Clark, Kathy Connely, Esther Coogle, Raphael C. Goetlieb, Suzanne McCullough, Suzanne M. Sasso, Bart Schutzman, Robert K. Turner, Wendy B. Zomlefer (in addition to the excellent drawings done specifically for this manual, she gave her kind permission to copy a few illustrations from her book *Common Florida Angiosperm Families*, 1990), and various artists (by permission from the University Press of Florida and University of Florida herbarium). Cover photography is by Fé C. Almira.

Note

All proceeds from this book have been donated to the University of Florida Environmental Horticulture Teaching and Research Tree Laboratory.

Horticultural Plant Nomenclature

One of the constant challenges for students of plant identification is to recognize and identify plants by their scientific and common names. This can be a daunting task, especially when one considers that for centuries horticulturists have selected plants for various desirable characteristics and these selections have expanded the number of flowering plant species to perhaps more than 500,000. Because it is human nature to characterize and bring order to the chaotic world around us, we have developed systems to organize and name plants. How do we classify so many plants? How do we name any of those plants so that a German horticulturist knows the plant by the same name as a Frenchman or an American?

Common Names

Common names often are those we associate with plants encountered in our daily lives. The names may refer to certain characteristics. Such characteristics may be morphological, such as leaf shape (arrowhead), flower shape (sunflower), fruit color (blueberry), and so on; based on one of the human senses, such as taste (bittersweet), smell (skunk cabbage), or touch (thornbush); places or situations in which they occur (mountain laurel, prairie coneflower, water hyacinth); or blooming time (Christmas cactus, Easter lily, four o'clock, morning glory). Common names tend to be simple words to pronounce and spell because of familiarity with the language and frequency of usage in conversation.

The use of common names is beset with several problems and disadvantages, however. With few exceptions, the meaning of common names is clear only in one language and not understood by all people. This is one of the primary reasons for the use of botanical names in scientific publications. Often a plant may be known by more than one, and perhaps several, common names. For example, the tree *Carpinus caroliniana* (American hornbeam) is variously called the water beech, blue beech, ironwood, and musclewood. Perhaps the greatest disadvantage of common names is that no laws or regulations control their application. Common names cannot be right or wrong, accurate or inaccurate. They can, however, lead to confusion.

Botanical (Scientific) Names

Carl von Linné (commonly known by his pen name of Linnaeus) is credited with bringing order to the often chaotic naming of plants. His book *Species Plantarum* (1753) introduced the binomial system of nomenclature. Briefly, in the binomial system plants are given two latinized names; one represents the **genus** and the other represents the **specific epithet**. Together, these two names become the name of the **species**. The latinized names are universal, and they are used to represent a given species regardless of where in the world it is found or in which language it is being discussed. The binomial system, therefore, lends precision and consistency to the naming of plants. Today, the use of botanical names is governed and regulated by the International Code for Botanical Nomenclature (ICBN) and is referred to as the "**Botanical Code.**" The principles and rules of the Botanical Code are uniformly applicable to cultivated as well as wild plants. The articles and recommendations of the code are intended to promote "uniformity, fixity and accuracy" in naming of plants and, at least in principle, have the force of international law.

Scientific names are often descriptive, frequently more so than common names. Learning a few simple Latin or latinized words will simplify the learning process considerably. At the rank of species (the specific epithet), morphological characteristics such as shape, number, and color; sensual features such as taste, smell, or touch; geography and ecological conditions; or the name of a person to be honored have all been used for designation.

Use of Botanical Names in Horticulture

The same botanical organization that sets the rules and amends or changes the Botanical Code once every five years is also responsible for the "International Code of Nomenclature for Cultivated Plants" or the "**Cultivated Code.**" Because we are obligated to accept and use the Botanical Code, a brief review of taxonomic or hierarchical classification of cultivated plants is appropriate.

Below is an abbreviated list of categories of taxonomic hierarchy in descending sequence. Each category is considered a rank, and each rank is subordinate to the one above it. For example, the rank of species is assignable to a genus, each genus to a family, each family to an order, and so on. The endings for appropriate ranks are also listed. Only ranks below the rank of "order" (family, genus, species, etc.) are of significance in classification of cultivated plants. The ranks in boldface type are those of greatest significance to the horticulture industry.

Rank	Endings
KINGDOM	
DIVISION	
CLASS	
ORDER	-ales
FAMILY	**-aceae**
TRIBE	-eae
GENUS	**-us, a, um, es, on, etc.**
SPECIES	**-us, a, um, es, on, etc.**
SUBSPECIES	-us, a, um, es, on, etc.
VARIETY	**-us, a, um, es, on, etc.**
FORM	-us, a, um, es, on, etc.

From this list, our focus in horticultural plant identification is typically on the genus and species. The **genus** (plural, genera) is one or a group of plants that have one or more major characteristics in common. The genus *Ginkgo* is **monotypic** in that it consists of only one species (*Ginkgo biloba*). Lime, lemon, grapefruit, orange, and others, for instance, are all in the genus *Citrus* because they share the characteristic fruit (a hesperidium), leaves with winged petioles, and so forth. The rose may be any of the approximately 200 species from the genus *Rosa*. The genus name is always capitalized and italicized (or underlined), and it always precedes the specific epithet.

The rank of **species** is the most important in classification. The species, for practical purposes of this book, may be defined as a group of interbreeding individuals that are morphologically similar but not necessarily identical. In this definition some degree of variation may exist among individuals of a given species, and their progeny are also fertile. As an analogy, races of humans (*Homo sapiens*) may differ in color or other features but are fully capable of interbreeding. By the same token, cultivars of plants may differ in growth habit or any other characteristics but in most cases retain the ability to cross with any other cultivar of the same species. For example, the yaupon hollies *Ilex vomitoria*, *I. vomitoria* 'Nana', and *I. vomitoria* 'Pendula' when grown together interbreed and have fertile progeny.

Based on the binomial system, the name of each species is a binary combination, consisting of a genus name and a specific epithet. The specific "species" name alone is meaningless without reference to the name of the genus. By way of analogy, the name "John" is a common name and may refer to thousands of persons, but the name "John Smith" refers to a specific individual about whom one may have considerable knowledge. The name "rubrum" simply means red, and as such it does not refer to any particular plant or it may refer to any and all red plants. *Acer rubrum*, however, specifically refers to a **species** we know as red maple.

For writing purposes, the specific epithet always follows the capitalized genus name and is always written in lower case and italicized (or underlined) as in the example given. If the specific name of a species is not known but the generic name is recognized, the word "species" is abbreviated as sp. if singular or spp. if plural. For example, a reference to a particular species from the genus *Rosa* when its exact identity is unknown would be written as *Rosa* sp. Several plants representing various species of *Rosa* would be referred to as *Rosa* spp.

Although not used in the examples in this manual, the name of the person (the **authority**) who described and named a given plant must be included with the plant's name when in print. For example, *Brassica oleracea* L. (abbreviation for Linnaeus) would be written in scientific literature. Sometimes more than one person may be the authorities for the plant, in which case both names would appear with the binomial. It has become customary in recent times not to abbreviate the name of the authorities, as in *Jatropha moranii* Dehgan and Webster.

The rank of **variety** represents individuals of a species that exhibit consistent major differences in a wild population of a given locality. Similarly, **subspecies** differ in one or more characteristics but are geographically or altitudinally isolated populations of a wild species. These differences are inheritable and should continue to appear in succeeding generations. *Acer negundo* var. *variegatum* differs from the typical species by its variegated leaves. Seed collected from the variety (the former) will yield predominantly seedlings having variegated leaves. In written form (see above example), the word "variety" is abbreviated as var. and the name is not capitalized but is underlined or italicized, the same as the genus and specific epithet.

Family is the highest taxonomic rank used in horticulture. A family consists of one or more related genera. A family consisting of only one genus is referred to as **monogeneric**, as in Ginkgoaceae (*Ginkgo*). Unlike generic and specific names, family names are not underlined or italicized but their first letter is always capitalized (Ginkgoaceae). Family names end in -aceae, except in eight cases where long-used names continue to be accepted by the Botanical Code. One example is the family Leguminosae, the old yet still accepted name for Fabaceae. Familial names are based on generic names. For example, Fabaceae is based on *Faba*, Poaceae (= Graminae) is based on *Poa*, Asteraceae (= Compositae) is based on Aster.

Horticultural Names

Cultivars (cultivated varieties) consist of uniform populations of cultivated plants that have distinguishing characteristics that are retained when the plants are reproduced (sexually or asexually). Most woody plant cultivars are **clones** and produced only through asexual propagation such as grafting, budding, cuttings, or micropropagation. For example, *Ilex vomitoria* 'Nana' (dwarf yaupon holly) is a cultivar of *I. vomitoria* that retains a dwarf growth habit.

To be valid, similar species cultivar names and plant descriptions must be published and distributed to the horticultural community. In short, a cultivar name is legitimate only if it is in accordance with the articles of the Cultivated Code. Cultivar names are written with single quotes with the first letter of each word of the cultivar capitalized, such as *Lonicera japonica* '**Purpurea**'. The alternative acceptable way is to abbreviate the word cultivar as **cv.** and omit the single quotation marks, for example, as *Lonicera japonica* cv. **Purpurea.**

Some horticultural plants are **hybrids**, or the offspring of two plants of different species or genera. **Interspecific hybrids** are hybrids between two species of the same genus. They may be designated by names or a formula and expressed by a multiplication sign (∞). For example,

Berberis × *mentorensis* L.M. Ames. [= *Berberis thunbergii* DC. × *Berberis julianae* Schneid.].

In this example the specific epithet was assigned for the interspecific hybrid according to the rules of the Botanical Code with the intent of brevity, clarity and simplicity.

By contrast, **intergeneric hybrids** are hybrids of species in two or more distinct genera. In this case names of the genera are either combined into a formula or condensed into a collective generic name preceded by a multiplication sign (×), and followed by a Latin specific epithet. For example, × *Cuppressocyparis leylandii* (A.B. Jackson & Dallim.) Dallim & A.B. Jackson [= *Cupressus macrocarpa* Hartw. × *Chamaecyparis nootkatensis* (D. Don) Spach.].

As in the case of interspecific hybrids, the intent of the collective generic name is brevity, clarity, and simplicity.

The term **Group** refers to large hybrid populations (cultigens) such as **Begonia**. **Grex** is a specific term that refers to orchid cultivars of multiparental hybrid origin.

Leaf Terminology

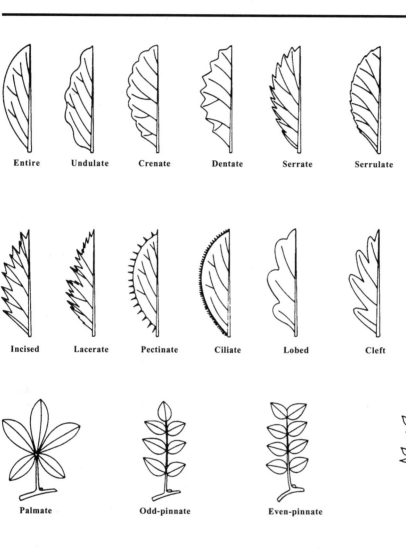

Entire Undulate Crenate Dentate Serrate Serrulate Doubly-serrate

Incised Lacerate Pectinate Ciliate Lobed Cleft Parted

Palmate Odd-pinnate Even-pinnate Bipinnate

Trifoliate

Trifoliolate

Pinnate

Palmate

Leaf Terminology

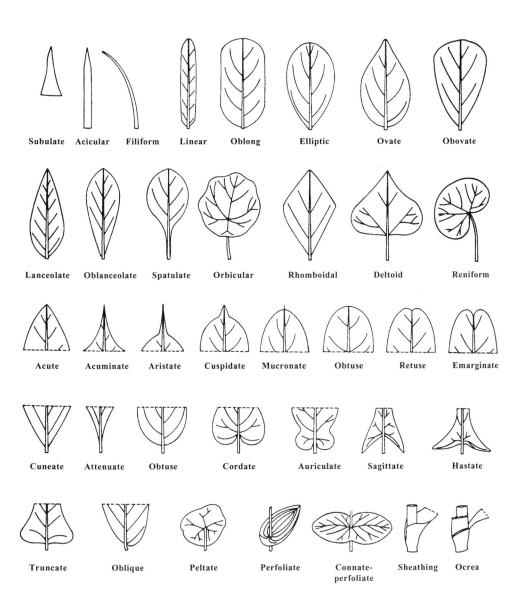

Inflorescences

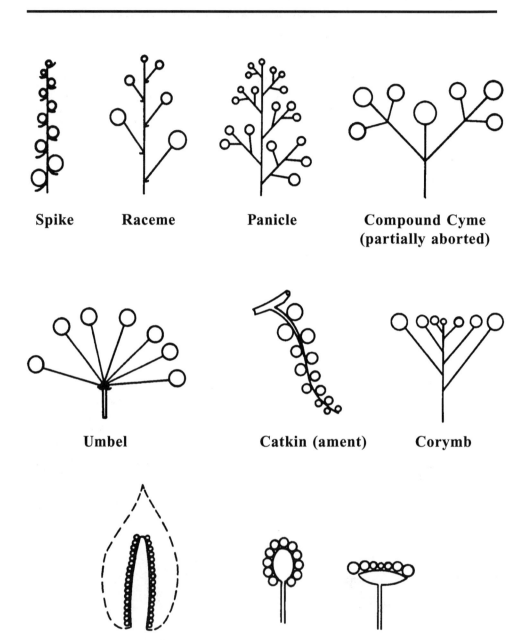

Spike   Raceme   Panicle   Compound Cyme
(partially aborted)

Umbel   Catkin (ament)   Corymb

Spadix   Head   or   Capitulum

Palm Terms

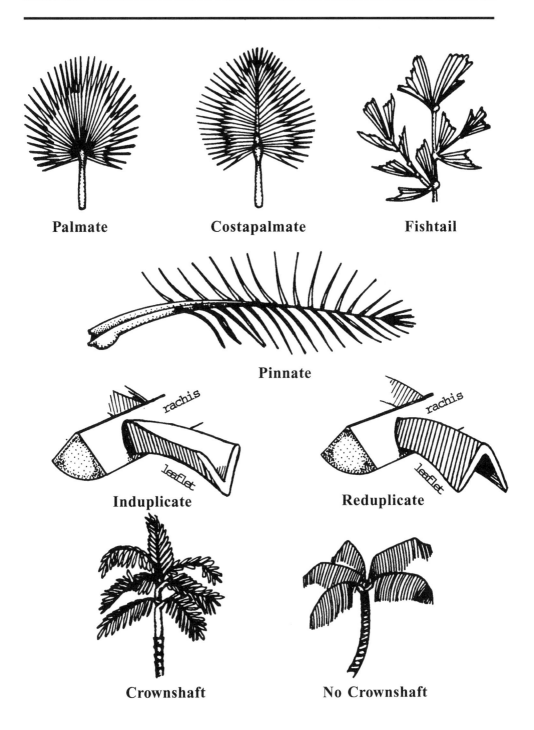

Palmate

Costapalmate

Fishtail

Pinnate

Induplicate

Reduplicate

Crownshaft

No Crownshaft

Tree Shapes

EXCURRENT

DECURRENT

Pyramidal or Conical

Weeping

Fastigiate

Globose

Columnar

Round

Ferns

ADIANTACEAE - MAIDENHAIR FAMILY

FERNS; ABOUT 30 GENERA WITH 150 TO 200 SPECIES

GEOGRAPHY:	Cosmopolitan but widespread and diversified in Central and South America; in damp, cool locations.
GROWTH HABIT:	Mostly terrestrial; small to medium; clump forming.
LEAVES:	Fronds clustered or spaced along creeping rhizomes; monomorphic, pinnately or palmately compound, with shiny-black, wiry stipes; pinnae variously shaped, from oblong rhomboid to often flabellate; veins free and dichotomously branched.
FLOWERS:	None; sori at terminus of veins at the margins of pinnae and covered by reflexed false indusia.
FRUIT:	None; spores tetrahedral or globose.
ECONOMIC USES:	Ornamentals: in rock gardens, along brooks, and as potted plants.

ORNAMENTAL GENERA: *Adiantum, Dryopteris, Pellaea, Pityrogramma.*

Adiantum spp.

MAIDENHAIR FERN

PRONUNCIATION - ˌæ dē ˈæn tə·m

TRANSLATION - [from Greek *adiantos* (= unwetted, dry), in reference to the pinnules which repel water (remain dry) if plunged in water].

FORM - Evergreen fern; terrestrial or rarely epiphytic; ground cover; short rhizomes; delicate, airy, foliage erect or drooping, graceful; fine texture.

SIZE - Variable with species to 3 feet tall, generally seen smaller.

HARDINESS ZONE - Varies with species. The commercially grown *A. raddianum* (Delta Maidenhair) is restricted to Zones 10-11, south Florida only. A Florida native, *A. tenerum* (Brittle Maidenhair), can be grown in Zone 9, south, central, and the warmest areas of north Florida.

LEAVES - Varies with species. From once to 4 times pinnate, generally 2 to 3 times pinnate; triangular to ovate to nearly orbicular; from 6 inches to 3 feet long. Pinnules 4-sided, oblong or wedge-shaped; without midribs, veins evenly forked. Size varies with species, ranging from 0.25 to 2.5 inches; margins more or less notched; light green.

STEM/BARK - Stemless; frond stipe and rachis slender, wiry; shiny black or purplish.

FLOWERS - None. Sori usually round or oblong; borne at pinnule upper margins; covered by recurved leaf margin (false indusium).

FRUIT - None. Minute spores.

CULTURE - Partial to full shade outdoors; inside in bright, indirect sunlight; moist but well-drained soils with high organic matter content. The Southern Maidenhair (*A. capillus-veneris*) and Brittle Maidenhair (*A. tenerum*) grow best in akaline soils; the other species grow best in acid soils. Plants do best in humid locations, requiring 60 percent or more humidity indoors to thrive. No salt tolerance.

PROBLEMS - Scale, mites, mealybugs, snails, slugs, root rots.

PROPAGATION - Division, spores.

LANDSCAPE USES - Outdoors as rock garden or border plants in shady, moist locations. The Southern and Brittle Maidenhairs do best in high-pH areas among limestone rocks, masonry walls, or along walks. Inside in pots or hanging baskets in high-humidity rooms or in terrariums.

COMMENTS - There are 200 or more species of *Adiantum,* and named cultivars of the most popular species are available but not common.

ASPLENIACEAE - SPLEENWORT FAMILY

FERNS; 7 TO 14 GENERA AND ABOUT 700 SPECIES

GEOGRAPHY: Cosmopolitan.

GROWTH HABIT: Small to medium size plants, mostly epiphytes or rocks
inhabitants
(= rupestral), with stems erect, long-creeping, stout to slender,
occasionally branched, and usually covered with scales and/or
hairs. Some species reproduce plantlets on the fronds.

LEAVES: Fronds simple forming a rosette or variously pinnately compound;
stipe rigid; stipules absent.

FLOWERS: None. Sori solitary, short or oblong-linear, along the upper
portion of branched veins; indusia oblong to linear.

FRUIT: None. Spores spheroid to ellipsoid.

ECONOMIC USES: Ornamentals, in moist locations or on trees or walls.

ORNAMENTAL GENERA: *Asplenium, Camptosorus, Ceterach, Sinephropteris* (= *Phyllitis*),
among others.

COMMENTS: As in other fern families and genera, there is much disagreement
on delimitation of taxa or their placement. Interested students
should consult appropriate references for additional information.

Asplenium nidus   BIRD'S NEST FERN

PRONUNCIATION - ə 'splē nē əm 'nī dəs

TRANSLATION - [from Greek *a* (= not) and *splen* (= the spleen), in reference to this fern's traditional virtues in afflictions of the spleen and liver] [nest].

FORM - Epiphytic; evergreen fern; erect stiff; fronds arising from the crown give a bird's-nest-like appearance to the center.

SIZE - Grows 2 to 4 feet tall, spread variable.

HARDINESS ZONE - Zone 10-11; outdoors only in south Florida; indoors in any location.

NATIVE HABITAT - Australia, tropical Asia, Polynesia.

LEAVES - Simple; arise from a crown on short stipes; 2 to 4 feet long, up to 8 inches wide; bright green; irregularly undulate; margins entire, sinuate, or irregularly lobed; light green.

STEM/BARK - Usually none visible.

FLOWERS - None. Spores produced in linear, elongate, black sori alongside secondary veins on frond undersides; lacking indusia or covered with false indusia.

FRUIT - None. Minute haploid spores.

CULTURE - Partial or full shade on a wide range of moist soils; high humidity; no salt tolerance.

PROBLEMS - Foliar nematodes, scale.

PROPAGATION - Spore or tissue culture.

LANDSCAPE USES - As epiphytes on trees, in containers for patios, or as foliage plant.

COMMENTS - Other species in the genus may be entire, pinnate, or lobed. Some are native to U.S., Europe, and temperate Asia and are hardier than the tropical species, which require greenhouse conditions. The genus includes both evergreen and deciduous species. A cold-hardy, smaller cultivar has recently been introduced.

DAVALLIACEAE - DAVALLIA FAMILY

FERNS; 9 OR 10 GENERA AND ABOUT 200 SPECIES

GEOGRAPHY: Except for *Nephrolepis* which is also in N. America, all other genera are native to the Old World, especially in tropical Asia.

GROWTH HABIT: Mostly epiphytic, with erect, decumbent, or creeping stem, sometime with stolons.

LEAVES: Fronds usually monomorphic; entire or variously pinnately compound, in a cluster or often spaced individually; stipe jointed near the base; pinnae entire or serrate, glabrous or pubescent; veins free.

FLOWERS: None; sori roundish or slightly elongate, indusia roundish, lunar (half moon-shaped), reniform, or orbicular; on terminus of veins near the margin.

FRUIT: None; spores ellipsoidal.

ECONOMIC USES: Ornamentals; used in hanging baskets and as ground covers.

ORNAMENTAL GENERA: *Davallia, Humata, Nephrolepis, Rumohra, Scyphularia,* and perhaps others in private collections.

Davallia fejeensis   RABBIT'S FOOT FERN

PRONUNCIATION - də ˈvæ lē ə ˌfē jē ˈen səs

TRANSLATION - [after Edmund Davall (1713-1798), Swiss botanist] [from Fiji Islands].

FORM - Evergreen fern; terrestrial or sometimes epiphytic; rhizomes stout, clumping, with long pubescence, appear furry.

SIZE - Grows 1.5 to 2 feet tall with a variable spread.

HARDINESS ZONE - Not sufficiently hardy to be grown permanently outdoors in the continental U.S.; hardy to 60 to 65°F.

NATIVE HABITAT - Fiji Islands.

LEAVES - Triangular; 4 times pinnate. Pinnules linear, terminal, single-veined.

STEM/BARK - Furry-appearing rhizomes; to 0.5 inch thick.

FLOWERS - None. Spores produced in sori along the pinnule margins.

FRUIT - None. Minute spores.

CULTURE - Partial or full shade on a wide range of soils; high humidity; no salt tolerance.

PROBLEMS - Leaf drop due to dry, hot air or cold; scales.

PROPAGATION - Division of old plants; tissue culture.

LANDSCAPE USES - Often grown as hanging basket plants or "fern balls."

COMMENTS - The genus consists of about 35 spp. of mostly epiphytic, tropical and subtropical plants of the Old World, which are mostly evergreen. One cultivar, **'Plumosa'**, has gracefully drooping, more feathery foliage.

Nephrolepis exaltata   BOSTON FERN, SWORD FERN

PRONUNCIATION - ˌnef rō 'le pəs   ˌek sɑl 'tā tə

TRANSLATION - [from Greek *nephros* (= a kidney) and *lepis* (= a scale), in reference to the kidney-shaped indusium] [very tall].

FORM - Evergreen, terrestrial or epiphytic fern; ground cover or often on palm trees; short rhizomes; foliage erect or drooping; medium-fine texture.

SIZE - Variable with cultivar, range 6 inches to 4 feet tall, commonly to 2 feet tall; variable spread; rapid growth rate.

HARDINESS ZONE - Zone 8b; south and central Florida, protected locations in north Florida.

NATIVE HABITAT - Tropics of the world.

LEAVES - Highly variable; 1 to 5 times pinnate in some cultivars; arching, flat, narrow, sword-shaped fronds to 5 feet long and 6 inches wide. Pinnae alternate, narrowly deltoid; to 3 inches long; numerous, close together; various shades of light green; not waxy, papery texture; entire or crenate to serrate margins.

STEM/BARK - Acaulescent; spreads by thin, green runners (stolons) from the crowns that root to form new plants.

FLOWERS - None. Spores are released from kidney-shaped brown sori that are submarginal on the underside of mature pinnae, terminal on veins.

FRUIT - None. Minute spores.

CULTURE - Partial to deep shade; moist but well-drained soil of some fertility; no salt tolerance.

PROBLEMS - Scale, mites, mealybugs, snails, slugs, fungus disease.

PROPAGATION - Division of rooted runners, spores.

LANDSCAPE USES - Makes a good, fast-spreading ground cover; requires frequent thinning once established. Gives tropical, lush effect to *Sabal, Butia, Phoenix,* and other palms when growing epiphytically on their trunks. Fancy cultivars used as pot or hanging basket plants.

COMMENTS - Historically the most common cultivar was ʹ**Bostoniensis,ʹ** which is more graceful, drooping, and compact than the species and has given rise to numerous sports. Today, hundreds of cultivars for leaf form have been selected; common ones are ʹ**Fluffy Ruffles', ʹRoosveltii',** and ʹ**Whitmanii.ʹ**

Rumohra adiantiformis   LEATHERLEAF FERN

PRONUNCIATION - rū 'mo rə   æ dē ˌæn tə 'for məs

TRANSLATION - [origin unknown] [like *Adiantum* or Maidenhair Fern].

FORM - Evergreen fern; terrestrial or sometimes epiphytic; rhizomes stout, clumping; symmetrical, compact, dense ground cover fern; medium-fine texture.

SIZE - Grows to 3 feet tall with a 4 to 5 foot spread; moderate growth rate.

HARDINESS ZONE - Zone 9; normally grown outdoors in south and central Florida. Can be grown in north Florida in very protected locations.

NATIVE HABITAT - Tropical and subtropical regions of the Southern Hemisphere.

LEAVES - Broadly triangular, to 3 feet long and 2.5 feet wide; 3 to 4 times pinnate at the base, less compound up the rachis; stiff, leathery, glabrous, waxy. Bottom pinnae triangular; pinnules oblong to narrowly ovate with a cuneate base and acute to acuminate apex; coarsely toothed margins; dark green.

STEM/BARK - Acaulescent; spreads by a stout creeping rhizome densely covered with brown, papery scales.

FLOWERS - None. Spores produced in large sori on the undersides of mature leaves.

FRUIT - None. Minute spores.

CULTURE - Partial or full shade on a wide range of soils; no salt tolerance.

PROBLEMS - Fern borers, scale, mites, mealybugs, snails, slugs, and fungus diseases.

PROPAGATION - Rhizome division, spores.

LANDSCAPE USES - Makes a durable, dependable ground cover. The stiff, harsh-feeling fronds are long-lasting when cut and popular in flower arrangements. Cut leatherleaf fern production is a major industry in central Florida. In the past, Florida produced nearly all the cut leatherleaf fern in the world. Labor costs are forcing production offshore.

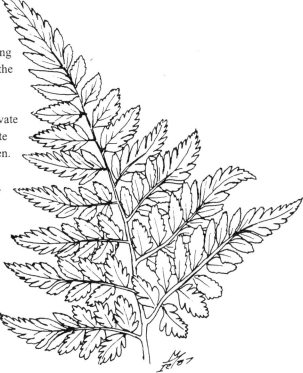

DICKSONIACEAE - DICKSONIA FAMILY

FERNS; 5 GENERA AND ABOUT 50 SPECIES

GEOGRAPHY: Tropical and subtropical Asia, Australia, C. America, and the Pacific Islands (including Hawaii).

GROWTH HABIT: Terrestrial; usually with an arborescent, unbranched, erect or creeping stem, covered with dense matted trichomes and/or fibrous roots.

LEAVES: Fronds usually monomorphic, in a loose cluster, to 4 m. long, variously pinnately compound or pinnatifid; pinnae usually much dissected; stipe covered with dense trichomes near the base; veins free.

FLOWERS: None; sori at the margins of pinnules on a somewhat elevated receptacle, on the terminus of veins and enclosed by the reflexed margins.

FRUIT: None; spores tetrahedral-globose.

ECONOMIC USES: Ornamentals; often used as garden or indoor plants; trunks of some species used for planting orchids; *Cibotium billardieri* is eaten like breadfruit in Hawaii.

ORNAMENTAL GENERA: *Cibotium, Dicksonia,* and perhaps others in private collections.

Dicksonia antarctica

AUSTRALIAN TREE FERN,
TASMANIAN TREE FERN,
TASMANIAN DICKSONIA

PRONUNCIATION - dik 'sō nē ə ant 'ark tə kə

TRANSLATION - [after James Dickson (1738-1822), a British botanist and nurseryman] [of the south polar region].

FORM - Terrestrial ferns with erect arborescent stems.

SIZE - To 50 feet, but usually considerably shorter in cultivation.

HARDINESS ZONE - 9-11.

NATIVE HABITAT - Australia, Tasmania.

LEAVES - Fronds to 4 feet long, more or less leathery, monomorphic or dimorphic, 2- to 4-pinnate-pinnatifid, with long, dense trichomes at the base of the petiole; pinnules to 2 inches long, with 5-7 teeth at margins, veins free.

STEM/BARK - Single, unbranched, densely covered with trichomes and fibrous roots.

FLOWERS - Indusium clam-shaped, consisting of an actual indusium attached to a segment tissue; sori marginal or rarely terminal.

FRUIT - None.

CULTURE - Moist, well-drained, shaded sites, preferably under large, evergreen trees.

PROBLEMS - Does not tolerate direct sun (sun scorch) or prolonged freezing temperatures; no salt tolerance.

PROPAGATION - By spores on screened peat moss or in sterile culture.

LANDSCAPE USES - Often used as landscape in warm, moist regions, or as indoor foliage plants. Attractive in mass plantings or as an accent plant.

COMMENTS - *Dicksonia fimbrosa* (wooly tree fern, with which *D. antarctica* is sometimes confused), *D. sellowiana, D. squarosa* (slender tree fern), and others are sometimes cultivated.

DRYOPTERIDACEAE - HOLLY FERN FAMILY

FERNS; 20 OR MORE GENERA AND ABOUT 500 SPECIES

GEOGRAPHY: Cosmopolitan.

GROWTH HABIT: Medium to large terrestrial, rupestral, or rarely epiphytic plants, with radially organized, clump-forming, creeping or erect stems, covered with large, usually reddish-brown scales.

LEAVES: Fronds mono- or occasionally dimorphic, simple and entire or pinnately compound or pinnatifid; stipe pubescent only at base or throughout; pinnae spinulose and/or leathery, entire or lobed; veins free or anastomosing.

FLOWERS: None; sori solitary or in pairs, roundish to elongate or orbicular; on terminus of veins; indusia reniform or orbicular.

FRUIT: None; spores ellipsoidal to spheroidal.

ECONOMIC USES: Ornamentals; used in shady, moist areas or extensively used in floral arrangements. Rhizomes of some species are roasted or eaten raw and some species are used for medicinal purposes.

ORNAMENTAL GENERA: *Dryopteris, Cyrtomium* (= *Phanerophelebium*), *Polystichum, Tectaria,* and others in private collections.

Cyrtomium falcatum

HOLLY FERN

PRONUNCIATION - sər ˈtō mē əm fal ˈkā təm

TRANSLATION - [from Greek *kyrtos* (= arched), from the habit of growth of these ferns] [sickle-shaped].

SYNONYM - *Phanerophlebium falcatum.*

FORM - Evergreen fern; terrestrial or rarely epiphytic; ground cover; rhizomes stout; clumping with a dense, spiral crown; arching; medium texture.

SIZE- Reaches a height of 3 feet with a 2 to 3 foot spread; moderate growth rate.

HARDINESS ZONE - Zone 8; grows well in all areas of Florida.

NATIVE HABITAT - Asia, South Africa.

LEAVES - Odd-pinnately compound; spirally arranged; to 2.5 feet long. Pinnae ovate to elliptic, to 5 inches long; dark green above, lighter beneath; glossy, waxy, leathery; netted veins; margins entire or weakly wavy or toothed. Frond rachis base densely covered with brown scales.

STEM/BARK - Acaulescent; rhizomes densely scaly, brown.

FLOWERS - None. Large, round, brown, spore-containing sori scattered on the undersides of mature leaflets.

FRUIT - None. Minute spores.

CULTURE - Can tolerate some direct sunlight and full shade; prefers partial shade; various,

moist, well-drained, fertile soils; no salt tolerance.

PROBLEMS - Scale, mites, mealybugs, snails, and slugs.

PROPAGATION - Division of clumps; rarely spores.

LANDSCAPE USES - Makes a good interior plant or a low-maintenance ground cover in shady locations.

COMMENTS - Several cultivars with varying frond forms and a dwarf form are available.

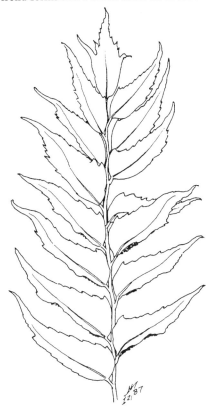

OSMUNDACEAE - OSMUNDA FAMILY

FERNS; 3 GENERA AND ABOUT 20 SPECIES

GEOGRAPHY: Cosmopolitan.

GROWTH HABIT: Terrestrials with erect or decumbent, often dichotomously
                      branched stems, or with a single arborescent trunk and wiry roots.

LEAVES: Fronds mono- or dimorphic, with the sterile ones once pinnate but
                      fertile ones bipinnate; glabrous at maturity; stipe with an expanded
                      stipular base; pinnae with free veins.

FLOWERS: None; sporangia separate or in loose clusters or in wholly fertile
                      bipinnate fronds; indusia absent.

FRUIT: None; spores tetrahedral-globose.

ECONOMIC USES: Ornamentals or cultivated specifically for trunks that are used
                      extensively for growing orchids, bromeliads, and other epiphytic
                      plants.

ORNAMENTAL GENERA: *Leptopteris, Osmunda, and Todea.*

Osmunda regalis   ROYAL FERN

PRONUNCIATION - ɑz ˈmun də   rə ˈga ləs

TRANSLATION - [derivation unknown but may be named for Osmundus (ca. 1025), a Scandinavian writer] [regal, royal].

FORM - Deciduous or evergreen (in southern Florida and warmer regions) terrestrial fern.

SIZE - To about 6 feet in height with equal spread.

HARDINESS ZONE - 3.

NATIVE HABITAT - Europe, Africa, and from Canada to South America. It is often found in moist woods, swamps, lake or stream banks. Also native to Florida, including *O. regalis* var. *spectabilis.*

LEAVES - Distinct fertile and sterile fronds: fertile fronds shorter and narrower, with brown sporangial clusters near the apex; the sterile fronds triangular to ovate, longer then the fertile fronds, with pinnae divided into 3-4 inch oblong-lanceolate pinnules with oblique bases and obtuse tips. Fronds have a long stipe and attached to a rhizome covered with root fibers.

STEM/BARK - Rhizomatous, acaulescent.

FLOWERS - None. Sporangia large, not in sori.

FRUIT - None.

CULTURE - Best grown in wet, acidic soils in shady locations. Requires a night temperature of about 45° F to remain green.

PROBLEMS - May be unsightly during winter months when dormant; caterpillars may also be a problem.

PROPAGATION - By division of the crown or spores.

LANDSCAPE USES - Hedge, specimen, and especially good for tropical effect.

COMMENTS - Related species, *O. cinnamomea, O. claytoniana,* and *O. spectabilis,* are also in cultivation.

POLYPODIACEAE - POLYPODIUM FAMILY

FERNS; A COMPLEX GROUP OF 40 OR MORE GENERA AND IN EXCESS OF 1000 SPECIES

GEOGRAPHY: Cosmopolitan.

GROWTH HABIT: Predominantly epiphytic, small to massive, slender to filiform
                    plants, with erect or short- or long-creeping stems, often with
                    many fibrous roots.

LEAVES: Fronds mostly monomorphic or sometimes dimorphic, in clusters
                    or individually spaced, simple and entire or variously pinnatifid or
                    forked; stipe jointed near the base; veins free or anastomosing.

FLOWERS: None; sori round to elongated, on an entire vein or only the vein
                    terminus; exindusiate (not covered with indusia).

FRUIT: None; spores ellipsoidal.

ECONOMIC USES: Commonly used as landscape or potted plants, with some of the
                    epiphytic species, such as *Platycerium*, extensively grown for
                    decorative purposes on walls and trees.

ORNAMENTAL GENERA: *Aglaomorpha, Campyloneurum, Drynaria, Lemmaphyllum,
                    Microgramma, Microsorium, Nephidium, Phlebodium,
                    Platycerium, Polypodium,* and *Pyrrosia,* among several others.

COMMENTS: This family included many taxa now recognized as distinct genera
                    and species. The Polypodiaceae family (in a strict sense) includes
                    the genera cited above and a few others.

Platycerium spp. STAGHORN FERN

PRONUNCIATION - ˌplæ tə ˈsē rē əm

TRANSLATION - [from Greek *platys* (= broad) and *keras* (= a horn), in allusion to the form of the fronds].

FORM - Evergreen ferns; epiphytic; large, spreading, or drooping, clasping; some forming large clumps; coarse texture.

SIZE - Variable with species, 1 to 4 feet but some fronds to 6 feet long; slow growth rate.

HARDINESS ZONE - Variable with species. Generally Zones 10-11, south Florida; a few species can be grown outside in central Florida.

NATIVE HABITAT - Old World tropics, subtropics (1 New World).

LEAVES - Dimorphic; sterile; rounded to oblong. Clasping leaves: shield-like, entire or lobed; turning brown. Fertile leaves: entire or typically dichotomously forked into antler-like lobes; covered with stellate hairs; upright or drooping.

STEM/BARK - Stemless.

FLOWERS - None. Spores formed in dense clusters on tips of lower surface of fertile leaves; no indusia.

FRUIT - None. Minute spores.

CULTURE - Partial to deep shade on organic well-drained fibrous materials; no salt tolerance.

PROBLEMS - Scale, ants, mites, snails, fungus diseases.

PROPAGATION - Spores, offsets, or "pups" from some spp.

LANDSCAPE USES - Use as a specimen or accent on a patio wall, palm trunk, or hanging from the branches of a tree.

COMMENTS - Many related species; some with several cultivars are available including *P. adenum* (South American Staghorn); *P. bifurcatum* (Common Staghorn); *P. coronarium*; *P. elephantotis* (Cabbage Fern); *P. grande* (Giant Staghorn Fern); *P. stemaria* (Triangular Staghorn Fern); *P. veitchii* (Silver Elkhorn Fern); and *P. willinckii* (Java Staghorn Fern), among a few others.

Polypodium polypodioides   RESURRECTION FERN

PRONUNCIATION - ˌpɑ lə ˈpō dē əm   ˌpɑ ləpō dē ˈoī dēz

TRANSLATION - [from the Greek name *Polypodion*: *polys* (= many) and *pons* (= a foot), in reference to the much-branched, spreading rhizomes] [resembling *Polypodium*].

FORM - Evergreen fern; epiphytic; with creeping rhizomes.

SIZE - To 7 inches tall; spread variable.

HARDINESS ZONE - Zone 7; can be grown in north, south, and central Florida.

NATIVE HABITAT - This Florida native can be found throughout the southeastern U.S. as far north as Delaware and west as Texas; it is also native to tropical America.

LEAVES - Oblong; to 7 inches long and 2 inches wide; pinnatifid, leathery, gray-scaly beneath; borne on stipes attached to the rhizomes with a distinct joint. Pinnae oblong, entire; medium green.

STEM/BARK - Stemless. Rhizomes; creeping, thin, wiry, much-branched.

FLOWERS - None. Sori; round; in rows along each side of the midvein; indusia absent.

FRUIT - None. Minute spores.

CULTURE - Partial to deep shade, will grow in light ranging from 300 to 6000 foot-candles. Naturally grows on the bark of oaks, magnolias, and some other trees; can be grown in an organic, very well-drained medium. A drought-resistant fern, the fronds fold and curl up during dry periods and revive again when moist (Resurrection Fern). No salt tolerance.

PROBLEMS - Generally pest-free.

PROPAGATION - Division or spores.

LANDSCAPE USES - Can be used in naturalistic landscapes on the bark of trees, rock crevices, and in terrariums.

COMMENTS: Many other *Polypodium* species are in cultivation, though primarily in private or botanical collections.

Gymnosperms

ARAUCARIACEAE - ARAUCARIA FAMILY

GYMNOSPERM: CONIFEROUS; 2 GENERA AND 38 SPECIES

GEOGRAPHY: Primarily tropical Southern Hemisphere, especially from Malaysia to eastern Australia and New Zealand, and also S. America.

GROWTH HABIT: Tall, resinous, columnar trees.

LEAVES: Lanceolate to ovate-oblong or needle-shaped or scale-like; in *Araucaria* compressed to the stem, spirally arranged and imbricate.

FLOWERS: Plants dioecious or rarely monoecious; male cones large, in catkins; female cones terminal on short branches; globose and often very large.

FRUIT: None; seeds without wings.

ECONOMIC USES: Planted as ornamentals and extensively used for timber production.

ORNAMENTAL GENERA: *Agathis* and *Araucaria*.

Araucaria bidwillii

FALSE MONKEY PUZZLE TREE,
BUNYA-BUNYA

PRONUNCIATION - ˌæ rə ˈkæ rē ə bid ˈwi lē ī

TRANSLATION - [after the Araucani Indians of central Chile] [in honor of the botanist John Carne Bidwill (1815-1853)].

FORM - Dioecious, coniferous, evergreen tree; single upright trunk (excurrent), tiered branching, pyramidal form; medium texture.

SIZE - To 80 feet tall; rapid growth rate.

HARDINESS ZONE - Zones 9-11, can be grown throughout Florida but needs a protected site in north Florida.

NATIVE HABITAT - Northeastern Australia.

LEAVES - Simple, spirally arranged; lanceolate to 2 inches long; sessile; rigid, terminates with a sharp spine; dark green; entire, translucent margins.

STEM/BARK - Rough, scars from old branches.

FLOWERS - Male cones 3 to 5 inches long and 0.5 inch in diameter; female cones globose 7 to 9 inches long and 6 to 8 inches in diameter.

FRUIT - None. One seed is produced per cone scale.

CULTURE - Full sun, varied soils; moderate salt tolerance.

PROBLEMS - Scale, sooty mold, and leaf spot.

PROPAGATION - Seeds or cuttings of erect shoot tips only.

LANDSCAPE USES - Use as a landscape specimen or urn subject.

COMMENTS - Often confused with *A. araucana*, the Monkey Puzzle Tree.

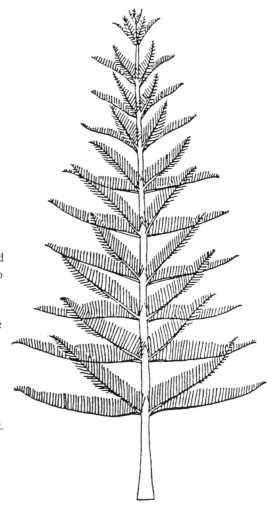

Araucaria heterophylla   NORFOLK ISLAND PINE

PRONUNCIATION - ˌæ rə ˈkæ rē ə   ˌhe tə rō ˈfi lə

TRANSLATION - [after the Araucani Indians of central Chile] [variable leaves].

FORM - Monoecious, coniferous, evergreen tree; single upright trunk (excurrent), tiered branching; pyramidal form; medium texture.

SIZE - To 200 feet tall, 80 feet in Florida; rapid growth rate in naturalized setting; slow growth as houseplant.

HARDINESS ZONE - Zones 9b-11, south and protected sites in central Florida.

NATIVE HABITAT - Norfolk Islands.

LEAVES - Simple, spirally arranged; subulate to 0.5 inch long; sessile, soft, curved toward stem, dark green.

STEM/BARK - Rough, scars from old branches.

FLOWERS - Male cones 1.5 to 2 inches long in clusters; female cones subglobose, 3 to 5 inches long and to 6 inches in diameter.

FRUIT - None. One seed produced per cone scale.

CULTURE - Full sun to partial shade; varied soils; moderate salt tolerance.

PROBLEMS - Scale, root rot, and bacterial diseases spread by rain.

PROPAGATION - Seeds, or cuttings of erect shoot tips only.

LANDSCAPE USES - Use as a landscape specimen or urn subject. Commonly grown as an interior plant and as a Christmas tree.

COMMENTS - Hortus III notes that most material grown as *A. excelsa* is *A. heterophylla*. Related species include *A. araucana* (Monkey-Puzzle Tree) and *A. cunninghamii* (Moreton Bay Pine).

CEPHALOTAXACEAE - PLUMYEW FAMILY

GYMNOSPERMS; CONIFEROUS; MONOGENERIC WITH 4 SPECIES

GEOGRAPHY:	Southeast Asia.
GROWTH HABIT:	Coniferous small trees or shrubs.
LEAVES:	Narrow-linear, regularly arranged in two ranks along short shoots or pseudowhorled.
FLOWERS:	Plants dioecious; male cones small, spherical to oval; female cones arillate, seeds enclosed within an aril, usually in two pairs or in clusters in the basal portion of shoots.
FRUIT:	None; seeds large and drupe-like.
ECONOMIC USES:	Ornamentals.

ORNAMENTAL GENERA: *Cephalotaxus*.

Cephalotaxus harringtonia   JAPANESE PLUM YEW

PRONUNCIATION - ˌse fə lō 'tæk səs   ˌhæ riŋ 'tō nē ə

TRANSLATION - [from Greek *kephale* (= a head), referring to the resemblance of the plant to *Taxus*] [Earl of Harrington].

FORM - Dioecious, evergreen, fine-textured shrub.

SIZE - Generally less than 8 feet in height with a variable spread. Rate of growth is slow.

HARDINESS ZONE - Zone 6. Grown in north Florida only.

NATIVE HABITAT - Japan.

LEAVES - Linear, 1 to 1.5 inches long, needle-like, with abruptly pointed apices soft to the touch. The leaves have two glaucous bands on the underside, one on each side of the midrib.

STEM/BARK - Gray fissured bark.

FLOWERS - Unisexual cones. Insignificant, small axillary.

FRUIT - None. Seeds drupe-like, green, almond-shaped, to 1 inch long. The seeds are usually not produced in Florida and take two years to mature.

CULTURE - Grown in partial to full shade on soils of reasonable fertility and drainage. It has no salt tolerance.

PROBLEMS - Nematodes and mushroom root rot.

PROPAGATION - Cuttings.

LANDSCAPE USES - Used in foundation plantings or in planters.

VARIETIES - *Cephalotaxus harringtonia* var. *drupacea* - low spreading shrub; two-ranked leaves form a V-shaped trough on horizontal arching branches; **'Fastigiata'** - upright columnar shrub; leaves dark green and spirally arranged on ascending vertical branches. Superficially resembles *Podocarpus macrophyllus*. Also reported from cultivation is *C. fortunii* (Chemise Plum Yew).

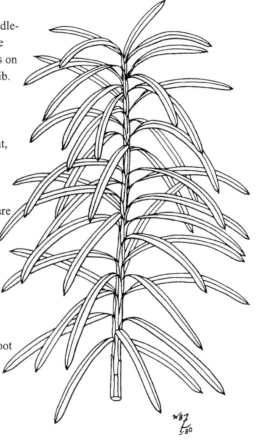

CUPRESSACEAE - CYPRESS FAMILY

GYMNOSPERMS; CONIFEROUS; 19 GENERA AND ABOUT 120 SPECIES

GEOGRAPHY:	Principally of temperate Northern Hemisphere but with a few in tropical mountains and temperate S. America.
GROWTH HABIT:	Coniferous erect, decumbent, or procumbent, much-branched coniferous trees and shrubs.
LEAVES:	Decussate or in opposite pairs or whorls of threes, juvenile leaves acicular but adult leaves scale-like and adpressed.
FLOWERS:	Plants mono- or dioecious; male cones small, solitary at the end of branchlets; female cones woody or fleshy and drupe-like, globose or elongated; cone scales imbricate or fused at margins so as to resemble a berry, without spines but often hooked.
FRUIT:	None; seeds winged or not winged.
ECONOMIC USES:	Ornamentals, timber, and *Juniperus* "berries" used for flavoring gin.

ORNAMENTAL GENERA: *Callitris, Chamaecyparis,* ↔ *Cupressocyparis, Cupressus, Juniperus, Platycladus* (= *Thuja*).

✕ *Cupressocyparis leylandii*   LEYLAND CYPRESS

PRONUNCIATION- kū ˌpre sə ˈsi pə rəs   lā ˈlan dē ī

TRANSLATION - [an intergeneric hybrid between *Cupressus macrocarpa* and *Chamaecyparis nootkatensis*, after C.J. Leyland who grew some of the first plants at Haggerston Hall, England].

FORM - Monoecious, evergreen, excurrent, more or less conical/pyramidal evergreen coniferous tree with a dense crown.

SIZE - Reaches a height of 100 feet or more with a fairly rapid growth rate.

HARDINESS ZONE - 6.

NATIVE HABITAT - Seeds collected from *C. macrocarpa* and grown by J.M. Naylor at Leighton Hall, Welshpool, England, in 1911.

LEAVES - Adult leaves opposite, entire, scale-like and juvenile leaves awl-shaped or acicular, spreading.

STEM/BARK - Branchlets flatter, finer, longer, and more slender than *Chamaecyparis* spp.

FLOWERS - Female cones to about 1 inch in diameter, most with 8 scales and 5 seeds under each scale.

FRUIT - None.

CULTURE - Tolerates a wide range of conditions but grows best in full sun and well-drained soils.

PROBLEMS - No major problems noted.

PROPAGATION - By cuttings that root relatively easily when treated with 5-10,000 ppm IBA.

LANDSCAPE USES - Useful as accent or specimen tree, for windbreak and screens, and as Christmas tree.

COMMENTS - Plant is used as timber and for resin, but includes several interesting cultivars, primarily involving shape and/or color variations:

'**Green Spire**' -Narrowly pyramidal, very dense, central leader often poorly developed; branch angles variable in relation to the stem; foliage bright green.

'**Haggerston Grey**' - Branches open, opposite, at right angles to one another and decussate. Foliage gray-green.

'**Leighton Green**' - With a distinct central leader, irregular branching arrangement, dense, and lying flat; foliage bright green to yellow-green; frequent cone producer.

'**Naylor's Blue**' - Similar to 'Lighton Green' but with gray-blue foliage and infrequent coning.

'**Robinson's Gold**' - Exceptionally fast grower but with more compact and conical shape; densely branched; foliage bronze-yellow in spring, turning gold-yellow in summer.

Cupressus sempervirens   ITALIAN CYPRESS

PRONUNCIATION - kū ˈpre səs ˌsem pər ˈvī rənz

TRANSLATION - [classical Latin name for *C. sempervirens*] [evergreen].

FORM - Monoecious, evergreen tree, coniferous, upright, narrow, strongly columnar (fastigiate) habit.

SIZE - To 80 feet, 3 to 6 feet in diameter, often much shorter, rapid growth.

HARDINESS ZONE - Zone 7. Grown throughout Florida.

NATIVE HABITAT - southern Europe, western Asia.

LEAVES - Small, scale-like, tightly compressed, whorled, obtuse, dark grey-green color.

STEM/BARK - Needle-like branchlets, round.

FLOWERS - Male cones small, female cones globose, to 1.5 inches in diameter, on separate branches.

FRUIT - None. 1.5 inch cones, many seeds per cone scale.

CULTURE - Full sun, various well-drained soils; moderately salt tolerant.

PROBLEMS - Spider mites, root rot, bacterial blight; cannot be pruned with success.

PROPAGATION - Seeds, cuttings of cultivars.

LANDSCAPE USES - Framing, strong accent around large buildings, formal landscape.

COMMENTS - Several cultivars: ´Glauca' (narrowly fastigiate, tinted blue leaves); ´Stricta' (narrowly fastigiate, leaves dark green); and others. Related species, such as *C. arizonica* (**Arizona Cypress**) and its cultivars and *C. lusitanica* (**Mexican Cypress**) and its cultivars, are also known from cultivation in Florida.

Juniperus chinensis   <small>CHINESE JUNIPER</small>

PRONUNCIATION - jū 'ni pɚ rəs   chi 'nen səs

TRANSLATION - [Latin name] [from China].

FORM - Dioecious, evergreen shrub, coniferous, horizontal and spreading, branch tips outward-pointing.

SIZE - To 60 feet, most cultivars 5 to 10 feet, medium to rapid growth.

HARDINESS ZONE - Zone 4. Planting in Florida varies with cultivar. Generally best in north and central regions.

NATIVE HABITAT - Temperate East Asia.

LEAVES - Adult leaves small (1/16 - 1/8 inch long), scale-like, tightly appressed, decussate, overlapping, obtuse, blue, grey, or green colors, depending on cultivar; juvenile leaves awl-shaped, 0.33 to 0.5 inch long, in whorls of 3 or opposite pairs, usually low on the plant.

STEM/BARK - Needle-like branchlets.

FLOWERS - Male cones yellow, catkin-like; female cones berry-like, with coalesced fleshy scales.

FRUIT - None. Subglobose cones; to 0.25 inch in diameter, 2-3 seeded, whitish-blue turning brown to purplish-brown, often glaucous. Seeds 1 to 12, not winged.

CULTURE - Full sun, fertile, well-drained soils; slight to moderate salt tolerance, good pollution tolerance. Will not tolerate wet feet. Frequently not given enough space, outgrows the site. Cannot be pruned severely.

PROBLEMS - Mites (especially in hot, dry sites), bagworms, root rot, *Phomopsis* blight, and others.

PROPAGATION - Cuttings (usually in winter), grafting.

LANDSCAPE USES - Variable with cultivar; ground cover, foundation, planter box, border, screening, specimen.

COMMENTS - Many varieties and cultivars. Some of the most popular in Florida are

var. *chinensis:* **'Armstrong Aurea'** (Old Gold Juniper);

'Blaauw' (Blue Vase Juniper);

'Blue Vase' - horizontal spreading to 8 feet, mostly adult foliage; blue-green, more upright and globose than **'Hetzii'**, feathery projecting branches densely foliated on all sides with a tufted "fox tail" appearance, used throughout Florida;

'Excelsa' (Tall Chinese Juniper);

'Hetzii' - horizontal, spreading to 15 feet, mostly adult foliage; blue-green, feathery branches project upward, form close to **'Mint Julep'** but color distinctly bluish, planted in north and central Florida;

'Hetz Columnaris';

'Humphrey's Pride' (Humphrey's Pride Juniper);

'Keteleeri' (Keteleer Juniper);

'Mint Julep' - horizontally spreading to 4 feet, mostly adult foliage; mint green,

(continued)

'Hetzii'

Juniperus chinensis (continued)

feathery branches project upward with foliage mostly on upper side of the branch, resembles **'Hetzii'** but color distinctly different, used throughout Florida;

'Parsonii' (Parson's Juniper) - prostrate ground cover to 3 feet, mostly adult foliage, grey-green, used throughout Florida, is actually *J. davurica* **'Parsonii'** but is sold in Florida as *J. chinensis* **'Parsonii'**;

'Pfitzerana' - horizontal spreading to 6 feet, mostly adult foliage, grey-green, resembles **'Mint Julep'** and **'Hetzii'** but foliage distinctly finer in texture, feathery branches not as upright, producing a flatter profile, planted only in north Florida;

'Pfitzerana Aurea' (Golden Pfitzer Juniper);

'Pfitzerana Glauca' (Blue Pfitzer Juniper);

'Pfitzerana Nick's Compact';

'Pyramidalis' (Pyramidal Juniper);

'San Jose' (San Jose Juniper);

'Sargentii Viridis';

'Sea Green';

'Shepparadii' (Sheppard Juniper);

'Spartan' and **'Spearmint'** are upright and pyramidal;

'Spiralis';

'Sylvestris' (Sylvester Juniper);

'Torulosa' - upright to 20 feet, predominantly adult foliage; light green; irregular branching produces a twisted, flame-like habit, planted throughout Florida;

var. *procumbens*: **'Nana'** and **'Variegata'** - prostrate ground cover to 2 feet, predominantly juvenile foliage; blue-grey-green, very dense foliage, often mounded, attacked seriously by mites and *Phomopsis*, planted only in north Florida.

'Torulosa'

var. *procumbens*

'Pfitzerana'

Juniperus conferta   SHORE JUNIPER

PRONUNCIATION - jū 'ni pə rəs   kən 'fər tə

TRANSLATION - [Latin name] [crowded, in reference to the leaves].

FORM - Dioecious, evergreen, coniferous ground cover, procumbent, creeping, branch tips verticillate.

SIZE - To 2 feet, with 6 to 9 foot spread; rapid growth rate.

HARDINESS ZONE - Zone 5. Grows well in north and central Florida.

NATIVE HABITAT - Japan.

LEAVES - Juvenile foliage only; linear, subulate, to 0.5 inch long, in whorls of 3, prickly, white bands on upper surface, light gray-green, often glaucous.

STEM/BARK - Young stems yellowish-green, older branches gray-brown.

FLOWERS - Male cones catkin-like; female cones blue-black, berry-like with coalesced fleshy scales.

FRUIT - None. Black glaucous cones; to 0.5 inch diameter, 3 seeds.

CULTURE - Full sun, well-drained soils. Salt and drought tolerant, but will not tolerate waterlogged conditions.

PROBLEMS - Mites (in hot, dry locations), bagworm, *Phomopsis* blight, root rot, and others. Tends to be short-lived due to insect and disease problems.

PROPAGATION - Seeds, cuttings of cultivars.

LANDSCAPE USES - Ground cover, embankments, planter boxes, draped over walls, seaside plantings. Plant in drier areas.

COMMENTS - Several cultivars offered: **'Blue Pacific'** - ocean blue-green color, usually less than 1 foot in height; **'Compacta'** - gray-green, dense with little upright branching, slower growing, 8 to 10 inches in height; **'Emerald Sea'** - USDA introduction, compact habit, blue-gray foliage, to 1 foot in height.

Juniperus horizontalis   CREEPING JUNIPER

PRONUNCIATION - jū 'ni pə rəs   ˌhɑ rə zɑn 'tæ ləs

TRANSLATION - [Latin name] [horizontal].

FORM - Dioecious, evergreen shrub, coniferous, horizontal and spreading.

SIZE - To 2 feet, most cultivars less than 1 foot, slow-growing.

HARDINESS ZONE - Zone 2. Plant only in north Florida.

NATIVE HABITAT - Northeastern United States.

LEAVES - Adult leaves small (about 0.25 inch long), scale-like, tightly appressed, opposite and decussate, bluish, grey or green depending on cultivar. Juvenile leaves awl-like. Foliage developing purplish cast in winter.

STEM/BARK - grey-brown, somewhat peeling bark.

FLOWERS - Male cones yellow, catkin-like; female cones berry-like, to 0.5 inch in diameter, blue-black, glaucous, scales 3 to 8, fleshy, coalescing.

FRUIT - None. Subglobose cones; to 0.5 inch in diameter, mostly 2 to 4 seeded, not winged, rarely seen.

CULTURE - Full sun, fertile, well-drained soils; slight to moderate salt tolerance (less so than *J. conferta*). Will not stand waterlogged conditions. Branches easily broken by foot traffic.

PROBLEMS - Mites, bagworm, root rot, *Phomopsis* blight (a major problem), and others.

PROPAGATION - Seeds, cuttings of cultivars.

LANDSCAPE USES - Planter box, border, ground cover; varies with cultivar.

COMMENTS - Many cultivars. Some of the most popular in Florida are **'Bar Harbor'** - prostrate ground cover to 8 inches. Predominantly adult foliage in plate-like clusters; blue-green. Fall color bluish-purple. Similar to **'Wiltonii'**; **'Wiltonii Blue Rug'** - prostrate ground cover to 6 inches. Predominantly adult foliage; blue-green. Extremely compact. Fall color bluish-purple. Difficult to tell from **'Bar Harbor'**; **'Plumosa'** (Andorra Juniper) - more upright ground cover to 18 inches. Mostly juvenile foliage; green. More erect than either **'Bar Harbor'** or **'Wiltonii'**, with plume-like branches. Fall color reddish-purple. **'Plumosa Compacta'** and **'Youngstown'** - compact selections of **'Plumosa'**.

'Bar Harbor'

'Plumosa'

Juniperus silicicola   SOUTHERN RED CEDAR

PRONUNCIATION - jū ˈni pə rəs ˌsi lə ˈsi kə lə

TRANSLATION - [Latin name] [growing in sand].

FORM - Dioecious, evergreen tree, coniferous, symmetrical, dense, oval to pyramidal, fine-textured.

SIZE - To 40 feet tall with a 20 foot spread. Grows at a fairly rapid pace.

HARDINESS ZONE - Zone 8. Grown throughout Florida.

NATIVE HABITAT - Coastal plain of the southeastern U.S.

LEAVES - Opposite or in whorls of 3. Juvenile leaves are needle-like, linear, to 0.25 inch long, green, sharp-pointed, prickly, with 2 silvery lines beneath. Adult leaves are dark green, scale-like and overlapping.

STEM/BARK - Thin, reddish, peeling bark, drooping branchlets. The wood repels insects and the tree was lumbered extensively for wood for chests and pencils. Cedar Key once had extensive red cedar forests.

FLOWERS - Staminate cones are yellowish, 0.25 inch long; pistillate cones are smaller, green. Flowering occurs in late winter.

FRUIT - None. Fleshy, drupe-like, one-seeded cones, 0.25 inch long, purple with a white bloom, ripen in late fall.

CULTURE - Plant in full or partial sun on a wide range of soils. Tolerates both calcareous soil and seashore salt. Difficult to transplant except when small. Transplanting shock may be avoided with initial frequent irrigation.

PROBLEMS - Juniper blight, spider mites, bagworms, cedar-apple rust.

PROPAGATION - By seed, which germinate faster if planted as soon as the cones mature or if given a stratification period. Tip cuttings will root.

LANDSCAPE USES - A specimen tree, also employed in windbreaks. Used in the Southeast as a Christmas tree, either grown in containers, cut from the wild, or planted in commercial tree farms.

COMMENTS - *Juniperus silicola* and *J. virginiana* are very similar species. The only difference between them is the greater height and straight branches of the latter, as opposed to drooping branches of the former.

Platycladus orientalis   ORIENTAL ARBORVITAE

PRONUNCIATION - ˌplæ tē ˈklā dəs   ˌo rē ən ˈtæ ləs

SYNONYM - *Thuja orientalis.*

TRANSLATION - [flat branch] [oriental].

FORM - Monoecious, evergreen tree, coniferous, densely branched, becoming more open with age, symmetrical, broad conical form; branchlets in vertical plane.

SIZE - To 40 feet, medium growth rate.

HARDINESS ZONE - Zone 6. Grown throughout Florida.

NATIVE HABITAT - China, Korea.

LEAVES - Small, scale-like, to 0.25 inch long, glandular, grooved, opposite, closely appressed, bright green.

STEM/BARK - Branchlets flat in vertical plane.

FLOWERS - Male cones catkin-like; female fleshy cones to 1 inch in diameter, erect, blue-green, becoming woody.

FRUIT - None. Woody cones; to 1 inch, hooked at apex of each scale; 1 to 2 wingless seeds per cone scale.

CULTURE - Full sun, various well-drained soils. Somewhat tolerant of heat and dry conditions, but will not tolerate salt or waterlogged soils. Easily transplanted. Survives in most locations.

PROBLEMS - Mites, *Phomopsis* blight, bagworms; none serious problems.

PROPAGATION - Seeds, cuttings of cultivars.

LANDSCAPE USES - Roadside plantings, barrier, large specimen. Extensively overplanted, especially in areas too small to accommodate the full-grown plant. Older plants are often open and ragged in appearance.

COMMENTS - Many cultivars exist in the trade: **'Aureus'** (Gold Tip Arborvitae) - low, compact, branchlet tips golden yellow; **'Aureus Nanus'** (Beckman Arborvitae) - same as **'Aureus'** except dwarf; **'Bakeri'** (Baker Arborvitae) - pale green; best adapted to hot, dry sites; **'Blue Cone'** (Blue Cone Arborvitae); **'Bonita'** - cone-shaped; leaves tipped golden yellow; **'Excelsus'** (Tall Arborvitae); **'Fruitlandii'** - dwarf, globose form; dark green foliage; **'Strictus'** (Pyramidal Arborvitae). Many others.

CYCADACEAE - CYCAD FAMILY

GYMNOSPERMS; CYCADS; MONOGENERIC WITH ABOUT 40 SPECIES

GEOGRAPHY: Widely distributed in mainland and islands surrounding the Indian Ocean, including northern Australia, southeast Asian islands, Japan, China, and eastern Africa and Madagascar.

GROWTH HABIT: Mostly evergreen, small trees or caudiciform, palmlike plants.

LEAVES: Numerous and often quite large, clustered atop the stem; pinnately compound; leaflets entire, with only a prominent central vein and no laterals.

FLOWERS: Dioecious plants; male cones (microstrobili) large and with spirally arranged microsporophylls which are covered with numerous pollen sacs; female cones (megastrobili) also often large but in rounded, clusters of leaf-like megasporophylls, each bearing 1 to 9 ovules.

FRUIT: None; seeds large, resemble a drupe, orange to reddish-brown.

ECONOMIC USES: Ornamentals; starch from trunk and seeds of some species.

ORNAMENTAL GENERA: *Cycas*.

Cycas revoluta   SAGO PALM, KING SAGO PALM

PRONUNCIATION - 'sī kəs   ˌre və 'lū tə

TRANSLATION - [Greek name for a palm, which *Cycas* spp. resemble in habit and leaf] [rolled backward, in reference to leaflet margins].

FORM - Dioecious, evergreen palm-like plant, upright, often suckering, sometimes branched.

SIZE - To 15 feet, usually shorter; slow growth.

HARDINESS ZONE - Zone 8b. Grown throughout Florida.

NATIVE HABITAT - Southern Japan.

LEAVES - Pinnately compound, 3 to 4 feet long in rosettes, leaflets to 7 inches long, 0.25 inch wide, glossy green, sharp apex, margins revolute, stiff, leaflets reduced to prickles at base of rachis; petiole spinose.

STEM/BARK - Leaf scars and persistent leaf bases. Male plants often branch but females only infrequently, though often sucker from base.

FLOWERS - Male cones cylindrical, to 24 inches tall; female with modified scale-like leaves, cream-brown felt-covered, grouped into a globose cane-like mass.

FRUIT - None. Ovate, orange-red seeds; to 2 inches in diameter, somewhat flattened.

CULTURE - Full sun to partial shade, various well-drained soils; moderately salt tolerant.

PROBLEMS - Scale, mealybugs, leaf spot, micronutrient deficiencies, especially Mn.

PROPAGATION - Seeds, rooting of "side shoots." (Cycads lack lateral buds; branching initiates from callus.)

LANDSCAPE USES - Specimen, accent, urn, used to create a tropical effect. Perhaps the most commonly cultivated cycad.

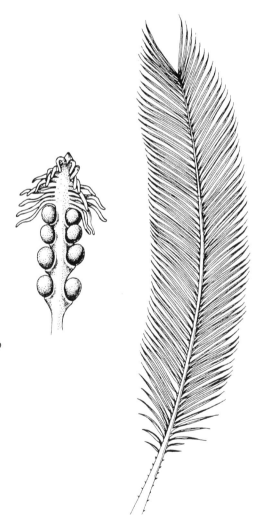

Cycas rumphii

QUEEN SAGO PALM

PRONUNCIATION - 'sī kəs   'rum fē ī

TRANSLATION - [Greek name for a palm, which *Cycas* spp. resemble in habit and leaf] [in honor of G.F. Rumphius].

FORM - Evergreen palm-like plant, upright, often suckering, occasionally branching on older plants.

SIZE - To 20 feet, commonly 8 to 15 feet in Florida; slow growth.

HARDINESS ZONE - Zone 9b. Grown in south and warmest parts of central Florida.

NATIVE HABITAT - Madagascar.

LEAVES - Pinnately compound, 5 to 8 feet long in rosettes, leaflets to 12 inches long and 0.75 inch wide, acuminate tip, margin flat, pliable, petiole variously spined or entire.

STEM/BARK - Pithy trunk, leaf scars and persistent leaf bases.

FLOWERS - Dioecious plants; male cone cylindrical to 25 inches long 8 inches in diameter; females without true cones but with a cluster of modified seed-bearing leaves (megasporophylls), brown felt-covered, bearing 4-9 seeds.

FRUIT - None. Ovate, initially green but reddish-brown when mature, seeds to 3 inches in diameter, somewhat flattened.

CULTURE - Full sun to partial shade, various well-drained soils; moderately salt tolerant.

PROBLEMS - Scale, mealybug (these two can be serious problems), leaf spot.

PROPAGATION - Seeds, rooting of "side shoots" (cycads do not possess lateral buds).

LANDSCAPE USES - Specimen, accent, urn, used to create a tropical effect.

COMMENTS - Several related species (including *C. circinalis* to which, until recently, cultivated *C. rumphii* were referred). *Cycas circinalis* is otherwise rare in cultivation. *Cycas media, C. normanbyana, C. siamensis,* and *C. wadei* are among the many other related species in cultivation.

Cycas taitungensis PRINCE SAGO OR EMPEROR SAGO PALM

PRONUNCIATION - 'sī kəs tī təŋ 'en səs

TRANSLATION - [Greek name for a palm which *Cycas* spp. resemble in habit and leaf] [after Taitung, Hsien, Taiwan].

SYNONYM - *Cycas taiwaniana, Cycas revoluta* var. *taiwaniana.*

FORM - Dioecious, palm-like gymnosperm, sometimes branching in male plants.

SIZE - To about 15 feet tall.

HARDINESS ZONE - Zone 9 (Zone 8 with some protection).

NATIVE HABITAT - Taitung, Taiwan, in full sun on rocky and steep slopes.

LEAVES - Pinnately compound, mostly upright; leaflets sequentially reduced from top to bottom so as to become spine-like at the base, 5-10 inches long and about ˘ inch wide, lanceolate-linear, straight, ending in a rigid, pungent point; margins thickened but not as revolute as *C. revoluta.*

STEM/BARK - Trunk with permanent leaf bases, to 20 inches or more in diameter. Male plants branch frequently.

FLOWERS - Male cones (microstrobilus) upright, to about 20 inches long, ovoid-cylindric, with triangular microsporophylls; female cones (megastrobilus) with leaf-like, yellowish-tomentose megasporophylls tightly grouped upon pollination, gradually becoming distinct as seeds mature.

FRUIT - None. Seeds 2-3 per sporophyll, narrowly obovate, to about 2 inches long, becoming purplish-red at maturity.

CULTURE - A more cold-hardy, faster-growing plant than *C. revoluta*, this species should be grown in a well-drained, fertile soil in full sun or partial shade. The leaves become somewhat long and curved when grown in shady locations.

PROBLEMS - None has been observed, although mealybugs and scales may become troublesome.

PROPAGATION - By seed or when possible by "side shoots." (Cycads do not possess lateral buds.)

LANDSCAPE USES - Specimen plants or in groups of three or more with a minimum of 6-8 feet spacing.

COMMENTS - This plant may be superior to *C. revoluta* because of its rapid growth, upright leaves, and trouble-free aspect, though each plant possesses positive features for the landscape.

GINKGOACEAE - GINKGO FAMILY

GYMNOSPERMS; GINKGO MONOGENERIC AND MONOTYPIC

GEOGRAPHY: China, but apparently not found in the wild.

GROWTH HABIT: Excurrent tree with long and short shoots; lateral branches arranged more or less horizontally.

LEAVES: Fan-shaped, incised, and with dichotomously branched veins.

FLOWERS: Dioecious plants; microsporophylls terminal on elongated axis; megasporophylls axillary with a branched or single stalk.

FRUIT: None; seeds hard, spherical.

ECONOMIC USES: Ornamental, noncommercial timber, seeds edible and considered a delicacy.

ORNAMENTAL GENERA: *Ginkgo.*

Ginkgo biloba   Maidenhair Tree

PRONUNCIATION - ˈgiŋ kō bī ˈlō bə

TRANSLATION - [a misrendering of the obsolete Japanese name *gin* (= silver) and *kyo* (= apricot)] [two-lobed].

FORM - Dioecious, deciduous tree of medium texture; irregular shape and branching pattern.

SIZE - To 120 feet (usually 65 to 100 feet), slow growing.

HARDINESS ZONE - Zone 5. Northern Florida best, marginal in central Florida. Best suited to temperate climate.

NATIVE HABITAT - Extinct in the wild; native to southeast China, where it was discovered growing in temple gardens.

LEAVES - Bilobed with parallel dichotomous venation; spiral or pseudoverticillate arrangement on short spur shoots.

STEM/BARK - Two kinds of shoots: long and spur shoots.

FLOWERS - None. Female trees bear pairs of sessile, naked ovules on a long peduncle; male trees bear clusters of microsporophylls on a similarly long peduncle. Both appear in early spring, ovules persisting until mature in autumn.

FRUIT - None. Megasporophylls with two ovules, usually develop only one yellowish, drupe-like fleshy seed, approximately 1 inch in diameter.

CULTURE - Easily grown. Initially somewhat slow but eventually rapid grower.

PROBLEMS - Female trees produce abundant quantities of seed with putrid fleshy seed coat when mature and fallen (the principal odoriferous component is butyric acid, the smell of rancid butter). The problem can be avoided by planting known males or grafting/budding known males onto seedling rootstocks. Very resistant to insect pests and diseases.

PROPAGATION - Grafting/budding, cuttings, layering, stratified seed. Usually grafted with known males to avoid seed production.

LANDSCAPE USES - Street, ornamental tree which is capable of withstanding hard-packed, poor soils and air pollution.

COMMENTS - Kernels of the seed are edible once the fleshy disagreeable portion is removed. Commonly used for food in the Orient. Several cultivars for growth habit (including fastigiate and weeping), leaf shape, color, and size have been reported, but none common in Florida.

PINACEAE - PINE FAMILY

GYMNOSPERMS; CONIFEROUS; 10 GENERA AND ABOUT 250 SPECIES

GEOGRAPHY: The entire Northern Hemisphere.

GROWTH HABIT: Coniferous trees, rarely shrubs.

LEAVES: Usually evergreen, acicular, spirally arranged in 1 (e.g., *P. monophylla*) or fascicles of 2, 3, 4, or 5.

FLOWERS: Usually monoecious; male cones with numerous spirally arranged microsporophylls (pollen-bearing scales); female cones woody, with numerous spirally arranged megasporophylls (ovuliferous), each with two ovules.

FRUIT: None; seeds winged only on one side or without wings.

ECONOMIC USES: Ornamentals, most important source of softwood timber, and numerous other uses, including chemicals.

ORNAMENTAL GENERA: *Cedrus, Pinus* are the only two genera cultivated in Florida. Other genera include *Abies, Keteleeria, Larix, Picea, Pseudolarix, Pseudotsuga,* and *Tsuga.*

Cedrus deodara

DEODAR CEDAR, HIMALAYAN CEDAR

PRONUNCIATION - ˈsē drəs ˌdē ə ˈdɑ rə

TRANSLATION - [Latin name for evergreen conifers] [old Indian name Deodar].

FORM - Monoecious, coniferous, narrowleaf, evergreen tree of excurrent, pyramidal growth habit and horizontally arranged, nodding branches.

SIZE - To 150 feet tall and with a trunk diameter of 10 feet, but often much smaller in cultivation.

HARDINESS ZONE - 7.

NATIVE HABITAT - The Himalayas.

LEAVES - Acicular, blue-green, grouped to about 30 in a cluster, 1.5-2 inches long.

STEM/BARK - Dark gray, smooth on young trees, fissured and scaly on older ones.

FLOWERS - Female cones one or two together on short shoots, more or less ovate, to 3 to 4 inches long and 2 to 2.5 inches wide, rounded at the apex.

FRUIT - None. Seeds whitish with light brown wings.

CULTURE - Should be planted in large spaces, in well-drained soil.

PROBLEMS- Difficult to transplant when mature. Tip dieback due to borer.

PROPAGATION - Primarily by seed but cuttings root with IBA treatment.

LANDSCAPE USES - In large spaces as specimen plant, particularly attractive because of its form and blue-green color.

COMMENTS - Many cultivars are known but none common in Florida. A few examples representing various growth forms or color include:
ʹArgenteaʹ - Fast-growing cultivar with silver-gray to bluish-gray foliage.
ʹAureaʹ - 10 to 15 feet tall with golden-yellow new growth.
ʹCompactaʹ - Globose-conical compact habit with dense branching habit.
ʹFastigiataʹ - Columnar habit, branches widely spaced.
ʹViridisʹ - Needles conspicuously glossy light green.

Two related species, *C. atlantica* (Atlantic cedar) and *C. libani* (Cedar of Lebanon), are well known and common in cultivation in the western states.

Pinus clausa

SAND PINE

PRONUNCIATION -ˈpī nə‑s   ˈklau sə

TRANSLATION - [Latin name] [closed].

FORM - Monoecious, evergreen, coniferous tree, upright, with dense foliage, irregular growth, and medium texture.

SIZE - Can reach a height of 70 feet, but more commonly in the 30-40 foot range with a 20-25 foot spread. It grows rapidly under favorable conditions.

HARDINESS ZONE - Zone 8. Thrives in all areas of Florida.

NATIVE HABITAT - Dry, white sand scrubs of Florida and adjacent states.

LEAVES - Needles, in fascicles of twos, to 3 inches long, often twisted or bent.

STEM/BARK - The 6- to 12-inch-thick trunks are gray and smooth when young, becoming reddish-brown with scaly plates when older.

FLOWERS - Yellowish male cones, to 1 inch; ovulate cones 0.5 inch in diameter at emergence. Borne in early spring at the base of new growth; at maturity, 2 to 4 inches long, brown, becoming gray with age. The cones frequently will not open until after a fire and persist on the tree for long periods.

FRUIT - None. It has 0.75 inch winged seeds.

CULTURE - Needs full sun; will grow in almost any soil except very wet ones. It tolerates poor, dry sands well and has marginal salt tolerance.

PROBLEMS - Pest-free.

PROPAGATION - Seed, extracted from cones, sown on the soil surface and covered with cut pine needles. Transplants very poorly from the wild.

LANDSCAPE USES - Leave old trees when clearing land for their picturesque leaning or twisted growth. Young trees are symmetrical, have been grown commercially as Christmas trees, and make excellent lawn specimens. However, the wood is of poor quality and not used as lumber.

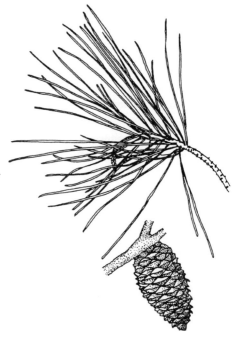

Pinus elliottii

PRONUNCIATION - ˈpī nəs   ˌe lē ˈɑ tē ī

TRANSLATION - [classical Latin name] [after Stephen Elliott (1771-1830), botanist at Charleston, South Carolina].

FORM - Monoecious, coniferous, evergreen tree, heavy horizontal branches clearing from lower portions of trunk with age, rounded open canopy.

SIZE - To 100 feet, rapid growth rate.

HARDINESS ZONE - Zone 8. Grown throughout Florida.

NATIVE HABITAT - Southeastern United States.

LEAVES - Needles, in fascicles of 2 or 3, to 8 inches long, clustered on ends of branches, deep green, stiff, straight.

STEM/BARK - To 3 feet in diameter, usually much smaller, tapering, bark dark brown, irregularly cracked, layered.

FLOWERS - Male cones catkin-like, clustered, to 3 inches long; ovulate cones globose. Female cones brown, woody, ovoid, to 6 inches long, stalked, mature second year, not persistent.

FRUIT - None. Seeds winged.

CULTURE - Full sun, various soils, moderately salt tolerant. More tolerant of wet sites than most pines.

PROBLEMS - Pine blister rust, borers, pine beetle.

PROPAGATION - Seed.

LANDSCAPE USES - Light shade, street plantings.

COMMENTS - Mainly used for lumber, pulp, etc. *Pinus elliottii* var. *densa*, a south Florida endemic, is considered by some to be a distinct species.

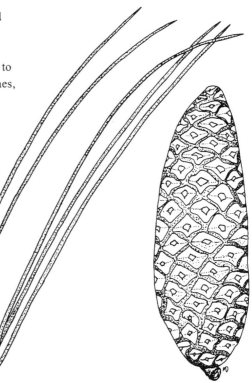

Pinus glabra

SPRUCE PINE

PRONUNCIATION - 'pī nəs   'glā brə

TRANSLATION - [Latin name] [glabrous, smooth].

FORM - Coniferous, monoecious, evergreen tree, heavily foliated, much-branched, bushy irregular canopy.

SIZE - To 80 feet, usually 30 to 50 feet, moderate growth rate.

HARDINESS ZONE - Zone 8. Grown in north and central Florida.

NATIVE HABITAT - Southeastern United States.

LEAVES - Needles, in fascicles of two, to 3 inches, clustered on ends of branches, light green when young turning deep green, soft, twisted.

STEM/BARK - Stem erect, slender, may curve or twist; bark finer than *P. elliottii.*

FLOWERS - Male cones catkin-like, female cones brown, globose, to 2.5 inches diameter, woody; remain on tree for 3 to 4 years.

FRUIT - None. Seeds winged.

CULTURE - Full sun, moist fertile soils, slightly salt tolerant. Retains branches near the ground when not shaded, therefore casts a heavy shade.

PROBLEMS - Pine blister rust, borers.

PROPAGATION - Seed.

LANDSCAPE USES - Specimen, street plantings, accent.

COMMENTS - Frequently used as Christmas trees because it is heavily foliated with short needles. Not very useful for timber.

Pinus palustris   LONGLEAF PINE

PRONUNCIATION - 'pī nəs pə 'lus trəs

TRANSLATION - [Latin name] [marsh-loving].

FORM - Coniferous, monoecious, evergreen tree, upright; sparse foliage concentrated in upper third on a few large irregular branches; coarse-textured.

SIZE - Can reach a height of 100 feet, though normally much smaller. The spread is 30 feet and growth rate is moderate.

HARDINESS ZONE - Zone 7. Grows in north and central Florida.

NATIVE HABITAT - Dry flatwoods and sand ridges of the southeastern United States; occasionally found in swampy areas.

LEAVES - Needles, in fascicles of threes, to 14 inches long, slender and flexible giving a weeping appearance. The winter buds are silvery-white and quite conspicuous.

STEM/BARK - The trunk is 1 to 2 feet wide and covered with thick brown plates of bark.

FLOWERS - Purplish staminate strobili, to 3 inches long; purplish developing ovulate cones, to 0.5 inch. Borne at the base of the current season's growth in early spring. Female cones brown, to 10 inches. Opening 1.5 years after pollination.

FRUIT - None. The winged seeds are 2 inches long.

CULTURE - Needs full sun; will grow in a wide range of soils. It is not salt tolerant. Very slow-growing for the first few years (often called grass stage because it looks like a clump of tall grass).

PROBLEMS - Borers; resistant to Fusiform Rust and pine bark beetle.

PROPAGATION - Extract seed from partially open cones, sow on soil surface, cover with cut pine needles, and protect from animals. Transplant poorly unless they have a good root ball of soil.

LANDSCAPE USES - An excellent specimen for giving an illusion of depth to a planting and for providing a light shade for azaleas and other shade-loving plants.

COMMENTS - This species may be distinguished from all other pines by its very long needles and conspicuous white winter bud.

Pinus taeda   LOBLOLLY PINE

PRONUNCIATION - ˈpī nəs   ˈtē də

TRANSLATION - [Latin name] [resinous wood].

FORM - Monoecious, evergreen tree, coniferous, upright, with a dense, rounded crown; medium-textured.

SIZE - Can reach 120 feet tall, though normally in the 40 to 70 foot range. Spread is about 30 feet. Growth rate is fast.

HARDINESS ZONE - Zone 7. Adapted to all areas of Florida.

NATIVE HABITAT - Southeastern United States.

LEAVES - Needles in fascicles of 3's, to 8 inches long, somewhat soft and flexible, especially in comparison to *P. elliottii.*

STEM/BARK - The straight, 1 to 2.5-foot-wide trunks are covered with plates of reddish-brown bark.

FLOWERS - Yellow-green microstrobili to 1.75 inches long, ovulate cones 0.5 inch wide, pale green with purplish tips. Borne at the base of new growth in early spring; at maturity, brown, to 5 inches long, often in pairs, mature in the fall, 1.5 years after pollination. The cones persist on the tree after opening.

FRUIT - None. The winged seeds are 1 inch long.

CULTURE - Loblolly pine grows in full sun in almost any soil of reasonable fertility. It has no salt tolerance.

PROBLEMS - Pine bark beetles, borers, Fusiform Rust.

PROPAGATION - Extract seed from partially opened cones, place on soil surface, and cover with cut pine needles.

LANDSCAPE USES - Employed as a screen/windbreak, for giving a depth effect to a planting and for providing light shade for azaleas, camellias, and other shade-loving plants.

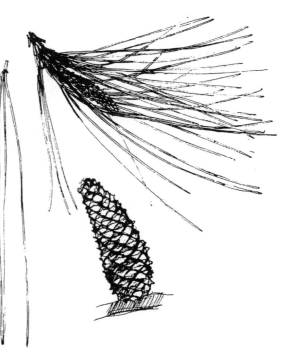

COMPARISON OF COMMON PINE CONES (LIFE-SIZE)

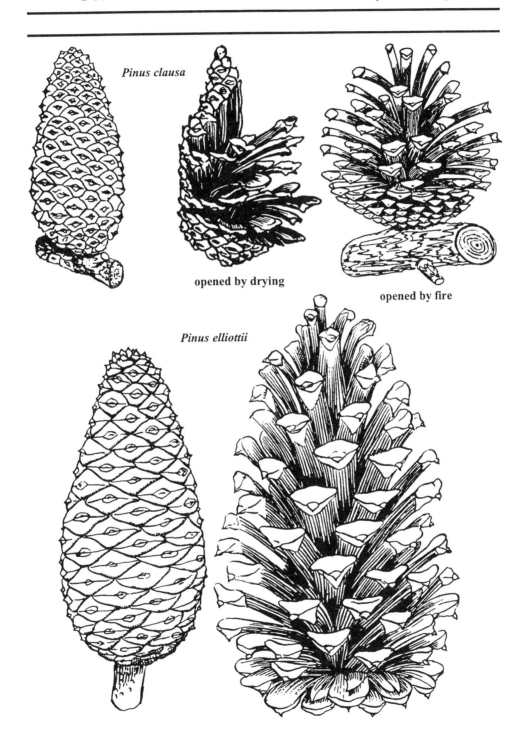

Pinus clausa

opened by drying

opened by fire

Pinus elliottii

COMPARISON OF COMMON PINE CONES (LIFE-SIZE)

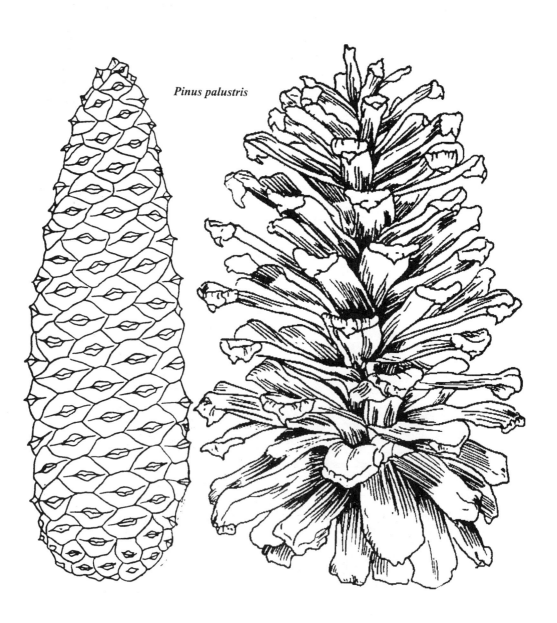

Pinus palustris

COMPARISON OF COMMON PINE CONES (LIFE-SIZE) AND PINE NEEDLES

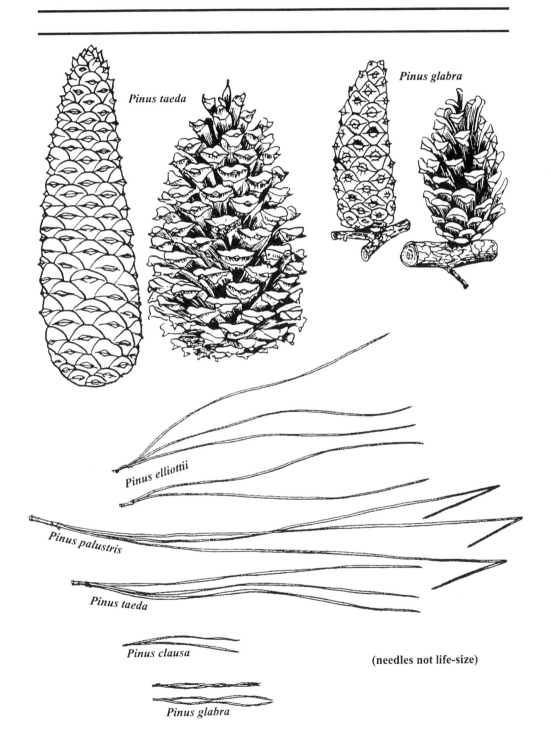

Pinus taeda

Pinus glabra

Pinus elliottii

Pinus palustris

Pinus taeda

Pinus clausa

(needles not life-size)

Pinus glabra

PODOCARPACEAE - PODOCARPUS FAMILY

GYMNOSPERMS; CONIFEROUS; 6 GENERA AND ABOUT 125 SPECIES

GEOGRAPHY: Tropical and subtropical regions, mostly in Southern Hemisphere, especially the mountains, extending north to Japan, Central America, and West Indies.

GROWTH HABIT: Coniferous evergreen trees and shrubs; sometimes with leaf-like short shoots (phylloclades).

LEAVES: Spirally arranged, decussate, scale- or needle-shaped or lanceolate to ovate.

FLOWERS: Monoecious or dioecious plants; microsporophylls (male cones), numerous, pendulous, on terminal or axillary branches; megasporangia with spiral, decussate, or whorled scales, each with one ovule, or expanded to an aril-like structure (epimatium) in which the single ovule is coated or enveloped.

FRUIT: None; seeds often subtended by a fleshy aril-like microstrobilus.

ECONOMIC USES: Ornamentals, important source of softwood timber.

ORNAMENTAL GENERA: *Dacrydium, Podocarpus.*

COMMENTS: There is some disagreement as to the generic limits of this family. Some authorities recognize up to 12 genera. Several *Podocarpus* species have been relegated to other genera (e.g., *Afrocarpus gracilior, Nageia nagi).*

Podocarpus gracilior

WEEPING OR FERN PODOCARPUS

PRONUNCIATION - ˌpō dǝ 'kɑr pǝs   grǝ 'si lē or

TRANSLATION - [from Greek [*podos* (= a foot) and *carpos* (= a fruit), referring to the aril-like stalk of the seed] [more graceful].

FORM - Dioecious, coniferous evergreen tree, upright, densely foliated, pyramidal, graceful, weeping branches. Fine-textured.

SIZE - Can reach heights of 40 feet, though normally smaller. Its spread is about 15 feet wide and it grows at moderate rates.

HARDINESS ZONE - Zone 9, grown in south Florida, and protected areas of central Florida.

NATIVE HABITAT - East Africa.

LEAVES - Simple, alternate, linear, to 4 inches long and 0.25 inch wide, arranged in spirals around the stem. New growth is bright green, standing out against dark green, mature leaves.

FLOWERS - Yellowish male catkins to 1 inch long, solitary or in clusters; ovulate cones drupe-like, solitary, more or less fleshy.

FRUIT - None. Seed 0.75 inch long, glaucous-blue, subtended by a purple, fleshy aril.

CULTURE - Not particular as to its light or soil conditions, but grows slowly under full shade. It has no salt tolerance.

PROBLEMS - Pest-free.

PROPAGATION - Seeds, cuttings.

LANDSCAPE USES - Makes a very beautiful and graceful specimen or screen.

COMMENTS - Some recent publications recognize *P. gracilior* as *Afrocarpus gracilior*.

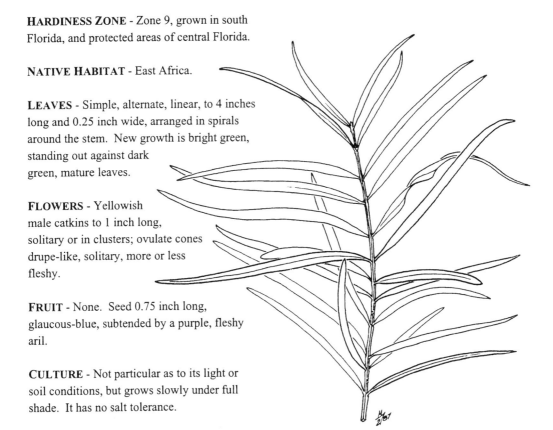

Podocarpus macrophyllus   PODOCARPUS

PRONUNCIATION - ˌpō də ˈkɑr pəs   ˌmæ krə ˈfi ləs

TRANSLATION - [from Greek [*podos* (= a foot) and *carpos* (= a fruit), referring to the aril-like stalk of the seed] [large-leaved].

FORM - Dioecious, evergreen, coniferous shrub or tree (depending on cultivar), upright, densely foliated, horizontal, branching, narrow columnar canopy. Medium-fine texture.

SIZE - To 45 feet, often maintained as a shrub 4 to 8 feet, slow growth rate.

HARDINESS ZONE - Zone 7. Grown throughout Florida.

NATIVE HABITAT - China.

LEAVES - Simple, spirally arranged, close on twigs, entire, linear to 4.5 inches long, glossy dark green above, lighter beneath, leathery, prominent midrib.

STEM/BARK - New growth green, woody with age, bark peeling.

FLOWERS - Male catkin-like cones, yellow, to 1.5 inches long, female scale-like, inconspicuous.

FRUIT - None. Seed drupe-like, green, ovoid to 0.5 inch long, on a fleshy purple, edible receptacle (aril).

CULTURE - Full sun to partial shade, various well-drained soils; poor salt tolerance.

PROBLEMS - Scale, sooty mold, mites, root rot; none serious.

PROPAGATION - Seeds, cuttings.

LANDSCAPE USES - Hedge, screen, accent, framing tree.

COMMENTS - Many cultivars for habit, leaf form, color, etc. **'Angustifolius'** (with narrow leaves), **'Crusty Drybread', 'Dwarf Pringles', 'Maki'** are commonly sold. A related species, *P. neriifolius*, with much longer leaves, is available for warmer areas.

Podocarpus nagi   NAGI PODOCARPUS

PRONUNCIATION - ˌpō də ˈkar pəs   ˈnæ gī

TRANSLATION - [from Greek [*podos* (= a foot) and *carpos* (= a fruit), referring to the aril-like stalk of the seed] [native Japanese name].

FORM - Dioecious, coniferous, evergreen tree, upright, heavily foliated, symmetrical, narrow columnar canopy. Medium texture.

SIZE - To 90 feet, commonly seen 20 to 30 feet, medium growth rate.

HARDINESS ZONE - Zone 7. Grown throughout Florida.

NATIVE HABITAT - Japan, Ryukyu Islands.

LEAVES - Simple, subopposite, entire, elliptic-ovate to 3 inches long, dark green, often glaucous, lighter beneath, many parallel veins, stiff, leathery, petiole short.

STEM/BARK - Young growth green, woody with age.

FLOWERS - Male cones catkin-like, female scale-like, inconspicuous.

FRUIT - None. Drupe-like seed, green, ovoid to 1 inch long, on a very small green receptacle. A conspicuous aril is not present.

CULTURE - Full sun to partial shade, various well-drained soils; moderately salt tolerant.

PROBLEMS - Scale, sooty mold, root rot, micronutrient deficiencies in alkaline soils.

PROPAGATION - Seed, cuttings.

LANDSCAPE USES - Hedge, screen, framing tree, specimen.

COMMENTS - Some recent publications have recognized *P. nagi* as *Nageia nagi*, based on the absence of a leaf midrib and absence of an aril.

TAXACEAE - TAXUS (YEW) FAMILY

GYMNOSPERMS; CONIFEROUS; 5 GENERA AND ABOUT 20 SPECIES

GEOGRAPHY: Northern Hemisphere, especially eastern Asia, western China.

GROWTH HABIT: Coniferous, much-branched shrubs or small trees; without resin ducts.

LEAVES: Spiral, occasionally decussate; acicular or sometimes linear-lanceolate.

FLOWERS: Plants monoecious or dioecious; microsporophylls (pollen-bearing organs) solitary or in small spikes in leaf axils; megasporophylls (ovulate scales) solitary or (in *Taxus* and *Torreya*) 2 or rarely more at the end of the short shoots.

FRUIT: None; seeds enclosed within a fleshy aril.

ECONOMIC USES: Ornamentals, but also used for medicinal purposes.

ORNAMENTAL GENERA: *Taxus, Torreya*.

COMMENTS: Some recent publications have included *Torreya* in Cephalotaxaceae.

Taxus floridana   FLORIDA YEW

PRONUNCIATION - ˈtæk səs ˌflo rə ˈdā nə

TRANSLATION - [Latin name of the plant] [from Florida].

FORM - Dioecious, evergreen shrub or small tree, spreading, drooping, densely foliated, and fine-textured.

SIZE - Can reach a height of 25 feet, but normally much smaller. The spread is variable and growth rate is slow.

HARDINESS ZONE - Undetermined, native to Zone 8. Florida yew succeeds in north Florida, but has not been tested in other areas of the state.

NATIVE HABITAT - Shade, moist, wooded ravines and slopes in a limited area as the Apalachicola River valley in western Florida.

LEAVES - Simple, narrowly linear, to 1 inch long, held in a horizontal plane. The leaves are dark green above, light green below, soft to the touch and occasionally curve downward. The new growth is bright green, and sometimes pinkish, making an attractive contrast to the mature leaves. The leaves are poisonous.

STEM/BARK - The short trunks have purplish brown, platy bark. Twigs green.

FLOWERS - Inconspicuous. Male - globose microsporophyll heads; female - bracted ovules, in March.

FRUIT - None. Aril fleshy, red, cup-like, partially enclosing bony 0.25 inch seeds, ripening in fall.

CULTURE - Plant in a partially shaded site with fertile, slightly acid, well-drained soil. It has no salt tolerance.

PROBLEMS - Scales, mushroom root rot.

PROPAGATION - Seed, if available, may require first warm, then cold stratification. Mature wood cuttings taken in winter root well under mist.

LANDSCAPE USES - Useful as a topiary or specimen shrub, hedge, or foundation planting. Should be planted more often to keep this rare native plant from extinction.

Torreya taxifolia   FLORIDA TORREYA, STINKING YEW

PRONUNCIATION - ˈto rē ə   ˌtæk sə ˈfō lē ə

TRANSLATION - [after Dr. John Torrey (1796-1873), American botanist] [leaves like yew, *Taxus*].

FORM - Dioecious, evergreen tree, upright, pyramidal, with drooping branches; fine-textured.

SIZE - Can reach a height of 40 feet and a spread of 20 feet. Grows at a slow rate.

HARDINESS ZONE - Zone 8, will grow in north Florida but hasn't been tested in other areas of the state.

NATIVE HABITAT - Wooded slopes and ravines along the eastern bank of the Apalachicola River in western Florida.

LEAVES - Simple, alternate, linear-lanceolate, to 1.5 inches long, held in a horizontal plane. The leaves, with sharp, prickly tips, are glossy dark green above and lighter green with two longitudinal grayish stripes below. They give off a strong turpentine (or tomato plant) odor when crushed.

STEM/BARK - The twigs are stiff and green and occur in whorls; the bark is blackish, thin, and shredding.

FLOWERS - Inconspicuous micro- and megastroboli appear in March.

FRUIT - None. Fleshy, drupelike, obovoid to 1.5 inches long, have one large bony seed, ripen in late summer.

CULTURE - Prefers partial shade and a well-drained, fertile, slightly acid soil. No salt tolerance.

PROBLEMS - Scales, blight, possibly mushroom root rot.

PROPAGATION - Mature wood cuttings taken in winter root well. Seeds, if available, germinate slowly and sporadically, stratification may help.

LANDSCAPE USES - Using this rare native tree as a specimen or framing tree will help keep it from extinction.

COMMENTS - In some recent publications, *Torreya* has been placed in Cephalotaxaceae. The plant is in danger of extinction due to natural causes.

TAXODIACEAE - TAXODIUM FAMILY

GYMNOSPERMS; CONIFEROUS; 10 GENERA AND ABOUT 17 SPECIES

GEOGRAPHY: Southeastern North America, northern California, Mexico, eastern Asia, and Tasmania.

GROWTH HABIT: Coniferous, tall, mostly excurrent trees.

LEAVES: Evergreen or sometimes deciduous; awl-shaped (subulate), scale-like, or acicular, usually spirally arranged on short shoots.

FLOWERS: Plants monoecious; male cones solitary, in paniculate groups; female cones solitary, terminal, open when mature, scales spirally arranged or fused, each with 2 to 9 ovules.

FRUIT: None. More or less woody cones; seeds winged.

ECONOMIC USES: Ornamentals, important softwood timber trees.

ORNAMENTAL GENERA: *Cryptomeria, Cunninghamia, Metasequoia, Sequoia, Sequoiadendron, Taxodium*, and others.

COMMENTS: In some recent publications, genera listed here have been included in Cupressaceae. This, however, may be an error since morphological differences between the two families are significant.

Taxodium distichum   BALD CYPRESS

PRONUNCIATION - tæk ˈsō dē əm   ˈdis tə kəm

TRANSLATION - [from *Taxus* and Greek *eidos* (= resemblance), in reference to the leaves] [2-ranked, in reference to leaf arrangement].

FORM - Monoecious, large deciduous coniferous tree, spreading; foliage sparse, pyramidal when young, irregular with age, often contorted canopy. Fine texture.

SIZE - To 150 feet, moderate growth rate.

HARDINESS ZONE - Zone 4. Grown throughout Florida.

NATIVE HABITAT - Eastern United States west to Texas; Florida native.

LEAVES - Simple needle-like, linear, appressed, to 0.5 inch long. Plants also possess deciduous branchlets that are flat, linear, 2-ranked, spreading, to 0.75 inch long. Both are light to dark green in spring, coppery brown in fall.

STEM/BARK - Base of trunk often flared (buttressed), bark gray-brown, peeling; aerating projections (pneumatophores or knees), often growing up from roots in wet sites (they do not develop significantly on dry sites). Wood is durable and decay resistant.

FLOWERS - Male catkin-like cones, clustered, to 4 inches long on branchlet tips; female cones globose, many woody scales to 1 inch in diameter, usually on branches.

FRUIT - None. Female cones to 1 inch in diameter, seeds irregularly 3-angled, 2 to each cone scale, and narrowly winged.

CULTURE - Full sun to partial shade, various soils including wet, muck-type; not salt tolerant. Will tolerate drier sites with sufficient irrigation until establishment.

PROBLEMS - No serious pests.

PROPAGATION - Seed.

LANDSCAPE USES - Specimen, light shade, street plantings, parks, primarily for large areas.

COMMENTS - Many regional variations in the wild. The var. *nutans,* Pond Cypress, is now believed to be a distinct species, *T. ascendens,* and has smaller, awl-shaped leaves that are closely appressed to the pendulous stems. The Mexican *T. mucro-natum,* an evergreen species, is also seen occasionally.

ZAMIACEAE - ZAMIA FAMILY

GYMNOSPERMS; CYCADS; 7 GENERA AND ABOUT 140 SPECIES

GEOGRAPHY: Florida, Central and South America, Australia, and Africa.

GROWTH HABIT: Palm-like small trees or caudiciform shrubs, sometimes with subterranean branches and usually with nitrogen fixing (through symbiotic relationship with blue-green algae), apogeotropic, dichotomously branched roots.

LEAVES: Once-pinnately compound; leaflets with parallel, dichotomously branched veins; entire or variously serrate or spinose.

FLOWERS: Plants dioecious; both male and female cones with well-organized, spirally arranged sporophylls which may be distinct or imbricate; microsporophylls each with numerous pollen sacs; megasporophylls each predominantly with 2 ovules.

FRUIT: None. Drupe-like seeds predominantly orange or red but may be cream or yellowish.

ECONOMIC USES: Ornamentals; starch is extracted from the stems and seeds, which when detoxified may be made into bread.

ORNAMENTAL GENERA: *Ceratozamia, Dioon, Encephalartos, Lepidozamia, Macrozamia, Microcycas,* and *Zamia.*

COMMENTS: The genus *Bowenia* is currently placed in Boweniaceae because it has bipinnately compound leaves, among other features. The seven genera currently included in Zamiaceae will, in the future, be divided into three distinct families. *Dioon,* in particular, is dissimilar to other genera in many respects.

Dioon edule   CHAMAL, CHESTNUT DIOON, MEXICAN SAGO

PRONUNCIATION - dī 'ūn   'e dyū lē

TRANSLATION - [from Greek *dis* (= twice) and *oon* (= an egg), in reference to the paired seeds on the megasporophyll] [edible].

FORM - Dioecious, palm-like plant, evergreen, with extremely slow-growing trunks. Similar to palms, leaves are borne only at the top of each stem.

SIZE - Ranging from 1 to 10 feet. Trunks become visible only after many years from the seedling stage.

HARDINESS ZONE - Zone 8b. A subtropical and tropical plant limited to the warmer regions of the United States Provenance is important in establishing hardiness of individual plants; plants from southernmost populations in Mexico barely tolerate frost, but those from northern populations, such as those in Tamaulipas, can stand much more freezing weather.

NATIVE HABITAT - Eastern Mexico, from the state of Tamaulipas southward to Veracruz.

LEAVES - Pinnately compound, glaucous or glabrous, green, bluish or reddish-brown when emerging, bluish to bright green at maturity, with sharp-pointed but smooth-margined leaflets.

STEM/BARK - Extremely slow-growing, a large specimen with approximately 10 feet of trunk length dated to more than 2600 years old. Specimens seldom branch aboveground, but frequently produce multiple stems at ground level.

FLOWERS - Male cones are relatively slender and have sporophylls bearing pollen in many small sacs; female cones are larger in diameter,

possessing large spade-shaped tomentose sporophylls, each bearing two naked ovules. Cones are densely tomentose and are cream to light brown in color.

FRUIT - None. Seeds covered with a fleshy layer (sarcotesta) which is cream to yellow at maturity.

CULTURE - Plants must have excellent drainage but otherwise grow well in a variety of soils. Plants survive adverse nutritional, soil, and light conditions for long periods of time but require full sun.

PROBLEMS - Scale and mealybug, and occasionally thrips during leaf emergence.

PROPAGATION - Seed germinate readily after the fleshy sarcotesta is removed.

LANDSCAPE USES - Grows into a magnificent specimen plant where under proper growing conditions it could potentially require a large area. Plants should not be planted close to walkways or areas where children play because leaflets are dangerously sharp.

COMMENTS - Emerging leaves and seeds contain carcinogens and may be poisonous, so seeds should be handled carefully during attempts at propagation. Leaves are commonly used in religious holidays in Central America to adorn crosses, hence the religious common name "Palma de la Virgen." Several related species are also in cultivation but grow outdoors in south Florida. These include *D. mejiae, D. purpusii, D. spinulosum*, among others.

Zamia fischeri   FERNLEAF ZAMIA, HELECHO, AMIGO DEL MAIZ

PRONUNCIATION -ˈzā mē ə   ˈfi shər ī

TRANSLATION - [name derived from *zamiae*, a false rendering for azaniae, referring to pine cones] [after Fischer, a gardener at St. Petersburg Botanical Garden].

FORM - Dioecious, shrubby, evergreen plant with subterranean stems, only the apex of which remains at ground level.

SIZE - From 1 to 4 feet; mature size is achieved slowly and clumps also spread very slowly.

HARDINESS ZONE - Zones 10 to11; a tropical plant limited to protected locations in the colder part of its range. Outdoor plantings limited to south-central and south Florida.

NATIVE HABITAT - Eastern Mexico, including the states of San Luis Potosi, Veracruz, and Hidalgo. Frequently, it is found growing in cornfields, hence the common name "amigo del maiz."

LEAVES - Pinnately compound, glabrous, with fernlike toothed leaflets, hence the common name "helecho" (Spanish for "fern").

STEM/BARK - Subterranean stems are contractile, continuously pulled into the ground, and infrequently branch dichotomously.

FLOWERS - Male cones are relatively slender and have sporophylls bearing pollen in many small sacs; female cones are larger in diameter, possessing larger megasporophylls, each bearing two ovules. Cones are densely tomentose and range from light to dark brown in color.

female

male

FRUIT - None. Seeds are covered with a fleshy layer which is scarlet at maturity. Cones ripen in the fall and release the seeds, which are attractive to birds.

CULTURE - Plants require good drainage but otherwise grow well in a variety of soils. Plants are adept survivors under tremendous adversity in nutritional, soil, and light conditions. Densely foliated in bright sun, progressively less under shadier conditions.

PROBLEMS - Insect infestations, notably scale and mealybug.

PROPAGATION - Seed germinate relatively quickly after the fleshy sarcotesta is removed. Division of large plants is risky but may be successful if the cuts are treated with fungicide and plants watered carefully to avoid rot.

LANDSCAPE USES - The fernlike foliage is attractive in foundation plantings, and individual plants are good specimen plants when in decorative containers.

COMMENTS - The fleshy seed layer contains carcinogenic agents so they should be handled carefully during attempts at propagation. Avoid planting in areas where livestock could graze because they often eat emerging foliage which can cause nerve disorders. This species is unique in its general appearance. See representative species listed with **Z. floridana.**

Zamia floridana

COONTIE, FLORIDA ARROWROOT,
SEMINOLE BREAD

PRONUNCIATION - 'zā mē ə   ˌflo rə 'dā nə

TRANSLATION - [name derived from *zamiae*, a false rendering for *azaniae*, referring to pine cones] [from Florida].

SYNONYMS - *Zamia pumila; Z. integrifolia; Z. silvicola.*

FORM - Dioecious, shrubby plant, evergreen, with subterranean stems, only the leaf-bearing tip exposed; densely foliated and, depending on the individual, may have arching to fully erect leaves.

SIZE - Overall height ranges from 1 to 3 feet; growth rate is variable, clumps spread slowly.

HARDINESS ZONE - Zone 8. Grows throughout Florida.

NATIVE HABITAT - East and west coast of Florida in pine and oak woodlands and hammocks, as far north as southern St. Johns County.

LEAVES - Pinnately compound, deep green, glossy, leathery leaflets. Leaflets are highly variable, ranging from (3 to 5 feet) in length, 0.15 to 0.5 inch in width. They may be variously twisted or in one plane, have parallel venation and possess a small amount of serration near the apex.

STEM/BARK - Subterranean, contractile; as the stems grow, they are continuously pulled into the ground; branching dichotomous.

FLOWERS - Male cones in which pollen is produced; in the female cones, each sporophyll possesses two naked ovules. Sporophylls of both sexes are shield-shaped and peltate. The cone stalk and sporophylls are heavily tomentose and are rusty to dark brown.

FRUIT - Naked seeds borne in female cones have a thick scarlet to orange fleshy seed coat; these ripen in fall-winter, at which time they fall apart, revealing the colored seeds.

CULTURE - No special requirements other than good drainage; variety of soils and light conditions. Perform best in partial shade.

PROBLEMS - Scales, mealybugs.

PROPAGATION - Seeds may be planted after the fleshy layer is removed and the stony layer scarified. Stems, often referred to as "tubers" or "bulbs," may be divided.

LANDSCAPE USES - Foundation or hedge planting or in mass as a subject in small gardens.

COMMENTS - Since this is such a variable species, selection may be made among the various forms that can be found in the trade: wider or narrower leaflets, arching to erect leaves, and leaflets that are twisted vs. those that lie in a single plane. Similar species include *Z. debilis, Z. portoricensis, Z. pumila* (restricted to the Dominican Republic), *Z. lucayana* (Bahamas), and the dwarf species *Z. pygmaea* (Cuba). *Zamia floridana* is often sold as *Z. pumila*. The true *Z. pumila* is endemic to the Dominican Republic and is commonly available in southern Florida.

Zamia furfuracea

CARDBOARD PLANT

PRONUNCIATION - ' zā mē ə   ˌfər fə ' rā sē ə

TRANSLATION - [name derived from *zamiae*, a false rendering for *azaniae*, referring to pine cones] [mealy, scurfy].

FORM - Large, dioecious, evergreen shrubby plant, with subterranean stems, only the upper portion that bears the leaves exposed;densely foliated.

SIZE - From 2 to 4 feet; achieves mature size in a few years in landscape plantings; clumps spread slowly.

HARDINESS ZONE - Zones 10-11, a tropical plant limited in outdoor plantings to southern regions of Florida, Texas, and California; an excellent houseplant elsewhere.

NATIVE HABITAT - East coast of Mexico in the state of Veracruz on sand dunes.

LEAVES - Pinnately compound, entirely glabrous to densely pubescent, extremely tough and leathery leaflets, hence the common name. A variable species, leaflets range from almost round to long linear, 2 to 6 inches in length, 0.5 to 3 inches wide. Serration may be present in the upper half of the leaf or

concentrated near the apex. Leaves may emerge green or deep bronze, eventually turning green.

STEM/BARK - Subterranean contractile stems are continuously pulled into the ground; dichotomously branching.

FLOWERS - Male cones are relatively narrow and have sporophylls bearing pollen; female cones are larger in diameter and possess larger sporophylls, each bearing two naked ovules. Cones are rusty brown to silvery gray tomentose.

FRUIT - None. Seeds have a scarlet, thick, fleshy outer seed coat at maturity, underneath which lies a stony inner seed coat; cones ripen in fall, releasing the colored seeds, which are attractive to birds.

CULTURE - Requires good drainage; otherwise, a variety of soils. Full sun is preferable to shadier conditions for best appearance. As a houseplant, the sunniest location available is preferred.

PROBLEMS - Scale and mealybug.

PROPAGATION - The fleshy seed coat should be removed, at which time the seeds can be scarified and planted. Seeds often germinate readily where they fall by the mother plant.

LANDSCAPE USES - Excellent specimen plant or foundation plant for larger buildings.

COMMENTS - Hybrids with other Mexican species, notably *Z. loddigesii,* are common in the trade, so individual plants should be hand-picked to accomplish the desired effect in one's landscape. This species is also visually unique in many respects, and few other similar taxa may be found.

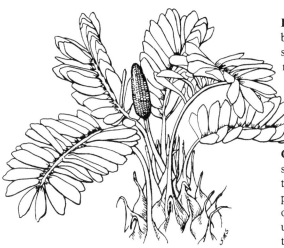

Angiosperms-Monocotyledons

AGAVACEAE - AGAVE FAMILY

MONOCOTYLEDONS; 20 GENERA; 700 SPECIES

GEOGRAPHY: Arid and semi-arid tropical and subtropical regions.

GROWTH HABIT: Most are robust woody rosette plants, a few are trees, sometimes
                  climbing; often rhizomatous.

LEAVES: Narrow, sharp, stiff, fleshy, and usually crowded at the end of the
                  stems.

FLOWERS: Usually bisexual, sometimes unisexual (monoecious or dioecious),
                  regular or slightly irregular; tepals united and tubular; stamens 6;
                  ovary of 3 fused carpels, superior or inferior.

FRUIT: A trilocular capsule or berry, with one or numerous seeds.

ECONOMIC USES: Economically important source of fibers; fermented sap of *Agave
                  americana* is the source of pulque (a national drink of Mexico),
                  which is consumed either fresh or distilled to make mescal.

ORNAMENTAL GENERA: *Agave, Cordyline, Dracaena, Furcraea, Nolina, Phormium,
                  Sansevieria, Yucca,* etc.

Agave americana

CENTURY PLANT

PRONUNCIATION - ə ˈgɑ vē   ə ˌme rə ˈkā nə

TRANSLATION - [noble, in reference to the tall inflorescence of *A. americana*] [from America].

FORM - Xerophytic evergreen rosulate shrub of coarse texture.

SIZE - To 8 feet tall with a 12 foot spread; fairly slow growth rate.

HARDINESS ZONE - Zone 9. Can be grown in all regions of Florida.

NATIVE HABITAT - Arid regions of Mexico.

LEAVES - In basal rosettes; sword-shaped, to 6 feet long and 10 inches wide; leaves are blue-green, thick, stiff, and fibrous with a sharp terminal black spine; held straight or recurved; often have sharp marginal teeth.

STEM/BARK - Acaulescent.

FLOWERS - Pale greenish-yellow, 3.5 inches long; in horizontal panicles borne on a stout terminal flower stalk up to 20 feet tall. This is a monocarpic plant, dying after the seed matures. The common name comes from the plant seeming to take 100 years to bloom in Mexico. Blooms and dies in 6 to 10 years in Florida, but new plants often arise from the base.

FRUIT - Capsules. Seeds are viviparous, germinating while still on the flower stalk, and grow into small plantlets that drop to the ground and root.

CULTURE - Plant in full sun on a wide range of well-drained soils; tolerates salt and poor sandy soil; extremely drought tolerant.

PROBLEMS - None of major importance. Sharp spines can be hazardous.

PROPAGATION - Seed or aerial plantlets and lateral offshoots.

LANDSCAPE USES - Distinctive, almost artificial-looking specimen. Requires plenty of room for wide spread. Keep out of areas where people frequent.

COMMENTS - 'Marginata' has yellow-white marginal stripes, **'Gainesville Blue'** has bright blue foliage. Others include **'Medio Picta'** and **'Variegata'**.

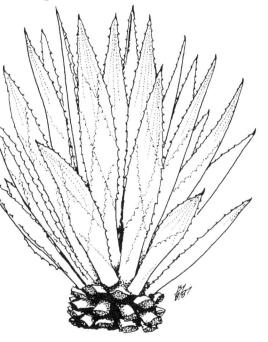

Agave angustifolia   CENTURY PLANT

PRONUNCIATION - ə ˈgɑ vē æŋ ˌgus tə ˈfō lē ə

TRANSLATION - [noble, in reference to the tall inflorescence of *A. americana*] [narrow leaves].

FORM - Xerophytic evergreen rosulate shrub; round or globose; medium texture.

SIZE - Rarely exceeds 5 feet in height or 6 feet in spread; fairly slow growth rate.

HARDINESS ZONE - Zone 9b. Can be grown in central and south Florida.

NATIVE HABITAT - Of unknown origin; widespread in tropical climates.

LEAVES - In basal rosettes; swordlike, to 3 feet long and 4 inches wide; gray-green, thick and stiff; leaves terminate in a sharp, conical, prominent black spine; the margins have black teeth every 0.75 inch.

STEM/BARK - Either acaulescent or forming a very short stem.

FLOWERS - Greenish, 2 inches long; in panicles on a stout, terminal, 9-foot-tall flower stalk. This plant is monocarpic, and the seeds are viviparous.

FRUIT - Dry dehiscent capsules.

CULTURE - Requires full or partial sun and well-drained soil; tolerates salt and poor sandy soils.

PROBLEMS - Generally pest-free; sharp terminal leaf spine can be hazardous.

PROPAGATION - By aerial plantlets, seeds, or basal sucker division if suckers are present.

LANDSCAPE USES - Same as *A. americana*, but this plant is more rigid and is only one-half to one-third as large.

COMMENTS - '**Marginata**' has a bold white stripe along the leaf margins. Several *Agave* species are listed by Florida nurseries: *A. attenuata* (Spineless Century Plant), *A. decipiens, A. desmettiana* (Dwarf Century Plant), *A. desmettiana* '**Variegata**', *A. deserti, A. fernandi-regis, A. filifera, A. huachucensis, A. miradorensis* (= *A. desmettiana*), *A. parryi, A. sisalana* (sisal, sisal hemp), *A. stricta,* and *A. victoriae-reginae* (a relatively small, compact, choice species).

Cordyline terminalis Tɪ Pʟᴀɴᴛ

PRONUNCIATION - ˈkor də lin ˌtər mə ˈnæ ləs

TRANSLATION - [from Greek *kordyle* (= a club), referring to the large, fleshy root of some species] [terminal, in reference to the terminal inflorescence].

FORM - Evergreen shrub with an unbranched or occasionally branched, slender, upright stem; medium texture.

SIZE - To 10 feet tall and 4 feet wide when grown outdoors.

HARDINESS ZONE - Zone 10, outdoor use restricted to south Florida.

NATIVE HABITAT - Eastern Asia and Australia.

LEAVES - Simple, clustered in close spirals at the ends of branches; narrow-oblong to 2.5 feet long and 5 inches wide; smooth, flexible, ranging in color from variegated light greens and pinks to reds to nearly black. Petioles deeply channeled, 2 to 6 inches long, clasping the stem.

STEM/BARK - Stem slender, ringed with leaf scars.

FLOWERS - Yellowish, white, or reddish, inconspicuous; 0.33 inch long; borne in 12-inch-long panicles; blooms in spring in Florida.

FRUIT - Berry; color changes from yellow to red; 0.25 inch wide; rarely produced in cultivation.

CULTURE - Grows well in partial to dense shade; well-drained soils; no salt tolerance. Best foliage color occurs in shade; discoloration results with exposure to full sun.

PROBLEMS - Mealybugs, mites, nematodes, leaf spot. Sensitive to fluoride damage, appearing as marginal necrosis.

PROPAGATION - Tip and cane cuttings, occasionally seed.

LANDSCAPE USES - Outdoors as a color accent for shaded areas; indoors in tubs or planters as a specimen plant.

COMMENTS - Many cultivars with foliage color variations available; commonly used as indoor foliage plant. Available *Cordyline* cultivars include **'Baby Doll', 'Black Magic', 'Black Prince', 'Bolero', 'Compacta', 'Fairchild Garden', 'Firebrand', 'Kilimanjaro', 'Kiwi', 'Mme. Eugene Andre', 'Nagi', 'Peter Buck', 'Red', 'Red Sister', 'Tricolor',** and **'Turkeytail'.**

Dracaena deremensis

PRONUNCIATION - drə ˈsē nə ˌde rə ˈmen səs

TRANSLATION - [from Greek *drakaina* (= a dragon), or it may have been named after Sir Francis Drake] [from Derma, Tanzania].

FORM - Evergreen shrub with an erect, single, unbranched stem; columnar form; medium texture.

SIZE - To 15 feet tall with a 4 foot spread.

HARDINESS ZONE - Zone 10. Outdoor use restricted to south Florida.

NATIVE HABITAT - Tropical Africa.

LEAVES - Simple, spirally arranged; linear to 2 feet long and 3 inches wide; sessile; leaf color ranges from green to gray-green with various white stripe patterns available.

STEM/BARK - Mature stems may become rigid, thick, and ringed with leaf scars. Leaves tend to persist longer than in *Cordyline terminalis*.

FLOWERS - Reddish adaxially (exterior), white abaxially (interior); 0.5 inch in diameter; borne in 1-foot-long panicles; rarely produced.

FRUIT - Berry; red.

CULTURE - Partial to dense shade; no direct afternoon sun; grows in wide variety of soils but prefers a well-aerated soil containing organic matter; drought tolerant; roots tolerate some salinity, but foliage has no salt tolerance.

PROBLEMS - Mites, thrips, chewing insects, leaf spot. Sensitive to fluoride damage.

PROPAGATION - Tip cuttings.

LANDSCAPE USES - Outside it can be used as a specimen in shaded areas. Makes a good, low-maintenance specimen for interiorscapes.

COMMENTS - There are two common cultivars of *Dracaena deremensis*. 'Janet Craig' has strap-like, dark green leaves with a prominent midrib; 'Warneckii' (Striped Dracaena) has linear leaves with two white stripes. Other cultivars include 'Bauei', 'Golden King', 'Green Stripe', 'Janet Craig Compacta', 'Lemon and Lime', and 'Warneckii Compacta'.

Dracaena fragrans

CORN PLANT

PRONUNCIATION - drə ˈsē nə ˈfrā grənz

TRANSLATION - [from Greek *drakaina* (= a dragon), or it may have been named after Sir Francis Drake] [fragrant].

FORM - Evergreen large shrub to small tree, with an unbranched stem; columnar form; medium-coarse texture.

SIZE - To 25 feet tall with a 15 foot spread.

HARDINESS ZONE - Zones 10-11. Outdoor use restricted to south Florida.

NATIVE HABITAT - Tropical Africa.

LEAVES - Simple, whorled in terminal clusters; linear to 3 feet long, 4 inches wide; sessile; dark, emerald green with a wide yellow-green center stripe; sun brings out center stripe; prominent midrib on the lower surface light green or yellowish.

STEM/BARK - Light brown stem ringed with leaf scars.

FLOWERS - Yellowish, extremely fragrant, nocturnal flowers; borne in terminal panicles to 1.5 feet long; not common.

FRUIT - Berry.

CULTURE - Grows best in partial to dense shade; leaf tips and margins will scorch in full sun. Excellent for low-light interiors; will tolerate light intensities as low as 25 to 35 foot-candles. Tolerates a wide variety of soils but prefers an organic soil. The foliage is not salt tolerant, but the roots will tolerate some salinity.

PROBLEMS - Mites, chewing insects, leaf spot, and fluoride toxicity.

PROPAGATION - Tip and cane cuttings.

LANDSCAPE USES - Outdoors as an accent plant because of its colorful foliage. An excellent interior specimen because of its durability.

COMMENTS - The common name derives from the yellow variegated, corn-like, arching leaves and trunk of the species cultivar 'Massangeana'. Other available cultivars include 'Lindenii' and 'Victoriae'. *Dracaena × masseffana* is *D. fragrans* 'Massangeana' × *D. surculosa.*

Dracaena marginata   DRACAENA

PRONUNCIATION - drə 'sē nə   ˌmar jə nā tə

TRANSLATION - [from Greek *drakaina* (= a dragon), or it may have been named after Sir Francis Drake] [margined, in reference to leaves].

FORM - Monoecious, evergreen shrub with multiple, irregular stems; upright, spreading form; fine texture.

SIZE - Up to 12 feet tall with a variable spread; frequently planted in clumps with about a 6 foot spread; moderate growth rate.

HARDINESS ZONE - Zone 10. Outdoor use restricted to south Florida.

NATIVE HABITAT - Madagascar.

LEAVES - Crowded into tufts at ends of branches; sessile, sword or strap-like leaves to 18 inches long; margins entire; leaves leathery, with a brownish-purple stripe along the margins.

STEM/BARK - Multiple stems are spindly and irregular; covered with distinctive scars where lower leaves have fallen.

FLOWERS - Bisexual, inconspicuous; in elongate panicles above the leaves.

FRUIT - Insignificant small berries.

CULTURE - Grows well in light conditions ranging from full sun to dense shade; needs a fertile, well-drained organic soil; no salt tolerance.

PROBLEMS - Spider mites when grown as an interior plant; leaf spot in outdoor locations; fluoride toxicity.

PROPAGATION - Normally grown from 2 to 4 inch long leafless stem sections laid horizontally on a well-drained medium. Stem tip cuttings and air layers are also commonly used.

LANDSCAPE USES - Commonly used as an elegant indoor or patio plant in tubs or planters to give a tropical effect. It also has been employed as a foundation planting and as an accent/specimen shrub, especially for a framing effect, usually near doorways.

COMMENTS - **'Tricolor'** has distinctly red margins, 2 white stripes, and a green center strip. Also available are **'Colorama'**, a truly colorful cultivar, **'Magenta'**, **'Braided'**, and probably others. Several other *Dracaena* species are available in Florida, including *D. americana*, *D. arborea* (True Dracaena), *D. cincta*, *D. concinna*, *D. draco* (Dragon Tree), *D. goldieana*, *D. hookeriana*, *D. reflexa* and its cultivars **'Angustifolia'**, **'Angustifolia Honoriae'**, **'Green Stripe'**, **'Song of India'**, and **'Song of Jamaica'**, *D. sanderana* and its cultivars **'Borinquensis'** and **'Celes'**, *D. surculosa* and its cultivar **'Florida Beauty'**, *D. thalioides*, and *D. umbraculifera*.

Nolina recurvata

PRONUNCIATION - nō ˈlī nə ˌrē kər ˈvā tə

TRANSLATION - [from *nola* (a small bell), in reference to shape of corolla] [curved backward or downward].

SYNONYM - *Beaucarnea recurvata.*

FORM - Evergreen tree; round, irregular; single-stemmed in youth, branching on older specimens; fine texture.

SIZE - Can reach 30 feet in height with a variable spread (6 to 15 feet) in old specimens; most plants don't exceed 10 feet in height; slow growth rate.

HARDINESS ZONE - Zone 10. Can be grown in south Florida and in protected locations in central Florida.

NATIVE HABITAT - Dry regions of Mexico.

LEAVES - Linear and recurved, sessile; up to 5 feet long, 0.75 inch wide at the base and tapering gradually to the long thin apex; margins have minute teeth, giving them a rough, bumpy feel; leaves are clustered at the tips of the branches, resembling a pony's tail.

STEM/BARK - Trunk woody, light brown; tapering from a large caudex to the leafy portions; remains unbranched until the plant becomes fairly old.

FLOWERS - White, small, in large erect panicles held above the leaves.

FRUIT - Small, long-pedicelled 3-winged capsules; rarely produced in cultivation.

CULTURE - Grown in full sun or partial shade on a wide range of well-drained soils; marginal salt tolerance. May be forced to branch by removal of top or chemically.

PROBLEMS - Chewing insects can disfigure the leaves; tends to develop root rot on poorly drained soils; micronutrient deficiences common.

PROPAGATION - By seed, which usually must be imported from its natural habitat in Mexico.

LANDSCAPE USES - A distinctive specimen for the unusual trunk and the arching, drooping leaves; mainly grown in containers on patios, decks, and in rock gardens; occasionally used as a lawn specimen; interiorscape plant under high light intensities.

Sansevieria trifasciata   SNAKE PLANT

PRONUNCIATION -   ˌsæn sə ˈvē rē ə   trī ˌfæ sē ˈā tə

TRANSLATION - [after Raimond de Sangro, prince of Sanseviero, eighteenth-century Italian patron of horticulture].

FORM - Monoecious, evergreen, herbaceous, perennial subshrub; upright, spreading; acaulescent, with stiff, erect leaves arising from a short, thick rhizome; medium texture.

SIZE - To 5 feet tall, spreads by means of an underground rhizome.

HARDINESS ZONE - Zone 10. South Florida only.

NATIVE HABITAT - Tropical Africa.

LEAVES - Simple, basal, erect; linear-lanceolate, to 5 feet long and 2.75 inches wide; conspicuously cross-banded with light and dark green; fibrous, flat, stiff, and fairly thick.

STEM/BARK - Acaulescent.

FLOWERS - Bisexual, greenish-white, tubular, and fragrant; to 0.5 inch long; borne in a racemose inflorescence to 2.5 feet tall.

FRUIT - Red berry.

CULTURE - Grows in light conditions ranging from full sun to dense shade; indoors will tolerate light intensities as low as 40 foot-candles; grows on a wide range of well-drained soils; very drought tolerant; moderate salt tolerance.

PROBLEMS - Mites, thrips, and chewing insects occasionally cause problems. Generally this plant has few insect or disease problems. Avoid overwatering as this induces root rot.

PROPAGATION - Division or leaf segment cuttings.

LANDSCAPE USES - Upright forms can be used as a vertical accent, while rosette forms make a good ground cover for very shady or dry areas in the landscape. Because of its tolerance to low light levels, *S. trifasciata* makes an excellent interior specimen.

COMMENTS - There are two commonly available cultivars of *Sansevieria trifasciata*. 'Hahnii' (Bird's Nest Sansevieria) is a dwarf cultivar to 8 inches tall; the short leaves form a funnel-shaped rosette. 'Laurentii' resembles the species except leaves bear golden yellow marginal stripes. *Sansevieria zeylanica* (Ceylanese Bowstring Hemp) and other species are offered.

Yucca aloifolia

SPANISH BAYONET

PRONUNCIATION - ˈyu kə ə ˌlō ə ˈfō lē ə

TRANSLATION - [Caribbean name for cassava] [aloe-like leaves].

FORM - Monoecious, evergreen shrub; upright, round; coarse texture.

SIZE - Can reach a height of 15 feet with the spread depending on the degree of clumping; fairly rapid growth rate.

HARDINESS ZONE - Zone 6. Can be grown in all areas of Florida.

NATIVE HABITAT - Coastal and dry areas of the southern United States and tropical America.

LEAVES - Spirally arranged, dagger-like, to 30 inches long and 2.5 inches wide, narrowing to a very sharp, terminal, conical, brown spine; leaf margins are denticulate.

STEM/BARK - Trunks about 4 inches wide; usually covered with a shag of brown dead leaves; frequently bend outward or arch with age; rarely branch, instead suckering from the base to form clumps.

FLOWERS - Bisexual, creamy-white, pendant, and bell-shaped; 1 inch long, in large showy panicles held above the leaves. Blooms May through November.

FRUIT - Capsules, turning black at maturity; oblong, 2 inches long.

CULTURE - Plant in full sun or partial shade on well-drained soils; tolerates salt and hot dry locations.

PROBLEMS - Scale and leaf spot can be a problem in areas with poor air circulation. Larvae of the yucca moth may bore through, weaken, and damage the terminal shoots.

PROPAGATION - Usually by sucker division; less commonly by seeds or large stem tip cuttings.

LANDSCAPE USES - A durable, maintenance-free plant for coastal areas and parking lots; sometimes seen as a foundation plant or rock garden specimen. Wicked leaf spines preclude use in areas with pedestrian traffic.

Yucca elephantipes   SPINELESS YUCCA

PRONUNCIATION - 'yu kə ‚e lə fən 'tī pēz

TRANSLATION - [Caribbean name for cassava] [like an elephant's foot].

FORM - Monoecious, evergreen tree; round, columnar, ascending, irregular; coarse texture.

SIZE - Can reach a height of 30 feet with a 15 foot spread, depending on degree of clumping; usually stays under 20 feet in height; fairly rapid growth rate.

HARDINESS ZONE - Zone 9b. Can be grown in south and central Florida.

NATIVE HABITAT - Mexico.

LEAVES - Simple, spirally arranged; shiny, strap-like, to 4 feet long and 3 feet wide; margins rough to the touch; leaves lack a sharp terminal spine.

STEM/BARK - Single, thick, rough trunk with a swollen base and usually a few short branches; there are multi-trunked specimens.

FLOWERS - Bisexual, creamy-white, bell-shaped and pendant; in upright, large, showy panicles held above the leaves; waxy petals are edible. Blooms May through November.

FRUIT - Capsule; black, oblong, pulpy.

CULTURE - Grows from full sun to dense shade on a wide range of well-drained soils; moderate salt tolerance.

PROBLEMS - Yucca moth borers and scale.

PROPAGATION - Seed; cuttings of any size.

LANDSCAPE USES - The tallest of yuccas, it is used as a framing plant for large buildings, in indoor malls and planters, and as a specimen, especially with other succulents. Lack of spines allows its use where people frequent. **'Variegata'**, a variegated cultivar, is offered.

Yucca gloriosa   Mound-lily Yucca, Spanish Dagger

PRONUNCIATION - ˈyu kə ˌglo rē ˈō sə

TRANSLATION - [Caribbean name of cassava] [glorious].

FORM - Monoecious, evergreen shrub; upright, round; coarse texture.

SIZE - Up to 8 feet tall with a 6 foot spread; fairly rapid growth rate.

HARDINESS ZONE - Zone 8. Can be grown throughout Florida.

NATIVE HABITAT - Coastal plain region of the southeastern United States.

LEAVES - Alternate, in spirals around the stem; sword-shaped, to 2.5 inches long; blue-gray with scabrous, brown margins and a stiff, sharp terminal spine.

STEM/BARK - Usually has multiple, thick, soft, green stems forming a clump; trunk, if present, is usually very short; suckers from the bases of stems or trunk.

FLOWERS - Bisexual, white with reddish tinges; 4 inches wide, in large, showy panicles held 2 to 4 feet above the leaves; fragrant; blooms in summer.

FRUIT - Capsules; black, 6-ribbed, many seeded, 3 inches long; ripen in late fall.

CULTURE - Requires full sun and well-drained soil; prefers hot, dry locations; marginal salt tolerance. Old flower stalks should be removed.

PROBLEMS - Scales in poorly ventilated areas.

PROPAGATION - Seed; division of suckers.

LANDSCAPE USES - A durable, maintenance-free plant, very good for parking lots and other hot, dry areas. Clumps less than other species of yucca and can be used in more confined areas. Terminal spines are not generally a safety problem for people.

COMMENTS - Spines are sharper when plants are young. Several other species of *Yucca* are available in Florida: *Y. baccata* (Spanish Bayonet), *Y. brevifolia* (Joshua Tree), *Y. carnerosana* (Spanish Dagger), *Y. filamentosa* ‘Bright Edge’, and ‘Variegata’, *Y. rigida, Y. rostrata*, and *Y. thompsoniana.*

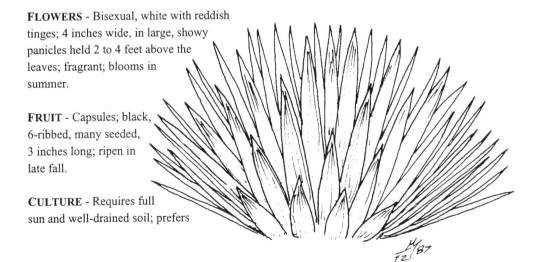

ALLIACEAE - ONION FAMILY

MONOCOTYLEDONS; 30 GENERA AND ABOUT 700 SPECIES

GEOGRAPHY: Cosmopolitan, except Australia.

GROWTH HABIT: Bulbous or rhizomatoous herbs.

LEAVES: Basal, linear, usually spirally arranged but may be 2-ranked.

FLOWERS: Bisexual, actinomorphic, or occasionally zygomorphic, with
                      perianth of 6 tepals in two whorls. This family is intermediate
                      between Amaryllidaceae and Liliaceae, having scapose, umbellate
                      inflorescences which are subtended by spathacious, membranous,
                      more or less imbricate bracts of the Amaryllidaceae and superior
                      ovary of the Liliaceae.

FRUIT: A trilocular fleshy capsule with numerous seeds.

ECONOMIC USES: Economically important vegetable crops, including *Allium* (onion,
                      garlic, etc.), as well as several ornamentals.

ORNAMENTAL GENERA: *Agapanthus, Allium, Tulbaghia*, etc.

COMMENTS: Species of this family have been variously included in
                      Amaryllidaceae or Liliaceae.

Agapanthus praecox ssp. *orientalis* AGAPANTHUS, LILY OF THE NILE

PRONUNCIATION - ˌæ gə ˈpæn thəs   ˌo rē ən ˈtæ ləs

TRANSLATION - [from Greek *agape* (= love) and *anthos* (= flower)] [eastern].

SYNONYM - *Agapanthus orientalis.*

FORM - Monoecious, evergreen, clumping, acaulescent perennial herb with thick fleshy rhizomes, low growing, lacking aerial stem.

SIZE - Variable with cultivar, generally 2 feet or more, rapid growing.

HARDINESS ZONE - Zone 8. Can be grown in all areas of Florida. Foliage is damaged by frost but plants will recover.

NATIVE HABITAT - South Africa.

LEAVES - Simple, basal, often 2-ranked, arching, straplike, leathery, linear-lanceolate to 2 feet long, 2 inches wide, entire margins, rounded apices, usually about 10 leaves per plant forming a mound-shaped clump.

STEM/BARK - Acaulescent, forms clumps by thick, fleshy, light brown to yellow rhizomes.

FLOWERS - Bisexual, blue, violet, white, some multicolored, corolla tubular to campanulate, 1.5 inches across, 6 exserted stamens, in terminal umbels, to 4 inches across and containing 40 to 100 flowers, on a solid, smooth, green, leafless stalk (scape)

about 2 feet tall. Flowers in summer to early fall.

FRUIT - A dehiscent, 3-chambered capsule.

CULTURE - Full sun to partial shade, on fertile, well-drained soils. Moderately salt tolerant.

PROBLEMS - Chewing insects, maggots, borers, botrytis.

PROPAGATION - By seed or clump division.

LANDSCAPE USES - Edging, bedding plant, pot plant, cut flowers.

COMMENTS - Many cultivars, hybrids and a few related species. Dwarf and white ('**Albus**') or lilac-flowered and dwarf ('**Nanus**') cultivars are available. *Agapanthus africanus* and its cultivar '**Peter Pan**' are gaining popularity in Florida.

Tulbaghia violacea

SOCIETY GARLIC

PRONUNCIATION - tūl 'bā gē ə   ‚vī ə 'lā sē ə

TRANSLATION - [after Rijk Tulbagh (1699-1771), Dutch governor of the Cape of Good Hope] [violet colored].

FORM - Monoecious, evergreen, perennial, tuberous herb, acaulescent, medium-textured.

SIZE - Reaches a maximum height of 30 inches with a variable spread. Growth rate is medium.

HARDINESS ZONE - Zone 8. Can be grown throughout Florida.

NATIVE HABITAT - South Africa.

LEAVES - Simple; 4 to 8, in basal rosettes; linear, grass-like, to 1 foot long, with an acute apex, and channeled at the base; distinct garlic odor when crushed.

FLOWERS - Bisexual, bright lilac to violet, salverform flowers, 0.75 inch long, in terminal umbels of 7 to 20 atop a long upright scape. Blooms in warm months of the year.

FRUIT - Insignificant capsules.

CULTURE - Flowers best in full sun, but can be grown in part shade. It prefers light, sandy soils and is not salt tolerant.

PROBLEMS - Pest-free.

PROPAGATION - Seeds, clump division.

LANDSCAPE USES - Makes a pleasant ground cover, but avoid planting in entryways. Works well massed in a naturalized area. Some people may find the odor objectionable, particularly if forced to smell it for a long period of time.

COMMENTS - The cultivars 'Tricolor' and 'Silver Lace' (large flowers) are offered.

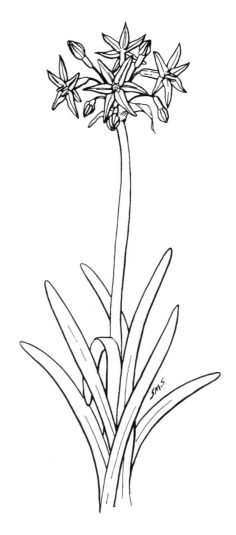

AMARYLLIDACEAE - AMARYLLIS FAMILY

DICOTYLEDONS; 75-85 GENERA AND 1100 SPECIES

GEOGRAPHY: Primarily warm temperate and subtropical, extending into tropical and cool temperate regions.

GROWTH HABIT: Deciduous or evergreen, mostly bulbous herbs.

LEAVES: Basal, linear, 2-ranked or spirally arranged, few to many.

FLOWERS: Scapose inflorescence with one to a few flowers subtended by a spathe; actinomorphic, perianth of 6 tepals in 2 whorls, free or fused, often showy; sometimes with a corona (in *Narcissus*) or staminal cup (in *Eucharis*), stamens 6; carpels usually 3, fused, inferior.

FRUIT: Loculicidally dehiscent fleshy capsule or a berry.

ECONOMIC USES: Horticulturally important ornamentals.

ORNAMENTAL GENERA: *Amaryllis, Clivia, Crinum, Cyrtanthus, Eucharis, Eucrosia, Haemanthus, Hippeastrum, Hymenocallis, Narcissus, Nerine, Pamianthe, Stenomesson, Sternbergia, Zephyranthes*, among others.

COMMENTS: Species of Amaryllidaceae differ from those of Liliaceae and Alliaceae by their inferior ovary.

Crinum spp.

CRINUM LILY, SPIDER LILY

PRONUNCIATION - 'krī nəm

TRANSLATION - [from Greek *crinon* (= a lily)].

FORM - Monoecious, large perennial herbs with tunicate bulbs, often with long necks, stalkless, often clump-forming. Coarse texture.

SIZE - Variable with species and cultivar, to 5 feet or more, rapid growth.

HARDINESS ZONE - Zones 8 to 10. Can be grown in all areas of Florida. Foliage is damaged by frost but plants recover rapidly.

NATIVE HABITAT - Tropics and subtropics worldwide, a few native to Florida.

LEAVES - Simple, mostly spirally arranged, basal or from bulb neck, sword shaped to strap shaped, to 5 feet long, 4 to 5 inches wide, light green, fleshy, thick, midrib often keeled beneath, entire and undulate margins.

FLOWERS - Bisexual, white, pinks, reds, some striped or multicolored, few or many-flowered, corolla funnelform to 6 inches across with a long slender tube that is straight or curved, lobes nearly equal, linear or lanceolate, in umbels on a 2-foot-long solid scape subtended by 2 bracts; flowers in summer-fall, some fragrant, especially at night.

FRUIT - Capsule, green, spherical, seeds globose.

CULTURE - Full sun, various soils; moderately salt tolerant.

PROBLEMS - Chewing insects, caterpillars, *Botrytis,* leaf spots (especially in south Florida).

PROPAGATION - Seed, division.

LANDSCAPE USES - Border, planter box, pot plant, bedding plant.

COMMENTS - Many cultivars, hybrids, and related species, including native taxa. *Crinum augustum* 'Purple Leaf' (Queen Emm) (= *C. amabile* var. *augustum*), *C. americanum* (String Lily, Florida Swamp Lily), *C. asiaticum* (Tree Crinum), *C. bulbispermum, C. jagus* (St. Christopher Lily), *C. zeylanicum* (Milk and Wine Lily) which has naturalized in Florida, and others.

Eucharis amazonica   AMAZON LILY, EUCHARIST LILY

PRONUNCIATION - 'yū kə rəs   ˌæ mə 'za nə kə

TRANSLATION - [Greek word meaning pleasing, charming] [from the Amazon River region].

SYNONYM - *Eucharis ⟷ grandiflora.*

FORM - Monoecious, semi-evergreen, clumping, bulbous perennial herb.

SIZE - 1 foot in foliage, 2 to 3 feet with flower scape.

HARDINESS ZONE - Zone 10. South Florida, central and north only with maximum protection. Houseplant anywhere.

NATIVE HABITAT - Andes of Colombia and Peru.

LEAVES - Ovate to ovate-lanceolate, blade to 6 inches wide and about twice as long, borne on 1 to 2 foot long succulent petiole, glossy dark green above, lighter green below, prominent midrib.

BULB - Tunicate, to 4 inches in diameter.

FLOWERS - Bisexual, white, 4 inches wide, nodding, 4 to 6 in umbel atop 1 to 2 foot scape, 6 recurved tepals surrounding staminal cup which is tinged green inside, fragrant, long-lasting. Appear in spring and intermittently throughout year. Very striking.

FRUIT - 3-chambered, leathery capsule; 0.5 to 1 inch diameter, green or yellow. Seeds black, seldom formed.

CULTURE - Shade (bright sun burns leaves), rich, moist soil. Plant bulbs 2 to 3 inches below soil, or grow in pots. Keep on dry side in winter to stimulate flowering.

PROBLEMS - Caterpillars, spider mite, bulb mites, virus, bulb rot.

PROPAGATION - Division, tissue culture.

LANDSCAPE USES - Highlight for shady perennial bed, bedding in shade, container or houseplant, interiorscapes, cut flower.

COMMENTS - Although several related species are in cultivation, none have become commonly available. *Eucharis × grandiflora* is a natural hybrid, often sold as *E. amazonica.*

Hippeastrum Hybrids and Cultivars   AMARYLLIS

PRONUNCIATION - ˌhi pē ˈæs trəm   ˈhī brə dəm

TRANSLATION - [from Greek *hippus* (= horse) or *hippeus* (= a rider) and *equestre* (belonging to a horseman)].

FORM - Monoecious, perennial herb with tunicate bulbs, stalkless, often clump-forming.

SIZE - Varies with cultivar, 1 to 2 feet tall, rapid growth.

HARDINESS ZONE - Zone 8. Can be grown in all areas of Florida. Foliage is damaged by frost, but plants recover.

NATIVE HABITAT - Horticultural origin; species native to tropical America.

LEAVES - Simple, basal, 2-ranked, linear to strap-shaped, to 2 feet long, light green, glabrous, entire margins, arising with or after flower stalk emergence.

BULB - Tunicate, globular, to 6 inches in diameter.

FLOWERS - Bisexual, predominantly reds, pinks, whites, often lined or striped, funnel-form, to 10 inches across, on umbels of 1-10 flowers (commonly 3 or 4) on a hollow leafless scape to 2 feet tall; flowers in spring.

FRUIT - Capsule; globular, often 3-lobed, seeds disk-shaped, winged, black.

CULTURE - Full sun to partial shade, various well-drained soils; moderately salt tolerant.

PROBLEMS - Chewing insects, caterpillars, Red Blotch Virus mosaic, *Botrytis*.

PROPAGATION - Seeds, division.

LANDSCAPE USES - Bedding plant, edging, pot plants, planter box.

COMMENTS - Many cultivars, hybrids, and related species. Much interbreeding. The true *Amaryllis bella-donna* has white to pinkish flowers and is native to South Africa. Most *Hippeastrum* in trade are cultivars of hybrid origin, too numerous to mention.

Narcissus Species, Hybrids, Cultivars

DAFFODIL, JONQUIL

PRONUNCIATION - nɑr ˈsi səs

TRANSLATION - [from Greek mythology, in honor of a beautiful youth who became so entranced with his own reflection that gods turned him into a flower].

FORM - Monoecious, perennial herb, tunicate bulb, low growing, stemless.

SIZE - Variable with cultivars ranging from 3 to 24 inches, rapid growth.

HARDINESS ZONE - Varies with cultivar, generally Zones 4 to 11. Can be grown in all areas in Florida.

NATIVE HABITAT - Horticultural origin; species native to southern Europe, Mediterranean region, and North Africa.

LEAVES - Simple, basal, entire, strap-shaped, rush-like or semi-terete in Jonquil, nearly flat in Daffodil, to 24 inches long, may be spirally twisted, generally dark green, leathery texture.

BULB - Tunicate, 1-2 inches in diameter.

FLOWERS - One or several on a 24-inch-tall scape, central corona long and tubular or reduced to a shallow cup, perianth segments 6 (petals + sepals); stamens 6, hidden in corona; flowers often nodding; colors prevailing are white, yellows, oranges, various shades and particolored; flowers in early spring.

FRUIT - A capsule; seeds globose, black.

CULTURE - Full sun to partial shade, various soils; slightly to moderately salt tolerant.

DISEASES/PROBLEMS - Nematodes, basal rot, leaf spot, mosaic virus.

PROPAGATION - Seeds, division.

LANDSCAPE USES - Bedding plant, border, planter box, pot or dish plant.

COMMENTS - Eleven basic types and thousands of named cultivars; much confusion over names due to extensive interbreeding. *Narcissus pseudonarcissus* is the original wild daffodil. The Royal Horticultural Dictionary recognizes 12 Divisions to accommodate the numerous known species, hybrids, and cultivars of *Narcissus* known from cultivation.

Zephyranthes spp.

RAIN LILY, ZEPHYR LILY

PRONUNCIATION - ˌze fə ˈræn thēz

TRANSLATION - [from Greek *zephyros* (the west wind) and *anthos* (a flower)].

FORM - Monoecious, small herbaceous perennial, tunicate bulb, low growing, stemless.

SIZE - Varies with species, ranges from 4 to 8 inches tall, rapid growth.

HARDINESS ZONE - Zones 7 to 11. Can be grown in all areas of Florida.

NATIVE HABITAT - Tropical America, a few species in Florida.

LEAVES - Simple, basal, narrow, more or less grass-like, evergreen in some, appearing after flowering in others, narrowly linear to 2 feet long, dark to light green, somewhat leathery texture, entire margins.

BULB - Tunicate; 0.75 to 1.5 inches in diameter.

FLOWERS - White, yellow, pink, rose, red, orange, some particolored, solitary, sessile, or pedicellate, on a hollow scape to 8 inches tall, corolla erect, funnelform, segments 6, to 5 inches across; stamens 6, flowers spring, summer, fall.

FRUIT - A capsule, 3 locules.

CULTURE - Full sun to partial shade, various soils; moderately salt tolerant.

PROBLEMS - Maggots, chewing insects, botrytis.

PROPAGATION - Seed, division.

LANDSCAPE USES - Bedding plant, edging, planter box, pot plant.

COMMENTS - About 70 species and many cultivars and hybrids. *Zephyranthes atamasco* (white, turning pink with age), *Z. simpsonii* (white, often with pink margin), and *Z. treatiae* (white to pinkish) are native to Florida. The common name "rain lily" refers to the flowering habit of some taxa which bloom after rain, if under dry conditions for a period of time.

ARACEAE - ARUM FAMILY

MONOCOTYLEDONS; ABOUT 110 GENERA AND 2000 SPECIES

GEOGRAPHY: Predominantly tropical with a few temperate.

GROWTH HABIT: Mostly herbaceous, cauline or with subterranean tubers or rhizomes, many epiphytic vines and one aquatic species (*Pistia*); roots adventitious, usually unbranched, growing downward or in epiphytic species clasping trees for support.

LEAVES: Simple or compound, pinnately or palmately divided, basal or on stems, with penni-parallel or palmate venation, and often petiolate.

FLOWERS: Small and numerous, stamens usually 6 but may be reduced to as few as 1 and perianth often lacking; unisexual or bisexual, with the male on the upper and the female on the lower part of the spadix which is situated in or enclosed within a petaloid, often brightly colored, conspicuous spathe. Flowers often have a disagreeable odor.

FRUIT: A berry, with one to many seeds.

ECONOMIC USES: The tuberous species are economically important as a source of starch in the tropics and subtropics: *Alocasia, Calocasia esculenta* (Taroor dasheen), *Amorphophallus*, etc.

ORNAMENTAL GENERA: *Aglaonema, Alocasia, Amorphophallus, Anthurium, Caladium, Colocasia, Dieffenbachia, Epipremnum, Monstera, Philodendron, Scindapsus, Spathiphyllum, Syngonium,* and *Zantedeschia*, among others.

Aglaonema commutatum   AGLAONEMA

PRONUNCIATION - ˌæ glō ˈnē mɚ   ˌkɑ myū ˈtā tɚm

TRANSLATION - [bright thread, in reference to stamens] [changeable].

FORM - Monoecious, evergreen, herbaceous perennial shrub; round, with leaves arranged at stem ends; medium texture.

SIZE - 2 to 5 feet tall with a variable spread.

HARDINESS ZONE - Zones 10-11. South Florida only.

NATIVE HABITAT - Malaysia.

LEAVES - Simple, oblong-elliptic to lanceolate; usually less than 12 inches long and 4 inches wide; obtuse to subcordate; dark glossy green, variously marked gray-green along primary veins. Petioles are equal to or shorter than blades, sheathing nearly to the apex.

STEM/BARK - Round, green, or variegated stems.

FLOWERS - Pale green spathe 1.5 to 3.5 inches long with shorter spadix. Monoecious; with inconspicuous male flowers at top of spadix; female, below. Blooms appear on peduncles, to 6 inches long, during the warm months.

FRUIT - Brown, glossy, oblong, to 2 inches wide; 1 to 3; turning yellow, then bright red in late summer; often hidden by leaves.

CULTURE - Low light preferred, down to 150 foot-candles. Leaves burn in direct sun. Fertile, nematode-free growing medium; no salt tolerance.

PROBLEMS - Nematodes, pythium root rot under some conditons, and mites.

PROPAGATION - Cuttage and air layers.

LANDSCAPE USES - Outstanding for areas of reduced light. They may be used in north side foundation schemes or as container specimens indoors.

COMMENTS - Several cultivars, exhibiting a range of leaf and petiole variegation, are available. 'Silver Queen' and 'Silver King' are popular cultivars. Also listed is 'Emerald Beauty'.

Aglaonema modestum   CHINESE EVERGREEN

PRONUNCIATION - ˌæ glə 'nē mə   mō 'des təm

TRANSLATION - [bright thread, in reference to the stamens] [modest, in reference to lack of leaf variegation].

FORM - Monoecious, evergreen herbaceous perennial; round, ascending, with leaves arranged at stem ends; medium texture.

SIZE - To 2 feet tall with a variable spread.

HARDINESS ZONE - Zones 10-11. South Florida only.

NATIVE HABITAT - China, Thailand.

LEAVES - Simple, ovate to more or less lanceolate; to 8.5 inches long and half as wide; long acuminate, obtuse, or rounded at base; dark green and glabrous; undulate margins. Petioles to 8 inches long, sheathing to above their middles.

STEM/BARK - Stems round and green.

FLOWERS - Light green spathe, to 3 inches long, with sessile spadix, 1.75 inches long. Monoecious; the inconspicuous male flowers appear on the upper spadix; females appear below. Peduncles, to 4 inches long, bear flowers during the warm months.

FRUIT - Berries, 1 inch long, orange; in late summer; hidden by leaves.

CULTURE - Low light preferred, will tolerate down to 40 foot-candles. Fertile, nematode-free growing medium and hydroculture. They are not tolerant of salt.

PROBLEMS - Nematodes, pythium root rot under some conditions, and mites.

PROPAGATION - Cuttings and tissue culture.

LANDSCAPE USES - Outstanding for areas of reduced light. They may be used in north side foundation plantings or as container specimens indoors.

COMMENTS - A variegated form is available.

Alocasia spp.

ELEPHANT'S EAR

PRONUNCIATION - ˌæ lō ˈkā shə

TRANSLATION - [without *Colocasia*, an allied genus from which it was separated].

FORM - Tuberous or rhizomatous perennial shrub; irregular form; coarse texture.

SIZE - Varies with species; to 15 feet tall with a variable spread. Some are rank growers.

HARDINESS ZONE - Varies with species; south, central, or north Florida.

NATIVE HABITAT - Tropical Asia.

LEAVES - Simple; entire to pinnatifid, often with basal lobes uppermost; frequently marked or colored; blades as long as 3 inches. Petioles cylindrical to 3.5 feet long. Size varies greatly among species. Medium green.

FLOWERS - Greenish spathe and spadix. Monoecious; both male and female flowers occupy the same spadix. Blooms during the warm months.

FRUIT - Fleshy berries if present.

CULTURE - Full sun or broken shifting shade, depending on the kind; soil should be moisture-retentive, rich and organic; no salt tolerance.

PROBLEMS - Soilborne fungus diseases.

PROPAGATION - Division of underground storage organs, from stem pieces, and seeds.

LANDSCAPE USES - Use outdoors as specimen or accent plants to enhance the feeling of the tropics. Indoors, smaller fancy-leaved types serve as container specimens.

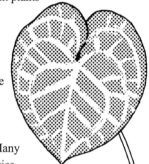

COMMENTS - Many species and varieties available: *Alocasia macrorhiza* (Taro, Poi) and the closely related *Colocasia esculenta* (Dasheen), are cultivated for their edible rhizome. *Alocasia* × *amazonica*, *A. cucullata* (Chinese Taro), *A. odora* and its cultivar **'California'**, as well as *Alocasia* **'Porfora'**, are listed.

Anthurium andraeanum

TAIL FLOWER,
FLAMINGO FLOWER

PRONUNCIATION - æn ˈthū rē əm   ˌæn drē ˈā nəm

TRANSLATION - [Greek for flower and tail, in reference to the tail-like spadix of the flower] [after Edouard F. Andre (1840-1911)].

FORM - Monoecious, herbaceous perennial shrub; compact, round, upright; medium-coarse texture.

SIZE - To 3 feet tall with a 4 foot spread.

HARDINESS ZONE - Zones 10-11. South Florida only.

NATIVE HABITAT - Colombia.

LEAVES - Simple, medium green, reflexed, ovate and sagittate; to 10 inches long and half as wide; petioles somewhat longer. Primary lateral veins are mostly connected by a well-defined vein running along inside and parallel to the margin.

FLOWERS - Bisexual, spathe and spadix on peduncle 15 to 20 inches long. Spathe is spreading, orbicular-ovate, 3 to 5 inches long, cordate, puckered, polished, and salmon-red. Basal lobes are semicircular, sometimes shortly united. The spadix is sessile, recurved, to 2.5 inches long, golden with an ivory zone, and densely covered with inconspicuous flowers.

FRUIT - Fleshy berries.

CULTURE - Prefers low light conditions, but will tolerate up to 5000 foot-candles. High humidity is necessary for flowering; soils should be moist, rich, and high in organic matter; no salt tolerance.

PROBLEMS - Mites, nematodes, scales, mealybugs, and grasshoppers.

PROPAGATION - Cuttage, seeds, and tissue culture.

LANDSCAPE USES - As a specimen in frostless, shady outdoor spots; accent plant in pots; interiorscapes.

COMMENTS - There are nearly 900 Anthurium species, including many epiphytic ones. This species is one of the parents of a group of hybrids with large, showy, puckered spathes from black-red to red, salmon, pink, and white, which are often incorrectly referred to as varieties of the species. A few listed cultivars include **'Julia', 'Kohara Double', 'Lady Ann', 'Lady Beth'** (patented), **'Lady Jane', 'Mary Jane', 'Royal', 'Southern Blush'**, and probably others. *Anthurium scherzerianum* and its cultivars of hybrid origin are referrable to *A.* × *hortulanum. Anthurium hookeri* (Bird's Nest Anthurium) is sold for outdoor landscape use.

Caladium bicolor   FANCY LEAFED CALADIUM

PRONUNCIATION - kə ˈlā dē əm   ˈbī ku lər

TRANSLATION - [from *Kaladi*, a Malaysian name] [two colors].

SYNONYM - *Caladium × hortulanum*.

FORM - Monoecious, perennial herb; ground cover; tuberous, stemless; upright, spreading; coarse texture. Cultivated for its beautiful foliage.

SIZE - Range 8 inches to 3 feet tall (12 inches typical), variable with cultivar; rapid growth rate.

HARDINESS ZONE - Tubers may be left in the ground throughout the year in Zones l0 and 11. In Zone 9 digging is recommended as tubers may be damaged in cold winters. In other areas of the country, tubers must be dug up each year before frost.

NATIVE HABITAT - Hybrid origin. Tropical America.

LEAVES - Simple, basal, sometimes peltate; ovate to cordate in outline; to 14 inches long; basally bifid, cordate, or truncate; flat, undulate, or ruffled; variously variegated red, rose, white, green, pink; entire margins. Petioles as long as or several times longer than blade.

TUBER - Irregular, dark brown.

FLOWERS - Unisexual, spathe and spadix arrangement; spathe white, pink, or green.

FRUIT - Berries, densely packed along spadix.

CULTURE - Full sun to partial shade, organic soils; no salt tolerance.

PROBLEMS - Mealybugs, caterpillars, fungal diseases.

PROPAGATION - Seeds, division.

LANDSCAPE USES - Bedding plant for foliage, planter box, edging, pot plants.

COMMENTS - Until recently, hybrids and cultivars of caladium were recognized under the name *Caladium × hortulanum*. The two main groups included "fancy leaf" (= *C. bicolor* ssp. *pictoratum*) and "strap leaf" (= *C. bicolor* ssp. *marmoratum*). Within each of the two groups, numerous cultivars are included. Florida grows more than 90 percent of the world's supply of caladium tubers.

Dieffenbachia amoena   GIANT DUMB CANE

PRONUNCIATION - ˌdē fən ˈbɑ kē ə   ˌæ mō ˈē nə

TRANSLATION - [in honor of J.F.Dieffenbach (1790-1863), who was in charge of the gardens of the royal palace of Schönbrunn, in Vienna] [pleasant].

FORM - Monoecious, herbaceous perennial shrub; ascending branches; coarse texture.

SIZE - To 8 feet in height with a 5 foot spread.

HARDINESS ZONE - Zones 10-11. South Florida only.

NATIVE HABITAT - Tropical America.

LEAVES - Simple, clustered at stem end; elliptic to oblong; up to 20 inches in length; typically dark green with irregular zones of creamy white along, between, or over the primary lateral veins. Petiole light   green, sheathing; about 12 inches long extending into the midrib.

STEM/BARK - Typically stout, unbranched, bright green, and ringed with leaf scars.

FLOWERS - Spathe and spadix; typical of the family in having male flowers at the apex of the spadix and female flowers basally. The greenish spathe may be up to 5 inches and is constricted in the middle. Flowers are not significant.

FRUIT - Reddish berries covered by a persistent bract.

CULTURE - Tolerates light intensities from 75 to 6000 foot-candles; foliage will burn if exposed to prolonged full sunlight. The plant will tolerate many soil types; prefers those with moderate moisture and freedom from nematodes; slight salt tolerance.

PROBLEMS - Mites, mealybugs, and bacterial stem rot.

PROPAGATION - Cuttings, cane sections, air layering, and tissue culture.

LANDSCAPE USES - As accents in outdoor plantings or as interior specimens; lends a tropical effect.

COMMENTS - The name "dumb cane" is given because the leaves and particularly the stem contain calcium oxalate crystals which, when combined with enzymes, cause irritation and swelling of tissues, especially vocal chords, if ingested. Excellent patented (**'Tropic Snow'**) and unpatented (**'Hi-Color'**) variegated cultivars are available. **'Alex'** (or **'Alix'**) is more compact. Plant is polyploid.

Dieffenbachia × bausei   DUMB CANE, DIEFFENBACHIA

PRONUNCIATION - ˌdē fən ˈbɑ kē ə· ˈbaū sē ɑī

TRANSLATION - [in honor of J.F.Dieffenbach (1790-1863), who was in charge of the gardens of the royal palace of Schönbrunn, in Vienna] [after Christian Frederick Bause (ca. 1839-1895), German nurseryman].

FORM - Monoecious, shrubby herbaceous perennial, suckering from an upright, ascending base; coarse texture.

SIZE - To 3 feet in height with a 3 foot spread.

HARDINESS ZONE - Zones 10-11. South Florida only.

NATIVE HABITAT - Tropical Americas for parent plants: *D. maculata × D. weiri.*

LEAVES - Simple; elliptic to oblong; with blades 6 to 8 inches in length. Dark green with creamy variegation.

STEM/BARK - Green, ringed stems.

FLOWERS - Monoecious; surrounded by a spathe which is constricted in the middle, covering the female portion of the inflorescence.

FRUIT - Reddish-orange berries.

CULTURE - Tolerates light intensities from 100 to 4500 foot-candles; foliage burns in full sun; prefers nematode-free, moderately moist soils; some salt tolerance.

PROBLEMS - Mites, mealybugs, and bacterial stem rot.

PROPAGATION - Tip and cane cuttings and tissue culture.

LANDSCAPE USES - Suitable for landscape plantings where it would fill in an area quickly; an excellent interior or exterior foreground plant.

COMMENTS - A number of cultivars are offered in the trade whose origins are uncertain at this time but are probably of hybrid origin: *Dieffenbachia* 'Compacta', 'Nelly', 'Parachute', 'Paradise', 'Sarah', 'Sparkles', 'Star Bright', 'Star White', and 'Triumph', among others. Although these are probably selections of *Dieffenbachia × bausei,* they may include other species.

Dieffenbachia maculata   SPOTTED DUMB CANE

PRONUNCIATION - ˌdē fən ˈbɑ kē ə ˌmæ kyū ˈlā tə

TRANSLATION - [in honor of J.F.Dieffenbach (1790-1863), who was in charge of the gardens of the royal palace of Schönbrunn, in Vienna] [spotted].

FORM - Monoecious, herbaceous perennial; upright, ascending branches; coarse texture.

SIZE - To 5 feet tall.

HARDINESS ZONE - Zones 10-11. South Florida only.

NATIVE HABITAT - Central America to northern South America.

LEAVES - Simple, to 12 inches long; ovate-elliptic, nearly cordate at base; many pairs of primary lateral veins; new growth cream-white or chartreuse-finely-splotched-white with green midrib and margins.

STEM/BARK - Stem may be green or mottled and striped.

FLOWERS - Greenish spathe and spadix bearing inconspicuous flowers.

FRUIT - Orange-red berries.

CULTURE - Tolerates light intensities from 100 to 4000 foot-candles; direct sun burns foliage; prefers nematode-free, moderately moist soils; some salt tolerance.

PROBLEMS - Mites, mealybugs, systemic diseases, and bacterial problems in late winter and spring.

PROPAGATION - Cuttings, cane sections, and air layering.

LANDSCAPE USES - An accent plant for tropical effect or, more frequently, an interior specimen.

COMMENTS - Numerous cultivars of this species are available, including **'Camilla'**, a mutation of **'Exotica Perfection'** (cream with white veins); **'Exotica'** (a compact form); **'Gigantea'** (large plant and leaves); **'Rudolph Roehrs'** (Yellow-Leaf Dieffenbachia); **'Tropic Snow'** (dense, tall with thick leaves and variegated cream and green); **'Tropic White'** (large leaves blotched white); and **'Viridis'** (leaves green), among others. Stems and leaves contain calcium oxalate crystals which cause irritation and swelling when touched and possibly death if chewed.

Epipremnum aureum   GOLDEN POTHOS

PRONUNCIATION - ˌe pə ˈprem nəm   ˈo rē əm

TRANSLATION - [up on trees] [golden].

FORM - Evergreen herbaceous vine; vigorous, climbs into trees. Juvenile has medium texture; mature has coarse texture.

SIZE - Climbs to 40 feet or more; rapid growth rate.

HARDINESS ZONE - Zones 10-11. May be grown outdoors in south Florida only.

NATIVE HABITAT - Southeast Asia.

LEAVES - Simple, alternate, ovate-cordate. Juvenile (most frequently seen): entire to 12 inches. Mature (tree-climbing): pinnatifid or perforate to 30 inches. Leaves glossy bright green or irregularly variegated with yellow or white. Petiole channeled at base, clasping.

STEM/BARK - Green or striped, somewhat flattened.

FLOWERS - Bisexual, densely packed on spadix; surrounded by white spathe.

FRUIT - Berries.

CULTURE - Full sun to dense shade, varied soils; slight to moderate salt tolerance.

PROBLEMS - Scale, mites, mealybugs.

PROPAGATION - Cuttings.

LANDSCAPE USES - Ground cover, potted foliage, hanging baskets, planters, totems, grown on trees.

COMMENTS - Several variegated cultivars. **'Marble Queen'** (with variegation) very popular. Often sold as *Scindapsus aureus.* However, **'Wilcoxii', 'Jade'**, and **'Marble Queen'** are selections of *E. aureum.*

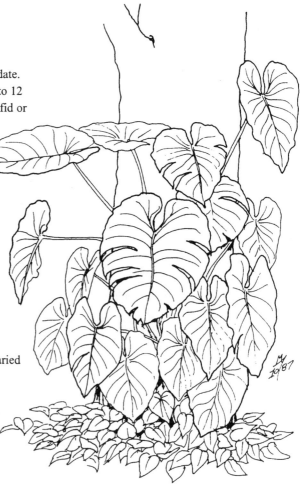

Monstera deliciosa   SPLIT-LEAF PHILODENDRON, CERIMAN, SWISS CHEESE PLANT

PRONUNCIATION - mɑn ˈste rə də ˌli shē ˈō sə

TRANSLATION - [monsterous, probably in reference to leaves] [delicious, in reference to its fruit].

FORM - Monoecious, evergreen herbaceous vine; vigorous, climbing; coarse texture.

SIZE - To 30 feet or more.

HARDINESS ZONE - Zones 10-11. May be grown outdoors in south Florida only.

NATIVE HABITAT - Mexico and Central America.

LEAVES - Simple, alternate, ovate, basally cordate; leathery. Juvenile: entire. Mature: pinnatifid halfway to midrib, perforate with oblong holes, 5 feet long to 3 feet wide. Petiole channeled at base, clasping. Dark green.

STEM/BARK - Ringed leaf scars; many aerial roots.

FLOWERS - Unisexual, creamy white; densely packed on spadix; spathe to 1 foot.

FRUIT - Densely packed berries, yellow; edible with pineapple/banana flavor. Dark area on fruit segment contains calcium oxalate.

CULTURE - Partial to deep shade; rich, moist soils; no salt tolerance.

PROBLEMS - Scale, mites, mealybugs.

PROPAGATION - Cuttings, seeds.

LANDSCAPE USES - Urn specimen, totems; grown on trees.

COMMENTS - Several variegated cultivars, usually creamy-white and/or yellow.

Philodendron bipennifolium

FIDDLELEAF OR HORSEHEAD PHILODENDRON

PRONUNCIATION - ˌfi lə ˈden drən   bī ˌpe nə ˈfō lē əm

TRANSLATION - [from Greek *philo* (= to love) and *dendron* (= a tree), in reference to their tree climbing habit] [with bipinnate leaves].

FORM - Monoecious, evergreen herbaceous vine; coarse texture.

SIZE - Of variable height depending on support.

HARDINESS ZONE - Zones 10-11. South Florida only.

NATIVE HABITAT - Southeastern Brazil.

LEAVES - Five-lobed, to 18 inches long; basal lobes extended and central lobes narrow towards the middle; dull olive green with a leathery texture.

STEM/BARK - Stems are green; aerial roots present.

FLOWERS - Unisexual; a greenish spathe 4.5 inches long encloses a spadix bearing inconspicuous unisexual flowers.

FRUIT - Berries.

CULTURE - Light intensities from 75 to 5000 foot-candles (partial shade); well-drained soil; slight salt tolerance.

PROBLEMS - A variety of pests including mites, scale, thrips, and mealybugs. There are several leaf spotting diseases and a bacterial soft rot in the nursery industry.

PROPAGATION - Cuttings or layering.

LANDSCAPE USES - As a totem subject on a bark slab, a focal point in dish gardens, or hanging on a trellis.

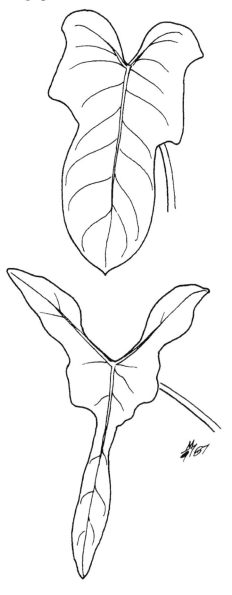

Philodendron bipinnatifidum   SELLOUM

PRONUNCIATION - ˌfi lə ˈden drən ˌbī pi nə ˈti fə dəm

TRANSLATION - [from Greek *philo* (= to love) and *dendron* (= a tree), in reference to their tree-climbing habit] [twice pinnately divided].

SYNONYM - *Philodendron selloum.*

FORM - Monoecious, evergreen shrub; densely foliated, stout, round, erect; arborescent (self-heading); coarse texture.

SIZE - To 15 feet tall with a 15 foot spread; rapid growth rate.

HARDINESS ZONE - Zones 8b-10, may be grown in south, central, and protected areas of north Florida.

NATIVE HABITAT - Southern Brazil.

LEAVES - Simple, spirally arranged; sagittate in outline, to 3 feet long; undulate; deeply pinnatifid, many segments overlapping; deep green, more or less leathery.

STEM/BARK - Leaf scars conspicuous; many adventitious roots.

FLOWERS - Unisexual; spadix with thick, green, boat-like spathe to 12 inches; persistent.

FRUIT - Berries; edible.

CULTURE - Full sun to partial shade, varied soils; slight salt tolerance.

PROBLEMS - Scale, mites, leaf spot.

PROPAGATION - Seed.

LANDSCAPE USES - Foundation planting for large buildings; screen, specimen, urn plant.

COMMENTS - Several cultivars, including **'German Selloum'** (graceful, finely cut leaves), **'Miniature Selloum'** (dwarf with small leaves), and **'Uruguay'** (leaves large and thick), **'Variegatum'** (leaves marbled light green to yellow), etc. Widely used as parent for arborescent hybrids.

Philodendron cannifolium   FLASK PHILODENDRON

PRONUNCIATION - ˌfi lə ˈden drən ˌka nə ˈfō lē əm

TRANSLATION - [from Greek *philo* (= to love) and *dendron* (= a tree), in reference to their tree climbing habit] [canna-like leaves].

SYNONYM - *Philodendron martianum.*

FORM - Monoecious, self-heading, evergreen, herbaceous, perennial vine or shrub; coarse texture. Growth vine-like but rate is so slow that plant functions as a shrub.

SIZE - To 2 feet tall; slow growth rate.

HARDINESS ZONE - Zones 10-11. South Florida only.

NATIVE HABITAT - Southeast Brazil.

LEAVES - Simple, lanceolate to ovate; to 18 inches long, 6 to 8 inches wide; acute-acuminate, basally cuneate to truncate. Petiole unusually full and spongy. Dark green. Internodes very short.

STEM/BARK - Green.

FLOWERS - Unisexual, spathe 5 to 6 inches long; green inside with cherry-red base; cream outside.

FRUIT - Berries.

CULTURE - 300-5000 foot-candles, shade; well-drained soils or soil-less mixes; some salt tolerance.

PROBLEMS - Mites, scale, mealybugs, and fungal leaf spot diseases.

PROPAGATION - Seeds and cuttings.

LANDSCAPE USES - Accent or specimen.

COMMENTS - Mainly used in breeding. Could be used in landscapes more frequently.

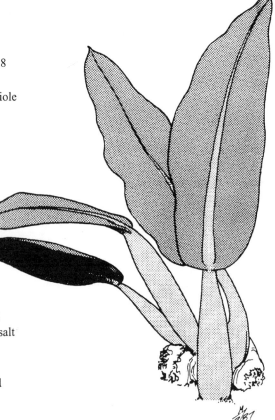

Philodendron Cultivars

PRONUNCIATION - ˌfi lə ˈden drən

TRANSLATION - [from Greek *philo* (= to love) and *dendron* (= a tree), in reference to their tree-climbing habit]

FORM - Monoecious, herbaceous evergreen perennials.

SIZE - Rosettes to 3 feet; vines variable depending on support.

HARDINESS ZONE - Zones 10-11, south Florida only.

NATIVE HABITAT - Probably mostly of hybrid origin.

LEAVES - Many have red stems and petioles; color variable, depending on hybrid. Red, burgundy, yellow, and variegated forms available.

STEM/BARK - Varies with cultivar.

FLOWERS - Typical Araceae spathe and spadix.

FRUIT - Berries.

CULTURE - Tolerate low light very well; slight salt tolerance.

PROBLEMS - Few, mainly mealybugs, scale, mites indoors.

PROPAGATION - Cuttings and tissue culture.

LANDSCAPE USES - Vining forms for trellises; rosettes as accents or small specimens; mass plantings.

COMMENTS - Younger leaves usually have most intense color. Many of the best cultivars are patented. A number of hybrids are often sold as cultivars: **'Black Cardinal', 'Emerald Prince', 'Imperial Green', 'Imperial Red', 'Kaleidoscope', 'Prince Albert', 'Red Empress', 'Royal Queen', 'Swiss Cheese Vine', and 'Xanadu',** among others.

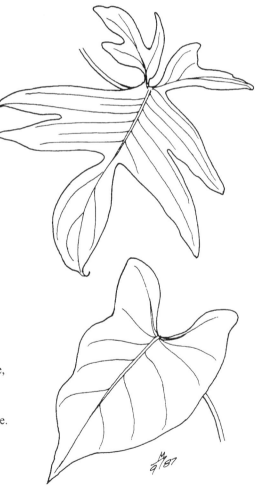

Philodendron scandens   HEART-LEAF PHILODENDRON

PRONUNCIATION - ˌfi lə ˈden drən   ˈskæn dənz

TRANSLATION - [from Greek *philo* (= to love) and *dendron* (= a tree), in reference to their tree-climbing habit] [climbing].

FORM - Monoecious, evergreen herbaceous vine; vigorous, climbing; medium texture.

SIZE - Climbs to 30 feet or more; rapid growth rate.

HARDINESS ZONE - Zones 10-11. May be grown outdoors in south Florida only.

NATIVE HABITAT - Tropical America.

LEAVES - Simple, alternate; cordate, to 12 inches; glossy-green; entire margins; leaf sheaths dry and persist on stem. Petiole round, not clasping.

STEM/BARK - Green, round.

FLOWERS - Unisexual, densely packed spadix; spathe greenish.

FRUIT - Berries.

CULTURE - Partial to deep shade; fertile, moist soils; slight salt tolerance.

PROBLEMS - Scale, leaf spots.

PROPAGATION - Cuttings.

LANDSCAPE USES - Ground cover, potted foliage, hanging baskets, totems.

COMMENTS - Many cultivars. *Philodendron scandens* often sold as *P. oxycardium* or *P.*

cordatum. In *P. scandens* f. *micans (= P. scandens* × *P. micans*, the underside of leaves is purple; **'Variegatum'** has marbled, off-white and green-gray on dark green leaves.

Scindapsus pictus   POTHOS

PRONUNCIATION - sin 'dæp sɚs 'pik tɚs

TRANSLATION - [Greek name for an ivy-like plant] [painted].

FORM - Monoecious, evergreen herbaceous vine; medium texture.

SIZE - To 40 feet depending on support; slow growth rate.

HARDINESS ZONE - Zones 10-11, south Florida only.

NATIVE HABITAT - Indonesia, Borneo.

LEAVES - Simple; obliquely ovate to oblong, to 6 inches long; deeply cordate; dark green splotched silvery-gray above and very pale beneath. Petioles short and sheathing.

STEM/BARK - Green, with aerial roots.

FLOWERS - Bisexual, inconspicuous, on spadix enclosed within a 3 inch, white spathe.

FRUIT - Berries.

CULTURE - Light intensities of 150 foot-candles to partial shade; well-drained soils; moderate salt tolerance.

PROBLEMS - Root rot.

PROPAGATION - Cuttings.

LANDSCAPE USES - A ground cover or more commonly as an interior foliage plant.

COMMENTS- The cultivar **'Argyraeus'** is known as Silver or Silver Pothos and is dark green with silver spots.

Spathiphyllum wallisii 'Clevelandii'

CLEVELAND
PEACE LILY

PRONUNCIATION - ˌspæ thə 'fi ləm   wɑ 'li sē ī

TRANSLATION - [from Greek *spathe* and *phylon* (= a leaf), in reference to the leaf like spathes] [in honor of President Cleveland].

SYNONYM - *Spathiphyllum clevelandii.*

FORM - Monoecious, evergreen, rhizomatous, perennial herb; acaulescent and clumping; medium-coarse texture.

SIZE - 3 feet tall, 3 foot spread.

HARDINESS ZONE - Zones 10-11, south Florida only.

NATIVE HABITAT - Unknown. Probably of hybrid origin.

LEAVES - Simple, narrow blades to 1 foot long and 4 to 6 inches wide; acuminate at apex, attenuate at base; glossy dark green with depressed venation. Petioles slender and longer than the blades.

FLOWERS - Bisexual; inconspicuous, densely covered spadix. Spathe is white, erect, and ovate, to 6 inches. Flowers are borne well above foliage on slender conspicuous penduncles during the warm months.

FRUIT - Berry-like, dry.

CULTURE - Light intensities between deep and partial shade; moist organic soil; no salt tolerance.

PROBLEMS - Mites, mealybugs, scale, foliar diseases, and *Cylindrocladium* root rot.

PROPAGATION - Division, tissue culture.

LANDSCAPE USES - Coarse herb in shaded areas of south Florida. It is also a good specimen for interiorscapes.

COMMENTS - Many other cultivars, mostly of unknown origin, of varying plant and flower sizes are available: **'Deneve', 'Leprechaun', 'Linda', 'Lynise', 'Petite', 'Sensation'** (patented), **'Starlight', 'Supreme', 'Symphony', 'Tasson', 'Viscount', 'Viscount Prima'.** Also available are *S. floribundum* (Snowflower) and its cultivars **'Mauna Loa'** and **'Mauna Loa Supreme'.**

Syngonium podophyllum   NEPHTHYTIS

PRONUNCIATION - sin 'gō nē əm   ˌpō də 'fi ləm

TRANSLATION - [in allusion to united ovaries] [foot-like leaf].

FORM - Monoecious, evergreen herbaceous vine; medium-coarse texture.

SIZE - Varies depending upon support, rapid growth rate.

HARDINESS ZONE - Zones 10-11, south Florida only.

NATIVE HABITAT - Mexico and Costa Rica.

LEAVES - In juvenile plant, arrow-shaped or saggitate, becoming palmately divided at maturity. The plant will have an odd number of leaflets or divisions; blade size ranges from 2 to 12 inches. The color may be green or variegated with silver, cream, or white.

FLOWERS - Whitish spathe to 4 inches with a shorter spadix appearing during the warm months.

FRUIT - Brownish berries.

CULTURE - Light intensities from deep to partial shade; fertile, fibrous, acid compost; no salt tolerance.

PROBLEMS - Mites, scale, and a host of different disease organisms.

PROPAGATION - Cuttings; primarily tissue culture.

LANDSCAPE USES - As a ground cover or vine in frost free areas. Juvenile forms are popular for interior use as hanging baskets and potted plants.

COMMENTS - 'White Butterfly' is the most commonly available cultivar but several others are often listed, for example, **'Emerald Gem'**, **'Emerald Gem Variegated'**, **'Lemon & Lime'**, **'Maya Red'**, **'Pink Allusion'**, **'Pixie'**, and probably others. Virtually all plants are produced by tissue culture.

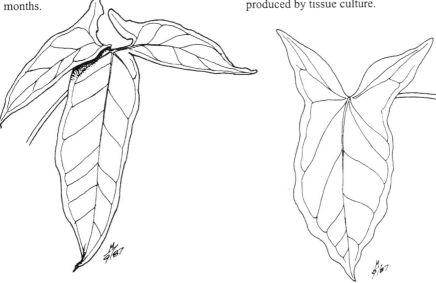

ARECACEAE (= PALMAE) - PALM FAMILY

MONOCOTYLEDONS; ABOUT 212 GENERA AND 2800 SPECIES

GEOGRAPHY: Chiefly tropical (especially eastern Asia and South America), with some subtropical, and very few temperate.

GROWTH HABIT: Solitary or clumped, branching very rare, small or large; trunks with leaf petiole bases or variously marked with leaf scars, occasionally with thorns, and sometimes with a distinct crownshaft; rarely monocarpic.

LEAVES: Terminal, clustered atop the trunk; pinnate (leaflets reduplicate or induplicate), palmate, or costapalmate; petiole entire or variously spine-toothed; with a distinct hastula in most palmate-leaved species.

FLOWERS: 3-merous, uni- or bisexual (plants mono- or dioecious, or polygamous), numerous (to several thousand), in lateral or terminal paniculate inflorescences which are enclosed within a large, boat-shaped bract.

FRUIT: One-seeded berries or drupes, ranging from pea-size to the large single coconut (*Cocos*) and double coconut (*Lodoicea*).

ECONOMIC USES: A vast majority of the species are ornamentals but many yield valuable economic products, including thatch, starch (from *Metroxylon* - the true sago palm), palm oil, fiber (coir, raffia), copra, dates (from *Phoenix dactylifera*) and other edible fruit.

ORNAMENTAL GENERA: *Acoelorrhaphe, Acrocomia, Aiphanes, Archontophoenix, Areca, Arenga, Arikuryroba, Asterogyne, Asterocaryum, Bactris, Bismarckia, Brahea, Brassiophoenix, Butia, Calypterocalyx, Calyptronoma, Carpentaria, Caryota, Chamaedorea, Chamaerops, Chambeyronia, Chrysalidocarpus, Coccothrinax, Cocos, Copernicia, Corypha, Cryosophila, Dictyosperma, Drymophloeus, Elaeis, Euterpe, Gastrococos, Gaussia, Geonoma, Hedyscepe, Heterospathe, Howea, Hyophorbe, Hyphaene, Jubaea, Latania, Lepidorrhachis, Licuala, Livistona, Mauritia, Microcoelum, Nannorrhops, Neodypsis, Normanbya, Nypa, Opsiandra, Orbignye, Phoenix, Pinanga, Polyandrococos, Pritchardia, Pseudophoenix, Ptychosperma, Ravenea, Reinhardtia, Rhapidophyllum, Rhapis, Rhopalostylis, Roystonea, Sabal, Salacca, Satakentia, Serenoa, Syagrus, Synechanthus, Thrinax, Trachycarpus, Veitchia, Wallichia, Washingtonia, Wodyetia, Zombia,* and probably many others.

Acoelorrhaphe wrightii

PRONUNCIATION - ə ͵sē lē ˈrā fē ˈrī tē ī

TRANSLATION - [in reference to the needle-like leaf segments] [after Charles Wright (1811-1855), a plant taxonomist].

SYNONYM - *Paurotis wrightii.*

FORM - Multitrunked cluster palm; bushy, dense; medium texture. Basal sprouts assure that there is always foliage at the base of the trunks.

SIZE - Up to 25 feet tall with a variable spread; large, old, mature specimens can reach 40 feet in height; moderate to slow growth rate.

HARDINESS ZONE - Zones 9b-11, central and south Florida.

NATIVE HABITAT - Low, moist areas in the Everglades region of south Florida, the West Indies, and Central America.

LEAVES - Palmate, orbicular in outline, 2 to 3 feet wide and long; leaf divided halfway toward center into pointed, stiff segments split at apex; lighter green undersides. Petioles 3 feet with orange teeth along the margins that point upward and often occur in pairs.

TRUNKS - The slender trunks are covered with old leaf bases and matted fiber, giving them a burlap-like appearance.

FLOWERS - Yellow-green, small, on erect panicles that arch as fruit matures. The flower stalks usually are around 3.5 feet long, extend beyond the leaves, and are borne in late winter/early spring.

FRUIT - Orange at first, then black at maturity; round, 0.25 inch wide; mature in December.

CULTURE - Grows in full sun to partial shade; any soil, but growth rate is slow in drier soils; thrives in low, moist, reasonably fertile soils; slight salt tolerance.

PROBLEMS - Pest-free, micronutrient deficiencies; resistant to lethal yellowing.

PROPAGATION - By seed.

LANDSCAPE USES - Good near pools or patios, as a screen plant, a specimen, or as a corner plant for houses.

Butia capitata   PINDO PALM, JELLY PALM

PRONUNCIATION - byū tē ə   ˌkæ pə 'tā tə

TRANSLATION - [Brazilian name] [dense-headed].

FORM - Monoecious, medium-sized single-trunked erect palm, stiff, strongly recurving canopy.

SIZE - To 30 feet, commonly seen 10 to 20 feet, slow growth rate.

HARDINESS ZONE - Zones 8-11. Can be grown in all areas of Florida.

NATIVE HABITAT - South America.

LEAVES - Pinnate, 8 to 10 feet long, strongly recurving toward trunk, leaflets stiff, standing upward from rachis in 1 rank, blue-green, reduplicate, petiole armed, thorns pointing toward leaf tip.

TRUNK - 1 to 2 feet diameter, persistent leaf bases along entire trunk.

FLOWERS - Unisexual, in groups of 3: 2 male and 1 female, small, stalk inflorescences, to 5 feet long.

FRUIT - Drupe; yellow to red, oblong-ovoid to 1 inch long and wide, dense clusters, pulpy, fibrous, edible.

CULTURE - Full sun, various soils; moderately salt tolerant. Tolerates hot, windy conditions, asphalt and concrete areas.

PROBLEMS - Palm leaf skeletonizer, scale, micronutrient deficiencies. Fruit can be messy on sidewalks.

PROPAGATION - Seed but germination difficult.

LANDSCAPE USES - Specimen, accent, street plantings, planters.

COMMENTS - *Butia capitata* var. *nehrlingiana* (smaller bright red fruit), var. *odorata* (glaucous leaves), and var. *strictior* (strongly ascending, bluish leaves) are available. Fruit is used in making jellies and jams.

Caryota mitis

PRONUNCIATION - ˌkæ rē 'ō tə   'mī təs

TRANSLATION - [a date-shaped nut] [without spines, soft].

FORM - Monoecious, large, multitrunked, cluster palm; coarse texture.

SIZE - Height ranges from 25 to 40 feet with variable spread; medium to rapid growth rate.

HARDINESS ZONE - Zones 10-11, south Florida only.

NATIVE HABITAT - Asian tropics.

LEAVES - Bipinnately compound, 4 to 9 feet long; leaflets 6 inches long by 5 inches wide, triangular, like a fish's tail. Leaflets have a jagged, toothed apex, with numerous parallel veins and are slightly induplicate. Petioles unarmed and round in cross section. Dark green.

TRUNKS - The slender trunks, 4 inches in diameter, are covered with gray leaf bases and black matted fibers.

FLOWERS - Monocarpic; each trunk blooms successively from top leaf axils to bottom axils and then dies, replaced by younger trunks in 5 to 7 years. Many-branched, hanging flower stalks resemble a horsetail, usually 2 feet long with whitish flowers. Blooms all year.

FRUIT - Black, globular, 0.5 inch fruit; ripening all year; stinging crystals in the outer pulp.

CULTURE - Full sun to partial shade; well-drained soils with reasonable fertility; no salt tolerance.

PROBLEMS - Red spider mites in interior use; lethal yellowing disease.

PROPAGATION - Seeds.

LANDSCAPE USES - Useful as an interior/patio tub specimen or as a specimen or screen planting.

COMMENTS - *C. urens* (Wine Palm) differs in having a thick, solitary, gray, smooth trunk to 80 feet and is larger overall.

Chamaedorea elegans

NEANTHE BELLA, PARLOR PALM

PRONUNCIATION - ˌkæ mə ˈdo rē ə   ˈe lə gə-nz

TRANSLATION - [low growing - a gift] [elegant].

FORM - Dioecious, small, single-trunked palm; medium-fine texture.

SIZE - Usually 4 feet high, occasionally reaching 6 to 8 feet with a spread of 2 to 3 feet; rapid growth rate.

HARDINESS ZONE - Zones 10-11, south Florida only.

NATIVE HABITAT - Understory plant of dense rain forests of Mexico, Guatemala.

LEAVES - Pinnately compound, 18 to 36 inches long;leaflets 20 to 40, lanceolate, to 1 inch wide and 8 inches long. Petioles short, unarmed. Dark green.

TRUNKS - Slender green trunks, 1 to 1.5 inches wide. Leaf scar rings.

FLOWERS - Unisexual; whitish, small; on branched, orange flower stalk to 2 feet long, in or below the leaves; flower stalks borne all year.

FRUIT - Black, globose, 0.25 inch wide; maturing all year long.

CULTURE - Requires partial to full shade and fertile, well-drained soil; no salt tolerance.

PROBLEMS - Spider mites in interior situations.

PROPAGATION - Seeds.

LANDSCAPE USES - An excellent houseplant or interiorscape plant; also useful for tubs and planters in shady locations; can be used as an accent plant on north side locations and in shady underplantings.

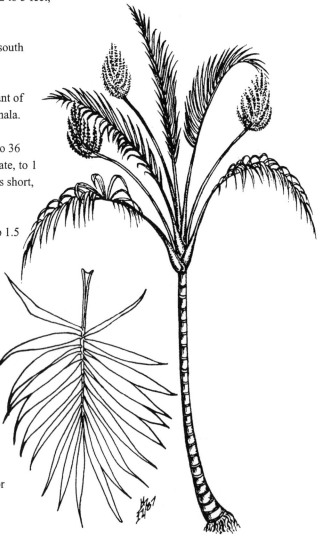

Chamaedorea erumpens   BAMBOO PALM

PRONUNCIATION - ˌkæ mə ˈdo rē ə   ē ˈrum pənz

TRANSLATION - [low growing - a gift] [breaking through, in reference to the inflorescence which ruptures the shoot as it emerges].

FORM - Dioecious, small, delicate, multiple-trunked palm; medium texture.

SIZE - Up to 12 feet high with variable spread (usually seen 8 feet); rapid growth rate.

HARDINESS ZONE - Zones 10-11, outdoor use limited to south Florida.

NATIVE HABITAT - Dense rain forests of Central America.

LEAVES - Pinnately compound, to 20 inches long; leaflets 20 to 30, lanceolate, 8 inches long and 1.5 inches wide; terminal leaflet pair united at base, generally twice as wide as other leaflets. Petioles short, smooth.

TRUNKS - Up to 40 green, stem-like trunks per clump; 0.5 inch diameter.

FLOWERS - Unisexual; whitish, small; on once-branched, 1 foot long, orange flower stalks, in or below the leaves; flower stalks borne all year.

FRUIT - Black, globose, 0.25 inch wide; maturing all year.

CULTURE - Requires partial to full shade and fertile, well-drained soil; no salt tolerance.

PROBLEMS - Spider mites in interior scapes.

PROPAGATION - Seed, division.

LANDSCAPE USES - Provides a tropical effect; used for screening or as an interior or exterior container plant.

Chamaedorea seifrizii   REED PALM

PRONUNCIATION - ˌkæ mə ˈdo rē ə   sē ˈfrit sē ī

TRANSLATION - [low growing - a gift].

FORM - Dioecious, small, delicate, multiple-trunked palm; medium-fine texture.

SIZE - Up to 12 feet tall with a variable spread (usually seen 8 feet); rapid growth rate.

HARDINESS ZONE - Zones 10-11, outdoor use limited to south Florida.

NATIVE HABITAT - Dense rain forests of Mexico.

LEAVES - Even-pinnately compound, to 2 feet long; leaflets 24 to 36, 10 inches long by 0.75 inch wide, narrowly lanceolate with ribbed margins. Petioles short, smooth.

TRUNKS - Slender green trunks are 0.75 inch thick.

FLOWERS - Unisexual; whitish, small; on once-branched, 1 foot long, orange flower stalks, in or below the leaves; flower stalks borne all year.

FRUIT - Green to black, globose 0.25 inch; fruit mature all year.

CULTURE - This species will endure more light than most Chamaedoreas, but still needs some shade part of the day; fertile, drained soil; no salt tolerance.

PROBLEMS - Susceptible to nematodes and spider mites in interiorscapes.

PROPAGATION - Seeds, division.

LANDSCAPE USES - Often used as a screen in shade locations; also used as a tub plant for patios and interiors. Several *Chamaedorea* species are used in Florida landscapes, a few proven cold hardy throughout the state. Examples include *C. arenbergiana, C. brachypoda, C. cataractarum, C. costaricana, C. elatior, C. ernesti-augusti, C. erumpens* × *C. seifrizii* ‘Florida Hybrid’, *C. glaucifolia, C. metallica, C. microspadix, C. oblongata, C. radicalis, C. stolonifera* (often incorrectly applied to plants of *C. brachypoda*), *C. tenella* (sometimes incorrectly applied to plants of *C. metallica*), and *C. tepejilote*.

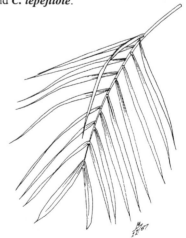

Chamaerops humilis   EUROPEAN FAN PALM

PRONUNCIATION - 'kæ mə raps   'hyū mə ləs

TRANSLATION - [low growing] [dwarf].

FORM - Dioecious or polygamodioecious, bushy, medium-sized, low-growing palm, forming a clump of several trunks, often reclining.

SIZE - To 20 feet, usually 3 to 8 feet with crown spread of 6 to 8 feet, slow growth rate.

HARDINESS ZONE - Zones 9-11; warmer areas of Zone 8. Can be grown in all areas of Florida.

NATIVE HABITAT - Mediterranean region of Europe and North Africa.

LEAVES - Palmately divided almost to base, segments sword-shaped, split at ends, to 3 feet across, green, gray-green or glaucous blue, often silvery beneath, very stiff (not drooping); petiole strongly spined, pointing toward leaf apex.

TRUNK - To 10 inches in diameter, persistent leaf bases burlap-like.

FLOWERS - Unisexual or occasionally bisexual, small, yellow, hidden among leaves; stalk short.

FRUIT - Drupe; brown or yellow, globose, 3-sided near base, to 1 inch in diameter, in short dense clusters.

CULTURE - Full sun to bright shade, various soils; slightly salt

tolerant. Slow growth makes it expensive to produce in nursery.

PROBLEMS - Scale.

PROPAGATION - Seed, division.

LANDSCAPE USES - Specimen, framing, urn or planter box, terrace, patio. Gives a tropical effect. Excellent small palm for homes.

COMMENTS - Several cultivars; var. *arborea* is single-trunked.

Chrysalidocarpus lutescens   YELLOW BUTTERFLY PALM

PRONUNCIATION - ˌkri sə ˌli də ˈkɑr pəs   lū ˈte sənz

TRANSLATION - [chrysalis-like fruit, in reference teo pupa (chrysalis) of a butterfly] [yellowish].

FORM - Dioecious, multiple-trunked palm; medium texture.

SIZE - Reaches a height of 30 feet with a variable spread; rapid growth rate.

HARDINESS ZONE - Zones 10-11, outdoor use limited to south Florida.

NATIVE HABITAT - Madagascar.

LEAVES - Pinnately compound, to 6 feet long; arching; leaflets linear, 80 to 120, narrowly induplicate, to 20 inches long and 1.5 inch wide, with tapering apices. Petioles smooth, to 2 feet, channeled on the upper side, expanded at the base to form a crownshaft, yellow with black streaks at the base. Light green.

TRUNKS - Yellow-green, prominently ringed; 4 to 6 inches wide; surmounted by the crownshaft.

FLOWERS - Unisexual; whitish, small; on many-branched, 3-foot yellowish inflorescence among the leaves; borne all year.

FRUIT - Yellow turning violet-black when mature; 0.75 inch long, oblong; ripens all year.

CULTURE - Full sun to partial shade; fertile, well-drained soil; no salt tolerance.

PROBLEMS - Pest-free in outdoor use.

PROPAGATION - Seed.

LANDSCAPE USES - Valued as a specimen, screen, corner, foundation plantings, and as a patio tub plant. Often seen as a potted decoration for commencement stages. Can be used in interior location if acclimated properly but quickly grows too large.

COMMENTS - Often incorrectly called *Areca* palm. Related species in Florida include *C. cabadae* and *C. madagascariensis*.

Coccothrinax argentata SILVER PALM

PRONUNCIATION - ˌkō kō 'thrī næks ˌar jən 'tā tə

TRANSLATION - [grinning face-trident, in reference to the appearance of the seed] [silvery].

FORM - Monoecious, small, single-trunked palm; medium-coarse texture.

SIZE - Can reach 20 feet tall, but 4 to 8 feet is the normal range; 6-foot spread; slow growth rate.

HARDINESS ZONE - Zones 10-11, limited to south Florida.

NATIVE HABITAT - Limestone pinelands of south Florida and the Bahamas.

LEAVES - Palmate, 2 to 3 feet long; divided nearly to the base, 30 to 40 slender, drooping segments; dark green on the upper surface, silvery below. Petioles 2.5 feet long, unarmed. Silver-green.

TRUNK - Trunk is usually 6 inches wide; smooth and gray or sometimes covered with woven-appearing fiber.

FLOWERS - Bisexual, small, white, numerous; borne on 2 foot flower stalks among the leaves in summer.

FRUIT - Purple to black, globose; 0.25 to 0.5 inch wide; ripening in late summer and fall.

CULTURE - Requires full sun to partial shade; tolerates any well-drained soil; moderate salt tolerance.

PROBLEMS - None of major importance.

PROPAGATION - Seed.

LANDSCAPE USES - Prized as a diminutive specimen for the silver flashing of leaves in the wind; especially good for coastal locations.

COMMENTS - Related species in south Florida landscapes include *C. alta, C. argentea* (Silver Thatch Palm), *C. crinita* (Old-Man Palm), *C. dussiana*, and *C. miraguama*.

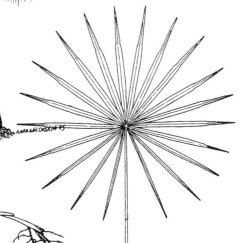

Cocos nucifera

COCONUT PALM

PRONUNCIATION - 'kō kōs   nū 'si fə rə

TRANSLATION - [a grinning face, in reference to appearance of the seed] [nut-bearing].

FORM - Large, single-trunked palm; arched, gracefully curving canopy; coarse texture.

SIZE - To 80 feet, commonly seen to 40 feet, with a 20 foot spread; rapid growth rate.

HARDINESS ZONE - Warmest areas of Zones 10-11, can be grown in south Florida only.

NATIVE HABITAT - Unknown, probably South Pacific. Floats with ocean currents, now widespread in tropics.

LEAVES - Pinnate to 15 feet long, 60 to 80 leaflets; leaflets stiff and leathery, in 2 ranks, green to yellow-green, reduplicate. Petiole unarmed, channeled above, with coarse woven fiber wrapped around base.

TRUNK - Enlarged at base to 3 feet in diameter, upper portion to 1 foot in diameter; irregularly ringed; vertical cracks present.

FLOWERS - Unisexual (plants monoecious); inconspicuous; inflorescence stalk to 6 feet long.

FRUIT - The coconut of commerce; obovoid to 1 foot long, somewhat 3-sided; fibrous husk; albumen lining the endocarp; fluid filling the cavity is known as "coconut milk."

CULTURE - Full sun, various soils; high salt tolerance.

PROBLEMS - Lethal yellowing disease; falling coconuts are a hazard.

PROPAGATION - Seed.

LANDSCAPE USES - Parks, large areas, street and seaside plantings; specimen plant.

COMMENTS - Some 1200 cultivars worldwide; '**Malayan Dwarf**' and the '**Maypan**' cultivars are resistant to lethal yellowing disease.

Howea forsteriana   SENTRY PALM

PRONUNCIATION - 'how ē ə   ˌfor stə 'rā nə

TRANSLATION - [from Lord Howe Islands] [after William Forster, a senator from New South Wales].

FORM - Monoecious, single-trunked palm; medium size; coarse texture.

SIZE - Can reach a height of 40 feet, but commonly much shorter, with a spread of 15 feet; slow growth rate.

HARDINESS ZONE - Zone 11, outdoor use limited to south Florida.

NATIVE HABITAT - Lord Howe Islands near Australia.

LEAVES - Pinnately compound; 9 to 12 feet long, stiff, arching only slightly;leaflets about 90, to 2 inches wide and 30 inches long with a prominent midrib and major veins; held horizontally out from the rachis giving the entire leaf a flat appearance. Petioles smooth to 5 feet long. Dark green leaves.

TRUNK - Trunk green; usually 5 inches thick; ringed with distinct leaf scars.

FLOWERS - Unisexual, whitish, small; on 1 to 3 hanging, 3-foot, spike-like rattails; borne all year among lower leaves.

FRUIT - Yellow-green, rounded-conical, 2 inches long; ripening all year. Fruit are not produced in Florida and take years to mature.

CULTURE - Requires partial to dense shade; fertile, well-drained soils; no salt tolerance.

PROBLEMS - Lethal yellowing disease.

PROPAGATION - Seed.

LANDSCAPE USES - Large specimens are rare and expensive, so this palm is rarely seen in landscapes. Very popular as an interior/patio tub plant.

COMMENTS - Incorrectly called Kentia palm. *Howea belmoreana* (Belmore Sentry Palm) is also in south Florida landscapes.

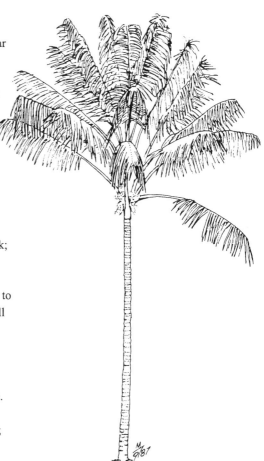

Latania spp.

PRONUNCIATION - lə 'tā nē ə

TRANSLATION - [from Mauritius, vernacular name].

FORM - Dioecious, single-trunked palms; extremely coarse texture.

SIZE - Up to 35 feet tall with a spread of 15 feet; moderate growth rate.

HARDINESS ZONE - Zones 10-11, limited to south Florida.

NATIVE HABITAT - The Mascarene Islands in the Indian Ocean.

LEAVES - Costapalmate; very thick and stiff, to 8 feet in diameter; divided into 3-inch-wide segments with finely toothed margins, undivided at base. Petioles 5 feet long, sometimes with basal marginal teeth. As the palms mature, whitish, glaucous, or waxy pubescence covers the undersides of leaves and petioles.

TRUNKS - All three latan palms have 10 inch thick trunks with swollen bases; ringed with leaf scars.

FLOWERS - Unisexual; whitish, small; on 3 to 6 foot long flower stalks with short branches; flower stalks borne within the leaves all year long.

FRUIT - Brown, glossy, oblong; to 2 inches wide; 1- to 3-seeded; ripening all year.

CULTURE - Prefers full sun, but tolerates partial shade; fertile, well-drained soil; moderate salt tolerance.

PROBLEMS - Susceptible to lethal yellowing disease.

PROPAGATION - Seed.

LANDSCAPE USES - Planted as a specimen for its leaves; especially useful in coastal situations.

COMMENTS - Species may be distinguished by leaf color; use only young leaves to make a determination asdifferences in color between the palms fade with age: *L. loddigesii* (Blue Latan) entire leaf blue-gray; *L. lontaroides* (Red Latan) petiole, leaf margins, veins reddish; *L. verschaffeltii* (Yellow Latan) petiole, leaf margins, veins deep orange-yellow.

Livistona chinensis   CHINESE FAN PALM

PRONUNCIATION - ˌli vi ˈstō nə   chī ˈnen səs

TRANSLATION - [after Patrick Murray, Baron of Livingston (died 1671), whose plant collection helped establish Edinburgh Botanical Gardens in 1670] [from China].

FORM - Single-trunked palm; coarse texture.

SIZE - Up to 30 feet high and 15 feet wide; moderate growth rate.

HARDINESS ZONE - Zones 9b-11, grown throughout Florida, except in the panhandle.

NATIVE HABITAT - Southern Japan, central China.

LEAVES - Palmate, 6 feet long and 4.5 feet wide. Mature leaves: divided one-third of the way toward the petiole into 60 to 100, 2 inch wide segments; segment tips are cleft for 8 inches, forming two slender sections which droop to form a fringe around the leaf. Juvenile leaves: palmate-orbicular with drooping, solid segment tips, giving a "footstool" appearance. Petiole 6 feet, curving toward the trunk, armed with stout spines at the basal end. Light green.

TRUNK - The trunk is ringed when young, smooth when mature, and 1 foot wide.

FLOWERS - Whitish, small; borne on yellowish, 6 foot flower stalks with many short branches; flower stalks appear all year among the leaves.

FRUIT - Blue-green, ellipsoidal, 0.75 inch long; ripening all year.

CULTURE - Prefers full sun or partial shade; young plants thrive in dense shade; fertile, well-drained soil; no salt tolerance.

PROBLEMS - Susceptible to lethal yellowing.

PROPAGATION - Seed.

LANDSCAPE USES - Makes an excellent freestanding specimen. Young plants are very popular as interior/patio tub plants, but tend to become too large with age.

COMMENTS - Other *Livistona* species in cultivation include *L. australis* (Australian Fan Palm), *L. decipiens*, and *L. rotundifolia.*

Phoenix canariensis CANARY ISLAND DATE PALM

PRONUNCIATION - 'fē niks   kə ˌnæ rē 'en səs

TRANSLATION - [Greek name for date palm] [from Canary Islands].

FORM - Dioecious, large single-trunked upright palm; stiff globular canopy.

SIZE - To 60 feet; slow growth rate.

HARDINESS ZONE - Zones 9-11. Can be grown in all areas of Florida.

NATIVE HABITAT - Canary Islands.

LEAVES - Pinnate, to 20 feet long, leaflets short, narrow, stiff, 2 to 3 ranked, green, induplicate, reduced to spines at base of petiole.

TRUNK - To 4 feet in diameter, dense diamond-shaped, persistent leaf bases; often large fibrous root mass at base.

FLOWERS - Unisexual, inconspicuous, inflorescence to 6 feet long, much-branched.

FRUIT - Drupe; elongate to 1 inch in diameter, in heavy clusters, orange.

CULTURE - Full sun, various well-drained soils, moderately salt tolerant.

PROBLEMS - Palm weevil, leaf spot, macro- and micronutrient element deficiencies, moderately susceptible to Lethal Yellowing Disease.

PROPAGATION - Seed.

LANDSCAPE USES - Specimen, large areas, street plantings. Too large for most residential sites.

COMMENTS - Easily hybridizes with other *Phoenix* spp. Relatively slow growing, hence expensive to purchase as mature plants.

Phoenix reclinata

SENEGAL DATE PALM

PRONUNCIATION - ˈfē niks ˌre klə ˈnɑ tə

TRANSLATION - [Greek name of date palm] [bent backward].

FORM - Dioecious, medium-sized clustering palm, often with reclining trunks, stiff recurving canopy.

SIZE - To 30 feet, slow growth rate.

HARDINESS ZONE - Zones 10-11, warmest areas of Zone 9. Can be planted in south, central, and protected areas of north Florida.

NATIVE HABITAT - Tropical Africa.

LEAVES - Pinnate, to 20 feet long, recurving; leaflets short, narrow, stiff, 2 to 3 ranked, green, induplicate, reduced to spines at base of petiole.

TRUNK - 4 to 7 inches thick, usually free of leaf bases, covered with fibers, often reclining.

FLOWERS - Unisexual, inconspicuous, stalk to 3 feet long, much branched.

FRUIT - Drupe; ovoid to 0.75 inch long, brown or orange.

CULTURE - Full sun, various well-drained soils; moderately salt tolerant.

PROBLEMS - Palm weevil, macro- and micronutrient deficiencies, somewhat susceptible to Lethal Yellowing Disease.

PROPAGATION - Seed, division.

LANDSCAPE USES - Specimen, accent, large areas for full development.

COMMENTS - Many hybrids with other *Phoenix* spp.

Phoenix roebelinii

PYGMY DATE PALM,
MINIATURE DATE PALM

PRONUNCIATION - 'fē niks   ‚rō bə 'le nē ī

TRANSLATION - [Greek name of date palm] [after M. Roebelin who collected in Southeast Asia].

FORM - Dioecious, diminutive, single-trunked palm; medium-fine texture.

SIZE - Up to 8 feet tall and 5 feet wide; slow growth rate.

HARDINESS ZONE - Zones 10-11, limited to south Florida.

NATIVE HABITAT - Laos.

LEAVES - Pinnately compound, to 4 feet long; graceful, arching; leaflets 90 to 100, induplicate, linear, 10 inches long; modified near the trunk to form long, straight, sharp spines. Light green.

TRUNKS - The slender, 5-inch-wide trunks are studded with knobs of old leaf bases.

FLOWERS - Unisexual, whitish, small; on numerous short branches at the end of a 1 foot stalk; flower stalks appear among the leaves all year.

FRUIT - Dark red when mature, ovoid, 0.5 inch long; ripening all year.

CULTURE - Requires full to partial sun and fertile, well-drained soil; no salt tolerance.

PROBLEMS - Chewing insects, leaf spot, and bud rot.

PROPAGATION - Seed.

LANDSCAPE USES - Excellent as a lawn specimen or group of three; very popular as a planter, tub, and pot plant; suitable for interiorscapes.

COMMENTS - Other Phoenix species include *P. dactylifera* (Date Palm), *P. rupicola,* and *P. sylvestris* (Wild Date Palm).

Ptychosperma macarthuri   MACARTHUR PALM

PRONUNCIATION - ˉˌtī kō ˈspər mə   mə ˈkɑr thə rī

TRANSLATION - [a folded seed] [after Sir W. Macarthur].

FORM - Monoecious, medium-size, multiple-trunked palm; medium texture.

SIZE - Can reach a height of 25 feet, but more commonly seen in the 12 foot range with a variable spread; rapid growth rate.

HARDINESS ZONE - Zones 10-11, outdoor use limited to south Florida.

NATIVE HABITAT - New Guinea.

LEAVES - Pinnately compound, to 6 feet long; leaflets 40 to 70, reduplicate, 1 foot long and 2 inches wide, with jagged, square-ended apex and a torn appearance. Petioles short, smooth, and expanded at the base to form a crownshaft.

TRUNKS - Slender, ringed gray trunks; 3 to 4 inches wide; surmounted by a crownshaft.

FLOWERS - Unisexual, whitish, small; on a branched, bushy flower stalk 2 feet long; flower stalks appear all year below the crownshaft.

FRUIT - Red, ovoid, 0.5 inch long, ripening all year.

CULTURE - Partial shade best, but tolerates full sun and dense shade; grows in any soil of reasonable drainage and fertility; no salt tolerance.

PROBLEMS - Relatively pest-free outdoor uses.

PROPAGATION - Seed.

LANDSCAPE USES - Valued as a specimen or in corner foundation plantings; makes a good indoor/patio tub plant, but becomes too large quickly.

COMMENTS - *Ptychosperma elegans* (Solitaire palm) is a related species which is single-trunked and reaches 20 feet.

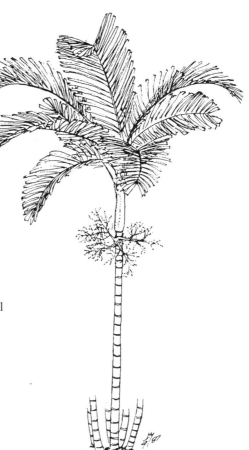

Ravenea glauca   MAJESTY PALM

PRONUNCIATION - rə ˈvē nē ə   ˈglaū kə

TRANSLATION - [Ravenea is probably a misspelling of Ran»vea which is named after Louis Ranev», a horticulturist at Berlin] [whitish, powdery coating].

FORM - Robust palm with a solitary trunk.

SIZE - 15-20 feet; reaches 10 feet quickly, then growth slows.

HARDINESS ZONES- Zones 10-11.

NATIVE HABITAT - Madagascar.

LEAVES- Pinnately compound, reduplicate, erect at first, then arching, twisted near apex; with numerous, crowded, narrow, ribbed leaflets. Petioles unarmed, fibrous margined, leaves medium green.

TRUNK - Gray, swollen at base and gradually tapering upward, ringed (caudiciform); no crownshaft.

FLOWERS - White, short inflorescence, borne among the leaves.

FRUIT - Drupe, red, 0.5 inch diameter.

CULTURE- Widely adaptable, requires moderate to high light (tends to yellow somewhat without some shade); moderate drought and salt tolerance.

PROBLEMS - None serious.

PROPAGATION - Seed, germinating in 2-3 months.

LANDSCAPE USES - Popular interiorscape palm or used in the landscape under a canopy of tall trees. Specimen plant, often grown in large contrainers. True identity of *Ravenea* in Florida landscapes is uncertain. The cultivated taxa may be either *R. glauca* or *R. rivularis.*

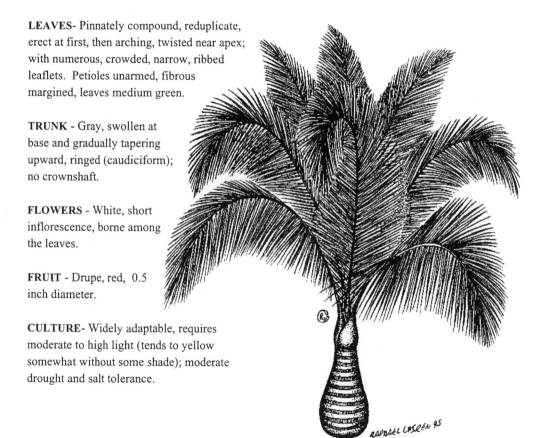

Rhapidophyllum hystrix   NEEDLE PALM

PRONUNCIATION - rə ˌpi də ˈfi ləm   ˈhis trəks

TRANSLATION - [needle-leaved] [porcupine].

FORM - Polygamodioecious, low, bushy palm with single or multiple trunks and medium texture.

SIZE - Reaches a maximum height of 8 feet, with a variable spread. Grows very slowly.

HARDINESS ZONE - Zone 7. Grows in all areas of Florida. It is the hardiest species of palm, surviving temperatures of -6° F.

NATIVE HABITAT - Low, moist areas of the southeastern United States; uncommon.

LEAVES - Palmate, to 3 feet wide, separated almost to the base into 7 to 20 spreading, stiff, 3-ribbed segments. The 1.5-inch-wide linear segments are toothed and 2-cleft at the apex, and are powdery below. The 2 to 3 foot petioles are slender and unarmed.

TRUNK - The trunk is very short and thick. Trunks may be solitary when young, but sucker with age and are covered with brown matting and long, slender, sharp, black, 6 to 8 inches, erect spines or needles, arising from the leaf bases.

FLOWERS - Flowers uni- or bisexual, reddish, small, on short flower stalks, hidden among the leaf bases and spines.

FRUIT - Drupe, brown, egg-shaped to 1 inch long, woolly.

CULTURE - Prefers partial to full shade, but tolerates full sun. Native to poorly drained soils, but will grow in moderately moist soils of reasonable fertility. It is not salt tolerant. Easily transplanted.

PROBLEMS - Pest-free.

PROPAGATION - Seed.

LANDSCAPE USES - Usually grown as a specimen if available.

COMMENTS - The plant is endangered because it is often collected from wild populations.

Rhapis excelsa   LADY PALM

PRONUNCIATION - ˈrā pəs   ek ˈsel sə

TRANSLATION - [needle, in reference to leaf segments] [tall, in reference to cane-like stems].

FORM - Dioecious, small delicate palm, forming dense clusters of cane-like trunks.

SIZE - To 15 feet, commonly 6 to 10 feet, moderate growth rate.

HARDINESS ZONE - Zones 9-11. Can be grown in all areas of Florida, but needs protection in north Florida during severe winters.

NATIVE HABITAT - Southern China.

LEAVES - Palmate, 5 to 10 segments, divided almost to base, to 1 foot across; segments with 2 to 4 strong ribs at tip; petiole unarmed.

TRUNK - Slender, covered with leaf bases and fiber at top, smooth, cane-like near base, green-ringed.

FLOWERS - Unisexual, inconspicuous, fragrant stalks to 12 inches, branched, hidden by leaves.

FRUIT -Drupe; oblong, white, to 3 inches long, sometimes several-seeded.

CULTURE - Partial to deep shade, fertile organic soils; not salt tolerant.

PROBLEMS - Scale, sooty mold, palm aphids.

PROPAGATION - Seed, division.

LANDSCAPE USES - Barrier, foundation for large buildings, accent, urn, planter box.

COMMENTS - Many cultivars for leaflet forms, variegations, etc., especially in Japan. However, *R. humilis* (fine-leaved Lady Palm, Dwarf Lady Palm) and *R. subtilis* (Thailand Lady Palm, Thai Dwarf Rhapis) are also in cultivation.

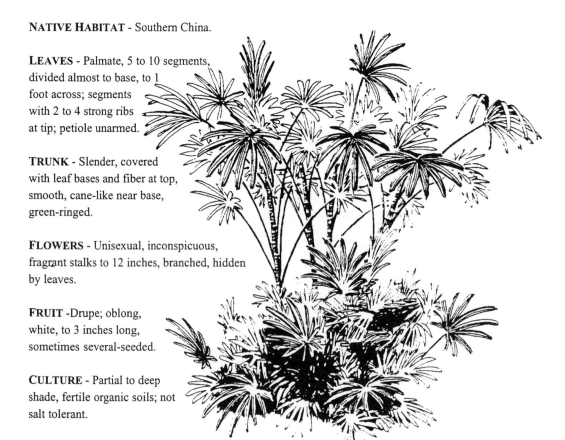

Roystonea spp.

PRONUNCIATION - roi ʹstō nē ə

TRANSLATION - [after General Roy Stone (1836-1905), American army engineer in Puerto Rico].

FORM - Monoecious, large, single-trunked, erect palm; majestic, gently drooping canopy; coarse texture.

SIZE - To 100 feet, commonly seen 50 feet; moderate growth rate.

HARDINESS ZONE - Zones 10-11, use limited to south Florida.

NATIVE HABITAT - Caribbean, South America, one to Florida.

LEAVES - Pinnate leaves, to 12 feet long; leaflets to 3 feet long, stoutly nerved on either side of midrib, 3 to 4 ranked, bright green, reduplicate. Petiole unarmed.

TRUNK - Smooth, grayish, irregularly bulged; large, glossy green crownshaft; leaf scars when young.

FLOWERS - Unisexual, born in spadices below crownshaft stalk; flower stalks to 3 feet long, much branched.

FRUIT - Drupe; purplish-black, oblong globose, 0.5 inch long.

CULTURE - Full sun; fertile organic soils; moderate salt tolerance.

PROBLEMS - Palm leaf skeletonizer, Royal Palm bug, micronutrient deficiencies.

PROPAGATION - Seed.

LANDSCAPE USES - Parks, large areas, street plantings.

COMMENTS - *Roystonea regia* (Cuban Royal Palm) and *R. elata* (Florida Royal Palm) are the most commonly cultivated spp. in Florida. Two other species, *R. borinquena* (Puerto Rican Royal Palm) and *R. oleracea* (Caribbean Royal Palm), are also used in landscapes.

Sabal palmetto

CABBAGE PALM

PRONUNCIATION - sā bəl   pɑl 'me tō

TRANSLATION - [from South American vernacular name] [small palm].

FORM - Monoecious, erect, medium-sized, single-trunked palm; dense, tight globular canopy.

SIZE - To 90 feet, commonly 20 to 40 feet, moderate growth rate.

HARDINESS ZONE - Zones 9-11 and warmer areas of Zone 8. Can be grown in all areas of Florida.

NATIVE HABITAT - Eastern United States (Carolinas to Florida).

LEAVES - Costapalmate, to 6 feet long, 3 feet wide, divided one-third of way to base, segments long, tapering, pointed, split at apex, many threads in sinuses, green or gray-green; petiole unarmed.

TRUNK - To 18 inches in diameter but quite variable, fibrous, rough; sometimes covered with old split leaf bases, often clean.

FLOWERS - Bisexual inflorescence; stalk to 4 feet, much-branched.

FRUIT - Drupe; brown-black, globose, to 0.25 inch in diameter, shiny.

CULTURE - Full sun to partial shade, various soils; highly salt tolerant. Easily transplanted.

PROBLEMS - Palm weevil, palm leaf skeletonizer.

PROPAGATION - Seed, which often germinate readily where they fall.

LANDSCAPE USES - Specimen, framing tree, street plantings.

COMMENTS - Several related species. Leaves often used in thatching; the terminal meristematic portion is removed and eaten as "heart of palm." Several related species also are seen in Florida landscapes: *S. causiarum* (Puerto Rican Hat Palm), *S. etonia* (Scrub Palmetto), *S. mexicana*, *S. minor* (Dwarf Palmetto, Blue Palm), and *S. yapa*.

Serenoa repens SAW PALMETTO

PRONUNCIATION - ˌse rə ˈnō ə ˈre pənz

TRANSLATION - [Sereno Watson (1826-1892), distinguished American botanist at Harvard] [creeping].

FORM - Monoecious, low, clumping palm, bushy with multiple trunks. It has a medium texture.

SIZE - Can reach heights of 20 feet, but normally in the 4 to 5 foot range; spread increases with age. Growth rate is moderate.

HARDINESS ZONE - Zone 8. Flourishes in all areas of Florida.

NATIVE HABITAT - Sandy areas and pinelands, coastal locations throughout the southeastern United States. It often forms extensive, dense colonies.

LEAVES - Palmate, to 3.5 feet wide, deeply divided into 25 to 30 stiff, tapering segments with cleft tips. The leaves are normally green, but there are bluish-silver varieties. The 3 to 4 foot petioles have small, sharp sawteeth covering the margins of the basal half.

TRUNK - The trunks normally creep along the ground and are rarely erect. They sucker in contact with the ground; 9 to 12 inches wide and covered with brown fiber and old leaf bases.

FLOWERS - Whitish, small, on a 3.5-foot-long flower stalk with numerous short branches. Flower stalks appear among the leaves in spring. The flowers are the source of a high-grade honey.

FRUIT - Drupe; yellowish, turning black at maturity, ellipsoidal, to 1 inch long, ripening August through October.

CULTURE - Needs full sun to partial shade, and will grow even in poor soils as long as they have good drainage. It is highly salt tolerant.

PROBLEMS - Pest-free.

PROPAGATION - Seed; seedlings grow very slowly. Transplants poorly from wild.

LANDSCAPE USES - Leave when clearing land to give a naturalistic effect.

COMMENTS - There is a form with bluish-gray foliage in central and south Florida.

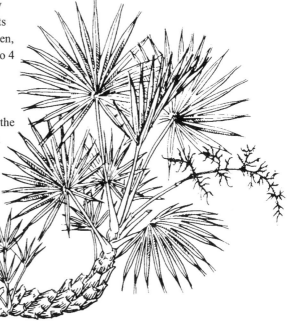

Syagrus romanzoffianum   QUEEN PALM

PRONUNCIATION - sī ˈa grəs ˌrō mən ˌzo fē ˈā nəm

TRANSLATION - [Greek word for a species of palm] [after Prince Nicholas Romanoff].

SYNONYMS - *Arecastrum romanzoffianum, Cocos plumosa.*

FORM - Large single-trunked erect palm, graceful drooping canopy.

SIZE - To 40 feet or more, rapid growth rate.

HARDINESS ZONE - Zones 9-11 and warmer areas of Zone 8b. Can be cultivated in central, south, and protected areas in north Florida.

NATIVE HABITAT - Southern Brazil to northern Argentina.

LEAVES - Pinnate, 8 to 15 feet long, glabrous leaflets to 3 feet long, soft, drooping, 2 to 3 ranked, dark green both sides, reduplicate; petiole unarmed.

TRUNKS - 1 to 2 feet in diameter, slightly and irregularly bulging, gray, smooth except for ring scars, crownshaft absent.

FLOWERS - Monoecious, cream-colored, arising in lower leaf axils, on stalk to 6 feet long, at first covered by long woody spathe.

FRUIT - Drupe; yellow, broad ovoid, short-beaked to 1 inch long, fleshy fibrous exterior.

CULTURE - Full sun, various well-drained soils (well adapted to sandy soils); moderately salt tolerant. Relatively short lived (35 to 40 years).

PROBLEMS - Palm leaf skeletonizer, scale, minor nutrient deficiency (Mn deficiency resulting in frizzle top symptoms); leaves are persistent after death and require pruning.

PROPAGATION - Seed.

LANDSCAPE USES - Accent, specimen, street plantings, commonly used in central Florida to line avenues. It can substitute for *Roystonea* **spp**. (Royal Palm) in areas that are too cold for the latter.

COMMENTS - Considerable seedling variation exists. Resistant to Lethal Yellowing. Related species include *S. comosa, S. coronata,* and *S. flexuosa.*

Trachycarpus fortunei   WINDMILL PALM

PRONUNCIATION - ˌtrā kē ʹkɑr pəs   for ʹtū nē ī

TRANSLATION - [rough fruit] [after Robert Fortune (1812-1880), Scottish horticulturist].

FORM - Monoecious, erect, small to medium sized, single trunked palm; compact globose canopy.

SIZE - To 40 feet, usually seen 5 to 15 feet; slow growth rate.

HARDINESS ZONE - Zones 9-11, warmer areas of Zone 8b. Can be grown in south, central, and protected areas of north Florida.

NATIVE HABITAT - China.

LEAVES - Palmate; to 3 feet across, divided almost to base, segments often drooping near tips, dark green above, glaucous beneath; petiole unarmed but bumpy, rough.

TRUNK - To 1 foot in diameter, usually much more slender; densely covered with brown fibers, old leaf bases.

FLOWERS - Unisexual, small, yellow, fragrant; stalk very short, branched. Not showy.

FRUIT - Drupe; blue when ripe, 3-lobed, to 0.5 inches long.

CULTURE - Full sun to partial shade, fertile well-drained soils; moderately salt tolerant. Also moderately drought and wind tolerant.

PROBLEMS - Scale, palm aphids, root rot; moderately susceptible to Lethal Yellowing Disease.

PROPAGATION - Seed.

LANDSCAPE USES - Framing tree, accent, specimen, urn. Does well in confined areas.

COMMENTS - Several related species, but only *T. takil* and *T. martianus* are reported in Florida.

Veitchia merrillii   CHRISTMAS PALM, MANILA PALM

PRONUNCIATION - 'vē chē ə   mə 'ri lē ī

TRANSLATION - [after James Veitch (1815-1869) and his son John Gould Veith, leading nurserymen of Exter and Chelsea, England] [Elmer Drew Merrill (1876-1956), a botanist].

FORM - Monoecious, small, single-trunked erect palm; rigidly arched canopy; medium-coarse texture.

SIZE - To 20 feet, usually 6 to l0 feet; moderate growth rate.

HARDINESS ZONE - Warmest areas of Zone l0, use limited to south Florida.

NATIVE HABITAT - Philippines.

LEAVES - Pinnate to 6 feet long; rigidly arched; bright green leaflets in 2 ranks, sword-shaped, reduplicate, to 30 inches long. Petiole short, unarmed.

TRUNK - Smooth; to l0 inches in diameter; faintly ringed; whitish-gray; tapering to green crownshaft.

FLOWERS - Unisexual, yellow-green to white, small; inflorescence stalk short, below crownshaft.

FRUIT - Drupe; green becoming red when ripe; elliptic to 2 inches long; pointed, glossy; very showy.

CULTURE - Full sun to partial shade; various well-drained soils; moderate salt tolerance.

PROBLEMS - Scale, lethal yellowing disease.

PROPAGATION - Seed.

LANDSCAPE USES - Specimen, framing tree, patio, terrace, small street plantings.

COMMENTS - Several related species, *V. arecina, V. joannis, V. montgomeryana,* and *V. winin*, are reported from cultivation in Florida.

Washingtonia robusta   WASHINGTON PALM

PRONUNCIATION - ˌwɑ shən 'tō nē ə   rō 'bus tə

TRANSLATION - [after George Washington (1732-1799)] [stout; strong].

FORM - Monoecious, large single-trunked erect palm; loose globose canopy.

SIZE - To 80 feet, commonly seen 40 to 50 feet, rapid growth.

HARDINESS ZONE - Zones 8b-11. Can be grown in all areas of Florida.

NATIVE HABITAT - Southwestern United States, Mexico.

LEAVES - Palmate; to 4 feet across, divided halfway to base, many threads in sinus when young, disappearing with age, segments bright green; petiole reddish-brown, armed, spines pointing in both directions; leaves often persist, forming a dense skirt.

TRUNK - To 2 feet in diameter, wider at base, angled rings, vertical cracks present, sometimes large root mass at base.

FLOWERS - Bisexual, small, numerous, white stalk to 12 feet, erect at first, then hanging. Not showy.

FRUIT - Drupe; black, ovoid, to 0.33 inch long.

CULTURE - Full sun, various well-drained soils; moderately salt tolerant.

PROBLEMS - Palm weevils, root rot, persistent leaves. Armed petioles on falling leaves are dangerous. Apparently resistant to Lethal Yellowing Disease.

PROPAGATION - Seed.

LANDSCAPE USES - Specimen, accent for tall buildings, street plantings.

COMMENTS - *W. filifera* similar but larger trunk. Hybrids between the two species are common.

Wodyetia bifurcata   FOXTAIL PALM

PRONUNCIATION - wōd ˈye tē ə   ˌbī fər ˈkā tə

TRANSLATION - [Wodyeti, an aboriginal name for a gentleman known as Johnny Flindor, the last surviving male with knowledge of the region] [in reference to the equally forked leaflets].

FORM - Monoecious, solitary with a canopy of 8-10 leaves.

SIZE - To 30 feet; fast growth rate.

HARDINESS ZONE - 10a-11.

NATIVE HABITAT- Queensland, Australia.

LEAVES - Pinnately compound, reduplicate, arching, several hundred leaflets attached in several ranks. Leaves 8-10 feet long; leaflets 6 inches long by 2 inches wide. Deep green above, silvery on underside. Common name reflects the full appearance of the leaves.

TRUNK - Slender, gray, swollen at base, ringed with leaf scars; crownshaft narrow, green with whitish waxy scales; leaf sheaths with dark brown scales at top.

FLOWERS - White, branched, borne below the crownshaft.

FRUIT- Red, 2 inches long.

CULTURE - Widely adaptable, requires moderate to high light; moderate drought and salt tolerance.

PROBLEMS - May develop fungal leaf spots if irrigated with overhead sprinklers.

PROPAGATION - Seed, germinating in 2-3 months.

LANDSCAPE USE - Popular specimen plant for the landscape. Although described in 1983 and introduced only recently, the plant has taken the palm world by storm.

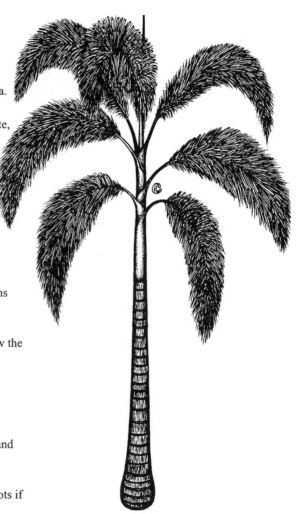

BROMELIACEAE - PINEAPPLE FAMILY

MONOCOTYLEDONS; ABOUT 50 GENERA AND 2100 SPECIES

GEOGRAPHY: Tropical and subtropical America, with only one species in West Africa.

GROWTH HABIT: Terrestrial and epiphytic herbs, often monocarpic.

LEAVES: Basal rosettes, often spinose and frequently forming a "tank" at their base from which water and nutrients are absorbed by specialized hairs. The "tank" is a mini-ecosystem where potentially many small animals and plants may thrive.

FLOWERS: Actinomorphic, 3-merous, in terminal racemose or paniculate inflorescences with showy bracts.

FRUIT: Berry or capsule.

ECONOMIC USES: Ornamentals, fruit (*Ananas comosus,* pineapple), fibers (*Tillandsia usneoides*, Spanish moss).

ORNAMENTAL GENERA: *Aechmea, Ananas, Billbergia, Bromelia, Cryptanthus,* × *Cryptbergia, Dyckia, Griegia, Guzmania, Neoregelia, Nidularium, Pitcairnia, Puya, Tillandsia, Vriesea,* and *Wittrockia*, among others.

Aechmea fasciata

SILVER VASE

PRONUNCIATION - ˈek mē ə   fæ sē ˈā tə

TRANSLATION - [from Greek, meaning spear tip] [banded].

FORM - Evergreen; epiphytic; round herbaceous perennial with leaves in a basal rosette; medium-coarse texture.

SIZE - To 2 feet tall.

HARDINESS ZONE - Zones 10-11; can be grown outside only in south Florida.

NATIVE HABITAT - Brazil.

LEAVES - Simple, in a tubular rosette, linear, inner leaves rounded and mucronate at the tip, to 2 feet long and 3 inches wide, green and may be banded with silver cross or covered with silvery scales, stiff, spiny margins.

STEM/BARK - Stemless.

FLOWERS - Pale blue, sessile; sepals mucronate, long-lasting, persistent (3 to 5 months) pink bracts are most noticeable; borne in a spike-like, pyramidal inflorescence. Blooms in March and April.

FRUIT - Berry.

CULTURE - Grown in partial shade, in interiors under light intensities down to 250 foot-candles; tolerates short periods of exposure to full sun; requires a well-drained, well-aerated medium; slight salt tolerance.

PROBLEMS - Scale; rots if kept too moist.

PROPAGATION - Seed, divison of offsets.

LANDSCAPE USES - Can be fastened to the branches of rough-barked trees; used as an interior or exterior potted plant or as a specimen.

COMMENTS - Several cultivars with different foliage variegation patterns are available.

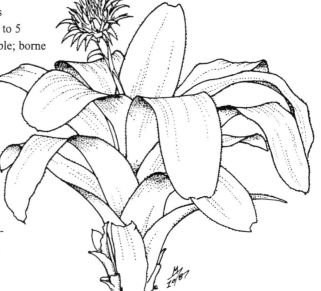

Ananas comosus   PINEAPPLE

PRONUNCIATION - ə ˈnæ nəs kō ˈmō səs

TRANSLATION - [Guarani Indian name] [tufted].

FORM - Evergreen; terrestrial; round herbaceous perennial; medium-coarse texture.

SIZE - To 4 feet tall.

HARDINESS ZONE - Zones 10-11; can be grown outside only in south Florida.

NATIVE HABITAT - Origin uncertain, probably Brazil.

LEAVES - Simple, in a basal rosette, to 3 feet long and 1.5 inches wide, stiff, bright green, channeled, with sharp spiny tips and margins.

STEM/BARK - Forms a short stem.

FLOWERS - Violet or reddish, to 0.5 inch long, individually inconspicuous; in a dense head, borne on a stout scape that rises from the center of the plant. After pollination, it forms a fleshy syncarp of inferior ovaries.

FRUIT - The pineapple of commerce; syncarp (fused carpels of many flowers); fleshy and juicy, globose to cylindrical, to 1 foot long and weighing 1 to 14 pounds. The fruit is topped with a small rosette of leaves that form a miniature plant.

CULTURE - Grown in light intensities ranging from full sun down to 250 foot-candles in interiors; well-drained soils with good aeration; slight salt tolerance. Pineapple is more attractive as an ornamental if given some protection from full sun.

PROBLEMS - Scales, mealy bugs, nematodes, and mites; root rots in poorly drained media.

PROPAGATION - Division of basal suckers, crowns of the fruit; seeds are used in experimental breeding programs.

LANDSCAPE USES - A horticultural curiosity, the plant is grown as a specimen in outdoor rock gardens, in tubs, or as an interior plant.

COMMENTS - The most important commercial cultivars are the nearly spineless **'Smooth Cayenne'** in Hawaii and **'Red Spanish'** in the West Indies. A few cultivars are available with variegated foliage: **'Porteanus'** has leaves with yellow stripes, **'Variegatus'** has longitudinal stripes of green, white, and pink.

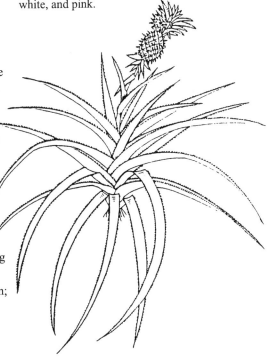

Bromelia balansae

HEART OF FLAME

PRONUNCIATION - brō ˈmē lē ə   bə ˈlæn sē

TRANSLATION - [after Olof Bromel (1629-1705), Swedish botanist] [after Benedict Balansa (1825-1891), French botanical collector].

FORM - Evergreen; terrestrial; round, herbaceous perennial; globose, spiny; coarse texture.

SIZE - To 4.5 feet tall with a 6 foot spread.

HARDINESS ZONE - Zone 9b-11; grown outside in south and central Florida; will survive in a protected location in north Florida.

NATIVE HABITAT-Argentina, Brazil, and Paraguay.

LEAVES - Simple; in basal rosettes; linear to 4.5 feet long and 1.25 inch wide; gray-green, stiff; spiny margins.

STEM/BARK - Spreads by means of underground offshoots.

FLOWERS - Maroon or violet; to 2 inches long subtended by scarlet bracts to 1.25 inches long; arranged in a massive, chalky-white, pedunculate head that rises from the center of the plant. As the inflorescence develops the central leaves turn a brillant red. Blooms in late spring and early summer.

FRUIT - Berry; orange; used to make a cooling drink in its native countries.

CULTURE - Tolerates full sun and will still produce an inflorescence down to 3000 f.c. Tolerates a wide range of well-drained soils; moderate salt tolerance.

PROBLEMS - Scale and root rot in poorly drained soils.

PROPAGATION - Seed or division of offsets.

LANDSCAPE USES - Use outdoors as a specimen for the dramatic red color and inflorescence in springtime. In its native environment the plant is used as a living fence. Not recommended as an indoor plant because of its large size and sharp spines.

COMMENTS - May spread and present a maintenance problem.

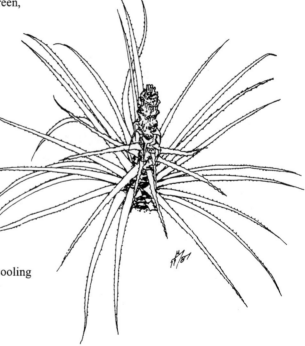

Cryptanthus spp.

EARTH STAR

PRONUNCIATION - krip ˈtæn thəs

TRANSLATION - [hidden-flower].

FORM - Evergreen; terrestrial or sometimes epiphytic; herbaceous perennial; medium-fine texture.

SIZE - From 2 to 10 inches tall with a 6 to 10 inch spread.

HARDINESS ZONE - Zone 10-11; can be grown outside only in south Florida.

NATIVE HABITAT - Brazil.

LEAVES - Simple; in crowded, flattened rosettes; linear, stiff, spreading; undulate with prickly margins; length varies with species from 2 to 18 inches long; generally 1 to 2 inches wide. Leaf colors vary with species from green to reddish to various striping or crossbanding patterns.

STEM/BARK - Usually with short stems or none; rarely with leafy stems; may produce suckers readily or not.

FLOWERS - White or greenish-white; inconspicuous, borne in small heads that nest in the center of the rosette.

FRUIT - Berry; tiny, dry.

CULTURE - Does best in partial shade ranging from 200 to 6000 foot-candles; well-drained, high organic matter soil; tolerant of some salt in the root zone; not tolerant of dune conditions (salt spray on the foliage).

PROBLEMS - Scale; root rot if overwatered.

PROPAGATION - Division of offsets.

LANDSCAPE USES - Use in little planters and dish gardens in interiors. Outdoors may be used to decorate limbs of rough-barked trees or as a ground cover or rock garden plant.

COMMENTS - At least 20 species and several hybrids are known. Among the most popular ones are *C. bivittatus, C. zonatus,* and a hybrid *Cryptanthus* × ʹIt'. There are also numerous cultivars of unknown or hybrid origin, including: **'Aloha'**, **'Cascade', 'Koko'**, **'Mirabilis',** and **'Pink Starlight'**, among others.

Dyckia brevifolia

MINIATURE AGAVE

PRONUNCIATION - ˈdi kē ə   ˌbre və ˈfō lē ə

TRANSLATION - [after Prince Joseph Salm-Reifferscheid-Dyck (1773-1861), author of outstanding books on succulents] [short leaves].

FORM - Evergreen; terrestrial; round, herbaceous perennial; medium texture.

SIZE - To 1.5 feet tall; clump-forming by production of suckers in the leaf axils.

HARDINESS ZONE - Zone 9b-11; can be grown outside in south and central Florida.

NATIVE HABITAT - Brazil.

LEAVES - Simple; in basal rosettes; stiff, succulent; with sharp spiny apex and margins; narrow, to 8 inches long and 0.75 inch wide; glossy green with white stripes on the undersurface.

STEM/BARK - Stemless; leaves in rosettes.

FLOWERS - Bright yellow to orange; campanulate to 0.5 inch long; borne in a simple, 12-inch-tall, racemose inflorescence.

FRUIT - Capsule.

CULTURE - Grown in light intenstities ranging from full sun to partial shade (500 f.c.); well-drained soils with good aeration; moderate salt tolerance.

PROBLEMS - Scale; root rot in poorly drained soils.

PROPAGATION - Division of offsets.

LANDSCAPE USES - Use as a ground cover or in succulent gardens; may also be used in dish gardens.

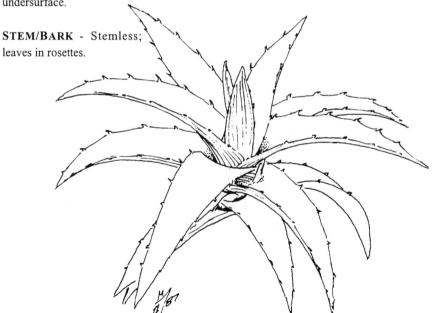

Guzmania lingulata var. *minor*   Guzmania

PRONUNCIATION - gūz ˈmā nē ə   ˈliŋ gyū ˈlā tə   ˈmī nor

TRANSLATION - [named in honor of the 18th-century Spanish naturalist Anastasio Guzman] [tongue-shaped] [smaller].

FORM - Epiphytic herb, clustering rosette to 12 inches.

SIZE - 2 feet; slow.

HARDINESS ZONE - 10a-11.

NATIVE HABITAT - Tropical America.

LEAVES - In basal rosettes, stiff, entire, thin-leathery, 12 to 18 inches long, 1 inch wide.

FLOWERS - Yellow or white, in vertical ranks in terminal spikes or panicles, long floral bracts, bright orange-red.

FRUIT - A capsule.

CULTURE - Adaptable in warm climates, requires part shade.

PROBLEMS - None serious; mites may be a problem in dry interiors.

PROPAGATION - Seed, tissue culture, division.

LANDSCAPE USES - Specimen plant, popular in interior and exterior landscapes.

COMMENTS - Many cultivars available: **'Empire'** popular in trade; **'Magnifica'** (selection from a hybrid between the typical species and var. *minor*) has red inflorescences and spreading bracts; var. *splendens* has longitudinal maroon stripes; and var. *cardinalis* has green leaves and scarlet floral bracts.

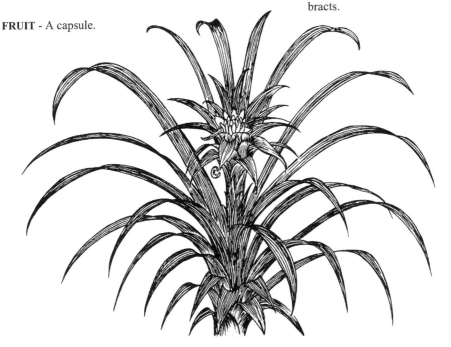

Neoregelia spectabilis PAINTED FINGERNAIL

PRONUNCIATION - ˌnē ō rə ˈjē lē ə spek ˈtæ bə ləs

TRANSLATION - [after Eduard Albert von Regel (1815-1892), director of the Imperial Botanical Garden at St. Petersburg] [spectacular].

FORM - Evergreen; epiphytic; round, herbaceous perennial; medium-coarse texture.

SIZE - To 1 foot tall.

HARDINESS ZONE - Zones 9b-11, can be grown outside in central and south Florida.

NATIVE HABITAT - Brazil.

LEAVES - Simple; in a basal rosette; stiff, strap-shaped to 16 inches long and 1.5 inches wide; olive green above, with transverse, gray bands beneath, and a red tip; inner leaves marked with maroon; margins almost spineless.

STEM/BARK - Forms large clumps by the production of offsets.

FLOWERS - Blue; tubular, to 1.5 inches long; borne in a dense head that nests in the center of the leaf bases.

FRUIT- Berry.

CULTURE - Can be grown in light levels from full sun to partial shade down to 200 foot-candles; more attractive if grown at 6000 foot-candles.In full sun or very high light the foliage will be bronze colored. Well-drained, well aerated soils; moderate salt tolerance.

PROBLEMS - Scale; mites in interiors; rots in poorly drained media.

Tillandsia cyanea TILLANDSIA

PRONUNCIATION - tə lan sē ə   sī 'a nē ə

TRANSLATION- [named in honor of Elias Til-Landz (died 1693), a Swedish botanist and professor of medicine at Abo, Finland] [blue, in reference to color of flowers].

FORM - Epiphytic, stemless herb, suckering rosette.

SIZE - 1 foot; slow.

HARDINESS ZONE - 10a-11.

NATIVE HABITAT - Ecuador.

LEAVES - Linear, channeled, recurved; to 14 inches long by 5/8-inch wide.

FLOWERS - Violet-blue, arising from a spike with broad, flattened, clear pink bracts.

FRUIT - A capsule.

CULTURE - Adaptable in warm climates, requires part shade.

PROBLEMS - None serious.

PROPAGATION - Seed, division, tissue culture.

LANDSCAPE USES - Specimen plant, popular in interior and exterior landscapes.

COMMENTS - With nearly 400 species, *Tillandsia* is, by far, the largest genus in the family and perhaps among the most common bromeliads. Many of the smaller taxa are used in dish gardens. These require little care and remain alive and attractive for a long time.

Tillandsia usneoides

SPANISH MOSS

PRONUNCIATION - tə 'lænd sē ə   ˌūs nē 'oi dēz

TRANSLATION - [named in honor of Elias Til-Landz (died 1693), a Swedish botanist and professor of medicine at Abo, Finland] [like a lichen of the genus *Usnea*].

FORM - Evergreen; epiphytic; herbaceous perennial; with slender, hanging stems; often seen festooned in masses over trees; fine texture.

SIZE - Stems to 20 feet long.

HARDINESS ZONE - Zone 8b; grows throughout Florida.

NATIVE HABITAT - A Florida native; ranges from eastern Virginia south to Argentina.

LEAVES - Simple; scattered at intervals along the stem; smooth, very narrowly linear, curved, to 2 inches long; silver-gray, peltate scales cover the leaves; entire margins.

STEM/BARK - Stems are slender, branched, much elongated, flexible and covered with silver-gray scales.

FLOWERS - Pale green or yellowish; inconspicuous to 0.5 inch long; borne singly in the leaf axils; fragrant, especially at night.

FRUIT - Capsule.

CULTURE - Tolerates full sun but grows better under 5000 f.c. (partial shade); will tolerate light down to 1000 f.c. This plant is rootless; the scales covering the stems and leaves absorb moisture. Moderate salt tolerance.

PROBLEMS - Spanish moss is not a parasite. If growing in massive quantities it may block sunlight and cause a reduction in the number of leaves on a tree. During hurricanes or periods of wet weather, the increased weight of large clumps of moss may contribute to breaking of tree limbs.

PROPAGATION - In nature by tiny, wind-borne seeds and by bird- or wind-borne festoons of the plant.

LANDSCAPE USES - Hanging from trees to create naturalistic settings, can also be used in hanging baskets.

COMMENTS - Has been used as a packing material, upholstery stuffing, cattle feed, and in air conditioner and oil filters. Can be used as sandpaper when green. Spanish moss is one of the characteristic natural features of the Southern United States.

CANNACEAE - CANNA FAMILY

MONOCOTYLEDONS; MONOGENERIC WITH 30-35 SPECIES

GEOGRAPHY:	In West Indies (including Florida) and C. America.
GROWTH HABIT:	Rhizomatous perennial herbs with aerial stems.
LEAVES:	Large, broad, with a strong central and penniparallel lateral veins, sheathing at base.
FLOWERS:	Showy, bisexual, 3-merous, on racemose inflorescences and subtended by a bract; sepals usually free, green; petals 3 with one smaller than the others and fused at base and to the staminal column; stamens 4-6, usually brightly colored; ovary inferior and consist of 3 fused carpels.
FRUIT:	A warty, 3-locular capsule containing several spherical black (when ripe) seeds.
ECONOMIC USES:	Primarily as ornamentals. The rhizome of the South American/West Indian *C. edulis* is the source of canna starch (Tous les Mois).

ORNAMENTAL GENERA:*Canna*.

Canna × *generalis*

PRONUNCIATION - ˈkæ nə ˌje nə ˈræ ləs

TRANSLATION - [from Greek *kanna* (= a reed)] [normal, common].

FORM - Monoecious, tall, erect perennial herb, thick branching rhizomes, mostly solitary or single main stems, upright, heavily foliated, vigorous. Coarse texture.

SIZE - Variable with cv. from l.5 to 5 feet tall. Rapid growth rate.

HARDINESS ZONE - Rhizomes may be left in the ground year round in Zone 7 to 11 (all areas of Florida). Farther north, rhizomes must be dug up each fall.

NATIVE HABITAT - Horticultural origin.

LEAVES - Simple, alternate to spirally arranged, ovate to elliptic-lanceolate, to 2 feet long, prominent veins, usually glaucous, entire margins, sheathing petioles. Color varies with cultivar from green to reddish-purple to bronze to variegated.

STEM/BARK - Unbranched, green or somewhat colored.

FLOWERS - Red, pink, yellow, white, striped or splashed; in spikes, terminal to 18 inches tall, flowers 3-merous, irregular, reflexed; to 6 inches across; flowers in summer and fall.

FRUIT - A capsule; 3-valved, rough.

CULTURE - Full sun or light shade, various well-drained, fertile soils; some cultivars moderately salt tolerant. Withstands summer heat if moisture is adequate.

PROBLEMS - Canna leaf roller (a major problem), borers, chewing insects.

PROPAGATION - Seeds, division of rhizome.

LANDSCAPE USES - Bedding plant, border, pot plant, planter box, mass plantings, formal or informal gardens.

COMMENTS - A large group of complex hybrids from which many cultivars have been selected for flower and foliage color and size. A few related species are also cultivated. *Canna flaccida* (Golden Canna), a Florida native, grows in swamps, marshes, ditches and flooded pinelands. Its yellow flowers may be seen throughout the spring and summer (year round in South Florida). This species is probably involved in hybridization and selection of taxa in cultivation.

COMMELINACEAE - SPIDERWORT FAMILY

MONOCOTYLEDONS; ABOUT 40 GENERA AND 600 SPECIES

GEOGRAPHY: Moist locations in tropical, subtropical, and warm temperate.

GROWTH HABIT: More or less succulent annual or perennial herbs, stemless or with jointed stems, rhizomatous and sometimes tuberous and with fibrous adventitious roots.

LEAVES: Alternate, entire, sheathing at base.

FLOWERS: Bisexual, actinomorphic or rarely zygomorphic, 3-merous with distinct green sepals and free or rarely fused petals; stamens 6, free, often with colorful hairs; ovary superior; in terminal or lateral cymes.

FRUIT: A capsule.

ECONOMIC USES: Ornamentals and a few locally used for medicinal purposes.

ORNAMENTAL GENERA:*Commelina, Cyanotis, Dichorisandra, Rhoeo, Setcreasea, Tradescantia, Zebrina,* etc.

Setcreasea pallida   PURPLE HEART

PRONUNCIATION - set ˈkrē sē ə   ˈpæ lə də

TRANSLATION - [derivation unclear] [pale].

FORM - Monoecious, evergreen perennial herb; sprawling, mat-forming, succulent ground cover; medium-coarse texture.

SIZE - Reaches a maximum height of 15 inches and spreads to cover large areas; fairly rapid growth rate.

HARDINESS ZONE - Zone 8b; can be grown in north, central, and south Florida, but needs a protected location in north Florida.

NATIVE HABITAT - Northeastern Mexico.

LEAVES - Simple; alternate; lanceolate and trough-shaped, to 7 inches long, clasping the stem; color varies from green to intense purple.

STEM/BARK - Succulent, reclining stems; break easily; root at the nodes in contact with the ground; have a watery sap that may irritate skin.

FLOWERS - Pink; petals 3, to 1 inch wide; usually terminal and subtended by two large, leaf-like bracts; last only one morning.

FRUIT - Small, inconspicuous capsules.

CULTURE - Grows in full sun or partial shade on a wide range of soils; marginal salt tolerance. Does well under trees.

PROBLEMS - Generally pest-free, although chewing insects may attack.

PROPAGATION - Cuttings root easily.

LANDSCAPE USES - Ground cover, occasionally used as a pot plant or hanging basket.

COMMENTS - '**Purple Heart**' is the most widely used cultivar and has purple leaves and stems when grown in full sun.

Tradescantia pendula WANDERING JEW

PRONUNCIATION - ˈtra də ˈskan tē ə   ˈpen dyə lə

TRANSLATION - [after John Tradescant (1608-1662)] [weeping].

SYNONYM - *Zebrina pendula.*

FORM - Monoecious, evergreen perennial herb; creeping, succulent ground cover; medium-fine texture.

SIZE - Reaches a maximum height of 10 inches with an indefinite spread; rapid growth rate.

HARDINESS ZONE - Zone 9; can be grown in central and south Florida, but requires protected locations in north Florida.

NATIVE HABITAT - Tropical America.

LEAVES - Simple; alternate; ovate to 2 inches long; sheathing leaf bases. The typical form has purple-green leaves with two longitudinal, silvery stripes and purple undersides. The cultivars have different coloring and variegation.

STEM/BARK - Fleshy stems break easily and root at the nodes if in contact with the ground.

FLOWERS - Pink; small, inconspicuous; in sessile clusters subtended by 2 unequal, spathelike bracts.

FRUIT - Capsules; 3-valved, small.

CULTURE - Grown in partial shade on a wide range of well-drained soils; marginal salt tolerance.

PROBLEMS - Sometimes mites, if grown indoors; weedy.

PROPAGATION - Stem cuttings root easily.

LANDSCAPE USES - A good ground cover for shady areas; it covers quickly, but tends to spread beyond bed boundaries quickly. Also grown as an indoor pot plant, hanging basket, or in shady planters.

COMMENTS - Cultivars **'Purpusii'** (mat-forming, with purple leaves and small pink flowers) and **'Quadricolor'** (leaves with pink, red, and white stripes) have been reported.

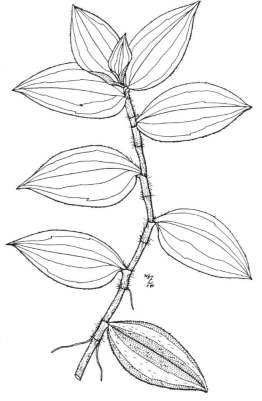

Tradescantia spathacea

OYSTER PLANT,
MOSES IN THE CRADLE

PRONUNCIATION - ˌtra də ˈskan tē ə   spæ ˈthā sē ə

TRANSLATION - [after John Tradescant (1608-1662)] [spathe-like].

SYNONYM - *Rhoeo spathacea.*

FORM - Monoecious, evergreen perennial herb; clumping, succulent, ground cover; medium texture.

SIZE - Grows to 18 inches tall with an indeterminate spread; moderate growth rate.

HARDINESS ZONE - Zone 9b-11, grown in south Florida and in protected locations in central Florida.

NATIVE HABITAT - Tropical America.

LEAVES - Simple, alternate, lanceolate and dagger-like, to 12 inches long, in tight rosettes; stiff, fleshy, upright, green on the upper surface, purple below.

STEM/BARK - Purple, succulent, erect stems fall over with age and form roots in contact with the ground; new, erect shoots follow.

FLOWERS - White, small, and inconspicuous; petals 3, in scorpioid cymes, enclosed by small, clam-like purple bracts.

FRUIT - Small, inconspicuous capsules within the bracts.

CULTURE - Grows under any light condition on a wide range of soils, including bare rock; marginal salt tolerance.

PROBLEMS - Caterpillars and mites.

PROPAGATION - Seeds, stem cuttings, or division.

LANDSCAPE USES - An easy to grow, low-maintenance ground cover, edging, or planter plant that spreads, but rarely gets out of control.

COMMENTS - Variegated and dwarf cultivars are available.

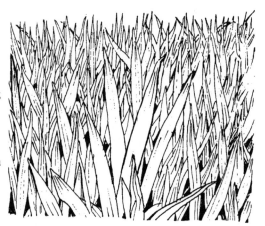

CYPERACEAE - SEDGE FAMILY

MONOCOTYLEDONS; ABOUT 100 GENERA AND 4,000 SPECIES

GEOGRAPHY:
Cosmopolitan, predominantly in poor wet soils of temperate zones.

GROWTH HABIT:
Rhizomatous, grass-like herbs with solid, often triangular stem.

LEAVES:
Basal, 3-ranked, grass-like and sheathing around the stem.

FLOWERS:
Small and inconspicuous, bi- or unisexual (plants monoecious); 3-merous, perianth absent or represented by bristles; ovary superior; situated in axil of a bract (glume), arranged in spikelets.

FRUIT:
Achene.

ECONOMIC USES:
Ornamentals; the source of papyrus paper, mat making, edible rhizomes, perfumes, and other uses such as hat and basket making and medicinal purposes.

ORNAMENTAL GENERA: *Carex, Cyperus, Eleocharis, Rhynchospora,* and *Scripus* are cultivated.

Cyperus alternifolius   UMBRELLA SEDGE

PRONUNCIATION - sī ˈpē rəs   ol ˌtər nə ˈfō lē əs

TRANSLATION - [Greek name] [alternate leaves].

FORM - Evergreen; herbaceous perennial shrub; rhizomatous, forms dense, tufted clumps; medium-fine texture.

SIZE - To 8 feet tall; clump forming; rapid growth rate.

HARDINESS ZONE - Zone 8b; can be grown throughout Florida.

NATIVE HABITAT - Madagascar.

LEAVES - Basal; reduced to sheaths at base of plant; reddish-brown.

STEM/BARK - Slender, green; triangular to rounded; finely grooved; end in a conspicuous, umbrella-shaped flowering head.

FLOWERS - Inflorescence a compound umbel, with 12 to 20 conspicuous, drooping, leaflike bracts, 4 to 12 inches long and 0.5 to 0.75 inch wide; bracts subtend by a shorter central cluster of rays bearing many minute flowers arranged in spikes to 0.5 inch long; dull brown.

FRUIT - Inconspicuous black achenes.

CULTURE - Grows in deep shade to full sun; varied soils; grows well in water; tolerates some salt drift.

PROBLEMS - Mites.

PROPAGATION - Division of clumps.

LANDSCAPE USES - Popular water garden plant; will also grow in garden soil; accent, screen. In interiors, used as a pot plant.

COMMENTS - The dwarf umbrella sedge (ˈGracilis') may be a cultivar of this species. Several related species and cultivars are in the trade, including *C. isocladus* (Dwarf Papyrus), *C. papyrus* (Papyrus), and ‘Giant’ and ‘Nanus'.

IRIDACEAE - IRIS FAMILY

MONOCOTYLEDONS; ABOUT 90 AND MORE THAN 1800 SPECIES

GEOGRAPHY: Cosmopolitan, but especially S. Africa and E. Mediterranean.

GROWTH HABIT: Perennial herbs with rhizomes, corms, or less often bulbs.

LEAVES: Narrow, linear, mostly 2-ranked and often appearing in one plane, resembling a fan.

FLOWERS: Terminal, in racemes or solitary; actinomorphic or zygomorphic; bisexual; 3-merous; perianth similar (tepals) or dissimilar with two whorls each of 3 segments each, the outer larger and deflexed and with a patch of hairs ("the falls"); stamens 3; ovary usually inferior.

FRUIT: Capsule with numerous seeds.

ECONOMIC USES: Ornamentals, saffron (from *Crocus sativus*), and perfumes from some *Iris* species.

ORNAMENTAL GENERA: *Crocus, Dietes, Freesia, Gladiolus, Iris, Ixia, Moraea, Sisyrinchium, Sparaxis,* and *Tigridia,* among others.

Dietes iridioides   AFRICAN IRIS

PRONUNCIATION - dī 'ē tēz ˌi ri 'doī dēz

TRANSLATION - [from Greek *dietesiae* (= perennial with short shoot), in reference to the rhizomes] [iris-like].

SYNONYM: *Dietes vegeta, Moraea iridioides, M. vegeta.*

FORM - Evergreen perennial clumping herb, of medium texture.

SIZE - Reaches a height of 2 feet with an equal spread. Grows at a medium rate.

HARDINESS ZONE - Zone 8b. Can be grown in all areas of Florida.

NATIVE HABITAT - South Africa.

LEAVES - Simple, sword-shaped, linear, rigid leaves, to 2 feet long, 2-ranked, are held in a vertical, fan-like plane.

STEM/BARK - Spreads by creeping, stout rhizomes.

FLOWERS - Flowers white, with yellow or brown spots toward tips of the outer petals to 3 inches, with 3 to 4 flowers/spathe. The style is marked with blue. Short-lived, flowers in the spring.

FRUIT - Capsules, small, 3-valved, ellipsoidal, 1 to 1.5 inches long.

CULTURE - Plant in full sun or partial shade on fertile, well-drained soil. It is not salt tolerant.

PROBLEMS - Nematodes.

PROPAGATION - Rhizome division or seed.

LANDSCAPE USES - A ground cover, used in foundation plantings, beds, and planters.

COMMENTS - 'Johnsonii' has erect leaves and tall flowering stems. Oakhurst Hybrids have spreading habit, cream-white flowers blotched brown-yellow with a purple center.

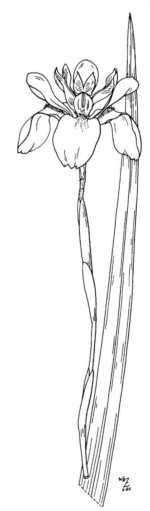

Gladiolus × hortulanus   GARDEN GLADIOLUS

PRONUNCIATION - ˈglæ dē ˈō ləs   ˌhor tyū ˈlā nəs

TRANSLATION - [small sword] [from horticulture].

FORM - Perennial caulescent herb with corm, stems erect, unbranched, leafy, sturdy.

SIZE - Variable with species and cultivar, to 5 feet tall, rapid growth rate.

HARDINESS ZONE - Varies with cultivar and species; generally Zones 7 to 10. Can be left in ground year-round in all areas of Florida, but plants flower more profusely if the corms are dug and reset annually.

NATIVE HABITAT - Horticultural origin; species primarily native to Tropical and South Africa.

LEAVES - Simple, basal and cauline, linear, sword-shaped or cylindrical to 2 feet long, often prominently veined or ribbed, light green, often rigid to somewhat papery texure.

STEM - Green, leafy, to 6 feet tall, stiff, unbranched.

FLOWERS - 28 recognized basic colors through yellow, whites, oranges, reds, lavenders, purples, browns, variously shaded and particolored; in 1-sided spikes, flowers irregular, tepals 6, united into a curved funnelform tube spread wide open to 8 inches across, upper 3 segments larger than lower 3; stamens 3, flowers in summer, fall, winter.

FRUIT - Capsule, usually flattened or winged, 3-valved.

CULTURE - Full sun, various fertile soils; not salt tolerant.

PROBLEMS - Thrips, scab, heart rot, *Fusarium, Penicillium* fungus diseases.

PROPAGATION - Seeds, more often separation of cormels.

LANDSCAPE USES - Cut flowers primarily, also bedding plant, planter box.

COMMENTS - About 10,000 cultivars and 180 related wild species. Important cut flower crop and garden plants. For an excellent treatment of *Gladiolus,* see "the American Horticultural Society A-Z Encyclopedia of Garden Plants". Three groups have been recognized: Grandiflorus Group (late spring to early fall), Nanus Group (early summer) and Primulinus Group (early to late summer).

Iris spp. and Hybrids

IRIS, FLEUR-DE-LIS

PRONUNCIATION - ˈī rəs

TRANSLATION - [after the Greek goddess of the rainbow].

FORM - Upright rhizomatous or bulbous herbaceous perennials.

SIZE - To about 2 feet.

HARDINESS ZONE - 5 to 9.

NATIVE HABITAT - Widespread in the north temperate regions.

LEAVES - Basal, but with a few on the flowering stalk, flat, linear, often sword-shaped and distichous, sometimes grass-like.

STEM/BARK - Caulescent, erect, simple or branched.

FLOWERS - Showy and of various sizes and colors, including nearly black; terminal on racemose or paniculate inflorescences, one to several on erect stems, usually of short duration but opening sequentially over a period of time. Segments of flowers united into a long or short tube; the three outer segments (= "falls") usually reflexed and with a row of hairs (= "bearded") on the upper surface in many species or sometimes a serrated crest ("crested" or "evansia"), or it may be smooth; the three inner segments (= "standards") erect and often narrowed to a "claw." Style branches are petal-like.

FRUIT - Oblong, 3 or 6-sided, 2-3 inch long capsule with numerous seeds.

CULTURE - Species dependent: in well-drained, loose soils or in moist to wet soils, in full sun or in partial shade.

PROBLEMS - None major, but it is imperative to know the requirements of the specific taxa being grown.

PROPAGATION - Seeds germinate readily when fresh; cultivars usually by separation of bulbs or division of rhizomes.

LANDSCAPE USES - Excellent in rock gardens, as ground covers, for spring or early summer flowering, or as accent plants for cluster of foliage.

COMMENTS - With more than 150 species and numerous hybrids and cultivars, irises are among the most popular garden plants around the world. The most commonly cultivated types are the lilac and purple forms are the **"bearded"** forms commonly known as the **"blue flag"** irises and sometimes referred to as the Japanese or German irises. The bulbous irises include **"Dutch"**, **"English"**, and **"Spanish"** irises and are members of the subgenera *Xiphium* and *Scorpiris* or their hybrids. The **"Bearded Iris"** are of the Mediterranean origin (*I.* × *germanica*) and are more adapted to drier regions. The **"Louisiana"** irises constitute several species including *I. fulvala, I. brevicaulis, I. nelsonii,* and *I. giganticaerulea*) and their hybrids which occur in the southern states, though they are known to perform well in other regions. These require moist to wet soils.

LILIACEAE - LILY FAMILY

MONOCOTYLEDONS; 250 TO 300 GENERA AND MORE THAN 4,000 SPECIES

GEOGRAPHY: Cosmopolitan.

GROWTH HABIT: Predominantly herbaceous perennials with bulbs, corms, rhizomes, or fleshy rootstocks; some are evergreen leaf succulents, and a few are more or less woody or herbaceous vines.

LEAVES: Variable; basal and linear and grass-like, broadly laminate and lanceolate to ovate, and in some cases reduced and scale-like; veins usually parallel but sometimes netted.

FLOWERS: Actinomorphic; bisexual; often solitary but sometimes in cymes or umbellate heads; tepals 6, occasionally readily distinguishable into sepals and petals; stamens usually 6; ovary superior and of 3 fused carpels.

FRUIT: Usually a dry capsule but sometimes a berry.

ECONOMIC USES: Many ornamentals, but a few vegetables (asparagus and lily flower buds).

ORNAMENTAL GENERA: *Aloe, Asparagus, Aspidistra, Chlorophytum, Convallaria, Fritillaria, Gloriosa, Haworthia, Hemerocallis, Hosta, Hyacinthus, Kniphofia, Lapageria, Lilium, Liriope, Ophiopogon, Scilla, Tulipa, Zigadenus,* among many others.

COMMENTS: Because of its diversity, Liliaceae has been variously split into several families and at times included some members of Alliaceae and Amaryllidaceae.

Aloe barbadensis   ALOE

PRONUNCIATION - ˈæ lō ˌbɑr bə ˈden səs

TRANSLATION - [from the Arabic name] [of Barbados, West Indies].

FORM - Monoecious, evergreen, herbaceous perennial; succulent rosette of leaves on a very short stem, clump-forming; coarse texture; ground cover.

SIZE - To 2 feet tall, generally seen about 1 foot; moderate growth rate.

HARDINESS ZONE - Zone 9; grown in south and warmest areas of central Florida.

NATIVE HABITAT - Mediterranean Region.

LEAVES - Simple; alternate but appearing whorled; thick and succulent; narrowly lanceolate to a long acuminate apex; 1 to 2 feet long and 2 to 3 inches wide at the base; glaucous green, often spotted; margins armed with white to reddish teeth.

STEM/BARK - Very short-stemmed, stoloniferous.

FLOWERS - Yellow; tubular; segments and stamens 6; to 1 inch long; borne in terminal racemes to 3 feet high.

FRUIT - Capsules; loculicidal, to 2 inches long.

CULTURE - Full sun to partial shade; various well-drained soils; moderate salt tolerance.

PROBLEMS - Caterpillars occasionally attack young leaves.

PROPAGATION - Division of suckers, cuttings, or seeds.

LANDSCAPE USES - Use as a specimen or accent plant or in succulent and rock gardens; a well-known pot plant for interior use; ground cover.

COMMENTS - A large genus of leafy succulents. A major source of drug aloe used in burn, sunburn remedies, skin creams, shampoos and soaps, etc. There are several hundred related species native primarily to Africa and Arabia.

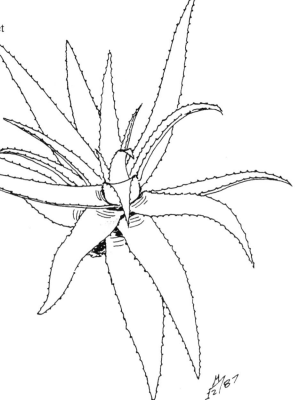

Asparagus densiflorus

ASPARAGUS FERN

PRONUNCIATION - ə ˈspæ rə gəs   ˌden sə ˈflo rəs

TRANSLATION - [ancient name] [densely-flowered].

FORM - Monoecious, evergreen; perennial herb; ground cover; tuberous, spreading, fine texture.

SIZE - To 3 feet tall, spreading; rapid growth rate.

HARDINESS ZONE - Zone 9; grown in south, central, and warmest areas of north Florida. Frost kills the foliage, but plants recover quickly.

NATIVE HABITAT - South Africa.

LEAVES - True leaves scale-like; subtending narrow, green, leaf-like branchlets called cladophylls: linear, 1-nerved, usually flattened, and slightly curved to 1.25 inches long; solitary or sometimes 3 or more at a node.

STEM/BARK - Somewhat woody and spiny.

FLOWERS - Bisexual; white or pale pink; to 0.25 inch long; borne in axillary racemes; relatively attractive when in full bloom.

FRUIT - Berry; red; ovoid to 0.25 inch long; seeds black, hard, 1 or 2 per fruit.

CULTURE - Full sun to partial shade; various well-drained soils; no salt tolerance.

PROBLEMS - Generally pest free.

PROPAGATION - Seeds which germinate in 4 to 6 weeks, cuttings, or division of clumps.

LANDSCAPE USES - Used as a border, ground cover, bedding plant, hanging basket, or in pots and urns.

COMMENTS - Two popular cultivars are grown in Florida: **'Myers'** - Stems stiffly erect, very densely short branched, forming narrow plumes to 2 feet tall and 2.5 inches wide, tapering to the apex, slow growing; **'Sprengeri'** - Stems drooping, loosely branched to 3 feet tall, branches to 5 inches long. The most commonly cultivated ornamental *Asparagus.*

Aspidistra elatior   CAST IRON PLANT

PRONUNCIATION - ˌæ spə ˈdis trə   ē ˈlā tē or

TRANSLATION - [a small, round shield; in reference to the shape of the stigma] [taller].

FORM - Monoecious, evergreen, rhizomatous perennial, herbaceous, clumping, of coarse texture.

SIZE - Reaches a height of 2 feet with a wider spread. Grows at a slow rate.

HARDINESS ZONE - Zone 7, grows well in all areas of Florida. Foliage injured by prolonged exposure to below freezing temperatures and direct sunlight.

NATIVE HABITAT - Eastern Asia.

LEAVES - Simple, oblong-elliptic, to 2.5 feet and 4 inches wide, entire. The dark green, leathery, glossy leaves are borne on thin, erect, long-channelled petioles, 8 to 12 inches long, arising from rhizomes.

STEM/BARK - Acaulescent, spreads slowly by a creeping rhizome.

FLOWERS - Brown-purple, campanulate, 1" wide, inconspicuous. Flowers are borne near the soil surface below the leaves.

FRUIT - Berries, small, 1-seeded, inconspicuous.

CULTURE - Grows in partial to very dense shade. If grown in full sun, foliage becomes yellowed and burned. Tolerates a wide range of soils (except heavily compacted soils) and marginal amounts of salt. Good drought tolerance. Withstands a wide range of conditions and abuse. Old leaves will need to be removed periodically.

PROBLEMS - Occasionally attacked by a leaf-spotting disease, mites in low humidity situations, scale insects; generally pest-free.

PROPAGATION - Clump division.

LANDSCAPE USES - Groundcover, planters, edging, massing, interiorscapes, textural contrast. As the common name implies, this is a tough plant that persists as a ground cover in areas where lack of light, water or ventilation causes other plants to die.

COMMENTS - 'Variegata' has striped green and white leaves; tends to lose variegation in high fertility situations.

Chlorophytum comosum   SPIDER PLANT

PRONUNCIATION - ˌklo rē ˈfī təm   kə mō səm

TRANSLATION - [from Greek *chloros* (= green) and *phyton* (= a plant)] [tufted].

FORM - Monoecious; evergreen herbaceous perennial; ground cover, spreading, very short-stemmed, medium-fine texture.

SIZE - To 1 foot tall; rapid growth rate.

HARDINESS ZONE - Zone 9b; grown outside in south and warmer areas of central Florida; grown elsewhere as an interior plant.

NATIVE HABITAT - South Africa.

LEAVES - Simple; alternate appearing whorled; linear-lanceolate to 1.5 feet long and 0.75 inch wide; in basal rosettes; sessile, soft, green; entire margins.

STEM/BARK - Stoloniferous.

FLOWERS - White, small; perianth rotate, segments and stamens 6; borne in a loose bracteate panicle on a cylindrical stolon. Small plantlets are formed and persist on the stolon terminus.

FRUIT - Loculicidal capsule.

CULTURE - Partial to dense shade, in interiors will tolerate light levels of 150 f.c.; rich organic but well-drained soils; no salt tolerance.

PROBLEMS - Spider mites, mealy bugs, root rot, sensitive to fluoride.

PROPAGATION - Seeds, offsets, or division.

LANDSCAPE USES - Used as a pot plant, hanging basket, or ground cover.

COMMENTS - Several cultivars are available: **'Variegatum'** (leaves margined with white) and **'Vittatum'** (leaves recurved, with a central white stripe; slower growing).

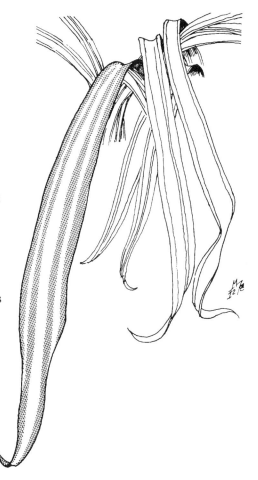

Gloriosa rothschildiana   GLORIOSA LILY, GLORY LILY

PRONUNCIATION - ˌglo rē ˈō sə   roth ˌshil dē ˈā nə

TRANSLATION - [from Latin, full of glory] [after Lionel Walter, 2nd Baron Rothschild (1868-1937)].

FORM - Monoecious, perennial herb, climbing, medium texture.

SIZE - To 8 feet, usually seen 4 to 5 feet, moderate growth rate.

HARDINESS ZONE - Zone 9. Grows in south and protected areas of central and north Florida.

NATIVE HABITAT - Tropical Africa.

LEAVES - Simple, alternate, opposite or whorled, ovate-lanceolate, 5 to 7 inches long, with a coiled, tendril-like (cirrhose) tip, margins entire.

STEM - Tuberous underground stem; above ground stem green, succulent, easily broken.

FLOWERS - Solitary in upper leaf axils, lily-like, crimson, yellow, and whitish on margins and at base, perianth segments 6, oblong-lanceolate to 3 inches long, strongly recurved, margins wavy and crisped. Very unusual and showy. From late spring throughout summer.

FRUIT - 3-valved, loculididal capsule. Seeds red.

CULTURE - Full sun to partial shade, various moisture-retentive, fertile soils; not salt tolerant.

PROBLEMS - Chewing insects, aphids.

PROPAGATION - Seeds, offsets, division of tuber.

LANDSCAPE USES - Fence, trellis, specimen, cut flowers.

COMMENTS - Plant of unusual growth habit; spectacular when in flower.

Haworthia fasciata

ZEBRA HAWORTHIA

PRONUNCIATION - hɑ 'wor thē ə ˌfæ sē 'ā tə

TRANSLATION - [in honor of Adrian Hardy Haworth (1768-1833), English authority on succulent plants] [bound together].

FORM - Monoecious, perennial herb, succulent, short-stemmed, clump-forming, medium texture.

SIZE - To 6 inches, usually smaller, slow growth rate.

HARDINESS ZONE - Grown as a greenhouse plant throughout Florida.

NATIVE HABITAT - South Africa.

LEAVES - Simple, alternate, appearing whorled, triangular-lanceolate, to 1.5 feet long, incurved toward apex, succulent, slightly glossy, lower surface with large, white tubercles confluent into transverse line.

STEM/BARK - Very short-stemmed.

FLOWERS - White, with green stripes, perianth tubular, 2-lipped, stamens 6, racemes on a scape to 12 inches.

FRUIT - Capsule, loculicidal, 3-valved.

CULTURE - Full sun or very light shade; sandy, very well-drained soils; not salt-tolerant.

PROBLEMS - Scales, root rot

PROPAGATION - Seeds, offsets

LANDSCAPE USES - Greenhouse pot plant.

COMMENTS - Many related species, cultivars. Indeed, an entire group of rosette plants, such as *Aloe, Gasteria,* etc., are much sought after by succulent collectors.

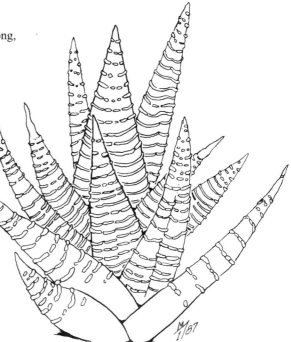

Hemerocallis Hybrids and Cultivars   DAYLILY

PRONUNCIATION - ˌhe mə rō ˈkæ ləs

TRANSLATION - [from Greek *himera* (= day) and *kallas* (= beauty), beautiful for a day].

FORM - Monoecious, perennial herbs, evergreen or deciduous, clumping, medium-textured.

SIZE - Reaches a height of 3 feet or less, depending on cultivar, with a wider spread. Growth rate is rapid.

HARDINESS ZONE - Zone 3, can be grown in all areas of Florida.

NATIVE HABITAT - Europe and Asia.

LEAVES - Simple, linear and strap-like, keeled, grasslike, arching, to 2 feet long. The leaves are 1.5 inches wide at the base, tapering gradually to a narrow apex, 2-ranked.

STEM/BARK - Acaulescent, spreads by fleshy rhizomes.

FLOWERS - Shades of yellow, orange, red and purple; funnelform to campanulate, 6-tepals to 5 inches wide, in clusters on long scapes up to 5 feet tall, subtended by a bract. The flowers only last one day, and appear in spring and throughout the summer, depending on cultivar.

FRUIT - Loculicidal capsules, 3-parted, few-seeded.

CULTURE - Grows in full sun or partial shade on a wide range of soils. Salt tolerance is moderate. Flowering declines with overcrowding; dig and divide every 5 to 7 years.

PROBLEMS - Aphids attack the leaf base, thrips may injure flower buds; generally pest-free.

PROPAGATION - Clump division for cultivars, or seed, if available, for species. High demand cultivars have been commercially propagated by tissue culture. Offset may develop on flowerstalks and can be used for propagation.

LANDSCAPE USES - A tall or compact ground cover, planter box, should be massed for greatest effect. Grows on poor soil; useful for erosion control on slopes and banks.

COMMENTS - 13-15 species, but 30,000 hybrids and cultivars. Many of the northern cultivars may not be suited for Florida conditions, especially south Florida. The more common cultivars have been recently grouped according to size: dwarf, medium, and tall. Specific cultivars are too numerous to mention. They are also grouped according to their flower shapes: triangular, circular, double, star-shaped, and spider-shaped.

Liriope muscari   LILYTURF, MONKEY GRASS, LIRIOPE

PRONUNCIATION - lē ′rī ō pē   mūs ′kɑ rē

TRANSLATION - [named in honor of a Greek woodland nymph, Liriope, the mother of Narcissus] [Greek musk, in reference to the sweet scent of the flowers].

FORM - Monoecious, perennial, evergreen, clumping herb, which forms dense, grasslike mats of medium texture.

SIZE - Reaches a height of 8 to 24 inches, depending on cultivar, with an indeterminate spread. Grows at a moderate pace.

HARDINESS ZONE - Zone 6, grown in all areas of Florida.

NATIVE HABITAT - Eastern Asia.

LEAVES - Simple, linear, arching, 8 to 24 inches long and 0.5 to 0.75 inches wide, dark green, leathery, grass-like, with parallel veins, tuft-forming.

STEM/BARK - Acaulescent, spreads by rhizomes, forms tubers.

FLOWERS - Purple, small (0.25 inch across), dense, hyacinth-like, in short spikes held on stalks several inches taller than the leaves. Flowers on some cultivars can be showy in full bloom in late spring to early summer.

FRUIT - Black, small, fleshy, berry-like, 0.5 inch wide in fall and winter, held above the foliage.

CULTURE - Prefers partial to deep shade. Some cultivars can tolerate full sun. In general, variegated cultivars revert to the green form in dense shade. Tolerates a wide range of soils and a moderate amount of salt. Moderately drought tolerant, but may develop tipburn in severely hot, dry locations. Can be heavily sheared (actually mowed) every few years to remove ragged old foliage. Highly competitive against weeds once established.

PROBLEMS - Scale; no serious pest problems. Fruiting stalks may be unsightly and require removal.

PROPAGATION - Seeds, clump division of cultivars.

LANDSCAPE USES - A ground cover for shady locations, especially useful where grass will not grow, and for edging woodland walkways. It will not withstand foot traffic.

COMMENTS - Numerous available cultivars: **'Big Blue'** - 18 to 20 inches tall, bold blue-green foliage; **'Evergreen Giant'** - 18 to 24 inches tall, white flowers; **'Lilac Beauty'** - prolific flowering, lilac; does well in sun or shade; **'Majestic'** - to 2 feet tall, rich lavender flowers; **'Monroe #2'** - white flowers; leaves tend to bleach in full sun; **'Silver Midget'** - 8 inches tall; variegated with white banding, slightly twisted foliage; **'Silvery Sunproof'** - lavender flowers; white variegation; does well in sun or shade (however, leaves lose some of variegation in dense shade); **'Variegata'** - variegated with yellow striping; and many others. *Liriope spicata* has narrower leaves, 0.25 inch wide, 8 to 16 inches tall, similar to *Ophiopogon japonicus* but flowers are borne above leaves; spreads vigorously and is difficult to confine as an edging.

Ophiopogon japonicus   MONDO GRASS, DWARF LILYTURF

PRONUNCIATION - ˌō fē ə ˈpō gən   jə ˈpɑ nə ˈkəs

TRANSLATION - [from Greek *ophis* (= a snake) and *pogon* (= a beard)] [from Japan].

FORM - Monoecious, perennial, evergreen, clumping herb which forms dense, fine-textured, grasslike mats.

SIZE - Height is 10 inches with an indeterminate spread. Growth rate is medium.

HARDINESS ZONE - Zone 7, can be grown in all areas of Florida.

NATIVE HABITAT - Japan and Korea.

LEAVES - Simple, linear, grass-like, 6 to 15 inches long, 0.25 inch wide, dark green and curving toward the ground, occurring in tufts.

STEM/BARK - Acaulescent, spreads by long, underground stolons.

FLOWERS - Lilac or white, 0.25 inch wide, inconspicuous in short, loose, few-flowered racemes below the leaves. Flowers in early summer.

FRUIT - Capsules, blue, pea-sized, fleshy.

CULTURE - Grows in partial to full shade on a wide range of soils. Good salt and drought tolerance. Requirements very similar to those of *Liriope muscari* but generally slower growing.

PROBLEMS - Generally pest-free.

PROPAGATION - Seeds, division of clumps of cultivars.

LANDSCAPE USES - Often used on walkway borders and in planters and foundation plantings. Makes an excellent, low maintenance ground cover in areas too shady for grass. It will not withstand foot traffic.

COMMENTS - Only a few cultivars are available: **'Nana'** - dwarf form, 2 to 3 inches tall, small white flowers; **'Variegatus'** - foliage with white and green striping. Recent introductions include: **'Kyote Super Dwarf'** - tightly clumped, to 4 inches; **'Silver Dragon'** has variegated leaves; the related *O. jaburan* **'Vittatus'** - leaves symmetrically arranged, pale green stripes and white margins; **'White Dragon'** has wide white stripes.

Tulipa × hybrida   TULIP

PRONUNCIATION - tū ˈlē pə   ˈhī brə də

TRANSLATION - [from Turkish *tulband* (= a turban), in reference to shape of the flowers] [hybrid].

FORM - Monoecious, herbaceous perennial, tunicate bulb, low growing, erect stem in some.

SIZE - Variable with cultivar, 12 inches to 3 feet tall, rapid growth.

HARDINESS ZONE - Zones 3 to 7. Can be grown in all areas of Florida, but must be dug annually and stored cool.

NATIVE HABITAT - Horticulture species native to Central Asia, particularly Turkey and Iran.

LEAVES - Simple, basal or a few on the stalk in some tall cultivars, smooth, undulate, or folded, to 18 inches long, strap shaped, generally bluish-green, thick, margins entire.

BULB - Generally pointed, tunics of various textures.

FLOWERS - Colors all except true blue, many combinations; campanulate to rotate, chiefly erect, petals and sepals indistinguishable, as such totaling - 6 except in double-flowered forms, 6 stamens; variously hairy to glabrous inside; usually solitary on smooth stalk with or without leaves to 3 feet; flowers in early spring.

FRUIT - Loculicidal, 3-valved capsule, seeds flat, many.

CULTURE - Full sun to partial shade, various soils; slightly salt tolerant.

PROBLEMS - Grey bulb rot, *Botrytis*, maggots, Mosaic Virus.

PROPAGATION - Seeds, separation of bulblets of cultivars.

LANDSCAPE USES - Bedding plant, planter box, pot plant, cut flowers.

COMMENTS - Over100 species and 4,000 named varieties and cultivars. Hybrids and cultivars have been divided into 15 groups based on their flowering time and morphological features. Inclusion of such groups is of little value since tulips are not particularly suited to warmer climates.

MARANTACEAE - ARROWROOT FAMILY

MONOCOTYLEDONS; 30 GENERA AND ABOUT 350 SPECIES

GEOGRAPHY: Predominantly tropical America, with a few species in Africa and Asia.

GROWTH HABIT: Rhizomatous or tuberous perennial herbs.

LEAVES: Often colorful and showy; distichously arranged; the blades variously narrow or broad, with penni-parallel venation (with many laterals parallel to the midrib); petiolate, with a swollen pulvinus at the point of attachment to the blade; sheathing at base.

FLOWERS: Usually small and not showy, zygomorphic, bisexual, each subtended and partially enclosed by a bract; perianth with a distinct series each of free sepals and tubular 3-lobed petals; stamens epipetalous, with usually only one fertile and functions as a trigger when touched by pollinating insects; ovary inferior and consist of 3 carpels.

FRUIT: A capsule.

ECONOMIC USES: Ornamentals (particularly as foliage plants), flowers and tubers of some eaten (arrow root), and leaves are used in roofing and basket making.

ORNAMENTAL GENERA: *Calathea, Ctenanthe, Maranta, Maranthocloa, Stromanthe, Thalia,* and others.

Calathea makoyana   PEACOCK PLANT

PRONUNCIATION - ˌkæ lə ˈthē ə   ˌmæ kə ˈyɑ nə

TRANSLATION - [from Greek *kalathos* (= a basket), in allusion to the flower cluster which looks like a flower in a basket] [in honor of Jacob Makoy (1790-1875), nurseryman of Li»ge].

FORM - Monoecious, evergreen; herbaceous perennial; clump forming, rhizomatous; coarse texture.

SIZE - To 3 feet tall, generally seen 20 inches tall; moderate growth rate.

HARDINESS ZONE - Zone 10-11; south Florida only, protect from cold; injured below 40°F.

NATIVE HABITAT - Brazil.

LEAVES - Simple; ovate to oblong; upper surface cream or olive green with dark green elliptic to oblong markings along the major lateral veins; border dark green and lower surface purple. Petioles reddish- purple.

STEM/BARK - Stemless; leaves and inflorescence arise directly from an underground rhizome.

FLOWERS - Whitish; small; irregular; 3-parted corolla with tube equal to or longer than sepals; borne in a raceme arising directly from the rhizomes.

FRUIT - Capsule; usually 3-seeded.

CULTURE - Partial to dense shade; at higher light intensities foliage color is lost; fast-draining, moisture-retentive soils with high organic matter content; high humidity; no salt tolerance; very sensitive to dissolved salts in the growing medium.

PROBLEMS - Nematodes, mites, and root rot.

PROPAGATION - Division.

LANDSCAPE USES - Primarily used as a container-grown specimen in interiors; can be used as an accent or specimen for its unusual foliage. May be grown as a specimen or ground cover outdoors if given cold protection.

Maranta leuconeura   PRAYER PLANT

PRONUNCIATION - mə ˈræn tə   ˈlū kə nū rə

TRANSLATION - [after Bartolommeo Maranti, 16th century Venetian botanist] [white veined].

FORM - Monoecious, evergreen; herbaceous perennial; ground cover; low growing, forms clumps with spreading or pendent branching stems; medium-coarse texture.

SIZE - To 2 feet tall, generally seen to 6 inches tall.

HARDINESS ZONE - Zone 10-11; south Florida only; protect from cold.

NATIVE HABITAT - Brazil.

LEAVES - Simple; alternate; elliptic to oblong, to 6 inches long and 3.5 inches wide; velvety; colorful, variegated; upper surfaces marked with dark green, light green, or brown; main and lateral veins sometimes gray or red; lower surfaces may be purple or reddish-purple; margins entire. Petioles sheathing.

STEM/BARK - Stems short and cylindrical with a zig-zag branching pattern.

FLOWERS - White marked with purple; small, irregular; 3 sepals, 3 petals; borne in loose racemes.

FRUIT - Capsule; 1-seeded.

CULTURE - Dense to partial shade; at higher light intensities the foliage will bleach; fast draining, moisture retentive, organic soils; high humidity; no salt tolerance.

PROBLEMS - Nematodes, mites, slugs, and root rots.

PROPAGATION - Division.

LANDSCAPE USES - Use primarily in interiors for its unusual foliage coloration; also in hanging baskets, containers, ground beds, or even on short totems.

COMMENTS - Several varieties are available: var. *erythroneura* (Herringbone Plant) with rose-red main lateral veins and a reddish-purple lower surface; var. *kerchoviana* (Rabbit's-Tracks) - with a row of dark brown or dark green blotches aligned on each side of the midrib on a light-green leaf); '**Massangeana**' - leaves tinted blue, dull rusty-brown toward center. A relatively large number of *Maranta* species have been relegated to other genera.

MUSACEAE - BANANA FAMILY

MONOCOTYLEDONS; 2 GENERA AND ABOUT 40 SPECIES

GEOGRAPHY: From lowlands of West Africa to the Pacific.

GROWTH HABIT: Large, laticiferous, sometimes rhizomatous, monocarpic or polycarpic perennial herbs, with the sheathing leaf bases forming a stem.

LEAVES: Very large, spirally arranged, penni-parallel venation.

FLOWERS: Zygomorphic, usually unisexual (plants monoecious: females on the lower portion and males on the upper portion of the terminal inflorescence); tepals in 2 whorls; stamens 5; ovary inferior and consist of 3 fused carpels.

FRUIT: Fleshy berry with numerous seeds.

ECONOMIC USES: Although used as ornamentals, banana is one of the most important commercial fruit crops.

ORNAMENTAL GENERA: *Ensete* and *Musa*.

COMMENTS: The genus *Strelitzia* which was previously included in Musaceae is currently recognized as the distinct monogeneric family Strelitziaceae.

Musa spp.

BANANA

PRONUNCIATION - ˈmyū sə

TRANSLATION - [from Arabic *mouz* or *moz*, but may be named after Antonio Musa (63-14 B.C.), physician to the first Roman Emperor].

FORM - Monoecious, evergreen; clumping; perennial, tree-like herb; with very large leaves clustered at the top of each stem; coarse texture.

SIZE - Heights range from 7 feet for dwarf species to 30 feet for the largest types; rapid growth rate with fertilizer.

HARDINESS ZONE - 9; can be grown in central and south Florida, but need a protected location in central Florida. Survives in north Florida, but damaged in winter.

NATIVE HABITAT - Originated in tropical Asia, but now worldwide.

LEAVES - Spirally arranged; arching or drooping; oblong, very large, to 9 feet long and 2 feet wide; entire at first, but become separated into many lateral, tattered segments with age; prominent midrib, deeply channelled on the upper surface. The deep channel continues into the short, stout, fleshy petioles.

STEM/BARK - Succulent pseudostems made of concentric layers of expanded petiole bases; suckers continuously at pseudostem bases.

FLOWERS - Terminal, on a peduncle which grows out of the top of the pseudostem; borne in a spicate or paniculate inflorescence often terminated by a large purple bud that peels away one bract at a time. Flowers are borne in the axils of the bracts; lower flowers female or bisexual, upper flowers male.

FRUIT - Berry; elongate, fleshy, edible; usually yellow and large.

CULTURE - Full sun or partial shade in fertile, moist soil; require wind and cold protection and heavy fertilization; no salt tolerance.

PROBLEMS - Sigatoka leaf-spot disease.

PROPAGATION - Division of thick, narrow-leaved suckers is best.

LANDSCAPE USES - Different species are grown for the flowers, variegated foliage, or fruit; also as specimens to give a tropical effect.

COMMENTS - *Musa acuminata*, ʹDwarf Cavendishʹ, a triploid form, is one of the best fruit cultivars. In addition, several species and hybrids are commonly planted in southern parts of the state, including: *M. acuminata, M. coccinea, M. ornata* (Flowering Banana), *M. × paradisiaca* (Banana, Plantain, Platano), *M. textilis, M. velutina*, among others in private and tropical fruit collections.

ORCHIDACEAE - ORCHID FAMILY

MONOCOTYLEDONS; 750 GENERA, MORE THAN 18,000 SPECIES,

AND A MULTITUDE OF INTERGENERIC AND INTERSPECIFIC HYBRIDS AND CULTIVARS.

GEOGRAPHY: Cosmopolitan, except in Antarctica, found in a diversity of habitats.

GROWTH HABIT: Perennial, terrestrial, epiphytic, or saprophytic herbs with rhizomes or pseudobulbs; aerial roots.

LEAVES: Alternate or rarely opposite, often distichous, sometimes reduced to scales, simple, fleshy, and in cauline species, sheathing at their base around the stem.

FLOWERS: Mostly very showy but some inconspicuous, bisexual, zygomorphic, solitary or in spikes or racemes or panicles; 3-merous, with the sepals similar but petals dissimilar: two lateral petals (wings) elongated but the dorsal petal (labellum or lip) of various shapes, sizes, and colors; reproductive organs represented in a column, with the stigmatic surface below and 1 or 2 pollinia-bearing stamens around it, though it may vary considerably among various taxa.

FRUIT: A capsule containing numerous minute seeds.

ECONOMIC USES: Except for fruit of vanilla (from *V. planifolia*), orchids are used only as ornamentals.

ORNAMENTAL GENERA: Too numerous to list, but those mentioned in sale catalogues include *Acacallis, Acampe, Acineta, Ada, Aerangis, Aeranthes, Aerides, Alamania, Amblostoma, Amesiella, Ancistrohynchus, Angraecopis, Angraecum, Anguloa, Ansellia, Arachnis, Arpophyllum, Arundina, Ascocentrum, Aspasia, Barbosella, Barkeria, Bifrenaria, Bletia, Bollea, Bolusiella, Brassavola, Brassia, Broughtonia, Bulbophyllum, Calanthe, Calyptrochilum, Capanemia, Catasetum, Cattleya, Caularthron, Chiloschista, Chysis, Cirrhopetalum, Cleisostoma, Cochleanthes, Cochlioda, Coleogyne, Coparettia, Cryptophoranthus, Cyclopogon, Cychnoches, Cymbidium, Cynorkis, Cypripedium, Cyrtopodium, Cyrtochis, Dendrobium, Dendrochilum, Diaphananthe, Diploprora, Disa, Doritis, Dressleria, Ellianthus, Encyclia, Epidendrum, Epigeneium, Eria, Erycina, Esmeralda, Euanthe, Eulophia, Galeandra, Gastrochilus, Gomesa, Gongora, Goodyera, Grammangis, Graphorkis, Haemeria, Hebenaria, Helcia, Hexisea, Huntleya, Ionopsis, Isochilus, Jummellea, Kefersteinia, Laelia, Lanium, Leochilus, Lepanthes, Leptotes, Leucohyle, Liparis, Listrostachys, Lockhartia, Ludisia, Luisia, Lycaste, Macodes, Macradenia, Masdevallia, Maxillaria, Meiracyllium, Microcoelia, Miltonia, Miltoniopsis, Mormodes, Mormolyca, Nageliella, Neobathiea, Neomoorea, Notylia, Octomeria, Odontoglossum, Oeceoclades, Oeonia, Oeoniella, Oncidium, Ophrys, Orchis, Ornithocephalus, Otoglossum, Pabstia, Palumbina, Paphiopedilum, Pectilis, Pelatantheria, Pescatoria, Phaius, Phalonopsis, Pholidota, Phragmipedium, Phisosiphon, Pleione, Pleurothallis, Polycycnis, Polystachya, Ponthieva, Porroglossum, Promenaea, Rangaeris, Renanthera, Restrepia, Rhynchostylis, Robiquetia, rodriguezia, Rodrigueziella, Rossioglossum, Rudolfiella, Sarchochilus, Sarcoglottis, Scaphosepalum, Schoenorchis, Schomburgkia, Scuticaria, Sigmatostalix, Sobralia, solenidium, Sophronitella, Sophronitis, Spathoglottis, Sphyrarhynchus, Stanhopea, Stenia, Stenoglottis, Stenorrhynchus, Symphyglossum, Tainia, Telipogon, Thunia, Trichocentrum, Trichoglottis, Trichopilia, Tridactyle, Vanda, Vandopsis, Vanilla, Xylobium,* and *Zygopetalum,* among others. It should be noted that not all the genera listed above are of general appeal. Several are primarily collector's items. Also, many intergeneric hybrids and grexes which are common in cultivation have not been included here.

Cattleya spp.

CATTLEYA

PRONUNCIATION - 'kat lē ə

TRANSLATION - [after William Cattley (died 1832), one of the first horticulturists to grow epiphytic orchids successfully.

FORM - Evergreen, sympodial, epiphytic. Sparse appearance.

SIZE - Overall: 3-18 inches, average: 12 inches. Growth rate slow.

HARDINESS ZONE - Greenhouse grown in Florida.

NATIVE HABITAT - Central and South America.

LEAVES - Unifoliate or bifoliate, 1-2, leathery leaves at apex of pseudobulb; 4-12 inches long, 1-4 inches wide.

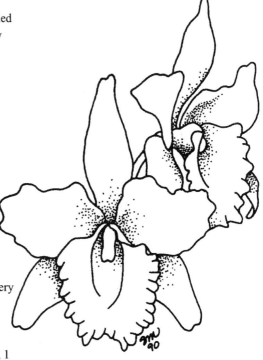

STEM - Pseudobulbs: average: 8 inches tall, 1 inch wide. One inch of rhizome between bulbs.

FLOWERS - Terminal; one to few flowered (3-7 inches across); sepals free and more or less equal; petals much broader than sepals, lip sessile, usually free; column long and semi-waxy; any season, most species flower in fall, winter and spring. Purple is dominant color, but white, yellow, red, and bicolors are also available. Some species are fragrant.

CULTURE - 2400-3500 foot-candles - medium light. Temperature: intermediate conditions. Media: bark; tree fern, or any free-draining epiphytic mix. Allow surface of the media to dry out briefly between waterings.

PROBLEMS - Botrytis spotting of flowers. Virus causing "flower break" - distorted flower shape and color. Brown rot, scale.

PROPAGATION - Division into clumps of 4 or more growths plus lead, meristem tissue culture; seed in 5-7 years, backbulbs.

LANDSCAPE USES - Decorative pot plant when in flower, popular corsage orchid.

COMMENTS - Sixty species and hundreds of intergeneric and interspecific hybrids, grexes, and cultivars commonly seen. *Cattleya labiata* - origin of common purple cattleyas; *C. dowiana* - origin of yellow/red lip hybrids; *C. skinneri* - purple flower 3 inches across, many (5-10) flowers per growth. Easter flowering.

Cymbidium spp.

PRONUNCIATION - sim 'bi dē əm

TRANSLATION - [from Greek *kymbe* (= a boat), referring to the hollowed lip].

FORM - Evergreen, sympodial, epiphytic and rarely terrestrial, dense clumps of grassy leaves.

SIZE - 2-3 feet tall; width depends on number of growing pseudobulbs.

HARDINESS ZONE - Standards can be grown in north Florida, if protected when nights go below 30°F. Miniature and warm types need greenhouses.

NATIVE HABITAT - Asian tropics and subtropics.

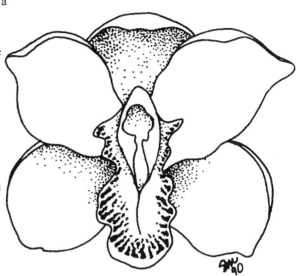

LEAVES - 7-12 alternate linear, grassy leaves, to 36 inches long, to 2 inches wide, on sheathing pseudobulb.

STEM - Pseudobulbs short or elongate, 2-4 inches around.

FLOWERS - On racemose 2- to many-flowered inflorescences. Pastel colors, including bi- and tricolors, semi-cup-shaped flower, sepals and petals free and "tongue" or "boat"-shaped lips - 2-6 inches across, 5-15 flowers on inflorescence arising from base of bulb, usually winter-spring. Not commonly fragrant.

CULTURE - 3500 foot-candles; partial shade to full sun. Media: bark/peat, peat/perlite; semi-terrestrial mix. Temperature: cool, night 45°-55° day 65°-70°. Miniatures: intermediate, nights to 50°, days 70°-75°. Keep relatively moist.

PROBLEMS - Cymbidium mosaic virus; not flowering due to insufficient low temperatures.

PROPAGATION - Division into 1-2 bulb clumps (once mature size). Meristem tissue culture; from seed in 4-6 years.

LANDSCAPE USES - Indoor/outdoor flowering pot plant. Outdoors, standards can take temperatures to 30°; must have cool nights in fall to initiate flowers.

COMMENTS - ±70 species, many hybrids. Species - only a few are seen in collections. *Cymbidium tigrinum, C. pumilum* (miniature). Hybrids and clones - larger flowers, more rounded shape, more colors. Miniatures - easier culture due to intermediate temperatures, smaller size.

Cyrtopodium punctatum

CIGAR ORCHID,
COW-HORN ORCHID

PRONUNCIATION - ˌsər tō ˈpō dē əm   puŋk ˈtā təm

TRANSLATION - [from Greek *kyrtos* (= curved swelling) and *podion* (= little foot), in reference to the shape of the column-foot, which curves upward] [from Latin *punctum* (= dark spots, pitted)].

FORM - Deciduous, sympodial, epiphytic and terrestrial, coarse texture.

SIZE - 2-3 feet or more tall, half as wide. Growth rate slow.

HARDINESS ZONE - Zones 10-11, native in south Florida.

NATIVE HABITAT - South Florida, Central and South America.

LEAVES - 5-7 soft, alternate, linear to elliptic lanceolate, pleated leaves, each up to 2 feet long and 6 inches wide. Leaves often have 3 prominent veins.

STEM - Pseudobulbs clustered, erect, to 3 feet and cigar shaped, covered with sheating leaf bases. Bases bearing "spines."

FLOWERS - Basal, branched inflorescences bearing many 1.5-inch flowers in spring and summer, grow to 3-4 feet. Large, colorful bracts subtend the flowers and the nodes. Both bracts and flowers are yellow-green with reddish brown markings. The sepals are similar, with undulating margins and markings. The petals are similar, short and broad, reflexed, with or without markings like the sepals, the lip is 3-lobed, mostly red-brown and bears a yellow callus.

CULTURE - 2400-3600 foot-candles, some found in full sun. Temperature: intermediate-cool (to 30°). Media: bark, tree fern, or any good epiphytic mix. Water: allow to dry briefly between waterings.

PROBLEMS - Relatively problem-free. Red spider mite.

PROPAGATION - Division; from seed in 4-5 years.

LANDSCAPE USES - Pot plant grown as a curiosity ("Florida orchid").

COMMENTS - *Cyrtopodium punctatum* is found in the woods of the Everglades and other similar areas in south Florida. Of the 30 species known, only a few are commonly cultivated.

Dendrobium spp.

DENDROBIUM

PRONUNCIATION - den ʹdrō bē əm

TRANSLATION - [from Greek *dendron* (= a tree) and *bios* (= life), in reference to their epiphytic habit].

FORM - Evergreen or deciduous; sympodial; mostly epiphytic; variable foliage density.

SIZE - 5 inches to 5 feet or more. Growth rate slow.

HARDINESS ZONE - Hardier species can be grown in south and central Florida but primarily greenhouse plants.

NATIVE HABITAT - Asia, Philippines, Australia.

LEAVES - Highly variable depending on type; 1 to many adult leaves; linear-lanceolate to loblong-ovate 1-15 inches long, 1-2 inches wide; leathery (evergreen), terete, or papery at the apex or distichously along stem.

STEM - Rhizomatous or pseudobulbous: vary from 1, small and rounded, to canes 5 feet tall.

FLOWERS - Terminal or axillary racemose inflorescences bearing 1 to many flowers from less than 1-3 inches. Uniform sepals; uniform petals may be broader than sepals, undulated, or helically twisted. 3-lobed lip with lateral lobes encircling column, apical lobe constricted and attached to spur at base of column. Colors of white, purple, and yellow. Not commonly fragrant.

CULTURE - 2400-3600 foot-candles. Temperature: *D. nobile* types - cool-growing. Deciduous, cool temperature in fall to initiate flowers. *Dendrobium phalaenopsis* types - warm-growing. Many others - intermediate. Media: epiphytic mix of bark and/or treefern. Water: allow surface of medium to dry briefly between watering.

PROBLEMS - Relatively problem-free.

PROPAGATION - Division, meristem tissue culture, from seed in 3-5 years, offsets from canes.

LANDSCAPE USES - Pot plant when in bloom.

COMMENTS - Hundreds of species, hybrids, and grexes. *Dendrobium aggregatum* - clustered 2-inch pseudobulbs, round yellow flowers in spring; *D. nobile* - deciduous; white and purple blooms in twos and threes at nodes in winter-spring; *D. phalaenopsis* - sprays of "butterfly" flowers in fall in colors of white through purple.

Epidendrum spp.   EPIDENDRUM, REED-STEM EPIDENDRUMS

PRONUNCIATION - ˌe pə ˈden drəm

TRANSLATION - [from Greek *epi* (= upon) and *dendron* (= a tree), in reference to their epiphytic habit].

FORM - Evergreen, sympodial, epiphytic, variable foliage density.

SIZE - Variable: from 1 inch to 5 feet tall, usually around 1 foot or less.

HARDINESS ZONE - Zone 9b; *E. conopseum*, native to Gainesville, can be grown in central and south Florida.

NATIVE HABITAT - North Carolina to south Florida; Central and South America.

LEAVES - Linear-lanceolate to ovate; alternate, thick and fleshy or leathery, to 4 inches long and 1 inch wide.

STEM - Caulescent, erect or creeping, sometimes branching, to 5 feet tall and 1 inch in diameter, bearing few to many leaves.

FLOWERS - Terminal inflorescence bearing few to many flowers, each ranging from less than 1-3 inches wide. Uniform sepals; uniform petals a little narrower than sepals, 3-lobed lip with lateral lobes attached to the column. Center lobe of lip may be broad, lobed, or fringed. Colors of green, brown, yellow, red, purple, and white. Many are fragrant.

CULTURE - Light: 2400-3600 foot-candles. Temperature: intermediate: nights to 50°, days 70°-75°. Media: epiphytic mix of bark and/or tree fern fiber. Water: allow surface of media to dry between watering.

PROBLEMS - Red spider, leaf spots, virus.

PROPAGATION - Division, offsets, meristematic tissue culture; from seed in 4-5 years.

LANDSCAPE USES - Naturalized on trees in areas with 45° or warmer nights. Pot plant when in bloom. Reed stem types can be grown in beds in south Florida.

COMMENTS - Hundreds of species and hybrids. *Epidendrum ibaguense (E. radicans)* - reed stem type; terminal inflorescence produces red/orange and yellow 1-inch flowers for months; *E. nocturnum* - stems to 3 feet tall bear few 3-4 inch greenish-white flowers that are fragrant at night. Florida native.

Ludisia discolor

PRONUNCIATION - lū 'di zē a 'dis ku ler

SYNONYM - *Haemaria discolor.*

TRANSLATION - [the origin and meaning of *Ludisia* are unknown, but it may refer to a personal name] [variegated, in reference to leaves].

FORM - Evergreen, sympodial, terrestrial. Moderate foliage density.

SIZE - To 10 inches tall (usually procumbent). Growth rate slow.

HARDINESS ZONE - Zones 10-11, can be grown in south Florida.

NATIVE HABITAT - Indonesia, Burma, southern China.

LEAVES - 4 to 6 tightly clustered, ovate leaves at apex of stem, each to 3 inches long and half as wide. Leaves are dark velvety-green (sometimes with red or yellow veins) on top and blood red underneath.

STEM/BARK - Succulent, dark red-brown, procumbent.

FLOWERS - Terminal hairy inflorescence bears up to 12 flowers in winter/spring. Each 3/4-inch white flower has a yellow anther cap and is subtended by a large bract. Sepals and petals are similar, and the lip has a sac at the base. Column twisted.

CULTURE - 2400-3600 foot-candles. Temperature: intermediate - cool. Media: peat moss, perlite, and soil in equal proportions. Water: keep relatively moist.

PROBLEMS - Relatively problem-free.

PROPAGATION - Division and cuttings.

LANDSCAPE USES - Attractive pot plant year-round because of its attractive foliage (but may lose foliage occasionally).

COMMENTS - One species and one variety currently recognized. *Ludisia discolor (H. discolor)* - velvety green leaves, sometimes with dark red veins. *Ludisia discolor* var. *dawsoniana (H. discolor* var. *dawsoniana)* has red or yellow veins.

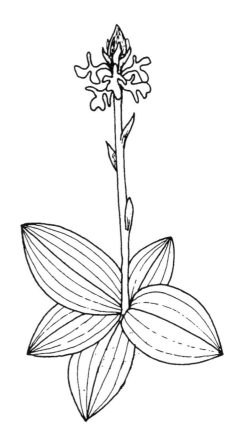

Oncidium spp.

DANCING LADY ORCHID, ONCIDIUM

PRONUNCIATION - ɑn ˈsi dē əm

TRANSLATION - [a diminutive of Greek *onkos* (= a tumor), in reference to the swelling on the lip of these orchids].

FORM - Evergreen, sympodial, epiphytic. Variable foliage density.

SIZE - 5 inches to 2 feet. Growth rate slow (some medium-fast).

HARDINESS ZONE - Zone 9b, some species may be grown in central and south Florida.

NATIVE HABITAT - Florida, West Indies, Central and South American tropics.

LEAVES - Small, soft and thin, papery, terete, or large, thick and leathery ("mule-ears"). Light green, dark green, or green with brown or red stippling. Equitant oncidiums - a fan of 6-8 succulent, V-shaped leaves to 6 inches long, toothed margins.

STEM - Pseudobulbs - very small to very large, subtended by sheaths (8 inches tall and 5 inches across).

FLOWERS - Terminal or axillary inflorescences bearing few to many 1-4 inch flowers, fall, winter, or spring flowering. "Dancing Lady" shape: sepals usually similar; petals similar to dorsal sepal. Lip usually large and spreading, attached to base of column. Primary colors are yellow and brown; also pink, white, and green tones.

CULTURE - Light - varies from 1500 footcandles to full sun depending on individual species. Temperature: mostly intermediate, some warm. Media: bark and/or tree fern mix. Water: 1-5 days (depending on growth type) between watering.

PROBLEMS - Red spider, virus, leaf spot.

LANDSCAPE USES - Pot plant. Some species may be naturalized on trees in south Florida.

COMMENTS - About 450 species and hundreds of hybrids and grexes. *Oncidium ampliatum* - "Turtle shell"-shaped pseudobulbs, many yellow "dancing ladies" in spring. *Oncidium lanceanum* - "Mule-ear-type" with pink, brown, and green fragrant flowers in summer. *Oncidium papilio* - (Butterfly Orchid) at end of 2-foot inflorescence. Attractive red stippled foliage. Equitant oncidiums - popular small, fast-growing, 4-inch plant that blooms profusely when growth is mature.

Paphiopedilum spp.

LADY'S SLIPPER ORCHID,
VENUS'S SLIPPER

PRONUNCIATION - ˌpa fē ō ˈpe də ləm

TRANSLATION - [from Greek *paphia* (an epithet of Aphrodite) and *pedilon* (= slipper), in reference to the slipper-shaped lip of the flower].

FORM - Evergreen, sympodial (fan-type), mostly terrestrial orchids, moderate foliage density.

SIZE - 6-18 inches tall with an equal or wider spread. Growth rate slow (some medium).

HARDINESS ZONE - Grown in greenhouses in Florida.

NATIVE HABITAT - Asia, Philippines.

LEAVES - Fans of 6-10 folded leathery leaves, alternate, elliptic to lanceolate, to 15 inches long and 2 inches wide, may be green or green with darker green mottlings.

STEM - Stemless, without pseudobulb.

FLOWERS - Terminal, single or few flowered scapes, any season, depending on spp. Hard, waxy, long-lasting flowers; dorsal sepal usually large and showy with spots, stripes, etc. Petals spread laterally, may have undulations, hairs, spots, or warts. Lip is slipper-shaped, hard and waxy, with inrolled or outrolled margin. Lateral sepals fused into a ventral "synsepalum" behind slipper. Colors of browns, greens, white, or pink. Not fragrant.

CULTURE - 1800-2400 foot-candles (low light). Temperature: green-leaved varieties generally intermediate-cool; mottled-leaved varieties tend to be warm-intermediate. Media: peat moss, tree fern, perlite, sphagnum, or any combination. Water: keep moist, not soggy.

PROBLEMS - Rots, due to low light and moist media.

PROPAGATION - Division, meristematic tissue culture, from seed in 3-5 years.

LANDSCAPE USES - Pot plant for both the showy flowers and the attractive mottled foliage.

COMMENTS - About 60 species and hundreds of hybrids. *Paphiopedilum callosum* - popular mottled-leaved species with brown/green/purple/white patterned flowers. *Paphiopedilum glaucophyllum* - bears flowers one at a time over several months. Flowers are white and green with a pink slipper.

Phaius tankervilliae   Nun's Orchid, Phaius

PRONUNCIATION - əfā əs   ˌtaŋ kər ɵvi lē ē

TRANSLATION - [from Greek *phaios* (= dusky or gray), in reference to the dark flowers of the type species or dark color of old or injured flowers] [after Emma Lady Tankerville (1750-1836)].

SYNONYM - *Phaius wallichii.*

FORM - Evergreen, sympodial, semi-terrestrial, densely foliated.

SIZE - 1.5-4 feet tall, half as wide. Growth rate: slow.

HARDINESS ZONE - Zone 9b, may be grown in Central and South Florida in protected areas.

NATIVE HABITAT - Tropical Asia

LEAVES - 2 to 10, alternate or appearing spiral, thin and broadly elliptic, ribbed and folded.

STEM - Pseudobulbs are 2-3 inches across, thick and stocky, hidden by sheathing leaf bases.

FLOWERS - The 3-4 foot tall inflorescence arises from a leaf axil near the rhizome, bearing many 2-3 inch flowers in the spring. Inflorescence bears large leafy bracts at the nodes and subtending the flowers. Sepals and petals are similar: creamy-white on the outside, yellow/rusty-brown on the inside. The 3-lobed lip has two lateral lobes encircling the column, the middle lobe spreading, giving a tubular appearance. The lip is yellow-brown and has a small spur at the base. Flowers darken with age.

CULTURE - 2400-3600 foot-candles. Temperature: intermediate-cool. Media: peat, perlite, and soil in equal amounts. Water: generally keep moist, although they do have pseudobulbs.

PROBLEMS - Relatively problem-free. Red spider, rust.

PROPAGATION - Division usually; also old inflorescence placed on moist sphagnum moss will produce offsets from nodes. Seed.

LANDSCAPE USES - Decorative pot plant, for flowers.

COMMENTS - *Phaius tankervilliae* is the most commonly grown genus member.

Phalaenopsis spp.

MOTH ORCHID, PHALAENOPSIS

PRONUNCIATION - ˌfæ lə ˈnɑp səs

TRANSLATION - [from the Greek *phalaina* (= moth) and *opsis* (= appearance), in reference to the delicate moth-like flowers of some species].

FORM - Evergreen, monopodial, mostly epiphytic.

SIZE - Less than 1 foot tall, wider than tall. Growth rate slow to medium.

HARDINESS ZONE - Grown in greenhouse, even in south Florida.

NATIVE HABITAT - Tropical Asia

LEAVES - 3 to several, leathery, succulent, usually 4-12 inches long and 2-5 inches wide. May be solid green or silver-green with dark green mottlings, purplish underside.

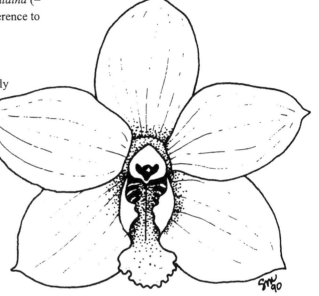

STEM - Very short, apparently stemless and lacking pseudobulbs; aerial adventitious roots common.

FLOWERS - Axial racemose or paniculate inflorescences produce many 1-6 inch flowers mostly in winter and spring. Sepals are uniform; petals uniform, equal to or broader than sepals. Lip is 3-lobed, lateral lobes upright, middle lobe may have two antennae at end; callus between lateral lobes. Colors of white, pink, yellow, and mottled. A few are fragrant.

CULTURE - 1500 foot-candles - low light. Temperature: warm conditions (do well as houseplants). Media: bark and/or tree fern. Water: keep moist.

PROBLEMS - Crown rot, caused by water in crown of plant. Bud blasting, due to change in environment or drafts. Mesophyll collapse, virus.

PROPAGATION - Offsets from lower "stem" or from some nodes on inflorescences; meristem tissue culture; from seed in 2-4 years.

LANDSCAPE USES - Pot plants with long-lasting display of flowers in winter-spring. After first set of flowers, inflorescence may branch and produce more flowers (only on *P. amabilis* types).

COMMENTS - About 40 species and numerous hybrids, grexes, and cultivars of small and large, solid or mottled leaves, rose, cream, yellow, red, and other colors.

Vanda spp.

PRONUNCIATION - ˈvan də

TRANSLATION - [from the Sanskrit or Hindi name for one of the species (*Vanda tessellata*)].

FORM - Upright, evergreen, monopodial, mostly epiphytic, coarse texture.

SIZE - 1-6 feet or more tall, 6 inches to 2 feet wide. Growth rate fast in sunny tropical environments.

HARDINESS ZONE - Zones 10-11, can be grown in south Florida.

NATIVE HABITAT - Tropical Asia.

LEAVES - Two types: distichous and strap-leaved - many, 2-12 inch folded, leathery leaves, clasping leaf base, "torn" apex; terete-leaved - size of a pencil, 4-6 inches long, sharp or blunt tip.

STEM - Sheathed by leaf bases; thick aerial roots present.

FLOWERS - Axial inflorescence produces two to many 1-4 inch flowers, any season. Flowers appear rounded with similar sepals and petals. Petals may have a 180° twist. Lip is commonly tongue-shaped with a spur at base of column. Column is short and cylindrical. Colors of lavendar, blue, pink, yellow, brown, white, green. Some are fragrant.

CULTURE - Greenhouse 3600 foot-candles. Outdoors 5000-6000 foot-candles. Terete-leaved varieties require brighter light than strap-leaved varieties. Temperature: warm conditions. Media: bark, charcoal, treefern. Requires very airy media. Water: abundant water when growing fast.

PROBLEMS - Leaf spot, brown rot, virus.

PROPAGATION - Tip cuttings: after removing top portion, bottom may produce offsets. Also meristem tissue culture. From seed in 4-7 years.

LANDSCAPE USES - Pot plant, specimen plant for patio and pool areas. Grown in large outdoor beds in full sun in Hawaii.

COMMENTS - Many species and hundreds of hybrids. *Vanda coerulea* - smaller-growing strap-leaved, produces many 2.5 inch lavender-blue flowers in the fall. *Vanda teres* - terete-leaves with delicate looking pink flowers, 3-4 inches across. *Vanda tricolor* - strap-leaved plant with many 2 inch, white, red/brown spotted flowers with a purple lip. Fragrant.

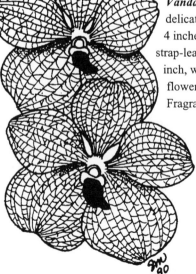

Vanilla planifolia   Vanilla

PRONUNCIATION - və ˈni lə   ˌpla nə ˈfō lē ə

TRANSLATION - [from the Spanish *vainilla* (= a small pod), in reference to the shape of the fruit] [with flat leaves].

FORM - Evergreen monopodial epiphytic vine of coarse texture.

SIZE - Variable length, to 1 foot wide.

HARDINESS ZONE - Zone 10, native in south Florida.

NATIVE HABITAT - Native to the West Indies and Central America, but widely cultivated throughout the tropics.

LEAVES - Alternate, ovate, fleshy, shiny, up to 9 inches long and 3 inches wide.

STEM - Green, succulent, and sheathed by leaf bases.

FLOWERS - Axillary clusters of few to many 3 inch yellow-green flowers appear in spring. Sepals and petals are similar. A ruffled tubular lip encircles the column. Flowers last but a day.

FRUIT - The 6 inches or more long, 1/2 inch wide seed pod is the original source of vanillin, or vanilla flavoring.

CULTURE - 2400-3600 foot-candles. Temperature: cool-intermediate conditions. Media: organic compost or epiphytic mix; being a vine, support is more important than potting material.

PROBLEMS - Relatively problem-free.

PROPAGATION - Cuttings.

LANDSCAPE USES - Grown as a curiosity and for vanilla "beans."

COMMENTS - Although there are about 100 species, only *V. planifolia* is most commonly grown; it is also available as a variegated cultivar.

PANDANACEAE - SCREW-PINE FAMILY

MONOCOTYLEDONS; 3 GENERA AND ABOUT 700 SPECIES

GEOGRAPHY: Tropics and subtropics of the Old World, usually in coastal or marshy areas.

GROWTH HABIT: Branched trees, shrubs, and vines, with distinct leaf base scars and aerial roots.

LEAVES: Appearing spirally arranged but 3-ranked, long and strap-shaped, often coriaceous, margins spinose-serrate.

FLOWERS: Unisexual (plants dioecious); spadix is subtended by a spade; flowers of both sexes apetalous and asepalous; male flowers with numerous free or fused stamens; female flowers with superior ovary consisting of usually numerous but rarely only one carpel.

FRUIT: Berry or cone-like multiple drupes that resemble pineapple.

ECONOMIC USES: Ornamentals, but several species of *Pandanus* are used as food and flowers of some used in perfumery.

ORNAMENTAL GENERA: *Freycinetia* and *Pandanus*; *Saranga* is not reported from cultivation.

Pandanus utilis   SCREW PINE

PRONUNCIATION - pan 'da nəs   yū 'ti ləs

TRANSLATION - [latinized form of the Malayan name *pandan*] [useful].

FORM - Dioecious, evergreen tree; multiple-branched; pyramidal; coarse texture.

SIZE - Up to 25 feet tall with a 15 foot spread; slow growth rate.

HARDINESS ZONE - Zones 10-11; limited to south Florida.

NATIVE HABITAT - Madgascar.

LEAVES - Simple; arranged in spiral tufts at the end of each stout branch; stiff, sessile, keeled; sword-shaped, to 3 feet long and 3 inches wide;margins lined with small, reddish spines.

STEM/BARK - Trunk and branches ringed by old leaf scars; stout, 8-10 inch trunk braced at the bottom by adventitious prop roots.

FLOWERS - Male, a 4-inch-long, branched spadix; female, a dense head 1 to 2 inches in diameter.

FRUITS - Spherical syncarp; to 8 inches; composed of 100 to 200 prismatic drupes, 1.5 inches long; drupes green with a red-banded basal end; fruit yellowish when ripe; contains a small amount of edible pulp.

CULTURE - Full sun for fruiting specimens, young plants endure shade; wide range of soils; high tolerance of soilborne salt, no tolerance of salt spray.

PROBLEMS - Scale insects.

PROPAGATION - Seed, which are soaked for 24 hours before planting; basal sucker division; large cuttings.

LANDSCAPE USES - Free-standing specimens give a tropical effect; used as potted patio plants. Native to tidal basins, plants could be used along intercoastal shorelines in Florida.

COMMENTS - Several species are available in Florida; taxonomy is confused. Leaves used to make mats and baskets in the tropics.

POACEAE (= GRAMINEAE) - GRASS FAMILY

MONOCOTYLEDONS; ABOUT 650 GENERA AND 9000 SPECIES

GEOGRAPHY: Truly cosmopolitan: from the Arctics to the equator and at all elevations.

GROWTH HABIT: Annual or perennial tillering rosettes or sometimes woody, with early fibrous but later adventitious roots, often rhizomatous and/or stoloniferous, usually with hollow cylindrical aerial stems.

LEAVES: Distichous, arising at the nodes and consisting of the blade and the sheath that covers the stem; the blade is long and usually narrow; a membranous or hairy ligule is located at the junction of the blade and the sheath.

FLOWERS: Florets usually bisexual or rarely unisexual (plants monoecious or rarely dioecious), in terminal spikes and/or spikelets on leafless stems; flowers lack a well-developed perianth, it is reduced to a very small structure called a lodicule; the androecium consist of 2-6 stamens; the gynoecium consist of 2 to 3 united carpels, with a single, one-seeded functional ovary.

FRUIT: Caryopsis or grain, rarely an achene or berry (in some bamboos).

ECONOMIC USES: Perhaps the single most important food source for man (e.g., wheat, rice, barley, corn, etc.), building materials from bamboos, and several species are used as ornamentals.

ORNAMENTAL GENERA: *Agrostis, Arundinaria, Axonopus, Bambusa, Cortaderia, Cynodon, Dendrocalamus, Eragrostis, Eremochloa, Festuca, Lolium, Panicum, Phragmites, Phyllostachys, Poa, Pseudosasa, Saccharum* (sugar cane)*, Sorghum, Stenotaphrum, Triticum* (wheat)*, Zea* (corn)*, Zoysia,* among others.

COMMENTS: The structure of inflorescence and flower in grasses is much too complex for detailed presentation in this manual. Interested students should consult one of several excellent plant taxonomy books for proper terminology or one of several books specifically written on grasses for treatment of additional taxonomic and morphological details.

Cortaderia selloana   PAMPAS GRASS

PRONUNCIATION - ˌkor tə ˈdē rē ə   ˌse lō ˈā nə

TRANSLATION - [from the Argentinian name] [in honor of Friedrich Sellow (1789-1831), German traveler and naturalist who made extensive collections in Brazil and Uruguay].

FORM - Dioecious, perennial grass, large, clumping.

SIZE - Reaches 6 to 8 feet in height with an equal spread. Grows rapidly.

HARDINESS ZONE - Zone 5, grows in all regions of Florida.

NATIVE HABITAT - South America.

LEAVES - Simple, 5 to 7 feet long, 0.5 inch wide at the base, tapering to a point at the drooping apex. The leaf margins are saw-toothed.

STEM/BARK - Dense, clumping, grass-like stem near ground.

FLOWERS - Silvery-white, tiny, in terminal panicles (plumes) 1 to 2 feet long and held 1 to 3 feet above the leaves. Plumes appear in August, persisting until January. Often used in dried arrangements; pampas grass plumes are grown commercially for this purpose in California, where it has become a weed.

FRUIT - Caryopsis, small, usually non-viable in Florida.

CULTURE - Grows and blooms best in full sun, but tolerates partial shade.

Grows well in most soils except very wet ones and tolerates drought and salt spray. Should be cut back to 18 inches high after blooms fade in late winter.

PROBLEMS - Relatively pest-free.

PROPAGATION - Seed, if available, or clump divison.

LANDSCAPE USES - Makes an attractive, showy specimen, looks especially good in seaside landscapes.

COMMENTS - Once planted, it is difficult to remove. One cultivar has pink plumes. Several cultivars selected for height or panicle color have been introduced, though none reported from Florida.

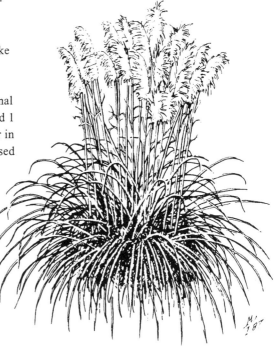

Cynodon dactylon   BERMUDA GRASS

PRONUNCIATION - ˈsi nə ˌdan   ˈdæk tə lan

TRANSLATION - [from Greek *Cyon* (= a dog) and *odos* (= a tooth)] [from Greek *dactylos* (= a finger)].

FORM - Low-growing, perennial grass, fine-textured, dense, vigorous.

SIZE - Cut to 0.5 to 1.5 inches tall, rapid growth.

HARDINESS ZONE - Warmer areas of Zone 6. May be grown in all areas of Florida.

NATIVE HABITAT - Warm regions of both hemispheres.

LEAVES - Simple, alternate at nodes, in 2 ranks, entire; linear to 1.5 inches long, sheathing at the base, folded in bud; green, often glaucous, turning brown in cold weather; ligule a fringe of hairs; leaves soft, somewhat pubescent on upper surface.

STEM/BARK - Spreads by stolons and rhizomes, internodes alternating long and short.

FLOWERS - In terminal spikes 4 to 7, to 2 inches long, flattened, stalk to 16 inches tall.

FRUIT - Seedlike grain (caryopsis).

CULTURE - Full sun, fertile soils; highly salt tolerant. Good drought tolerance if nematodes controlled. Poor shade tolerance, therefore not for shady sites. Tolerates a lot of wear; recovers quickly when injured. High-maintenance grass: must be mowed closer and

more often than other grasses, requires frequent fertilization and spraying to control insect and disease problems.

PROBLEMS - Numerous insect and disease problems: mites, nematodes, sod webworms, armyworms, scale, many fungal diseases, mole crickets.

PROPAGATION - Seed of "improved" common types and cultivars.

LANDSCAPE USES - Lawns, golf course greens, athletic fields.

COMMENTS - Cultivar 'Ormond' and several cultivars of *C. dactylon* × *C. transvaalensis*, such as 'FLoraTeX' |, 'Tifdwarf', 'Tifgreen', 'Tifgreen II', 'Tiflawn', 'Tifway', and 'Tifway II' are used in golf greens.

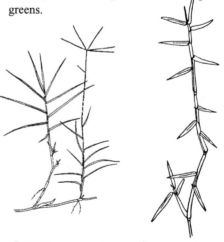

Eremochloa ophiuroides

CENTIPEDE GRASS

PRONUNCIATION -ˌe rə mō ˈklō ə ˌō fē yū ˈroi dēz

TRANSLATION - [from Greek *eremia* (= desert) and *chloris* (= green)] [from *ophis* (= snake) and *uris* (= tail), probably in reference to the cylindrical infloresences].

FORM - Low-growing, perennial grass, somewhat coarse textured, dense, vigorous.

SIZE - Cut to 2 inches tall, slow growth rate.

HARDINESS ZONE - Warmer areas of Zone 8. May be grown in all areas of Florida.

NATIVE HABITAT - Southeast Asia.

LEAVES - Simple, alternate at nodes, 2-ranked, entire, linear to 2 inches long; sheathing at the base, folded in bud; green, turning brown in cold weather; ligule a purple membrane; leaves soft, pubescent margins

STEM/BARK - Spreads by stolons, internodes short, more or less equidistant.

FLOWERS - Spikes, solitary, cylindrical to 2.5 inches long, terminal and axillary.

FRUIT - Seedlike grain (caryopsis).

CULTURE - Full sun to partial shade, various soils; slightly salt tolerant. Fair to good shade tolerance; good drought tolerance if nematodes controlled. Adapted to low-fertility soils. Iron chlorosis on soils with pH greater than 6.2, therefore, not well suited to south Florida. Does not withstand heavy foot traffic.

PROBLEMS - Nematodes (highly susceptible), mole crickets, sod webworms, scale insects

called ground pearls (serious problem), brown patch and dollar spot (fungal diseases).

PROPAGATION - Sod of cultivars, seeds.

LANDSCAPE USES - Lawn; low-maintenance grass.

COMMENTS - A few cultivars: **'Oaklawn'** and **'Centennial'** are selected specifically for cold tolerance.

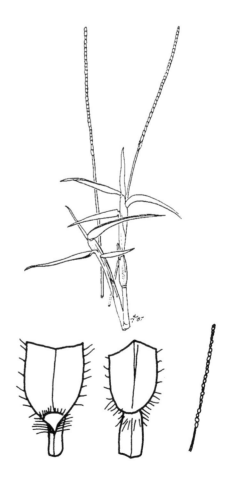

Paspalum notatum   BAHIA GRASS

PRONUNCIATION - pæs 'pā ləm   nō 'tā təm

TRANSLATION - [Greek name for a kind of millet] [spotted, marked].

FORM - Tall-growing, perennial grass, coarse-textured, moderately dense, vigorous.

SIZE - Cut to 2.5 to 4 inches, rapid growth.

HARDINESS ZONE - Zone 8b. Can be grown in all areas of Florida.

NATIVE HABITAT - Paraguay, Argentina.

LEAVES - Simple, alternate at nodes, 2-ranked, entire, soft, somewhat papery, tough, slightly hairy, linear to l2 inches long, sheathing at base, rolled in bud; light green, browning only below 30°F, ligule-membranous.

STEM/BARK - Spreads by stout rhizomes, internodes short, compressed.

FLOWERS - Spike-like raceme, 2 to 3 or rarely 5 per stalk, to 2 inches long, stalk to 20 inches tall, terminal.

FRUIT - Caryopsis (seed-like grain).

CULTURE - Full sun to partial shade, various soils; slightly salt tolerant. Withstands drought better than most grasses due to its extensive root and thick rhizome system. Relatively good shade tolerance. Withstands heavy foot traffic. Not well adapted to high pH soils.

PROBLEMS - Sod webworms, armyworms, mole crickets, brown patch, dollar spot. Less susceptible to nematodes than most grasses, fewer insect and disease problems, tall, unsightly seed heads.

PROPAGATION - Seed (which is abundant and relatively inexpensive), sod.

LANDSCAPE USES - Lawn, road-sides, forage, parks, athletic fields, minimum maintenance grass.

COMMENTS - Several cultivars including 'Argentine', 'Paraguay', 'Paraguay Z-2' (short, narrow, hairy leaves), 'Pensacola', 'Tifton-9 Pensacola' (greater vigor in seedling stage), and 'Wilmington' (more cold hardy than others). Extensively planted on disturbed sites and for erosion control.

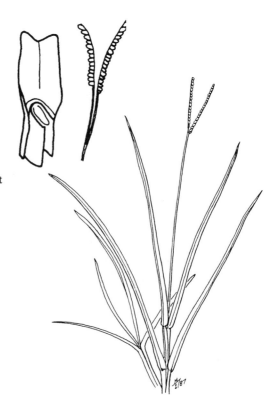

Stenotaphrum secundatum ST. AUGUSTINE GRASS

PRONUNCIATION -ˌste nə ˈtæf rəm ˌse kun ˈdā təm

TRANSLATION - [from Greek *stenos* (= narrow) and *taphrus* (= a trench), in reference to the cavities on the inflorescence peduncles] [one-sided].

FORM - Low-growing lawn grass, coarse-textured, very dense, vigorous.

SIZE - Cut l to 2 inches tall, rapid growth.

HARDINESS ZONE - Warmer areas of Zone 8. Can be grown in all areas of Florida.

NATIVE HABITAT - Tropical America.

LEAVES - Simple, alternate or opposite at nodes, 2-ranked, linear, green turning purple with cold weather; ligule a fringe of hairs; leaves soft, smooth, folded in the bud.

STEM/BARK - Spreads by thick fleshy stolons, branching, internodes equidistant, leaf sheaths are flattened.

FLOWERS - Fleshy raceme, solitary, to 4 inches long, stalk to 3 inches tall, terminal.

FRUIT - Seed-like grain (caryopsis), sterile.

CULTURE - Full sun to moderately deep shade (tolerates shade better than most warm season grasses), various soils; highly salt tolerant. Not drought tolerant therefore requires frequent irrigation. Poor wear tolerance.

PROBLEMS - Chinch bugs (a major problem), armyworms, sod webworms, mole crickets, nematodes, several fungal diseases, thatch build-up, St. Augustine Decline (SAD virus).

PROPAGATION - Sod of cultivars. New seeded types but not widely available and expensive.

LANDSCAPE USES - Lawn; moderately high-maintenance grass.

COMMENTS - 'Bitterblue' (fine, dense texture and darker color), 'Floratine' (finer texture, denser grasses), 'Floratam' (resistant to nematodes and SAD virus), 'Raleigh' (coarse texture, cold-hardy), Seville' (dwarf, dark green). Common and 'Roseland' are pasture grasses. 'Floralawn' (resistant to SAD virus, chinch bug, and webworm), 'Jade' and 'Delmar' (both with improved shade tolerance), 'FX-10' (chinch bug resistant and deep roots), etc.

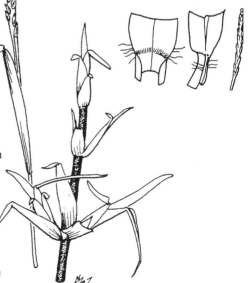

Zoysia spp.

ZOYSIA GRASS

PRONUNCIATION - 'zoi shə

TRANSLATION - [in honor of Karl von Zoys (1756-1800), Austrian botanist].

FORM - Low-growing lawn grass, fine-textured, dense.

SIZE - Cut to 0.5 to 1.5 inches tall, slow growth rate.

HARDINESS ZONE - Warmer areas of Zone 6. May be grown in all areas of Florida.

NATIVE HABITAT - Asia, Japan.

LEAVES - Simple, alternate at nodes, 2-ranked, entire; linear, length varies with species 1 to 5 inches long, sheathing at the base, rolled in the bud; green, turning brown with cold weather, ligule a fringe of hairs; leaves stiff, prickly.

STEM/BARK - Spreads by stolons and rhizomes, internodes equidistant.

FLOWERS - Terminal spike-like racemes, solitary, to 2 inches long.

FRUIT - Seed-like grain (caryopsis).

CULTURE - Full sun to partial shade (good shade tolerance), adapted to wide variety of soils; moderately salt tolerant. Good wear resistance, dense coverage. Moderate maintenance: requires frequent fertilization and irrigation, slow growing, therefore, slow to establish and slow to recover from damage (however, it needs less mowing).

PROBLEMS - Nematodes (a serious problem), mole crickets, sod webworms, armyworms, several fungal diseases.

PROPAGATION - Sod.

LANDSCAPE USES - Lawn; moderate maintenance grass not widely used in Florida.

COMMENTS - Several related species and varieties, including *Z. japonica* (Japanese or Korean lawngrass), has a coarse texture and hairy light green leaves; **'Meyer'** (= **'Z-52'** or **'Amazoy'**), a *Z. japonica* cultivar, has deep green leaves and medium texture; *Z. matrella* (Manila grass), finer and dense than *Z. japonica* but less cold-hardy; *Z. tenuifolia* (Mascarene grass), is the finest textured *Zoysia* grass. **'Emerald'**, a hybrid cultivar, has faster growth and is cold-hardy. Other cultivars include **'Belaire'**, **'El Toro'**, and **'Cashmere'**.

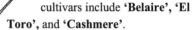

STRELITZIACEAE - STRELITZIA FAMILY

MONOCOTYLEDONS; 4 GENERA AND ABOUT 55 SPECIES

GEOGRAPHY: Tropical America, Madagascar, Guiana, and South Africa, respectively, as the four genera listed below.

GROWTH HABIT: Herbaceous to tree-like,; stems formed by sheathing leaf bases.

LEAVES: Often quite large, alternate, distichous (distinctively fan-shaped), with a well-defined midrib and penniparallel laterals.

FLOWERS: Zygomorphic, bisexual, born on long-stalked inflorescences which are enclosed in a boat-shaped bract; perianth in two series of 3 segments, the outer (sepals) equal in size but two of the inner series (petals) unequal and the third narrow and elongated; stamens usually 5; ovary inferior and consists of 3 fused carpels.

FRUIT: Woody, loculicidally dehiscent capsule or a fleshy schizocarp; seeds with or without aril.

ECONOMIC USES: No uses other than ornamentals reported.

ORNAMENTAL GENERA: *Heliconia, Ravenala, Phenakospermum,* and *Strelitzia.*

Ravenala madagascariensis   TRAVELER'S TREE

PRONUNCIATION - ˌræ və ˈnæ lə   mæ də ˌgæs kə rē ˈen səs

TRANSLATION - [native Madagascar name] [from Madagascar].

FORM - Monoecious, evergreen tree; vase-shaped; large-leaved; palm-like appearance; coarse texture.

SIZE - Reaches heights of 30 feet and spreads of 18 feet; moderate growth rate.

HARDINESS ZONE - Zones 10-11; limited to south Florida.

NATIVE HABITAT - Madagascar.

LEAVES - Very large, banana-like, to 9 feet long; torn into many parallel segments; 2-ranked; arranged to give a fan-like appearance. Petioles long; enlarged basal sheath that collects rain water; thirsty travelers tap this water, giving this plant its common name.

STEM/BARK - Trunk stout, ringed, unbranched, gray; numerous suckers at the base.

FLOWERS - White; small; borne in large, axillary inflorescences in an erect series of up to 12 boat-shaped bracts.

FRUIT - Capsules; woody, 4 inches long; 3-valved; contain many black, 0.25 inch seeds with indigo arils.

CULTURE - Full sun on fertile soils with high organic matter; no salt tolerance.

PROBLEMS - A *Cercospora* leaf-spotting disease can cause problems.

PROPAGATION - Division of basal suckers; seeds slow to germinate.

LANDSCAPE USES - An excellent specimen or accent tree for its unique appearance and tropical effect.

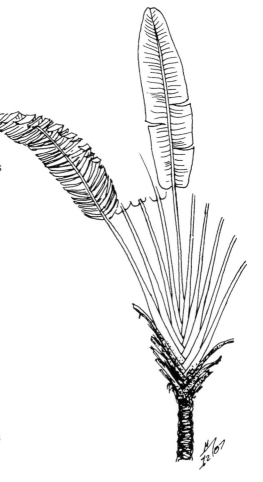

Strelitzia nicolai

**GIANT BIRD OF PARADISE,
WHITE BIRD OF PARADISE**

PRONUNCIATION - strə ˈlit sē ə   ˈni kə lī

TRANSLATION - [after Charlotte of Mecklenburg-Strelitz (1744-1818), who in 1761 became queen of George III] [after Czar Nicholas I (1796-1855) of Russia].

FORM - Monoecious, evergreen tree; upright, large-leaved; palm-like appearance; coarse texture.

SIZE - Reaches a height of 20 feet with a spread of 10 feet, commonly much smaller; medium growth rate.

HARDINESS ZONE - Zone 9; can be grown only in south and protected locations in central Florida.

NATIVE HABITAT - South Africa.

LEAVES - Banana-like; 2-ranked; to 5 feet long and 2 feet wide; dark green; less drooping and tattered than *Ravenala;* midribs channeled on the upper side.

STEM/BARK - Solitary trunk; gray, stout, ringed; suckers at the base.

FLOWERS - White sepals and purple-blue petals; borne in a compound inflorescence of several reddish-brown, boat-shaped bracts.

FRUIT - Capsules; 3-valved; split to reveal many seeds with filamentous arils.

CULTURE - Partial shade on fertile, moist, acid soil; no salt tolerance.

PROBLEMS - Scales can be a problem in poorly ventilated areas.

PROPAGATION - Division of suckers; seeds germinate slowly.

LANDSCAPE USES - Use as a specimen plant for an exotic, tropical effect.

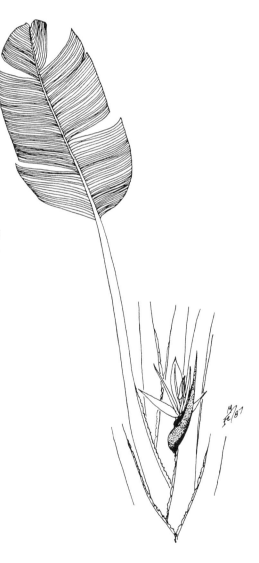

Strelitzia reginae   BIRD OF PARADISE

PRONUNCIATION - strə ˈlit sē ə   ˈre jə nī

TRANSLATION - [after Charlotte of Mecklenburg-Stelitz (1744-1818), who in 1761 became queen of George III] [of the queen, in reference to Queen Marie of Belgium, wife of Leopold II].

FORM - Monoecious, evergreen; herbaceous perennial or shrub; clump-forming, trunkless; coarse texture.

SIZE - Reaches a height of 4 feet with spread increasing with age; old clumps may measure 10 feet across; slow growth rate.

HARDINESS ZONE - Zone 9; can be grown in south and central Florida, but should be planted in protected locations in central Florida.

NATIVE HABITAT - South Africa.

LEAVES - Basal, simple; oblong to lanceolate; somewhat 2-ranked; thick, waxy; grayish glaucous below; not separated into segments; undulate basal margins. Petioles long and channeled, to 1.5 feet long and 6 inches wide.

STEM/BARK - Acaulescent.

FLOWERS - Blue fused petals, long orange sepals; borne in solitary, boat-shaped, green, 8 inch bracts on stout scapes; bracts subtend flowers like flying birds; up to 6 flowers per bract; one opening daily. Blooms periodically throughout the year.

FRUIT - 3-valved capsules containing many 0.25 inch black seeds with orange filamentous arils; ripen all year.

CULTURE - Light, drifting shade on fertile, acid, moisture-retentive soils; no salt tolerance.

PROBLEMS - Scales.

PROPAGATION - Division of clumps; seeds germinate slowly.

LANDSCAPE USES - Use as a specimen for the curiosity of its flowers. Also often grown for cut flowers. Several cultivars are listed: **'Farinosa'** - oblong glaucous leaves with long petiole; **'Humilis'** (= **'Pygmaea'**) - dwarf, clump-forming; **'Kirstenbosch Gold'** - has orange-gold flowers; and **'Rutilans'** - has leaves with red-purple midrib.

ZINGIBERACEAE - GINGER FAMILY

MONOCOTYLEDONS; ABOUT 45 GENERA AND 1,300 SPECIES

GEOGRAPHY: Strictly tropical, especially in Indomalaysia.

GROWTH HABIT: Rhizomatous perennial herbs, often with tuberous roots; cauline stems, when present, usually short and leafless or sometimes foliated.

LEAVES: Often large, distichous, sheathing, with a distinct ligule at base, and with parallel veins arising from a distinct midrib.

FLOWERS: Zygomorphic, bisexual, subtended by a bract, with a conspicuous 2- or 3-lobed labellum; stamens 1-3 but only 1 fertile; perianth segments fused into a tubular calyx and 3 more or less fused petal-like showy corolla segments; ovary inferior and consists of 3 fused carpels.

FRUIT: Brightly colored, often fleshy capsule; seeds frequently arillate.

ECONOMIC USES: Ornamentals, condiments (e.g., ginger from *Zingiber officinale*, turmeric from *Curcuma angustifolia,* etc.), herbs (e.g., cardamom from *Eletaria cardamomum*), dyes (from several genera, including *Curcuma* and *Hedychium*), perfumes (e.g., abir from the rhizome of *Hedychium spicatum*), and medicinal (e.g., arrowroot from *Curcuma* spp.).

ORNAMENTAL GENERA: *Alpinia, Costus, Curcuma, Eletaria, Hedychium, Kaempferia,* and *Zingiber,* among many others.

COMMENTS: The family Costaceae is sometimes included in this family. Most recent classifications, however, no longer combine the two.

Alpinia zerumbet SHELL FLOWER

PRONUNCIATION - æl ˈpi nē ə zə ˈrum bət

TRANSLATION - [after Prospero Alpino (1553-1616), Italian botanist, professor of botany at Padua, who wrote on plants of Egypt] [aboriginal vernacular name].

FORM - Monoecious, evergreen; herbaceous perennial shrub; densely foliated, clump forming; coarse texture.

SIZE - To 12 feet tall; spreading; rapid growth rate.

HARDINESS ZONE - Zone 8b, can be grown in south, central, and north Florida. Plant may freeze back to the ground in north Florida, but grows from the roots in spring.

NATIVE HABITAT - East Asia.

LEAVES - Simple; alternate; 2-ranked; elliptic-oblong to 2 feet long and 5 inches wide; deep green; pinnately veined; smooth with hairy margins. Sheathing bases are a source of fiber for rope in southeastern Asia.

STEMS/BARK - Stems arch gracefully.

FLOWERS - Bisexual; white tipped with red; yellow lip variegated with red and brown, broad, curved, crinkled, to 2 inches long; irregular, bell-shaped; borne in the axils of obtuse bracts; inflorescence terminal, pendulous, hairy; fragrant. Blooms in summer and fall.

FRUIT - Capsule; red; globose; to 0.75 inch in diameter.

CULTURE - Full sun or partial shade on moist, fertile soil; slight salt tolerance; not recommended for dune plantings.

PROBLEMS - Mites.

PROPAGATION - Division of clumps.

LANDSCAPE USES - Use as a specimen or accent plant for the unusual flowers and lush effect of the foliage.

COMMENTS - A cultivar with white variegated leaves, **'Vittata',** is available.

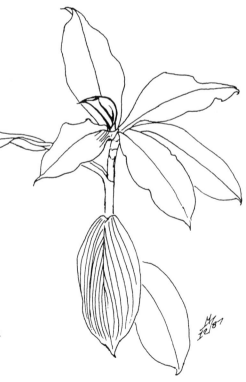

Costus igneus   SPIRAL FLAG

PRONUNCIATION - 'kɑs təs 'ig nē əs

TRANSLATION - [the Latin name derived from an Oriental name for an imported aromatic root] [fiery red].

FORM - Monoecious, evergreen; herbaceous perennial shrub or ground cover; rhizomatous; spreading to form dense mounds; clumping; medium-coarse texture.

SIZE - To 3 feet tall, commonly 1 foot, with a variable spread.

HARDINESS ZONE - Zone 9, can be grown in central and south Florida. In protected locations in north Florida it is killed to the ground by freezing temperatures, but comes from the roots in spring.

NATIVE HABITAT - Brazil.

LEAVES - Simple; spirally arranged; oblong-lanceolate, to 6 inches long and 2 inches wide; smooth, dark green; reddish beneath; tubular sheathing bases.

STEMS/BARK - Stems spirally twisted.

FLOWERS - Bisexual; orange-red; calyx tubular, 3-lobed, borne terminally in few flowered spikes. Showy part of the flower a staminoidal lip: nearly circular, petal-like, shallowly 4-lobed, to 2-inch-diameter; broad orange stamen with a petal-like filament protrudes from the center of the lip. Blooms in the warm months.

FRUIT - Capsule.

CULTURE - Full sun or partial shade, on fertile, moist soil; moderate salt tolerance.

PROBLEMS - Mites and nematodes.

PROPAGATION - Division of clumps, offsets, or stem cuttings.

LANDSCAPE USES - As a ground cover or specimen; frequently planted near water.

Hedychium coronarium   BUTTERFLY GINGER, GARLAND FLOWER, CINNAMON JASMINE

PRONUNCIATION - hə 'di kē əm   ˌko rə 'næ rē əm

TRANSLATION - [from Greek *hedys* (= sweet) and *chion* (= snow), in reference to the color and fragrance of the flower] [used in garlands].

FORM - Monoecious, monocotyledonous clumping herbaceous perennial of coarse texture.

SIZE - 4-6 feet.

HARDINESS ZONE - Zones 10-11 (9 with some protection).

NATIVE HABITAT - Tropical Asia but naturalized in tropical America.

LEAVES - Alternate, simple, entire margins, clasping the stem, to 24 inches long and 5 inches wide.

STEM/BARK - Stiff, erect, mostly unbranched stems to 6 feet, which droop with age after flowering.

FLOWERS - Several white, zygomorphic, fragrant terminal flowers subtended by large stiff bracts, on a spike. Corolla tube about 3 inches long; staminodial lip large, sometimes with a yellow tinge.

FRUIT - A 3-locular capsule.

CULTURE - Partial shade, in moist fertile soil.

PROBLEMS - Requires removal of older stems and may become too large if not periodically divided.

PROPAGATION - Division of the rhizome which should be done once every 3-4 years to keep the plant under control.

LANDSCAPE USES - Outdoors or in greenhouse as specimen or accent plant for its tropical effect and large, showy, fragrant flowers.

COMMENTS - One cultivar ('**Angustifolium**') and several varieties have been listed. Also several related species, such as *H. coccineum* (scarlet ginger) and *H. flavum* (= f. *flavescens*) (yellow ginger), are commonly offered for sale.

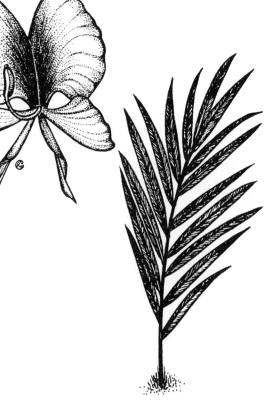

Zingiber zerumbet   PINE CONE LILY, WILD GINGER

PRONUNCIATION - ˈzin jə bər   zə ˈrum bət

TRANSLATION - [probably from pre-Roman *srnga* (= a horn) and *ver* (= a root), giving the Latin Zingiber] [aboriginal vernacular name].

FORM - Monoecious, herbaceous perennial shrub; rhizomatous; heavily foliated; inclined stems form dense clumps; coarse texture.

SIZE - To 6 feet tall, spread is variable.

HARDINESS ZONE - Zone 8b, can be grown throughout Florida. Plants die back to ground in response to the short days of autumn, but grow from the root in spring.

NATIVE HABITAT - India and the Malay Peninsula.

LEAVES - Simple; alternate; 2-ranked; long and narrow, to 12 inches long and 3 inches wide; thin; hairy beneath; sheathing bases.

STEM/BARK - Leaf stems arise from a tuberous, aromatic rhizome.

FLOWERS - Bisexual; white or yellowish with a yellow lip; tubular, 3-lobed; inconspicuous; arise from overlapping bracts to 1.25 inches long; bracts showy, green when young, becoming red with age, 2 to 3 inches long; dense, pine cone-like inflorescence borne on a stalk to l2 inches long, separate from the leaves. The bracts develop maximum color in fall and winter.

FRUIT - Capsule; 3-valved.

CULTURE - Full sun or partial shade on moist, fertile soil; moderate salt tolerance.

PROBLEMS - Mites.

PROPAGATION - Division of clumps.

LANDSCAPE USES - As a specimen for its unusual inflorescence, may be used as a ground cover. The inflorescence is popular in arrangements.

COMMENTS - *Zingiber officinale*, the ginger of commerce, is much like *Z. zerumbet*.

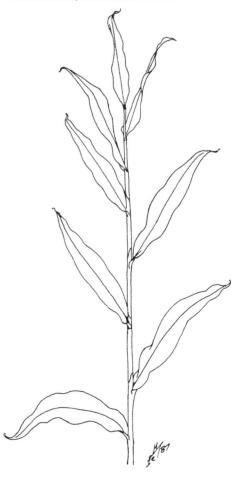

Angiosperms -
Dicotyledons

ACANTHACEAE - ACANTHUS FAMILY

DICOTYLEDONS; 357 GENERA; 4350 SPECIES

GEOGRAPHY: Mostly tropical with a few temperate.

GROWTH HABIT: Predominantly shrubs, a few vines, and some herbaceous.

LEAVES: Simple, opposite and discussate, leaf pairs often of unequal size.

FLOWERS: Bisexual, zygomorphic, 4- or 5-merous, sepals and petals fused, often subtended by a showy bract, stamens 2-4, epipetalous; ovary superior.

FRUIT: Bilocular capsule with numerous seeds, explosively dehiscent when mature and exposed to moisture.

ECONOMIC USES: Ornamentals, minor medicinal uses.

ORNAMENTAL GENERA: *Acanthus, Anisacanthus, Aphelandra, Asystasia, Barleria, Crossandra, Dicliptera, Eranthemum, Fittonia, Graptophyllum, Justicia, Mackaya, Megaskepasma, Odontonema, Pachystachys, Peristrophe, Pseuderanthemum, Ruellia, Ruspolia, Ruttya, Sanchezia, Sciaphyllum, Strobilanthes, Thunbergia,* etc.

Aphelandra squarrosa   ZEBRA PLANT

PRONUNCIATION - ˌæ fə ˈlæn drə   skwəˈrō sə

TRANSLATION - [from Greek *apheles* (= simple) and *aner* (= male), in reference to the one-celled anthers] [with parts spreading horizontally].

FORM - Monoecious, evergreen herbaceous shrub; upright growth habit; medium-coarse texture.

SIZE - To 5 feet tall and 3 feet wide but usually considerably smaller; rapid growth rate.

HARDINESS ZONE - Zone 10. Grown outdoors only in south Florida.

NATIVE HABITAT - Tropical America.

LEAVES - Simple, opposite; ovate to ovate-elliptic, 6 to 12 inches long; glossy dark green above, veins marked in white; glabrous; margins entire.

STEM/BARK - Stems round, green, and succulent; become semi-woody and brown with age.

FLOWERS - Bisexual, yellow, tubular flowers with yellow to orange-yellow 1 to 1.5 inch bracts; borne on 4 to 6 inch terminal spikes in summer. Showy.

FRUIT - Capsule.

CULTURE - Prefers partial shade, well-drained soil, high humidity; frequently drops lower leaves under low humidity culture; no salt tolerance.

PROBLEMS - Mites, nematodes, and crinkle-leaf syndrome.

PROPAGATION - Cuttings.

LANDSCAPE USES - A specimen or accent plant; more commonly seen as a houseplant.

COMMENTS - Several cultivars for compact growth habit and variegation, as **'Dania'**. Other species include *A. aurantiaca*, and its cultivar **'Roezlii'**, *A.sinclairiana*, and *A. tetragona.*

Fittonia verschaffeltii   NERVE PLANT

PRONUNCIATION -   fi 'tō nē ə   vər shə 'fel tē ī

TRANSLATION - [after Elizabeth and Sarah Mary Fitton, authors of *Conversations on Botany* (1817)] [after Ambrose Colleto Alexander Verschaffelt (1825-1886), Belgian nurseryman and author of a book on *Camellia*].

FORM - Monoecious, evergreen, herbaceous ground cover, spreading; medium-fine texture.

SIZE - To 6 inches tall, spread variable.

HARDINESS ZONE - Zone 11. Grown outdoors only in the Keys. Suffers cold damage at 45 to 50°F.

NATIVE HABITAT - Colombia to Peru.

LEAVES - Simple, opposite; ovate or elliptic to 4 inches long; medium green with red veins; pubescent; margins entire.

STEM/BARK - Creeping stems root at the nodes.

FLOWERS - Bisexual, yellowish-green, inconspicuous, tubular flowers with persistent, light-green bracts; borne in spikes. Blooms during periods of active growth.

FRUIT - Capsule.

CULTURE - Requires filtered shade (maximum light level is 50 percent sun), organic soil, high humidity; no salt tolerance.

PROBLEMS - Mites and nematodes.

PROPAGATION - Cuttings.

LANDSCAPE USES - Ground cover, houseplant, hanging basket, terrarium plant, interiorscape.

COMMENTS - *Fittonia verschaffeltii* var. *argyroneura* (Silver-Nerve Plant) is a white-veined variety considered easier to grow by most producers. Variegated cultivars are also available.

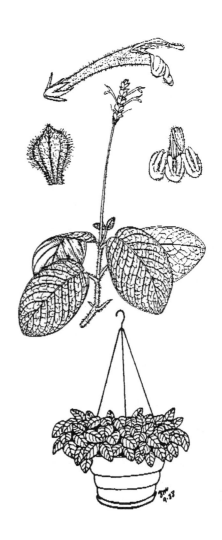

Justicia brandegeana

SHRIMP PLANT

PRONUNCIATION - jus 'ti shə ˌbran də jē 'ā nə

TRANSLATION - [after James Justice (1730-1763), a Scottish horticulturist] [after Townsend Stith Brandegee (1843-1925), American civil engineer, noted for his studies of Californian and Mexican plants].

SYNONYM - *Beloperone guttata* Hort.

FORM - Monoecious, evergreen, irregular, leggy, herbaceous shrub; sprouts from base; medium texture.

SIZE - To 4 feet tall and 6 feet spread; rapid growth rate.

HARDINESS ZONE - Zone 9. Can be grown in south and central Florida; killed to ground in some winters in north Florida.

NATIVE HABITAT - Mexico; locally naturalized in peninsular Florida.

LEAVES - Simple, opposite; ovate to 4 inches long; tomentose.

STEM/BARK - Stems cylindrical, green, with purple ring at each node; turning brown with age.

FLOWERS - Bisexual, white tubular flowers with reddish-brown 1 inch bracts; borne in 4 to 6 inch terminal, drooping spikes. Blooms in summer.

FRUIT - Capsule.

CULTURE - Full sun for more compact growth, better flowering; requires high soil moisture and high fertility; no salt tolerance.

PROBLEMS - Caterpillars, becomes leggy when grown in shade.

PROPAGATION - Cuttings, division.

LANDSCAPE USES - Accent, facer material, small specimen.

COMMENTS - Hummingbirds are particularly attracted to *Justicia brandegeana*. Cultivar **'Yellow Queen'** is probably *Justicia lutea* which is a small plant with upright flower spikes bearing yellow bracts. Related species in cultivation include *J. adhatoda, J. aurea, J. betonica, J. carnea* (Brazilian-plume), *J. cydoniifolia, J. fulvicoma,* and *J. spicigera.*

Thunbergia erecta   BUSH CLOCK VINE, KING'S MANTLE

PRONUNCIATION - thun ˈbər jē ə ē ˈrek tə

TRANSLATION - [in honor of Karl Pehr Thunberg (1743-1822), a plant explorer in Japan and later professor of botany at Uppsala] [erect, upright, in reference to the growth habit of the plant].

FORM - Monoecious evergreen upright shrub.

SIZE - Reaches a maximum height of 6 feet and about 4 feet wide, but somewhat smaller in cultivation.

HARDINESS ZONE - Zones 9b-11, does well in south Florida but requires some protection in central Florida.

NATIVE HABITAT - Tropical to southern Africa.

LEAVES - Opposite, ovate to oblong, mostly 1.5 to 2.5 inches long; glabrate, margins toothed, base cuneate; shortly petiolate.

STEM/BARK - Shoots glabrous, erect and upright but with a tendency to grow rapidly and appear vine-like.

FLOWERS - Solitary in the leaf axils; calyx small and enclosed within the bracts; corolla tube conspicuous, widened on one side (zygomorphic), dark blue with orange throat and yellow tube.

FRUIT - A leathery, thick, globose capsule, violently explosive when ripened and in the presence of moisture.

CULTURE - Requires a well-drained but rich soil. Regular light pruning keeps the fast-growing, leggy shoots under control.

PROBLEMS - None serious, but overwatering and overfertilization result in leggy, soft growth. Leaves may drop in colder areas.

PROPAGATION - By seed which germinate readily or by semi-hardwood cuttings.

LANDSCAPE USES - In warmer areas may be grown outdoors as specimen or in groups or as potted flowering plants on patios.

COMMENTS - The cultivar 'Alba' (sometimes listed as var. *alba*) has white flowers with yellow throat. A few related species such as *T. batiscombei, T. gregori, T. grandiflora,* and others mostly have a viny growth habit. Other species, such as *T. alata, T. capensis,* and *T. primulina,* are annuals used as bedding plants.

ACERACEAE - MAPLE FAMILY

DICOTYLEDONS; 2 GENERA; 102-160 SPECIES

GEOGRAPHY:	Cosmopolitan, mostly north temperate regions of Old (especially China) and New Worlds (especially eastern U.S.), with a few on tropical mountains.
GROWTH HABIT:	Polygamous trees and shrubs with branches in opposite pairs.
LEAVES:	Deciduous or less often evergreen, opposite, simple or less commonly pinnately compound, palmately lobed, toothed, or entire, palmately veined.
FLOWERS:	Unisexual or bisexual, 5-merous, regular; petals and sepals free; stamens 4-10; ovary superior, carpels fused.
FRUIT:	Pair of winged samaras.
ECONOMIC USES:	Ornamentals, timber, and sugar maple (*Acer saccharum*).

ORNAMENTAL GENERA: *Acer; Dipteronia* (2 spp. in China, not known from cultivation in Florida) .

Acer negundo

BOX ELDER

PRONUNCIATION -ˈā sʀ   nə ˈgun dō

TRANSLATION - [classical Latin name] [from *nirgundi*, a Sanskrit word rendered by Acosta as *negundo* for *Vitex negundo*].

FORM - Dioecious, deciduous tree, spreading, open habit, low branching; medium texture.

SIZE - Irregular, 50 to 70 feet with 40 to 50 foot spread, rapid growth.

HARDINESS ZONE - Zone 2. Grows well only in north Florida.

NATIVE HABITAT - Temperate North America; from Canada to southeastern U.S. to California.

LEAVES - Odd-pinnately compound, opposite, with 3 to 5 leaflets, terminal leaflet often 3-lobed, 2 to 5 inches long, coarsely toothed, scented when young, little fall color.

STEM/BARK - Young stems green to reddish-brown, often glaucous, malodorous when crushed.

FLOWERS - Unisexual; staminate flowers in corymbs, pistillate flowers in racemes, flowers in spring before and during leaves. Not showy.

FRUIT - Pairs of winged samara; red-brown 1 to 1.5 inches long. Not showy.

CULTURE - Full sun, fertile soils; no salt tolerance. Tolerates wet or dry sites, drought; pH adaptable. Will grow in sites where few other plants can survive.

PROBLEMS - Cottony maple scale, borers, aphids, wilt, fall mites; very brittle wood. Can become a weed due to abundant seedlings. Short-lived.

PROPAGATION - Seed.

LANDSCAPE USES - Shade tree, large screen, naturalized areas.

COMMENTS - Several subspecies and cultivars: ‘**Auratum**’ with golden leaves, ‘**Elegans**’ leaves edged bright yellow, ‘**Variegatum**’ leaves marbled white and cream, etc. Also, *A. negundo* ssp. *californicum*, ssp. *mexicanum*, etc., are known from cultivation.

Acer palmatum   Japanese Maple

PRONUNCIATION - 'ā sʀ   pɑl 'mā təm

TRANSLATION - [classical Latin name] [palmate, in reference to the leaf lobes].

FORM - Polygamous, deciduous tree, rounded to irregular in shape, weeping, densely foliated, fine-textured, lacy.

SIZE - Seldom exceeds 20 feet in both height and spread. Grows slowly.

HARDINESS ZONE - Zone 5. Should be grown only in north Florida.

NATIVE HABITAT - Korea, China, Japan.

LEAVES - Simple, opposite, circular in outline, with 5 to 11 deeply cut narrow palmate lobes, papery texture, green to reddish-purple (depending on cultivar). The leaves range from 2 to 4 inches wide, have doubly serrate margins and turn red in the fall. Some cultivars red to purple all year.

STEM/BARK - Older branches and the trunk have smooth, gray-brown bark. Slender green twigs create a lacy winter appearance.

FLOWERS - Uni- or bisexual, red, small, inconspicuous flowers in dense racemes, appear in spring.

FRUIT - Pairs of winged samaras, red, to 1 inch long, ripen in fall and persist.

CULTURE - Grows in full sun or partial shade on fertile, moisture-retentive soils with good drainage. It requires high air humidity and is not salt tolerant. Purple-leaved cultivars require full sun or they will revert to green form.

PROBLEMS - Suffers from mushroom root rot on poorly drained soils, leaf scorch if moisture inadequate.

PROPAGATION - Rooting softwood cuttings or grafting of desired cultivars is best as seedlings are variable and not true to type.

LANDSCAPE USES - An excellent specimen or accent plant, in planters, formal gardens, good for giving an "oriental" effect and for focal points at the end of a path or vista.

COMMENTS - There are many cultivars of various growth forms, some with reddish or purple leaf color and some with very dissected leaves. Cultivars of *A. palmatum* have been classified into five Groups: **Palmatum Group** - leaves palmately 5-7-lobed; **Elegans Group** - leaves 5-9-lobed, narrowly divided to near the base; **Dissectum Group** - leaves 5-9-lobed, narrowly divided to the base and coarsely serrate; **Linearilobum Group** - leaves divided into 5-7 narrow lobes nearly to the base, lobes denticulate; **Variegated Cultivars** - leaves mostly 5-7-lobed and variously variegated. The actual number of cultivars in Florida is limited by humid, warm climate.

Acer rubrum

RED MAPLE

PRONUNCIATION - ˈā sʁ   ˈrū brəm

TRANSLATION - [classical Latin name] [red, in].

FORM - Polygamous, deciduous tree, oval canopy, open habit, low branching; medium texture.

SIZE - To 120 feet, in Florida usually 35 to 40 feet, rapid growth.

HARDINESS ZONE - Zone 3. Grows throughout Florida.

NATIVE HABITAT - Temperate North America, including Florida.

LEAVES - Simple, opposite, palmately 3 to 5 lobed, lobes triangular, 3 to 6 inches across, unequally crenate-serrate; petiole usually pink-red and longer than the blade; emerging leaves yellowish-brown to dark red; red to yellow fall color (quite variable among seedlings and between cultivars), showy.

FLOWERS - Uni- or bisexual; red to yellow-ish, in dense racemes, flowers in early spring before leaves. Showy.

FRUIT - Pair of winged samaras, red, 1.0 to 2.5 inches long. Showy.

CULTURE - Full sun or partial shade, variety of soils, well suited to organic, wet areas; not salt tolerant. Generally not pollution tolerant; only moderately drought tolerant. Minor element deficiencies on high pH soils.

PROBLEMS - Cottony maple scale, borers, aphids, wilt, gall mites.

PROPAGATION - Seed, cuttings, graftage of cultivars.

LANDSCAPE USES - Street, parks, speci-men, woodland and water areas. Consideration should be given to shallow root system.

COMMENTS - Many cultivars; some are crosses with *A. saccharinum,* and some with *A. saccharum* subsp. *floridanum.* There are many outstanding red maple selections (color of leaves and shape) that do not perform well in Florida. Several cultivars are also available, including **'Columnare'** - to 50 feet, broadly columnar; **'October Glory'** - shiny green leaves, turn crimson in fall; and **'Red Sunset'** - upright, dense growth habit. A number of other cultivars are more suited to cooler climates.

Acer saccharinum   SILVER MAPLE

PRONUNCIATION -   ˈā sʀ   ˌsæ kə ˈrī nəm

TRANSLATION - [classical Latin name] [sugary, in reference to the sap].

FORM - Polygamous, deciduous tree, upright globose crown, drooping branches. Coarse texture.

SIZE - 90 to 130 feet, rapid growth.

HARDINESS ZONE - Zone 3. Grows best in extreme north Florida.

NATIVE HABITAT - Temperate North America.

LEAVES - Opposite, deeply and palmately 5-lobed, sinuses round, long central lobe, 4 to 6 inches across, pale green above, silvery beneath, pubescent when young, doubly serrate margins, petiole green; some yellow fall color. Silvery underside of leaves very apparent when wind blows.

STEM/BARK - Gray trunk.

FLOWERS - Uni- or bisexual; pinkish, in dense racemes, flowers in early spring before leaves.

FRUIT - Pair of obtuse-angled, winged samara; brownish-red, 1.5 to 2.5 inches long, not showy.

CULTURE - Full sun, rich moist soil; no salt tolerance. Adapted to poorly drained sites, even periodic flooding. Minor element deficiencies on high-pH soils.

PROBLEMS - Cottony maple scale, borers, aphids, *Verticillium* wilt, gall mites, cankers, anthracnose. Weak, brittle wood, easily broken in storms. Shallow roots heave sidewalks and invade septic tanks. Generally short-lived.

PROPAGATION - Seed, softwood cuttings, grafting.

LANDSCAPE USES - Shade tree, specimen, not a good street tree. Some communities have ordinances forbidding further planting of this species.

COMMENTS - Many naturally pendulous and pyramidal forms and cultivars; some are crosses with *A. rubrum*. Several other maples, some native, are grown in Florida, including *A. buergerianum* (Trident Maple), *A. japonicum* (Moonleaf Maple), *A. oblongum, A. paxii, A. platanoides* (Norway Maple) and its cultivar '**Crimson King**', and *A. sieboldianum.*

Acer saccharum subsp. *floridanum*

FLORIDA MAPLE,
SOUTHERN SUGAR MAPLE

PRONUNCIATION - ˈā sʁ ˌsæ kə ˈrī nəm ˌflo rə ˈdā nə

TRANSLATION - [classical Latin name] [sugar] [Florida].

SYNONYM - *Acer barbatum.*

FORM - Monoecious, deciduous tree, oval canopy, densely foliated, medium texture.

SIZE - To 60 feet, usually seen 20 to 30 feet; rapid growth.

HARDINESS ZONE - Zone 7. Grows best in north and central Florida.

NATIVE HABITAT - Southeastern United States; Florida native.

LEAVES - Simple, opposite, palmately 3 to 5 lobed, 1.5 to 4 inches long and wide, lobes squarish, pubescent and glaucescent beneath, petiole green (or occasionally pinkish-red); yellow fall color, leaves ultimately turn brown and frequently persist in the central portion of the canopy for much of the winter.

STEM/BARK - Twigs grayish to purplish.

FLOWERS - Uni- or bisexual; flowers greenish-yellow with conspicuous long beard projecting from the throat, in dense racemes.

FRUIT - Pairs of winged samaras; to 1.5 inches long.

CULTURE - Full sun or partial shade, variety of soils; not salt tolerant.

PROBLEMS - Cottony maples scale, borers, aphids, wilt, gall mites; persistent leaves give a somewhat "trashy" appearance.

PROPAGATION - Seed, cuttings.

LANDSCAPE USES - Street, park, specimen, woodland area.

COMMENTS - There is some disagreement in the literature concerning correct identity and nomenclature of this taxon. The name *A. barbatum* is apparently misapplied. Subspecies *grandidentatum* (to 35 feet tall, deep brown bark, and leaves to 3 inches) and *leucoderme* (to 25 feet, pale gray bark, and leaves 3 inches, dark above, pale-whitish below) are also native to northern Florida.

ANACARDIACEAE - CASHEW FAMILY

DICOTYLEDONS; ABOUT 77 GENERA AND 600 SPECIES

GEOGRAPHY: Predominantly tropical and subtropical with a few temperate representatives in North America and Eurasia.

GROWTH HABIT: Trees, shrubs, and a few vines.

LEAVES: Alternate or rarely opposite, pinnately compound or less often simple (as in *Cotinus, Anacardium,* and *Mangifera*).

FLOWERS: Monoecious, uni- or bisexual; regular, usually with 5 fused sepals; 5 free petals; 5-10 or more stamens; carpels of 5 usually united, 1-3-lobed stigmata; ovary superior.

FRUIT: A drupe, with a single seed.

ECONOMIC USES: Major sources of tannins and resins, important nut crops, including cashew (*Anacardium occidentale*), pistachio (*Pistacia vera*), Dhobi's nut (*Semecarpus anacardium*), and fruits such as mango (*Mangifera indica*), hog plum, Jamaica plum, and others (*Spondias* spp.), as well as several timber species and various other uses.

ORNAMENTAL GENERA: *Anacardium, Bouea, Cotinus, Herpephyllum, Mangifera, Pistacia, Pleiogynium, Pseudospondias, Rhus, Schinus, Spondias,* among others.

COMMENTS: This family includes poison oak and poison ivy (*Toxicodendron*). Some people may show allergic reactions to *Pistacia, Rhus, Schinus*, as well as other genera.

Mangifera indica   MANGO

PRONUNCIATION - mæŋ 'gi fə rə   'in də kə

TRANSLATION - [*Mangot* - Indian vernacular, *fero* - to bear] [from India].

FORM - Monoecious, evergreen tree; densely foliated, rounded, symmetrical; coarse texture.

SIZE - Very old trees may reach 100 feet in height and spread, but a 50 foot height and 40 foot spread is more common; medium growth rate.

HARDINESS ZONE - Zone 10-11. Limited to south Florida.

NATIVE HABITAT - Northern India, Burma, and the Malay Peninsula.

LEAVES - Simple, alternate; lanceolate, to 16 inches long; dark green, leathery, and stiff; new growth wine red; leaves have a turpentine smell when crushed.

STEM/BARK - Forms a stout trunk with corrugated brown bark. The sap and even the fruit cause rashes in some people.

FLOWERS - Pinkish-white, very small and numerous; in showy terminal panicles to 18 inches long. Flowering occurs in late winter (March) and is triggered by cool weather.

FRUIT - Large fleshy drupe, ovoid-pointed to elliptic; weighs 1 to 4 pounds; with delicious, edible, deep yellow flesh; large flattened hairy seeds; borne singly or in 2's or 3's on long, hanging peduncles; ripen in summer, ranging in color from green to combinations of yellow, pink, red, or purple.

CULTURE - Plant in full sun in fertile, drained soils; no salt tolerance.

PROBLEMS - Scales followed by sooty mold; anthracnose on fruit and leaves. Fallen leaves are messy.

PROPAGATION - By budding or veneer grafting on seedling rootstocks.

LANDSCAPE USES - Basically a shade or dooryard fruit tree.

COMMENTS - Among the many cultivars, *'Keitt', 'Hent', 'Edward', 'Glenn',* and *'Haden'* are best. The fruit is of considerable commercial value.

Pistacia chinensis

CHINESE PISTACHE

PRONUNCIATION - pə 'stæ shə   chī 'nen səs

TRANSLATION - [from Greek *pistake* - originally derived from the Persian name *pesteh*] [of China].

FORM - Dioecious, deciduous tree, oval canopy, densely foliated, medium-fine texture.

SIZE - To 60 feet with 25 to 35 foot spread, usually seen 20-30 feet, fast growth rate.

HARDINESS ZONE - Zone 6b. Grown in north and central Florida.

NATIVE HABITAT - China, Taiwan, Philippine Islands.

LEAVES - Even-pinnate, alternate, to 1.5 feet long, leaflets in 6 to 10 pairs, acuminate, 1 to 2.5 inches long, to 0.75 inch wide, base oblique, margins entire, petiole puberulent, distinct odor when crushed; red to reddish-orange fall color.

STEM/BARK - Gray-brown, fissured bark; flakes off to reveal salmon inner bark, attractive. Young stems have prominent orange lenticels. Wood is extremely durable.

FLOWERS - Unisexual, small, petals 0, stamens 5; male flowers in compound racemes, female flowers in panicles. Flowers before leaves emerge but not showy.

FRUIT - Drupes; reddish-brown, globose, dry to 1.5 inches long, in large showy panicles in autumn.

CULTURE - Full sun to partial shade, sandy, well-drained soils; not salt tolerant. Withstands heat and drought.

PROBLEMS - Oak root fungus, verticillium wilts, no serious insect problems, copious fruits somewhat messy.

PROPAGATION - Seeds.

LANDSCAPE USES - Street tree, park, specimen, shade tree. An all-around good tree for urban sites.

COMMENTS - Several cultivars. Used as the understock on which the commercial Pistachio nut (*P. vera*) is grafted. In China, young shoots and leaves eaten cooked as vegetable.

Rhus copallina

SHINING SUMAC, WINGED SUMAC,
FLAMELEAF SUMAC

PRONUNCIATION - rūs   ˌkō pə ˈlī nə

TRANSLATION - [Greek name for *Rhus coriaria*, the edible sumac] [resinous].

FORM - Monoecious, rhizomatous, slender shrub or small tree, deciduous, with a rounded, open crown. Medium texture.

SIZE - Reaches a height of 20 to 30 feet with a similar spread, usually seen as a shrub under 8 feet tall. Fast-growing but short-lived.

HARDINESS ZONE - Zone 5. Can be grown throughout Florida.

NATIVE HABITAT - Native to eastern North America from southeastern Maine to southern Florida, west to eastern Texas, Oklahoma, and eastern Kansas.

LEAVES - Alternate, odd-pinnately compound, to 12 inches long, leaflets 9 to 21, to 4 inches long, oblong-lanceolate, usually entire, base oblique, dark green and nearly glabrous above, paler and usually pubescent below, rachis winged between the leaflets, petiole and rachis pubescent. Foliage turns an attractive red in autumn.

STEM/BARK - Trunk short, slender, to 6 inches in diameter. Bark smooth when young becoming roughened and developing large thin scales with age; light brown. The twigs are closely pubescent and have conspicuous wart-like reddish lenticels.

FLOWERS - Greenish-yellow, tiny. Borne in a compact, broadly ovate, terminal panicle during the summer months. Inflorescence conspicuous but flowers not showy.

FRUIT - Fuzzy-red, ovoid or depressed globose, about 0.25-inch in diameter, in compact, dense clusters at ends of branchlets. Fruiting clusters persist into the winter. Quite showy.

CULTURE - Generally grows in dry soils on hillsides, along margins of woodlands, roads, and rights-of-way, and in abandoned fields. Plant in a dry (well-drained) soil with plenty of sunlight.

PROBLEMS - Generally pest-free.

PROPAGATION - In nature, sumacs multiply prolifically by underground rhizomes, thus they tend to form thickets that provide excellent cover for birds and small and large animals.

LANDSCAPE USES - Best of the sumacs for ornamental planting because of its lustrous dark green foliage. Planted to attract birds and other wildlife and for its brilliant red and orange-red autumn foliage. A coarse-growing, suckering shrub not at all suited for the small garden; best used for naturalizing where there is plenty of space, especially on poor, sandy soils in sunny situations. *Rhus glabra* (Smooth Sumac) and *R. lancea* (Willow Sumac) are also sometimes offered for sale.

Schinus terebinthifolius

**BRAZILIAN PEPPER TREE,
CHRISTMAS BERRY TREE**

PRONUNCIATION - 'shī nəs ˌte rə ˌbin thə 'fō lē əs

TRANSLATION - [Greek name for *schinos*, the mastic tree which it resembles] [turpentine leaf].

FORM - Dioecious, evergreen shrub or tree; low branching; vase form, heavily foliated, with a weedy, open habit; medium texture.

SIZE - To 30 feet, usually 15 to 20 feet; rapid growth rate.

HARDINESS ZONE - Zones 9b to 11. Can be grown in central and south Florida.

NATIVE HABITAT - Brazil, widely naturalized in peninsular Florida, Hawaii, southern California, and in several countries.

LEAVES - Odd-pinnately compound, alternate; with 5 to 13 oblong leaflets to 2.5 inches long; shallow toothed, undulate margins; red rachis; strong turpentine odor when crushed. Light green.

STEM/BARK - Young branches smooth, becoming rough with age.

FLOWERS - Unisexual, white-green, inconspicuous; borne in panicles. Blooms in fall.

FRUIT - Bright red berries in dense clusters; very ornamental during fall and winter.

CULTURE - Grows in full sun to partial shade on a variety of soils; moderate salt tolerance.

PROBLEMS - Scale, thrips, galls; caustic sap may cause irritations.

PROPAGATION - Seeds, cuttings, layers.

LANDSCAPE USES - Use with caution; can be a shade tree if trained; often used as a barrier or windbreak.

COMMENTS - Brazilian pepper has escaped from cultivation in Florida and has become a noxious weed. Its use is forbidden in Florida by law. Two other species, however, may be grown: *S. molle* (California Pepper Tree) and *S. polygamous* (Huigen).

APOCYNACEAE - DOGBANE FAMILY

DICOTYLEDONS; ABOUT 180 GENERA AND 1500 SPECIES

GEOGRAPHY: Throughout tropics, particularly rain forest regions, with a few temperate and desert representatives.

GROWTH HABIT: Evergreen and deciduous small to large trees, shrubs, and vines, often caudiciform succulents, and frequently with milky latex.

LEAVES: Simple, opposite or whorled, usually with entire margins.

FLOWERS: Bisexual, regular, pinwheel-shaped or sepals and petals fused to form a tube; often large, showy, and fragrant; stamens 5, anthers usually connate; ovary mostly superior, with 2 free or united carpels.

FRUIT: Fleshy or woody, single or paired follicles.

ECONOMIC USES: Several important drugs (cardiac glucosides), minor rubbers, fruit (e.g., *Carrisa*), and several ornamentals.

ORNAMENTAL GENERA: *Acokanthera, Adenium, Allamanda, Alstonia, Beaumontia, Carrisa, Catharanthus, Chonemorpha, Conopharyngia, Fosteronia, Kopsia, Mandevilla, Mascarenhasia, Nerium, Ochrosia, Pachypodium, Plumeria, Rauvolfia, Tabernaemontana, Thevetia, Tracheleospermum, Vallaris, Vinca,* and others.

Adenium obesum

DESERT ROSE

PRONUNCIATION - ə ′dē nē əm   ō ′bē səm

TRANSLATION - [from Aden, Yemen, where the species is native] [obese, in reference to the fleshy caudex].

FORM - Monoecious, deciduous, caudiciform, upright stem succulent.

SIZE - Reaches a maximum height of 6 feet and about 4 feet wide, but in cultivation 3 to 4 feet tall and about 3 feet wide.

HARDINESS ZONE - Zones 10-11, does well only in south Florida.

NATIVE HABITAT - Dry, warm southern Arabia and northeastern Africa.

LEAVES - Opposite, arranged in clusters at branch tips, to 3 inches long, ovate to oblong, narrowing at the base, upper surface glossy green, lower surface dull green, pubescent when young but glabrous at maturity.

STEM/BARK - Caudex short, thick, and fleshy, often irregularly shaped because of swollen surface roots; branches often dichotomous, appearing spiral, also thick and fleshy.

FLOWERS - In cymes of 2-10; bisexual, pinkish-crimson, funnel- or salver-form; free flowering and very attractive.

FRUIT - Follicles, usually in pairs.

CULTURE - Primarily a greenhouse crop, requiring a well-drained soil. Must be grown as a succulent, requiring minimal irrigation when dormant.

PROBLEMS - None serious; overwatering, overfertilization, and low light conditions result in excessive "soft" growth.

PROPAGATION - Preferably by seed. Cuttings root relatively easily but a normal caudex is unlikely to develop.

LANDSCAPE USES - In succulent rock gardens, as specimen plant in drier sites, but primarily as a flowering foliage plant. Sap is said to be extremely poisonous, so avoid planting where children frequent.

COMMENTS - A few related taxa such as subsp. *multiflorum* (numerous, dark red flowers), subsp. *socotranum* (large, erect branches and bright pink flowers), *A. boehmianum* (smaller but numerous pink flowers), *A. oleifolium* (much branched and few-flowered), and several hybrid cultivars, selected primarily for flower size and color.

Allamanda cathartica

YELLOW ALLAMANDA,
CANARIO

PRONUNCIATION - ˌæ lə mæn də   kə ˈθɑr tə kə

TRANSLATION - [after Frederick Allamand, eighteenth-century Swiss botanist] [purging].

FORM - Monoecious, clambering vine that may be maintained as a shrub; an erect climber, sprawling without support, sprouting from base; medium-coarse texture.

SIZE - To 20 feet if trained and supported; rapid growth rate.

HARDINESS ZONE - Zones 9b to 11. Grown in central and south Florida.

NATIVE HABITAT - Northern South America.

LEAVES - Simple, opposite or in whorls of 3 to 4; elliptic-oblong, 4 to 6 inches long; light green; caustic, milky sap. Petiole attenuate to very short (subsessile).

STEM - Slender green stems become woody with age.

FLOWERS - Yellow; corolla funnelform with 5 united, rounded petals; to 5 inches across; in few-flowered cymes; blooms during the warm season.

FRUIT - Dehiscent follicle with 0.25 inch spines.

CULTURE - Full sun is required for best flowering; various soil types; moderate salt tolerance.

PROBLEMS - Caterpillars, mites, nutrient deficiencies.

PROPAGATION - Cuttings or division.

LANDSCAPE USES - As a vine on a trellis, wall, arbor, or on a tree; as a freestanding specimen shrub if properly pruned.

COMMENTS - Related species and cultivars are available for floral variation and compact growth habit: *A. williamsii* (yellow-brown throat - may be a variant of *A. cathartica*), **'Cherry's Jubilee'**, **'Chocolate Cherry'**, **'Chocolate Swirl'**, **'Dwarf Discovery'**, **'Grandiflora'**, **'Hendersonii'** (Brown-Bud Allamanda), **'Hendersonii Compacta'**, **'Hendersonii Dwarf'**, **'Silver Dwarf Discovery'**, and **'Stanstill's Double'** (double yellow flowers).

Allamanda violacea   PURPLE ALLAMANDA

PRONUNCIATION - ˌæ lə mæn də   ˌvɪ ō ˈlā sē ə

TRANSLATION - [after Frederick Allamand, eighteenth-century Swiss botanist] [violet-colored].

FORM - Evergreen climbing-clambering vine; medium-coarse texture.

SIZE - Variable, depending on size of the support; fairly rapid growth rate.

HARDINESS ZONE - Zones 10-11. Can be grown in south Florida and in protected locations in central Florida.

NATIVE HABITAT - Brazil.

LEAVES - Simple, whorled, usually in fours; oblong to obovate with an acuminate apex; to 6 inches long; light green; leaves and new growth are scabrous and densely pubescent.

STEM/BARK - Weak, sprawling stems exude milky sap when injured.

FLOWERS - Funnelform; 3 inches long; reddish-purple fading to pink. The throat of the flower is usually intense in color. Blooms appear in few-flowered cymes during warm months of the year, peaking in summer.

FRUIT - Dehiscent, globose, spiny follicle; rarely seen.

CULTURE - Plant in full sun on a wide range of soils; no salt tolerance.

PROBLEMS - Scale and mites.

PROPAGATION - By cuttings of any age wood, but grown best when grafted on *A. cathartica.*

LANDSCAPE USES - A specimen plant that is primarily a vine but may be a shrub, depending on the training and amount of pruning. This plant is poisonous and should not be used in areas where children frequent.

COMMENTS - *Allamanda schottii* (= *A. neriifolia* -Bush Allamanda) is also frequently offered.

Carissa macrocarpa   NATAL PLUM

PRONUNCIATION - kə 'ri sə   ˌmak rə 'kɑr pə

TRANSLATION - [African aboriginal name] [large fruit].

SYNONYM - *Carissa grandiflora.*

FORM - Evergreen shrub; round, much branched, dense, broad canopy; medium-fine texture.

SIZE - To 18 × 18 feet; most cultivars grown are much smaller; medium growth rate.

HARDINESS ZONE - Zones 9b to 11. Can be grown in south and central Florida.

NATIVE HABITAT - South Africa.

LEAVES - Simple, opposite, ovate, to 3 inches long and 2 inches wide; leathery, dark green; entire with mucronate tip; bifurcate stipular spines to 1.5 inches long; milky sap.

STEM/BARK - Green stems on new growth, becoming woody with age.

FLOWERS - White, star-shaped, to 2 inches across; corolla united; solitary, pseudoaxillary; blooms from early spring to summer.

FRUIT - Berry; red, plum-shaped, to 2 inches long; edible, primarily used for jellies and preserves.

CULTURE - Full sun to light shade, well-drained soil; high salt tolerance.

PROBLEMS - Scale, foliar bacteria, root rots, and nutrient deficiencies.

PROPAGATION - Seeds or cuttings.

LANDSCAPE USES - Use in borders, impenetrable screens or foundation plantings; an excellent hedge plant or specimen. Because of its salt tolerance, it is highly recommended for seaside use. Compact cultivars good for ground cover.

COMMENTS - Several cultivars for compact and spreading growth habits. Some cultivars grow to only 2 feet tall. Listed cultivars of *C. macrocarpa* include 'Bonsai', 'Boxwood Beauty' - compact, semi-upright, but mound forming, 'Dainty Princess', 'Emerald Blanket', 'Hendrii', 'Horizontalis' and 'Prostrata' - low and spreading, among others. Planting close to pedestrian traffic should be avoided. Several species and cultivars are available: *C. bispinosa, C. carandas* (Karanda), *C. edulis,* and *C. spinarum.*

Catharanthus roseus MADAGASCAR PERIWINKLE

PRONUNCIATION - ˌka thə ˈran thəs ˈrō zē əs

TRANSLATION - [from Greek *katharos* (pure) and *anthos* (flower)] [rose-colored].

SYNONYM - *Vinca rosea.*

FORM - Monoecious, perennial often cultivated as an annual. Bushy, but not very dense.

SIZE - Height: 1.5-2 feet; spread: 2 feet.

HARDINESS ZONE - Zone 10, as a perennial, does not tolerate freezing.

NATIVE HABITAT - African origin, naturalized in waste or disturbed areas in south Florida.

LEAVES - Simple, opposite, entire, oblong-lanceolate, 1-2 inches long, glossy, short petioled.

STEM/BARK - Thin, branching.

FLOWERS - 5-merous, typically rose-pink, varying to mauve and white, to 1.5 inches across; tube about 1 inch long.

FRUIT - Inconspicuous follicle to 1.5 inches long.

CULTURE - Best in full sun, but stands light shade. Resistant to parched, dry conditions. Will not tolerate freezing.

PROBLEMS - Micronutrient deficiencies may develop. Fungal problems may occur in wet weather.

PROPAGATION - Seed or stem cuttings at any time of the year.

LANDSCAPE USES - Often grown as a ground cover using dwarf varieties for dense cover. Border plant, also good for hanging baskets.

COMMENTS - 'Bright Eyes' is a dwarf white cultivar. 'Coquette' is a dwarf cultivar with rose-colored flowers.

Mandevilla splendens

PINK ALLAMANDA

PRONUNCIATION - ˌmæn də ˈvi lə   ˈsplen dənz

TRANSLATION - [after Henry J. Mandeville (1773-1861), a minister in Buenos Aires] [splendid].

SYNONYM - *Dipladenia splendens.*

FORM - Monoecious, evergreen woody vine; densely foliated, twining; medium-coarse texture.

SIZE - Variable, depends on size of the support; rapid growth rate.

HARDINESS ZONE - Zones 10-11. Can be grown in south Florida and in protected locations in central Florida.

NATIVE HABITAT - southeastern Brazil.

LEAVES - Simple, opposite; broadly elliptic with an acuminate apex and subcordate base; to 8 inches long; subsessile, dark green; thin, soft, and translucent with a rumpled appearance.

STEM/BARK - Brownish-red slender stems; finely pubescent; twine very readily; have milky sap and swollen nodes.

FLOWERS - Light pink on opening, rose-pink with age; very showy, funnelform; to 4 inches wide and 2 inches long; in 3 to 5 flowered axillary racemes. The flower throat is usually deeper in color, and bloom occurs in warm months of the year, peaking in summer.

FRUIT - Paired follicles; slender, 8 inches long; rarely produced.

CULTURE - Requires full sun and well-drained soils; marginal salt tolerance.

PROBLEMS - Mealybugs and scales, especially in enclosed areas.

PROPAGATION - By stem cuttings under mist.

LANDSCAPE USES - An excellent long-blooming screening vine which climbs and covers readily; hanging basket; ground cover for large areas.

COMMENTS - Often sold as **'Mrs. DuPont'**. **'Red Riding Hood'** is also a popular cultivar. The related species include *M.* × *amabilis,* *M. laxa,* and *M. sanderi.*

Nerium oleander OLEANDER

PRONUNCIATION - ˈnē rē əm ˈō lē ˌæn dər

TRANSLATION - [the original Greek name] [the Italian name].

FORM - Monoecious, evergreen shrub, erect, much-branched usually from base; lower portions of stems become leafless. Fine to medium texture.

SIZE - To 20 feet tall with 6 to 12 foot spread; rapid growth rate.

HARDINESS ZONE - Zones 8b-11. Grows in south, central, and north Florida with some cold damage in the north.

NATIVE HABITAT - Mediterranean region to Japan.

LEAVES - Simple, mostly in whorls of 3, sometimes opposite, lanceolate to 10 inches long, smooth and leathery, dark green above and lighter green below, prominent midrib, nearly penni-parallel-veined, short petiole, entire; all parts are highly toxic and exude a sticky sap.

STEM/BARK - Young stems green at first, stout and glabrous, becoming gray-brown with age. Older branches have raised lenticels and prominent leaf scars.

FLOWERS - Reds, pinks, yellows, white, single and double forms, funnelform corolla with 5 obovate petals, to 2 inches across, borne in terminal cymes, throughout the warm season. Some cultivars scented. Very showy.

FRUIT - A pair of follicles 4 to 7 inches long.

CULTURE - Full sun (for best flowering) to partial shade, tolerant of many soils; highly drought, wind, and salt tolerant. Easily transplanted. Withstands severe pruning. A very durable plant.

PROBLEMS - Oleander caterpillar (can completely defoliate plant if left untreated, but easily controlled by insecticide sprays), scale, mealybug, root rot in wet locations. All parts are highly toxic (even inhaled smoke is toxic); ingestion of a single leaf is reportedly sufficient to kill an adult human. Leaves used to prevent moth damage to clothing.

PROPAGATION - Cuttings and seed.

LANDSCAPE USES - Use as a screen, barrier, windbreak, or specimen. Its salt tolerance makes oleander an excellent seaside shrub. Good container or tub plant. Commonly used in highway plantings in western states.

COMMENTS - Many cultivars selected for flower color, scent and form are available: **'Calypso'**, **'Dwarf'**, **'Hawaii'**, **'Ice Pink'**, **'Morocco'** (Dwarf White), **'Petite'**, **'Saman Dwarf'**, **'Sister Agnus'**, and **'Variegata'** are among those listed.

Ochrosia elliptica   KOPSIA, OCHROSIA, POKOSOLA

PRONUNCIATION - ō ˈkrō zhə   ē ˈlip tə kə

TRANSLATION - [pale yellow, in reference to flower color] [elliptic, in reference to the leaves].

SYNONYM - Frequently and erroneously called "Kopsia," which is the generic name of a similar plant.

FORM - Evergreen shrub; large, upright; becoming a small tree with age; medium-coarse texture.

SIZE - Reaches a height of 20 feet with a 10 foot spread; medium growth rate.

HARDINESS ZONE - Zones 10-11. Limited to south Florida.

NATIVE HABITAT - Coastal areas of Australia, New Guinea, and adjacent islands.

LEAVES - Simple, in whorls of 3 to 4; obovate-oblong to elliptic with obtuse apices; to 6 inches long; glossy, leathery, with transverse veins; entire margins. Medium green.

STEM/BARK - The stems bleed copious milky sap when cut or injured.

FLOWERS - Yellowish-white, not showy; 0.5 inch long, in dense, flat, sessile cymes. The fragrant flowers are borne terminally and in the upper leaf axils from late summer into winter.

FRUIT - Bright red elliptical drupes; 2 inches long, usually borne end to end in pairs. The white, mealy flesh around the large, teardrop-shaped seed is poisonous.

CULTURE - Grown in full sun or partial shade on a wide range of soils; moderate salt tolerance.

PROBLEMS - Scales and occasionally mites.

PROPAGATION - Scarified seed or cuttings.

LANDSCAPE USES - In seaside hedges; also makes an attractive specimen for planters and shrub groupings.

COMMENTS - A related cultivated species is *O. borbonica.*

Plumeria rubra   FRANGIPANI

PRONUNCIATION - plū 'me rē ə   'rū brə

TRANSLATION - [after Charles Plumier (1646-1704), French monk and botanist] [red].

FORM - Monoecious, deciduous tree; vase-shaped to round; wide-spreading; coarse texture.

SIZE - Reaches a height of 25 feet with an equal spread; fairly rapid growth rate on good soils.

HARDINESS ZONE - Zones 10-11. Can be grown only in south Florida.

NATIVE HABITAT - Seasonally dry areas of Central America and the Caribbean.

LEAVES - Simple, alternate; elliptic, to 20 inches long; with prominent midrib and many parallel lateral veins at right angles to the midribs; leaves clustered at tips of the branches on stout, 4-inch-long petioles; shed in winter and during prolonged dry periods; exude milky sap when damaged. Medium green.

STEM/BARK - Succulent, blunt-tipped, 1 inch thick, green turning gray; crooked branches are soft and weak; exude copious milky sap when cut.

FLOWERS - White, red, pink, or yellow; salverform, to 3 inches wide; in dense terminal clusters; fragrant, showy, waxy; blooms mainly in summer.

FRUIT - Paired follicles; leathery, brown, 10 inches long; rarely seen in cultivation.

CULTURE - Plant in full sun on a wide range of well-drained soils; does poorly on wet soils; marginal salt tolerance.

PROBLEMS - Scale is the major pest; mites in greenhouse situations.

PROPAGATION - By cuttings. Large hardwood cuttings should be allowed to dry several days. Leafy tip cuttings should be planted immediately.

LANDSCAPE USES - A specimen tree for the fragrant, showy flowers. In Hawaii, the blooms are used for leis.

COMMENTS - *Plumeria rubra* ssp. *acutifolia* with narrowly lanceolate leaves and ssp. *lutea* with yellow flowers are also offered. Related species listed include *P. alba* (West India Jasmine), *P. obtusa* (White Frangipani, Arbolde Novia) and *P. obtusa* var. *sericifolia* (Lily of the Coast, with pubescent leaves and inflorescences).

C. CONNELLY '79

Tabernaemontana divaricata
CREPE JASMINE,
PINWHEEL FLOWER

PRONUNCIATION - tə ˌbər nē mɑn 'tā nə   də ˌvæ rə 'kɑ tə

TRANSLATION - [after Jakob Theodor von Bergzabern, who latinized his name to Tabernaemontanus. He was the author of the herbal *Neuw Kreuterbuch* (1588-1591)] [species].

FORM - Monoecious, evergreen shrub; round, symmetrical, dense, spreading, much-branched; medium-fine texture.

SIZE - To 10 feet tall.

HARDINESS ZONE - Zones 9b to 11. Grown in south Florida and protected areas of central Florida.

NATIVE HABITAT - India.

LEAVES - Simple, opposite; oblong-lanceolate to obovate, to 6 inches long; acuminate to subcaudate. Leaves of each pair are unequal, thin, dark green, and glabrous.

STEM/BARK - New growth is green, becoming woody with age. Milky sap.

FLOWERS - Waxy white, salverform; to 1.5 inches across; borne in few-flowered cymose clusters; fairly showy; blooms during the warm months; especially fragrant at night.

FRUIT - Paired follicles; oblong with recurved beak; to 3 inches long.

CULTURE - Full sun to partial shade; tolerant of various soil types; no salt tolerance.

PROBLEMS - Scale, mites, nematodes, and sooty mold.

LANDSCAPE USES - Use in shrub border or as a specimen plant.

COMMENTS - Double-flowered and large-flowered cultivars are available: **'Flore Pleno'** (Double Flower Crepe Jasmine) and **'Cashmere'** are commonly available. Related species listed include *T. coronaria* is the same as *T. divaricata.*

Trachelospermum asiaticum

SMALL-LEAF CONFEDERATE JASMINE, JAPANESE STAR JASMINE

PRONUNCIATION - ˌtrā kə lō ˈspər məm   ˌā zhē ˈæ tə kəm

TRANSLATION - [from Greek *trachelos* (= a neck) and *sperma* (= a seed)] [from Asia].

FORM - Monoecious, evergreen vine, twining but usually not climbing too far, fine-textured.

SIZE - Grows to 14 inches tall as a ground cover and to 12 feet tall as a traveling vine with support. Spread is up to 15 feet and growth rate is moderate.

HARDINESS ZONE - Zone 7b. Can be grown in all regions of Florida. Slightly hardier than *T. jasminoides*.

NATIVE HABITAT - Korea and Japan.

LEAVES - Simple, opposite, ovate to elliptic, entire, to 1 inch long, acute apex. The shiny dark green leaves have prominent, lighter green (almost white) main veins and pale green undersides.

STEM/BARK - Dark brown stems very wiry and slender; do not readily develop aerial roots.

FLOWER - Yellowish-white, slightly fragrant, salverform, 0.75 inch long, in axillary and terminal cymes. Rarely produced, in May.

CULTURE - Full sun or partial shade. Tolerates a wide range of light and soil conditions; moderately salt tolerant. Resists trampling.

PROBLEMS - Scale insects, whiteflies, sooty mold; no serious pests.

PROPAGATION - Softwood - semi-hardwood cuttings placed in mist beds with rooting hormone treatment.

LANDSCAPE USES - Primarily a ground cover as it does not climb readily. Also works well hanging over a wall or planter edge; good for banks and slopes.

COMMENTS - Often mislabeled and sold as *T. jasminoides* 'Nana', 'Minima' or 'Microphylla'. *T. asiaticum* 'Nortex' has a more lance-shaped leaf, but is otherwise similar (may be the same as 'Longleaf'). Other available cultivars include 'Mini Mound' and 'Variegation'.

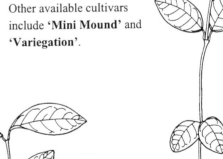

Trachelospermum jasminoides CONFEDERATE JASMINE, STAR JASMINE

PRONUNCIATION - ˌtrā kə lō ˈspər məm ˌjæz mə ˈnoi dēz

TRANSLATION - [from Greek *trachelos* (= a neck) and *sperma* (= a seed)] [jasmine-like].

FORM - Monoecious, evergreen vine or ground cover, irregular, climbing, of medium texture.

SIZE - Grows 12 to 16 inches tall as a ground cover or 60 feet tall on a tree or other support as a climbing vine. Growth rate is fairly rapid.

HARDINESS ZONE - Zone 8b. Can be grown throughout Florida.

NATIVE HABITAT - Eastern India to China and Japan.

LEAVES - Opposite, simple, ovate, thick and shiny, to 4 inches long, entire. Leaves are larger, the apex more acuminate and veins not as distinctly white as *T. asiaticum*.

STEM/BARK - Thin, wiry, dark brown, twining stems develop aerial roots when climbing and root when in contact with moist soil. Exudes milky sap when broken.

FLOWERS - White, very fragrant, salverform, 1 inch wide, in axillary and terminal cymes that extend beyond the leaves. Season of bloom is April-May.

FRUIT - Paired follicles; slender, cylindrical, 3 inches long, containing small seeds with a tuft of hairs, usually inviable.

CULTURE - Best in partial to full shade (flowers well even in shade), fair in full sun; moderately wet to moderately dry soil. Moderately salt tolerant. Tolerates only a small amount of foot traffic.

PROBLEMS - Scale insects, sooty mold; no serious pests.

PROPAGATION - Softwood-semi-hardwood cuttings under mist with rooting hormone dip.

LANDSCAPE USES - Trellis, good for banks and slopes. Not as good a ground cover as *T. asiaticum*. Used mainly to cover the trunks of tall pines and oaks, pergolas, trellises, and other supports. Available cultivars include **'Dwarf'**, **'Star'**, and **'Variegata'**.

Vinca major

PERIWINKLE

PRONUNCIATION - ˈviŋ kə   ˈmā jər

TRANSLATION - [winding around] [larger].

FORM - Monoecious, evergreen subshrub, trailing, medium-textured, forming a dense, irregular ground cover.

SIZE - Reaches a maximum height of 18 inches with an indeterminate spread. Growth rate is fairly rapid.

HARDINESS ZONE - Zone 6. Does well only in central and north Florida.

NATIVE HABITAT - Europe and western Asia.

LEAVES - Simple, opposite, ovate with a subcordate base to 2 inches long, margins entire.

STEM/BARK - Green, trailing, has no aerial roots and does not climb, but roots at nodes when in contract with the ground.

FLOWERS - Bluish-purple, showy, salverform to 2 inches wide, axillary and solitary, showy. Appear in March and sporadically over the growing season.

FRUIT - Insignificant, cylindrical follicles, rarely seen.

CULTURE - Requires partial to full shade and moist, well-drained soil. It does not tolerate salt or hot, dry conditions.

PROBLEMS - None serious; leaf scorch in hot, dry sites.

PROPAGATION - Stem cuttings or division at any time of year.

LANDSCAPE USES - A ground cover for shaded banks and wooded areas. Naturalizes well and can compete successfully with surface tree roots. Also used sometimes in window boxes and hanging baskets.

COMMENTS - *Vinca major* 'Variegata' has irregular white or cream-colored markings on foliage. *Vinca minor,* a hardier, smaller, related species resembles *Trachelospermum asiaticum* when not in flower.

AQUIFOLIACEAE - HOLLY FAMILY

DICOTYLEDONS; 3 GENERA AND ABOUT 400 SPECIES

GEOGRAPHY: Distributed in temperate and tropical regions.

GROWTH HABIT: Trees and shrubs.

LEAVES: Alternate, coriaceous, often evergreen, entire to variously and
                      conspicuously spinose, serrate, serrulate, or crenate.

FLOWERS: Small, greenish-white, unisexual (plants dioecious) or rarely
                      bisexual, actinomorphic; usually in spikes or panicles; 4-merous;
                      stamens often represented as staminodes in female flowers.

FRUIT: A berry with four pyrenes, each containing one seed.

ECONOMIC USES: Primarily as ornamentals; the hard white wood is used in carving
                      and for inlays, and leaves of *I. paraguariensis* (Maté, Yerba
                      Matá) are used as tea.

ORNAMENTAL GENERA: *Ilex*, with 400 species, constitutes nearly all cultivated members
                   of the family; *Nemopanthus* (2 species) and *Phelline* (10 species)
                   are only rarely cultivated.

Ilex × *attenuata*   COMMON NAMES VARY WITH CULTIVAR

PRONUNCIATION - 'ī leks   ə ˌte nyū 'ā tə

TRANSLATION - [Latin name for *Quercus ilex*] [interspecific hybrid between *Ilex cassine* and *I. opaca*].

FORM - Dioecious, more or less dense, evergreen trees of pyramidal growth form.

SIZE - Varies with cultivar, from about 20 to 50 or more feet in height and various dimensions.

HARDINESS ZONE - Zone 7.

NATIVE HABITAT - Various forms may be found where the range of the two parental species overlap.

LEAVES - Alternate, simple, entire, or, similar to *I. opaca*, spinose though spines less sharp and equidistant, light to dark green depending on the cultivar.

STEM/BARK - Smooth, gray, often covered with lichens.

FLOWERS - Unisexual; 4-merous white, individually inconspicuous but collectively attractive.

FRUIT - Red berries (pyrenes) similar to *I. opaca*, often produced profusely.

CULTURE - Similar to its parental species, it requires well-drained, moist, slightly acid soil.

PROBLEMS - None serious but scale and occasionally sooty mold may become troublesome.

PROPAGATION - Semi-hardwood cuttings.

LANDSCAPE USES - Popular hollies, used as specimen plants, street trees, and in public landscapes such as parks and parking lots.

COMMENTS- Cultivars of this hybrid have potential for use as cut foliage particularly when bearing abundant fruit.

'East Palatka' - A densely foliated, oval to more or less pyramidal tree with mostly entire leaves but a terminal spine. An increasingly common plant in the urban landscapes for specimen, street tree, or public landscapes.

'Fosteri' - Very attractive, comparatively slow growing, densely foliated, conical small tree with a height of about 20 feet and dark, ovate-lanceolate, spinose foliage.

'Sunny Foster' - Similar to 'Fosteri' but with variegated foliage.

'Savannah' - Similar to *I. opaca* in its growth form and foliar characteristics, with conical growth form, spinose leaves (though spines not as sharp and are equidistant) but lighter color foliage.

Ilex cassine   DAHOON HOLLY

PRONUNCIATION - 'ī leks   kə 'sēñ

TRANSLATION - [Latin name for *Quercus ilex*, a California native oak species] [American Indian name].

FORM - Evergreen tree, erect, compact, of medium texture.

SIZE - Can reach a height of 40 feet and a spread of 20 feet, typically 20 to 30 feet in height and 8 to 15 feet crown. Growth rate is medium.

HARDINESS ZONE - Zone 7b. Can be grown in all regions of Florida.

NATIVE HABITAT - Swamps, low hammocks and other moist areas in the coastal plain of the southeastern United States, Cuba, and the Bahamas.

LEAVES - Alternate, leathery, glossy, elliptic to oblong, to 4 inches long, petiole often reddish. The margins are either entire or have several tiny teeth near the apex, more or less pubescent on midrib on the lower side.

STEM/BARK - Young stems remain green for 1 to 2 years. The bark is grayish and often covered with lichens.

FLOWERS - Unisexual (plants dioecious); yellowish-white, few and usually inconspicuous, in axillary cymes in spring.

FRUIT - Pyrenes, bright red, persistent through winter, to 0.25 inch wide, occur on female plants in clusters of 1 to 3 and ripen in late fall. Quite attractive.

CULTURE - Grown in full to partial sun on moist soils. Withstands poor drainage and marginal amounts of salt.

PROBLEMS - None of major importance.

PROPAGATION - Cuttings root easily and are the preferred method since they give plants of known sex. Seeds germinate readily when stratified or soaked in GA_3.

LANDSCAPE USES - Generally a specimen or street tree. Can be used as a tall hedge as it tolerates close clipping. Fruit attracts wildlife.

COMMENTS - Some recent cultivars have more and larger fruit. *Ilex cassine* **'Myrtifolia'** is considered to be a distinct Florida native species, *I. myrtifolia.* Cultivars with larger leaves and profuse fruit are offered.

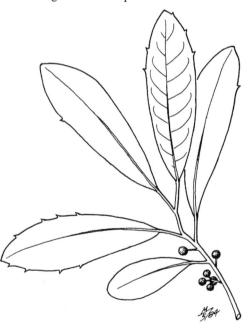

Ilex cornuta

PRONUNCIATION - 'ī leks   kor 'nū tə

TRANSLATION - [Latin name for *Quercus ilex,* a California oak species] [horned, in reference to the leaves].

FORM - Dioecious, evergreen, large shrub or small tree, densely branched, pyramidal to rounded; medium texture.

SIZE - To 20 feet, variable with cultivar, slow growing.

HARDINESS ZONE - Zone 7. Grows throughout Florida, but does best in northern regions.

NATIVE HABITAT - Eastern China.

LEAVES - Simple, alternate, dark green, glossy, stiff and leathery, short petiole, margins translucent, spines 0 to 5; variable with cultivar.

STEM/BARK - Smooth, gray, often covered with lichens.

FLOWERS - Unisexual; white to 0.25 inch, 4-merous, not showy, in axillary cymes, fragrant; flowers in spring.

FRUIT - Pyrenes; red, shiny, to 0.5 inch in diameter, in axillary clusters, very ornamental in fall and winter.

CULTURE - Full sun to partial shade, fertile well-drained soils; not salt tolerant. Withstands drought; pH adaptable.

PROBLEMS - Severe tea scale problem (especially in cool, shady areas), leaf miner.

PROPAGATION - Cuttings, grafting.

LANDSCAPE USES - Screening, foundation, hedge, specimen, excellent barrier plant. Fruit attracts wildlife.

COMMENTS - Many cultivars. Some of the most popular in Florida are: **'Burfordii'** - vigorous female, leaves are very glossy, oblong, entire but with a terminal spine, usually 10 to 12 feet in height, but can reach 20 to 25 feet; **'Burfordii Compacta'** (= **'Burfordii Nana', 'Dwarf Burford'**) - smaller leaves, more compact growth than **'Burfordii'**, usually 6 to 8 feet in height and smaller leaves and fruit, reduced scale problem; **'Dazzler'** - spectacular female , with copious red fruits to 0.5 inch in diameter; **'Rotunda'** - dwarf, compact male, spreading habit, lower growing, very spiny, usually 4 to 5 feet tall and 6 to 8 feet across; **'Carissa'** is more compact, low growing, and has only a terminal spine; **'Needle Point'** - dense, upright form with only a terminal spine and excellent fruiting; **'Nellie R. Stevens'** has dark green glossy foliage and superior berries. Other listed cultivars include **'Avery Island'**, **'Azusa', 'Decambre', 'Foemina', 'O' Spring',** and **'Willowleaf'** (Willowleaf Holly) has a narrower leaf.

Ilex crenata   JAPANESE HOLLY

PRONUNCIATION - 'ī leks krə 'nā tə

TRANSLATION - [Latin name for *Quercus ilex*, a California native oak species] [scalloped, crenate, in reference to the leaf margins].

FORM - Dioecious, evergreen shrub, rounded, spreading, compact, densely foliated, and fine-textured.

SIZE - Quite variable depending on cultivar. Generally 5 to 10 feet tall with an equal or greater spread. Grows at a medium rate.

HARDINESS ZONE - Zone 6. Should be grown only in north Florida.

NATIVE HABITAT - Japan.

LEAVES - Alternate, elliptic to obovate, lustrous dark green above, glandular-dotted below, to 1 inch long. The nearly sessile leaves have crenate-serrate margins, cuneate bases and are crowded on the twigs.

STEM/BARK - Heavily branched, with many stiff twigs that can remain green for several years.

FLOWERS - Unisexual, greenish-white, small and inconspicuous in the leaf axils, in spring; male flowers in cymes of 3 to 7; female flowers are solitary.

FRUIT - Berries (pyrenes); black, globose to 0.25 inch wide, in fall, often hidden by the foliage.

CULTURE - Grown in full to partial sun on fertile, well-drained soil that is moisture-retentive. Salt tolerance is marginal.

PROBLEMS - Scale, spider mites, and nematodes (a major problem, especially in the Florida panhandle).

PROPAGATION - Semi-hardwood cuttings treated with rooting hormones.

LANDSCAPE USES - Dwarf forms are used in foundation planting; larger forms are employed as clipped hedges, topiaries, and background shrubs.

COMMENTS - There are numerous cultivars. Some of the most popular in Florida are 'Helleri' - a male dwarf, compact cultivar, rarely larger than 3 feet, twigs typically red for most of their length, leaves to 0.5 inch long, serrate margins, superficially resembles *I. vomitoria;* 'Hetzii' - dwarf cultivar, spreading, larger than 'Helleri', but rarely more than 6 feet; twigs typically green, leaves glossy, cupped slightly downward, crenate margins; 'Rotundifolia' - upright cultivar, usually 5 to 6 feet, leaves flat, glossy to 1.25 inches long, slightly toothed; 'Green Cushion' is a dwarf cultivar; 'Convexa' (= 'Buxifolia', 'Bullata') is low growing and compact. Other cultivars listed include 'Compacta' and 'Green Luster'.

Ilex latifolia   LUSTERLEAF HOLLY

PRONUNCIATION - ˈī leks   ˌlæ tə ˈfō lē ə

TRANSLATION - [Latin name for *Quercus ilex,* a California native oak species] [broad-leaved].

FORM - Dioecious, evergreen tree, pyramidal, dense round canopy, of coarse texture.

SIZE - Reaches a height of 40 feet with 20-foot spread. Growth rate is medium.

HARDINESS ZONE - Zone 7. Can be grown in north and central Florida.

NATIVE HABITAT - Eastern China and Japan.

LEAVES - Simple, alternate, thick and leathery, oblong, dark green, to 6 inches long. The glossy leaves have marginal black teeth that form sharp serrations.

STEM/BARK - The stout, heavy branches and trunk are covered with gray bark. Twigs remain green for several years.

FLOWERS - Unisexual; yellowish-white, small and inconspicuous in axillary cymes in spring.

FRUIT - Berries (pyrenes); brick-red, globose, to 0.25 inch wide, ripen in fall and persist through winter.

CULTURE - Grown in full to partial sun on fertile, well-drained soil that is moisture retentive. It is not salt tolerant.

PROBLEMS - Generally pest-free.

PROPAGATION - Difficult to propagate. Hardwood cuttings taken in fall and winter sometimes root. Seeds take several years to germinate. Often grafted onto *I. opaca* seedlings.

LANDSCAPE USES - An elegant, formal specimen tree.

COMMENTS - 'Emily Bruner' is a selection from *Ilex cornuta* ✕ *I. latifolia* and is said to have outstanding features.

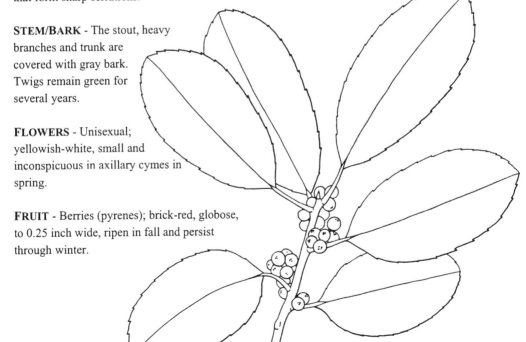

Ilex opaca   AMERICAN HOLLY

PRONUNCIATION - 'ī leks   ō 'pā kə

TRANSLATION - [Latin name for *Quercus ilex,* a California native oak species] [opaque].

FORM - Dioecious, evergreen tree, conical to columnar, branches short, spreading; medium texture.

SIZE - To 50 feet, usually 15 to 25 feet, slow growth.

HARDINESS ZONE - Zone 5. Grown in north and central Florida.

NATIVE HABITAT - Temperate North America, including Florida.

LEAVES - Simple, wide spiral arrangement, elliptic, to 4 inches long; leathery, pliable, margins entire or with varied number of spines, dull green above, sometimes slightly twisted.

STEM/BARK - Smooth, gray, often with lichens.

FLOWERS -Unisexual; creamy white, solitary or in axillary cymes, not showy, flowers in the spring.

FRUIT - Berries (pyrenes); red, to 0.25 inch in diameter, in axillary clusters, persisting through the winter, very ornamental.

CULTURE - Full sun to broken shade; fertile, well-drained soils; slightly salt tolerant. Will not tolerate wet feet. Best on acid soils. Pollution tolerant.

PROBLEMS - Scale, leaf miners.

PROPAGATION - Cuttings, grafting, and seed.

LANDSCAPE USES - Street tree, framing tree, specimen, hedge, barrier planting. Fruit attracts wildlife.

COMMENTS - Over 1000 cultivars, including several compact, cone-shaped (e.g., 'Howardii'), yellow fruiting (e.g., 'Calloway' and 'Canary'), and various foliage qualities (e.g., 'Amy' and 'Miss Helen'). A complete and extensive list of Opaca cultivars may be found in the *International Checklist of Cultivated Ilex,* Part I. *Ilex opaca.* U.S.D.A. *Ilex opaca* var. *arenicola* (Scrub Holly), a native Florida taxon, is also available.

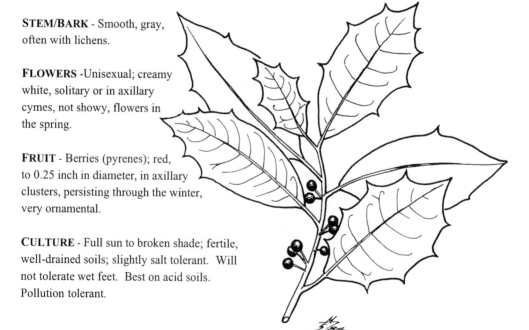

Ilex rotunda

KUROGANE HOLLY, ROUND HOLLY

PRONUNCIATION - ˈī leks rō ˈtun də

TRANSLATION - [Latin name for *Quercus ilex,* a California native oak species] [rounded, in reference to the leaves].

FORM - Dioecious, evergreen tree, pyramidal to globose in habit, compact, dense. Medium texture.

SIZE - To 60 feet with trunk 3 feet in diameter, in Florida usually 20 feet in height; slow-growing.

HARDINESS ZONE - Zone 8. Grown throughout Florida, but may be hurt during severe winters in north Florida.

NATIVE HABITAT - Japan, Korea, Southeast Asia.

LEAVES - Simple, spirally arranged, ovate to 3.5 inches long, leathery, glossy, margins entire, translucent, and apex acuminate.

STEM/BARK - Smooth, gray, often covered with lichens.

FLOWERS - Unisexual; white, solitary or in axillary cymes arranged around stem, large number, flowers in spring. Individually not showy, but collectively attractive.

FRUIT - Berries (pyrenes); red, to 0.25 inch, in clusters arranged around stem, very showy in fall and winter.

CULTURE - Full sun to partial shade; fertile, well-drained soils; no salt tolerance.

PROBLEMS - Generally pest-free.

PROPAGATION - Seeds, cuttings (difficult).

LANDSCAPE USES - Border, specimen.

COMMENTS - Several cultivars. Perhaps one of the best plants for attracting wildlife. Because of propagation difficulty, only infrequently found in the trade.

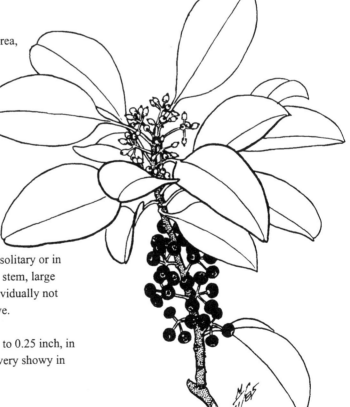

Ilex vomitoria   YAUPON HOLLY

PRONUNCIATION - 'ī leks   ˌvɑ mə 'to rē ə

TRANSLATION - [Latin name for *Quercus ilex*, a California native oak species] [emetic, in reference to its use by Indians].

FORM - Dioecious, evergreen shrub or small tree, irregularly shaped, stiffly branched, suckering habit. Fine texture.

SIZE - To 25 feet, rapid growth.

HARDINESS ZONE - Zone 7. Can be grown throughout Florida.

NATIVE HABITAT - Temperate North America, Florida native.

LEAVES - Simple, alternate or spirally arranged, elliptic, to 1.5 inches long, leathery, glossy above, new growth often pinkish, margin crenate.

STEM/BARK - Smooth, gray-brown. Young twigs very slender.

FLOWERS - Unisexual; white, 4 petals, solitary or in axillary cymes, not showy.

FRUIT - Berries (pyrenes); red or sometimes yellow to 0.25 inch in diameter, in axillary clusters.

CULTURE - Full sun to partial shade, various well-drained soils; highly salt tolerant. Also tolerates heat and drought as well as wet sites. One of the toughest hollies.

PROBLEMS - Scale, leaf miners, aphids, rampant growth, suckers and seedlings.

PROPAGATION - Seeds, cuttings.

LANDSCAPE USES - Screen, hedge, foundation, topiary.

COMMENTS - Many cultivars. Some of the most popular in Florida are **'Nana'** - dense growing, compact, dwarf male, leaves smaller; **'Schelling's Dwarf'** and **'Stokes Dwarf'** - extremely compact, low-growing male, usually less than 2 feet, leaves small; **'Pendula'** (= **'Folsom's Weeping'**) - sparsely foliated, with pendulous branches, beautiful weeping habit, numerous shiny berries; **'Gray's Littleleaf'** has very small leaves. Several other species are reported from cultivation in Florida, including *I. ambigua* (Carolina Holly), *I.* × *aquipernyi* (= *I. aquifolium* × *I. pernyi*), *I. aquipernyi* **'Brilliant'**, *I. chinensis, I. coriacea* (Large Gallberry), *I. integra, I. krugiana* (Krug Holly), *I. paraguariensis* (Yerba Matá, Paraguay Tea), and probably other species and cultivars. Indians used infusion of the leaves to induce vomiting to cleanse impurities of body and soul.

LEAF SHAPES OF *ILEX*

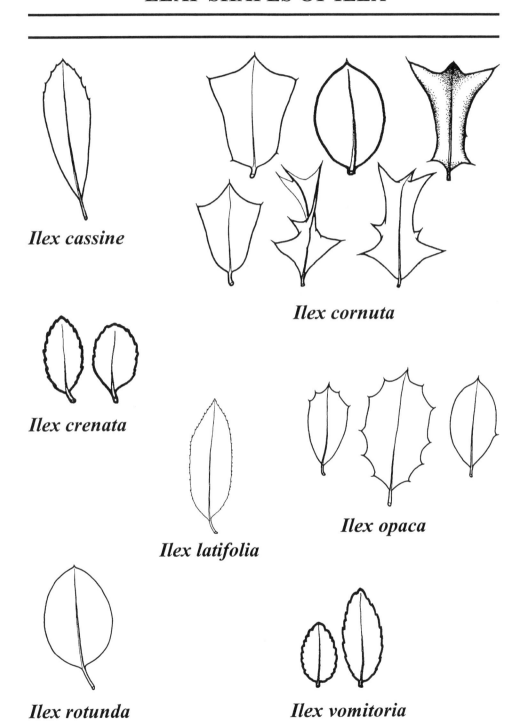

Ilex cassine

Ilex cornuta

Ilex crenata

Ilex latifolia

Ilex opaca

Ilex rotunda

Ilex vomitoria

ARALIACEAE - GINSENG FAMILY

DICOTYLEDONS; ABOUT 58 GENERA AND 700 TO 800 SPECIES

GEOGRAPHY: Cosmopolitan, but predominantly tropical in Indomalaysia and tropical America.

GROWTH HABIT: Pachycaulous trees and shrubs, vines clinging by aerial roots, and few herbs.

LEAVES: Alternate or rarely opposite or whorled; usually large, often pinnately or palmately compound.

FLOWERS: Regular, small and numerous, 4- or 5-merous, unisexual or bisexual (plants monoecious), usually epigynous, greenish or whitish, on compound umbels.

FRUIT: A 5-seeded drupe.

ECONOMIC USES: Ginseng (from roots of *Panax quinquefolia*), rice-paper (from *Tetrapanax papyriferus*), and medicinal extracts from several *Aralia* species.

ORNAMENTAL GENERA: *Acanthopanax, Aralia, Boerlagiodendron, Cussonia, Dizygotheca, × Fatshedera, Fatsia, Hedera, Polyscias, Schefflera, Tetrapanax, Trevisia, Tupidanthus,* among others.

Dizygotheca elegantissima   FALSE ARALIA

PRONUNCIATION - ˌdi zə ˈgɑ thə kə   ˌe lə gən ˈti sə mə

TRANSLATION - [refers to double number of anther lobes] [most elegant].

FORM - Monoecious, evergreen shrub or small tree; upright, ascending. Juvenile foliage fine texture, adult foliage medium-coarse.

SIZE - To 20 feet tall with an 8 foot spread.

HARDINESS ZONE - Zones 10-11, south Florida only.

NATIVE HABITAT - Pacific Islands.

LEAVES - Dimorphic, palmately compound, alternate; juvenile leaves are composed of 7 to 11 thin, notched, reddish-gray leaflets about 0.5 inch wide. As plants mature, leaflets become wider and change color to dark grayish-green. Petioles mottled white.

STEM/BARK - Stems have prominent lenticels.

FLOWERS - Small, borne in large terminal compound umbels.

FRUIT - Drupe, black, small.

CULTURE - Full sun to deep shade (to 100 foot-candles indoors); various well-drained soils;no salt tolerance.

PROBLEMS - Scale, nematodes, and mites indoors.

PROPAGATION - Cuttings, air layers, and seeds.

LANDSCAPE USES - Outdoors use as a specimen for vertical accent or as an urn subject for patio or terrace. In interiors, small specimens can be used as table or desk plants, while large specimens can be used as small indoor trees.

COMMENTS - Large mature plants will have both juvenile and adult foliage. A related species, *D. kerchoveana* (False Aralia), is also available.

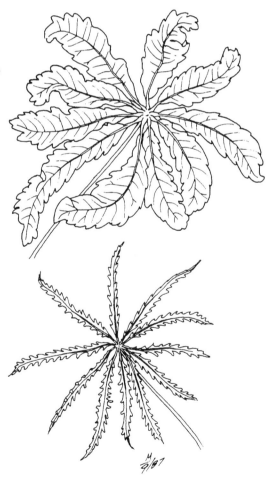

× *Fatshedera lizei*

BUSH IVY

PRONUNCIATION - fæts 'he də rə   'lī zē ī

TRANSLATION - [intergeneric hybrid name: *Fatsia × Hedera*] [after Lizé Fr»res, a French nurseryman].

FORM - Monoecious, evergreen vining shrub, clambering, medium-textured.

SIZE - Reaches a height of 8 feet with an indeterminate spread. Growth rate is fairly rapid.

HARDINESS ZONE - Zone 7. Can be grown in all areas of Florida.

NATIVE HABITAT - A hybrid between *Fatsia japonica* '**Moseri**' and *Hedera helix* var. *hibernica,* discovered in nursery of Lizé Fr»res of Nantes, France.

LEAVES - Alternate, with 5, rarely 7, palmate lobes, to 8 inches long and 12 inches wide, sheathing petiole. The pointed lobes may be indented more than halfway into the leathery, glossy leaves.

STEM/BARK - The thick stems have no aerial roots and need support. They are rusty-pubescent when young, becoming glabrous with age.

FLOWERS - Pale green, 0.25 inch wide, in 1 inch globular umbels in terminal panicles to 6 inches long. The flowers, sterile and rarely produced, appear in fall.

FRUIT - None produced.

CULTURE - Plant in full or partial shade on a wide range of soils. Salt tolerance is marginal.

PROBLEMS - Aphids and scale.

PROPAGATION - Cuttings, air layering.

LANDSCAPE USES - Usually grown as an espalier plant or in interior or exterior planter boxes, giving a tropical appearance.

Fatsia japonica

FATSIA, FALSE CASTOR OIL PLANT

PRONUNCIATION - ˈfæt sē ə   jə ˈpɑ nə kə

TRANSLATION - [original Japanese name] [from Japan].

FORM - Monoecious, irregular, rounded to semi-upright evergreen shrub of coarse texture.

SIZE - Reaches a height of 7 feet with an almost equal spread. Rate of growth is moderate.

HARDINESS ZONE - Zone 8. Can be grown in all regions of Florida. Hardy to about 10° F.

NATIVE HABITAT - Japan.

LEAVES - Alternate, with 7 to 11 deep, palmate lobes, up to 16 inches long and wide. The glossy, dark-green, leathery leaves are held horizontally on 12-inch petioles. Leaf margins are variously smooth or serrate.

STEM/BARK - The thick, green stems with prominent, crescent-shaped leaf scars are weak, easily damaged, seldom branched.

FLOWERS - Creamy-white, small, rounded, pedicellate, arranged in 18-inch terminal compound umbels in fall.

FRUIT - Drupes; black, 0.25 inches wide, in winter.

CULTURE - Requires partial or full shade, but tolerates a wide range of soils. Will not tolerate salt or hot, dry sunny locations.

PROBLEMS - Wax scale in subtropical areas.

PROPAGATION - By seed, which should be kept cool, or softwood cuttings.

LANDSCAPE USES - An interior or patio pot plant, also used in planters and foundation plantings. Gives a tropical or oriental effect.

COMMENTS - 'Moseri' - vigorous but compact.

Hedera canariensis   ALGERIAN IVY

PRONUNCIATION - ˈhe də rə   kə ˌnā rē ˈen səs

TRANSLATION - [classical Latin name for ivy] [of the Canary Islands].

FORM - Monoecious, evergreen woody vine, prostrate, creeping; medium-coarse texture.

SIZE - Varied length to 40 feet, rapid growth.

HARDINESS ZONE - Zone 9. Can be grown in south, central, and protected areas in north Florida.

NATIVE HABITAT - Canary Islands, North Africa.

LEAVES - Simple, alternate; juvenile leaves ovate to 6 inches, entire or shallowly 3 to 7 lobed, few stellate hairs, leathery, dark green, petioles reddish; adult leaves ovate-lanceolate.

STEM/BARK - Round, few aerial roots, reddish on juvenile growth.

FLOWERS - In compound umbels, white, inconspicuous, only on mature stage.

FRUIT - Drupe, black, to 0.25 inch, poisonous.

CULTURE - Full sun to deep shade, varied soils, slightly salt tolerant.

PROBLEMS - Scale, sooty mold.

PROPAGATION - Cuttings of juvenile shoots only.

LANDSCAPE USES - Ground cover. Provides solid cover under trees where grass will not grow.

COMMENTS - **'Variegata'** has leaves edged with yellowish white, as does **'Gloire-de-Marengo'**.

Hedera helix   ENGLISH IVY

PRONUNCIATION - ˈhe də rə   ˈhē ləks

TRANSLATION - [classical Latin name of the plant] [spiral].

FORM - Monoecious, evergreen woody vine, climbing; medium texture.

SIZE - Climbing to 40 feet or more as a vine, 6 to 8 inches as ground cover; rapid growth.

HARDINESS ZONE - Zone 5. Can be grown throughout Florida.

NATIVE HABITAT - Europe, North Africa. Naturalized in United States.

LEAVES - Simple, alternate, highly variable in shape, size, color (over 40 forms); juvenile and adult foliage typically variable; juvenile leaf 3 to 5 lobed, with the terminal lobe largest, 3 to 5 inches, dark green or variegated, leathery stellate hairs; mature leaf rounded to rhombic; petiole pink to green.

STEM/BARK - Round; aerial roots at nodes on juvenile growth.

FLOWERS - White; umbels arranged in panicles, inconspicuous, only on mature stage.

FRUIT - Drupe; black, to 0.25 inch, poisonous.

CULTURE - Full sun to deep shade, various soils, acid or alkaline, slightly salt tolerant. Withstands city conditions, acid or alkaline soils. Transplants readily. May need some pruning to keep it in bounds.

PROBLEMS - Scale, sooty mold, leaf spots.

PROPAGATION - Cuttings of young shoots only.

LANDSCAPE USES - Ground cover, closely trimmed on walls, potted foliage plant; will not damage walls.

COMMENTS - Hundreds of cultivars exist with a variety of leaf shapes, color, and variegation patterns. Most used in hanging baskets. Examples of cultivars intended for landscape-groundcover use include 'Ann Marie' with predominantly white margins, 'Baltica' whitish-yellow speckled, 'Gold Child' with golden-yellow margins, 'Hahns' 5-lobed and whitish veins, 'Ingelise' 5-lobed and elongated central lobe and white margins, 'Ivalace' more or less irregularly shaped and spotted leaves, and 'Needlepoint' with exceptionally large, 5-lobed leaves and white-spotted, to mention a few.

Polyscias filicifolia

FERN-LEAF ARALIA

PRONUNCIATION - pǝ 'li sē ǝs   fǝ ˌli sǝ 'fō lē ǝ

TRANSLATION - [refers to the numerous inflorescence umbels] [fern-like leaves].

FORM - Monoecious, evergreen shrub to small tree; stiff upright growth habit; medium-fine texture.

SIZE - Typically to 8 feet tall with a 4-5 foot spread; moderate growth rate.

HARDINESS ZONE - Zones 10-11, limited to south Florida.

NATIVE HABITAT - Polynesia and tropical Asia.

LEAVES - Even pinnately compound, leaflets varying, sometimes on the same plant, from oblong and entire to 7 inches long, to very narrow, pinnatifid, sharply toothed and to 1 foot long.

STEM/BARK - Young stems green with many prominent lenticels and large, circular leaf scars.

FLOWERS - Flowers very small in umbels, usually arranged in panicles.

FRUIT - Small drupes, smooth round.

CULTURE - Full sun to deep shade; prefers moist, well-drained soil, but will tolerate a wide variety of soils; moderate salt tolerance.

PROBLEMS - Mites, scale, and nematodes.

PROPAGATION - Seeds, cuttings, and air layers.

LANDSCAPE USES - In the landscape, use as a tall, narrow hedge or potted specimen for patio or terrace. Good interior plant, tolerates low light (to 100 foot-candles).

COMMENTS - Two cultivars, **'Marginata'** and **'Variegata'** have leaves with white margins. Other available cultivars include **'California Gold'**, **'Fernleaf'**, **'Tomatoleaf'**.

Polyscias fruticosa   MING ARALIA

PRONUNCIATION -   pə 'li sē əs   ˌfrū tə 'kō sə

TRANSLATION - [in reference to the numerous inflorescence umbels] [shrubby, bushy].

FORM - Monoecious, densely foliated evergreen shrub freely branching with many twisted willowy, slender stems.

SIZE- 6 to 8 feet; moderate growth rate.

HARDINESS ZONE - Zones 10a-11.

NATIVE HABITAT - South Florida, the Bahamas, and West Indies.

LEAVES - Evergreen; simple; to 6 inches long, bright green and glossy with prominent veins.

STEM - New growth glossy green; old stems tan to dark brown.

FLOWERS - White, 3/16 inch wide in short-stalked axillary and terminal umbels.

FRUIT - Scarlet, oval, up to 3/8 inch long, drupe-like with 2 seeds similar to coffee beans but not similarly used; harmless and attractive to wildlife.

CULTURE - Adaptable, full sun to partial shade; prefers moist, well-drained soil but will tolerate a variety of soils.

PROBLEMS - Mites, scale, and nematodes.

PROPAGATION - Seed, cuttings.

LANDSCAPE USES- Good plant for naturalizing, wildlife habitat, low-maintenance situations.

COMMENTS - 'Emerald Globe', 'Plumata', and 'Silver Queen' are examples of available cultivars. *Polyscias* 'Elegans' is considered a distinct species, *P. elegans* (Celery Wood).

Polyscias scutellaria   DINNERPLATE ARALIA

PRONUNCIATION - pə ˈli sē əs   ˌskū tə ˈla rē ə

TRANSLATION - [refers to the many inflorescence umbels] [a small dish, probably in reference to the leaflet shape].

SYNONYM - *Polyscias pinnata.*

FORM - Evergreen shrub to small tree; stiffly upright growth habit; medium-coarse texture.

SIZE - Typically to 10 feet tall with a 5 foot spread; moderate growth rate.

HARDINESS ZONE - Zones 10-11, definitely limited to south Florida.

NATIVE HABITAT - New Caledonia.

LEAVES - Compound, commonly trifoliolate; alternate; the 3 leaflets are broadly ovate to orbicular, to 4 inches wide; glossy green; margins crenate to dentate.

STEM/BARK - Young stems green with many prominent lenticels and large, circular leaf scars.

FLOWERS - Small umbels usually arranged in panicles.

FRUIT - Drupes, smooth, round.

CULTURE - Full sun to deep shade (to 100 foot-candles in interiors); prefers moist, well-drained soil but will tolerate a wide variety of soils; moderate salt tolerance.

PROBLEMS - Mites, scale, and nematodes.

PROPAGATION - Seeds, cuttings, and air layers.

LANDSCAPE USES - In the landscape use as a tall, narrow hedge or potted specimen for patio or terrace. In interiors, small plants can be used on tables, while larger ones can be used as small trees.

COMMENTS - Common cultivar '**Marginata**' has leaves with irregular, milky-white variegations at the margins. '**Pennockii**' and '**Tricochleata**' (Evergreen Aralia; Geranium Leaf Aralia) are cultivars of *P. scutellaria.* Other species and cultivars in cultivation include *P. crispa* '**Crispata**', '**Palapala**', *P. grandifolia, P. guilfoylei* (Roseleaf Aralia) and its cultivars '**Blackie**', '**Fishtail**', '**Laciniata**' (Lace-Edge Aralia), '**Marginata**' (Variegated Roseleaf Aralia), and '**Victoriae**', *P. obtusa* (Oakleaf Aralia) '**Fabian**'. There is considerable confusion in the identity of *Polyscias* species. Delimitations of species and cultivars are difficult to determine.

Schefflera actinophylla

SCHEFFLERA

PRONUNCIATION - shəf 'le rə   ˌæk tə nə 'fi lə

TRANSLATION - [after J.C. Scheffler, nineteenth-century botanist of Danzig] [with rayed leaves, in reference to radiating leaflets].

FORM - Monoecious, evergreen tree, upright, oval; low branching, often multiple-trunked; branches leafless at base; coarse texture.

SIZE - To 30 feet tall by 15 feet wide; rapid growth rate.

HARDINESS ZONE - Zones 9b-11, can be grown in south and the warmest areas of central Florida.

NATIVE HABITAT - Queensland, Australia.

LEAVES - Palmately compound; 7 to 15 oblong leaflets spirally arranged, radiating from apex of elongate petiole (to 12 inches long); glossy green; entire or sparsely dentate on juvenile plants.

STEM/BARK - Large leaf scars, lenticels.

FLOWERS - Red, crowded in terminal umbels arranged in stiff racemes; to 4 feet long; very prominent.

FRUIT - Drupes, purplish to 0.5 inch.

CULTURE - Full sun to partial shade; varied soils; moderate salt tolerance.

PROBLEMS - Scale, mites, sooty mold.

PROPAGATION - Seeds, cuttings, layers.

LANDSCAPE USES - Small tree, framing plant, specimen, urn, potted foliage; fairly good indoor plant.

COMMENTS - 'Amate' is a commonly sold cultivar.

Schefflera arboricola   DWARF SCHEFFLERA

PRONUNCIATION - shəf 'le rə   ˌar bə 'ri kə lə

TRANSLATION - [after J. C. Scheffler, nineteenth-century botanist of Danzig] [growing on trees].

FORM - Monoecious, round, evergreen shrub or small tree; compact habit; medium texture.

SIZE - To 18 feet tall with a 10 foot spread.

HARDINESS ZONE - Zones 9b-11, can be grown in south and the warmest areas of central Florida.

NATIVE HABITAT - Taiwan.

LEAVES - Palmately compound; leaflets spirally arranged, radiating from apex of elongate petiole; to 6 inches across; glossy green; 7 to 9 leaflets in mature foliage.

STEM/BARK - Stems flexible; green with corky brown patches when young, grayish-brown as stems mature.

FLOWERS - Whitish green in terminal umbels.

FRUIT - Berry-like drupe.

CULTURE - Full sun to partial shade; best looking plants grown in partial shade; will tolerate 50 foot-candles. indoors (150-1,000 foot-candles recommended); well-drained soils; some salt tolerance.

PROBLEMS - Scale; mites indoors.

PROPAGATION - Seeds, cuttings, air layers.

LANDSCAPE USES - Specimen, foundation plant, urn, potted foliage, small shrub, interiorscapes.

COMMENTS - Variegated and other cultivars available include **'Braided', 'Coveen', 'Covette', 'Gold Capella', 'Hawaiian Elf', 'Trinette', 'Variegata'**, and probably others. In Southeast Asia the plant is used for medicinal purposes.

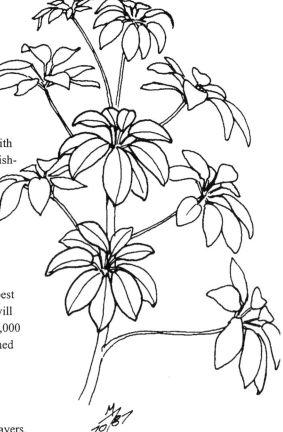

Tetrapanax papyriferus　　　RICE PAPER PLANT

PRONUNCIATION - ˌte trə ˈpæ næks ˌpæ pə ˈri fə rəs

TRANSLATION - [four-panacea, in reference to the medicinal properties of *Panax* (= ginseng)] [bearing paper, in reference to "rice paper"].

FORM - Monoecious, stoloniferous, rhizomatous, evergreen shrub or small tree of coarse texture.

SIZE -Reaches a maximum height of 30 feet, but usually does not exceed 10 feet in height. Spread is variable and growth rate is rapid.

HARDINESS ZONE - The aboveground portion is killed by frost, but the roots are hardy to Zone 8. This shrub can be grown throughout Florida.

NATIVE HABITAT - South China or Taiwan.

LEAVES - Orbicular, more or less whorled, to 15 inches long, palmately lobed. The corrugated, deeply incised, 5 to 14 lobes have toothed, undulate margins. The upper surface is dark green, lower surface and new growth is felty white (canescent). The leaves are borne on stout petioles 24 inches long.

STEM/BARK - Plants form from rhizomes, often at great distances from the trunk. Rice paper was made from the trunk pith.

FLOWERS - White, fuzzy, small, in globose umbels, of large, woolly, terminal panicles, to 3 feet long, in fall.

FRUIT - Small globular drupes.

CULTURE - Grown in full sun or partial shade on a wide range of soils. Salt tolerance is marginal.

PROBLEMS - Mealybugs.

PROPAGATION - Sucker division, seed, or cuttings.

LANDSCAPE USES - A good specimen plant for giving a tropical look. It is best to grow this plant in planters or containers where its suckering habit is easier to control or it may otherwise become a serious problem.

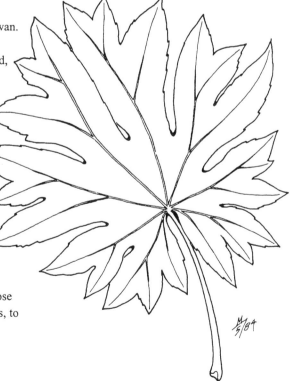

ASCLEPIADACEAE - MILKWEED FAMILY

DICOTYLEDONS; ABOUT 250 GENERA AND 2000 SPECIES

GEOGRAPHY: Mainly tropical and subtropical, especially South America and South Africa.

GROWTH HABIT: Twining or erect perennial herbs or large shrubs, sometimes with succulent (including cactoid) stem, and often with white sap.

LEAVES: Opposite or whorled, usually simple and entire, very small and often early deciduous in succulent forms.

FLOWERS: Actinomorphic, bisexual, 5-merous, the sepals partly connate, petals contorted and often with appendages that form the corona; stamens often with a pair of united pollinia containing granular pollen or a waxy pollen mass (the pollinium).

FRUIT: A pair of follicles containing flattened seeds covered with long, silky hairs.

ECONOMIC USES: Primarily as ornamentals, but the silky seed hairs are used as down in pillows and several species are used for medicinal purposes.

ORNAMENTAL GENERA: *Araujia, Asclepias, Calotropis, Caralluma, Ceropegia, Dischidia, Duvalia, Echidnopsis, Edithcolea, Fockea, Hoodia, Hoya, Huernia, Oxypetalum, Periploca, Sarcostemma, Stapelia, Stephanotis, Tavaresia, Trichocaulon*, among others.

COMMENTS: Very interesting and unusual plants with a complex floral structure and often fetid odor, attracting carrion flies as pollinators.

Hoya carnosa

WAX PLANT

PRONUNCIATION - ' hoi ə   kɑr ' nō sə

TRANSLATION - [after Thomas Hoy (1750-1872), gardener at Syan House] [fleshy].

FORM - Monoecious, evergreen vine, climbing and twining; flexible stems, wiry to woody; medium texture.

SIZE - To 10 feet tall depending upon support; slow growth rate.

HARDINESS ZONE - Zone 10-11, can be grown outside in south Florida only; sensitive to temperatures below 40°F.

NATIVE HABITAT - Southern China to Australia.

LEAVES - Simple, opposite; ovate to oblong-ovate or obovate to 3 inches long;thick, waxy. Petioles short and thick.

STEM/BARK - New growth green;aerial roots on stem; bleeds milky sap when wounded.

FLOWERS - Pink and white, waxy; star-shaped to 0.5 inch across; inflorescence is an umbellate cyme; borne on a specialized flowering stem that persists for many years in the leaf axil.

FRUIT - Follicle, rarely produced.

CULTURE - Partial shade (interiors from 75 to 3000 foot-candles), requires at least 250 foot-candles to bloom; well-drained soil; moderate salt tolerance.

PROBLEMS - Nematodes, mealybugs, and root rots if kept too wet.

PROPAGATION - Layers or cuttings.

LANDSCAPE USES - Outside as a vine on a trellis, an excellent hanging basket plant; aerial roots enable it to be grown on a totem.

COMMENTS - Several cultivars, e.g., **'Variegata'** (Hindu Rope), for foliage variegation (patterns with red, pink, or cream), shortened internodes, or variously contorted leaves, such as **'Krinkle Kurl'**. In addition, a few species with exceptionally attractive flowers are also available, including *H. australis, H. bella* (= *H. lanceolata* ssp. *bella*) (white flowers), *H. imperialis* (flowers large), and *H. purpureofusca* and *H. purpurea-fusca* **'Silver Pink'**.

Stapelia nobilis

CARRION FLOWER

PRONUNCIATION - stə ˈpē lē ə   ˈnō bə ləs

TRANSLATION - [after Johannes Bodaeus van Stapel] [notable].

FORM - Evergreen, succulent, herbaceous perennial. A mat-forming ground cover with fleshy stems and no leaves.

SIZE - To 8 inches tall.

HARDINESS ZONE - Zone 10. Can be used outside only in south Florida.

NATIVE HABITAT - South Africa.

LEAVES - Absent, except minute leaves at tips of actively growing shoots.

STEM - Velvety green, 4-angled, the angles toothed, the thick, fleshy stems branch from the base. The stems are not strong enough to grow more than 8 inches tall before bending back to the ground.

FLOWERS - Purplish, barred and mottled with darker colors, open-campanulate flower to 12 inches across. Flowers with ciliate, recurved petals are borne singly or in twos at the middle or base of stems. Stapelias are usually grown for their flowers which have an odor similar to rotting meat.

FRUIT - Follicle.

CULTURE - In the landscape prefers light shade; in full sun the stem turns a bronze color and is not attractive. Will bloom at 500 foot-candles. in an interior. Well-drained soil. Moderate salt tolerance.

PROBLEMS - Scale, mealybugs, mites, stem rot if overwatered.

PROPAGATION - Seed, division of clumps, or stem cuttings.

LANDSCAPE USES - As a ground cover in south Florida landscapes; as a container novelty plant throughout the U.S. because it is easy to grow on a windowsill.

COMMENTS - Several related species with variously colored or mottled flowers are also grown: *S. gigantea, S. grandiflora, S. hirsuta, S. pillansii,* among others.

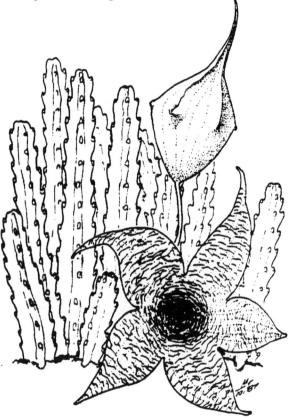

ASTERACEAE (COMPOSITAE) - DAISY FAMILY

DICOTYLEDONS; 1100 GENERA AND ABOUT 20,000 SPECIES
(ARGUABLY THE SECOND LARGEST PLANT FAMILY, AFTER ORCHIDACEAE)

GEOGRAPHY: Cosmopolitan, but predominantly in temperate regions.

GROWTH HABIT: A few arborescent, but mostly subshrubs and annual and perennial herbs, sometimes rhizomatous or tuberous, some are succulents, and a few are twining vines; sometimes with milky latex.

LEAVES: Alternate or opposite, simple or infrequently compound, sessile or petiolate, usually lobed or toothed, and sometimes succulent.

FLOWERS: Variously consist of individual small disk and/or ray florets grouped into a head (= capitulum), resembling a solitary flower; the heads are subtended by an involucre (a row of bracts resembling the calyx); the florets consist of disk and ray florets; corolla are strap-shaped (ligulate) or tubular; the calyx may be lacking or modified into a pappus of hairs, scales, or bristles which usually assists in seed dispersal; stamens are joined into a tube; disk flowers are usually bisexual while ray florets are commonly female.

FRUIT: Achene or achene with pappus (= bristles).

ECONOMIC USES: In addition to numerous ornamental and weedy species, the family includes valuable eco0nomically important food plants (such as *Lactuca sativa* - lettuce and *Helianthus tuberosus* - Jerusalem artichoke), oil-producing plants (such as *Carthamus tinctorius* - safflower and *Helianthus annus* - sunflower), salsify (*Tragopogon porrifolius*), insecticides (pyrethrum), medicines and drugs, etc.

ORNAMENTAL GENERA: *Aster, Baccharis, Calendula, Centaurea, Centratherum, Chrysanthemum, Cosmos, Dahlia, Euryops, Felicia, Gamolepis, Gazania, Gerbera, Gynura, Helianthus, Iva, Montanoa, Santolina, Senecio* (the largest genus of flowering plants with more than 2000 species, including many ornamentals), *Tagetes, Tithonia, Wedelia, Zinnia,* and numerous others in cooler regions.

*Chrysanthemum morifolium**   CHRYSANTHEMUM

PRONUNCIATION - krə ˈsæn thə məm   ˌmo rə fō lē əm

TRANSLATION - [gold flower] [mulberry-leaved].

FORM - Herbaceous perennial; erect, stout, generally much branched.

SIZE - Varies with cultivar, generally 2 to 5 feet, rapid growth.

HARDINESS ZONE - Highly variable with cultivar. May be grown in all areas of Florida.

NATIVE HABITAT - Horticultural origin; related spp. from China, Japan.

LEAVES - Simple, alternate, widely variable, lobed; lobes entire to coarsely toothed; outline lanceolate to ovate, to 3 inches long, often pubescent; lower surface often gray-pubescent, thick, strongly scented.

STEM/BARK - Green, slightly woody with age, often ribbed, angular.

FLOWERS - Many shades of white, yellow, pink, bronze, red-purple; heads of various sizes and shapes, typically clustered; disk and ray florets, ranging from 1 to 8 inches across, form quite variable; some fragrant; flowers in fall, winter (short-day plants).

FRUIT - Achenes, nearly cylindrical, ribbed to angled, winged.

CULTURE - Full sun, various well-drained soils; not salt tolerant.

PROBLEMS - Aphids, mites, thrips, caterpillars, wilt, leaf spot, *Botrytis*.

PROPAGATION - Seeds, cuttings of cultivars.

LANDSCAPE USES - Cut flowers, potted plant, bedding plant, planter box.

COMMENTS - A hybrid of *C. indicum* and one or more other species. Numerous related species, varieties, cultivars, and hybrids of all shapes, sizes, and colors. One of the most important floriculture crops.

*The name *Dendranthema*, according to several authorities, is the correct genus for the common chrysanthemum (*D. morifolia*). However, this controversy has not been fully resolved and awaits a decision by ICBN. The name *C. morifolium* is retained in this publication until further notice.

Gerbera jamesonii

GERBERA DAISY

PRONUNCIATION - 'gər bə rə   ˌjā mə 'sō nē ī

TRANSLATION - [after Traugott Gerber, a German naturalist, died in 1743] [after W. William Jameson (1815-1882), plant explorer of India].

FORM - Monoecious, acaulescent, herbaceous perennial, rosette habit.

SIZE - To 1.5 feet, slow growth rate.

HARDINESS ZONE - Zone 8. May be grown in all areas of Florida.

NATIVE HABITAT - Transvaal, South Africa.

LEAVES - Simple, arranged in a basal rosette, blade to 10 inches long, deeply lobed to lyrate-pinnatifid, hairy, very woolly beneath; petioles to 6 inches long, hairy.

STEM/BARK - Stemless (acaulescent).

FLOWERS - Many color forms ranging through yellows, salmon, pinks, and reds, singles and doubles; to 4 inches across, disk and ray florets, the latter long and strap-shaped; solitary on long, hairy scapes arising from the ground, flowers spring through fall.

FRUIT - Achenes, flattened, ribbed, often beaked.

CULTURE - Full sun, various well-drained soils; not salt tolerant.

PROBLEMS - Mealybugs, chewing insects, caterpillars. Subject to crown rot if planted too deeply.

PROPAGATION - Seeds, division.

LANDSCAPE USES - Edging, bedding plant, planter box, cut flower.

COMMENTS - Many cultivars and hybrids for various flower colors, shapes (singles and doubles), and scape height. Much of the material in cultivation, according to *Index of Garden Plants*, is **G. jamesonii** × **G. viridifolia.**

Gynura aurantica   PURPLE PASSION, VELVET PLANT

PRONUNCIATION - jī ˈnū rə   o ˌræn tē ˈā kə

TRANSLATION- [refers to long, rough stigma] [orange-colored].

FORM - Monoecious, evergreen, herbaceous perennial; clambering, vine-like, or decumbent ground cover; medium-fine texture.

SIZE - Stems to 12 inches tall, spread to 10 feet; rapid growth rate.

HARDINESS ZONE - Zones 10-11, can be grown outside only in south Florida.

NATIVE HABITAT - Java.

LEAVES - Simple, alternate; blade ovate to broadly elliptic to 8 inches long and 4.5 inches wide; coarsely dentate margins; velvety with purple hairs and deeper purple veins.

STEM/BARK - Angular stems covered with purple hairs.

FLOWERS - Bisexual, orange-yellow fading to purple; not showy; borne in heads 0.5 to 0.75 inch long. Only disk flowers are present.

FRUIT - Achenes, linear, 5 to 10 ribbed with a pappus of white bristles.

CULTURE - Partial shade; moist, fertile soil; no salt tolerance. In interiors needs high light intensity for optimal foliage color.

PROBLEMS - Mealybugs.

PROPAGATION - By cuttings, which root easily.

LANDSCAPE USES - Outdoors as a hanging basket or ground cover plant in south Florida. Common as an interior plant in high light situations.

COMMENTS - The chief value of this plant is its purple color, which is most striking on the new leaves. In interiors, branch tips can be pinched back to encourage dense, brightly colored new growth. Plant can become leggy if not pinched or provided with sufficient light.

Senecio confusus

MEXICAN FLAME VINE

PRONUNCIATION - sə ˈnē sē ō   kən ˈfyū səs

TRANSLATION - [old man, in reference to the hoary pappus] [confused].

FORM - Evergreen, semi-woody, perennial vine; twining; medium texture.

SIZE - Capable of climbing 25 feet, depending on the size of the support; rapid growth rate.

HARDINESS ZONE - Zones 10-11, can be grown in south Florida and protected locations in central Florida.

NATIVE HABITAT - Mexico.

LEAVES - Simple, alternate; narrowly ovate, up to 4 inches long; medium green, thick; margins slightly dentate.

STEM/BARK - Green, fleshy; root at the nodes when in contact with the ground.

FLOWERS - Daisy-like with ray and disk florets; orange-red; 1 inch across; borne in terminal cymes 6 to 8 inches across. Blooms in spring and summer.

FRUIT - Small, bristled achenes in the old, dry flower heads.

CULTURE - Plant in full sun or partial shade on a wide range of soils; no salt tolerance. Best flowering occurs in full sun.

PROBLEMS - Nematodes, mites, scales, and caterpillars.

PROPAGATION - By seed or stem cuttings.

LANDSCAPE USES - An easy-to-grow vine to cover palm trunks, fences, and sides of buildings. Used sparingly as a ground cover because of rampant growth. Some people develop a rash after pruning this vine.

COMMENTS - As the largest and most diverse genus of flowering plants, it is natural that species be available for any given area. The number of species in Florida landscapes is surprisingly few and includes *S. hoffmannii*, *S. petasitis* (Velvet Groundsel), and *S. salignus*.

Tagetes erecta   MARIGOLD

PRONUNCIATION - tə ˈjē tēz   ē ˈrek tə

TRANSLATION - [after the Etruscan god Tages] [erect].

FORM - Monoecious, bushy herbaceous annual, freely branching, densely foliated, compact.

SIZE - Variable with cultivar, range 6 to 36 inches tall, rapid growth.

HARDINESS ZONE - Zone 8. Can be grown in all areas of Florida year-round, but usually as summer annual.

NATIVE HABITAT - Mexico, naturalized in many warm regions.

LEAVES - Odd-pinnately compound, opposite, to 12 inches long; leaflets with serrate margin, lanceolate, to 2 inches long; dark green, glandular dotted; strongly aromatic-pungent.

STEM/BARK - Green, woody at base with age, purplish-brown cast in some cultivars.

FLOWERS - Yellows, oranges, reds, browns, or particolored; often 2-lipped or quilled in cultivars; dense heads to 5 inches across, solitary, peduncle long, slightly enlarged upward; ray florets few to many; flowers in spring, summer.

FRUIT - An elongate, club-shaped achene, usually bristle-like, numerous.

CULTURE - Full sun, various soils; not salt tolerant.

PROBLEMS - Leaf miners, downy mildew.

PROPAGATION - Seed.

LANDSCAPE USES - Cut flowers, edging, bedding plant, planter box.

COMMENTS - Many related species, varieties, and cultivars, ranging from single to double and light yellow to brown flower color. Also selected for height and leaf characteristics. An extract from the roots is antagonistic to soil nematodes, hence often planted around vegetable gardens.

Wedelia trilobata   WEDELIA

PRONUNCIATION - wə 'dē lē ə ˌtrī lō 'bɑ tə

TRANSLATION - [after George Wolfgang Wedel (1645-1721), professor of botany at Jena] [three-lobed, in reference to the leaves].

FORM - Herbaceous, creeping perennial, mat-forming. Medium textured.

SIZE - Reaches a maximum height of 12 inches with an indeterminate spread. Growth rate is fairly rapid.

HARDINESS ZONE - Zones 8b-11. Can be grown in south and central Florida.

NATIVE HABITAT - Tropical America, naturalized in south Florida.

LEAVES - Simple, opposite, elliptic to obovate, to 4 inches long, fleshy and scabrous. The leaves have serrate to dentate margins and are frequently 3-lobed at the apex.

STEM/BARK - Succulent, decumbent, purplish stems root at the nodes when in contact with the ground to form mats.

FLOWERS - Yellow, daisy-like, axillary heads, 1.5 inches across, with 10 to 12 ray florets. The flowers are solitary and appear all year on erect stalks of up to 6 inches long.

FRUIT - Achenes, conical, 0.25 inch long, in the dry, brown flower heads.

CULTURE - Grows well in full sun or partial shade on a wide range of soils. Salt tolerance is good. Will not tolerate long periods of drought. Should be periodically clipped or mowed when plants begin to look straggly.

PROBLEMS - Chewing insects.

PROPAGATION - By tip cuttings or layering, which root readily.

LANDSCAPE USES - A ground cover for beds and planters, covering rapidly and providing color with the flowers. It is especially useful in coastal locations. Good ground cover for banks and slopes. Should be clipped or mowed occasionally. Do not plant in shrub beds, since stems quickly grow up into shrubs, lending a weedy appearance to the landscape.

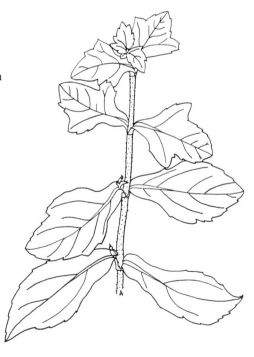

Zinnia elegans   ZINNIA

PRONUNCIATION - 'zi nē ə   'e lə gənz

TRANSLATION - [after Johann Goftfried Zinn (1727-1759), professor of botany, Göttingen] [elegant].

FORM - Monoecious, herbaceous annual.

SIZE - Variable with cultivar, range from 7 to 36 inches tall; rapid growth rate.

HARDINESS ZONE - Warmer areas of Zone 8. Can be grown in all areas of Florida.

NATIVE HABITAT - Mexico.

LEAVES - Simple, opposite, lanceolate, ovate or oblong, to 5 inches long, dark green, pubescent, prominently veined, entire, usually sessile and clasping the stem.

STEM/BARK - Erect, stiff, covered with hairs, woody at base.

FLOWERS - In every color but blue, some multicolored; heads solitary, terminal, to 6 inches across; disk and ray florets, often elongate, twisted, tubular; flowers spring through summer.

FRUIT - Achenes, compressed, obovate.

CULTURE - Full sun, various soils; not salt tolerant.

PROBLEMS - Stem borers, chewing insects, downy mildew.

PROPAGATION - Seed.

LANDSCAPE USES - Cut flowers, bedding plants, planter box, edging (using dwarf cultivars).

COMMENTS - Many cultivars of varying colors and flower sizes, as well as plant height and mildew resistance.

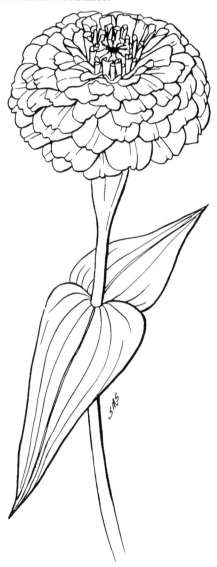

BALSAMINACEAE - BALSAM FAMILY

DICOTYLEDONS; 2 GENERA AND ABOUT 600 SPECIES

GEOGRAPHY:	Temperate and tropical regions, especially Asia and Africa.
GROWTH HABIT:	Annual and perennial herbs with brittle translucent stems.
LEAVES:	Simple, alternate or opposite, toothed.
FLOWERS:	Bisexual, zygomorphic, 5-merous, with three free sepals of which the rear one is large, spurred, and petaloid; the upper petal larger than others and the lower ones connate in pairs.
FRUIT:	Explosively dehiscent capsules.
ECONOMIC USES:	Ornamentals only.

ORNAMENTAL GENERA: *Impatiens* and *Hydrocera* (a monotypic aquatic plant).

Impatiens wallerana

IMPATIENS

PRONUNCIATION - im ˈpā shənz   ˈwɑ lə ˈrā nə

TRANSLATION - [from Latin, referring to sudden bursting of ripe pods when touched, "touch-me-not"] [after Rev. Horace Waller (1833-1896), a missionary in central Africa].

FORM - Monoecious, succulent branching annual, erect, spreading, brittle.

SIZE - Variable with cultivar, range from 8 to 36 inches tall, rapid growth.

HARDINESS ZONE - Zones 9-11. Not frost hardy. Grown throughout Florida and much of the United States as an annual bedding plant.

NATIVE HABITAT - Africa to Southeast Asia, but naturalized in many subtropical and tropical areas.

LEAVES - Simple, alternate, sometimes opposite, ovate-lanceolate to elliptic-oblong, to 6 inches long, acute to cuspidate tip, green or reddish-green on both surfaces, glabrous, margin serrate.

STEM - Green or reddish-green, succulent, smooth.

FLOWERS - Many colors: purple, whites, yellows, reds, oranges, variegated; solitary or in axillary to terminal racemes, many forms, double, semi-double, etc., to 2.5 inches across; nectariferous spur usually present.

FRUIT - Capsule; 5-valved, explosively dehiscent.

CULTURE - Partial shade, although some newer hybrids tolerate full sun; various moist, well-drained soils; requires frequent watering during hottest months. Not salt tolerant.

PROBLEMS - Scale, mealybugs, aphids, brittle. Various stem and root rots if kept overly wet.

PROPAGATION - Seeds, cuttings.

LANDSCAPE USES - Edging, bedding plant, planter box.

COMMENTS - Tendency to become a weed in warmer areas. Two of the more common cultivars are 'Accent' and 'Super Elfin'. The single and double "New Guinea Hybrids" (originated from *I. hawkeri*) with their multitude of flower and foliage colors are largely replacing the typical *I. wallerana*. A common bedding plant, *I. balsamina* is also planted in Florida. There is a tendency for some seed-producing taxa to become weedy.

BEGONIACEAE - BEGONIA FAMILY

DICOTYLEDONS; 2 GENERA AND ABOUT 900 SPECIES

GEOGRAPHY: Mostly tropical with a few subtropical.

GROWTH HABIT: Herbaceous succulents, often with jointed stems, many with thick
                      rhizomes or tubers, a few climbers, and some with fibrous roots.

LEAVES: Alternate, simple, 2-ranked, often asymmetrical, with large
                      membranous stipules.

FLOWERS: Unisexual (plants monoecious); mostly zygomorphic, four petal-
                      like segments in opposite pairs, the larger lower ones are the
                      calyx and upper ones are the corolla; born in cymes and often
                      showy, especially in the tuberous taxa.

FRUIT: Capsule or berry.

ECONOMIC USES: As ornamentals.

ORNAMENTAL GENERA: *Begonia* and *Hillebrandia* (only one Mexican species).

COMMENTS: Cultivars of Begonia have been classified into eight groups, each
                      containing subgroups of numerous cultivars: **Cane-like, Shrub-
                      like, Thick-stemmed, Semperflorens, Rhizomatous, Rex-
                      Cultorum, Tuberous,** and **Trailing Scandent.** A detailed
                      discussion of these Groups is beyond the scope of this manual.
                      Interested readers are referred to *Index to Garden Plants* by Mark
                      Griffiths, Macmillan, 1994, or *The New Royal Horticultural
                      Society Dictionary of Gardening,* 1992. Also see the *American
                      Horticultural Society A-Z Encyclopedia of Garden Plants,* D.K.
                      Publishing, Inc., 1997.

Begonia Rex-Cultorum Hybrids   Rex Begonia

PRONUNCIATION - bə ˈgō nyə

TRANSLATION - [after Michael Begon (1638-1710), governor of French Canada] [king-cultivated].

SYNONYM - *Begonia × rex-cultorum.*

FORM - Monoecious, evergreen herbaceous perennial; round, compact, and densely foliated, commonly rhizomatous; medium-coarse texture.

SIZE - Variable, to 4 feet tall.

HARDINESS ZONE - Zones 10-11, south Florida only.

NATIVE HABITAT - Of hybrid origin (primarily between *B. rex* and related Asian species), parents native to tropics and subtropics of both hemispheres.

LEAVES - Simple, alternate, variable shape; mostly obliquely ovate to ovate-lanceolate; unlobed to sinuately or sharply lobed; boldly or subtly zoned, marbled, blotched, or spotted in various patterns of green, purple, reddish brown, bronze, gray, or silver.

FLOWERS - Unisexual (plants monoecious); white or pink; usually not showy. Bloom during warm months.

FRUIT - Angled pods, often green with red markings.

CULTURE - Partial shade preferred; fibrous, organic, slightly acid, fertile, well-drained soil; no salt tolerance.

PROBLEMS - Mealybugs, mites, and nematodes.

PROPAGATION - Stem and leaf cuttings, division, seeds.

LANDSCAPE USES - Typically porch or interior specimens; require protection from direct sun, and more warmth and humidity than other types. Used to give a mass color or tropical effect to landscapes.

COMMENTS - There are hundreds of named cultivars, varying in habit, plant and leaf size, shape, pubescence, and coloration. May be mass-produced by making small notches on leaf veins and laying it flat on moist soil.

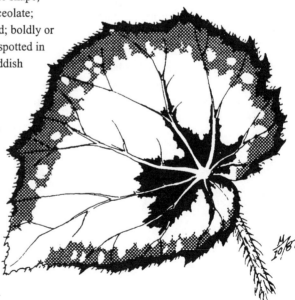

Begonia Semperflorens Hybrids   WAX BEGONIA

PRONUNCIATION - bə ˈgō nyə   ˌsem pər ˈflo rənz

TRANSLATION - [after Michael Begon (1638-1710), governor of French Canada] [everblooming].

SYNONYM - *Begonia × semperflorens-cultorum.*

FORM - Monoecious, compact, and bushy, herbaceous perennial; with fibrous roots; medium-fine texture.

SIZE - Variable.

HARDINESS ZONE - Zones 10-11, south Florida only.

NATIVE HABITAT - Of hybrid origin (originally from *B. cucullata* var. *hookeri* and *B. schmidtiana*); parents native to South America.

LEAVES - Simple, alternate; ovate to broad-ovate; glossy; usually glabrous, occasionally sparsely pubescent. Color depends on cultivar; can be green to bronzy-red or mahogany-red, or green variegated with white.

STEMS/BARK - Stems are branching and succulent.

FLOWERS - White to shades of pink or red; single or double; in small axillary clusters. Bloom almost continuously.

FRUIT - Capsule.

CULTURE - Partial shade, fertile organic soil; no salt tolerance.

PROBLEMS - Nematodes.

PROPAGATION - Cuttings and seeds.

LANDSCAPE USES - Edging, planter box, bedding plants, hanging baskets. Use in mass to add annual color to the landscape.

COMMENTS - Cultivars available adapted to full sun. Several newer cultivars are gaining popularity as bedding plants.

BERBERIDACEAE - BARBERRY FAMILY

Dicotyledons; 4-14 genera and about 570 species

Geography: North temperate regions and South American mountains.

Growth Habit: Perennial shrubs, evergreen or deciduous, with inner yellow bark.

Leaves: Alternate, usually spiny, simple or compound.

Flowers: In racemes or panicles, regular, bisexual, 2- or 3-merous, free, in two or more similar or dissimilar whorls.

Fruit: A berry.

Economic Uses: Ornamentals, fruit, dye, and medicines.

Ornamental Genera: *Berberis* and *Mahonia* are commonly cultivated but *Epimedium* and *Vancouveria* are uncommon.

Comments: Some authorities include Nandinaceae and Podophyllaceae in Berberidaceae. Except Nandinaceae, taxonomy of the group is not well-defined.

Berberis julianae   WINTERGREEN BARBERRY

PRONUNCIATION - ˈbər bə rəs   ˈjū lē ˈæ nē

TRANSLATION - [from the Arabic name] [given by Schneider, in honor of his wife, Juliana].

FORM - Monoecious, evergreen shrub, oval, rounded, densely foliated, with medium texture and somewhat weeping growth habit.

SIZE - Reaches 6 feet tall with an equal or greater spread. Growth rate is fairly slow.

HARDINESS ZONE - Zone 6. Should be grown only in north Florida.

NATIVE HABITAT - Central China.

LEAVES - Alternate; in rosettes on short shoots, narrowly elliptic, to 3 inches long, dark green. Leaves have 12 to 20 sharp, marginal, spiny teeth; new growth is a bright purple-green. In winter, leaves develop slight purple color when grown in full sun.

STEM/BARK - Stiff, slender, arching stems are brownish-yellow with yellow inner bark and have thin, stiff thorns to 1 inch long, usually in groups of 3 at base of each node. Young stems often zigzag.

FLOWERS - Lemon yellow, 0.5 inch wide, somewhat showy, in axillary fascicles of 15 to 20, in May.

FRUIT - Ovoid berries, blue-black with a heavy, waxy bloom, ripen in fall and persist into winter.

CULTURE - Full sun or partial shade in fertile soil with good moisture-holding capacity. Salt tolerance is marginal. Some pruning is required to maintain best form.

PROBLEMS - None serious.

PROPAGATION - By semi-hardwood cuttings, rooted under mist with IBA treatment.

LANDSCAPE USES - Barberry species best adapted to Florida. Employed as a specimen, border, or background shrub, or more commonly as dense, impenetrable barrier hedge. Too spiny to use in areas children frequent.

COMMENTS - The cultivar 'Nana' grows to about half the height of the species, forming a compact mound. It is not commonly available, however.

Berberis × *mentorensis*

PRONUNCIATION - ˈbər bə rəs   ˌmen to ˈren səs

TRANSLATION - [from the Arabic name] [Mentor, Ohio].

FORM - Monoecious, semi-evergreen shrub, upright, rounded, of medium texture.

SIZE - Can reach a height of 7 feet with an almost equal spread. Growth rate is medium.

HARDINESS ZONE - Zone 5. Grows well only in north Florida.

NATIVE HABITAT - A hybrid between *B. thunbergii* and *B. julianae* originating in Mentor, Ohio.

LEAVES - Alternate, in rosettes on short shoots, rhombic-ovate, to 1 inch long. Leaf margins are sparingly spiny-toothed near apex. Leaves turn red in fall.

STEM/BARK - Reddish stems have yellow inner bark and slender, stiff, 0.5-inch-long thorns at each node, in groups of 1 to 3, usually 2.

FLOWERS - Yellow, 0.5 inch wide, axillary, in solitary or sub-umbellate fascicles in spring; not as showy as other barberries.

FRUIT - Dull, dark red berries, rarely formed.

CULTURE - Grows in full sun or partial shade on soils of good fertility and drainage. Salt tolerance is marginal. Easily transplanted.

PROBLEMS - Generally pest-free.

PROPAGATION - By softwood cuttings in spring or hardwood cuttings in fall, both with rooting hormone treatments.

LANDSCAPE USES - Barrier, hedge, or foundation plantings.

WBJ
5-80

Berberis thunbergii   JAPANESE BARBERRY

PRONUNCIATION - ˈbər bə rəs   thun ˈbər jē ī

TRANSLATION - [Arabic name] [Carl Peter Thunberg (1743-1828), a student of Linnaeus and professor of botany at Uppsala].

FORM - Monoecious, deciduous shrub, densely foliated, compact, rounded, medium-textured.

SIZE - Obtains a height of 6 feet with an equal spread. Grows at a moderate rate.

HARDINESS ZONE - Zone 4. Should be grown in north Florida only.

NATIVE HABITAT - Japan.

LEAVES - Alternate, obovate to spatulate with a terminal spine, to 0.75 inch long. Leaves are yellow-green to maroon, depending on cultivar, and glaucous below. Leaves are often clustered on short spurs, appearing whorled, and turn red to reddish-purple in fall.

STEM/BARK - Dark red, grooved stem has yellow wood and a single (usually), flexible thorn, 0.5 inch long, at each node.

FLOWERS - Yellow, 0.5 inch wide, in 2- to 5-flowered axillary umbels in March, noticeable but not showy.

FRUIT - Berries; red, shiny, ellipsoidal, 0.5 inch long, attractive; ripen in fall and persist into winter.

CULTURE - Full sun or partial shade on a wide range of well-drained soils. Salt tolerance is marginal. Easily transplanted. Withstands dry conditions.

PROBLEMS - Generally no serious pest problems. Root rot in wet locations; host to wheat rust.

PROPAGATION - Softwood cuttings in spring or hardwood cuttings in fall, both with rooting hormones. Seed must be separated from the pulp and stratified.

LANDSCAPE USES - Makes an excellent, durable clipped hedge or barrier. Red-leaved cultivars can be used as specimen or accent plants.

COMMENTS - Many cultivars have been selected: 'Aurea', 'Nana', 'Atropurpurea' - foliage reddish-purple throughout growing season if grown in full sun; in shaded sites, foliage is reddish-green; 'Crimson Pygmy' (also sold as 'Little Gem', 'Atropurpurea Nana', 'Little Beauty') - low, dense growing to 2 feet tall and 3 feet wide, reddish-purple foliage; 'Erecta' - similar to 'Atropurpurea' but more upright, 'Rosy Glow' (Rosy Glow Barberry), and many others.

Mahonia bealei

LEATHERLEAF MAHONIA

PRONUNCIATION - mə ˈhō nē ə   ˈbē lē ī

TRANSLATION - [Bernard McMahon, American horticulturist who died in 1816] [Thomas C. Beale, who grew plants collected by Robert Fortune in his garden in Shanghai, China].

FORM - Monoecious, evergreen shrub, upright, irregular habit, clumping, of coarse texture.

SIZE - Can reach 7 feet tall but has little horizontal spread. Grows at a fairly moderate rate.

HARDINESS ZONE - Zone 6. Can be grown throughout Florida.

NATIVE HABITAT - China.

LEAVES - Alternate, dull blue-green, odd-pinnately compound, to 16 inches long. The 9 to 15 stiff, glabrous, leathery leaflets are ovate, to 5 inches long with 5 to 9 large, sharp, marginal teeth; sessile on the rachis. Terminal leaflet is larger and wider than the rest.

STEM/BARK - The upright, unbranched, stout stems have yellow wood with foliage clustered at the tips. A weak rhizome gives rise to multiple stems.

FLOWERS - Lemon yellow, small, on 3 to 6 inch racemes, in dense terminal clusters, quite showy, fragrant; in February.

FRUIT - Berries; dark blue with a glaucous bloom, ovoid, 0.5 inch long, and held in attractive, erect, grape-like clusters throughout the summer.

CULTURE - Requires partial shade and soils with good drainage; will not tolerate wet sites. Salt tolerance is marginal. Moderately drought tolerant.

PROBLEMS - Pest-free.

PROPAGATION - Generally by seed, which should not be allowed to dry out. Tip cuttings will root with hormone treatment, but this method normally is not used.

LANDSCAPE USES - Specimen shrub used in foundation plantings, shrubbery borders, and planters. Gives an "oriental" effect; can be pruned to create a series of tier-like sections of leaves.

Mahonia fortunei   FORTUNE'S MAHONIA

PRONUNCIATION - mə ˈhō nē ə   for ˈtū nē ī

TRANSLATION - [Bernard McMahon, American horticulturist who died in 1816] [after Robert Fortune, who introduced the species in 1846].

FORM - Monoecious, evergreen shrub, upright, multistemmed, mounding, of medium texture.

SIZE - May reach a height of 6 feet with an equal spread. Grows at a moderate rate.

HARDINESS ZONE - Zone 8. Can be grown throughout Florida.

NATIVE HABITAT - China.

LEAVES - Alternate, odd-pinnately compound, to 15 inches, long dark green above, yellow-green below. The 5 to 9 lanceolate leaflets and 6 to 10 marginal teeth are soft and flexible; not as lethal as *M. bealei*. Leaflets are about 5 inches long, 0.5 to 0.75 inch wide, and sessile on rachis. Foliage has fern-like appearance.

STEM/BARK - Slender, unbranched stems, occurring in clusters, arise from a weak rhizome. The inner bark is yellow.

FLOWERS - Lemon yellow, small, in 2-inch-long, erect racemes, in February. Not as showy as *M. bealei*.

FRUIT - Berries, purple-black with a waxy bloom, small, in late spring, seldom develop.

CULTURE - Grows in partial shade on a wide range of well-drained soils. Will not tolerate excessively wet or hot sites; not salt tolerant. Requires little pruning or maintenance.

PROBLEMS - Generally pest-free.

PROPAGATION - By seed, which should not be allowed to dry out, or by semi-hardwood cuttings.

LANDSCAPE USES - Forms a thick, mounded or oval shrub, unlike the tiered appearance of other mahonias. A specimen or accent plant with dark color which gives a contrast in foundation planting. Occasionally grown as a houseplant.

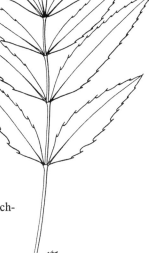

Mahonia lomariifolia   CHINESE HOLLYGRAPE

PRONUNCIATION - mə 'hō nē ə   lō 'mɑ rē ə 'fō lē ə

TRANSLATION - [Bernard McMahon, American horticulturist who died in 1816] [leaves like the fern *Lomaria* (now known as *Blechnum*)].

FORM - Monoecious, evergreen shrub, upright, multistemmed, of medium texture.

SIZE - Can reach 12 feet tall, but more typically 3 to 4 feet tall. Growth rate is medium.

HARDINESS ZONE - Zone 8. Grown in all areas of Florida.

NATIVE HABITAT - China.

LEAVES - Closely alternate, odd-pinnately compound, to 20 inches long, appearing to be in horizontal tiers. The 13 to 27 rigid, lanceolate-oblong, sessile leaflets are about 3 inches long and have 3 to 7 spiny teeth.

STEM/BARK - The erect, unbranched stems have scaly bark and yellow inner wood. The multiple stems arise from a weak rhizome.

FLOWERS - Lemon yellow, small, in clustered racemes to 6 inches long. The moderately showy blooms, appearing in February, are held erect above the terminal leaves.

FRUIT - Berries; black with a bluish bloom, ovoid, ripening late spring.

CULTURE - Requires partial shade and soil of moderate fertility and drainage. Does not tolerate salt, poor drainage or light, sandy soils. Moderately drought tolerant.

PROBLEMS - Generally pest-free.

PROPAGATION - Mainly by seed, which should not be allowed to dry out, or by semi-hardwood cuttings.

LANDSCAPE USES - A good specimen plant for formal gardens, it is also used in foundation plantings and shrubbery borders. Gives a tiered or layered effect. Interesting effect in gardens viewed from above.

COMMENTS - *Mahonia trifoliolata* (= *M. trifoliata*) is also reported from cultivation in Florida.

BETULACEAE - BIRCH FAMILY

DICOTYLEDONS; 6 GENERA AND ABOUT 150-170 SPECIES

GEOGRAPHY: North temperate, on tropical mountains, and South America.

GROWTH HABIT: Deciduous trees and shrubs, often with peeling bark.

LEAVES: Alternate, simple, stipulate, usually with serrate margins.

FLOWERS: Unisexual (plants mostly monoecious), the male in pendulous catkins, the female in groups of two to several, subtended by bracts; stamens 2-10; ovary of two inferior, fused carpels.

FRUIT: A single-seeded, winged samara.

ECONOMIC USES: Ornamentals, timber, and filberts.

ORNAMENTAL GENERA: *Alnus, Betula, Carpinus, Corylus* (hazel nuts), and *Ostrya.*

Betula nigra   RIVER BIRCH

PRONUNCIATION - ˈbe chə lə   ˈnī grə

TRANSLATION - [Latin name] [black].

FORM - Monoecious, deciduous tree; upright, rounded, oval or vase-shaped, single or multistemmed. Medium texture.

SIZE - Reaches a height of 60 feet with 25-foot spread. Grows rapidly in good soils.

HARDINESS ZONE - Zone 4. Can be grown in north and central Florida.

NATIVE HABITAT - Riverbanks and moist areas of the eastern U.S., from Massachusetts to north Florida.

LEAVES - Alternate, simple, rhombic-ovate, to 3 inches long, margins doubly serrate, acute apices, bases broadly truncate to wide-angled cuneate, 7 to 9 pairs of impressed veins, pubescent when young becoming glabrous above but retaining pubescence along veins beneath, pubescent petiole 0.25 to 0.5 inch long.

STEM/BARK - Generally has several large, irregular limbs instead of one main trunk. Attractive tan bark peels off in large, curly, papery patches, exposing coppery inner bark. Twigs are flexible and drooping. Young twigs pubescent.

FLOWERS - Male flowers are slender, drooping catkins, 3 inches long, usually in clusters of threes, developing partially in fall and persisting throughout winter. Female flowers appear in February and are short, thick, woolly catkins, 0.25 inch long, usually not clustered. Not showy.

FRUIT - Winged nutlets, light brown, 1 inch long, in conelike clusters, ripening in April, not showy.

CULTURE - Full sun to partial shade on moist, acid soil. Tolerates periodic flooding (after all, it is the River Birch) but does not tolerate salt or prolonged drought. Easily transplanted but requires frequent irrigation to survive.

PROBLEMS - Generally pest-free.

PROPAGATION - Seed, which must be sown as soon as it ripens. Germination is rapid, but low due to a large percentage of inviable seeds. Softwood cuttings will root under mist with rooting hormone treatment.

LANDSCAPE USES - A handsome specimen/shade tree for estates, parks, golf courses, and other large areas.

COMMENTS - Several cultivars are available: **'Heritage'** - leathery, dark green leaves and salmon/white bark; **'Gulf Stream'** - larger leaves and a lighter, more showy bark than the species.

Carpinus caroliniana American Hornbeam, Musclewood, Ironwood, Blue Beech

PRONUNCIATION - kɑr ˈpī nəs   ˈkæ rə ˌli nē ˈā nə

TRANSLATION - [the Latin name] [from the Carolinas].

FORM - Monoecious, deciduous tree, irregular, rounded-spreading, single or multistemmed. Fine to medium texture.

SIZE - Reaches a height of 35 feet with nearly equal spread. Growth rate is slow.

HARDINESS ZONE - Zone 4. Should be grown only in north and central Florida.

NATIVE HABITAT - An understory tree of moist woods and riverbanks of eastern North America from Nova Scotia and Ontario to north Florida and Texas.

LEAVES - Alternate, simple, ovate, to 4 inches long, glabrous above, tufts of hair in vein angles below, 2-ranked, doubly serrate margins, acute to acuminate apices, rounded bases, veins seldom forking at ends, petiole pubescent to 0.5 inch long.

STEM/BARK - Smooth, thin, bluish-gray bark covers the crooked, fluted, "muscular" trunk (hence, Musclewood). Wood heavy and hard (hence, Ironwood). Lower branches drooping. Young twigs reddish-brown, often zigzag. Wide-angle branching contributes to its wind resistance.

FLOWERS - Inconspicuous, separate male and female catkins, borne with the new growth in spring.

FRUIT - 2-inch-long pendant clusters of 0.25 inch, ridged nutlets, each subtended by a 3-lobed, leafy bract. Bracts turn brown in early fall as the fruit mature.

CULTURE - Full sun or partial shade (tolerates heavier shade than most trees) on a wide range of moist soils. Tolerates poor drainage, but not salt. Difficult to transplant from the wild.

PROBLEMS - Relatively pest-free.

PROPAGATION - By seeds, which require stratification before germination.

LANDSCAPE USES - An interesting specimen tree, usually not used as a shade or street tree due to slow growth rate; however, this trait can be used to advantage in narrow swales and small lots. Ideal for naturalized settings.

COMMENTS - The common name, referring to the wood, comes from "horn," meaning tough, and "beam" (similar to German "baum") for tree.

Ostrya virginiana   AMERICAN OR EASTERN HOP HORNBEAM

PRONUNCIATION - ɑ ˈstrī ə   vər ˌji nē ˈā nə

TRANSLATION - [Latinized Greek name] [from Virginia].

FORM - Monoecious, upright deciduous tree, somewhat pyramidal when young, rounded with age, irregular. Medium texture.

SIZE - Reaches 40 feet (rarely 60 feet) in height with 20 to 25 foot spread. Growth rate is slow to medium.

HARDINESS ZONE - Zone 4. Should be grown in north and central Florida.

NATIVE HABITAT - An understory tree of dry woodlands of eastern North America from Ontario to Minnesota, to north Florida and Texas.

LEAVES - Alternate, simple, ovate with acute to acuminate tip and subcordate base, to 4 inches long, granular texture; doubly serrate, with veins forking near margins. They turn dull yellow in fall (not particularly showy), then brown and persist into winter.

STEM-BARK - Dark brown bark splits into short, narrow, shaggy strips. Strong, hard wood combined with stout branches at right angles make this tree vandal- and wind-resistant. Young twigs reddish-brown, often zigzag.

FLOWERS - Catkins: the female borne in spring with the new growth; the male formed in threes the fall before and visible throughout the winter.

FRUIT - Hoplike, pendant, light brown clusters, to 3 inches long, composed of 0.25 inch long bladderlike, bristly bracts each containing a single, slender seed. Fruit matures in September.

CULTURE - Full sun or partial shade on wide range of soils, including poor, dry soils. It is not salt tolerant; grows poorly in wet soils. Fairly drought tolerant, tough and durable. Transplants poorly from the wild due to deep taproot.

PROBLEMS - Pest-free.

PROPAGATION - By seed, which should be removed from the bladders and stratified.

LANDSCAPE USES - A tough, durable medium-sized street/background tree, also as shade tree for parks, lawns, golf courses. Ideal for naturalized areas.

BIGNONIACEAE - BIGNONIA FAMILY

DICOTYLEDONS; ABOUT 120 GENERA AND 650 SPECIES

GEOGRAPHY:	Predominantly northern South America, otherwise tropical, only a few temperate (*Catalpa*).
GROWTH HABIT:	Chiefly woody vines, climbing by tendrils or aerial roots, and some trees and shrubs.
LEAVES:	Opposite, decussate, often pinnately compound; usually exstipulate, in some trifoliolate genera the terminal leaflet is modified into a tendril.
FLOWERS:	Showy, born in cymose clusters; zygomorphic, hypogynous, 5-merous with fused sepals and petals; bilabiate, funnelform, or campanulate, stamens 2 or 4; ovary superior.
FRUIT:	Usually a loculicidal capsule with numerous, flattened, small, winged seeds.
ECONOMIC USES:	Minor timbers and many ornamentals.

ORNAMENTAL GENERA: *Amphitecna, Anemopaegma, Bignonia, Campsis, Catalpa, Clytostoma, Crescentia, Cybistax, Cydista, Distictis, Doxantha, Eccremocarpus, Enallagma, Jacaranda, Kigelia, Macfadyena, Mansoa, Markhamia, Newbouldia, Oroxylum, Pandorea, Parmentiera, Pithecoctenium, Podranea, Pyrostegia, Radermachera, Saritaea, Spathodea, Stereospermum, Tabebuia, Tecoma, Tecomaria, Techomella,* among others.

Amphitecna latifolia

BLACK CALABASH

PRONUNCIATION - ˈam fēˈtek nə   ˌlæ tə ˈfō lē ə

TRANSLATION - [from Greek *amphi* (=both) and *tecna* (=hidden or covered)] [broad leaved].

SYNONYM - *Enallagma latifolia.*

FORM - Monoecious, evergreen tree; upright, oval, densely foliated; medium texture.

SIZE - Can reach a height of 30 feet with a variable spread; medium growth rate.

HARDINESS ZONE - Zones 10-11, can be grown in south Florida only.

NATIVE HABITAT - South Florida and tropical America.

LEAVES - Alternate; elliptic to obovate, to 7 inches long; dark green, glossy, leathery; usually have abruptly acuminate tips and entire margins.

STEM/BARK - Gray, rough, and furrowed bark.

FLOWERS - Purplish-white, nonshowy, solitary; to 2 inches long; tubular; borne irregularly on short axillary stalks throughout the year.

FRUIT - Shiny green, oval, four-ridged, and smooth; to 4 inches long; gourd-like fruit with thin, hard shell; contains numerous, edible, 0.5 inch long black seeds in white pulp.

CULTURE - Grown in full sun or partial shade on a wide range of soils; poor wind resistance; marginal salt tolerance.

PROBLEMS - Pest-free. Tends to get top-heavy and blow over in high winds; needs pruning yearly to prevent windthrow.

PROPAGATION - By seed, cuttings, or air layers.

LANDSCAPE USES - A tall hedge or small-scale, specimen/shade tree.

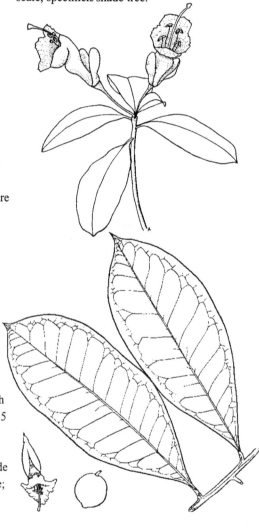

Campsis radicans

TRUMPET VINE, TRUMPET CREEPER

PRONUNCIATION - ˈkæmp səs ˈræ də kənz

TRANSLATION - [Greek for curved, referring to the curved stamens] [with rooting stems].

FORM - Deciduous woody vine of medium texture, climbs by aerial rootlets and spreads by rooting where branches touch the ground.

SIZE - Rampant-growing, self-attaching, or sprawling vine. A fast grower to 20 feet, sometimes 40 feet high.

HARDINESS ZONE - Zone 4. Grows in north and central Florida.

NATIVE HABITAT - Moist woods and thickets of southern New Jersey and Pennsylvania to central Florida and Texas.

LEAVES - Odd-pinnately compound, opposite, not tendril-bearing, to 15 inches long; leaflets 7 to 11, ovate to ovate-oblong, to 3 inches long, acuminate, yellow-green above, pale and pubescent beneath (at least along the midrib), margins coarsely serrate.

STEM/BARK - Glabrous, twining stems produce aerial roots that cling to almost anything. Old branches become woody, covered with cinnamon-brown bark.

FLOWERS - Orange-red, trumpet-shaped, 3 inches long, in 4- to 12-flowered, terminal clusters. Showy for several months in summer.

FRUIT - Capsules about 5 inches long, keeled and beaked. Not showy.

CULTURE - Grows in full sun to partial shade, in any soil. Not salt tolerant. Tolerates dry conditions but grows vigorously when ample water is available. An extremely durable plant that will grow almost anywhere; potentially a weed because of this ability.

PROBLEMS - Pest-free.

PROPAGATION - By seed or layering; vines root where they touch the ground.

LANDSCAPE USES - Bold vine for rustic or large-scale situations. Excellent cover for pine trunks, a wall, trellis, arbor, or fence. Best suited for naturalized sites; will need pruning to keep it in bounds in a more refined setting. Flowers attract hummingbirds.

COMMENTS - Vigorous plants may become rank and invasive. Difficult to eradicate once established. Contact with foliage may cause a skin rash in some people. The cultivar **'Flava'** has yellow flowers; **'Crimson Trumpet'** has large velvety red flowers; **'Praecox'** has scarlet flowers; and **'Speciosa'** has shrubby habit. *Campsis* × *tagliabuana* **'Mme. Galen'**, a cross between *C. radicans* and *C. grandiflora*, is more compact and has larger, showier, orange-red flowers. *Campsis grandiflora* (Chinese Trumpet Creeper) is also offered.

Clytostoma callistegioides

PAINTED TRUMPET VINE,
ARGENTINE TRUMPET VINE

PRONUNCIATION - klī 'tɑ stə mə   'kæ lə 'ste jē 'oi dēz

TRANSLATION - [beautiful mouth] [covered calyx, resembling *Calystegia*].

SYNONYM - *Bignonia violacea.*

FORM - Monoecious, evergreen, woody vine, climbing by means of tendrils. Medium texture.

SIZE - Variable, depends on size of support. Growth rate is rapid.

HARDINESS ZONE - Zone 8b. Can be grown in all areas of Florida, south-facing location in northern counties.

NATIVE HABITAT - Southern Brazil and Argentina.

LEAVES - Opposite, trifoliolate, with the terminal leaflet modified into a tendril; leaflets elliptic-oblong, dark-green, glabrous, undulate margins, to 4 inches long.

FLOWERS - Lavender streaked with purple, funnelform, to 3 inches long. The trumpet-like flowers are borne in axillary and terminal pairs in April.

FRUIT - Capsules, insignificant, broad, prickly, 5 inches long.

CULTURE - Full sun or partial shade on soils of good fertility and drainage. It is not salt or drought tolerant.

PROBLEMS - Scales and mites.

PROPAGATION - By cuttings, or layering,

forming roots where stems touch the ground.

LANDSCAPE USES - Excellent for covering fences and arbors. It is slightly less rampant and more cold-hardy than most evergreen vines.

COMMENTS - Flowers resemble those of *Pandorea jasminoides* 'Rosea' and *Podranea ricasoliana* (both in Bignoniaceae), vines that are hardy in south Florida only.

Jacaranda mimosifolia   JACARANDA

PRONUNCIATION - ˈjæ kə ˈræn də   mə ˌmō sə ˈfō lē ə

TRANSLATION - [Latinized Brazilian name] [mimosa-like leaves].

FORM - Monoecious, deciduous tree; spreading, vase-shaped, open-crowned; fine texture.

SIZE - Reaches a height of 45 feet with a 30 foot spread; rapid growth rate.

HARDINESS ZONE - Zone 9b, can be grown in central and south Florida, but is better adapted to south Florida.

NATIVE HABITAT - Northwest Argentina.

LEAVES - Bipinnately compound; opposite; fern-like, to 18 inches long; numerous oblong-rhombic leaflets about 3/8 inch long. Medium green.

STEM/BARK - Trunks often bent or arching; covered with light gray bark.

FLOWERS - Blue to violet; funnelform, very showy; 2 inches long; in terminal or axillary panicles. Blooms in April to June and sometimes again in August.

FRUIT - Two-celled capsules, tardily dehiscent; 2 inches wide; resembling hard, brown, flattened disks.

CULTURE - Does best in full sun on soil of reasonable fertility; no salt tolerance.

PROBLEMS - Mushroom root rot on poorly drained soils.

PROPAGATION - By seed sown on the surface of sterile, well-drained media (i.e., sand); softwood cuttings or grafting. Seedlings often take a very long time to bloom in south Florida, so grafted trees or those rooted from cuttings are preferred.

LANDSCAPE USES - Best used as a flowering street tree; tends to get too big for use on city lots. Spectacular in full bloom; fallen flowers may be beautiful on a lawn or pavement.

COMMENTS - *Jacaranda caerulea* and *J. cuspidifolia* are also cultivated in southern Florida.

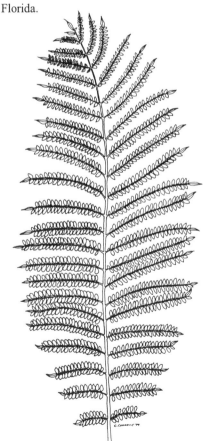

Macfadyena unguis-cati

CAT-CLAW VINE,
CAT-CLAW CREEPER

PRONUNCIATION - mək ˌfæ dē ˈyā nə   ˈun gwəs   ˈkɑ tē

TRANSLATION - [Dr. James MacFadyen] [cat-like claws].

SYNONYM - *Bignonia unguis-cati, Doxantha unguis-cati.*

FORM - Monoecious, evergreen woody vine, climbing by means of tendrils. Medium texture.

SIZE - Climbs up to 30 feet or more if given a support. A rampant grower.

HARDINESS ZONE - Zone 8b. Grown in south and central Florida and protected locations in north Florida.

NATIVE HABITAT - Central and South America; naturalized in Florida.

LEAVES - Opposite, compound, with 2 leaflets and a terminal, 3-parted, clawlike tendril, leaflets elliptic to 2 inches long with entire margins and acute apices, papery texture.

STEM/BARK - Develops woody trunks and climbs by claw-like tendrils.

FLOWERS - Bright yellow, funnelform, 3 inches long and 4 inches wide, in showy axillary clusters. Blooms for several weeks in March and April, generally on the uppermost branches, therefore, flowers appear to be high atop the tree(s) supporting the vine.

FRUIT - Capsules; brown, linear, 2-parted, dehiscent, leathery, to 12 inches long with many winged seeds, not showy. Superficially resembles a legume.

CULTURE - Full sun or partial shade on a wide range of soils. It is not salt tolerant. Easily grown.

PROBLEMS - None of importance. Will kill trees by strangling and covering them.

PROPAGATION - By seed, cuttings, or ground layers. Roots where stems come into contact with the ground.

LANDSCAPE USES - To cover fences or sides of buildings; becomes difficult to keep under control once established because it is both a rampant grower and a prolific producer of seedlings. Best for naturalized areas. Plant is considered a weed in Florida and should not be planted.

Pandorea jasminoides

BOWER PLANT

PRONUNCIATION - pæn ˈdo rē ə   ˈjæz mə ˈnoi dēz

TRANSLATION - [Pandora of mythology] [jasmine-like].

FORM - Monoecious, evergreen twining vine; medium texture.

SIZE - May climb up to 30 feet if given support; rapid growth rate.

HARDINESS ZONE - Zones 9b-11, can be grown in south Florida and in protected central Florida locations.

NATIVE HABITAT - Australia.

LEAVES - Odd-pinnately compound; opposite; to 1 foot long; 5 to 9 ovate to lanceolate leaflets, more than 2 inches long; glossy green; margins entire.

STEM/BARK - Vine becomes woody; climbs by twining.

FLOWERS - White with a pink throat; campanulate; 2 inches wide; borne in summer and fall.

FRUIT - Oblong, woody capsule.

CULTURE - Requires full sun and fertile, rich soil; no salt tolerance.

PROBLEMS - None of consequence.

PROPAGATION - By seed or softwood cuttings.

LANDSCAPE USES - To cover fences, arbors, and other structures.

COMMENTS - Several cultivars have been introduced, including **'Alba'**, with white flowers; **'Lady Di'**, with white flowers and cream throat; **'Rosea'**, flowers pink with darker throat; and **'Rosea Superba'**, large pink flowers with darker throat spotted purple.

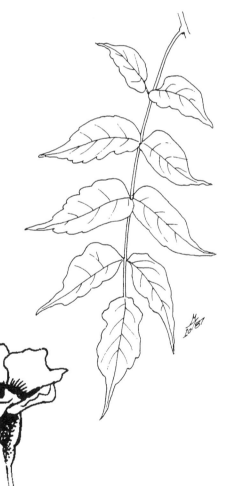

Pyrostegia venusta FLAME VINE

PRONUNCIATION - 'pī rə 'stē jə   və 'nū stə

TRANSLATION - [fire roof] [handsome].

FORM - Monoecious, evergreen woody vine; vigorous, high climbing.

SIZE - To 30 feet or taller; rapid growth rate.

HARDINESS ZONE - Zones 9b-11, can be grown in south and central Florida.

NATIVE HABITAT - Brazil, Paraguay.

LEAVES - Palmately compound; opposite; 2 to 3 leaflets, to 3 inches long; acuminate tip, pliable, leathery; often with a terminal, 3-parted tendril; entire margins. Dark green.

STEM/BARK - Round, branchlets often 6- to 8-ribbed.

FLOWERS - Reddish-orange; tubular to 3 inches long; corolla 5-lobed, reflexed, stamens protrude; borne in axillary or terminal panicled cymes. Blooms profusely in winter, sparsely in summer.

FRUIT - Capsule; linear to 1 foot long.

CULTURE - Grows in full sun on a wide range of soils; no salt tolerance.

PROBLEMS - Scale, caterpillars, mites. *Pyrostegia* can strangle trees with its rampant growth.

PROPAGATION - Cuttings.

LANDSCAPE USES - Use as an arbor, roof vine, or on a fence or trellis.

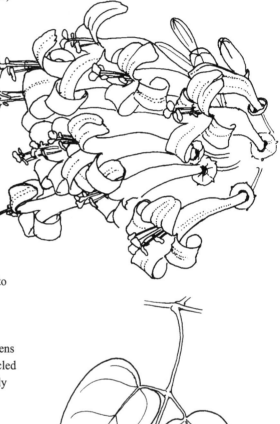

Spathodea campanulata   AFRICAN TULIP TREE

PRONUNCIATION - spæ ˈthō dē ə   kəm ˈpæ nyə ˈlā tə

TRANSLATION - [spathe-like or boat-shaped calyx] [bell-shaped].

SYNONYM - *Spathodea nilotica.*

FORM - Monoecious, evergreen tree; upright, round; densely foliaged, narrow-crowned; medium texture.

SIZE - To 60 feet with a 40 foot spread; rapid growth rate.

HARDINESS ZONE - Zones 10b-11, should be planted in a protected location in south Florida as it is severely damaged by subfreezing temperatures.

NATIVE HABITAT - Forests of equatorial Africa.

LEAVES - Odd-pinnately compound; opposite, to 1.5 feet long; 9 to 19 elliptic leaflets about 4 inches long with entire margins; new growth orangeish, then green.

STEM/BARK - Wood is soft, brittle, and easily broken by high winds.

FLOWERS - Striking orange-red, campanulate, 5 inches long; in terminal clusters held above the leaves. Flowers open several at a time from curved, 2 inch long, banana-like, fuzzy, brown flower buds filled with water. Blooms any time of the year, but maximum bloom is in late winter.

FRUIT - Capsule; brown, upright, narrowly cylindrical, dehiscent; to 8 inches long, with many membranous seeds; rarely produced.

CULTURE - Needs full sun and soil of reasonable fertility and drainage; no salt tolerance.

PROBLEMS - Generally pest-free. Subject to cold and wind damage but recovers quickly.

PROPAGATION - By seed, sown on the surface of well-drained, sterile media such as sand; softwood cuttings; root suckers.

LANDSCAPE USES - A specimen tree or shade tree.

COMMENTS - One of the world's most beautiful flowering trees and a common plant throughout the tropics.

Tabebuia argentea   TRUMPET TREE

PRONUNCIATION - ˈta bə ˈbū yə   ɑr ˈjen tē ə

TRANSLATION - [from the native Brazilian name] [silvery, in reference to the leaves].

FORM - Deciduous or semi-evergreen shrubs and trees; multi-branched, irregular form; medium-coarse texture.

SIZE - Variable, often to 40 feet tall with a 25 foot spread; rapid growth rate.

HARDINESS ZONE - Zones 10-11, restricted to south Florida.

NATIVE HABITAT - Tropical America.

LEAVES - Palmately compound; opposite; 3 to 7 leaflets, usually oblong-elliptic, green to gray-green.

STEM/BARK - Varied; cork-like in some species.

FLOWERS - Red, pink, purple, white, or yellow; funnelform, usually 2 to 3 inches long; profuse; borne in terminal clusters. Blooms in spring before or concurrent with leaf growth.

FRUIT - Capsule; linear or oblong-linear to 10 inches long.

CULTURE - Grows in full sun to partial shade on a wide range of soils; salt tolerance varies with the species.

PROBLEMS - The wood becomes brittle with age.

PROPAGATION - Seeds or layers.

LANDSCAPE USES - Used as a specimen or patio tree and in street plantings.

COMMENTS - Several other species of *Tabebuia* of various flower colors are cultivated in southern Florida, including *T. bahamensis, T. caraiba* (Silver Trumpet Tree), *T. chrysantha, T. chrysotricha* (Golden Trumpet Tree), *T. donnell-smithii* (Primavera), *T. guayacan, T. heptaphylla (= T. impetiginosa), T. heterophylla, T. impetiginosa, T. lepidota, T. ochracea, T. rosea, T. serratifolia, T. umbellata* (Yellow Trumpet Tree), and probably others. Two cultivated *Tabebuia* species have recently been transferred to *Cybistax: C. chrysea (= T. chrysea)* and *C. donnell-smithii (= T. donnell-smithii-primavera).*

Tecoma stans

YELLOW ELDER

PRONUNCIATION - tə ˈkō mə stænz

TRANSLATION - [from Mexican name *Tecomaxochitl*] [erect, upright].

FORM - Monoecious, evergreen shrub or tree; vase-shaped; spreading, weedy, bushy; medium texture.

SIZE - Reaches a height of 20 feet with a l5 foot spread; rapid growth rate.

HARDINESS ZONE - Zones 9b-11, can be grown in south and in protected locations in central Florida.

NATIVE HABITAT - A pioneer or weed tree of tropical America, naturalized in south Florida.

LEAVES - Odd-pinnately compound; opposite, to l0 inches long; 5 to l3 papery, light green, lanceolate leaflets to 5 inches long; serrate margins.

STEM/BARK - Branches are flexible, willowy, and remain green for a long time before becoming gray. Supposedly, the wood of this tree was used for bows by the Carib Indians.

FLOWERS - Yellow, funnelform-campanulate, to 2 inches long; in terminal, many-flowered racemes. Flowers with each flush of new growth; main bloom is in the fall.

FRUIT - Capsules; tan, narrow, to 8 inches long, papery, dehiscent; seeds thin, papery, double-winged. Fruits mature mainly in winter and are persistent and unattractive.

CULTURE - Plant in full sun on any soil of good drainage. Does not tolerate standing water or salt.

PROBLEMS - Chewing insects and scale are minor problems.

PROPAGATION - By seed, sown on the surface of a sterile, well-drained medium such as sand. Seedlings bloom in 2 years. Can also be propagated by softwood cuttings under mist.

LANDSCAPE USES - Specimen plant, easy to grow, but somewhat weedy. Also in cultivation is *T. castaneifolia.*

Tecomaria capensis   CAPE HONEYSUCKLE

PRONUNCIATION - 'tē kə 'mæ rē ə   kə 'pen səs

TRANSLATION - [from the Mexican name *Tecomaxochit*] [from the Cape of Good Hope, South Africa].

FORM - Monoecious, evergreen, rambling shrub.

SIZE - To 12 feet or more, frequently less; rapid growth rate.

HARDINESS ZONE - Zones 9b-11, can be grown in central and south Florida.

NATIVE HABITAT - South Africa.

LEAVES - Odd-pinnately compound; opposite, to 6 inches long; 5 to 9 elliptic leaflets, to 2 inches long; serrate except at base, papery; no tendrils.

STEM/BARK - Grayish-green when young; becomes woody with age; prominent lenticels.

FLOWERS - Orange-red, scarlet or yellow; funnelform to 3 inches long; calyx 5-lobed, borne in terminal racemes. Blooms in the spring and fall.

FRUIT - Capsule; flattened, to 2 inches long.

CULTURE - Grow in full sun on well-drained soils; slight salt tolerance.

PROBLEMS - Scale, mites, nematodes, root rot.

PROPAGATION - Seeds or cuttings.

LANDSCAPE USES - Use as a vine with the support of a fence or post; can be trimmed to a freestanding shrub.

COMMENTS - Cultivars **'Lutea'** and **'Aurea'** have yellow flowers, **'Coccinea'** has scarlet flowers, and **'Salmonea'** has pale pink to orange flowers.

BISCHOFIACEAE - BISCHOFIA FAMILY

DICOTYLEDONS; A MONOGENERIC AND MONOTYPIC (*BISCHOFIA JAVANICA*) FAMILY

GEOGRAPHY: Eastern to central China, Malaysia, and the Pacific Islands.

GROWTH HABIT: Large deciduous or semi-evergreen trees.

LEAVES: Trifoliolate, with 3 serrate leaflets; stipules, early deciduous.

FLOWERS: Small, unisexual (plants dioecious), 5-merous, apetalous, in cymes.

FRUIT: Trilocular, tardily dehiscent capsule, with 2 seeds per locule and a thin endocarp.

ECONOMIC USES: Ornamentals and timber.

ORNAMENTAL GENERA: *Bischofia.*

COMMENTS: This family was previously placed in Euphorbiaceae and the monotypic genus *Bischofia* is now sometimes placed in Staphylleaceae.

Bischofia javanica

TOOG TREE

PRONUNCIATION - bə 'shō fē ə jə 'vɑ nə kə

TRANSLATION - [after Gottlieb Wilhelm Bischoff (1797-1854), professor of botany at Heidelberg] [from Java].

FORM - Dioecious, evergreen or partly deciduous tree; heavy trunk, dense, round, symmetrical canopy; medium-coarse texture.

SIZE - To 75 feet, usually 40 feet tall in Florida with a 30 foot spread; rapid growth rate.

HARDINESS ZONE - Zones 9b-11, can be grown in central and south Florida.

NATIVE HABITAT - Tropical Asia.

LEAVES - Alternate, trifoliolate; long-petioled; ovate-acuminate, 2 to 5 inches long, dark green, sometimes bronzy, leathery, with serrulate margins.

STEM/BARK - Bleeds sticky sap when wounded.

FLOWERS - Greenish, small, inconspicuous; borne in racemes.

FRUIT - A fleshy capsule; reddish or blue-black to 0.25 inch in diameter; drops and can stain walks.

CULTURE - Grows in full sun on various soil types; moderate salt tolerance.

PROBLEMS - Suffers from severe scale infestations, especially false oleander scale. Surface roots and brittle wood also cause problems.

PROPAGATION - Seeds and cuttings.

LANDSCAPE USES - Use as a shade or specimen tree in street plantings and parks.

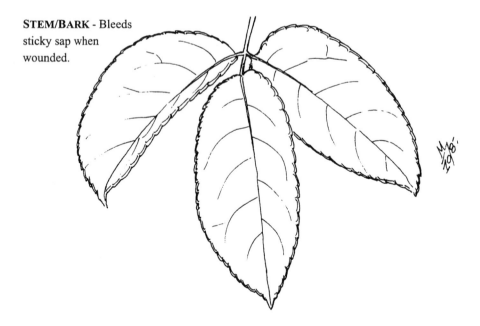

BOMBACACEAE - BOMBAX FAMILY

DICOTYLEDONS; ABOUT 30 GENERA AND 200 SPECIES

GEOGRAPHY: Tropics, primarily South America.

GROWTH HABIT: Deciduous or evergreen trees, some with peculiarly enlarged, bottle-shaped trunks adapted for water storage.

LEAVES: Palmately compound, usually stipulate.

FLOWERS: Large and showy, often appearing during dry season when plants are leafless; bisexual; 5-merous with numerous stamens; ovary superior.

FRUIT: Large, woody capsule containing many seeds which are covered with white, silky fibers.

ECONOMIC USES: Ornamentals, kapok (silk cotton), durian fruit from *Durio zibethinus*.

ORNAMENTAL GENERA: *Adonsonia, Bombax, Cavanillesia, Ceiba, Chorisa, Durio, Eriotheca, Matisia, Ochroma, Pachira, Pseudobombax, Quararibea,* and probably others.

Chorisia speciosa

SILK FLOSS TREE

PRONUNCIATION - kə ˈri sē ə   ˈspē sē ˈō sə

TRANSLATION - [after Ludwig Choris (1795-1859), Swiss botanist and professor of philosophy at Geneva] [showy].

FORM - Deciduous tree; upright, rounded, with wide-spreading branches; coarse texture.

SIZE - Can reach 50 feet in height with an equal or lesser spread; rapid growth rate on good soil.

HARDINESS ZONE - Zones 9b-11, can be grown in south Florida and in central Florida if protected when young.

NATIVE HABITAT - Brazil and Argentina.

LEAVES - Palmately compound; alternate; 5 to 7 narrowly elliptic, serrate leaflets, to 5 inches long. Petioles are long and slender.

STEM/BARK - The buttressed trunk and large branches are covered with green bark and stout, conical spines. The bark slowly turns gray with age and the spines may be lost.

FLOWERS - Colors range from white to lavender, with pink predominating; some have white centers and dark streaks; 5-petaled, spreading to 5 inches wide; borne in short clusters. Blooms in fall when the tree is bare.

FRUIT - Capsules; woody, pear-shaped, to 8 inches long; filled with silky, white, kapok-like floss and pea-like seeds. The capsules are only occasionally produced in Florida.

CULTURE - Plant in full sun on soil of reasonable fertility and drainage; no salt tolerance.

PROBLEMS - None of importance. May have surface roots and can be messy.

PROPAGATION - By seed or grafting. Grafted trees are preferred as they bloom earlier and at a smaller size.

LANDSCAPE USES - A specimen tree or novelty plant; spectacular in bloom, but needs plenty of room.

COMMENTS - **'Majestic Beauty'** and **'Los Angeles Beautiful'** are offered as grafted trees.

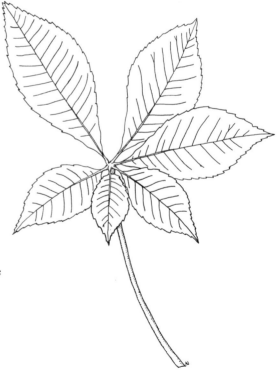

Pseudobombax ellipticum

SHAVING BRUSH TREE, PACHIRA

PRONUNCIATION - ˈsū dō ˈbɑm baks   ē ˈlip tə kəm

TRANSLATION - [*pseudo* (= false) *bombax* (= silk), in reference to silky hairs in the fruit] [*elliptic*, in reference to leaflet shape].

FORM - Monoecious, deciduous tree; upright, rounded, with wide-spreading branches; medium texture.

SIZE - To 25 feet tall.

HARDINESS ZONE - Zones 10b-11, can be grown outside only in south Florida.

NATIVE HABITAT - Tropical America and West Indies.

LEAVES - Palmately compound; alternate; 5-7 elliptic leaflets.

STEM/BARK - Bark on younger limbs green, "wrinkled" where branch joins trunk. Bark slowly turning gray with age.

FLOWERS - Colors from pink to red; having numerous stamen, very showy. Flowers in winter and spring.

FRUIT - Capsule, only occaisonally produced in Florida.

CULTURE - Plant in full sun on well-drained soil; no salt tolerance.

PROBLEMS - None of importance.

PROPAGATION - Air layers; large cuttings.

LANDSCAPE USES - Specimen tree. Allow plenty of room.

COMMENTS - Damaged by hard frosts. Very attractive when in flower. The related *P. grandiflorum* has also been reported.

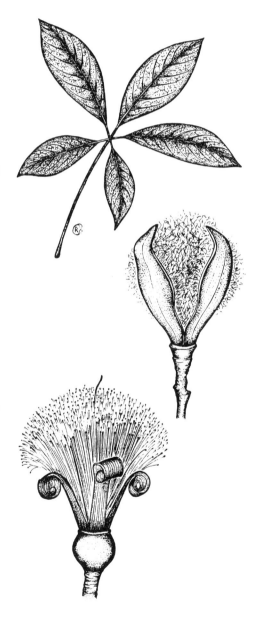

BORAGINACEAE - BORAGE FAMILY

DICOTYLEDONS; ABOUT 100 GENERA AND 2000 SPECIES

GEOGRAPHY: Cosmopolitan but centered in southern Europe and eastern Asia.

GROWTH HABIT: Annual and perennial herbs and less commonly trees and shrubs; stems covered with hispid pubescence.

LEAVES: Alternate, simple, entire, exstipulate.

FLOWERS: Actinomorphic or rarely zygomorphic, salverform to campanulate, usually bisexual (plants sometimes polygamous, with female flowers. occurring on separate plants), 5-merous, in characteristic helicoid cymes.

FRUIT: Consist of 4 nutlets or sometimes a drupe.

ECONOMIC USES: Several ornamentals, herbs (such as comfrey and alkanet), and red dyes.

ORNAMENTAL GENERA: *Borago, Bourreria, Carmona, Cordia, Echium, Ehretia, Heliotropium, Mallotonia, Mertensia, Myosotis, Pulmonaria,* among others.

Cordia sebestena   GEIGER TREE

PRONUNCIATION - kor dē ə ͵se bəs 'tē nə

TRANSLATION - [after Euricius Cordus (1486-1535) and his son Valerus (1515-1544), German botanists and pharmacists] [Arabic name].

FORM - Monoecious, evergreen tree; rounded, densely foliated, medium-coarse texture.

SIZE - Reaches a maximum height of 25 feet with a 20 foot spread; fairly slow growth rate.

HARDINESS ZONE - Zones 10b-11, can be grown in south Florida, but should have a protected location as it is damaged by frost.

NATIVE HABITAT - Dry, coastal areas of extreme south Florida and tropical America.

LEAVES - Simple, alternate; ovate, to 7 inches long; dark green, with undulate margins; stiff, rough and hairy, feeling like sandpaper (scabrous). New growth and young flower buds are dark gray and wooly.

STEM/BARK - Irregular, crooked trunk and branches covered with ridged, dark brown bark.

FLOWERS - Burnt orange to vermilion; funnelform and crepe-papery to 2 inches wide; borne in terminal, flattened, showy, branched cymes. Blooms nearly all year, with peak flowering in June and July.

FRUIT - Drupe; white, pear-shaped, 1.5 inches long. The flesh has a pleasant smell, is edible, but not especially good.

CULTURE - Requires full sun and well-drained soil. Tolerates alkalinity, poor sandy soils, and fair amounts of salt spray.

PROBLEMS - Chewing insects occasionally attack the leaves.

PROPAGATION - Seeds or air layers work well. Cuttings will not root.

LANDSCAPE USES - A very good specimen or street tree, especially for coastal areas. Several species of *Cordia* are valued for their attractive flowers and grown in southern Florida. These include *C. africana, C. alliodora, C. boissieri* (Texas Wild Olive), *C. dentata* (Jackwood), *C. globosa, C. lutea, C. nitida, C. obliqua* (Sticking Tree), and probably others.

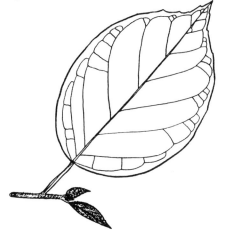

BURSERACEAE - TORCHWOOD FAMILY

DICOTYLEDONS; ABOUT 18 GENERA AND 500 SPECIES

GEOGRAPHY: Tropical Asia (especially Malaysia), Africa, and America.

GROWTH HABIT: Resiniferous trees, often with smooth, copper-colored trunk.

LEAVES: Odd-pinnately compound, spirally arranged but often crowded at the branch tips.

FLOWERS: Unisexual (plants often dioecious), small, 3- to 5-merous, sepals often connate; petals usually free; ovary superior.

FRUIT: A drupe or sometimes a capsule.

ECONOMIC USES: Important source of timber, aromatic resins (including frankincense and myrrh), and perfumes and soaps.

ORNAMENTAL GENERA: *Boswellia, Bursera, Canarium, Commiphora, Dacrodes, Tetragastris,* etc.

Bursera simaruba   GUMBO-LIMBO

PRONUNCIATION - ˈbər sə rə   ˌsi mə ˈrū bə

TRANSLATION - [after Joachim Burser (1583-1649), German physician and botanist] [after the genus *Simaruba*, in reference to the pinnate leaves].

FORM - Dioecious, deciduous tree; irregular; medium texture.

SIZE - A large tree that may reach 60 feet in height with an equal or wider spread; commonly seen to 30 feet; rapid growth rate on good soil.

HARDINESS ZONE - Zones 10-11, can be grown only in south Florida.

NATIVE HABITAT - Coastal and interior hammocks of south Florida and tropical America.

LEAVES - Odd-pinnately compound; alternate, to 8 inches long; 3 to 7 ovate to elliptic leaflets about 2 inches long; margins entire. Leaves are shed during prolonged dry weather.

STEM/BARK - The trunk and the large, irregular, crooked branches are covered with resinous, smooth, peeling copper-colored bark with an attractive, shiny, varnished appearance.

FLOWERS - Unisexual, greenish-yellow, small, nonshowy; in 5-inch-long axillary racemes. Blooms with the new leaves, generally in May.

FRUIT - Berry; red, three-sided, ovoid, 0.5 inch long; splits into three sections at maturity

to reveal a 0.25-inch-long, triangular red seed. The fruit take a year to mature and ripen in June.

CULTURE - Plant in full sun or partial shade on a wide range of well-drained soils. Tolerates calcareous soils and marginal amounts of salt but grows poorly on deep white sands.

PROBLEMS - Generally pest-free.

PROPAGATION - By seed, which germinate readily if fresh; cuttings of any size, up to huge truncheons for living fence posts.

LANDSCAPE USES - A superb shade/specimen/street tree, but needs room to grow.

COMMENTS - The wood, which is soft, lightweight, and easily carved, was used for making carousel horses before the advent of molded plastics. *Bursera microphylla*, a small-leaved species, is also cultivated in Florida.

BUXACEAE - BOXWOOD FAMILY

DICOTYLEDONS; 4 OR 6 GENERA AND ABOUT 100 SPECIES

GEOGRAPHY: Temperate and tropical regions.

GROWTH HABIT: Mostly evergreen shrubs, rarely trees and herbs.

LEAVES: Opposite or alternate, simple, often leathery, exstipulate.

FLOWERS: Actinomorphic, unisexual (plants mono- or dioecious); with 4 connate sepals and apetalous; ovary superior.

FRUIT: Loculicidal capsule or drupe, with shiny black seeds.

ECONOMIC USES: Ornamentals and high-grade timber used for carvings.

ORNAMENTAL GENERA: *Buxus, Pachysandra,* and *Sarcococca.*

COMMENTS: The two genera *Simondsia* (jojoba) and *Styloceras* are recognized as distinct families: Simondsiaceae and Styloceraceae, respectively.

Buxus microphylla

PRONUNCIATION - ˈbuk səs ˌmī krō ˈfi lə

TRANSLATION - [the classical Latin name for *B. sempervirens*] [small-leaved].

FORM - Evergreen shrub, compact, multi-stemmed, erect, densely foliated. Medium-fine texture.

SIZE - To 5 feet, more frequently 2 to 3 feet, with equal spread. Slow growing.

HARDINESS ZONE - Zone 5. Grows best in central and north Florida.

NATIVE HABITAT - Japan.

LEAVES - Simple, opposite, obovate to 1 inch, stiff, leathery, short petiole, entire margins, silver line down midrib on underside, apex rounded or emarginate, medium green in color; some cultivars and varieties developing a yellowish-brown cast during the winter months in colder climates.

STEM/BARK - Not round, often quadrangular, slender, green, glabrous.

FLOWERS - Greenish, inconspicuous, in terminal or axillary clusters in early spring.

FRUIT - Capsule, inconspicuous.

CULTURE - Full sun to partial shade, fertile, acid soils, not salt tolerant. Shallow-rooted, therefore avoid deep cultivation around root system. Avoid excessively hot, dry conditions. At the other extreme, will not tolerate poor drainage.

PROBLEMS - Root rot (if kept too wet), nematodes, and mites can cause serious damage. Leaf miners, scale insects, mealybugs, and other insects are lesser problems.

PROPAGATION - Cuttings.

LANDSCAPE USES - Hedges, foundation, planter, edging, excellent closely clipped material (topiary, parterres, and knot gardens) for formal gardens.

COMMENTS - Leaves and bark are reportedly poisonous if eaten in quantity. Many cultivars: **'Compacta'** - even slower growing than species, dark green foliage; var. *japonica* (Japanese Boxwood); var. *koreana* - hardier, more loose and open than species; foliage develops yellowish-brown cast in winter; **'Tide Hill'** - a cultivar of var. *koreana* with green foliage in winter; **'Winter Green'** - cultivar of var. *koreana* with green winter foliage, hardier; *B. sempervirens* (common boxwood) is a different species, can reach 15 to 20 feet in height, has elliptic to ovate leaves; not well adapted to Florida conditions.

CACTACEAE - CACTUS FAMILY

DICOTYLEDONS; 85-220 GENERA AND ABOUT 2000 SPECIES

GEOGRAPHY: Semi-deserts of North, Central, and South America.

GROWTH HABIT: Spiny perennial, xerophytic, succulents, some epiphytes, and rarely leafy vines.

LEAVES: Much reduced or absent, except in *Pereskia* and *Persekiopsis* where they are ovate, entire, and more or less succulent; spines and glochids (barbed hairs) arise from areoles on ribs or tubercles (fingerlike projections).

FLOWERS: Very showy, solitary, sessile, bisexual; 5-merous but usually in spirally arranged multiples; ovary inferior.

FRUIT: A juicy or leathery berry with many seeds.

ECONOMIC USES: Primarily as ornamentals by collectors, but the fruit is used for making jellies or jams and some species have narcotic properties.

ORNAMENTAL GENERA: Probably all known genera are in cultivation, the most common of which include *Acanthocalycium, Acanthocereus, Acanthorhipsalis, Ancistrocactus, Aporocactus, Aporoheliocereus, Ariocarpus, Aprophyllum, Astrophytum, Aztekium, Blossfeldia, Borziacactus, Buiningia, Cephalocereus, Cereus, Cleistocactus, Copiapoa, Coryphantha, Cryptocereus, Denmoza, Discocactus, Echinocactus, Echinocereus, Echinomastus, Echinofossulocactus, Echinopsis, ' Epicactus, Epiphyllum, Epithelantha, Eriosyce, Erythrorhipsalis, Escobaria, ' Ferocactus, Frailea, Gymnocactus, Gymnocalycium, Hatiora, Heliocereus, Homalocephala, Hylocereus, Lamaireocereus, Lepismium, Leuchtenbergia, Lobivia, ' Lobivopsis, Lophophora, Lymanbensonia, Mammillaria, Matucana, Melocactus, Neolloydia, Neoporteria, Neowerdermannia, Nopalxochia, Notocactus, Obregonia, Opuntia, Oroya, Ortegocactus, Parodia, Pediocactus, Pelecyphora, Pereskia, Pereskiopsis, Pigmaeocereus, Pfeiffera, Rebutia, Rhipsalis, Rhipsalidopsis, Schlumbergera, Sclerocactus, Seleliocereus, Selenicereus, Strombocactus, Strophocactus, Thelocactus, Trichocereus, Turbinicarpus, Uebelmannia, Weingartia, Wittiocactus,* among others.

COMMENTS: The number of genera vary according to various authorities. The name "cactus" was applied by ancient Greeks to some spiny plant unrelated to the members of Cactaceae, but it has since been adopted as the type genus for the family. In common usage, "cactus" (pl. cacti) is sometimes incorrectly applied to all succulent plants.

Astrophytum myriostigma　BISHOP'S CAP CACTUS

PRONUNCIATION - æs trō fī təm ˌmē rē ō ˈstig mə

TRANSLATION - [from Greek *astron* (= a star) and *phyton* (= a plant)] [with many stigmas].

FORM - Cylindrical, few-ribbed, unbranched cactus.

SIZE - To 24 inches, commonly seen 3 to 6 inches, slow growth.

HARDINESS ZONE - Grown throughout the U.S. as a greenhouse plant.

NATIVE HABITAT - North-central Mexico.

LEAVES - None; areoles brown, wooly, spineless.

STEM - Globose to cylindrical, ribs 4-10 (usually 5), broad, covered with grayish scales.

FLOWERS - Yellow, short-funnelform, many tepals and stamens, to 2.5 inches long and wide, subapical, opening on successive days.

FRUIT - Globose berries, vertically dehiscent; seeds glossy black.

CULTURE - Full sun to light shade; sandy, well-drained soils; allow to become moderately dry between waterings.

PROBLEMS - Scale, root rot.

PROPAGATION - Seeds.

LANDSCAPE USES - Pot plant.

COMMENTS - Many related species, hybrids.

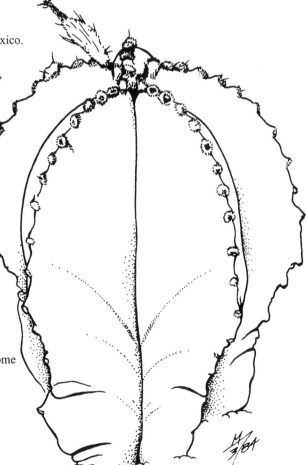

Cereus peruvianus   HEDGE CACTUS

PRONUNCIATION - ˈsē rē əs   pə ˌrū vē ˈā nəs

TRANSLATION - [a wax taper, in reference to the plant's shape] [Peruvian].

FORM - Cylindrical cactus, ribbed, erect, many-branched.

SIZE - To 25 feet, may form huge clumps, rapid growth.

HARDINESS ZONE - Zones 9b-11. Can be grown in central and south Florida.

NATIVE HABITAT - West Indies, South America.

LEAVES - None. Areoles, straight spines to 0.75 inch long.

STEM/BARK - Ribbed (4 to 8) stems to 8 inches in diameter, more or less octagonal shape, dark green, become woody with age, suckering.

FLOWERS - White to pinkish, nocturnal, funnelform, to 12 inches long, polypetalous, many stamens.

FRUIT - Berry, to 4 inches, many-seeded, white, pink, red, purple, yellow, many edible.

CULTURE - Full sun to partial shade; varied, well-drained soil; moderately salt-tolerant; requires little care.

PROBLEMS - Woodpeckers, sharp spines.

PROPAGATION - Seed, cuttings.

LANDSCAPE USES - Specimen, urn, accent.

COMMENTS - Many related species in cultivation. A recent publication considers *C. uruguayanus* to be the correct name for this species.

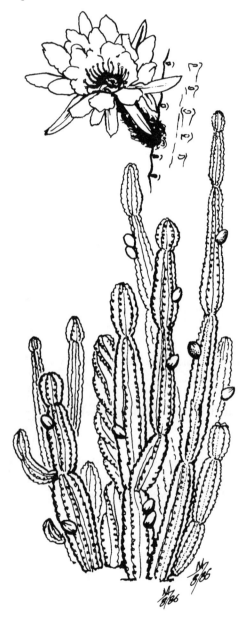

Epiphyllum ×

ORCHID CACTUS

PRONUNCIATION - ˌe pə ˈfi ləm

TRANSLATION - [from Greek *epi* (= upon) and *phyllon* (= a leaf), in reference to the leaf-like flattened green stems].

FORM - Epiphytic cactus, 2- to 3-winged, much-branched.

SIZE - To 20 feet long, commonly seen 5 to 6 feet, rapid growth.

HARDINESS ZONE - Zones 10-11. Grown outside only in south Florida. Grown throughout the U.S. as a greenhouse plant.

NATIVE HABITAT - Tropical America; horticultural origin.

LEAVES - None; areoles marginal in the indentations, spines bristle-like and mostly absent on mature plants.

STEM - Stems cylindrical and woody or flattened; branches elongate, flat, 2- or 3-winged, 5 inches wide, crenate or lobed, with prominent midrib.

FLOWERS - Various shades of white, yellow, pink, red, and many combinations, many tepals and stamens, to 12 inches long and 10 inches across, sometimes nocturnal, lasting 1 to 3 days, often fragrant.

FRUIT - Berries (varying with cultivar) from green to purplish-red, ovoid, to 4 inches long, with low ridges or scales, splitting at maturity.

CULTURE - Partial shade; fertile, well-drained soils; keep evenly moist to slightly dry.

PROBLEMS - Slugs, snails, root rot.

PROPAGATION - Seeds, cuttings of stem sections of cultivars.

LANDSCAPE USES - Greenhouse, window garden, or specialty plant grown on trellises, palms, driftwood, etc.

COMMENTS - About 15 species and hundreds of cultivars, advanced hybrids.

Gymnocalycium spp.

CHIN CACTUS

PRONUNCIATION - ˌjim nō kə ˈlē sē əm

TRANSLATION - [from Greek *gymnos* (= naked) and *calyx* (= a bud), in reference to the naked flower buds].

FORM - Globose cactus.

SIZE - To 8 inches high, 10 inches in diameter; but usually seen much smaller.

HARDINESS ZONE - Grown throughout the United States as a greenhouse plant.

NATIVE HABITAT - South America.

LEAVES - None; spines 3 to 13 (mostly 7 to 9), needle-shaped, to 2 inches long, yellow, brown or gray.

STEM - Stems simple or caespitose, usually globose, with tubercled ribs 5 to 16 (usually 10), often with a protrusion (chin) below each areole.

FLOWERS - White to pink, rarely yellow, campanulate to short-funnelform, to 3 inches long, many tepals and stamens, opening several days in succession.

FRUIT - Berries; red, oblong, seeds dome-shaped.

CULTURE - Full sun to light shade; sandy, well-drained soils; allow to become moderately dry between waterings.

PROBLEMS - Scale, root rot.

PROPAGATION - Seeds.

LANDSCAPE USES - Pot plant.

COMMENTS - Many related species, several cultivars. Variegated cultivars often grafted on other cactus species as novelties.

Hylocereus undatas   NIGHT-BLOOMING CEREUS

PRONUNCIATION - ˌhī lō 'sē rē əs   un 'dā təs

TRANSLATION - [from Greek *hyle* (= a wood) and *cereus* (= a wax taper), in reference to their epiphytic habit] [undulate].

FORM - Vining cactus, 3-angled, vigorous, often epiphytic.

SIZE - To 20 feet, often forms large mass in trees, rapid growth.

HARDINESS ZONE - Zones 10-11. Can be grown only in south Florida.

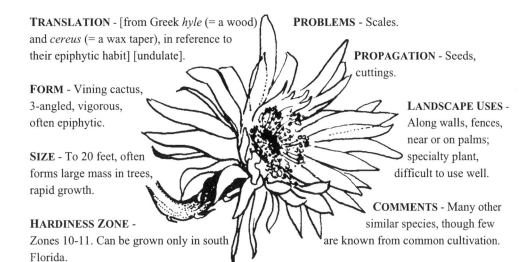

PROBLEMS - Scales.

PROPAGATION - Seeds, cuttings.

LANDSCAPE USES - Along walls, fences, near or on palms; specialty plant, difficult to use well.

COMMENTS - Many other similar species, though few are known from common cultivation.

NATIVE HABITAT - Tropical America.

LEAVES - None. Areoles about 1.5 inches apart, small spines to 0.25 inch, usually 1 to 5.

STEM - Three-winged, triangular, to 4 inches in diameter, margins undulate, many aerial roots, usually apple-green.

FLOWERS - White, nocturnal, funnelform, to 14 inches long, polypetalous, many stamens, fragrant; flowers in summer.

FRUIT - Berry, red, to 4 inches, many-seeded, edible.

CULTURE - Full sun to partial shade; varied, well-drained soils, boots of palms; highly salt-tolerant.

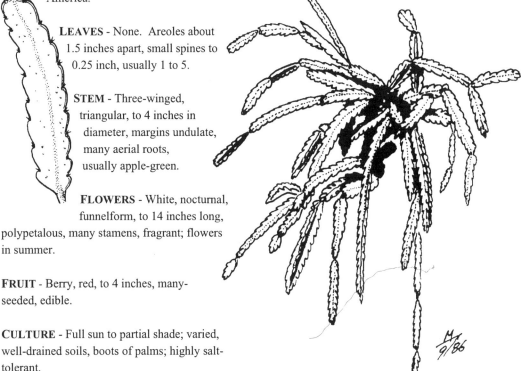

Mammillaria elongata   Golden Star Cactus

PRONUNCIATION - ˌma mə ˈlæ rē ə   ˌē loŋ ˈgā tə

TRANSLATION - [from Latin *mammila* (= a nipple), in reference to the shape of tubercles] [elongated].

FORM - Oblong cactus, tubercled, much-branched.

SIZE - To 4 inches high, forming large clumps.

HARDINESS ZONE - Grown throughout the U.S. as a greenhouse plant.

NATIVE HABITAT - Central Mexico.

LEAVES - None; radial spines 15 to 20, slightly spreading and recurved, needle-shaped, yellow, to 0.5 inch long, central spine rarely borne from spine-bearing areoles at the apex of the tubercles.

STEM - Caespitose; to 4 inches high and 1.5 inches thick, covered with tubercles in 3 and 5 or 5 and 8 spirals, to 0.25 inch long; axils (flower-bearing areoles) naked or slightly woolly.

FLOWERS - Yellowish-cream-colored, short-funnelform, to 0.75 inch long, stamens few and mostly lateral, diurnal, usually many at one time.

FRUIT - Berries; red, club-shaped, exserted, to 1 inch long.

CULTURE - Full sun to light shade; sandy, well-drained soils; allow to become moderately dry between waterings.

PROBLEMS - Scale, root rot.

PROPAGATION - Seed, cuttings.

LANDSCAPE USES - Greenhouse pot plant.

COMMENTS - Many related species. Several cultivars, such as **'Longispina'** and **'Minima'**. *Mammilaria* is a large and complex genus of about 300 species, nearly all of which are in cultivation, primarily by private collectors.

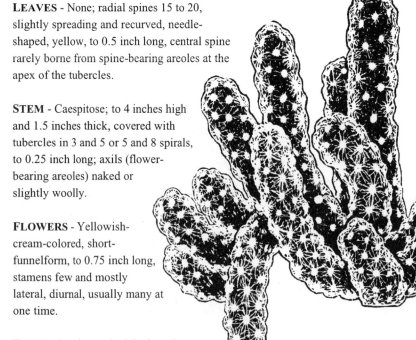

Opuntia spp.

PRICKLY PEAR CACTUS

PRONUNCIATION - ō ˈpun tē ə

TRANSLATION - [name of a plant that grew near Opus (= *optunis*) in ancient Greece].

FORM - Jointed cactus, usually flattened, many-branched.

SIZE - Variable with species. Some tree-like to 20 feet, others less than 1 foot. Rapid growth.

HARDINESS ZONE - Highly variable with species. Many species hardy throughout the country.

NATIVE HABITAT - Western Hemisphere from British Columbia to the Straits of Magellan. Several are native to Florida, many naturalized.

LEAVES - Cylindrical to conical, small and early-deciduous in most species, but in some relatively large and persistent; spines naked or sheathed to 3 inches long; very minute spines (glochids) usually in the upper part of the areole; rarely spineless.

STEM - Mostly divided, at least distally, into determinate segments, which are commonly flattened and obovate, some cylindrical to globose.

FLOWERS - Commonly yellow, but range from white to purple, except blue, to 5 inches across, tepals and stamens many, stamens shorter than tepals, light-sensitive.

FRUIT - Berry; dry, or juicy and green, yellow, red, or purple, to 5 inches long, many edible; seeds flattened with a bony covering.

CULTURE - Full sun to light shade; sandy, well-drained soils; allow to become moderately dry between waterings.

PROBLEMS - Root rot, spines, glochids.

PROPAGATION - Cuttings of segments; seeds of many species difficult to germinate.

LANDSCAPE USES - Exposed and rocky banks, rock gardens, neglected areas, pot plants.

COMMENTS - Over 300 species, including *O. microdasys,* the popular "Bunny Ears" pot plant. *Opuntia ficus-indica* (Indian-Fig Cactus, Tuna), *O. littoralis* (Prickly Pear), *O. stricta* (Prickly Pear), and *O. stricta* var. *dillenii,* are but a few examples of those grown in Florida.

Pereskia aculeata   BARBADOS GOOSEBERRY

PRONUNCIATION - pə 'res kē ə   ə kyū lē ā tə

TRANSLATION - [after Nicholas Claude Fabre de Peiresc (1580-1637), French naturalist] [prickly].

FORM - Monoecious, vining cactus, erect at first, often bushy, leafy.

SIZE - To 20 feet long, commonly much shorter; rapid growth.

HARDINESS ZONE - Zones 10-11. Grown outdoors only in south Florida.

NATIVE HABITAT - Tropical America.

LEAVES - Deciduous under natural conditions, alternate, thick, lanceolate to ovate, to 3 inches long, apex acute, margin entire, short-petioled; areoles with 1 to 3 spines, recurved, without glochids.

STEM/BARK - Herbaceous at first, becoming woody, unjointed.

FLOWERS - Yellowish-green, to 2 inches across, tepals and stamens many, in panicles or corymbs.

FRUIT - Berry; yellow, to 1 inch in diamenter, spiny, edible.

CULTURE - *Pereskia* uses more water throughout its period of active growth than other cacti, but still requires full sun to light shade and well-drained soils.

PROBLEMS - Chewing insects, root rot.

PROPAGATION - Cuttings root very easily, seeds.

LANDSCAPE USES - Along walls, fences; specialty plant difficult to use in landscape; frequently grown as a pot plant.

COMMENTS - Related species, several cultivars. "Lemon Vine" has leaves blotched with yellow and mottled. Pereskias are often used as stock on which other cacti are grafted. The related genus *Pereskiopsis*, another leafy taxon, is only rarely seen in cultivation.

Rhipsalis spp.

PRONUNCIATION - 'rip sə ləs

TRANSLATION - [from Greek *rhips* (= wicker-works), in reference to jointed supple shoots].

FORM - Elongate or jointed cactus, mostly pendant and epiphytic or rock-dwelling.

SIZE - Highly variable with species, to 30 feet in some, many less than 1 foot; rapid growth.

HARDINESS ZONE - Zones 9b-11. Grown outdoors in central and south Florida.

NATIVE HABITAT - Tropical America, naturalized in Africa and Ceylon; one native to Florida.

LEAVES - None; areoles small, with hairs or bristles, rarely spiny.

STEM - Cylindrical, angled or flattened, elongate or jointed, 0.25 to 1 inch in diameter, often branched laterally or from the apex of the joints, often with aerial roots.

FLOWERS - White, yellow, or pinkish, less than 1 inch across, mostly lateral, 1 to 5 in an areole, perianth segments few.

FRUIT - Berry; white to red or purple, globose, typically 0.25 to 0.5 inch in diameter, nearly transparent, mucilaginous; seeds black.

CULTURE - Partial shade; fertile, well-drained soils, allow to become slightly dry between waterings.

PROBLEMS - Root rot.

PROPAGATION - Cuttings, seeds.

LANDSCAPE USES - Pot plant, hanging basket.

COMMENTS - Many related species. *Rhipsalis baccifera,* the Mistletoe Cactus, is native to Florida.

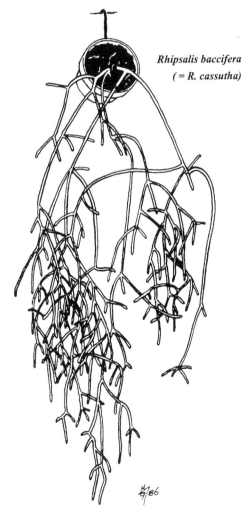

Rhipsalis baccifera
(= R. cassutha)

Schlumbergera ✕   CHRISTMAS CACTUS, EASTER CACTUS

PRONUNCIATION - shlum 'bər gə rə

TRANSLATION - [after Frederick Schlumberger (1804-1865), Belgian horticulturist, explorer, and plant collector].

FORM - Jointed cactus, flattened, many-branched, epiphytic.

SIZE - To 12 inches, typically seen 6 to 8 inches, slow growth.

HARDINESS ZONE - Zones 10-11. Grown outdoors in south Florida and throughout the U.S. as a greenhouse potted plant.

NATIVE HABITAT - Horticultural origin. Species native to Brazil.

LEAVES - None; areoles marginal and bearing short bristles.

STEM - Cladophylls jointed, flattened, thin, obovate-truncate, to 1 inch wide and 2 inches long, segments crenate to serrate, green, becoming woody with age. New growth produced apically.

FLOWERS - Variable with species and hybrids, regular or irregular, shades and combinations of white, pink, and violet, to 3 inches long, inner perianth segments united in a tube, inner stamens united in a tube around the style.

FRUIT - Berry.

CULTURE - Partial shade; fertile, well-drained soils; keep evenly moist to slightly dry.

PROBLEMS - Snails, slugs, root rot.

PROPAGATION - Cuttings of cultivars, seeds.

LANDSCAPE USES - Pot plant, hanging basket.

COMMENTS - Two commonly cultivated species: *S.* ✕ *buckleyi (= S. bridgesii)* Christmas Cactus - arching; segment margins 2-3 crenate, flowers nearly regular; *S. truncata* - Easter Cactus - more erect; segment margins sharply 2-serrate, flowers irregular. Many hybrids and cultivars. *S.* ✕ *buckleyi* is a hybrid between *S. truncata* and *S. russeliana.*

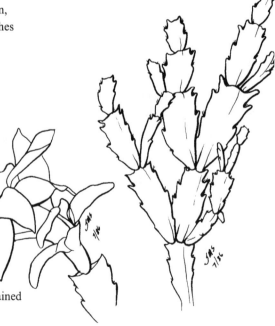

CAPRIFOLIACEAE - HONEYSUCKLE FAMILY

DICOTYLEDONS; 18 GENERA AND ABOUT 450 SPECIES

GEOGRAPHY:	Cosmopolitan but predominantly Northern Hemisphere.
GROWTH HABIT:	Small trees, shrubs, woody vines, and rarely herbs.
LEAVES:	Usually opposite, simple, and exstipulate but rarely (in *Sambucus*) with pinnately compound leaves and stipulate.
FLOWERS:	Actinomorphic or zygomorphic, bisexual, in cymose inflorescences, 4- but mostly 5-merous; tubular and sometimes bilabiate; ovary inferior, carpels united.
FRUIT:	A berry or sometimes a capsule.
ECONOMIC USES:	Common as ornamentals but fruit of *Sambucus* (elderberry) is used for making jellies and jams.

ORNAMENTAL GENERA: *Abelia, Diervilla, Kolkwitzia, Leycesteria, Lonicera, Sambucus, Symphoricarpos, Viburnum, Weigelia,* and others.

Abelia × grandiflora   GLOSSY ABELIA

PRONUNCIATION - ə ˈbē ə   ˌgræn də ˈflo rə

TRANSLATION - [after Dr. Clarke Abel (1780-1826), who introduced *A. chinensis*] [large-flowered].

FORM - Monoecious, evergreen or partly deciduous shrub, many-branched, arching, spreading.

SIZE - To 8 feet, moderately fast growth rate.

HARDINESS ZONE - Zone 5. Grows well only in north Florida.

NATIVE HABITAT - A hybrid between *A. chinensis* and *A. uniflora*.

LEAVES - Simple, opposite or whorled, ovate, acuminate, to 1.5 inches long, glossy surface, serrate margin, may have reddish color in cool weather, new growth reddish.

STEM/BARK - Reddish-brown, fine-textured young stems, exfoliating bark on older stems.

FLOWERS - Funnelform, united corolla, to 0.75 inch long, white tinged with pink, in loose terminal panicles, pinkish-red calyces persist for much of the year; prolific flowering throughout spring and summer.

FRUIT - A leathery achene, not showy.

CULTURE - Full sun to light shade, moist, fertile soils; not salt tolerant, tends to become spindly with age and therefore requires regular pruning.

PROBLEMS - Needs rich soils, no serious insect or disease problems.

PROPAGATION - Cuttings.

LANDSCAPE USES - Clipped (needs frequent pruning) or unclipped hedge, foundation, border, bank cover.

COMMENTS - Several cultivars: 'Prostrata' - prostrate growth habit, sometimes used as ground cover; 'Sherwoodii' - dwarf, to 3 feet, somewhat smaller leaves and flowers; 'Confetti' is a dwarf with variegated leaves; 'Edward Goucher' is a hybrid between *A. × grandiflora* and *A. schumannii;* abundant lavendar-pink flowers and showy red calyces, to 5 feet in height.

Lonicera japonica   JAPANESE HONEYSUCKLE

PRONUNCIATION - lō 'ni sə rə   jə 'pɑ nə kə

TRANSLATION - [Adam Lonitzer (1528-1586), German naturalist] [from Japan].

FORM - A twining, evergreen vine, medium-textured, forming dense, tangled mats.

SIZE - Variable, depending on size of the support. Growth rate is rapid.

HARDINESS ZONE - Zone 5. Can be grown in all areas of Florida.

NATIVE HABITAT - Eastern Asia, widely naturalized in woodlands of the southeastern United States.

LEAVES - Opposite, ovate to oblong-ovate, to 3 inches long, apex acute to short-acuminate, dark green. The leaves have entire margins, pubescent undersides (both sides pubescent when young) and turn purplish in subfreezing weather.

STEM/BARK - The slender, hairy, light brown to reddish-brown stems are hollow and climb by twining. A shredding bark develops on older stems.

FLOWERS - White, fading to yellow, 1.5 inches long, two-lipped (zygomorphic) with long, funnel-shaped throat. The flowers appear in pairs in the axils of new growth in summer. Has nectar on the style and stigma; very fragrant.

FRUIT - Berries, 0.25 inch wide, globose and shiny black, in late summer to early fall.

CULTURE - Plant in full sun or partial shade on a wide range of soil types. Moderately tolerant of soil salinity and salt spray. So easily grown that it has become a noxious weed in the South.

PROBLEMS - Pest-free.

PROPAGATION - Cuttings of any age root well, except in winter. Can also be grown from seed.

LANDSCAPE USES - Mainly used as a ground cover as it covers bare ground rapidly. Useful for stablilizing and preventing erosion on steep soils. Occasionally grown on fences and trellises, but requires heavy pruning to keep its rampant growth under control.

COMMENTS - Cultivars include **'Halliana'** (Hall's Japanese Honeysuckle) - common form, very vigorous, flowers white, fading to yellow; **'Purpurea'** - purplish leaves, red flowers, fading to yellow, probably the best one for landscaping; **'Variegata'** - yellow variegation on leaves. A number of other *Lonicera* species are in cultivation though, for the most part, restricted to north Florida. Among these, the very fragrant *L. fragrantissima, L. hildebrandiana* (Giant Burmese Honeysuckle), *L. maackii,* and *L. maackii* f. *podocarpa* are well known.

Lonicera sempervirens   CORAL HONEYSUCKLE

PRONUNCIATION - lō 'ni sə rə   'sem pər 'vī rənz

TRANSLATION - [Adam Lonitzer (1528-1586), German naturalist] [evergreen].

FORM - Monoecious, climbing, semi-evergreen vine of medium texture.

SIZE - Variable, depends on size and shape of the support. Rate of growth is fairly rapid.

HARDINESS ZONE - Zone 5. Can be grown in north and central Florida.

NATIVE HABITAT - Edges of woods, fence rows, and thickets throughout the southeastern United States.

LEAVES - Opposite, oblong to ovate, connate-perfoliate near apex of flowering shoots, to 3 inches long, apex obtuse to acute. The leaves are blue-green with glaucous undersides.

STEM/BARK - Climbs by twining; glabrous, light brown stems.

FLOWERS - Orange-red with yellow insides, narrowly funnelform, to 2 inches long. The flowers are borne in whorls of 2 to 4 on short, terminal spikes in April and May and sporadically thereafter. Not fragrant.

FRUIT - Berries; red, ovoid, 0.25 inch long, in late summer through fall.

CULTURE - Grown in partial shade or full sun. Tolerates most soils except poor sands but prefers fertile, well-drained soil. It has good salt tolerance.

PROBLEMS - Pest-free.

PROPAGATION - softwood cuttings, which root easily.

LANDSCAPE USES - An attractive non-rampant vine to grow on mailbox supports, fences, and trellises. Probably the best native vine in the state, excellent for naturalizing. Several species of birds feed on fruit, while flowers attract hummingbirds.

COMMENTS - Several cultivars exist: **'Sulphurea'** - completely yellow flowers; **'Superba'** - scarlet flowers; **'Magnifica'** - large, bright red flowers, later flowering. Undoubtedly one of the most attractive Florida native plants.

Viburnum odoratissimum   SWEET VIBURNUM

PRONUNCIATION - vī 'bər nəm   ˌō də rə 'ti sə məm

TRANSLATION - [ancient Latin name for *V. lantana*] [most fragrant].

FORM - Monoecious, evergreen, large erect shrub or small tree, multibranched round canopy.

SIZE - To 20 feet, frequently much smaller; rapid growth.

HARDINESS ZONE - Zone 8b. Can be grown in all regions of Florida.

NATIVE HABITAT - Himalayas to Japan.

LEAVES - Simple, opposite, elliptic to 6 inches long, obtuse base, leathery; margin may be toothed at apex or entire; smooth upper surface, veins not deeply impressed, tomentum in vein axils on underside, "bacon" aroma when crushed.

STEM/BARK - Prominent raised lenticels.

FLOWERS - White, tubular to 0.25 inch, in showy terminal, broadly pyramidal panicles to 4 inches long, extremely fragrant; flowers in spring.

FRUIT - Drupe; to 0.25 inch, red becoming black, one-seeded, can be moderately showy.

CULTURE - Full sun to partial shade, varied soils; moderately salt tolerant.

PROBLEMS - Aphids, scale, stem canker, severe sooty mold problem.

PROPAGATION - Cuttings.

LANDSCAPE USES - Border, screen, hedge, foundation plantings for large buildings, small specimen tree.

COMMENTS - Several cultivars: 'Nanum' - dwarf form; var. *awabuki* (Mirror-leaf Viburnum) - large leaves, very glossy on upper surface; large inflorescences; ultimate height about 12 feet.

Viburnum rufidulum   RUSTY BLACK HAW

PRONUNCIATION - vī 'bər nəm   rū 'fi dyə ləm

TRANSLATION - [ancient Latin name for *V. lantana*] [pale reddish-brown, in reference to indumentums on young shoots].

FORM - Monoecious, deciduous multiple or single trunk tree or shrub; broad, flat-topped and open, of medium texture.

SIZE - Can reach a height of 25 feet with a nearly equal spread. Grows at a moderate pace.

HARDINESS ZONE - Zone 6. Should be grown only in north and central Florida.

NATIVE HABITAT - Upland, well-drained woods of the southeastern United States, including north Florida.

LEAVES - Opposite, broadly elliptical, to 3 inches long, dark green on the upper surface, paler below, leathery and shiny with finely toothed margins. The buds, petioles, young twigs, and occasionally the leaf undersides are rusty-tomentose. Scarlet red   to   purple fall color.

STEM/BARK - Generally forms several slender trunks covered with dark brown bark, divided into small blocks (similar to *Cornus florida)*.

FLOWERS - White, small, in showy, flat-topped cymes, 5 inches across; in April, about the time when leaves are fully expanded; unpleasant odor.

FRUIT - Dark blue drupe with a waxy bloom. Ellipsoidal, to 0.5 inch long, in attractive clusters from September throughout autumn.

CULTURE - Grows in full sun or partial shade on any soil of reasonable fertility and drainage. It is not salt tolerant. Somewhat drought tolerant, but will not tolerate soil compaction.

PROBLEMS - Generally pest-free.

PROPAGATION - By seed, which may require warm followed by cold stratification periods. Cuttings may also root.

LANDSCAPE USES - A specimen tree, hedge or mass plantings, attractive in all seasons.

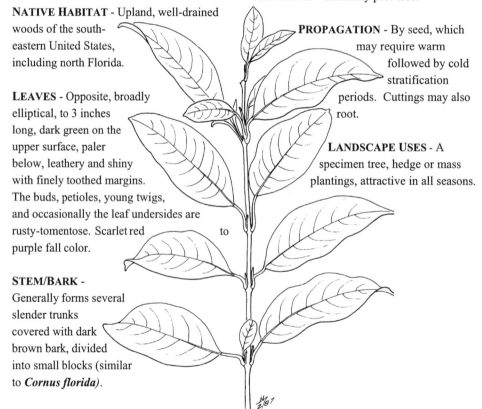

Viburnum suspensum   SANDANKWA VIBURNUM

PRONUNCIATION - vī ˈbər nəm   sə ˈspen səm

TRANSLATION - [ancient Latin name for *V. lantana*] [hanging].

FORM - Monoecious, evergreen shrub, freely branching, compact, densely foliated.

SIZE - To 12 feet, commonly smaller; moderate growth rate.

HARDINESS ZONE - Zone 8. Grown throughout Florida.

NATIVE HABITAT - Japan: Ryukyu Islands.

LEAVES - Simple, opposite, ovate to elliptic to 4 inches long, acute to obtuse apex, shallowly serrate, leathery, deeply impressed veins make upper surface appear verrucate (= puckered), bacon odor when crushed.

STEM/BARK - Stems green, maturing to light brown, covered with numerous rough, wartly lenticels (much more pronounced than on *V. odoratissimum*).

FLOWERS - White, faintly tinged with pink, tubular to 0.25 inch, in dense corymbose panicles to 1.5 inches across; flowers in spring.

FRUIT - Drupe; ovoid, 0.25 inch long, red, sparingly produced in Florida.

CULTURE- Full sun to partial shade, varied soils; moderate to good tolerance of soil salinity. Will tolerate some heat, but does not perform well in hot, exposed sites such as parking lots.

PROBLEMS - Scale, whitefly, nematodes, none serious.

PROPAGATION - Cuttings.

LANDSCAPE USES - Foundation, clipped or unclipped hedge, border, planter.

Viburnum tinus   LAURUSTINUS

PRONUNCIATION - vī 'bər nəm   'tī nəs

TRANSLATION - [ancient Latin name for *V. lantana*] [Tinus, pre-Linnaean name for the plant].

FORM - Monoecious, evergreen shrub, upright, columnar, dense, compact, and medium-textured.

SIZE - Reaches a height of 10 feet and a spread of 4 feet. A moderate grower.

HARDINESS ZONE - Zone 7. Should be grown in north Florida only.

NATIVE HABITAT - Mediterranean region.

LEAVES - Opposite, ovate to oblong, to 3 inches long, margins entire and often revolute, acute apex. The very dark green (almost blue-green) leaves, petioles, and leaf margins are pubescent.

STEM/BARK - The young twigs are pubescent and the buds, both terminal and axillary, are prominent.

FLOWERS - Profuse, white to pinkish, 0.25 inch across, in many-flowered terminal cymes, 2 to 3 inches wide. The slightly fragrant flowers are showy and appear in late winter.

FRUIT - Drupe, blue-black, ovoid, small, with an attractive metallic sheen for several weeks in the fall.

CULTURE - Plant in full sun or partial shade on soils of moderate fertility and drainage. Will not tolerate wet feet. It is not salt tolerant.

PROBLEMS - Nematodes, root rot (in areas with poor drainage), aphids, and thrips.

PROPAGATION - Mature wood cuttings.

LANDSCAPE USES - A shrub for background, barrier, or screen plantings. Makes a good clipped or unclipped hedge. A very good plant for giving a vertical line effect.

COMMENTS - Several cultivars exist: **'Compactum'** - dwarf, upright form with dark green foliage; **'Eve Price'** - compact form with smaller leaves and pink-tinged flowers; **'Lucidum'** - larger leaves and inflorescences; **'Robustum'** - mid-sized, with dense, dark green foliage, heavy bloomer; **'Variegatum'** - leaves variegated with yellow markings. Several other *Viburnum* species, including native taxa, are in cultivation in Florida. These include *V. cassinoides, V. japonicum, V. nudum* (Possum Haw), *V. obovatum* (Black Haw), *V. rhytidophyllum, V. setigerum,*

CASUARINACEAE - CASUARINA FAMILY

DICOTYLEDONS; ONE GENUS AND ABOUT 70 SPECIES

GEOGRAPHY:	Southeast Asia to Australia.
GROWTH HABIT:	Xeromorphic trees with somewhat weeping, slender, cylindrical, jointed, and grooved green branches with short internodes, resembling *Equisetum* (the horsetails).
LEAVES:	Minute scale leaves in whorls at nodes.
FLOWERS:	Much reduced, apetalous, unisexual (plants monoecious); male flowers near top of the plant in terminal spikes, in aggregate groups; female flowers subtended by a bract, in dense heads, lateral on lower branches; stamen 1, ovary superior.
FRUIT:	Single samaroid nuts enclosed within a bract, aggregated in cone-like woody structures.
ECONOMIC USES:	Wood is hard and used for furniture manufacturing; also used as ornamentals but have a tendency for weediness in areas of significant rainfall.

ORNAMENTAL GENERA: *Casuarina.*

Casuarina spp.

AUSTRALIAN PINE

PRONUNCIATION - ˌkæ zhū ə ˈrī nə

TRANSLATION - [like cassowary feathers, in reference to long drooping branches].

FORM - Monoecious, evergreen tree; erect, pyramidal; fine texture with many jointed branchlets resembling horsetail; suckering or nonsuckering depending on species.

SIZE - To 70 feet tall with a 40 foot spread; rapid growth rate.

HARDINESS ZONE - Zones 9b-11; can be grown outside in south and central Florida.

NATIVE HABITAT - Pacific Islands and Australia.

LEAVES - Reduced to minute scales; in whorls of 6 or 7 on jointed, dark green, wiry branchlets to 0.03 inch in diameter.

STEM/BARK - Bark becomes rough, exfoliating with age.

FLOWERS - Inconspicuous; male flowers in spikes, female flowers in dense heads that become woody, cone-like, to 0.75 inch long and 0.5 inch in diameter.

FRUIT - One-seeded samara to 0.25 inch long.

CULTURE - Grow in full sun to partial shade on various soils; high salt tolerance.

PROBLEMS - Root rot; brittle; one species suckers profusely.

PROPAGATION - Seeds or division.

LANDSCAPE USES - Windbreaks, screens; erosion prevention along roads or canals; clipped hedges, topiary.

COMMENTS - Several similar species are cultivated in Florida. *Casuarina equisetifolia,* a seashore pioneer tree, does not sucker from the roots. *Casuarina cunninghamiana* suckers from the roots and is the most cold-tolerant species. Australian pines have naturalized and become noxious pests in parts of south Florida. Several species grow throughout California and southwestern states.

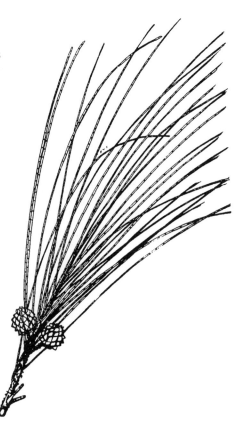

CELASTRACEAE - EUONYMUS FAMILY

DICOTYLEDONS; ABOUT 94 GENERA AND 1300 SPECIES

GEOGRAPHY:	Cosmopolitan except arctics, mainly tropical and subtropical.
GROWTH HABIT:	Trees and shrubs.
LEAVES:	Opposite or alternate, simple, leathery.
FLOWERS:	Small, greenish, actinomorphic, uni- or bisexual, 5-merous; ovary superior; usually in cymose inflorescences.
FRUIT:	Loculicidal or indehiscent capsule, a samara, a berry, or a drupe; seeds often covered by a colorful aril.
ECONOMIC USES:	Many are ornamentals, source of khat leaves (*Catha edulis* - Arabian tea), timber, seed oil, and a dye.

ORNAMENTAL GENERA: *Cassine, Catha, Celastrus, Elaeodendron, Euonymus, Hippocratea, Maytenus, Paxistima,* and probably others.

Euonymus fortunei

CREEPING EUONYMUS,
WINTERCREEPER

PRONUNCIATION - yū ˈɑ nə məs   for ˈtū nē ī

TRANSLATION - [based on the ancient Greek name *euonymon dendron*, meaning "wood of good name"] [Robert Fortune (1812-1880), Scottish horticulturist and collector in China].

FORM - Monoecious, evergreen creeping vine or small shrub, densely foliated and branched, of medium texture.

SIZE - Can reach a height of 6 feet as a shrub form, spreads up to 15 feet as a vining ground cover. Grows at a moderate pace.

HARDINESS ZONE - Zone 4. Grown in north Florida. Can also be grown in central Florida, but performs marginally there.

NATIVE HABITAT - Central and western China.

LEAVES - Opposite, elliptic, ovate or obovate, 1 to 2 inches long. The dark green leaves have crenate to serrate margins.

STEM/BARK - The twigs remain green for several years and often produce aerial rootlets. Has both juvenile and adult growth; the adult fruiting form is shrublike, while the juvenile form is sprawling or vining. Juvenile growth will become adult if allowed to climb on a support.

FLOWERS - Greenish-white, small, inconspicuous, in long-peduncled axillary cymes in late spring.

FRUIT - Capsule; pinkish, 4-parted, splits in fall to reveal whitish seed covered by red-orange arils. Borne only on adult forms.

CULTURE - Grows under almost all light conditions on a very wide range of soils. It has good salt tolerance.

PROBLEMS - Euonymus scale and powdery mildew can be serious problems.

PROPAGATION - Semi-hardwood cuttings root easily. Stock plant's juvenile or adult form is transmitted to its cuttings.

LANDSCAPE USES - Depends on cultivar and form. Trailing forms are used as ground covers or vines; shrub forms in foundation plantings, etc.

COMMENTS - There are hundreds of cultivars, many variegated. Unfortunately, its usefulness may be limited by its disease problems. The variety *radicans* and cultivar **'Silver Queen'** are also grown.

I·M·B

Euonymus japonicus JAPANESE EUONYMUS

PRONUNCIATION - yū ˈɑ nə məs   jə ˈpɑ nə kə

TRANSLATION - [based on the ancient Greek name *euonymon dendron*, meaning "wood of good name"] [from Japan].

FORM - Monoecious, evergreen shrub, upright, compact, of medium texture.

SIZE - Can reach a height of 15 feet with a 6 foot spread. Grows at a fairly rapid rate.

HARDINESS ZONE - Zone 7. Should be grown only in north Florida.

NATIVE HABITAT - Japan.

LEAVES - Opposite, elliptic to ovate, 1 to 3 inches long, leathery, apex obtuse to acute, glossy dark green above and light green below with slightly serrate margins. Leaves are held upright at about a 45 ° angle from the vertical stem.

STEM/BARK - The stout, glabrous twigs, which remain green for several years, have prominent green axillary buds.

FLOWERS - Greenish-white, small, inconspicuous, in axillary cymes in late spring.

FRUIT - Capsules; pinkish, 3- to 4-valved, splits in fall to reveal whitish seeds enclosed by orange arils. Rarely in sufficient quantity to be ornamental.

CULTURE - Grows under any light condition (full sun to dense shade) on a very wide range of soils. Most variegated cultivars require full sun for maximum variegation. It has moderate to good salt and drought tolerance. Easily transplanted. Difficult to maintain a dense, full plant due to pest problems.

PROBLEMS - Euonymus scale is a very serious problem; powdery mildew, leaf spots, aphids, whitefly.

PROPAGATION - Semi-hardwood and hardwood cuttings root easily.

LANDSCAPE USES - A tough, durable plant, employed as a specimen shrub or in hedges. Tolerates heavy pruning well.

COMMENTS - There are many cultivars, most with some degree of yellow, white or silver variegation: **'Albo-marginata'** - leaves with narrow white border; **'Argenteo-variegata'**, **'Aureo-marginata'** - bright gold leaf margin; **'Aureo-variegata'** - medium green leaf with yellow patches; **'Duc d' Anjou'**, **'Macrophylla'** - larger green leaves; **'Mediopicta'**, **'Microphylla'** - dwarf form, 1 to 3 feet tall, with smaller leaves; **'Silver King'** - pale green leaf with creamy white blotches.

CHRYSOBALANACEAE - CHRYSOBALANUS FAMILY

DICOTYLEDONS; 17 GENERA AND ABOUT 400 SPECIES

GEOGRAPHY:	Tropical and subtropical lowlands of the Old World and the New World.
GROWTH HABIT:	Trees and shrubs.
LEAVES:	Alternate, simple, stipulate.
FLOWERS:	Predominantly zygomorphic, mostly bisexual, but sometimes unisexual; 5-merous, with 2 to numerous stamens; perigynous with superior ovary.
FRUIT:	Dry or fleshy drupe.
ECONOMIC USES:	The wood of some species is used in construction and for charcoal. Several species are cultivated for their edible fruit, and oil is extracted from seeds of many species.

ORNAMENTAL GENERA: *Chrysobalanus, Couepia, Licania, Parinari,* and probably others.

Chrysobalanus icaco

COCO PLUM

PRONUNCIATION - ˈkrī sō ˈbæ lə nəs   i ˈkɑ kō

TRANSLATION - [golden acorn, in reference to the yellow fruit of some species] [Spanish for cocoplum].

FORM - Monoecious, evergreen shrub; rounded vase, spreading, dome-shaped, densely foliated; medium texture.

SIZE - Reaches a height of 15 feet with a 20 foot spread; medium growth rate.

HARDINESS ZONE - Zones 10-11, can be grown in south Florida and coastal areas of central Florida. Severely damaged by sub-freezing temperatures.

NATIVE HABITAT - Coastal beaches and dunes, hammocks and edges of freshwater swamps of south Florida and tropical America.

LEAVES - Simple; alternate; suborbicular to broadly obovate, to 3 inches long; shiny, leathery with obtuse or emarginate apices; new growth often red-tinged. Dark green.

FLOWERS - White; in short, axillary cymes 0.25 inch long, inconspicuous. Main bloom period is late spring, but some flowering occurs all year.

FRUIT - Pulpy drupes; dark purple or pinkish-white; 1.5 inches long. Fruit and the large, angled, obovoid seed are edible but not very good. Maximum fruiting is in late summer.

CULTURE - Grows in full sun or partial shade on a wide range of soils; medium salt tolerance.

PROBLEMS - Pest-free.

PROPAGATION - Seed germinate readily if not allowed to dry out. Leafy cuttings root well under mist.

LANDSCAPE USES - Makes a very good background, screen, or specimen shrub for its unusual, dense, low, symmetrically spreading form. Also makes a handsome clipped hedge.

COMMENTS - 2 common varieties: the typical var. *icaco* (round, pinkish-white fruit; yellow-green new growth) and var. *pellocarpus* (ellipsoidal, dark purple fruit; burgundy new growth; more ornamental; marginal salt tolerance). Cultivars **'Greentip'**, **'Red Tip'**, **'Horizontal'** and *C. oliviforme* (Satin Leaf) are commonly grown.

CLUSIACEAE (= GUTTIFERAE) - GARCINIA FAMILY

DICOTYLEDONS; ABOUT 40 GENERA AND MORE THAN 1000 SPECIES

GEOGRAPHY: Cosmopolitan but predominantly tropical.

GROWTH HABIT: Trees and shrubs.

LEAVES: Opposite, simple, entire, exstipulate, often with oil glands.

FLOWERS: Bisexual or unisexual (plants dioecious or polygamous); 4- or 5-merous; stamens numerous; ovary superior.

FRUIT: A capsule, but may be berry- or drupe-like.

ECONOMIC USES: Ornamentals, timber, drugs, dyes, and fruit.

ORNAMENTAL GENERA: *Calophyllum, Clusia, Garcenia, Hypericum, Mammea, Platonia, Rheedia, Symphonia,* and others.

Calophyllum brasiliense

BRAZILIAN BEAUTY LEAF, CALABA TREE, SANTA MARIA

PRONUNCIATION - ˈkæ lə ˈfi ləm   brə ˌsi lē ˈen sē

TRANSLATION - [beautiful leaf, in reference to the venation pattern] [from Brazil].

FORM - Polygamous, evergreen tree; upright oval, bushy and densely foliated; medium-coarse texture.

SIZE - May reach 60 feet in height, but tends to be a small tree about 20 to 30 feet tall with a 15 to 20 foot spread; slow growth rate.

HARDINESS ZONE - Zones 10-11, can be grown only in south Florida.

NATIVE HABITAT - The West Indies and ttropical America.

LEAVES - Simple; opposite; elliptic or oval to 4 inches long; leathery; rounded apices; numerous, parallel lateral veins at right angles to the midrib; entire margins. Medium green.

STEM/BARK - Stems bleed yellow latex when injured. The wood is valuable for shipbuilding and cabinet work.

FLOWERS - Uni- or bisexual, white; 0.25 inch wide; in few-flowered axillary racemes to 1.5 inches long; fragrant.

FRUIT - Drupe; globose, long.

CULTURE - Plant in full to partial sun on well-drained soil; good salt tolerance.

PROBLEMS - Relatively pest-free.

PROPAGATION - Seeds or cuttings.

LANDSCAPE USES - Street or shade tree, especially for coastal areas; can be used as a screen if maintained as a shrub.

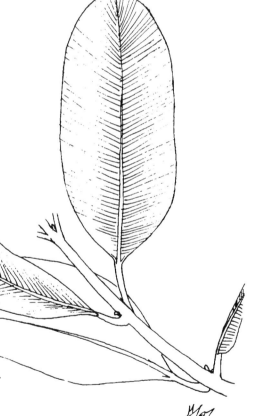

Calophyllum inophyllum

BEAUTY LEAF

PRONUNCIATION - ˈkæ lə ˈfi ləm   ˈin ə ˈfi ləm

TRANSLATION - [beautiful leaf, in reference to the venation pattern] [fibrous-leaved].

FORM - Polygamous, evergreen tree; upright, pyramidal; densely foliated; becomes twisted and misshapen when exposed to constant wind; coarse texture.

SIZE - Can reach 60 feet in height with a 20 to 40 foot spread, but generally is much smaller; slow growth rate.

HARDINESS ZONE - Zones 10b-11, can be grown only in south Florida, but must be planted in a protected location to avoid severe damage in freezes.

NATIVE HABITAT - Coastal regions from India to the Malay Peninsula.

LEAVES - Simple; opposite; oval to oblong, to 7 inches long; dark green, glossy, stiff, leathery; numerous, distinct parallel veins at right angles to the midrib; entire margins.

STEM/BARK - Trunks have light gray, shallowly ridged bark. The wood is valued for boat building and cabinetwork.

FLOWERS - Uni- or bisexual, white; 0.75 inch across; showy and very fragrant; in axillary racemes to 8 inches long. Blooms in summer.

FRUIT - Drupe; yellow; globose to 1.5 inches wide; contains a single seed with a nutlike kernel that may be poisonous.

CULTURE - Grown in full sun or partial shade on well-drained soils; wind and salt tolerant.

PROBLEMS - Generally pest-free.

PROPAGATION - Seeds or cuttings.

LANDSCAPE USES - A specimen/street/shade tree, especially useful in coastal locations; sometimes used as a tall hedge around tennis courts and public spaces.

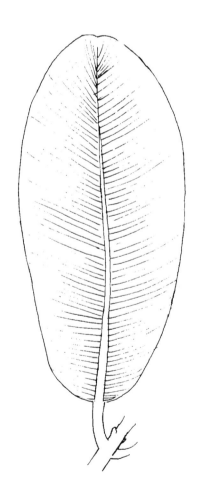

Clusia major

BALSAM APPLE,
PITCH APPLE

PRONUNCIATION - ˈklū zē ə ˈmā jər

TRANSLATION - [in honor of Carolus Clusius (1526-1609), a Flemish botanist] [large].

SYNONYM - *Clusia rosea.*

FORM - Dioecious, evergreen tree; irregular branching, horizontal canopy, wide-spreading, densely foliated; coarse texture.

SIZE - To 50 feet, commonly 10 to 15 feet; rapid growth rate.

HARDINESS ZONE - Zones 10-11, can be grown outside only in south Florida.

NATIVE HABITAT - West Indies; in Florida, possibly the Keys.

LEAVES - Simple; opposite; obovate to 8 inches long; truncate tip; dark green, stiff, leathery; no conspicuous lateral veins.

FLOWERS - Unisexual, pink and white; to 2 inches across; solitary, terminal, glossy; plastic appearance.

FRUIT - Capsule; spherical to 3 inches across; fleshy; resinous, inedible.

CULTURE - Full sun to partial shade; various well-drained soils; high salt tolerance.

PROBLEMS - Scale.

PROPAGATION - Seeds and cuttings.

LANDSCAPE USES - Used as a specimen tree, in informal borders and screens, or in urn plantings.

COMMENTS - A variegated cultivar is occasionally seen, as well as **'Nana'** (Dwarf Pitch Apple). A related species with small leaves, *C. guttifera* (Small Leaf Clusia), is becoming increasingly popular.

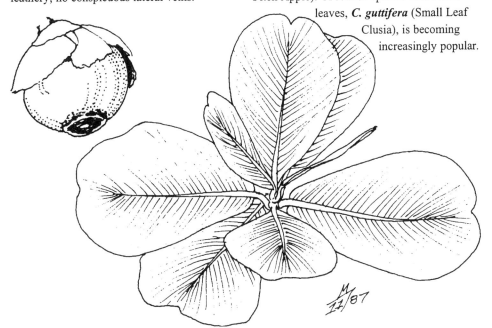

COMBRETACEAE - COMBRETUM FAMILY

DICOTYLEDONS; 20 GENERA AND ABOUT 500 SPECIES

GEOGRAPHY:	Primarily tropical, with a few species extending into the subtropics.
GROWTH HABIT:	Large to small trees, shrubs, woody vines, some with rhizomes and a few are mangrove plants.
LEAVES:	Alternate or opposite, simple, entire, and lack stipules.
FLOWERS:	Small, actinomorphic, usually bisexual, in many-flowered clusters; 5-merous, sometimes apetalous; stamens in two rows of 4 or 5; ovary inferior, surrounded by a disk.
FRUIT:	Fleshy or dry with wings: viviparous in mangrove species, water, animal or wind dispersed in others.
ECONOMIC USES:	Ornamentals and an important source of timber in the tropics.

ORNAMENTAL GENERA: *Buchenavia, Bucida, Combretum, Conocarpus, Laguncularia, Quisqualis, Terminalia,* and others.

Bucida buceras   BLACK OLIVE

PRONUNCIATION - byū ˈsē də   byū ˈsē rəs

TRANSLATION - [crooked horn] [ox-horned]. Both names in reference to the long twisted galls into which the fruit becomes converted by a small mite.

FORM - Monoecious, evergreen or partly deciduous tree, tiered branching, open canopy, fine-textured.

SIZE - To 50 feet, rapid growth rate.

HARDINESS ZONE - Zones 10-11; limited to south Florida only.

NATIVE HABITAT - Central America, West Indies.

LEAVES - Simple, alternate or spirally arranged in pseudowhorls, usually crowded on swollen ends of branches, obovate to 3 inches long, light green, leathery, entire margins; some specimens show red leaf color during cool weather.

STEM/BARK - Branches often bearing 1 inch long spines. The bark becomes checkered into regular squares.

FLOWERS - Greenish-yellow, borne in axillary spikes to 4 inches long, inconspicuous; flowers in late spring and summer.

FRUIT - Drupe; to 1/3 inch long, black, hard, and nut-like. Remnants of calyx present.

CULTURE - Full sun to partial shade, various well-drained soils; highly salt tolerant; wind resistant.

PROBLEMS - Scale, whiteflies, and sooty mold.

PROPAGATION - Seed.

LANDSCAPE USES - As a street, shade, or specimen tree. Because of its resistance to salt and wind, *Bucida* makes an excellent windbreak.

COMMENTS - There is a great deal of seedling variation for such characteristics as height, form, leaf size, and spines. Cultivars with varying growth characteristtics include **'Iron Mike', 'Shady Lady',** and **'Table Top'.**

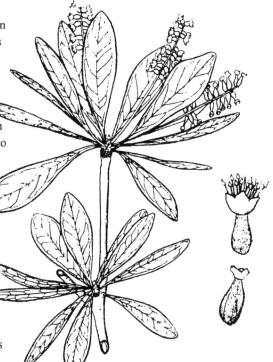

Bucida spinosa   SPINY BLACK OLIVE

PRONUNCIATION - bū ˈsē də   spī ˈnō sə

TRANSLATION - [crooked horn, in reference to twisted galls] [having spines].

FORM - Monoecious, evergreen or semi-deciduous shrub or small tree; rounded; tiered branching, open canopy; fine texture.

SIZE - To 20 feet tall with a 15-foot spread; slow growth rate.

HARDINESS ZONE - Zones 10-11, limited to south Florida only.

NATIVE HABITAT - Bahamas, Cuba.

LEAVES - Simple, alternate or spirally arranged, usually crowded on swollen ends of branches; obovate to 1 inch long; light green, leathery, entire margins.

STEM/BARK - Branches often bear 1/4 inch spines; spines in groups of three. Branches exhibit crooked, zigzag growth.

FLOWERS - White, borne in axillary spikes to 1 inch long; inconspicuous. Blooms year-round.

FRUIT - Drup to 1/4 inch long, black.

CULTURE - Full sun to partial shade, various well-drained soils; high salt, drought, and wind resistance.

PROBLEMS - No major problems; susceptible to some of the same insect and disease problems arising on *B. buceras*: scale, white flies, sooty mold. Medium nutritional requirements.

PROPAGATION - Seeds.

LANDSCAPE USES - As a small tree or shrub. Does not seem to have the same problem of staining masonry as does its larger relative *B. buceras*.

COMMENTS - Small leaves and irregular branches make this species an excellent specimen for bonsai.

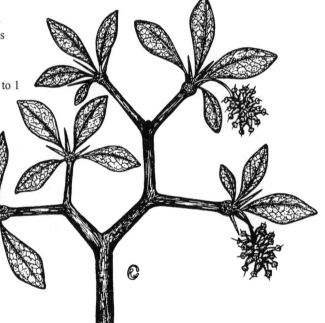

Conocarpus erectus

BUTTONWOOD

PRONUNCIATION - ˈkō nə ˈkɑr pəs   ə ˈrek təs

TRANSLATION - [cone-like fruit] [erect].

FORM - Monoecious, evergreen tree, upright, rounded, narrow-crowned, medium-textured and often contorted where exposed to seashore winds.

SIZE - Reaches a height of 40 feet with a 20-foot spread. A moderate grower.

HARDINESS ZONE - Zones 10-11, can be grown only in south Florida.

NATIVE HABITAT - Coastal swamps of south Florida, tropical America, and West Africa.

LEAVES - Simple, alternate, ovate to elliptic, with entire margins and cuneate bases, to 4 inches long, leathery.

STEM/BARK - The dark brown, attractive bark is ridged and scaly. The wood was formerly used for firewood, cabinetwork, and charcoal making.

FLOWERS - Greenish, conelike heads in terminal panicles appearing throughout the year, 1/3-inch long, not showy.

FRUIT - Conelike, red/brown, 1/2 inch long, disintegrating at maturity into small winged seeds and chaff.

CULTURE - Plant in full sun or partial shade on a wide range of soils. Tolerates salt, wet brackish areas, and alkaline soils.

PROBLEMS - Sooty mold caused by sucking insect secretions.

PROPAGATION - Seed or cuttings.

LANDSCAPE USES - A specimen or street tree, especially useful in coastal locations and sometimes used as a screen or clipped hedge.

COMMENTS - Variety *sericeus* (Silver Buttonwood) has a silvery (canescent) appearance due to silky hairs covering the leaves. Usually a shrub, it must be propagated by cuttings and is the most commonly used Buttonwood. Also the cultivar **'Silver Sheen'** is available in the trade.

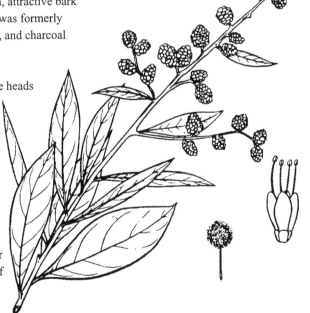

Terminalia catappa   INDIAN ALMOND, TROPICAL ALMOND

PRONUNCIATION - ˈtər mə ˈnæ lē ə   kə ˈtæ pə

TRANSLATION - [leaves at ends, in reference to leaves crowded at the branch tips] [Malayan name].

FORM - Monoecious, deciduous tree, pyramidal, coarse-textured, with branches arranged in horizontal tiers.

SIZE - Generally only reaches 50 feet tall with a 30 foot spread in Florida. Grows at a fairly rapid rate.

HARDINESS ZONE - Zones 10b-11; should be planted only in protected locations in south Florida, as it is severely damaged in freezes.

NATIVE HABITAT - Malay peninsula, mainly along the coast.

LEAVES - Simple, alternate, obviate and crowded at the tips of branches, to 1 foot long and 6 inches wide. The stiff leaves turn bright red and fall in winter, but the tree is bare for only a short while.

FLOWERS - Greenish, tiny, inconspicuous, borne in long, slender "rattail" recurved, terminal spikes to 6 inches long. Blooms mainly in the spring.

FRUIT - Drupes, green, flattened, ellipsoidal, to 2.5 inches long; ripen mainly in summer. The fruit is mainly corky fiber, with thin, green flesh and a slender, edible, almond-like kernel. The fruits were once used in tanning due to high tannic acid content.

CULTURE - Needs full sun, but grows in a wide range of soils and is both wind and salt tolerant. Somewhat messy due to litter from large leaves and fruit.

PROBLEMS - Thrips may cause earlier leaf drop in fall and winter.

PROPAGATION - By seed.

LANDSCAPE USES - A shade, street, or specimen tree, valued for its pagoda-like form and tolerance to seaside conditions.

COMMENTS - Several related species are also in Florida landscapes: *T. arjuna* (Arjan), *T. bellirica, T. mulleri* (Mueller Terminalia, Black Olive), and *T. prunoides.*

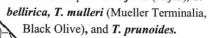

CORNACEAE - DOGWOOD FAMILY

DICOTYLEDONS; 12 OR 13 GENERA AND ABOUT 100 SPECIES

GEOGRAPHY: Mostly north temperate with a few in tropical and subtropical Africa, Central and South America, New Zealand, and Southeast Asia.

GROWTH HABIT: Trees, shrubs, and a few herbaceous.

LEAVES: Opposite or rarely alternate, deciduous or evergreen, simple, entire or serrate.

FLOWERS: Small, actinomorphic, bisexual or unisexual (plants dioecious); 5-merous, occasionally asepalous and apetalous; ovary inferior; in corymbs or umbels, usually surrounded by a series of large, often showy bracts.

FRUIT: Drupe or berry.

ECONOMIC USES: Ornamentals, alcoholic beverage (vin de cornouille) from fruit of *Cornus mas*, and wood for furniture and various implements.

ORNAMENTAL GENERA: *Aucuba, Cornus, Griselinia*, and others.

Aucuba japonica

AUCUBA, GOLD DUST PLANT

PRONUNCIATION - o ˈkū bə   jə ˈpɑ nə kə

TRANSLATION - [Latinized Japanese name] [from Japan].

FORM - Dioecious, evergreen shrub, upright, many-branched, leafless on basal portions of branches. Coarse texture.

SIZE - To 15 feet, commonly 2 to 4 feet in Florida, slow growth.

HARDINESS ZONE - Zone 7. Grows well in north and central Florida only.

NATIVE HABITAT - Himalayas to Japan.

LEAVES - Simple, opposite, ovate to elliptic to 7 inches long, dark green, often variegated with white or yellow spots, leathery, glossy, coarsely toothed above the middle, apex acute to acuminate.

STEM/BARK - Stout, glabrous, green stems with shield-shaped leaf scars joined by stipular scar, large terminal bud.

FLOWERS - Purple, clustered in terminal panicles, not showy.

FRUIT - Drupe, oblong, red, rarely yellow or white, to 0.5 inch in diameter, ripens in early winter. Hidden by the foliage, therefore not particularly ornamental.

CULTURE - Partial to deep shade, well-drained, fertile soils; slightly salt tolerant. Easily transplanted. Drought tolerant if shaded, but will not tolerate high heat situations, such as parking lots. Also makes a good houseplant.

PROBLEMS - Scale, nematodes, sooty mold, none serious.

PROPAGATION - Roots easily from cuttings.

LANDSCAPE USES - Mass plantings, urn, patio use, shaded border plantings. Good substitute for *Codiaeum variegatum* (croton) in the northern part of the state.

COMMENTS - Many cultivars with different leaf shapes, variegation: **'Crotonifolia'** - white-spotted leaves; **'Dentata'** (**'Serratifolia'**)- smaller, coarsely toothed leaves; **'Fructo Albo'** - pale pinkish fruit, silver-variegated foliage; **'Goldeana'**; **'Longifolia'** (**'Angustifolia'**, **'Salicifolia'**) - leaves narrow, to 5 inches, deep green. True **'Longifolia'** and **'Salicifolia'** are female; **'Angustifolia'** is male. **'Macrophylla'** - large, broad leaves; female; **'Nana'** - dwarf, compact form; probably a collective name for several clones; better fruit display since fruits are held above the foliage (female selections only); **'Picturata'** - large yellow blotch in center. **'Sulfurea'** - dark green leaf with golden margins; **'Variegata'** - yellow flecked foliage; female; compact form. Note: nomenclature of cultivars is somewhat confused. Also reported is *A. himalaica*.

Cornus florida   FLOWERING DOGWOOD

PRONUNCIATION - ˈkor nəs   ˈflo rə də

TRANSLATION - [Latin for horn, in reference to the toughness of the wood] [floriferous].

FORM - Deciduous tree, small, symmetrical, central leader with broad, rounded canopy. Medium texture.

SIZE - To 40 feet, medium growth rate.

HARDINESS ZONE - Zone 4. North and central Florida.

NATIVE HABITAT - Temperate eastern United States, including Florida.

LEAVES - Simple, entire, opposite, ovate, to 6 inches long, acute to short-acuminate, surface crinkled, light green, arcuate venation, fine silky threads visible when veins broken; some fall color (red to maroon) in Florida, but more outstanding farther north; new growth pubescent beneath.

STEM/BARK - Sympodial branching, slender young twigs green or greenish-purple often with waxy bloom. Older stems grayish-brown; trunks developing scaly bark with "alligator hide" effect. Two types of buds present for much of year--larger, globose, terminal, flower buds and smaller, valvate, terminal, or lateral vegetative buds.

FLOWERS - Small, dense heads subtended by 4 showy petal-like bracts; bracts white, obovate, notched; actual flowers greenish-yellow, not showy. Flowers in early spring (late Feb. to Mar., in Fla.), before leaves expand.

FRUIT - Drupe; red, to 0.5 inch long, in clusters of 3 to 4, showy in autumn.

CULTURE - Full sun to partial shade, fertile, well-drained acid soils; slightly salt tolerant. Will not tolerate drought, waterlogged conditions, pollution, or compacted soils.

Extremely sensitive to herbicides. Flowers best in full sun, but will not tolerate hot, dry sites, such as parking lots. Prune, if neccessary, shortly after flowering to avoid removing flower buds set during the summer.

PROBLEMS - Borers (generally attack weakened plants), root rot, thrips, micronutrient deficiencies (on alkaline soils), leaf spots; generally problem-free if proper planting site is chosen.

PROPAGATION - Seed, grafting; difficult to root cuttings.

LANDSCAPE USES - Specimen, framing tree, patio use, small shade tree; birds attracted by the fruit.

COMMENTS - Several cultivars, including some with pink bracts. These, however, do not receive sufficient winter chilling to grow well in Florida. Tremendous variation in flowering and fall color among seedlings. **'Cherokee Princess'** - large white bracts, blooms at early age; **'Cloud 9'** - heavy-blooming white, heavy fruiting, patented; **'First Lady'** - yellow-green variegated leaves; **'Weaver'** is resistant to leaf spot; **'White Cloud'**- heavy-blooming, old cultivar; **'Xanthocarpa'** - yellow fruit. Many more. Several other species of *Cornus* are native to Florida and are becoming increasingly popular: *C. foemina (= C. stricta)* (Stiff Cornel).

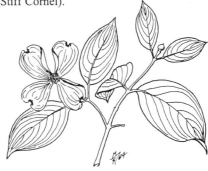

CRASSULACEAE - ORPINE FAMILY

DICOTYLEDONS; 33-35 GENERA AND ABOUT 1,500 SPECIES

GEOGRAPHY:	Predominantly in South Africa but cosmopolitan in warm, dry regions.
GROWTH HABIT:	Perennial or rarely annual or biennial succulent herbs and subshrubs.
LEAVES:	To a greater or lesser extent fleshy, usually entire or infrequently serrate and sometimes with plantlets on leaf margins (*Kalanchoe* sect. *Bryophyllum*), commonly clustered in rosettes at branch tips, and usually variously pubescent and/or glaucous.
FLOWERS:	Small but often numerous, in large corymbs or panicles; usually 5-merous, all parts free, perigynous; stamens in 1 or 2 rows; ovary superior.
FRUIT:	Groups of follicles.
ECONOMIC USES:	Important ornamentals, especially in rock gardens, some of considerable importance in floriculture.

ORNAMENTAL GENERA: *Aeonium, Crassula, Echeveria, Kalanchoe, Rochea, Sedum, Sempervivum,* and several others.

Crassula argentea

JADE PLANT

PRONUNCIATION - ˈkræs yū lə   ɑr ˈgen tē ə

TRANSLATION - [from Latin *crassus* (= thick), in reference to the fleshy leaves] [silvery].

FORM - Monoecious, evergreen shrub; irregular, stout, succulent, glabrous; compact habit; medium texture.

SIZE - To 10 feet tall and 8 feet wide. Very slow growth.

HARDINESS ZONE - Zones 10-11; requires cold protection, although it does well in cool but frost-free areas.

NATIVE HABITAT - South Africa.

LEAVES- Simple; opposite; 4-ranked, obovate, thick, fleshy pads to 2 inches long; glossy medium green; under high light edges become red-tinged; subsessile.

STEM/BARK - Young stems are green, herbaceous, and cylindrical; with time develop ringed bark.

FLOWERS - Small; pink or white; star-shaped; in terminal cymes. Blooms from November to April in California; does not seem to flower well in Florida.

FRUIT - Follicles.

CULTURE - Full sun or deep shade, indoors down to 50 foot-candles; prefers soil on the dry side; moderate salt tolerance.

PROBLEMS - Few; scale sometimes a problem. Overwatering results in excessive growth and loss of proper growth.

PROPAGATION - Leaf or stem cuttings.

LANDSCAPE USES - Container plant, patio garden specimen; common houseplant.

COMMENTS - 'Tricolor' is an attractive variegated cultivar. *Crassula falcata* (Airplane Plant) is also commonly sold for indoor use.

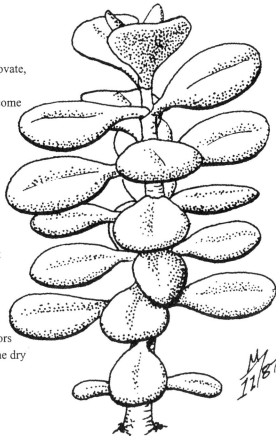

Echeveria spp.

HEN-AND-CHICKENS

PRONUNCIATION - ˈe chə ˈvā rē ə

TRANSLATION - [after Athanasio Echeverriay Godoy, eighteenth-century Mexican botanical illustrator].

FORM - Monoecious, rosetting, perennial, succulent herbs and shrubs.

SIZE - Variable; usually under 1 foot; flowering stalks usually under 3 feet.

HARDINESS ZONE - Zones 10-11 for outdoor use; greenhouse or indoor plants anywhere. Plant grows well in frost-free areas.

NATIVE HABITAT - Texas to Argentina; most of the more or less 150 species from Mexico.

LEAVES - Spirally arranged along a short stem creating a rosette effect; fleshy, sessile, usually glaucous.

STEM/BARK - Green fleshy stems, usually very short and not seen due to crowded, sessile leaves.

FLOWERS - Yellow to red; campanulate or urceolate; borne on axillary branched inflorescences of various types (cincinnus, thyrse, raceme, spike).

FRUIT - Capsule.

CULTURE - Allow soil to dry well before watering. Greenhouse and houseplants require good sunlight to prevent stretching of stems.

PROBLEMS - Plants are prone to overwatering and root rot.

PROPAGATION - Leaf cuttings will root and produce plantlets at their bases.

LANDSCAPE USES - Good rock garden subjects in frost-free areas. With more than 100 species, mostly popular among succulent fanciers.

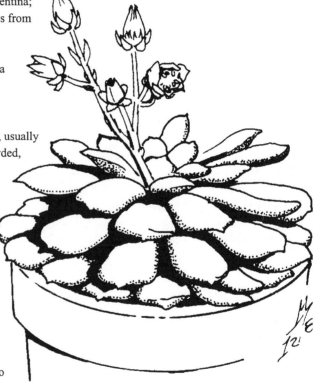

Kalanchoe blossfeldiana   KALANCHOE

PRONUNCIATION - ˈkæ lən kō ē   ˈblos fel dē ˈā nə

TRANSLATION - [from Chinese name of one species] [after Robert Blossfeld, German nurseryman].

FORM - Monoecious, evergreen; herbaceous perennial; succulent, glabrous, upright, much branched; medium-fine texture.

SIZE - Usually to 12 inches, many cultivars 6 to 18 inches. Medium growth rate.

HARDINESS ZONE - Zones 10-11, in protected sites; sensitive to chilling.

NATIVE HABITAT - Madagascar.

LEAVES - Simple; opposite; elliptic-oblong, 1 to 3 inches long, obtuse; waxy; green or bronze depending on light intensities; margins crenate and midrib conspicuous on upper leaf surface. Petioles to 1 inch long.

FLOWERS - Yellow, pink, orange and red; corolla tube to 0.25 inch long, lobes to 0.25 inch long; borne in many-flowered, terminal cymes. Blooms in response to short day lengths.

FRUIT - Follicles.

CULTURE - Full sun to partial shade on a wide variety of soils; temperatures above 40°F; moderate salt tolerance.

PROBLEMS - Caterpillars, mealybugs, yellowing of lower leaves.

PROPAGATION - Cuttings, seeds.

LANDSCAPE USES - Indoors as a table or shelf plant; outdoors as a bedding plant.

COMMENTS - A common florist pot plant. Many excellent cultivars are available for compact form and flower color. Most of the plants grown as commercial floriculture crops are hybrids with *K. flammea* and *K. pumila.*

Kalanchoe tomentosa   PANDA PLANT

PRONUNCIATION - 'kæ lən kō ē   ˌtō mən 'tō sə

TRANSLATION - [from Chinese name of one species] [densely woolly].

FORM - Monoecious, evergreen; herbaceous perennial; succulent; medium-coarse texture.

SIZE - Grows to 10-30 inches tall, depending on soil moisture; fast growth rate.

HARDINESS ZONE - Zones 10-11; grown outside only in south Florida.

NATIVE HABITAT - Madagascar.

LEAVES - Simple; alternate; variable in shape but mostly oblong-ovate to 3 inches long; sessile; thick; densely covered with silvery, 3-branched hairs; margins entire at base, becoming crenate toward tip; the crenate edges are covered with brown hairs.

STEM/BARK - Succulent, densely hairy (tomentose).

FLOWERS - Yellow; tubular corolla to 0.5 inch long; borne in a cyme on a 1 to 2.5-foot-tall terminal inflorescence. Blooms in winter; rarely flowers in Florida.

FRUIT - Follicle.

CULTURE - Grown in full sun to partial shade in light, well-drained soils. Tolerates drought and moderate amounts of wind or soilborne salt.

PROBLEMS - Leaf spot diseases can be a problem under humid conditions.

PROPAGATION - Leaf and stem cuttings.

LANDSCAPE USES - Use outdoors in specialized areas such as succulent or rock gardens or in planters. Occasionally grown as an interior pot or dish garden plant.

COMMENTS - *Kalanchoe tomentosa* is grown for its foliage characteristics. It is not well adapted to conditions of high humidity. With about 125 species, *Kalanchoe* is a large genus of various sizes, leaf shapes, and colors, and popular in rock gardens.

Sedum morganianum BURRO'S TAIL, DONKEY'S TAIL

PRONUNCIATION - 'sē dəm mor ˌgæ nē 'ā nəm

TRANSLATION - [classical Latin name for several succulent plants, from *sedo* (= to sit)] [in honor of Dr. Meredith Morgan who grew the plant soon after its discovery].

FORM - Monoecious, evergreen; herbaceous perennial; succulent, trailing; medium-fine texture.

SIZE - Trailing or hanging stems to 3 feet in length.

HARDINESS ZONE - Zones 10-11; protected locations in Zone 9b.

NATIVE HABITAT - Mexico.

LEAVES - Simple; oblong-lanceolate to 1 inch long; 0.5 inch thick; acute, nearly cylindrical; turgid, light gray-green; sessile.

STEM/BARK - Pendulous; branching at base; persistent-leafy.

FLOWERS - Pink to deep red; 0.5 inch long; borne in a terminal corymbose, 6 to 12 flowered, inflorescence. Blooms in spring; rarely seen.

FRUIT - Follicle.

CULTURE - Partial shade; protect from cold and mechanical damage; rich, well-drained soil; slight salt tolerance.

PROBLEMS - Loses leaves in low-humidity environment.

PROPAGATION - Cuttings; individual leaves root readily.

LANDSCAPE USES - Handsome basket or planter specimen; also used in rock gardens and as ground cover.

COMMENTS - Many other species of *Sedum* are available in California and areas of lower humidity. A few other species, however, are sold in Florida, including *S. acre* (Mossy Stonecrop - a Florida native) and *S. sarmentosum* (Star Sedum). With more than 300 species, *Sedum* is a large genus with several potentially useful plants for garden and hanging basket planting.

ELAEAGNACEAE - OLEASTER FAMILY

DICOTYLEDONS; 3 GENERA AND ABOUT 50 SPECIES

GEOGRAPHY: North temperate, south Asia, and Australia.

GROWTH HABIT: Much branched, often thorny shrubs in which all parts are covered with scale-like silvery or sometimes golden patches of pubescence.

LEAVES: Alternate, opposite or whorled, simple, entire, and usually coriaceous.

FLOWERS: Small, solitary or clustered or in racemes; bi- or unisexual (plants dioecious); 4-merous, apetalous, ovary superior.

FRUIT: An achene or drupe-like.

ECONOMIC USES: Primarily as ornamentals but minor uses of the edible fruits.

ORNAMENTAL GENERA: *Elaeagnus* and *Hippophaë.*

Elaeagnus pungens   SILVER THORN

PRONUNCIATION - 'e lā 'æg nəs   'pun jənz

TRANSLATION - [from Greek *helodes* (= marshy) and *hagnos* (= pure), in reference to the white fluffy masses of fruit in some species of willow, to which the name was originally applied] [spiny, in reference to thorns on branches].

FORM - Monoecious, evergreen shrub, large, sprawling, drooping, and spreading. Medium-coarse texture.

SIZE - To 15 feet, very rapid growth.

HARDINESS ZONE - Zone 7. Grown in all regions of Florida.

NATIVE HABITAT - China, Japan.

LEAVES - Simple, spirally arranged, ovate-elliptic, to 3 inches long, entire, margin undulate, acute apex, underside silvery with brown dots, scurfy.

STEM/BARK - Young growth covered with silvery scales, branches often thorny.

FLOWERS - To 0.5 inch in length, silvery-white, tubular, inconspicuous in axillary clusters, pleasantly fragrant, blooming in late autumn (Oct.-Nov.).

FRUIT - Drupe; red, to 1 inch long, seldom seen, edible, ripens in spring.

CULTURE - Full sun to partial shade, varied soils; highly salt, drought, and heat tolerant. Appears also to be pollution tolerant. So easily grown that it is almost a weed. Requires frequent pruning due to very rapid growth of the individual shoots. Needs lots of space.

PROBLEMS - Mites (during dry weather), scale, micronutrient deficiencies (on alkaline soils); none serious.

PROPAGATION - Seeds, cuttings.

LANDSCAPE USES - Screen, barrier plant, highway plantings (where it flourishes), embankments (its tendency to sucker helps stabilize soil), accent planting, hedge. Frequently used as clipped hedge, requiring endless pruning; develops an attractive arching form if left alone. Fruit attracts wildlife.

COMMENTS - Several cultivars are available: **'Aurea'** - yellow margins on leaves; **'Fruitlandii'** - rounded, undulate leaves; dense; **'Maculata'** (**'Aureo-maculata'**) - green leaf with yellow center; **'Simonii'** - pink and yellow variegation on leaves; **'Variegata'** - leaf margins yellowish-white; and others. Nomenclature of the cultivars is somewhat confused. The origin of **'Clemsonii'** and **'Coral Silver'** are unknown. Related species available for sale include: *E.* × *ebbengei* (*E. macrophylla* × *E. pungens*), *E. latifolia* (Chinese Silverberry), *E. philippinensis* (Lingaro), and *E. macrophylla.*

ERICACEAE - HEATH FAMILY

DICOTYLEDONS; ABOUT 100 GENERA AND 3500 SPECIES

GEOGRAPHY: Cosmopolitan, but chiefly in Asia, New Guinea, and southern Africa; largely absent from Australia.

GROWTH HABIT: Shrubs and small trees of acid soil habitats and often mycorrhizae dependent for their growth.

LEAVES: Alternate, simple, usually evergreen, sometimes xeromorphic and needle-shaped.

FLOWERS: Solitary or in various inflorescence types; actinomorphic, usually bisexual, 4- or 5-merous; sepals often fused (synsepalous), petals fused (sympetalous) or sometimes free; stamens 4-10 but may be reduced to 4-5; ovary usually superior but sometimes inferior.

FRUIT: In genera with superior ovary (e.g., *Rhododendron*), a capsule; in genera with inferior ovary (e.g., *Vaccinium*), a berry.

ECONOMIC USES: Widely cultivated ornamentals.

ORNAMENTAL GENERA: *Agarista, Arbutus, Cavendishia, Cladothamnus, Enkianthus, Erica, Gaultheria, Kalmia, Ledum, Leucothoë, Lyonia, Oxydendrum, Pieris, Rhododendron, Vaccinium,* and others.

Kalmia latifolia

MOUNTAIN LAUREL

PRONUNCIATION - 'kæl mē ə   ˌlæ tə 'fō lē ə

TRANSLATION - [after Pehr Kalm (1715-1779), Finnish student of Linnaeus] [broad-leaved].

FORM - Monoecious, evergreen shrub or small tree, rounded, upright, symmetrical, compact, of medium texture.

SIZE - Becomes 20 feet tall in the wild, but generally is around 7 feet tall and 5 feet in spread in cultivation. Rate of growth is slow.

HARDINESS ZONE - Zone 5. Grown only in north Florida.

NATIVE HABITAT - Understory shrub of moist woods in eastern North America and the panhandle region of Florida.

LEAVES - Alternate, or sometimes in pseudo-whorls, elliptic and leathery, to 5 inches long, glabrous, entire, acute to short-acuminate apices with whitish calluses at extreme leaf tip, reddish petioles 0.25 to 1 inch long. The leaves are poisonous.

STEM/BARK - Multiple trunks are irregular, crooked, and have reddish-brown, shredding bark. Young twigs are reddish.

FLOWERS - White to pink to rose, saucer-shaped and angled, to 1 inch wide, 10 stamens held in pouches formed by the corolla lobes. The intricate, showy flowers are borne in terminal corymbs, 4 to 6 inches across, in late March to April. Even the star-like buds are attractive.

FRUIT - Capsules; round, 0.25 inch wide, dry, 5-celled, contain many seeds and ripen in fall. Not ornamental.

CULTURE - Plant in partial shade on moist, acid soils of moderate fertility and drainage. It is not salt tolerant. Will not tolerate hot, dry conditions or alkaline soils. Mulch to keep soil moist and cool. Rather choosy about growing conditions.

PROBLEMS - Leaf miners, lace bug, scale, borers, flower blight, and leaf spot disease (usually associated with plants under stress).

PROPAGATION - Veneer grafting or layering for cultivars, or seed, which should be sown on the surface of sphagnum moss and exposed to cold temperatures. Difficult to root cuttings. Now being commercially produced by tissue culture.

LANDSCAPE USES - A specimen shrub, more effective when massed. Occasionally used on the north side in large foundation and corner plantings. Naturalized settings.

COMMENTS - Cultivars are available with flowers from pure white to red. *Kalmia latifolia* '**Myrtifolia**' is a dwarf selection with leaves only 1.5 inches long.

Rhododendron austrinum   FLORIDA FLAME AZALEA

PRONUNCIATION - ˈrō də ˈden drən   o ˈstrī nəm

TRANSLATION - [the Greek name for *Nerium oleander*, from *rhodo* (= red) and *dendron* (= a tree)] [southern].

FORM - Monoecious, deciduous, upright, vase-shaped shrub, medium-textured, sparingly branched.

SIZE - Reaches a height of 10 feet and a spread of 8 feet. Growth is medium.

HARDINESS ZONE - Zone 6. Should be grown only in north and central Florida.

NATIVE HABITAT - Woods in the Panhandle area of Florida and adjacent areas of Georgia and Alabama.

LEAVES - Alternate, broadly elliptic to obovate, to 3.5 inches long, acute; finely pubescent with ciliate margins.

FLOWERS - Yellow-orange, funnelform, 1.25 inches long, with exserted stamens and styles. The flowers are slightly fragrant and appear in early April in showy, terminal, umbel-like clusters of 8 to 15 blooms, before the leaves emerge.

FRUIT - Dehiscent capsule; brown, cylindrical, not ornamental; ripen in fall.

CULTURE - Plant in partial shade on a well-drained, fertile, acid soil that is moisture-retentive. Not suited to hot, dry sites. It is not salt tolerant and does not tolerate compacted soils. Does not flower well in heavy shade. Extended drought during mid-summer, when flower buds are formed, reduces flowering the following spring. Pruning, if needed, should be done shortly after flowering to avoid removal of flower buds.

PROBLEMS - Iron deficiencies and mushroom root rot.

PROPAGATION - Softwood cuttings root well under mist if taken early in spring. Seed germinate readily if sown in late fall on moist peat moss.

LANDSCAPE USES - Specimen shrub, best when massed in woodland areas. A traffic stopper when in full bloom.

COMMENTS - Considerable variation in flower color exists within seedling populations, from pure yellow to deep orange.

Rhododendron canescens   FLORIDA PINXTER AZALEA, PIEDMONT AZALEA, WILD HONEYSUCKLE

PRONUNCIATION - ˈrō də ˈden drən   kə ˈne sənz

TRANSLATION - [the Greek name for *Nerium oleander*, from *rhodo* (= red) and *dendron* (= a tree)] [whitish-gray, soft hairs].

FORM - Monoecious, deciduous, upright shrub, vase-shaped, sparingly branched and medium-textured.

SIZE - Can grow up to 15 feet in height with a 12 foot spread. Growth rate is medium.

HARDINESS ZONE - Zone 7. Can be grown in north and central Florida only.

NATIVE HABITAT - Wooded areas near water in the southeastern United States and north Florida.

LEAVES - Alternate, obovate to oblanceolate, to 4 inches long, acute, ciliate. The leaves are grayish-pubescent on the underside.

FLOWERS - Pinkish-white, funnelform, with exserted stamens and style, 1.5 inches long, delicate fragrance, in showy, terminal, umbel-like clusters of 6 to 15 in March, before the leaves appear.

FRUIT - Dehiscent capsule; brown, cylindrical, about 1 inch long, contain many small seeds and ripen in the fall.

CULTURE - Does best in partial shade on a fertile, acid, well-drained soil that is moisture-retentive. Not suited to hot, dry sites. Has no salt tolerance and does not tolerate compacted soils. Becomes very open and flowers poorly in heavy shade. Since flower buds form in midsummer, extended drought during that period reduces flowering the following spring. Pruning, if needed, should be done shortly after flowering, to avoid removal of flower buds.

PROBLEMS - Mushroom root rot and iron deficiencies.

PROPAGATION - Softwood cuttings under mist in spring or seed sown on the surface of moist peat moss in fall.

LANDSCAPE USES - Specimen shrub, usually massed in woodland areas. Has a tendency to be stoloniferous, forming colonies. Magnificent in full bloom.

COMMENTS - Tremendous variation in flower color, from pure white to pink to rose, within seedling populations. Hybridizes readily with other species. A number of other native *Rhododendron* species are also available in the trade, including *R. calendulaceum* (Flame Azalea), *R. chapmanii* (Chapman Rhododendron - endangered), *R. flammeum* (Oconee Azalea), *R. serrulatum* (Swamp Honeysuckle), among others.

Rhododendron × obtusum   KURUME AZALEA

PRONUNCIATION - ˈrō də ˈden drən   αb ˈtū səm

TRANSLATION - [the Greek name for *Nerium oleander*, from *rhodo* (= red) and *dendron* (= a tree)] [obtuse, rounded, in reference to leaves].

FORM - Monoecious, evergreen, much-branched shrub, densely foliated, twiggy with horizontal branching pattern. Fine texture.

SIZE - 4 to 6 feet with equal spread; slow growth rate.

HARDINESS ZONE - Zone 6. Grown in north and central Florida.

NATIVE HABITAT - Japan.

LEAVES - Simple, alternate, elliptic to 1 inch long, deep green, very pubescent, entire, some bronzing during cool weather. Smaller leaf than *R. simsii*.

STEM/BARK - New growth pubescent. Stiff, slender stems, green, turning light brown with age. Sympodial branching habit.

FLOWERS - Many colors (white, pink, red, rose, lavender, salmon), single or double, widely funnelform to 1.5 inch across, in terminal umbel-like clusters of 2 to 6 flowers, 5 stamens; flowers in spring (late Feb. to April, depending on cv.).

FRUIT - Woody capsule; not ornamental.

CULTURE - Partial shade, fertile, well-drained soils of lower pH (pH 4.5 to 5.5); not salt tolerant. Will not tolerate excessive dry or wet conditions, heat, or soil compaction. Prune, if needed, shortly after flowering to avoid removal of flower buds, which are set in midsummer.

PROBLEMS - Mites, mealybugs, lacebug, whitefly, scale, thrips, stem borers, leaf gall, petal blight, root rot, nematodes, micronutrient deficiencies (especially on higher pH soils); although the list is long, most are not serious problems on vigorously growing plants located on suitable sites.

PROPAGATION - Cuttings.

LANDSCAPE USES - Massing, border, foundation, specimen, urn, rock garden, pot plant for greenhouse production.

COMMENTS - Hundreds of cultivars and hybrids. Some of the more common ones: **'Apple Blossom'** - pink with white throat, semi-double, late flowering; **'Bridesmaid'** - salmon single, early flowering; **'Coral Bells'** - pink single, mid-season flowering; **'Hershey's Red'** - bright red double, late flowering; **'Hino-crimson'** - crimson red single, mid-season flowering; **'Hino-degiri'** - brick red single, mid-season flowering; **'Snow'** - white single, mid-season flowering.

Rhododendron simsii   FORMOSA AZALEA, INDIAN AZALEA

PRONUNCIATION - ˈrō də ˈden drən   ˈsim zē ī

TRANSLATION - [the Greek name for *Nerium oleander*, from *rhodo* (= red) and *dendron* (= a tree)] [after John Sims (1749-1831)].

FORM - Monoecious, evergreen, much-branched shrub, densely foliated, horizontal branching, somewhat spreading. Medium texture.

SIZE - To 10 feet with an equal spread; rapid growth rate.

HARDINESS ZONE - Zone 7. Grown in north and central Florida.

NATIVE HABITAT - Burma, China, Taiwan.

LEAVES - Simple, alternate, ovate to 3 inches long, dark green, pubescent but less so than *R.* × *obtusum*, entire margins, ciliate.

STEM/BARK - Less pubescence on new growth than *R.* ∞ *obtusum*. Stiff, slender stems generally green turning sandy brown with age. Sympodial branching habit.

FLOWERS - Many colors (white, pink, rose, red, lavender), singles and doubles, widely funnelform, 2 to 2.5 inches across, in umbel-like clusters of 2 to 6 flowers, 10 stamens, flowers in spring (late Feb. to April, depending on cultivar).

FRUIT - Woody capsule; not ornamental.

CULTURE - Partial shade, fertile, well-drained soils of lower pH (pH 4.5 to 5.5); not salt tolerant. Not suited for excessively dry or wet sites, high heat, or compacted soils. Prune, if needed, shortly after flowering to avoid removal of flower buds, which are set in midsummer.

PROBLEMS - Mites, thrips, lacebug, leaf miner, whitefly, scale, stem borers, leaf gall, petal blight, root rot, minor element deficiencies (on alkaline soils, especially); although the list is long, vigorously growing plants on suitable sites are not usually affected.

PROPAGATION - Cuttings.

LANDSCAPE USES - Border, hedge, foundation for large buildings, specimen.

COMMENTS - Hundreds of cultivars and hybrids. Some common ones are **'Elegans'** - light pink, single, early flowering; **'Elegans Superba'** (**'Pride of Mobile'**) - light pink, single, mid-season flowering; **'Formosa'** - rose-purple, single, early to mid-season flowering, most popular cv. in the south; **'George L. Taber'** - lavender-pink, single, mid-season flowering; **'Mrs. G.G. Gerbing'** - white, single, mid-season flowering; **'Southern Charm'** - pink, single, early to mid-season flowering, a sport of **'Formosa'**.

EUPHORBIACEAE - SPURGE FAMILY

DICOTYLEDONS; ABOUT 300 GENERA AND 7,000 SPECIES

GEOGRAPHY: Cosmopolitan but primarily tropical.

GROWTH HABIT: Trees, shrubs, and herbs; some xerophytic or cactoid succulents;
                    sometimes with milky latex and some genera with clear or cloudy
                    latex.

LEAVES: Usually alternate, simple, and stipulate.

FLOWERS: Actinomorphic, unisexual (plants mono- or dioecious); 5-merous,
                    often apetalous and asepalous; stamens 1 to many, distinctive
                    glands; ovary superior; conspicuous nectariferous glands
                    prominent in many genera; inflorescence of some genera is a
                    cyathium, others are dichasium.

FRUIT: A 1- to 3-locular, often explosively dehiscent capsule; seeds
                    sometimes caranculate.

ECONOMIC USES: Source of rubber (especially *Hevea brasiliensis*), cassava
                    (*Manihot esculenta*), Castor oil (*Ricinus communis*), commercial
                    oils (*Aleurites* spp., *Sapium* spp., etc.), dyes, and other products,
                    and ornamentals. Many species are used for medicinal purposes.

ORNAMENTAL GENERA: *Acalypha, Aleurites, Baccaurea, Breynia, Cnidoscolus,*
                    Codiaeum, Euphorbia, Fluggea, Garcia, Glochidion,
                    Gymnanthes, Homalanthus, Hura, Jatropha, Joannesia,
                    Mallotus, Manihot, Pedilanthus, Phyllanthus, Putranjiva,
                    Ricinus, Sapium, Synadenium, among others.

COMMENTS: Euphorbia with nearly 2,000 species worldwide is one of the
                    largest and taxonomically most difficult genera of flowering
                    plants.

Acalypha wilkesiana

PRONUNCIATION - ˌæ kə ˈli fə ˌwilk sē ˈā nə

TRANSLATION - [classical name for the nettle with similar leaves] [after Admiral Charles Wilkes (1798-1877), explorer of the South Pacific].

FORM - Monoecious, evergreen, vigorous shrub, highly branched, often suckering from the base, irregular, upright to sprawling, densely foliated.

SIZE - To 15 feet, commonly less, rapid growth

HARDINESS ZONE - Zones 9b-11. Grown in south and the warmest areas of central Florida.

NATIVE HABITAT - Pacific Islands.

LEAVES - Simple, spirally arranged, ovate to 8 inches long, acuminate tip, many combinations of bronzy-green, copper, red, often variegated, serrate margins.

STEM/BARK - Brittle.

FLOWERS - Inconspicuous axillary spikes, drooping, flowers during warm months.

FRUIT - 3-celled capsule.

CULTURE - Full sun, various well-drained soils; moderately salt tolerant.

PROBLEMS - Mites, scale, caterpillars, cold sensitive.

PROPAGATION - Cuttings.

LANDSCAPE USES - Border, hedge, accent, mass planting, specimen, urn.

COMMENTS - Several cultivars, colors, variegation, including **'Ceylon'**, **'Godseffiana'**, **'Marginata'**, **'Musaica'**, and **'Tricolor'**. A related species, *A. hispida* (cattail, redhot cattail, etc.) has long, bright red inflorescences.

Breynia nivosa

SNOW BUSH

PRONUNCIATION - 'brā nē ə   ni 'vō sə

TRANSLATION - [in honor of Jacob Breyne (1637-1697), merchant in Danzig and his son Johann Philipp Breyne (1680-1764), authors of works on rare and little-known plants] [from Latin *niveus* = snow].

SYNONYM - *Breynia disticha.*

FORM - Monoecious, evergreen, rounded shrub, clump-forming, of medium texture.

SIZE - Reaches a height of 8 feet with a 4 foot spread. Grows at a moderate pace.

HARDINESS ZONE - Zones 9b-11, can be grown in central and south Florida, but needs a protected location in central Florida.

NATIVE HABITAT - Pacific islands.

LEAVES - Alternate, elliptic, ovate or obovate, to 2 inches long. The leaves are variegated with white and other colors and are somewhat 2-ranked, appearing pinnately compound, on short branches. Petioles are short.

STEM/BARK - The slender, wiry, dark red branches often appear to zigzag. Suckers from the base of trunk and roots often occur.

FLOWERS - Greenish and apetalous, small and inconspicuous, in short, axillary clusters on long peduncles.

FRUIT - Berries, red, 3/8 inch wide.

CULTURE - Grows best in full sun on a wide range of soils. Tolerates light, sandy soils but is not salt tolerant.

PROBLEMS - Caterpillars and mites.

PROPAGATION - Cuttings and sucker divisions.

LANDSCAPE USES - A specimen/accent shrub, also used in hedges. It is not suitable for foundation plantings.

COMMENTS - 'Roseo-picta' - Jacob's Coat, leaves mottled white, green, red, and pink. 'Atropurpurea' - leaves dark purple.

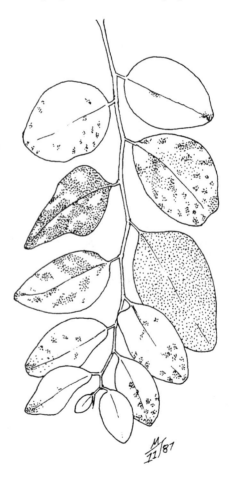

Codiaeum variegatum

CROTON

PRONUNCIATION - kō ˈdē əm ˌvæ rē ə ˈgā təm

TRANSLATION - [from Latinized vernacular name *kodiho*] [variegated].

FORM - Monoecious, evergreen shrub, vigorous, freely and irregularly branched, height and size variable.

SIZE - To 12 feet, commonly 3 to 5 feet in south Florida, rapid growth.

HARDINESS ZONE - Zones 9b-11. Can be grown in south and warmest areas of central Florida.

NATIVE HABITAT - Malaysia Pacific islands.

LEAVES - Simple, spirally arranged, often clustered at ends of branches, entire to deeply lobed, often undulate, wide variation in shade and coloration; greens, reds, yellows; leathery, glabrous; sap poisonous and staining.

STEM/BARK - Leaf scars on young wood, basal portions of branches often leafless.

FLOWERS - Unisexual, many small inconspicuous flowers, axillary racemes to 10 inches long.

FRUIT - Capsule, 3-celled.

CULTURE - Full sun for best color, varied well-drained soils; moderately salt tolerant.

PROBLEMS - Mites, scale, mealybugs, root rot if not in well-drained soil.

PROPAGATION - Cuttings.

LANDSCAPE USES - Accent, specimen, foundation, planter.

COMMENTS - Hundreds of cultivars with an amazing variety of leaf shapes, sizes, and colors. The most common in cultivation include '**Appendiculatum**' - leaf blade separated by midrib; '**Aureomaculatum**' - small leaves, spotted yellow; '**Cornutum**' - compact, with hornlike processes at the apex; '**Dayspring**' - common type in tropical landscapes; '**Disraeli**' - trilobed leaves marked and blotched with yellow; '**Eberneum**' - broad, marbled and blotched with white and cream; '**Interruptum**' - variegated blade, separated by midrib; '**Irregulare**' - variable size leaves, spotted with yellow; '**Maculatus Kantonii**' - trilobed leaves with scattered yellow spots; '**Majesticum**' - long, narrow leaves (to 18 inches or more), drooping habit, and change from yellow to crimson spots with age; '**Multicolor**' - leaves irregular in shape, blotched with yellow and red; '**Picturatum**' - long narrow leaves, yellow midrib, bright red; '**Punctatum**' - leaves 3 inches long and 1/2 inch wide, resembles *Podocarpus* leaves dusted with gold; '**Queen Victoria**' - large, dark green leaves, mottled red; '**Roseo-Pictus**' - medium-length leaves, spotted cream, rose, and yellow; '**Tortilis**' - leaf blade twisted spirally around midrib; '**Undulatum**' - leaf margins undulate; '**Variegatum**' - typical form, to 6 inches long, 1 inch wide, and green blotched with yellow; '**Warenii**' - leaves long, linear, twisted, midrib extends beyond the blade.

Euphorbia lactea   CANDELABRA CACTUS

PRONUNCIATION - yū 'for bē ə   'læk tē ə

TRANSLATION - [classical name in honor of Euphorbus, physician to Juba, king of Mauritania] [milk-white, in reference to the milky latex].

FORM - Monoecious, evergreen, succulent tree, upright, vigorous; medium texture.

SIZE - To 20 feet, often seen 6 to 8 feet; slow growth.

HARDINESS ZONE - Zones 10-11. Can be grown only in south Florida.

NATIVE HABITAT - East Indies.

LEAVES - Early-deciduous, minute, suborbicular to 1/8 inch long, between the pair of stipular spines; on the ridges of the stems.

STEM/BARK - Branches green, 3 to 4 angles, the sides with a white band down the center; succulent with a white milky latex.

FLOWERS - Yellow cyathium, in vertical rows along the stem ribs.

FRUIT - 3-celled, explosively dehiscent.

CULTURE - Full sun to light shade, various well-drained soils; not salt tolerant.

PROBLEMS - Bacterial spot, root rot.

PROPAGATION - Cuttings.

LANDSCAPE USES - Specimen, accent, patio tub plant; an unusual plant difficult to use well.

COMMENTS - Sap may be irritating. Many related species, a few cultivars; **'Cristata'** - popular "Brain Cactus." Contortion produced by infection of a mycoplasma; shoots sometimes revert to the species form, necessitating pruning. *Euphorbia*, with nearly 2,000 species, is one of the largest genera of flowering plants. Numerous species are cultivated primarily by succulent collectors. However, several cactoid or leafy species are more or less commonly grown in southern Florida, including *E. acrurensis* (= *E. abyssinica*), *E. antiquorum*, *E. cotinifolia*, and *E. cotinifolia* 'Sanguinea', *E. fulgens*, *E. grandicornis*, *E.* × *keysii* and *E.* × *keysii* 'Flamingo', *E. leucocephala*, *E. leuconeura*, *E. lophogona*, *E. neglecta*, *E. neriifolia*, and *E. neriifolia* 'Cristata' and its variegated form *'Crista Variegata'*, *E. punicea*, and *E. viguieri*, among many others.

Euphorbia milii   Corona de Cristo, Crown of Thorns

PRONUNCIATION - yū 'for bē ə 'mi lē ī

TRANSLATION - [classical name in honor of Euphorbus, physician to Juba, king of Mauritania] [Baron Milius, governor of the Island of Borbon].

FORM - Monoecious, evergreen, dwarf shrub, sprawling, sparsely foliated and fine to medium-textured.

SIZE - Can reach 4 feet in height, but is generally about 2 feet tall with an equal or greater spread. Growth rate is fairly slow.

HARDINESS ZONE - Zones 9b-11, can be grown in south and protected locations in central Florida.

NATIVE HABITAT - Madagascar.

LEAVES - Obovate with a mucronate tip, to 2.5 inches long. The sparse leaves are found only on the new growth at branch tips.

STEM/BARK - Gray, woody-succulent stems, 0.5-inch thick, and armed with numerous sharp, slender, stipular paired spines. The 0.5 inch long spines are arranged in spirals or vertical rows.

FLOWERS - Axillary, long-peduncled, upright branched cymes appear during warm months. Flowers themselves are small and inconspicuous, but are flanked by two pink to red, showy, rounded bracts, 0.5 inch wide.

FRUIT - Capsules, 3-valved, not normally produced in Florida.

CULTURE - Requires full sun and sandy, well-drained soils. Salt tolerance is marginal and watering and fertilization should be kept to a minimum.

PROBLEMS - Pest-free outdoors, bothered by mealybugs indoors.

PROPAGATION - Cuttings taken in spring and summer and allowed to dry for a while before planting.

LANDSCAPE USES - Grown in planters or as a ground cover, especially useful on poor, sandy soils. Used as a houseplant in high light situations.

COMMENTS - Several cultivars, including one which is yellow-flowered. These are represented by **'Compacta'**, **'Fireball'**, as well as var. *hislopii* (listed as *E. hislopii*), var. *splendens*, and others. In general, several species with various flower sizes and colors and some with exceptionally large and attractive leaves constitute an interesting and unique group of plants, nearly all endemic to Madagascar.

Euphorbia pulcherrima   POINSETTIA

PRONUNCIATION - yū 'for bē ə   pul 'ke rə mə

TRANSLATION - [classical name in honor of Euphorbus, physician to Juba, king of Mauritania] [very pretty].

SYNONYM - *Poinsettia pulcherima.*

FORM - Monoecious, evergreen shrub, many unbranched stems, upright to sprawling.

SIZE - To 12 feet, rapid growth

HARDINESS ZONE - Zones 9b-11. Grown as a perennial in central and south Florida.

NATIVE HABITAT - Central America, tropical Mexico.

LEAVES - Simple, alternate, ovate, sometimes fiddle-shaped to 7 inches long, entire or lobed, prominent veins, milky sap, long petiole.

STEM/BARK - Leaf scars on young wood.

FLOWERS - Terminal, cyathia in umbel-like cymes, subtended by many large showy bracts, many shades of red, white, some variegated.

FRUIT - Capsule, 3-celled.

CULTURE - Full sun for best color, various well-drained soils; not salt tolerant.

PROBLEMS - Mites, scale, thrips, caterpillars, root rot.

PROPAGATION - Cuttings.

LANDSCAPE USES - Border, accent, pot plant.

COMMENTS - Many cultivars, including **'Annette Hegg'** - compact habit, free branching, broad, bright red bracts; **'Barbara Ecke Supreme'** - stems heavy, more freely branching, bracts broad and blood red; **'Ecke's White'** - stems wiry, bracts membranous, cream; **'Henrietta Ecke'** - bracts broad, horizontal, vermillion; **'Oakleaf'** - vigorous, tall, lobed leaves, narrow, dark red bracts; **'Rosea'** - leaves pale with darker veins and petioles, bracts pale pink with darker veins; **'Ruth Ecke'** - dwarf and compact, leaves and bracts small and deep red, among many others.

Euphorbia tirucalli   PENCIL TREE

PRONUNCIATION - yū ˈfor bē ə   tē rə ˈkɑ lē

TRANSLATION - [classical name in honor of Euphorbus, physician to Juba, king of Mauritania] [young branches, in reference to the numerous branches].

FORM - Dioecious, evergreen, succulent shrub or small tree, upright but often sprawly, many-branched, vigorous; medium texture.

SIZE -To 30 feet.

HARDINESS ZONE - Zones 10-11. Grown only in south Florida.

NATIVE HABITAT - Tropical and South Africa.

LEAVES - Early deciduous, minute, suborbicular to 1/16 inch long, spineless.

STEM/BARK - Branches many, green, to 0.5-inch diameter, often clustered irregularly in a crown; succulent with a milky latex.

FLOWERS - Minute, in sessile cyathia in clusters at ends of ultimate branchlets.

FRUIT - Capsule, 3-valved.

CULTURE - Full sun to light shade, various well-drained soils; not salt tolerant.

PROBLEMS - Root rot, irritating sap.

PROPAGATION - Cuttings, seeds.

LANDSCAPE USES - Specimen, accent, patio tub plant; an unusual plant, difficult to use well. Much planted in the tropics as living fence and in recent years as a source of hydrocarbons.

COMMENTS - The milky latex is irritating and may cause severe allergic (dermatitis) reactions. Plant should be used with caution.

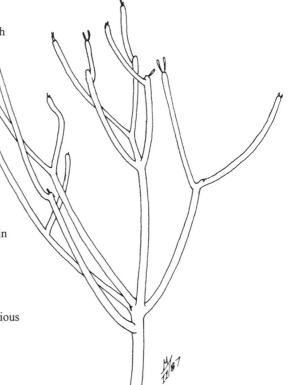

Jatropha integerrima FIRECRACKER

PRONUNCIATION - jə 'trō fə   ˌin tə 'ge rə mə

TRANSLATION - [from Greek *latros* (= a physician) and *trophe* (= food), in reference to medicinal properties of most species] [entire, in reference to leaf margins].

SYNONYM - *Jatropha hastata.*

FORM - Monoecious, evergreen shrub, rarely a small tree, medium-textured.

SIZE - Obtains a height of 10 feet with an equal spread. Grows at a medium rate.

HARDINESS ZONE - Zones 9b-11, can be grown only in south Florida or in central Florida with some protection.

NATIVE HABITAT - Cuba.

LEAVES - Alternate, oblong-obovate, with 0 to 3 large, acuminate lobes. The leaves are variable, often hastate and/or fiddle-shaped, depending on the degree of lobing.

STEM/BARK - Often forms multiple, slender trunks.

FLQWERS - Unisexual, scarlet to vermillion, 1 inch wide, in showy, upright cymes appearing all year on new growth.

FRUIT - 3-locular capsule, ovoid, six-lobed, 3/4 inch long, bursting when dry to scatter 3 smooth, speckled, toxic seeds.

CULTURE - Grown in full sun to partial shade on a wide range of soils. It is not salt tolerant.

PROBLEMS - Mites and scale.

PROPAGATION - Cuttings or seeds.

LANDSCAPE USES - Specimen or accent plant; should not be used in areas children frequent because of its poisonous properties. A variable species, it is also represented in cultivation by var. *hastata* and cultivar **'Compacta'**.

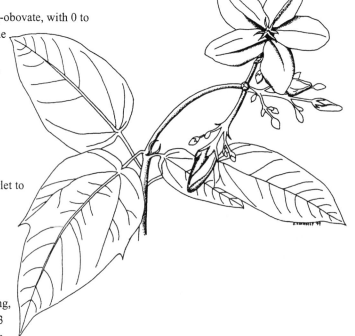

Jatropha multifida

CORAL PLANT

PRONUNCIATION - jə ˈtrō fə   mul ˈti fə də

TRANSLATION - [from Greek *jatros* (= a physician) and *trophe* (= food), in reference to medicinal properties of most species] [divided many times, in reference to the leaves].

FORM - Monoecious, semideciduous shrub, upright, irregular, of medium texture.

SIZE - Reaches 15 feet in height with a 10-foot spread. Grows at a fairly rapid pace.

HARDINESS ZONE - Zones 10-11, can be grown only in south Florida.

NATIVE HABITAT - Seasonally dry areas of tropical America. The specific origin is unknown but may be the island of Barbados.

LEAVES - Alternate, orbicular in outline, and deeply palmately 9 to 11-lobed, to 12 inches long and wide. Lobes often have smaller lobes of their own with glaucous undersides. The entire leaf resembles the marijuana leaf. The long petioles have stipules divided into brown, hairlike segments.

STEM/BARK - Forms a single, stout, soft-wooded trunk covered with smooth, brown bark and prominent, round leaf scars. Injured stems exude cloudy (but not milky) sap.

FLOWERS - Unisexual, red, small, in showy branched cymes on an 8 inch long terminal stalk. Blooms periodically during warm months.

FRUIT - Capsules, yellow 2- or 3-lobed, 1 inch long, contains 1 to 3 large, light brown, poisonous seeds.

CULTURE - Planted in full sun to partial shade on a wide range of soils. It is not salt tolerant and prefers to be kept on the dry side. Becomes invasive due to self-seeding ability.

PROBLEMS - Scales and mites.

PROPAGATION - By seeds or cuttings.

LANDSCAPE USES - A specimen/accent plant. Use should be considered carefully because it is both poisonous and weedy. Many species of *Jatropha*, such as *J. cathartica* and *J. podagrica*, are caudiciform succulents and are found in private collections. A few, such as *J. curcas* (Physic Nut) and *J. gossypiifolia* (Bellyache Bush), are used for medicinal purposes and are grown or occur naturally throughout the tropics. Several other species are either in cultivation or have potential as landscape plants in warmer regions.

Sapium sebiferum   CHINESE TALLOW TREE, POPCORN TREE

PRONUNCIATION - ˈsā pē əm   sə ˈbi fə rəm

TRANSLATION - [Latin name for resinous pine] [tallow-bearing].

FORM - Monoecious, deciduous tree, erect, irregular, medium-textured.

SIZE - Can grow to 30 feet tall with a 15 foot spread. Rate of growth is rapid.

HARDINESS ZONE - Zone 8. Can be grown in all regions of Florida.

NATIVE HABITAT - China and Japan. Naturalized in Florida and other southern states.

LEAVES - Alternate, broadly rhombic-ovate and abruptly acuminate, to 3 inches long, entire, glabrous, petiole 1 to 2 inches long. The new growth is reddish and leaves turn bright red and yellow in fall; this tree exhibits good fall color even in Florida.

STEM/BARK - Exudes milky poisonous sap from injured stems. Young stems are wispy, glabrous, and green, turning brown with age.

FLOWERS - Monoecious, yellowish, very small, in slender, terminal 2 to 4 inch spikes in spring.

FRUIT - Capsules; brown, round, 0.5 inch wide, splitting in fall to reveal 3 white, wax-covered seeds (hence the common name, Popcorn Tree); seeds persist into winter, after leaves have fallen. The waxy coating is used for making candles and soap in China.

CULTURE - Plant in full sun on a wide range of soils. Moderately salt tolerant. Performs well in tough sites, such as parking lots. Also tolerates drought, wet sites, and compacted soils. Easily transplanted when small; larger trees (trunks over 1.5 inch diameter) are more difficult. Canopy is open and airy, allowing grass to grow beneath the tree.

PROBLEMS - Pest-free. Seeds, which are produced in abundance, germinate readily; as a result, this tree has become a nuisance weed in some areas and may be considered a noxious weed. A relatively short-lived tree (15 to 25 years).

PROPAGATION - Generally by seed, which need a short stratification period. Cuttings will also root.

LANDSCAPE USES - Specimen, shade, or street tree, which provides dependable fall color in Florida. The leaves and fruit are messy, however. This tree resembles a northern poplar. It has become a noxious weed, and is not recommended for planting in the southern states.

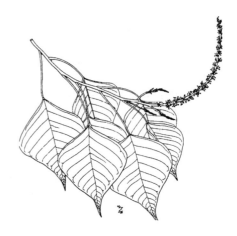

FABACEAE (LEGUMINOSAE) - PEA FAMILY

DICOTYLEDONS; ABOUT 700 GENERA AND 17,000 SPECIES

GEOGRAPHY: Cosmopolitan: woody species primarily tropical but herbaceous species mostly in temperate regions.

GROWTH HABIT: Trees, shrubs, subshrubs, vines, and annual and perennial herbs, including aquatics; usually with nitrogen-fixing root nodules.

LEAVES: Usually alternate, pinnately or bipinnately compound and stipulate; in some species leaves may be simple and in some the blade is not developed but the petiole assumes the function of the leaf (phyllodes of *Acacia*); in some species leaflets fold at night while in others they are sensitive to the stimuli, such as touch or wind, and fold (as in *Mimosa pudica*).

FLOWERS: 5-merous; actino- or zygomorphic, sometimes apetalous; stamens 5 to numerous, sometimes with long, colorful filaments, constituting a showy, 00dense head.

FRUIT: A legume or loment.

ECONOMIC USES: Numerous species are important as food, fodder, timber, drugs, dyes, fiber, etc. The family is second only to Poaceae in its importance to man as a source of food.

CLASSIFICATION AND CHARACTERISTICS OF SUBFAMILIES:

CAESALPINIODEAE (or CAESALPINACEAE): Mainly tropical and subtropical trees and shrubs, with about 180 genera and 3000 species. Leaves are usually pinnately but sometimes bipinnately compound or rarely simple; flowers slightly zygomorphic with the standard petal interior to the wings (lateral petals); stamens 10 or fewer, free or united.

ORNAMENTAL GENERA: *Bauhinia, Brownea, Caesalpinia, Cassia, Ceratonia, Cercis, Colvillea, Cynometra, Delonix, Gleditsia, Gymnocladus, Haematoxylum, Hymenaea, Lysiloma, Parkinsonia, Peltophorum, Saraca, Schizolobium, Schotia, Tamarindus,* etc.

(continued)

FABACEAE (LEGUMINOSAE) - PEA FAMILY - *(continued)*

PAPILIONOIDEAE (or Faboideae, = Papilionaceae): Temperate, tropical, and subtropical herbs, but with a few trees and shrubs; about 500 genera and 10,000 species. Leaves usually pinnate but sometimes palmate or simple; flowers zygomorphic, with standard petal exterior to the usually clawed wings (lateral petals), and the two basal petals often united into a boat-shaped structure called the keel; stamens 10 which are usually 9 united and one free, and the carpel inside the keel.

ORNAMENTAL GENERA: *Abrus, Andira, Bolusanthus, Butea, Cajanus, Camoensia, Castanospermum, Clitoria, Dalbergia, Derris, Erythrina, Gliricidia, Lathyrus, Lonchocarpus, Millettia, Ougeinia, Phyllocarpus, Pongamia, Pterocarpus, Pueraria, Robinia, Sabinea, Sesbania, Sophora, Tipuana, Wagatea, Willardia, Wisteria,* etc.

MIMOSOIDEAE (or Mimosaceae): Mainly tropical and subtropical trees and shrubs, with about 56 genera and 3000 species; leaves usually bipinnately compound; flowers actinomorphic, petals small or lacking, and have 10 or more stamens with long filaments, in showy dense heads.

ORNAMENTAL GENERA: *Acacia, Adenanthera, Albizia, Calliandra, Enterolobium, Inga, Leucaena, Lysiloma, Mimosa, Parkia, Pithecellobium, Wallaceodendron,* etc.

Acacia auriculiformis

EARLEAF ACACIA

PRONUNCIATION - ə 'kā shə   o 'ri kyū lə 'for məs

TRANSLATION - [the Greek name for the tree *Acacia arabica*, derived from *akis* (= sharp point)] [ear-like appendage, in reference to the ear-shaped fruit].

FORM - Monoecious, evergreen tree; rounded; medium texture.

SIZE - Can reach a height of 40 feet with a spread of 25 feet; very rapid growth rate.

HARDINESS ZONE - Zones 10-11; can be grown only in south Florida.

NATIVE HABITAT - Tropical northern Australia.

LEAVES - Does not have true leaves, but flattened petioles called phyllodes. Phyllodes: alternate, 6 inches long, curved-oblong, resembling flattened bananas or ears; entire margins; parallel, longitudinal veins.

STEM/BARK - Weak, brittle stems.

FLOWERS - Yellow; small, not showy; in 3 inch long spikes.

FRUIT - Legume; tan; coiled and twisted like an ear; to 4 inches long.

CULTURE - Grows in full sun on almost any soil; slight salt tolerance.

PROBLEMS - Generally pest-free. Breaks badly in high winds, is short-lived, and has messy leaves.

PROPAGATION - Seeds.

LANDSCAPE USES - A shade tree; use only if rapid growth and shade are desired; underplant with slower-growing, more desirable trees.

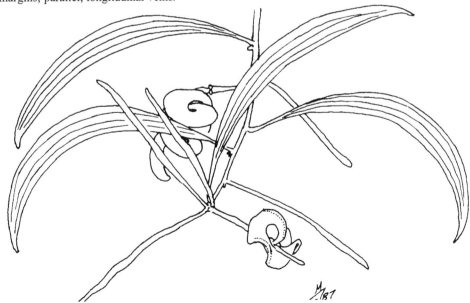

Acacia farnesiana   SWEET ACACIA

PRONUNCIATION - ə ˈkā shə   fɑr ˌnē sē ˈā nə

TRANSLATION - [the Greek name for the tree *Acacia arabica*, derived from *akis* (= sharp point)] [from the gardens of the Farnese Palace, Rome].

FORM - Monoecious, semideciduous shrub or small tree, rounded, spreading, much-branched, of fine texture.

SIZE - Can reach a height of 20 feet and a spread of 15 feet. Growth rate is rapid, but life span is short.

HARDINESS ZONE - Zone 9b. Can be grown in central and south Florida.

NATIVE HABITAT - Dry, sandy areas of tropical America. Naturalized in parts of south Florida.

LEAVES - Alternate, bipinnately compound, feathery, to 6 inches long, 2 to 8 pairs of primary divisions each with 10 to 25 pairs of linear leaflets, 0.25 inch long, oblique, glabrous.

STEM/BARK - The long, arching branches have a pair of thin, short, sharp, stipular spines at the base of each leaf. The trunks are covered with thin brown bark.

FLOWERS - Yellow, stalked, globose heads, 0.5 inch across, in axillary clusters with each new flush of growth. The flowers are very fragrant and are made into perfume in southern France.

FRUIT - Legumes, black, thick stubby, cylindrical, to 3 inches long, often in clusters.

CULTURE - Plant in full sun on a wide range of well-drained soils. Salt tolerance is moderate. Will defoliate during periods of drought. Will not tolerate waterlogged conditions. Generally easy to grow.

PROBLEMS - Caterpillars, if not controlled, can defoliate this plant.

PROPAGATION - By seed, which germinate readily, or semi-hardwood cuttings with a heel attached.

LANDSCAPE USES - A barrier shrub or trained to a freestanding specimen tree. Flowers and cut foliage are used in florist trade.

COMMENTS - Hundreds of *Acacia* species are native to warmer, drier areas of the world. Accordingly, many species are reported from cultivation in Florida and an even much larger number in California. A few of the notable species in Florida (including two native species) are *A. baileyana, A. choriophyllos, A. cornigera* (Bullhorn Acacia), *A. dealbata* (Silver Wattle), *A. decurrens* (Green Wattle), *A. macracantha, A. melanoxylon* (Blackwood Acacia), *A. nilotica* (Gum-Arabic Tree), and *A. simplicifolia*, among others.

Albizia julibrissin   MIMOSA, SILK TREE

PRONUNCIATION - æl ˈbi zē ə   ˌjū lə ˈbri sən

TRANSLATION - [in honor of F. del Albizzi, a Florentine nobleman who in 1749 introduced *A. julibrissin* into cultivation] [from the Persian name].

FORM - Monoecious, deciduous tree, horizontally branching, often multitrunked or leaning, widely spreading, flat-topped crown, not dense. Fine texture.

SIZE - To 40 feet, commonly seen 20 feet, rapid growth.

HARDINESS ZONE - Zone 7. Grows best in north and central Florida.

NATIVE HABITAT - Widespread, Iran to Japan. Naturalized in wooded areas of southeastern U.S.

LEAVES - Alternate, even-bipinnately compound, to 20 inches long, 8 to 24 primary divisions, each with 40 to 60 leaflets, leaflets oblong, asymmetrical with small point at tip, to 0.25 inch long, leaflets attached by a corner (not in the center). Late to leaf out in the spring.

STEM/BARK - Gray-brown with many prominent lenticels, angled, glabrous. Terminal bud absent.

FLOWERS - Bisexual, globose powderpuff heads, 1.5 to 2 inches across, many pink stamens form the showy part of the flower, crowded toward ends of branches; flowers in late spring and sporadically into summer. Can be messy on sidewalks and patios.

FRUIT - Legume to 6 inches long, brown, papery. Rather unattractive, remain on tree throughout autumn.

CULTURE - Full sun for best flowering, varied soils; moderately salt tolerant. Withstands drought and alkaline soils.

PROBLEMS - Mimosa (vascular) wilt is becoming more widespread, can kill tree; Mimosa webworm, also becoming more of a problem; brittle wood (easily broken during storms), messy, has become a weed in Florida (produces numerous seeds that germinate everywhere). Usually short lived (10 to 20 years).

PROPAGATION - Seeds, cuttings.

LANDSCAPE USES - Specimen, terrace tree, light shade, creates a tropical effect. Did well in highway plantings before the spread of Mimosa wilt. Despite its picturesque growth habit and its beauty when in bloom, some cities have passed ordinances outlawing further planting of this species due to its weed potential and wilt disease problem.

COMMENTS - Several cultivars exist: 'Alba' - flowers white; 'Charlotte' (= 'Tyron'?) - reported to be wilt-resistant clones; 'Rosea' (= 'E.H. Wilson'?) - dark pink flowers; 'Union' - released by Georgia Experiment Station; reportedly wilt-resistant. A few other Albizia species reported from cultivation in south Florida, including *A. calcora, A. lebbeck* (Woman's Tongue), *A. lucida, A. odoratissima,* and *A. procera* (White's Iris).

Bauhinia spp.   ORCHID TREE

PRONUNCIATION - baū 'hi nē ə

TRANSLATION - [after brothers Johann (1560-1624) and Caspar (1560-1624) Bauhin, Swiss botanists who were responsible for the monumental work *Historia Plantarum* and an index of plant names and synonyms. The two lobes of the leaves exemplify the two brothers.]

FORM - Monoecious, deciduous trees; many-branched; round; single-trunked, often crooked; densely foliated; medium-coarse texture.

SIZE - To 40 feet, commonly 15 to 25 feet; rapid growth rate.

HARDINESS ZONE - Zone 9b; can be grown in south and warmest areas of central Florida.

NATIVE HABITAT - 150 species in the Old and New World tropics.

LEAVES - Simple; alternate; 2-lobed, deeply cleft; light green, papery texture; entire margins.

FLOWERS - Many colors: pink, lavender, white, red, yellow; orchid-like, 3 to 6 inches across; borne in short terminal racemes. Blooms during warm months.

FRUIT - Legume; brown; to 12 inches long; woody; many.

CULTURE - Full sun to partial shade; various well-drained soils; moderate salt tolerance.

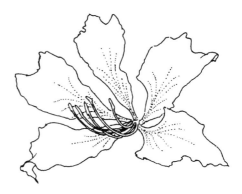

PROBLEMS - Borers, chewing insects; micronutrient deficiencies; pods may be messy.

PROPAGATION - Seeds, cuttings.

LANDSCAPE USES - Small shade tree, specimen, framing tree.

COMMENTS - Many species, varieties and cultivars are cultivated. *Bauhinia blakeana* is seedless. A few species are small shrubs; some are vining. The species of *Bauhinia* reported in cultivation include *B. aculeata, B. acuminata, B. binata, B.* × *blakeana* (Hong Kong Orchid Tree), *B. corymbosa, B. divericata, B. faberi, B. fassoglensis, B. forficata, B. galpinii* (Red Bauhinia), *B. glabra* (Turtle Vine), *B. lunarioides, B. malabarica, B. monandra* (Pink Orchid Tree), *B. multinervia, B. pauletia, B. purpurea* (Orchid Tree), *B. racemosa, B. roxburgiana, B. rufescens, B. tomentosa* (St. Thomas Tree), *B. vahlii* (Malu Creeper), *B. variegata* (Orchid Tree, Poor-Man's Orchid), *B. variegata* 'Candida' (White Orchid Tree), *B. viridescens,* and *B. yunnanensis.*

Caesalpinia pulcherrima   BARBADOS FLOWER-FENCE,
CLAVELLINA, DWARF POINCIANA

PRONUNCIATION - sē zæl 'pi nē ə   pul 'ke rə mə

TRANSLATION - [after Andreas Cesalpini (1519-1603), Italian botanist, philosopher, and physician to Pope Clement VIII] [pretty].

FORM - Irregular, evergreen shrub or small tree; open-branched; fine texture.

SIZE - Reaches a maximum height of 15 feet with a 10 foot spread; rapid growth rate; short life span.

HARDINESS ZONE - Zone 9b, can be grown in central and south Florida, but requires a protected location in central Florida.

NATIVE HABITAT - West Indies.

LEAVES - Bipinnately compound; alternate; soft and feathery, to 2 feet long; numerous oval leaflets to 0.75 inch long.

STEM/BARK - Stems are slightly thorny.

FLOWERS - Red with yellow petal margins; exserted stamens and pistil, 2.5 inches wide; borne in erect, pyramidal, large, showy racemes. Blooms almost year-round with peak displays in spring and fall.

FRUIT - Legumes; brown; flat, to 4 inches long.

CULTURE - Flowers best in full sun; grows on a wide range of soils; slight salt tolerance.

PROBLEMS - Scales, mushroom root rot.

PROPAGATION - Seeds, which germinate faster if scarified or soaked in hot water.

LANDSCAPE USES - A specimen or screen shrub which will tolerate drought and poor soil.

COMMENTS - Several other species of *Caesalpinia* are also used in the landscape, though none equal the beauty of *C. pulcherrima*. These include *C. cassioides, C. decapetala, C. fernea, C. gilliesii* (Paradise Poinciana), *C. granadello* (Bridalveil Tree), *C. mexicana, C. reticulata, C. sappan, C. spinosa,* and *C. vesicaria.*

Calliandra haematocephala   POWDERPUFF BUSH

PRONUNCIATION - ˌkæ lē ˈæn drə   hē ˌmæ tə ˈse fə lə

TRANSLATION - [beautiful stamen, in reference to the conspicuous stamens] [blood-red head].

FORM - Monoecious, evergreen shrub or small tree; round; multiple-trunked, low branching, dense, mound-like canopy; medium-fine texture.

SIZE - To 15 feet; rapid growth rate.

HARDINESS ZONE - Zone 9; can be grown in south Florida and warmest areas of central Florida.

NATIVE HABITAT - Bolivia.

LEAVES - Even-bipinnately compound; alternate; leaflets 8 to 10, asymmetrical, to 4 inches long; terminal pair often largest; pubescent when young.

STEM/BARK - Green on new growth.

FLOWERS - Bisexual; globular, powderpuff-like heads; many stamens, filaments white basally, red toward apex. Blooms in summer.

FRUIT - Legume with thickened margins; red (attractive) turning brown; to 5 inches long.

CULTURE - Full sun; various well-drained soils; no salt tolerance.

PROBLEMS - Mites, chewing insects.

PROPAGATION - Seeds, cuttings, layering.

LANDSCAPE USES - Barrier plantings, specimen.

COMMENTS - Adequate space must be provided for this large shrub. Exceptionally attractive when in full bloom.

Calliandra surinamensis   PINK POWDERPUFF

PRONUNCIATION - ˈkæ lē ˈæn drə   ˈsū rə nə ˈmen səs

TRANSLATION - [beautiful stamen, in reference to the conspicuous stamens] [from Surinam].

FORM - Monoecious, evergreen; spreading, irregular shrub or bushy tree with long arching branches; medium-fine texture.

SIZE - May reach 10 feet in height with an equal spread.

HARDINESS ZONE - Zones 10-11; restricted to south Florida.

NATIVE HABITAT - Native to northeastern South America.

LEAVES - Bipinnate; alternate; borne on short side twigs, 3 to 7 inches long, each main division having 8 to 12 pairs of oblong leaflets, 0.5 to 0.75 inch long. Medium green.

STEM/BARK - Light gray; trunk to 6 inches in diameter.

FLOWERS - Fragrant; showy flower heads nearly 2 inches long and broad; axillary; with numerous pink and white stamens resembling a powderpuff. Blooms more or less continually.

FRUIT - Legume; dark brown; single, flat with raised border, to 4 inches long and 0.5 inch wide.

CULTURE - Flowers best in sunny locations; needs well-drained soil; suitable for dry locations. Pink powderpuff has no salt tolerance.

PROBLEMS - None of significance.

PROPAGATION - Seeds.

LANDSCAPE USES - May be used as a flowering hedge. Often seen as a small, flowering specimen tree with the lower branches pruned off. The long, arching branches form an attractive canopy suitable for patio or tub plantings.

COMMENTS - Among other species in cultivation are *C. anomala, C. emarginata, C. schultzei, C. selloi, C. tweedii* (Mexican Flamebush), and probably others.

Cassia fistula

GOLDEN SHOWER, PUDDING-PIPE TREE

PRONUNCIATION - ˈkæ sē ə   ˈfis tyū lə

TRANSLATION - [ancient Greek name] [hollow].

FORM - Monoecious, semideciduous tree; upright, open-crowned; medium-coarse texture.

SIZE - Reaches a height of 30 feet with a spread of 20 feet; moderate growth rate.

HARDINESS ZONE - Zones 10-11; should be grown only in south Florida; will survive in protected locations in central Florida, but is badly damaged by freezes.

NATIVE HABITAT - India.

LEAVES - Even-pinnately compound; alternate; to 1.5 feet long; 8 to 16 ovate leaflets to 6 inches long.

STEM/BARK - The bark is smooth and gray.

FLOWERS - Yellow; 2 inches wide; very showy; borne in hanging axillary racemes to 18 inches long. Trees tend to become somewhat bare just before the profuse bloom in June or July.

FRUIT - Legumes; black, long, cylindrical, septate; 1 inch wide and 2 feet long; take one year to mature.

CULTURE - Grows in full sun or partial shade on well-drained soils; no salt tolerance.

PROBLEMS - Cassia caterpillars attack new growth.

PROPAGATION - By seed, which must be scarified and planted in sterile soil.

LANDSCAPE USES - A specimen or street tree, magnificent in full bloom.

COMMENTS - Many species of *Senna* and *Cassia* are used as landscape plants, particularly in the warmer southern Florida. Some of the more common include *Senna pallida (C. biflora), Senna corymbosa (C. corymbosa), Senna floribunda (C. floribunda), C. grandis* (Pink Shower), *C. roxburghii, Senna spectabilis (C. spectabilis)* (Carnival), among others.

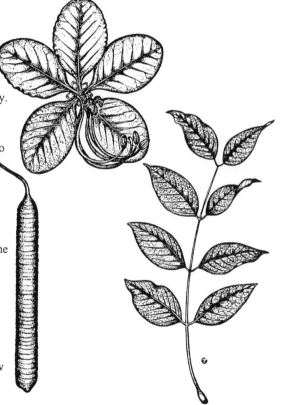

Cercis canadensis

EASTERN REDBUD

PRONUNCIATION - 'sər səs   'kæ nə 'den səs

TRANSLATION - [ancient Greek name *kerkis* for a European species, probably *C. siliquastrum*] [Canadian].

FORM - Monoecious, deciduous single- or multitrunk tree, much-branched, twiggy, broadly ovate canopy. Medium-coarse texture.

SIZE - To 40 feet, commonly 20 to 30 feet with 25 to 35 foot spread, moderate growth rate.

HARDINESS ZONE - Zone 5. Can be grown in north and central Florida.

NATIVE HABITAT - Eastern U.S.

LEAVES - Simple, alternate, ovate to nearly orbicular, base cordate, to 6 inches across, palmately veined, veins often pink underside, entire margins, papery texture, long petiole is somewhat bulbous where attached to blade.

STEM/BARK - Dark reddish-brown bark. Young stem zigzagging, somewhat slender, rough to the touch due to prominent lenticels. Cauliflorous clusters of small (0.25 inch), dark purplish-red flower buds present on stems, large branches, and even the trunk during late summer until flowering in spring.

FLOWERS - Rosy pink clusters, pea-like, petals 5, about 0.5 inch long, some cultivars fragrant; flowers in spring before or with leaves (late Feb. to March), effective for 2-3 weeks. Plants begin flowering young, about 4-6 years.

FRUIT - Legume, brown, to 4 inches long, persist after leaf fall. Not ornamental.

CULTURE - Full sun (for best flowering) to partial shade; fertile, well-drained soils; not salt tolerant. Tolerates hot, dry conditions, acid or alkaline soils, but not waterlogged sites. Difficult to transplant from the wild.

PROBLEM - Borers, chewing insects, stem canker, leaf spots.

PROPAGATION - Seeds, cuttings, graftage of cultivars.

LANDSCAPE USES - Street tree, framing, as a specimen or in groups, good residential tree for small lots, naturalized areas.

COMMENTS - 'Alba' - flowers white; 'Oklahoma' - deep purple flowers; dark, glossy foliage; 'Pansy Forest' - young foliage intensely purple; apparently less drought tolerant; 'Pinkbud' - pure, bright true pink flowers; 'Silver Cloud' - foliage with creamy-white variegation; best grown in partial shade; 'Wither's Pink Charm' - soft, true pink flowers. *Cercis chinensis* (Chinese Redbud) is also planted in Florida.

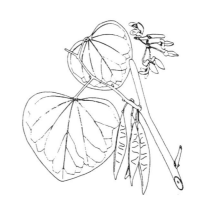

Dalbergia sissoo

SISSOO TREE (INDIAN ROSEWOOD)

PRONUNCIATION - dæl ꞌbər jē ə   ꞌsi sū

TRANSLATION - [after Nils Dalberg (1736-1820), Swedish botanist and royal physician, and Carl Gustav Dalberg (1754-1775), Swedish officer who owned an estate in Surinam from which he sent specimens to Linnaeus] [Indian name].

FORM - Semideciduous tree, upright, irregular, rounded, of coarse texture.

SIZE - Reaches a height of 60 feet with a 40 foot spread. Grows at a rapid rate.

HARDINESS ZONE - Zone 9b. Grows well in central and south Florida. Survives in north Florida in protected locations, but is defoliated by subfreezing temperatures.

NATIVE HABITAT - India.

LEAVES - Pinnately compound, alternate, to 8 inches long, light green. The 3 to 5 leaflets, orbicular with an acuminate apex, are arranged alternately along the rachis and can reach a length of 3 inches.

STEM/BARK - The young stems zigzag between leaves. The trunks yield a prized cabinet wood and it is an important timber tree in India.

FLOWERS - White, small, inconcpicuous but fragrant, in short, axillary panicles in spring.

FRUIT - Legumes, brown, thin, flat, papery, l- to 3-seeded, 2 to 4 inches long, and mature in winter.

CULTURE - Grows in full sun on a very wide range of soils; has marginal salt tolerance.

PROBLEMS - Pest-free.

PROPAGATION - By seed, which germinate better if planted when still within the pod.

LANDSCAPE USES - A handsome specimen, shade, street, framing tree, easily grown with a minimum of problems.

Delonix regia

FLAMBOYANT, ROYAL POINCIANA

PRONUNCIATION - də ˈlɑ nəks   ˈrē jē ə

TRANSLATION - [from Greek *delos* (= conspicuous) and *onux* (= a claw), in reference to the long clawed petals] [royal].

FORM - Monoecious, deciduous tree; large-branched, drooping, wide-spreading canopy, often twice the height, vase-shaped; fine texture.

SIZE - To 40 feet; rapid growth rate.

HARDINESS ZONE - Zones 10-11; can be grown only in south Florida.

NATIVE HABITAT - Madagascar.

LEAVES - Even-bipinnately compound; alternate; leaflets oblong, symmetrical, to 0.5 inch long. Medium green.

STEM/BARK - Bark gray-brown, smooth, often ribbed. Trunk often developing buttresses with age.

FLOWERS - Scarlet; terminal corymbose racemes; flowers 3 to 4 inches across, very showy. Blooms May through July.

FRUIT - Legume; large, woody; to 4 inches wide, 2 feet long.

CULTURE - Full sun; varied well-drained soils; slight salt tolerance.

PROBLEMS - Borers; brittle, very cold sensitive; large pods can be dangerous.

PROPAGATION - Seed.

LANDSCAPE USES - Parks, street plantings, specimen.

COMMENTS - Leaflets are somewhat allelopathic to turf. One of the most prized flowering trees in south Florida, and one of the most gorgeous trees in cultivation anywhere.

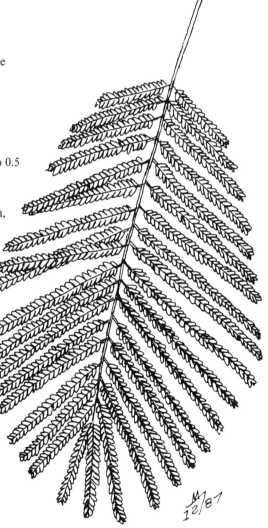

Erythrina herbacea   CORALBEAN, CHEROKEE BEAN

PRONUNCIATION - ˌe rə ˈthrī nə   hər ˈbā sē ə

TRANSLATION - [from Greek *erythros* (= red), referring to the color of the flowers] [herbaceous].

FORM - Monoecious, semi-evergreen perennial herb, or shrub of medium texture, clumping, irregular.

SIZE - Can reach 10 to 15 feet in height with 8 to 10 foot spread in south Florida, more typically 2 to 4 feet in height with equal spread in north and central Florida. Medium to rapid growth rate.

HARDINESS ZONE - Zone 8b. Can be grown in all areas of the state.

NATIVE HABITAT - Hammocks and coastal areas of the southeastern U.S. coastal plain region.

LEAVES - Alternate, trifoliolate, to 7 inches long. The 3-inch-long deltoid leaflets are thin, glabrous, and hastate with spines on the midrib underside.

STEM/BARK - The stems are armed with short, broad, recurved spines. Young stems are green. In south Florida, spongy, fibrous trunks are formed which are multiple, slender, spreading, erect, and covered with pale, thick bark.

FLOWERS - Scarlet, tubular, to 2 inches long, borne in long, terminal racemes to 2 feet long from April to   June. Showy flowers open in sequence from base to tip (indeterminate inflorescence).

FRUIT - Loment constricted between seeds; brown, hanging, to 6 inches long. The pods split open in fall to reveal 0.5-inch-long, shiny, bright red to scarlet seeds. Showy.

CULTURE - Grown in full sun or partial shade on a wide range of soils, but prefers fertile, well-drained soils. Salt tolerance is marginal.

PROBLEMS - Pest-free.

PROPAGATION - By scarified or hot-water-treated seed in sterile soil or by cuttings, which root very easily.

LANDSCAPE USES - An accent or specimen plant, useful for giving a naturalistic, informal effect to woodland plantings.

COMMENTS - *Erythrina* spp. are among the most popular flowering trees in the tropics, including south Florida. A few of the other species include *E. crista-galli* (Coral Tree, Cockspur Coral Tree), *E. fusca* and *E. fusca* '**Fastigiata**', *E. variegata* and *E. variegata* var. *orientalis*, *E. vespertilio* (Batwing Coral Tree), among others.

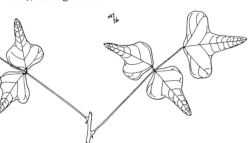

Parkinsonia aculeata

JERUSALEM THORN TREE, MEXICAN PALO VERDE, RATAMA

PRONUNCIATION - ˌpɑr kən 'sō nē ə   ə ˌkyū lē 'ā tə

TRANSLATION - [after John Parkinson (1567-1650), apothecary of London and author of two important books] [prickly].

FORM - Monoecious, deciduous single or multitrunked tree, asymmetrical, low-branching, often drooping, moundlike open canopy. Fine texture.

SIZE - To 25 feet with 20 to 25 foot spread; rapid growth.

HARDINESS ZONE - Zone 8. Can be grown in all areas of Florida.

NATIVE HABITAT - Tropical America.

LEAVES - Even bipinnately compound, spirally arranged, 8 to 16 inches long, 2 to 4 twig-like rachilla each with numerous small, linear leaflets, to 0.5 inch long, alternate on the rachilla, entire, rachilla persist after leaflets have fallen.

STEM/BARK - Green, smooth; brown, cracked with age. Twigs armed with short thorns at each node.

FLOWERS - Yellow with orange markings, in axillary racemes 4 to 6 inches long, flowers, to 1 inch across; fragrant, petals 5, flowering in spring and in cycles with a new flush of growth in the summer after dry periods.

FRUIT - Few-seeded loment, gray-brown, pointed to 6 inches long. Not ornamental.

CULTURE - Full sun, varied well-drained soils; highly salt tolerant. Tolerates high heat and drought, but does not like wet feet. A tough plant.

PROBLEMS - Scale, root rot, witches'-broom disease, thorns.

PROPAGATION - Scarified seed.

LANDSCAPE USES - Specimen, terrace or patio, good residential tree (if located where thorns will not pose a hazard). Provides light shade due to fine texture of foliage. Well adapted to arid landscapes.

COMMENTS - An extremely rugged and adaptable species. Despite its rapid growth rate, not a particularly weak-wooded plant but tends to be short-lived (15 to 20 years).

Peltophorum pterocarpum

**COPPERPOD,
YELLOW POINCIANA**

PRONUNCIATION - ˈpel tə ˈfo rəm ˌte rə ˈkɑr pəm

TRANSLATION - [from Greek *pelte* (= a shield) and *phoreo* (= to bear), in reference to the shape of stigma] [winged fruit].

FORM - Monoecious, semi-evergreen tree; upright, vase-shaped; densely foliated; fine texture.

SIZE - Reaches a height of 50 feet with a spread of 35 feet; rapid growth rate.

HARDINESS ZONE - Zone 9b, can be grown in central and south Florida, but requires a protected location in central Florida.

NATIVE HABITAT - Tropical coasts of Asia.

LEAVES - Bipinnately compound; alternate; to 1.5 feet long; many dark green, oblong leaflets, to 0.5 inch long; slightly larger than *Delonix;* lighter on the underside.

STEM/BARK - Young stems, new growth, and flower buds brown-downy; trunks have smooth, gray bark.

FLOWERS - Bright yellow; with crinkly petals; 1.5 inches wide; borne in 1.5 foot long, erect, terminal, branched panicles; with a grape-like fragrance. Blooms throughout summer.

FRUIT - Legume; coppery, wide, flat, persistent; to 4 inches long; 4- to 5-seeded.

CULTURE - Full sun on well-drained soils; marginal salt tolerance.

PROBLEMS - Pest-free. Problems are encountered with surface roots. Trees are often blown down in hurricanes.

PROPAGATION - By seed, which must be scarified. Seedlings bloom in 4 to 5 years.

LANDSCAPE USES - A handsome shade or specimen tree, magnificient in full bloom.

COMMENTS - Two related species, *P. africanum* and *P. dubium* (Yellow Poinciana), are also cultivated.

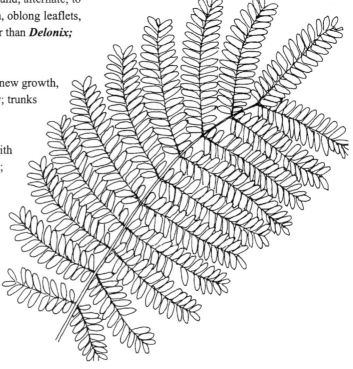

Senna alata   CANDLEBUSH, RINGWORM CASSIA

PRONUNCIATION - ˈse nə   ə ˈlā tə

TRANSLATION - [Greek name] [winged].

SYNONYM - *Cassia alata.*

FORM - Semi-evergreen, irregular shrub; medium-coarse texture.

SIZE - Reaches a height of 10 feet with an equal spread; rapid growth rate.

HARDINESS ZONE - Zone 9b, can be grown in central and south Florida, but is killed to the ground in central Florida in winter.

NATIVE HABITAT - Tropical America.

LEAVES - Even-pinnately compound; alternate; to 2 feet long; 16 to 28 obovate-oblong leaflets; prominently veined; to 6 inches long. Medium green.

STEM/BARK - New growth green, pubescent.

FLOWERS - Yellow; borne in terminal, elongate, stout, spike-like racemes which open from bottom to top and look like golden candles when covered with unopened flower buds. Showy blooms in late summer to fall.

FRUIT - Legume; black, slender, winged; 6 inches long.

CULTURE - Grows in full sun on a wide range of soils; marginal salt tolerance; should be pruned back after flowering.

PROBLEMS - Generally pest-free, rarely bothered by cassia caterpillars. Leaf miners may affect foliage.

PROPAGATION - Seed or cuttings. Seedlings bloom the first year from seed.

LANDSCAPE USES - Specimen shrub, shrub border accent, small tree for patios.

Senna bicapsularis   BUTTERFLY BUSH, CHRISTMAS SENNA

PRONUNCIATION ˈse nə ˈbī kap sə ˈla rəs

TRANSLATION - [ancient Greek name] [paired capsules].

SYNONYM - *Cassia bicapsularis.*

FORM - Monoecious, evergreen shrub, upright, sprawling, medium-textured.

SIZE - Reaches a height of 12 feet with an equal spread. Growth rate is rapid.

HARDINESS ZONE - Zone 9. Remains evergreen in central and south Florida, killed back in north Florida during severe winters, but regrows and blooms the next year.

NATIVE HABITAT - Tropical America.

LEAVES - Even-pinnately compound, alternate, to 6 inches long, 6 to 10 leaflets, oval to nearly orbicular, 1.25 inches long, obtuse apex, prominent gland at base of rachis. When partially folded, the leaf creates a "lobster-tail" effect.

STEM/BARK - Upright, weak, straggling, flexible stems. Usually multistemmed with most of foliage on upper sections of stems.

FLOWERS - Bright yellow with recurved stamens, showy, 0.5 inch wide, in axillary clusters of 4 to 8 flowers in October or November. Very showy.

FRUIT - Legume, brown, slender, cylindrical, septate, to 6 inches long. Not ornamental.

CULTURE - Grown in full sun on a wide range of soils. Salt tolerance is marginal.

PROBLEMS - Caterpillars attack new growth and can destroy flower buds. Twig borers can also be a problem.

PROPAGATION - By seed or cuttings.

LANDSCAPE USES - A specimen shrub, grown for its late fall floral display. Use in the back of a border to hide straggly, leafless lower stems.

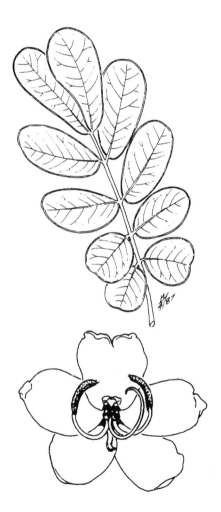

Tamarindus indica

PRONUNCIATION - tæ mə 'rin dəs   'in də kə

TRANSLATION - [from the Arabic name *tamar* (= date) and *hindi* (= Indian)] [from India].

FORM - Monoecious, evergreen tree; spreading, vase-shaped; densely foliated; fine texture.

SIZE - Can reach a height of 65 feet with a spread of 50 feet, but usually is smaller; slow growth rate.

HARDINESS ZONE - Zones l0b-11, should be planted only in frost-free locations in south Florida.

NATIVE HABITAT - India.

LEAVES - Even-pinnately compound; alternate; to 4 inches long; 20 to 40 oblong leaflets, to 1 inch long.

STEM/BARK - Bark brownish-gray, flaking with age; furrowed on young stems.

FLOWERS - Yellow and red; about 1 inch wide; born in few-flowered racemes. Blooms periodically in warm weather.

FRUIT - Legumes; cinnamon-brown; straight or curved, thick, 3 to 6 inches long. These hard-shelled pods contain a sweet, acid, edible brown pulp surrounding the seeds. Main fruit season is May and June.

CULTURE - Grows in full sun on a wide range of soils, but prefers deep, moist sands; no salt tolerance.

PROBLEMS - Fungi and beetles attack ripe fruit.

PROPAGATION - Seeds germinate readily and are satisfactory for ornamental purposes. If quality fruit is desired, superior types are air-layered, grafted, or shield-budded.

LANDSCAPE USES - An excellent, handsome specimen or shade tree; very wind-resistant and durable.

COMMENTS - The acid pulp of the seed pod is used for medicinal purposes and cooking and it is sometimes eaten raw, but is more commonly used in chutneys or curries or as an ingredient for soft drinks and Worcestershire sauce. It is grown commercially for the pulp in the tropics.

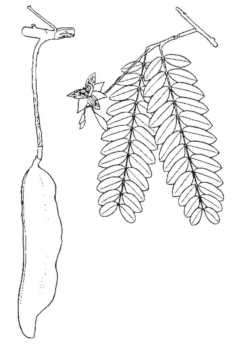

Wisteria sinensis

CHINESE WISTARIA

PRONUNCIATION - wˌ 'stē rē ə   sī 'nen səs

TRANSLATION - [after Caspar Wistar (1761-1818), professor of anatomy at University of Pennsylvania and one of the owners of Vernon Park in Philadelphia] [Chinese].

FORM - Monoecious, deciduous woody vine, climbing by twining. Medium texture.

SIZE - To 60 feet or more, rapid growth.

HARDINESS ZONE - Zone 5. Can be grown in north and central Florida.

NATIVE HABITAT - China but naturalized in Florida.

LEAVES - Odd-pinnately compound, alternate, leaflets 7 to 13, to 3 inches long, ovate to ovate-lanceolate, entire margins, acuminate, pubescent when young, becoming glabrous or nearly so with age. New growth often with pinkish tinge.

STEM/BARK - Large diameter, corky with age; new growth pubescent, slender, twining.

FLOWERS - Bluish-violet, pea-like, to 1 inch long; in dense, pendant terminal racemes 8 to 12 inches long, before leaves appear (March in north Florida); may be fragrant. Seedlings flower at 5-6 years.

FRUIT - Legume to 6 inches long, velvety. Not showy.

CULTURE - Full sun (for best flowering) to partial shade; varied soils, from somewhat poorly drained to dry, compacted soils, especially once established; not salt tolerant. Heavy fertilization (especially nitrogen) favors vegetative growth at the expense of flowering. A vigorously growing vine that may become difficult to eradicate if not kept confined.

PROBLEMS - Thrips, mites, none serious; rampant growth can strangle trees.

PROPAGATION - Seeds, cutttings, grafting.

LANDSCAPE USES - Trellis, fence, trained to freestanding specimen shrub (high-maintenance item). Puts on a spectacular show when in bloom.

COMMENTS - Many cultivars and related species: **'Alba'** - flowers white, fragrant; **'Black Dragon'** - double, deep purple flowers; **'Caroline'** - blue-violet flowers, heavy flowering; **'Plena'** - double, lilac flowers; *Wisteria floribunda* - (Japanese Wisteria) - differs from *W. sinensis* in several respects: flower clusters longer (20+ inches) and more fragrant, leaf consists of 13 to 19 slightly smaller leaflets. Many cultivars also available. Cultural conditions same as above. *Wisteria frutescens* (American Wisteria), a Florida native species, is also occasionally cultivated and is often represented by cultivars **'Magnifica'** (lilac flowers with a sulfur blotch) and **'Nivea'** (white flowers).

FAGACEAE - BEECH FAMILY

DICOTYLEDONS; 8 GENERA AND ABOUT 1000 SPECIES

GEOGRAPHY: Predominantly temperate and tropical forests of the Northern Hemisphere and to a lesser extent in Southern Hemisphere, but absent from Africa. Widespread and dominant feature of many broadleaf forests.

GROWTH HABIT: Excurrent and decurrent trees or rarely shrubs.

LEAVES: Deciduous, semi-evergreen, or evergreen, usually alternate, simple, entire, serrate, or pinnately lobed; pinnately veined; stipules early deciduous.

FLOWERS: Unisexual (plants monoecious), usually in catkins or small spikes; apetalous; stamens numerous; female flowers 1 to 3 in a group, surrounded by a basal involucre, ovary inferior.

FRUIT: Single-seeded calybium (acorn) surrounded or enclosed within a cupule.

ECONOMIC USES: Ornamentals, hardwood timber, cork, tannin, and edible fruit.

ORNAMENTAL GENERA: *Castanea, Castanopsis, Chrysolepis, Fagus, Lithocarpus, Nothofagus, Quercus,* and *Trigonobalanus.*

Quercus laevis   TURKEY OAK

PRONUNCIATION - ˈkwər kəs   ˈlē vəs

TRANSLATION - [ancient Latin name] [smooth].

FORM - Monoecious, deciduous tree, contorted irregular branching, narrow canopy, irregularly shaped. Coarse texture.

SIZE - To 60 feet, commonly 20 to 30 feet.

HARDINESS ZONE - Zone 8. Grows well in north and central Florida.

NATIVE HABITAT - Eastern United States, Florida native, in very well-drained sandy soils.

LEAVES - Simple, alternate, obovate to 12 inches long with 3 to 5 pointed lobes, bristle-tipped, wide sinuses, lateral lobes spreading, terminal lobe elongated, large veins, tomentose in vein axils on underside, otherwise glabrous on both surfaces, very short petiole that is twisted so that leaf surface is oriented vertically to the ground; fall color red to orange-red. The narrowly 3-lobed form of leaf suggests a turkey foot, hence the common name.

STEM/BARK - Dark brown, rough, deeply corrugated. Stems pubescent when young, becoming smooth and dark red-brown with age.

FLOWERS - Monoecious plants, male, slender catkins to 8 inches, female, axillary spikes. Not ornamental.

FRUIT - Nut (acorn), ovoid, to 1 inch long, 0.75 inch wide, deep cup enclosing one half; Black Oak group.

CULTURE - Full sun; sandy, well-drained soils; not salt tolerant.

PROBLEMS - Root rot.

PROPAGATION - Seeds.

LANDSCAPE USES - Shade tree, natural plantings.

COMMENTS - Best when part of the native landscape; does not respond well to cultivation. Tolerates dry conditions once established. Usually short lived (15 to 20 years).

Quercus laurifolia   LAUREL OAK

PRONUNCIATION - ˈkwər kəs   ˌlo rə ˈfō lē ə

TRANSLATION - [ancient Latin name] [bay-leaved].

FORM - Monoecious, semi-evergreen tree, large, upright, symmetrical, height greater than spread, oval canopy. Medium-fine texture.

SIZE - To 60 feet with 40 to 50 foot spread; rapid growth.

HARDINESS ZONE - Zone 8. Can be grown in all areas of Florida.

NATIVE HABITAT - Eastern United States, Florida native.

LEAVES - Simple, spirally arranged, elliptic-oblanceolate, occasionally young leaves shallowly 3-lobed at tip, otherwise obtuse, 2 to 5 inches long, glossy green above, light green below, flat (not revolute).

STEM/BARK - Grayish bark, tan vertical cracks.

FLOWERS - Slender male catkins, drooping, to 3 inches long; female catkins axillary, short stalked.

FRUIT - Nut (acorn) rounded, to 0.75 inch long, shallow cup enclosing one-fourth; Black Oak group.

CULTURE - Full sun; varied soils; moderately salt tolerant.

PROBLEMS - Root rot.

PROPAGATION - Seeds, cuttings - hardwood.

LANDSCAPE USES - Parks, street plantings.

COMMENTS - Not as long lived as *Q. virginiana*, usually 30 to 50 years. Hybridizes with *Q. nigra* and *Q. virginiana*. *Quercus hemisphaerica* differs from *Q. laurifolia* by its acute-triangular leaf apex, as opposed to obtuse.

Quercus michauxii

BASKET OAK,
SWAMP CHESTNUT OAK

PRONUNCIATION - ˈkwər kəs   mə ˈshō ē ī

TRANSLATION - [ancient Latin name] [in honor of André Michaux (1746-1803), French collector, explorer, and plantsman].

FORM - Monoecious, excurrent, with oval shape, more or less dense growth and coarse texture.

SIZE - Large tree, to 100 or more feet tall and 50 or more feet wide.

HARDINESS ZONE - Zone 4. Suitable for north and central Florida.

NATIVE HABITAT - Eastern United States, from Delaware to Florida, east to Louisiana. Grows in seasonally wet sites.

LEAVES - Alternate, simple, obovate to elliptic, 4-6 inches long or sometimes longer and 2-5 inches wide, green above, lighter tomentose below; margins coarsely serrate-dentate. Turn bright red in fall.

STEM/BARK - Clean trunk with shredding gray-brown bark; branches arising at sharp angles in relation to the trunk.

FLOWERS- Unisexual, apetalous; staminate flowers numerous and in drooping catkins; pistillate flowers few and in clusters.

FRUIT- Acorn to 1.5 inches long, enclosed to about one-third within the cup; cup scaly.

CULTURE - Best in moist but well-drained, fertile soils, in full sun, although it tolerates shady locations when young.

PROBLEMS - Although the plant defoliates nearly simultaneously, the large leaves may be considered a problem.

PROPAGATION - By seed, which usually germinate without difficulty.

LANDSCAPE USES - Suitable for shade, street, and public landscape situations.

COMMENTS - This is a long lived but much underused tree, with superior form, attractive coarse leaves, and splendid fall leaf color.

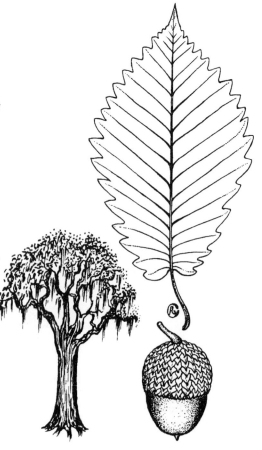

Quercus nigra

WATER OAK

PRONUNCIATION - ˈkwər kəs   nī grə

TRANSLATION - [ancient Latin name] [black].

FORM - Monoecious, semi-evergreen tree, large, symmetrical, open, vase-shaped (oval) canopy. Medium-coarse texture.

SIZE - To 80 feet with 50 to 60 foot spread, rapid growth.

HARDINESS ZONE - Zone 6. Grows best in north and central Florida.

NATIVE HABITAT - Eastern United States, Florida native.

LEAVES - Simple, alternate, extremely variable, spatulate to obovate, narrowed at base, to 3 inches long, apex unlobed, or shallowly 3-lobed, with 1 or more bristle tips, often undulate, bluish-green above, glabrous on both surfaces. No fall color.

STEM/BARK - Glabrous, brownish-gray branches. Trunk shallowly and irregularly furrowed.

FLOWERS - Staminate catkins to 3 inches long, pistillate axillary spikes. Not ornamental.

FRUIT - Acorn to 0.5 inch long, shallow cup enclosing one-fourth; Black Oak group.

CULTURE - Full sun, varied soils, moderately salt tolerant. Native to swampy areas, therefore adapted to wet sites. Tolerates compacted soils. Easily transplanted from root-pruned nursery stock.

PROBLEMS - Mites, borers, brittle wood (common problem with rapid growers), shallow rooted, little resistance to wind.

PROPAGATION - Seeds, cuttings - hardwood.

LANDSCAPE USES - Shade tree, street plantings (questionable), naturalized sites, wet sites (ponds, stream banks, etc.).

COMMENTS - Usually lives 20 to 30 years. A comparatively short-lived tree with little wind resistance.

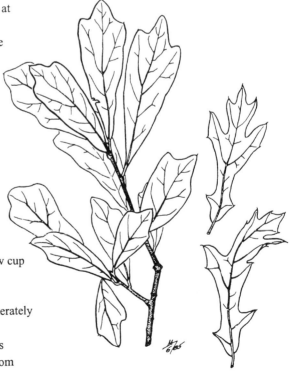

Quercus shumardii   SCHNECK RED OAK, SHUMARD OAK

PRONUNCIATION - ˈkwər kəs   shū ˈmɑr dē ī

TRANSLATION - [ancient Latin name] [after Benjamin Franklin Shumard (1820-1869), state geologist of Texas].

FORM - Monoecious, deciduous tree, tall, vigorous, excurrent, stout, wide-spreading branches, oval canopy when young, globose when older. Coarse texture.

SIZE - To 75+ feet with 50 to 60 foot spread, moderate growth rate.

HARDINESS ZONE - Zone 5. Can be grown in all areas of Florida.

NATIVE HABITIAT - Southeastern United States.

LEAVES - Simple, alternate, obovate, 4 to 8 inches long, with 7 to 9 bristle-tipped lobes each with several secondary lobes, primary lobes spread at nearly right angles, shallow sinuses, bases truncate on crown and broadly cuneate on lower limbs, glabrous, dark green, tomentose in vein axils on underside; red to red-orange fall color (even in Florida).

STEM/BARK - Grayish-brown trunk to 5 feet in diameter, shallowly fissured. Young stems relatively stout, glabrous, reddish-tan. Tough, durable wood.

FLOWERS - Slender male catkin to 6 inches long; pistillate, on short pubescent peduncles. Not ornamental.

FRUIT - Nut to 1.25 inches long, ovoid, shallow cup enclosing one-fourth; Black Oak group.

CULTURE - Full sun, varied soils, not salt tolerant. Tolerates urban conditions well. Transplants fairly easily.

PROBLEMS - Mites, root rot; none serious.

PROPAGATION - Seed, hardwood cuttings.

LANDSCAPE USES - Shade tree, street plantings, specimen. Good tree for large sites.

COMMENTS - A beautiful deciduous oak; becoming more popular. This species has been noted as the tallest oak, reaching a height of 200 feet.

Quercus virginiana   LIVE OAK

PRONUNCIATION - ˈkwər kəs   vər ˌji nē ˈā nə

TRANSLATION - [ancient Latin name] [virginian].

FORM - Monoecious, evergreen tree, large, symmetrical, spreading crown, spread greater than height, branches low, horizontal, drooping. Medium-fine texture.

SIZE - To 60 to 80 feet with 60 to 100 foot spread, slow to moderate growth.

HARDINESS ZONE - Zone 8. Can be grown in all areas of Florida.

NATIVE HABITAT - Eastern United States, Florida native.

LEAVES - Simple, spirally arranged, elliptic to ovate, 1.5 to 5 inches long, margin revolute and entire on mature branches, vigorous shoots may have sharply toothed (similar to *Ilex opaca*) or 3-lobed leaves, underside with whitish-gray tomentose, leathery, stiff, and crisp.

STEM/BARK - Deeply furrowed bark, cracks black. Young stems gray, glabrous or pubescent toward tips. Very strong wooded.

FLOWERS - Male catkins to 3 inches long, pistillate, few on long peduncles. Not ornamental.

FRUIT - Nuts, ovoid, solitary or sometimes paired to 1 inch long, shallow cup enclosing one-fourth; White Oak group.

CULTURE - Full sun, varied soils, moderately to highly salt tolerant. Also tolerates heat and dry conditions, even moderately wet conditions. Good wind resistance. Tolerates urban conditions and moderate soil compaction once established. Generally, a tough, durable tree. Growth rate can be enhanced considerably with good fertilization and adequate irrigation.

PROBLEMS - Root rot, galls, mushroom root rot; none serious.

PROPAGATION - Seed.

LANDSCAPE USES - Shade tree, street planting, parks, specimen. Definitely needs a large area. When grown in the open, the form of a mature specimen is truly majestic.

COMMENTS - Many forms within its native range. Commonly lives over 100 years. Perhaps the most commonly planted landscape tree in southeastern U.S. Many other oaks, predominantly native species, are planted in Florida and should be considered for wider use. A few examples include *Q. acuta* (Japanese Evergreen Oak), *Q. acutissima* (Sawtooth Oak), *Q. alba* (White Oak), *Q. austrina* (Bluff Oak), *Q. chapmanii* (Chapman Oak), *Q. coccinea* (Scarlet Oak), *Q. durandii* (Durand Oak), *Q. falcata* (Southern Red Oak), *Q. geminata* (Scrub Tree Oak), *Q. georgiana* (Georgia Oak), *Q. lyrata* (Overcup Oak), *Q. muehlenbergii* (Yellow Chestnut Oak), *Q. myrtifolia* (Myrtle Oak), *Q. nuttallii* (Nuttal's Oak), *Q. palustris* (Pin Oak), *Q. phellos* (Willow Oak), *Q. prinus* (Chestnut Oak), *Q. rubra* (Red Oak), *Q. stellata* (Post Oak), *Q. velutina* (Black Oak), among others.

FLACOURTIACEAE - FLACOURTIA FAMILY

DICOTYLEDONS; 88 OR 89 GENERA AND ABOUT 850 SPECIES

GEOGRAPHY: Predominantly tropical and subtropical, with a few in the
                     temperate regions.

GROWTH HABIT: Trees or rarely shrubs, sometimes with spiny branches.

LEAVES: Alternate, opposite, or sometimes whorled, simple, entire or
                     serrate.

FLOWERS: Small, actinomorphic, bisexual or unisexual (plants dioecious),
                     solitary or in terminal or axillary inflorescences; perianth
                     numerous and free; stamens numerous and free; ovary usually
                     superior.

FRUIT: Berries, drupes, capsules, or dry-indehiscent with wings or
                     prickles; seeds arillate or with hairs.

ECONOMIC USES: Ornamentals, otherwise of little or no economic value.

ORNAMENTAL GENERA: *Casearia, Dovyalis, Flacourtia, Olmediella, Oncoba, Xylosma,*
                     and others.

Xylosma congestum

XYLOSMA

PRONUNCIATION - zī 'lɑz mə   kən 'jes təm

TRANSLATION - [from Greek *xilos* (= wood) and *asme* (= fragrance), in reference to the fragrant wood] [congested, brought together].

FORM - Dioecious, evergreen shrub or small tree, graceful, spreading, of medium texture.

SIZE - Reaches a height of 20 feet with a 15 foot spread. Growth rate is medium.

HARDINESS ZONE - Undetermined, but grows well in all areas of Florida.

NATIVE HABITAT - China.

LEAVES - Simple, alternate, ovate-acuminate, to 3.5 inches long, glossy green. The shining, teardrop-shaped leaves have serrate margins.

STEM/BARK - Stems are armed with short, sharp, slender axillary thorns. Thornless types also exist. The bark is thin, light brown, and split by vertical fissures.

FLOWERS - The greenish-white, small, inconspicuous but usually numerous flowers are borne in axillary racemes in fall.

FRUIT - Berries, black, globose, two-seeded, 0.25 inch wide, in winter.

CULTURE - Grown in partial shade or full sun on a wide range of soils. It is not salt tolerant.

PROBLEMS - Pest-free.

PROPAGATION - Seed germinate readily without special treatments. Leafy cuttings taken in late summer and treated with rooting hormones will root under mist.

LANDSCAPE USES - Use as a specimen, patio, or framing tree for a small area. Also as clipped hedge, barrier planting.

COMMENTS - *Xylosma flexuosum* and *X. japonicum* are also reported, though the latter species is obscure.

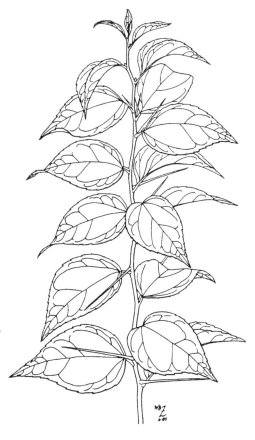

GESNERIACEAE - GESNERIA FAMILY

DICOTYLEDONS; 120-125 GENERA AND ABOUT 2000 SPECIES

GEOGRAPHY: Tropical and subtropical, Old and New Worlds.

GROWTH HABIT: Herbs, small shrubs or climbers, often prostrate epiphytes, sometimes with tubers, scaly stolons, or rhizomes.

LEAVES: Basal, opposite or whorled, sometimes unequal or rarely the cotyledons enlarge to form the only leaves (in *Streptocarpus*), simple, entire or toothed, occasionally purple or variously blotched; pinnately veined.

FLOWERS: Very showy, bisexual, zygomorphic; in cymes, racemes or solitary; 5-merous, petals and also sepals united to form bilabiate or sometimes pouched corolla; stamens 2 or 4; carpels 1, ovary superior or half inferior.

FRUIT: Loculicidally dehiscent capsule or a berry; seeds small and numerous.

ECONOMIC USES: Ornamentals.

ORNAMENTAL GENERA: *Achimenes, Aeschynanthus, Chirita, Codonanthe, Columnea, Episcia, Kohleria, Nematanthus, Saintpaulia, Sinningia, Smithiantha, Streptocarpus,* among others, including several artificial intergeneric and interspecific hybrids.

Episcia cupreata

FLAME VIOLET

PRONUNCIATION - ə 'pi shə ˌkū prē 'ā tə

TRANSLATION - [from Greek *episkios* (= shaded), in reference to the natural habit of the plants] [copper-colored].

FORM - Monoecious, evergreen; herbaceous perennial; ground cover, creeping or trailing, hairy; medium texture.

SIZE - To 6 inches tall as a ground cover; will trail to 2 feet in a hanging basket.

HARDINESS ZONE - Zones 10b-11; south Florida only; injured by temperatures below 40°F.

NATIVE HABITAT - Colombia and Venezuela.

LEAVES - Simple; opposite; elliptic to round, to 5 inches long and 3 inches wide; coppery or reddish-green to green or with silver variegations depending on cultivar; fleshy, more or less rugose, hairy; crenate margins. Petioles short.

STEM/BARK - Stems herbaceous, weak, spreading or hanging, rooting at the nodes.

FLOWERS - Red, orange-red, or yellow; tubular, to 1 inch long and 0.75 inch in diameter; solitary; borne on short axillary peduncles. Blooms continuously during the warm months.

CULTURE - Partial to deep shade, will tolerate brief exposures to full sun; interior light requirements similar to African violets; prefer fibrous, fast draining, slightly acid soil and high humidities; no salt tolerance.

PROBLEMS - Mealybugs, mites, nematodes, and root rots.

PROPAGATION - Cuttings or runners.

LANDSCAPE USES - In interiors as a hanging basket or on a pedestal for the cascading effect of stems. Sometimes used as a ground cover.

COMMENTS - Several cultivars for foliar variegation and flower color are available: 'Acajoa' (leaves dark mahogany with contrasting veins), 'Chocolate Soldier' (large leaves, brown with gray band), 'Frosty' (silver-white blotches), 'Silver Sheen', 'Metallica', 'Tetra' (large flowers), and 'Tropical Topaz' (flowers yellow).

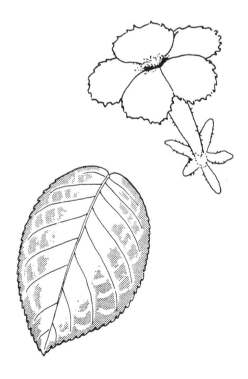

Saintpaulia ionantha   AFRICAN VIOLET

PRONUNCIATION - sānt 'po lē ə ˌī ō 'næn thə

TRANSLATION - [after Baron Walter von Saint Paul-Illaire (1860-1910), the discoverer of the African Violet in East Africa] [with violet-colored flowers].

FORM - Monoecious, evergreen; herbaceous, succulent, perennial; forms rosettes; medium texture.

SIZE - To 6 inches tall.

HARDINESS ZONE - Zones 10b-11, very sensitive to cold, primarily used as an interior plant.

NATIVE HABITAT - Tropical East Africa.

LEAVES - Simple; arranged in a basal rosette; orbicular to ovate to 2.5 inches long; green, fleshy; upper surface covered with intermixed long and short hairs; lower surface paler green or often purple, densely hairy; margins shallowly crenate to entire. Petioles long.

STEM/BARK - Acaulescent, nearly stemless.

FLOWERS - Light blue to violet, white, or pink; to 1 inch across; 1 to 10 flowers borne on a 1 to 4-inch-long peduncle. If given proper care the new cultivars bloom continuously.

FRUIT - Capsule; cylindrical, 0.5 inch long.

CULTURE - Partial to deep shade; for maximum bloom, light intensities of 600 to 1500 foot-candles required; light, well-drained soils; no salt tolerance.

PROBLEMS - Mealybugs, mites, chewing insects, and root rots.

PROPAGATION - Seed, cuttings, or division.

LANDSCAPE USES - African violets are perhaps the most common flowering house plants in the United States. They are normally used as window plants in east or north windows or in other windows if protected from full sun; also used in hanging baskets.

COMMENTS - Thousands of cultivars exist for colors, single, double, frilled, or ruffled flowers, leaf form, and size. The cultivars are registered with the African Violet Society of America, Inc. However, a vast majority of the cultivars are selections of *S. velutina*, which have been grouped into Standard, Dwarfs and Miniatures, and Trailing.

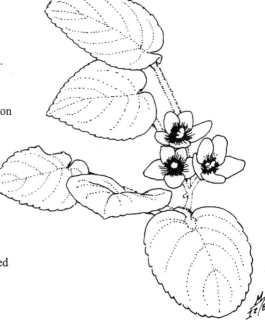

Sinningia speciosa   GLOXINIA

PRONUNCIATION - sə ˈnin jē ə ˌspē sē ˈō sə

TRANSLATION - [after Wilhelm Sinning (1794-1874), head gardener, University of Bonn] [showy].

SYNONYM - *Gloxinia speciosa.*

FORM - Monoecious, evergreen; herbaceous perennial; hairy, low-growing, tuberous; medium texture.

SIZE - Short stems; plants rarely to 1 foot tall.

HARDINESS ZONE - Zones 10b-11; cold sensitive, mainly an interior plant.

NATIVE HABITAT - Brazil.

LEAVES - Simple; either basally congested on short stems or arising directly from the tuber; ovate to oblong to 8 inches long and 6 inches wide; upper surface green, lower surface green or green tinged with red; finely hairy, more or less succulent; crenate margins. Petioles short.

STEM/BARK - Stem short or entirely underground and tuberous.

FLOWERS - White, pink, red, lavender, purple or spotted; bell-shaped, to 3 inches long; borne on axillary pedicels to 6 inches long. Free flowering, takes 6 to 7 months to flower from seed and about 3 months to flower from tubers.

FRUIT - Capsule; 2-valved.

CULTURE - Does not tolerate full sun, grows in deep shade up to 2400 foot-candles; light, well-drained soil; moist; no salt tolerance.

PROBLEMS - Mealybugs, mites, chewing insects, and root rots.

PROPAGATION - Seed, leaf cuttings, or tuber division.

LANDSCAPE USES - Normally used as container specimens for the flowers. A popular florist plant.

COMMENTS - The species is highly variable as to flowers, stems, and leaves. Based on flower characteristics the species is divided into 3 groups:(1) the **Speciosa** Group includes the wild forms; (2) the **Maxima** Group has larger and more colorful flowers than the wild forms; (3) the **Fyfiana** Group, which is the florist's gloxinia, contains many cultivars.

GOODENIACEAE - GOODENIA FAMILY

DICOTYLEDONS; 14 OR 16 GENERA AND 300 TO 400 SPECIES

GEOGRAPHY:	Predominantly Australian, with a few species of *Scaevola* widespread in the tropical and subtropical regions.
GROWTH HABIT:	Herbs or sometimes shrubs.
LEAVES:	Alternate, basal, or rarely opposite; entire to pinatisect; stipules absent.
FLOWERS:	Zygomorphic, bisexual, solitary or borne on axillary racemose or cymose inflorescences; 5-merous, corolla tube split almost to the base to form a bilobed tube; stamens 5, usually free; style with an outgrowth surrounding the stigma, ovary usually inferior and of 2 fused carpels.
FRUIT:	A drupe, a nut, or a capsule; seeds often winged.
ECONOMIC USES:	Ornamentals.

ORNAMENTAL GENERA: *Dampiera, Goodenia, Leschenaultia, Scaevola, Selliera,* and perhaps others.

Scaevola frutescens   SCAEVOLA, BEACH NAUPAKA

PRONUNCIATION - sē ˈvō lə   frū ˈte sənz

TRANSLATION - [*scaevus* (= left), in honor of Gaius Mucius, 507 B.C., left-handed king of Chisicom; in reference to the form of the corolla] [shrubby].

FORM - Evergreen shrub; round, densely foliated; medium texture.

SIZE - Grows to 5 feet tall with an equal or greater spread; moderate to rapid growth rate.

HARDINESS ZONE - Zones 10-11; limited to south Florida.

NATIVE HABITAT - Islands and coasts of the Indian and Pacific Oceans.

LEAVES - Simple; alternate; obovate to spatulate, to 6 inches long; fleshy, light green, glossy; clustered at the tips of the branches, resembling heads of lettuce; margins entire.

STEM/BARK - Fleshy stout branches.

FLOWERS - White with purple streaks; 0.75 inch long; usually solitary in the leaf axils; not showy, but are unusual in having the 5 petals (the corolla) arranged in a half-circle.

FRUIT - Drupes; fleshy, white, ovoid; 0.75 inch long.

CULTURE - Plant in full sun or partial shade on well-drained soil; high salt tolerance.

PROBLEMS - Chewing insects attack the leaves; mites can be a serious problem.

PROPAGATION - Mainly by cuttings; rarely by seed.

LANDSCAPE USES - Low hedge and/or erosion control on beachfront properties. Shrub borders.

COMMENTS - *S. plumieri* (Inkberry) has black fruit and is native to south Florida beaches, but is less ornamental. *Scaevola taccada* (Half-Flower) and *S. taccada* var. *sericea* are also reported in cultivation.

HAMAMELIDACEAE - WITCH HAZEL FAMILY

DICOTYLEDONS; 23 GENERA AND ABOUT 100 SPECIES

GEOGRAPHY: Temperate and subtropical regions of Northern and Southern Hemispheres but centered in eastern Asia.

GROWTH HABIT: Trees and shrubs, sometimes with winged branches.

LEAVES: Alternate, simple or palmately compound; stipulate.

FLOWERS: Bi- or unisexual (plants mono- or dioecious), 4- or 5-merous, sepals united; petals free or sometimes apetalous; stamens 2 to 14; ovary ranges from hypogynous to epi- and perigynous (superior or inferior), with 2 ovules and 2 styles; in spike or head, and often subtended by colorful bracts.

FRUIT: A capsule with woody and sometimes horny exocarp and brittle endocarp; seeds numerous.

ECONOMIC USES: Ornamentals, useful timbers, aromatic gums, resins, and pharmaceuticals.

ORNAMENTAL GENERA: *Distylium, Hamamelis, Liquidambar, Loropetalum, Rhodoleia, Sycopsis.*

Liquidambar styraciflua   SWEET GUM

PRONUNCIATION - ˈli kwə ˈdæm bɑr   stī ˌræ sə ˈflū ə

TRANSLATION - [from Latin *liquidus* (= liquid) and *ambar* (= amber), in reference to the resin obtained from the bark of *L. orientalis*] [flowing with storax, an aromatic balsam used in medicine and perfumery].

FORM - Monoecious, deciduous tree, upright, pyramidal canopy when young, globose with age. Medium-coarse texture.

SIZE - To 120 feet, often seen 60 to 70 feet with 40 to 50 foot spread in Florida; rapid growth.

HARDINESS ZONE - Zone 5. Grown throughout Florida.

NATIVE HABITAT - Eastern U.S., Central America.

LEAVES - Simple, spirally arranged, palmately 5- or 7-lobed, pointed, to 7 inches wide, finely serrate margins, aromatic "witch-hazel" smell when crushed, dark glossy green above, lighter green below, long-petioled, fall color variable (yellow, red, purplish-red, sometimes all on same tree).

STEM/BARK - Bark becomes corky with age, dark brown and fissured. Young stems reddish to yellowish brown, glabrous, aromatic, often (but not always) developing corky wings.

FLOWERS - Monoecious-unisexual; male flowers in terminal racemes, yellow-green; female flowers in globular heads, below staminate, or on separate branches. Not ornamental.

FRUIT - Round, woody head, composed of many 2-beaked capsules, to 1.5 inches diameter, spiny, persists through the winter, good identification feature. Hazardous to bare feet, littering pavement when they fall (do not decay rapidly).

CULTURE - Full sun to partial shade, various soil types, moderately salt tolerant. Avoid polluted areas and dry sites. Being native to somewhat swampy areas, it will tolerate fairly wet sites. Not easily transplanted when large.

PROBLEMS - Borers, caterpillars, spiny fruits. Brittle wood subject to wind damage.

PROPAGATION - Seeds; cuttings or grafting of selected cultivars.

LANDSCAPE USES - Shade tree, street plantings (questionable), parks, naturalized area, requires lots of room. 100+ years.

COMMENTS - Several cultivars selected for fall color and shape: **'Burgundy'** - deep red to purplish red fall color; **'Festival'** - yellow and red fall color, narrow upright form; **'Moraine'** - dark green foliage, brillant red fall color, upright oval form; **'Palo Alto'** - deep green foliage, orange-red fall color, pyramidal form; **'Purple Majesty'** - purple fall color. The other known species of *Liquidambar*, *L. formosona* (Formosa Sweet Gum) and *L. orientalis* (Oriental Sweet Gum), are both grown in Florida. The Formosa Sweet Gum, with its orange and golden-yellow fall color, is uniquely attractive.

Loropetalum chinense   CHINESE FRINGE BUSH

PRONUNCIATION - ˈlo rō ˈpe tə ləm   chī ˈnen sē

TRANSLATION - [from Greek *loron* (= strap) and *petalon* (= petal), in reference to the strap-shaped petals] [from China].

FORM - Monoecious, evergreen shrub or small tree, slender, freely branching, densely foliated. Medium-fine texture.

SIZE - To 12 feet with equal spread, usually much shorter, moderate growth rate.

HARDINESS ZONE - Zone 7. Grows best in north and central Florida.

NATIVE HABITAT - China, Japan.

LEAVES - Simple, alternate, 2-ranked, ovate to nearly rounded, to 2 inches long, oblique base, entire margins, interveinal region crinkled, pubescent, underside lighter coloration; petiole pubescent, 0.25 inch long; new growth pinkish.

STEM/BARK - New growth pubescent, slender, reddish-brown. Bark exfoliating in large strips on older stems.

FLOWERS - Whitish-yellow, axillary clusters, 4 strap-like petals slightly curled, to 1 inch long, fragrant; flowering in early spring.

FRUIT - Capsule, brown, woody, 2-beaked. Not ornamental.

CULTURE - Full sun to partial shade, various well-drained, acid soils; not salt tolerant. Easily transplanted from containers. Easy to grow.

PROBLEMS - Mites, nematodes, root rot; none serious. Minor element deficiencies on high pH soils.

PROPAGATION - Cuttings.

LANDSCAPE USES - Foundation plantings, clipped or unclipped hedge, barrier, small tree, singly or in groups. Not a widely known plant, but deserving of more widespread use. Interesting textural effect of foliage; showy when in flower. New cultivar **'Pizzazz'** has dark purple foliage; **'Razzelberi'** has purple foliage which becomes green; some cultivars have red flowers.

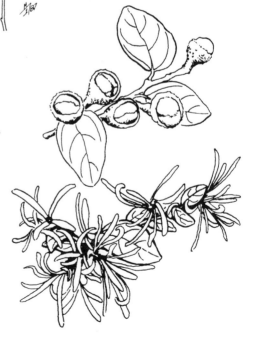

HYDRANGEACEAE - HYDRANGEA FAMILY

DICOTYLEDONS; 10 GENERA AND ABOUT 115 SPECIES

GEOGRAPHY:	Temperate and subtropical mountains, especially Himalayas to Japan and the Philippines.
GROWTH HABIT:	Shrubs, small trees, woody climbers, and sometimes herbs.
LEAVES:	Opposite, simple, often serrate.
FLOWERS:	Showy and numerous, in clusters, racemes, or panicles; bisexual; stamens numerous [in *Hydrangea* fertile flowers are inconspicuous but sterile flowers are apetalous but possess conspicuous colorful petaloid sepals].
FRUIT:	Capsule.
ECONOMIC USES:	Ornamentals: garden and potted plants.

ORNAMENTAL GENERA: *Deutzia, Hydrangea, Kirengeshoma,* and *Philadelphus*.

COMMENTS:	The family is sometimes included in the Saxifragaceae and it limits are not well-defined. *Philadelphus* and *Deutzia* are often placed in Philadelphaceae and, together with *Kirengshama*, sometimes placed in Saxifragaceae.

Hydrangea macrophylla

HYDRANGEA

PRONUNCIATION - hī 'dræn jə   ˌmæ krə 'fi lə

TRANSLATION - [from Greek *hydor* (= water) and *aggos* (= a jar), in reference to the cup-shaped fruit] [large-leaved].

FORM - Monoecious, deciduous shrub, rounded, suckering, compact, symmetrical. Coarse texture.

SIZE - To 8 feet with equal spread, commonly 3 to 5 feet; rapid growth.

HARDINESS ZONE - Zone 5. Grown in north and central Florida.

NATIVE HABITAT - Japan.

LEAVES - Simple, usually opposite/subopposite, ovate to 9 inches long, thick, flexible, often pubescent, coarsely serrate margins, short acuminate, fleshy texture, glabrous, stout petiole.

STEM/BARK - Stout, hollow with soft pith, large axillary buds. Young stems green, turning straw-brown with age, scarcely branching. Killed to the ground most winters in north Florida, but comes back from the base the following spring.

FLOWERS - Large, flat-topped branched cymes, terminal or occasionally axillary; calyx of sterile outer flowers is the showy portion, white (neutral), pink (alkaline soils), or blue (acid soils); fertile inner flowers not showy, small; flowers May-June in north Florida.

FRUIT - Dehiscent capsules, many small seeds.

CULTURE - Partial to fairly deep shade, fertile organic soils; not salt or drought tolerant. Soil pH 5.0 to 5.5 for blue flowers, 6.0 to 6.5+ for pink flowers.

PROBLEMS - Scale, aphids, mites, chewing insects, nematodes, powdery mildew.

PROPAGATION - Cuttings, tissue culture.

LANDSCAPE USES - Specimen, hedge, shaded patio, pot plant.

COMMENTS - Two groups of cultivars have been recognized: **Mopheads** (single or double sterile flowers, inflorescences compact or loose but usually rounded) and **Lacecaps** (sterile flowers usually peripheral, inflorescences flattened). Several other species have been reported for Florida: *H. arborescens* (Smooth Hydrangea), *H. paniculata* (and *H. paniculata* **'Grandiflora'** - Peegee Hydrangea), among others.

Hydrangea quercifolia   OAK-LEAF HYDRANGEA

PRONUNCIATION - hī 'dræn jə   ˌkwer sə 'fō lē ə

TRANSLATION - [from Greek *hydor* (= water) and *aggos* (= a jar), in reference to the cup-shaped fruit] [oak-like leaves].

FORM - Monoecious, deciduous shrub, erect, stout branches, asymmetrical canopy, stoloniferous, forming colonies. Coarse texture.

SIZE - To 8 feet with equal spread; moderate growth rate.

HARDINESS ZONE - Zone 5. Grown only in north Florida.

NATIVE HABITAT - Southeastern U.S.

LEAVES - Opposite, mostly 5-lobed, nearly orbicular or elliptic in outline, to 12 inches long, serrate, coarse papery texture, pubescent especially beneath; petioles densely rusty pubescent, 1 to 2 inches long. Red, orange-brown, to purplish fall color.

STEM/BARK - New growth rusty pubescent; pubescent axillary buds. Older stems with exfoliating bark and prominent lenticels. Large triangular leaf scars. Seldom branching above ground. Stems easily broken.

FLOWERS - Terminal, pyramidal panicles to 12 inches long. Outer sterile flowers (showy): white calyces turning purplish-pink, then brown, 1 to 1.5 inch diameters. Inner fertile flowers: not showy, numerous, small. Flowers in spring (May to June in north Florida) on previous year's wood.

FRUIT - Capsule, papery, dehiscent, 2 to 5-celled.

CULTURE - Partial to fairly deep shade, fertile acid, well-drained soils; not salt tolerant. When stressed (lack of water, full sun sites, etc.), plants tend to show premature fall color around August.

PROBLEMS - Scale, chewing insects; none serious.

PROPAGATION - Seeds, cuttings, root suckers.

LANDSCAPE USES - Wooded areas, hedge, mass plantings.

COMMENTS - Grown in sunnier and drier locations than most other hydrangeas. Several cultivars are available: **'Harmony'** - larger inflorescence, mostly sterile flowers that weigh branches down; **'Snow Queen'** - larger, denser inflorescence, mostly sterile flowers, borne upright; **'Snowflake'** - double "flowered" (actually multiple sepals), pure white, very showy, weigh branches down.

ILLICIACEAE - ILLICIUM FAMILY

DICOTYLEDONS; MONOGENERIC WITH 42 SPECIES

GEOGRAPHY: Southeast Asia, North America, and the West Indies.

GROWTH HABIT: Evergreen shrubs and small trees.

LEAVES: Alternate but sometimes occur in pseudowhorls at branch tips, simple, entire, leathery, and highly aromatic.

FLOWERS: Actinomorphic; bisexual; parts numerous, free, and spirally arranged; solitary in leaf axils.

FRUIT: Spreading, star-shaped, follicles (follicetum), each containing a single seed.

ECONOMIC USES: Ornamentals, oil, and spice (from unripe fruit of *I. verum*).

ORNAMENTAL GENERA: *Illicium.*

Illicium floridanum   FLORIDA ANISE, PURPLE ANISE

PRONUNCIATION - i 'li sē əm   ˌflo rə 'dā nəm

TRANSLATION - [allurement, referring to the agreeable odor] [from Florida].

FORM - Monoecious, evergreen shrub, many slender branches, rounded, more open canopy than *I. parviflorum*. Medium texture.

SIZE - To 10 feet with 6 to 8 foot spread; moderate growth.

HARDINESS ZONE - Zone 7. Grows best in north and central Florida.

NATIVE HABITAT - Southeastern United States, Florida native.

LEAVES - Simple, spirally arranged, elliptic to lanceolate, to 6 inches long, usually clustered at end of stems, apex acuminate, 0.5 inch long petiole often pink, entire margins, glabrous, dark green upper surface, lighter green below; oil aroma when crushed.

STEM/BARK - New growth reddish-pink.

FLOWERS - Reddish-purple to 2 inches across, numerous slender petals, nodding on 2-inch peduncles, axillary, solitary or clustered, somewhat showy, unpleasant odor, flowers in early spring over an extended period.

FRUIT - Star-shaped ring of follicles, many-seeded to 0.75 inch in diameter.

CULTURE - Full sun to partial shade, various well-drained soils; not salt tolerant. Not drought tolerant but will accept moderately wet conditions.

PROBLEMS - Mites, scale, none serious.

PROPAGATION - Seed, cuttings.

LANDSCAPE USES - Border, clipped or unclipped hedge, foundation planting, specimen, naturalized areas. A white flowering form, (*I. floridanum* f. *alba*) is available in the trade.

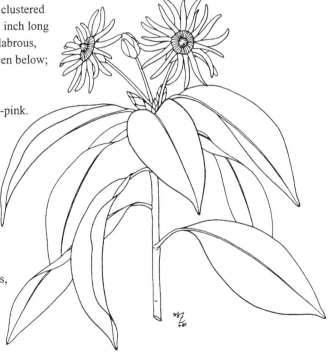

Illicium parviflorum   STAR ANISE

PRONUNCIATION - i ˈli sē əm   ˈpɑr və ˈflo rəm

TRANSLATION - [allurement, referring to the agreeable odor] [small flowered].

FORM - Monoecious, evergreen shrub or small tree, multiple stemmed, low branched, densely foliated. Medium texture.

SIZE - To 25 feet, commonly 6 to 12 feet with 4 to 8 foot spread; rapid growth.

HARDINESS ZONE - Zone 8. Grows best in north and central Florida.

NATIVE HABITAT - Doubtfully native to Japan and South Korea. This species occurs in the wild in Florida and is most likely confused with *I. anisatum*.

LEAVES - Simple, spirally arranged, obovate to elliptic to 4 inches long, apex obtuse, margins entire, leathery, olive-green color, short green petiole; licorice (or root beer) aroma when crushed.

STEM/BARK - New growth green.

FLOWERS - White-yellow, cup-shaped corolla, solitary, axillary, inconspicuous, fragrant.

FRUIT - Pod-like ring of follicles, many-seeded, star-shaped, to 0.75 inch in diameter.

CULTURE - Full sun to dense shade, various soils; not salt tolerant. Easily grown.

PROBLEMS - Mites, scale; none serious.

PROPAGATION - Seed, cuttings.

LANDSCAPE USES - Border, clipped or unclipped hedge, foundation for large buildings; good noise buffer due to dense foliage.

COMMENTS - Often sold as *Illicium anisatum*. *Illicium parviflorum* is said to be a Florida native. *Illicium anisatum*, native to China and Japan, has large star-shaped flowers.

JUGLANDACEAE - WALNUT FAMILY

DICOTYLEDONS; 7 GENERA AND ABOUT 55 SPECIES

GEOGRAPHY:	Predominantly north temperate with only a few extending into the subtropics.
GROWTH HABIT:	Deciduous trees, with brown-pubescent winter buds.
LEAVES:	Usually alternate, pinnately compound, and without stipules.
FLOWERS:	Small, unisexual (plants monoecious); male flowers with 3 to 40 free stamens, in catkin-like, pendulous inflorescences on previous year's branchlets; female flowers consist of 2 fused carpels and inferior ovary, in erect spikes on current year's branchlets.
FRUIT:	Drupe or nut.
ECONOMIC USES:	Ornamentals, but extensively grown as nut and oil crops, as well as timber.

ORNAMENTAL GENERA: *Carya, Engelhardtia, Juglans, Pterocarya*, etc.

Carya glabra

PIGNUT HICKORY

PRONUNCIATION - ˈkær yə   ˈglā brə

TRANSLATION - [Greek name for walnut] [smooth].

FORM - Monoecious, deciduous tree, massive branching, oval canopy, medium texture.

SIZE - To 120 feet, usually seen 20 to 40 feet, slow growth rate.

HARDINESS ZONE - Zone 5. Grown in north and central Florida.

NATIVE HABITAT - Eastern North America, Florida native.

LEAVES - Odd-pinnately compound, alternate, to 1 foot long, leaflets 3 to 9, mostly 5, acuminate, oblong to somewhat oblanceolate, uppermost leaflet largest, to 6 inches long, margins serrate, glabrous.

STEM/BARK - Bark close, not shaggy. Wood durable, not subject to wind damage.

FLOWERS - Plants monoecious; male flowers in drooping catkins, female flowers in 2 to 10 flowered terminal racemes. Not ornamental.

FRUIT - Drupes, green, obovoid, to 1 inch long, enclosing a ridged nut. The thick husk eventually splits into 4 valves. Edible but bitter.

CULTURE - Full sun to partial shade, various well-drained soils; not salt tolerant.

PROBLEMS - Borers, bagworms, scab, minor element deficiencies on high pH soils.

PROPAGATION - Stratified seed, root sprouts; not easily transplanted.

LANDSCAPE USES - Shade tree, street plantings, park, specimen, naturalized areas, needs lots of room. Fruit attracts wildlife.

COMMENTS - Related native species in cultivation include *C. aquatica* (Bitter Pecan, Water Hickory), *C. floridanum* (Scrub Hickory), *C. ovalis* (Sweet Pignut), *C. ovata* (Shagbark Hickory), and *C. tomentosa* (Mockernut Hickory).

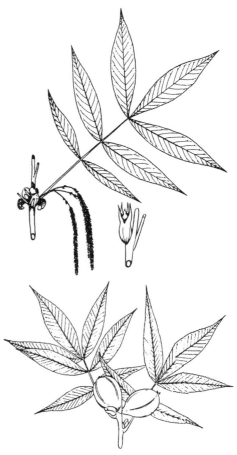

Carya illinoinensis   PECAN

PRONUNCIATION - ˈkær yə   ˌi lə noī ˈnen səs

TRANSLATION - [Greek name for walnut] [from Illinois].

SYNONYM - *Carya illinoensis, C. olivaeformis.*

FORM - Monoecious, deciduous tree, massive branching, wide-spreading, oval to round canopy. Medium texture.

SIZE - To 150, typically 70 to 100 feet with 40 to 75 foot spread, slow to moderate growth rate.

HARDINESS ZONE - Zone 5. Grows best in north Florida.

NATIVE HABITAT - Midwestern U.S. south to Mexico.

LEAVES - Odd-pinnately compound, alternate, 10 to 18 inches long, leaflets 11 to 17, of nearly uniform size, oblong-lanceolate to 7 inches long, asymmetrical, serrate margins, long acuminate, almost sessile, young leaves pubescent becoming glabrous at maturity, aromatic when crushed.

STEM/BARK - Gray-brown exfoliating bark on trunk. Young stem stout, olive-brown, pubescent. Large terminal bud (0.5 inch), yellowish-brown, pubescent. On older trees, lower branches become wide-sweeping, almost touching ground.

FLOWERS - Plants monoecious, male flowers in drooping catkins 3 to 5 inches long, female flowers in terminal racemes, inconspicuous; flowers April, May.

FRUIT - Drupe, oblong; brown nut is enclosed in a thick husk that splits into 4 valves; edible.

CULTURE - Full sun; fertile, well-drained soils; not salt tolerant. Difficult to transplant due to long taproot. Not well adapted to urban sites.

PROBLEMS - Tent caterpillars are a major pest; also borers, scale, aphids, bagworms, nut weevils, scab, minor element deficiencies (especially zinc) on high-pH soils. A high-maintenance plant because of these problems. Leaves and husks, during rains or as result of damage, release a substance that stains clothes, pavement, cars, etc.

PROPAGATION - Budding, grafting.

LANDSCAPE USES - Large landscapes, parks, fruit tree. Wildlife attracted by the fruit.

COMMENTS - Many cultivars for nut quality, disease resistance, regions. Be sure to select a cultivar suitable for your particular area of the country. **'Desirable'** and **'Stuart'** among the most popular in Florida. Wood used for flooring, cabinets, furniture.

LAMIACEAE (= LABIATAE) - MINT FAMILY

DICOTYLEDONS; ABOUT 220 GENERA MORE THAN 3000 SPECIES

GEOGRAPHY: Cosmopolitan.

GROWTH HABIT: Herbs, subshrubs, and rarely trees, with square stem.

LEAVES: Opposite and decussate, usually simple; stipules lacking; characteristically aromatic.

FLOWERS: Strongly zygomorphic; usually bisexual; scpals 5; petals 5, fused, mostly bilabiate; stamens 2 or 4, epipetalous; ovary superior, with 2 fused carpels and 4 locules.

FRUIT: Four 1-seeded nutlets.

ECONOMIC USES: Ornamentals, many herbs (mints, sage, oregano, basil, and others), source of several essential oils, etc.

ORNAMENTAL GENERA: *Ajuga, Iboza, Lavandula, Ocimum, Plectranthus, Rosmarinus, Salvia, Solenostemon, Westringia.*

COMMENTS: *Coleus* is no longer recognized as a distinct genus. The species previously assigned to *Coleus* are now included in the two genera *Plectranthus* and *Solenostemon.*

Ajuga reptans

PRONUNCIATION - ə ˈjū gə ˈrep tənz

TRANSLATION - [bugle-origin obscure] [creeping].

FORM - Monoecious, perennial herb, stoloniferous, coarse-textured, forming compact, dense, low mats with a flaccid appearance.

SIZE - Reaches a height of 10 inches with an indeterminate spread. Grows at a fairly rapid rate.

HARDINESS ZONE - Zone 6. Should be grown only in north Florida.

NATIVE HABITAT - Europe.

LEAVES - Opposite, in basal rosettes, oblong to ovate to spatulate, 3 inches long and 1 inch wide, rounded apex. The nearly sessile leaves often have wavy margins and range in color from dark green to bronze-purple, depending on cultivar.

STEM/BARK - Acaulescent, spreads by above-ground stolons.

FLOWERS - Blue, small, tubular, in compact whorls (verticillasters) on erect, terminal, 8-inch-tall spikes in March; showy when massed.

FRUIT - Four very small, obovoid nutlets within the withered remains of each pollinated flower.

CULTURE - Grows best in partial shade but tolerates full sun or shade. Requires fertile soil which is moist but not soggy. It is not salt or foot traffic tolerant; moderately drought tolerant. Not a good competitor against weeds, especially in sunny situation.

PROBLEMS - Crown rot on soggy soils; nematodes on sandy soils; spider mites in hot, dry locations; southern blight in moist, shady sites in southeast U.S. These may make this species a high maintenance or short-lived planting, especially in poorly suited sites.

PROPAGATION - By division, or less commonly, by seed.

LANDSCAPE USES - A ground cover, rock garden plant, showy when in bloom, durable and fast-covering when cultural requirements are met. One of the few ground covers to perform well under trees producing dense shade. Can be interplanted with *Liriope muscari* or *Ophiopogon japonicus* to give quick coverage while the *Liriope* or *Ophiopogon* becomes established.

COMMENTS - Many cultivars are listed, varying in leaf and flower color, variegation and adaptability to full sun: **'Alba'** - white flowers; **'Atropurpurea'** - blue flowers, bronze foliage; **'Burgundy Lace'** - rose flowers, rose and white variegated foliage; **'Rubra'** - dark purple foliage; **'Variegata'** - mottled and edged with creamy-white.

Solenostemon scutellarioides COLEUS

PRONUNCIATION - ˌsō lə ˈnɑ stə mən ˌskū tə la rē ˈoī dēz

TRANSLATION - [from Greek *soleno* (= a tube) and stamen] [*scutel* (a salver), platter-like, in reference to the first formed leaf].

SYNONYM - *Coleus ✕ hybridus.*

FORM - Monoecious, evergreen; herbaceous annual or perennial; freely branching, succulent, densely foliated, spreading; medium-coarse texture.

SIZE - Varies with cultivar; ranges from 6 inches to 3 feet in height; rapid growth rate.

HARDINESS ZONE - Zones 10-11; can be grown as a perennial only in south Florida; cultivated as a summer annual elsewhere.

NATIVE HABITAT - Old World tropics.

LEAVES - Simple; opposite; generally ovate in outline to, 8 inches long; mostly acuminate tips; soft-textured; margins crenate, serrate, often undulate, ruffled, or lobed. The leaves come in many colors and color combinations: patterns of pink, white, yellow, red, green, and maroon are available.

STEM/BARK - Square in cross section; green or brown-green or sometimes red-purple; becoming woody with age.

FLOWERS - Corolla pale to dark blue; not showy; borne in terminal panicles crowded at apex, progressively farther apart toward the base.

FRUIT - Nutlets; 4, smooth; seeds many, minute.

CULTURE - Grows in full sun to partial shade on various soils; no salt tolerance.

PROBLEMS - Mealybugs, caterpillars, fungus diseases.

PROPAGATION - Seeds, cuttings.

LANDSCAPE USES - Used as a bedding plant, in planter boxes or as edging material.

COMMENTS - More than 200 named cultivars with a tremendous variety of plant heights and leaf shapes and colors are available. Non-flowering cultivars also available. A related species, *S. shirensis (= C. shirensis)*, is also available.

Plectranthus australis

PRONUNCIATION - plek 'træn thəs   o 'stræ ləs

TRANSLATION - [from Greek *plectron* (= a spur) and *anthos* (= flower)] [southern].

FORM - Monoecious, evergreen; herbaceous perennial; ground cover, trailing, spreading, soft-stemmed; medium texture.

SIZE - To 1 foot tall; rapid growth rate.

HARDINESS ZONE - Zone 9b; grown outside in central and south Florida.

NATIVE HABITAT - Australia.

LEAVES - Simple; opposite; 4-ranked; broadly ovate to 1.5 inches across; waxy, dark green, somewhat fleshy, rugose; glaucous gray-green beneath and have purplish veins if grown under reasonable light intensity; crenate margins.

STEM/BARK - Stem is 4-angled.

FLOWERS - Pale purple or whitish; campanulate, 2-lipped, to 0.25 inch long; borne in 8 inch long racemes.

FRUIT - Nutlets.

CULTURE - Requires partial to full shade; foliage will burn if exposed to full sun; requires relatively high light in interiors; various soils; no salt tolerance.

PROBLEMS - Mites, mealybugs, chewing insects.

PROPAGATION - Cuttings root readily even in tap water.

LANDSCAPE USES - Used as a ground cover or in hanging baskets.

COMMENTS - *Plectranthus* is closely related to *Solenostemon (= Coleus)* and includes several species in cultivation. Some species previously placed in *Coleus* are now included in this genus.

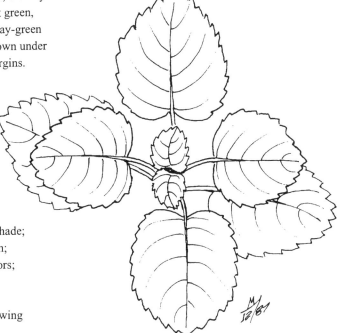

Salvia splendens   SCARLET SAGE

PRONUNCIATION - ˈsæl vē ə   ˈsplen dənz

TRANSLATION - [from Latin *salvus* (safe, unharmed), referring to medicinal properties of some species] [splendid].

FORM - Monoecious, herbaceous perennial subshrub, erect, freely branching, vigorous (grown as an annual in Florida).

SIZE - Variable with cultivar, from 8 inches to 8 feet (to 30 inches in Florida) rapid growth.

HARDINESS ZONE - Zone 9b. Grown throughout Florida as an annual bedding plant.

NATIVE HABITAT - Southern Brazil.

LEAVES - Simple, opposite, ovate to 4 inches long, acuminate tip, interveinal areas often puckered, bright green, glabrous, crenate-serrate margins.

STEM/BARK - Square, green, succulent.

FLOWERS - Terminal raceme, 2 to 6 flowers per whorl, bracts red, deciduous, corolla campanulate, 2-lipped, to 1.5 inches long, scarlet, lower lip much reduced, stamens 2, flowers summer to frost.

FRUIT - Nutlet, ovoid, 3-angled.

CULTURE - Full sun to partial shade, various well-drained soils; not salt tolerant.

PROBLEMS - Scale, caterpillars, chewing insects.

PROPAGATION - Seeds, cuttings of cultivars.

LANDSCAPE USES - Bedding plants, planter box. Flowers attract hummingbirds.

COMMENTS - Many cultivars with different flower colors (white, violet, rose, salmon, blue), plant habit, size, etc. A related native species, *S. coccinea*, a larger plant than *S. splendens*, is available in the trade.

LAURACEAE - LAUREL FAMILY

DICOTYLEDONS; 45 GENERA AND ABOUT 2,500 SPECIES

GEOGRAPHY:	Mostly tropics and subtropics, centered in the Amazonia and Southeast Asia, but with a few genera in the warm temperate areas.
GROWTH HABIT:	Predominantly trees and shrubs but a few leafless twining parasites.
LEAVES:	Evergreen; alternate or rarely opposite, leathery, simple, without stipules, and usually aromatic.
FLOWERS:	Small, actinomorphic, bisexual or unisexual (plants monoecious); 3-merous or in multiples; perianth of tepals and inconspicuous; stamens in whorls of threes or fours; ovary superior and surrounded by a cup-like receptacle.
FRUIT:	Berry or drupe, enclosed by a fleshy cupule.
ECONOMIC USES:	Ornamentals, cinnamon and camphor, oil of sassafras, avocado, timber, and medicinal uses.

ORNAMENTAL GENERA: *Cinnamomum, Laurus, Licaria, Lindera, Nectandra, Persea, Sassafras, Umbellularia,* and others.

Cinnamomum camphora   CAMPHOR TREE

PRONUNCIATION - ˌsi nə ˈmō məm kæm ˈfo rə

TRANSLATION - [ancient Greek name] [resembling camphor].

FORM - Monoecious, evergreen tree, single or multitrunked, closely branched, symmetrical, rounded canopy, spreading. Medium texture.

SIZE - To 100 feet, commonly 30 to 50 feet with 40 to 60 foot spread in Florida, rapid growth.

HARDINESS ZONE - Zone 8b. Grown in all areas of Florida. Severe freeze injury occurs when temperatures drop to 18° F for several days; crowns were severely damaged in north Florida during the 1983 and 1984 winters.

NATIVE HABITAT - China, Taiwan, Japan. Has escaped from cultivation throughout Florida and the lower South.

LEAVES - Simple, alternate, entire, often undulate, ovate to 5 inches long, acuminate apex, glossy-green above, blue-green below, thin but leathery, oil glands in vein axils near leaf base; camphor aroma when crushed.

STEM/BARK - Trunks dark gray-brown with deep, irregular furrows, rugged-looking; young stems up to 2 inch diameter bright green and glabrous. Youngest stems may be tinged red. Wood is moderately strong, not easily damaged by storms.

FLOWERS - Yellow, in axillary panicles, inconspicuous.

FRUIT - Drupe black, globose, 0.25 inch diameter in clusters. Somewhat showy.

CULTURE - Full sun to partial shade; varied soils; slightly salt tolerant. May develop minor element deficiencies on alkaline soils. Highly tolerant of urban conditions but does not like waterlogged situations.

PROBLEMS - Mites, scale; none serious. Tree casts a deep shade, making it impossible to grow grass beneath the canopy. Fruit can be messy near pavement. Seedlings resulting from the prolific fruit production can cause a weed problem.

PROPAGATION - Seed.

LANDSCAPE USES - Shade tree, street tree, parks. Too large for most city lots. Fruits serve as a food source for wildlife.

COMMENTS - The commercial source of camphor, which is extracted from the twigs, leaves, and wood. Dried bark of *Cinnamomum zeylanicum* yields cinnamon. *Cinnamomum camphora* has become much too widespread and weedy in many areas of Florida. Other species in cultivation in Florida include *C. aromaticum* (= *C. cassia* - Chinese Cinnamon, Cassia Bark) and *C. massoia.*

Persea americana

PRONUNCIATION - pər 'sē ə   ə ˌme rə 'kā nə

TRANSLATION - [from the Greek name *Persea*, in reference to the Egyptian tree *Cordia mixa*] [American].

FORM - Evergreen tree, low-branching, variously shaped open canopy. Coarse texture.

SIZE - To 60 feet, usually seen 35 to 40 feet, rapid growth.

HARDINESS ZONE - Zone 9b. Grown in south and protected areas of central Florida.

NATIVE HABITAT - Tropical America.

LEAVES - Simple, spirally arranged, entire, elliptic with acuminate tip, to 8 inches long, glossy-green above, light green below, yellow venation, undulate, glabrescent, aromatic when crushed.

STEM/BARK - Young stems green, angled at nodes.

FLOWERS - Greenish-gray, small, in large terminal panicles, pubescent, not showy; flowers in late winter to spring.

FRUIT - Drupe, pear-shaped, to 10 inches long, fleshy, edible.

CULTURE - Full sun to partial shade, varied well-drained soils; not salt tolerant.

PROBLEMS - Mites, scale, root rot (major problem in poorly drained sites), fire blight. Brittle wood subject to storm damage.

PROPAGATION - Seed, graftage.

LANDSCAPE USES - Dooryard fruit, shade tree, urn.

COMMENTS - Many cultivars for fruit production. Three races are recognized: Guatemalan and West Indian are typical for var. *americana*, while Mexican belongs to var. *drymifolia*.

Persea borbonia   RED BAY

PRONUNCIATION - pər sē ə   bor 'bō nē ə

TRANSLATION - [from the Greek name *Persea*, in reference to the Egyptian tree *Cordia mixa*] [after Gaston de Bourbon (1608-1660), Duke of Orleans and son of Henry IV of France].

FORM - Monoecious, evergreen tree, upright, rounded, columnar, densely foliated, of medium texture.

SIZE - Can reach a height of 50 feet and a spread of 20 feet. Growth rate is medium.

HARDINESS ZONE - Zone 8, can be grown in all areas of Florida.

NATIVE HABITAT - Hammocks, pine woods, and moist areas throughout Florida and the southeastern U.S. coastal plain.

LEAVES - Alternate, broadly lanceolate, to 6 inches long. The leathery, glossy leaves are dark green and glabrous above, glaucous below, entire to slightly undulate, with acute to obtuse apices. Emit spicy odor when crushed.

STEM/BARK - Twigs are slender, somewhat angled, smooth, and green or reddish green. The bark is purplish-brown, thick and ridged.

FLOWERS - Creamy, small, inconspicuous, in few-flowered axillary clusters on the new growth in spring.

FRUIT - Drupes, dark blue, subglobose, 0.25 inch wide, subtended by small cupule, on 1-inch, orange peduncles, ripening in fall.

CULTURE - Grows in full sun or partial shade on a wide range of soils. Tolerates poor drainage and moderate amounts of salt.

PROBLEMS - Generally pest-free, but insect-caused galls can distort and disfigure the leaves and are quite common.

PROPAGATION - By seed, which germinate readily after several months in the ground.

LANDSCAPE USES - A tough tree, used as a specimen or for shade. Does well in hot, harsh situations like parking lots. Works well as a background plant for a naturalistic effect. Wildlife feed on fruit.

COMMENTS - A rugged, adaptable plant. *Persea borbonia* var. *humilis*, *Persea palustris* and *Persea indica* are also offered.

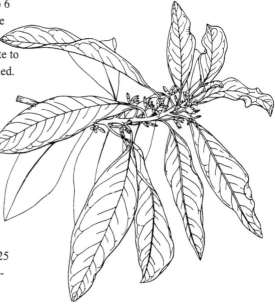

LEEACEAE - LEEA FAMILY

DICOTYLEDONS; MONOGENERIC WITH ABOUT 70 SPECIES

GEOGRAPHY: Tropics of the Old World.

GROWTH HABIT: Trees, shrubs, and herbaceous perennials, sometimes with prickly stems.

LEAVES: Pinnately to tripinnately compound, rarely ternate or simple, alternate or very rarely opposite, usually dentate, exstipulate.

FLOWERS: Inflorescence usually terminal, corymbose, many-flowered, often tomentose; bisexual; sepals, petals, and stamens usually five, anthers usually opposite to and adnate to the petals; carpels 3-8, with each locule containing 1 ovule.

FRUIT: Berry.

ECONOMIC USES: Ornamentals.

ORNAMENTAL GENERA: *Leea.*

COMMENTS: *Leea* was previously included in Vitidaceae (= Vitaceae), from which it differs in the number of carpels and its locules and several other technical characteristics.

Leea coccinea

WEST INDIAN HOLLY

PRONUNCIATION - 'lē ə   kαk 'si nē ə

TRANSLATION - [after James Lee (1715-1795), nurseryman of Hammersmith, London] [scarlet].

FORM - Evergreen shrub, glabrous.

SIZE - To 8 feet tall.

HARDINESS ZONE - Zones 10-11. Can be grown outside only in south Florida.

NATIVE HABITAT - Burma.

LEAVES - Bipinnately compound, alternate, to 1 foot long, leathery, glossy green. Leaflets elliptic to obovate, to 4 inches long, with undulate or wavy margins. New growth has a reddish cast.

STEM/BARK - Stem has a slightly zigzag growth pattern. New stems are green, becoming brown with age. The terminal bud is protected during its initial development by a covering which splits allowing the stem to elongate.

FLOWERS - Red, tubular, small, borne in flat-topped, terminal cymes to 5 inches in diameter.

FRUIT - Berry.

CULTURE - Tolerates full sun and grows under light levels down to 250 foot-candles. Various well-drained soils, drought tolerant. Moderately salt tolerant.

PROBLEMS - Occasionally chewing insects are a problem.

PROPAGATION - Cuttings.

LANDSCAPE USES - Used in interiors for its foliage, as a patio or specimen plant; outdoors used in shrubbery borders or as a freestanding specimen.

COMMENTS - A red leaf cultivar with more appeal as an interior plant is available. A few related species, including *L. manillensis* (flowers green-white) and *L. sambucina* (flowers yellow-pink) are also grown in Florida.

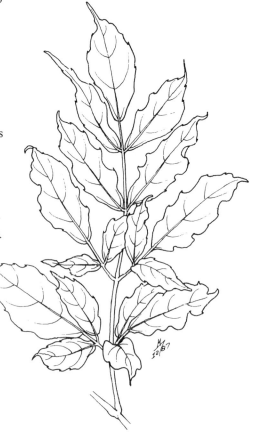

LOGANIACEAE - LOGANIA FAMILY

DICOTYLEDONS; 29 OR 30 GENERA AND ABOUT 600 SPECIES

GEOGRAPHY: Temperate, subtropical, and tropical regions.

GROWTH HABIT: Trees, shrubs, and vines.

LEAVES: Opposite, entire, pinnately veined, stipules small.

FLOWERS: Actinomorphic, bisexual; 4- or 5-merous; sepals imbricate, petals
                  usually imbricate and tubular; stamens 4-5, epipetalous; ovary
                  superior and consists of 2 carpels.

FRUIT: Capsule or berry.

ECONOMIC USES: Ornamentals; many members of this family are highly poisonous
                  and contain strychnine; several species are sources of timber.

ORNAMENTAL GENERA: *Buddleja, Fagraea, Gelsemium, Nicodema*, and others.

COMMENTS: Loganiaceae is sometimes split into several families, such as
                  Budliaceae, Antoniaceae, and Spigeliaceae.

Gelsemium sempervirens

CAROLINA JESSAMINE,
YELLOW JESSAMINE

PRONUNCIATION - jel ˈse mē əm   ˌsem pər ˈvɪ rənz̄

TRANSLATION - [from *gelsomino*, Italian for jasmine] [evergreen].

FORM - Monoecious, climbing evergreen vine of fine texture.

SIZE - Variable, depends on size of support. A moderate grower.

HARDINESS ZONE - Zone 7. Can be grown in all areas of Florida.

NATIVE HABITAT - Southeastern United States and Central America.

LEAVES - Opposite, lanceolate, to 3 inches long, acute to acuminate, dark green and glossy with entire margins, short-petioled. The leaves take on a red-purple tinge during the winter.

STEM/BARK - The slender, tough, wiry stems are reddish-brown and climb by twining.

FLOWERS - Bright yellow, funnelform with 5 short lobes, about 1 inch long, in axillary cymes. Flowers are very fragrant and appear in late January to early February, making them the earliest of spring blooms.

FRUIT - Capsules, brown, two-parted, ovoid, release winged seeds in late summer. Not ornamental.

CULTURE - Grows in full sun (best flowering) to partial shade on a wide range of acid or alkaline soils. It is not salt tolerant.

PROBLEMS - Pest-free.

PROPAGATION - Mature wood cuttings in fall, ground layers, or seed.

LANDSCAPE USES - Used to cover walls, fences, and arbors. Often planted near trees to allow it to grow among their branches. Occasionally used as a ground cover. This vine tends to be less rampant and needs less pruning than most vines.

COMMENTS - All parts of this plant are poisonous if ingested, so avoid using where animals graze or where there is high contact with children. Honey from this plant's flowers is inedible. The cultivar **'Plena' ('Pride of Augusta')** has double flowers.

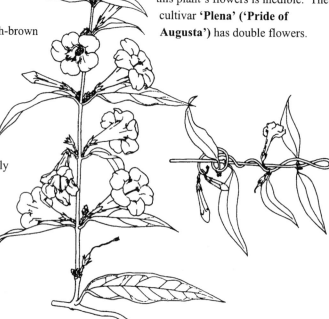

LYTHRACEAE - LOOSESTRIFE FAMILY

DICOTYLEDONS; 22 GENERA AND ABOUT 450 SPECIES

GEOGRAPHY:	Pantropical but with a few annual and perennial herbs in temperate areas.
GROWTH HABIT:	Predominantly herbaceous but includes several shrubs and trees.
LEAVES:	Opposite or whorled; simple, entire, usually without stipules.
FLOWERS:	In racemose, paniculate, or cymose inflorescences; actinomorphic, bisexual, 4- or 6-merous; epicalyx is sometimes present; perigynous, with free petals on the rim of the calyx tube and stamens inserted within the calyx tube; ovary is superior.
FRUIT:	Capsule.
ECONOMIC USES:	Ornamentals, source of several important dyes (e.g., henna from *Lawsonia inermis*) and valuable timber.

ORNAMENTAL GENERA: *Cuphea, Heimia, Lagerstroemia, Lawsonia, Woodfordia.*

Cuphea hyssopifolia   FALSE HEATHER, MEXICAN HEATHER

PRONUNCIATION - kū 'fē ə   hī ˌsɑ pə 'fō lē ə

TRANSLATION - [from Greek *kyphos* (curved), in reference to curved cupule] [*Hyssopus*-leaved].

FORM - Monoecious, evergreen shrub; small, erect, round; low-branching, compact and dense; fine texture.

SIZE - To 2 feet, commonly to 1 foot; moderate growth rate.

HARDINESS ZONE - Zone 9; can be grown in central and south Florida.

NATIVE HABITAT - Mexico and Guatemala.

LEAVES - Simple; opposite or whorled; linear or lanceolate to 0.75 inch long; acute apices; crowded on stem; margins entire; dark green.

STEM/BARK - Peeling bark.

FLOWERS - Purple, pink, or white; axillary; 6 petals, to 0.25 inch across; solitary or in clusters. Blooms much of the year, especially during warm seasons; showy.

FRUIT - Capsule; small, papery; to 0.25 inch. Viable seeds fall to ground and germinate, forming thick masses.

CULTURE - Grow in full sun or partial shade on varied soils; requires 2 to 3 hours direct sun for best form; no salt tolerance.

PROBLEMS - Nematodes.

PROPAGATION - Seeds, cuttings.

LANDSCAPE USES - Effective in mass plantings, as an edging material, or ground cover.

COMMENTS - A cultivar, **'Alba'**, with white flowers, is available. Also, a related species, *C. ignea* (Cigar Plant), is available in Florida.

Lagerstroemia indica   CREPE MYRTLE

PRONUNCIATION - ˈlæ gər ˈstrō mē ə   ˈin də kə

TRANSLATION - [after Magnus von Lagerströem (1696-1759), Swedish merchant and friend of Linnaeus] [from India].

FORM - Monoecious, deciduous shrub or small tree, erect, freely branching, often suckering. Medium-fine texture.

SIZE - To 40 feet, commonly 20 feet (dwarf cvs. to 6 feet and semi-dwarf cvs. 6 to 15 feet), rapid growth.

HARDINESS ZONE - Zone 7. Grown in all regions of Florida.

NATIVE HABITAT - China, Korea.

LEAVES - Simple, subopposite (may be alternate on vigorously growing branches), oblong-elliptic to rounded, to 3 inches long, short-petioled or sessile, acute or obtuse, entire, growth pubescent beneath especially when young, some fall color (red, orange, yellow - variable with cultivar and among seedlings).

STEM/BARK - Bark smooth, brown, peeling in patches, very showy; new growth 4-angled or ribbed, pinkish. Wood is moderately durable.

FLOWERS - White, pink, red, purple; in terminal and axillary panicles 6 to 12 inches long; petals 6, crinkled, to 1.25 inches long, flowers in late spring, early summer and effective for much of the summer.

FRUIT - Brown globose capsule, to 0.5 inch in diameter.

CULTURE - Full sun, varied well-drained soils, not salt tolerant. Drought tolerant. Easily transplanted. To avoid powdery mildew problem, plant in sunny, open site with good air circulation.

PROBLEMS - Aphids, powdery mildew (a major problem), sooty mold, root rot.

PROPAGATION - Cuttings to maintain cultivar integrity.

LANDSCAPE USES - Border, street plantings, framing tree, in groups or as specimen, patio.

COMMENTS - Many cultivars for color, habit, etc. Powdery mildew resistant cvs. (many are *L. indica* × *L. fauriei*), listed below, are becoming so common that there is virtually no reason to use a nonresistant cultivar. 'Apalachee' - to 12 feet, light lavender; 'Biloxi' - to 25 feet, pale pink; 'Comanche' - to 12 feet, coral pink; 'Hopi' - to 7 feet, medium pink; 'Miami' - to 20 feet, dark pink; 'Muskogee' - to 24 feet, light lavender; 'Natchez' - to 30 feet, white; 'Osage' - to 12 feet, clear pink; 'Potomac' - to 20 feet, clear pink; 'Sioux' - to 15 feet, medium pink; 'Tuscarora' - to 16 feet, coral to dark pink; 'Tuskegee' - to 15 feet, coral to dark pink; 'Wichita' - to 20 feet, lavender; 'Yuma' - to 15 feet, medium lavender; 'Zuni' - to 10 feet, medium lavender.

Lagerstroemia speciosa

REINA DE LAS FLORES,
QUEEN'S CREPE MYRTLE

PRONUNCIATION - ˌlæ gər ˈstrō mē ə   ˈspē sē ˈō sə

TRANSLATION - [after Magnus von Lagerströem (1696-1759), Swedish merchant and friend of Linnaeus] [showy].

FORM - Monoecious, deciduous tree; vase-shaped (oval); densely foliated; coarse texture.

SIZE - Reaches a height of 45 feet with a spread of 35 feet; medium growth rate.

HARDINESS ZONE - Zones 10-11; can be grown only in south Florida.

NATIVE HABITAT - Asian tropics.

LEAVES - Simple; alternate to subopposite; oblong to 1 foot long and 4 inches wide; veins prominent; glabrous, leathery; turn red and drop with winter cold.

STEM/BARK - Smooth, mottled, peeling bark. The wood is used for railroad ties and construction in India.

FLOWERS - Pink or lavender; to 3 inches wide; the flowers have 5 to 9 ruffled, crepy petals and more than 100 yellow stamens; borne in 1 foot or longer terminal panicles. Blooms in June and July.

FRUIT - Dehiscent capsules; round, brown; 1 inch wide; releasing 0.5-inch-long winged seeds in fall.

CULTURE - Grows in full sun on a wide range of soils; no salt tolerance.

PROBLEMS - Cottony cushion scale and aphids, followed by sooty mold.

PROPAGATION - Seed germinate readily and seedlings flower the second year; cuttings, division or root suckers.

LANDSCAPE USES - Use as a specimen, shade, or street tree.

COMMENTS - In addition to the species described here several others are, to a greater or lesser extent, grown in Florida, including *L. duperreana, L. floribunda, L. hirsuta, L. loudonii, L. siamica, L. subcostata, L. tomentosa, L. villosa,* and probably others.

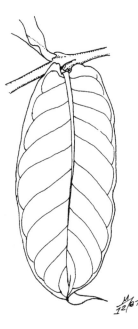

MAGNOLIACEAE - MAGNOLIA FAMILY

DICOTYLEDONS; 12 GENERA AND ABOUT 220 SPECIES

GEOGRAPHY: Temperate and tropical Asia and North and South America.

GROWTH HABIT: Trees and shrubs with aromatic bark.

LEAVES: Alternate, simple, entire, petiolate, and with distinctly large
                    stipules which enclose the apical bud and leave a marked stipular
                    scar.

FLOWERS: Solitary, often large and very showy; parts numerous, free, and
                    spirally arranged; tepals enclosed within a pair of bracts before
                    expansion; carpels may be partially fused to form a cone-like
                    structure.

FRUIT: Follicetum (fused or separate single-seeded follicles, as in
                    Magnolia) or samaracetums (single-seeded samaras, as in
                    Liriodendron).

ECONOMIC USES: Ornamentals, timber, and medicinal uses.

ORNAMENTAL GENERA: *Liriodendron, Magnolia, Michelia.*

Liriodendron tulipifera   TULIP TREE, YELLOW POPLAR

PRONUNCIATION - ˌlē rē ō 'den drən   ˌtū lə 'pi fə rə

TRANSLATION - [from Greek *leiron* (= a lily) and *dendron* (= a tree)] [tulip-bearing, in reference to the flowers and/or leaf shape].

FORM - Deciduous tree, upright, excurrent, symmetrical branching, dense oval canopy. Coarse texture.

SIZE - To 200 feet, commonly 50 to 75 feet with 40 to 60 foot spread; rapid growth.

HARDINESS ZONE - Zone 4. Grows well only in north Florida.

NATIVE HABITAT - Eastern United States.

LEAVES - Simple, alternate, lobed, somewhat tulip-shaped in profile (hence the common name), to 6 inches wide, apex broad and truncate, entire margins, 2 to 4 inches long petiole thickened at base. Called Yellow Poplar due to yellow fall color and the leaves that dance in the wind like cottonwood or aspen (*Populus* spp.).

STEM/BARK - Gray, rough bark. Young stems green or reddish-green, aromatic, sometimes glaucous, with stipular scars surrounding stem at each node. Terminal bud distinctively "duck-bill"-shaped. Wood is brittle, easily broken during storms.

FLOWERS - Petals greenish-yellow with broad orange band at base to 2 inches long. Terminal, solitary, cup-shaped flowers are held erect, above leaves high in the tree (frequently overlooked unless viewed from overhead) in spring.

FRUIT - Cone-like aggregate of samaras (samaracetum) brown to 3 inches long.

CULTURE - Full sun to partial shade; moist, fertile, well-drained soils; not salt or drought tolerant. Newly transplanted trees prone to leaf yellowing and leaf drop if moisture inadequate.

PROBLEMS - Borers, chewing insects, aphids, leaf spots, root and stem rot. Weak-wooded.

PROPAGATION - Seed, grafting of cultivars.

LANDSCAPE USES - Parks, street plantings (exhibits leaf scorch unless roots have plenty of room), shade, naturalized areas, for large areas only.

COMMENTS - Several cultivars for leaf shape, canopy habit, etc., are widely available: **'Aureomarginatum'** - yellow leaf margins; **'Aureo-picta'** - yellow blotch in center of leaf; **'Compactum'** - dwarf form with leaves 1/2 size of species; **'Fastigiatum'** - narrow, upright form. Also the very similar Chinese species, *L. chinense.*

Magnolia grandiflora   SOUTHERN MAGNOLIA, BULL BAY

PRONUNCIATION - mæg 'nō lē ə   'græn də 'flo rə

TRANSLATION - [after Pierre Magnol (1638-1715), French professor of botany] [large-flowered].

FORM - Monoecious, evergreen tree, upright, large-trunked, pyramidal when young, asymmetrical with age. Coarse texture.

SIZE - To 100 feet with 50 to 60 foot spread, slow to moderate growth rate.

HARDINESS ZONE - Zone 7. Grown in north and central Florida.

NATIVE HABITAT - Eastern United States.

LEAVES - Simple, alternate, ovate-oblong to 8 inches long, margins often undulate, thick, leathery, glossy-green above (looks polished), often rusty and tomentose below, especially when young, entire margins, petioles stout and pubescent.

STEM/BARK - Trunk pale gray, mottled, often with lichens. Young stems green, stout, often with rusty pubescence, becoming smooth, very brittle. Older wood more durable.

FLOWERS - White, waxy, to 8 inches across, solitary, terminal, fragrant, very showy, flowers in early spring and sporadically throughout summer. Can be used as cut flower.

FRUIT - Cone-like aggregate of follicles (follicetum) to 4 inches long, brown, tomentose, many red fleshy seeds exposed when ripe (October to November).

CULTURE - Full sun (for best flowering) or partial shade, varied soils, moderately salt tolerant. Once established, tolerates moderately wet or dry soils. Sensitive to soil compaction. Growth can be accelerated considerably by fertilization.

PROBLEMS - Scale can be a severe problem, bacterial leaf spot. Large leaves create litter problem when they fall.

PROPAGATION - Seed, cuttings, graftage of cultivars.

LANDSCAPE USES - Shade tree, specimen, street plantings, framing tree, long-lived. Needs lots of room.

COMMENTS - Several cultivars available: **'Glen St. Mary'** (**'St. Mary'**) - compact form, slow-growing, bronze underside of leaf; **'Gloriosa'** - large flowers and leaves; **'Goliath'** - flowers to 12 inches across; **'Lanceolata'** - narrow pyramidal form, narrower leaves with rusty pubescence below; **'Little Gem'** - dwarf upright form, smaller leaves, and compact growth habit, slower growing than **'Glen St. Mary'**, bronze underside of leaf, heavy flowering; **'Majestic Beauty'** - profuse flowering, large dark green leaves, pyramidal shape. Patented. **'Samuel Sommer'** - flowers to 14 inches across, upright growth habit.

Magnolia × soulangiana   SAUCER MAGNOLIA

PRONUNCIATION - mæg ˈnō lē ə   sū ˌlæn jē ˈā nə

TRANSLATION - [after Pierre Magnol (1638-1715), French professor of botany] [after Chevalier Etienne Soulange-Bodin, French cavalry officer and director of Institute of Horticulture].

FORM - Monoecious, deciduous small tree, upright, irregular, open-branched, spreading, of coarse texture.

SIZE - Reaches 25 feet high with an equal spread. Growth rate is medium.

HARDINESS ZONE - Zone 5b. Should be grown only in north Florida.

NATIVE HABITAT - A natural hybrid between *M. denudata (= M. heptapeta)* and *M. liliiflora (= M. quinquepeta)*, discovered in the garden of M. Soulange-Bodin in Paris, in 1826.

LEAVES - Alternate, obovate, to 7 inches long and 4 inches wide, abrupt acuminate. The young leaves are often woolly and have entire margins.

STEM/BARK - Young twigs are woolly at first, becoming glossy brown with age. The bark is smooth and silvery-gray, with numerous low, stout, spreading branches. Large (0.5 to 0.75 inch long) terminal flower buds, densely pubescent, present from early summer until flowering the following spring. Vegetative buds much smaller. No fall color.

FLOWERS - Tulip-like, purplish on the outside, whitish on the inside, to 6 inches wide, only slightly fragrant. The solitary, terminal flowers emerge before the leaves in February, can be killed by late freezes.

FRUIT - Cone-like aggregate of follicles, red, 4 inches long, usually few-seeded, ripening in fall.

CULTURE - Grows in full sun or partial shade on fertile, acid, well-drained but moisture-retentive soils. No salt or drought tolerance. Pruning should be done shortly after flowering to avoid removal of flower buds.

PROBLEMS - Scales, nematodes, leaf spots, and mushroom root rot; generally none of these are major problems.

PROPAGATION - Softwood cuttings under mist with IBA treatments, grafting.

LANDSCAPE USES - A flowering specimen, obscure when not in bloom.

COMMENTS - Many cultivars, differing mainly in flower characteristics: ‘Alexandrina’ - larger, later flowering; ‘Burgundy’ - burgundy wine flowers, early flowering; ‘Lilliputian’ - smaller, shrub-like habit. Many others.

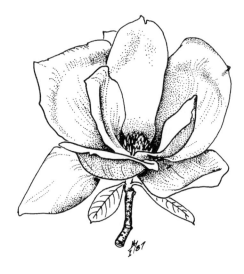

Magnolia stellata   STAR MAGNOLIA

PRONUNCIATION - mæg ′nō lē ə   stə ′lɑ tə

TRANSLATION - [after Pierre Magnol (1638-1715), French professor of botany] [star-like].

FORM - Monoecious, deciduous shrub or small tree, compact, rounded, and medium-textured.

SIZE - Can reach a height of 15 feet with a spread of 10 feet. Growth rate is slow.

HARDINESS ZONE - Zone 5b. Should be grown in north Florida only.

NATIVE HABITAT - Central Japan.

LEAVES - Alternate, oblong to obovate, to 5 inches long, entire, obtuse, dull green and glabrous above, light green and glabrous or appressed-pubescent along veins.

STEM/BARK - Either single- or multiple-trunked and densely branched. Young twigs are densely pubescent. Large (0.33 to 0.5 inch long) terminal flower buds densely pubescent.

FLOWERS - Showy, white, to 3 inches wide, with 12 to 18 spreading, finger-like petals. The solitary, terminal, fragrant flowers appear in February before the leaves. May be damaged by late freezes.

FRUIT - Cone-like aggregate of follicles, red, 2 inches long and few-seeded, in fall.

CULTURE - Grows in full sun or partial shade on fertile, acid, well-drained but moisture-retentive soils. It has no salt tolerance.

PROBLEMS - Scales and nematodes, generally none serious.

PROPAGATION - By softwood cuttings under mist with hormone treatments.

LANDSCAPE USES - As a specimen or accent shrub.

COMMENTS - Pink-flowered cultivars are available. Other deciduous magnolias reported from cultivation in Florida include *M. ashei* (Ashe Magnolia), *M. kobus, M. macrophylla, M. liliiflora,* and *M. tripetala.*

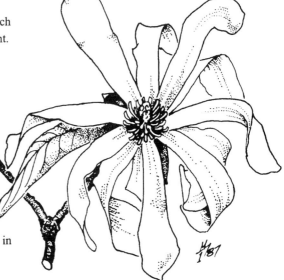

Magnolia virginiana   SWEET BAY

PRONUNCIATION - mæg 'nō lē ə   vər ˌji nē 'ā nə

TRANSLATION - [after Pierre Magnol (1638-1715), French professor of botany] [from Virginia].

FORM - Monoecious, evergreen tree, upright, columnar, with an open, rounded crown of irregular branches. Texture is coarse.

SIZE - Reaches a height of 75 feet and a spread of 35 feet, but much smaller in cultivation. Growth rate is medium.

HARDINESS ZONE - Zone 5. Can be grown throughout Florida.

NATIVE HABITAT - Swamps and low areas throughout Florida and the southeastern states.

LEAVES - Alternate, elliptic, to 6 inches long, thin, leathery and shining, entire, acute to obtuse. Leaf undersides are smooth and silvery-white. Aromatic.

STEM/BARK - The trunk, which can get 3 feet wide, is covered with smooth, gray bark. Young stems green, glaucous, with stipular scar encircling stem at each node.

FLOWERS - Cream-colored, 9 to 12 petaled, to 3 inches wide. The solitary, terminal flowers are very fragrant and appear in May or June and sporadically throughout summer.

FRUIT - Cone-like aggregate of follicles, red, ovoid, 2 inches long. The cones open

in September and October to reveal scarlet seeds hanging on threads.

CULTURE - Grows in partial shade or full sun on fertile, moist soils. Tolerates waterlogged conditions very well, but is not salt tolerant. Will not tolerate severe drought conditions but once established it survives short periods of dryness.

PROBLEMS - Scales and borers, usually none serious.

PROPAGATION - By seed, which need a chilling period plus sterile media to avoid rotting. Cuttings can be rooted under mist with rooting hormone treatment. Transplants from the wild with difficulty.

LANDSCAPE USES - A specimen/street tree. The silvery leaf undersides flash attractively in a wind.

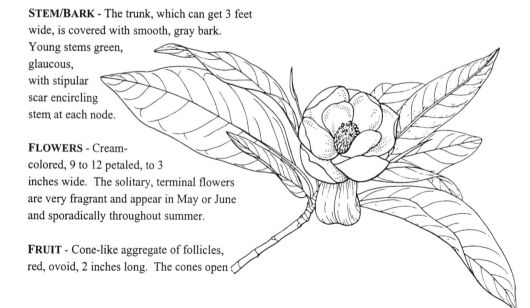

Michelia figo

Banana Shrub

PRONUNCIATION - mə ′she lē ə   ′fē gō

TRANSLATION - [after Pietro Antonio Micheli (1679-1737), Florentine botanist] [Chinese name].

SYNONYM - *Michelia fuscata.*

FORM - Monoecious, evergreen shrub, rounded, dense, multibranched, of medium texture.

SIZE - Reaches a maximum height and spread of 20 feet, but usually smaller. Growth rate is slow.

HARDINESS ZONE - Zone 7. Should be grown in north Florida only.

NATIVE HABITAT - China.

LEAVES - Alternate, elliptic to obovate, to 3 inches long, young leaves covered with rusty pubescence, becoming glabrous and dark green at maturity, petiole 0.25 inch long and also rusty pubescent.

STEM/BARK - Both the young branchlets and oval flower buds are brown-tomentose.

FLOWERS - Cream-yellow with purple edges, solitary, axillary, to 1.5 inches wide. Flowers appear in late March to early April and have a delightful, banana-like fragrance.

FRUIT - Cone-like aggregate of follicles, red, small, rarely produced.

CULTURE - Prefers partial shade but also grown in full sun. Requires fertile, well-drained soil and is not salt tolerant. Foliar chlorosis on alkaline soils.

PROBLEMS - Scales are a major pest; mushroom root rot can also cause problems.

PROPAGATION - Since the seeds, if produced, are nonviable, cuttings are the main method of propagation.

LANDSCAPE USES - This somewhat formal shrub can be used as a specimen or in corner plantings.

COMMENTS - *Michelia champaca* is reported from cultivation in Florida.

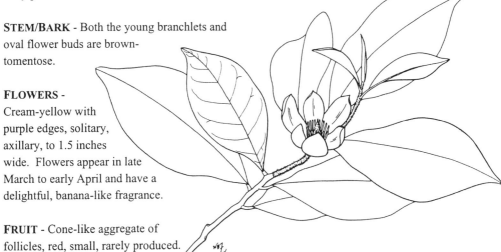

MALPIGHIACEAE - MALPIGHIA FAMILY

DICOTYLEDONS; ABOUT 60 GENERA AND 1000 SPECIES

GEOGRAPHY: World tropics, especially South America.

GROWTH HABIT: Trees, shrubs, and woody vines.

LEAVES: Opposite, simple, and with petiolar and lower side glands.

FLOWERS: Actinomorphic or zygomorphic; usually bisexual or rarely unisexual (plants monoecious); 5-merous with 5 imbricate sepals, 5 imbricate and clawed petals, and 10 basally fused stamens; ovary is superior and consists of 3 fused carpels.

FRUIT: Schizocarp or drupe.

ECONOMIC USES: Ornamentals, medicinal, and minor edible fruits.

ORNAMENTAL GENERA: *Acridocarpus, Banisteria, Bunchosia, Byrosonima, Galphimia, Heteropterys, Hiptage, Malpighia, Stigmaphyllon, Triopteris, Tristellateia,* etc.

Galphimia glauca   THRYALLIS, RAIN OF GOLD

PRONUNCIATION - gæl 'fi mē ə   'glau kə

TRANSLATION - [anagram of Malpighia)] [glaucous].

FORM - Monoecious, evergreen shrub; rounded, compact, densely foliated; medium-fine texture.

SIZE - Reaches a height of 8 feet with a 6 foot spread; rapid growth rate on good soils.

HARDINESS ZONE - Zone 9; can be grown in all areas of the state, but needs a protected location in north Florida.

NATIVE HABITAT - Central America.

LEAVES - Simple; opposite; oblong or elliptic, to 2 inches long; light green, becoming reddish-purple in winter. Petioles and stipules burgundy.

STEM/BARK - Slender, young twigs have many red hairs and appear reddish.

FLOWERS - Yellow; very showy; 0.5 inch wide; borne in densely flowered, terminal racemes to 4 inches long. Blooms almost continuously during warm months of the year.

FRUIT - Capsules; small, brown, dehiscent; 3-lobed; 0.25 inch wide.

CULTURE - Full sun for maximum flowering; any well-drained soil; no salt tolerance.

PROBLEMS - Caterpillars and mites occasionally.

PROPAGATION - By seeds or cuttings taken in July. Seed capsules should be planted when mature but still slightly green and unopened; seedlings bloom when 1 foot tall (6 months old).

LANDSCAPE USES - Use as a specimen, border accent, or foundation shrub.

COMMENTS - It has been noted that plants grown under the name *G. gracilis* may be *G. glauca.*

Malpighia coccigera

FLORIDA HOLLY, HOLLY MALPIGHIA,
MINIATURE HOLLY

PRONUNCIATION - mæl ˈpi gē ə   kɑk ˈsi jə rə

TRANSLATION - [after Marcello Malpighi (1628-1694), famous Italian professor of anatomy] [scarlet].

FORM - Monoecious, evergreen shrub; dwarf; upright, weeping or prostrate growth, depending on cultivar; fine texture.

SIZE - Reaches a maximum height of 3 feet with a variable spread; slow growth rate.

HARDINESS ZONE - Zones 9b-11; can be grown only in south Florida.

NATIVE HABITAT - West Indies.

LEAVES - Simple; opposite; elliptic in outline, to 0.75 inch long; leathery, glossy; usually with 5 to 9 large, spiny, marginal teeth; resemble miniature holly leaves.

FLOWER - Light pink; delicate; with 5 fringed, spatulate petals; 0.5 inch wide; borne in axillary cymes. Blooms periodically during warm months of the year.

FRUIT - Drupes; red, globose; 0.25 inch wide.

CULTURE - Does best in partial shade on a fertile, nematode-free soil; marginal salt tolerance.

PROBLEMS - Nematodes and scale.

PROPAGATION - Seeds or mature wood cuttings for cultivars.

LANDSCAPE USES - Used in foundation planting, massing, and dwarf hedges and as a facer plant or planter/pot plant. Prostrate forms have been used as ground covers.

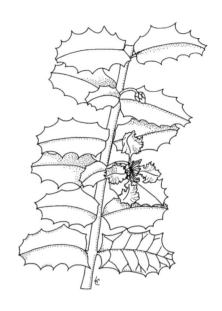

Malpighia glabra

ACEROLA, BARBADOS CHERRY

PRONUNCIATION - mæl 'pi gē ə 'glā brə

TRANSLATION - [after Marcello Malpighi (1628-1694), famous Italian professor of anatomy] [glabrous].

FORM - Monoecious, evergreen shrub; upright, vase-shaped; medium-fine texture.

SIZE - Reaches a height of 12 feet with a spread of 10 feet; moderate growth rate.

HARDINESS ZONE - Zone 9; can be grown in central and south Florida but needs a protected location in central Florida.

NATIVE HABITAT - Central America and the West Indies.

LEAVES - Simple; opposite; elliptic-lanceolate, to 3 inches long; margins entire; dark green.

STEM/BARK - Branches and twigs are very slender and densely branched.

FLOWERS - Pink; delicate; with 5 spatulate petals; 0.5 inch wide; borne in axillary umbels of 3 to 5. Blooms every 6 weeks from April to October.

FRUIT - Drupe; red, oblate, lobed; 1 inch wide, edible but tart; ripens about 1 month after bloom. The fruits have an extremely high vitamin C content.

CULTURE - Plant in full sun or partial shade on a fertile, well-drained soil; no salt tolerance.

PROBLEMS - Nematodes, whiteflies, scale. Plant bugs attack and deform fruit.

PROPAGATION - By mature wood cuttings taken in spring or summer with IBA treatments; air layers; avoid seedlings.

LANDSCAPE USES - Mainly grown as a fruiting specimen, but can be incorporated in shrub groupings.

COMMENTS - 'Florida Sweet' is the best fruit cultivar; 'Fairchild' has weeping habit. Fruit cultivars may be hybrids between *M. glabra* and *M. emarginata,* rather than pure *M. glabra.* A related species, *M. suberosa*, is also reported.

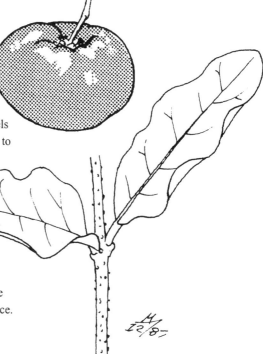

MALVACEAE - MALLOW FAMILY

DICOTYLEDONS; 121 GENERA AND ABOUT 1,500 SPECIES

GEOGRAPHY:	Cosmopolitan (except in colder regions), but especially in South America.
GROWTH HABIT:	Herbs, shrubs, and a few trees.
LEAVES:	Alternate, simple, often lobed, palmately veined, and stipulate.
FLOWERS:	Showy, actinomorphic, bisexual, 5-merous; sepals usually free but sometimes connate, and often subtended by an epicalyx; petals free; stamens united with the corolla at the base and form an "staminal column"; superior and consists of usually 5 united carpels.
FRUIT:	Capsule or schizocarp, or rarely a berry.
ECONOMIC USES:	Ornamentals, cotton (*Gossypium*), okra (*Hibiscus esculenta*), and fibers. Many species are weeds.

ORNAMENTAL GENERA: *Abutilon, Althaea, Gossypium, Hibiscus, Kydia, Lagunaria, Malvaviscus, Montezuma, Thespesia, Ulbirichia,* and others.

Hibiscus rosa-sinensis   HIBISCUS, ROSE-OF-CHINA

PRONUNCIATION - hī 'bis kəs   'rō zə   sī 'nen səs

TRANSLATION - [Greek for mallow] [Chinese rose].

FORM - Monoecious, evergreen shrub; large, upright, oval, many-branched, densely foliated; medium texture.

SIZE - To 20 feet tall, seldom seen over 10 feet in cultivation; rapid growth rate.

HARDINESS ZONE - Zone 8b; grown outside in central and south Florida, with some protection in the northern limits.

NATIVE HABITAT - Tropical Asia.

LEAVES - Simple; alternate or spirally arranged; ovate, to 6 inches long; with an acute tip; glossy-green; serrate margins. Petioles long and reddish.

STEM/BARK - New growth is reddish-brown.

FLOWERS - White, red, yellow, orange; bell-shaped; 5 petals; to 6 inches wide; solitary; hang from the leaf axils on long peduncles and have a conspicuous staminal column with an exserted pistil. Blooms during the warm months.

FRUIT - Capsule; 5-celled, ovoid.

CULTURE - Grows in full sun to partial shade on slightly acid, fertile soils; moderate salt tolerance.

PROBLEMS - Scale, mites, thrips, nematodes, and minor element deficiencies.

PROPAGATION - Seeds, cuttings, or graftings of named cultivars.

LANDSCAPE USES - Use as a border, hedge, specimen, small tree if pruned properly, or foundation plant for large buildings.

COMMENTS - Many cultivars for flower color, form, and variegation are available. **‘Cooperi’** has variegated foliage. Most named cultivars are presumed to be selections of *H. rosa-sinensis* but *H. schizopetalus* (Fringed Hibiscus) and other species have undoubtedly been used in the hybridization-selection process. A few of the frequently offered cultivars include **‘Anderson Crepe’, ‘Bride’, ‘Bridal Veil’, ‘Brilliant Red’, ‘Carnation Red’, ‘Double’, ‘El Capitala Sport’, ‘Fort Myers’, ‘Full Moon’, ‘Hula Girl’, ‘Itsy Bity’, ‘Jimmy Spankler’, ‘Joann’, ‘Kona’, ‘La France’, ‘Lutea’, ‘Nairobi’, ‘Painted Lady’, ‘President’, ‘Red Dragon’, ‘Scarlet Red’, ‘Seminole Pink’, ‘Snow Queen’, ‘White Wings’**, among others.

Hibiscus syriacus   ROSE OF SHARON, SHRUB ALTHAEA

PRONUNCIATION - hī 'bis kəs   ˌsē rē 'ā kəs

TRANSLATION - [Greek for mallow] [Syrian].

FORM - Monoecious, deciduous shrub upright, bushy, of medium texture.

SIZE - Reaches a maximum height of 20 feet and a spread of 10 feet but generally seen in the 10-foot range. Growth rate is rapid.

HARDINESS ZONE - Zone 5. Should be grown only in north Florida.

NATIVE HABITAT - Eastern Asia.

LEAVES - Alternate, rhombic-ovate in outline, to 3 inches long. The leaves are generally deeply 3-lobed, with 3 main palmate veins and coarsely toothed.

STEM/BARK - The round, gray twigs have leaf scars crowded at the tips.

FLOWERS - Shades of white, pink, rose, lavender, blue; solitary, in upper leaf axils on short pedicels; to 4 inches wide, showy. Flowers have flaring petals and a staminal column surrounding the style; can be either single or double. Blooms continually from June to October.

FRUIT - Capsule, to 1 inch long, ovoid, 5-celled, dehiscent, and persistent in fall.

CULTURE - Grows in full sun or very light shade; prefers fertile, well-drained soil. Not adapted to extremely wet or dry conditions. Has moderate salt tolerance. Blooms on new growth; prune only during dormant period. Easy to grow.

PROBLEMS - Nematodes, aphids, mites (in hot, dry locations) and scale; usually not serious.

PROPAGATION - Softwood cuttings under mist with IBA treatment.

LANDSCAPE USES - Can be used as a large hedge or as an accent or specimen shrub. Occasionally trained as a small tree. Useful for late summer flowering.

COMMENTS - Many cultivars selected for flower color: **'Admiral Dewey'** - single, white flowers; **'Ardens'** - semi-double, light purple flowers; **'Bluebird'** - large, single, pale blue flowers; **'Diana'** - triploid with large white flowers, remaining open at night; **'Hél»ne'** - white with reddish-purple center; and many, many others. Florida natives *H. coccineus, H. elatus* (Mountain Mahoe), and *H. mutabilis* (Confederate Rose, Cotton Rose) are also cold hardy in north Florida.

Hibiscus tiliaceus

SEA HIBISCUS, MAHOE

PRONUNCIATION - hī ˈbis kəs   ˌti lē ˈā sē əs

TRANSLATION - [Greek for mallow] [linden-like].

FORM - Monoecious, evergreen tree; spreading; round, densely foliated; medium-coarse texture.

SIZE - On inland sites, this tree reaches a height and spread of 35 feet; seashore specimens tend to be smaller; rapid growth rate.

HARDINESS ZONE - Zones 10-11; can be grown in central and south Florida, but survives only in coastal areas of central Florida.

NATIVE HABITAT - Tropical seashores of the world, including Puerto Rico and south Florida; considered to be naturalized rather than native.

LEAVES - Simple; alternate; heart-shaped, to 8 inches long and 6 inches wide; leathery, dark green; glabrous on the upper side, whitish downy on the underside.

STEM/BARK - Long, snaky, drooping, branches root where they touch the ground. The fibrous bark has been made into ropes, nets, and mats.

FLOWERS - Yellow with a maroon center upon opening in the mornings, changing gradually to dark maroon and falling in the evenings; broadly campanulate to 4 inches wide; solitary; borne in the leaf axils; showy. Bloom year-round.

FRUIT - Capsules; pointed, silky, ovoid, woody; 1 inch wide, 5-parted and dehiscent; maturing all year.

CULTURE - Grows in full sun on almost any soil; highly salt tolerant.

PROBLEMS - Generally pest-free.

PROPAGATION - Large cuttings, air layers, or seeds all give good results.

LANDSCAPE USES - Because of huge size, rank growth, dense shade, and messiness, this tree is recommended only for seaside locations where tree choice is limited or where quick shade is of paramount consideration.

COMMENTS - *H. platanifolius* is a more or less smaller species with yellow flowers.

Malvaviscus arboreus   Turk's Cap, Wax Mallow

PRONUNCIATION - ˌmɑl və 'vis kəs   ɑr 'bo rē əs

TRANSLATION - [from Latin *malva* (= mallow) and *viscus* (= glue), in reference to the pulp around the seed] [treelike].

FORM - Monoecious, evergreen shrub, rampant, densely foliated, sprawling, may be arborescent or somewhat vine-like if given support.

SIZE - To 12 feet, very rapid growth.

HARDINESS ZONE - Zone 8b, south and central Florida, protected locations in north Florida.

NATIVE HABITAT - Mexico to Brazil.

LEAVES - Simple, alternate, generally ovate but shape varies somewhat with conditions, apex acute, to 5 inches long, papery texture, usually densely pubescent, margins serrate.

STEM/BARK - Gray, smooth.

FLOWERS - Red, corolla funnelform, to 2 inches long, petals 5, not flaring, column protruding, solitary or in few-flowered racemes, borne in upper leaf axils. Blooms during warm months.

FRUIT - Schizocarp, red, fleshy at first, not common in Florida.

CULTURE - Grow in full sun on varied soils, no salt tolerance.

PROBLEMS - Scale, caterpillars, chewing insects, and the plant's rampant growth habit.

PROPAGATION - Cuttings.

LANDSCAPE USES - Use as a barrier, hedge, or foundation shrub for large buildings.

COMMENTS - This is a polymorphic species with several variants that have previously been recognized as distinct species. Two notable varieties are *M. arboreus* var. *drummondii* and *M. arboreus* var. *mexicanus.*

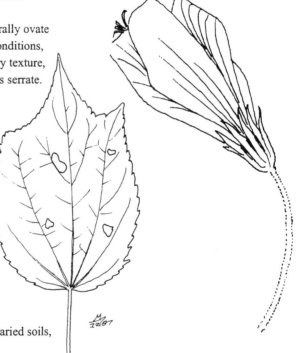

MELASTOMATACEAE - MELASTOMA FAMILY

DICOTYLEDONS; 240 GENERA AND ABOUT 3,000 SPECIES

GEOGRAPHY:	Predominantly tropical and subtropical, especially in South America.
GROWTH HABIT:	Shrubs and small trees, as well as a few climbing and herbaceous plants; stem usually 4-angled.
LEAVES:	Opposite and decussate, sometimes with alternating smaller and larger pairs, and without stipules; venation most distinctive feature of the family, palmate with 3 to 9 parallel pairs of primary veins.
FLOWERS:	Showy, actinomorphic, 5-merous; perianth of 5 each distinct sepals and petals; stamens usually 10 and with an appendage; ovary superior or inferior, with 1 to numerous fused carpels.
FRUIT:	A berry or a loculicidal capsule.
ECONOMIC USES:	Ornamentals and fruit of a few species eaten locally.

ORNAMENTAL GENERA: *Arthrostema, Dissotis, Medinilla, Melastoma, Tetrazygia, Tibouchina,* etc.

Tibouchina urvilleana   PRINCESS FLOWER

PRONUNCIATION - ˌti bū ˈchē nə ər ˌvi lē ˈā nə

TRANSLATION - [from the native Guianon name] [in honor of Jules S»bastian C»sar Dumont d' Urville (1790-1844), a French naval officer].

FORM - Monoecious, evergreen shrub or small tree; irregular, somewhat vine-like, often sparsely foliated; coarse texture.

SIZE- To 15 to 20 feet tall with a 20 foot spread; rapid growth rate.

HARDINESS ZONE- Zone 9b; grows in south and central Florida.

NATIVE HABITAT - Brazil.

LEAVES - Simple; opposite; elliptic-ovate, to 4 inches long and 1.5 inches wide; 3 to 7 prominent, parallel veins; pubescent above and below; entire margins; dark green.

STEM/BARK - Stems square; pubescent; green when young, corky with age.

FLOWERS - Rosy purple to violet; very showy; 5 inches across; 5 petals with 10 purple stamens and 2 circular bracts at the base; borne in terminal panicles. Blooms in warm months.

FRUIT - Capsule, to 0.5 inch long.

CULTURE- Grow in full sun on various well-drained soils; no salt tolerance.

PROBLEMS - Scale, nematodes, and root rot.

PROPAGATION - Cuttings.

LANDSCAPE USES - Use in borders, as a specimen, or patio shade tree.

COMMENTS - There are several related species. At least two related species, *T. clavata* and *T. granulosa* (Glory Bush), are cultivated in Florida.

MELIACEAE - MELIA FAMILY

DICOTYLEDONS; 50 GENERA AND ABOUT 550 SPECIES

GEOGRAPHY: Tropical and subtropical.

GROWTH HABIT: Trees and shrubs, sometimes unbranched.

LEAVES: Alternate, usually pinnately compound but sometimes bipinnate and rarely simple; stipules absent.

FLOWERS: Paniculate, cauliflorus, in leaf axils, or terminal at branch tips; actinomorphic; bisexual or unisexual (plants dioecious); 5-merous, with usually 3-5 free sepals and usually 3-5 free petals; stamens usually 10, free or often united into a tube; ovary superior.

FRUIT: Capsule, berry, or drupe; seeds often winged.

ECONOMIC USES: Ornamentals, an important source of timber (*Swietenia, Khaya,* etc.), soaps, insecticides, etc. Source of a natural insecticide from *Azadirachta indica*.

ORNAMENTAL GENERA: *Aglaia, Azadirachta, Cedrela, Chisochetom, Dysoxylum, Khaya, Lansium, Melia, Sandoricum, Swietenia, Turraea,* among others.

Melia azedarach   CHINABERRY TREE

PRONUNCIATION - ˈmē lē ə   ə ˈze də ræk

TRANSLATION - [Greek name for *Fraxinus* (= ash), in reference to similar leaves] [from the native name, noble tree].

FORM - Deciduous tree, low branching, spreading, broad, dense umbrella-shaped canopy. Medium texture.

SIZE - To 50 feet, commonly 20 to 30 feet, rapid growth rate.

HARDINESS ZONE - Zone 7. Grown in north, central, and south Florida.

NATIVE HABITAT - Iran, Himalaya, China; naturalized in tropical America and Florida.

LEAVES - Odd-bipinnately compound, alternate, 1 to 2.5 feet long; leaflets many, with a short petiolule, to 4 inches long, serrate margins, round rachis, dark green.

STEM/BARK - Dark, deeply furrowed trunk. Younger stems with conspicuous transverse lenticels.

FLOWERS - Purplish, small, fragrant, 5- to 6-lobed; borne in axillary panicles to 8 inches long. Blooms in spring and summer.

FRUIT - Berry, to 0.75 inch in diameter, yellow, sticky, poisonous, persisting after leaf fall.

CULTURE - Grows in full sun on various soils, not salt tolerant. In general, can withstand total neglect.

PROBLEMS - Scale, whitefly, sooty mold, brittle wood, toxic seeds, messy fruit, "weedy" seedlings.

PROPAGATION - Seeds, cuttings.

LANDSCAPE USES - Use as a shade tree, in parks, or street plantings. Not recommended, however, because of its weediness.

COMMENTS - Several cultivars for growth habit and profuse flowering are available. 'Umbraculifera' has an umbrella-shaped tree canopy.

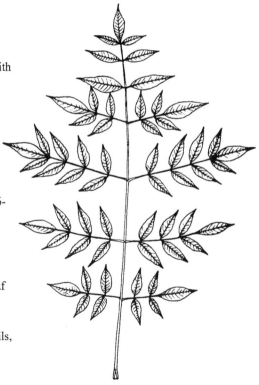

Swietenia mahogani   MADEIRA, MAHOGANY, CAOBA

PRONUNCIATION - swə ˈtē nē ə   mə ˈhæ gə ˌnī

TRANSLATION - [after Gerard van Swieten (1700-1772), Dutch botanist who settled in Vienna and became physician to Empress Maria Theresa] [Latinized aboriginal American name].

FORM - Dioecious, semideciduous tree; upright, symmetrical, loose, round canopy; medium-fine texture.

SIZE - To 75 feet, commonly 40 feet with a 40 foot spread; moderate growth rate.

HARDINESS ZONE - Zones 10-11; can be grown only in south Florida.

NATIVE HABITAT - West Indies, Florida.

LEAVES - Even-pinnately compound; alternate; to 8 inches long; leaflets 4 to 10, ovate to lanceolate, stalked, asymmetrical, to 3 inches long; shiny, glabrous; brownish-green with yellowish veins; margins entire.

STEM/BARK - Scaly, dark, furrowed.

FLOWERS - Greenish-white; small; 5-petals; borne in axillary panicles; inconspicuous. Blooms with leaf emergence in spring.

FRUIT - Woody capsule to 5 inches long; 5-celled; inverted pear shape; dehiscent.

CULTURE - Grow in full sun on various soils; moderate salt tolerance.

PROBLEMS - Tent caterpillars, scale, sooty mold. Large woody capsules a hazard.

PROPAGATION - Seed, although considerable seedling variation exists in this species. Cutting propagation proven difficult.

LANDSCAPE USES - Use for shade and street tree plantings or as a framing tree. This native tree casts a light shade and is notably resistant to strong winds.

COMMENTS - *Swietenia mahogani* is the original mahogany of commerce. Today *S. macrophylla* (Bigleaf Mahogany) has largely replaced it as the major source of true mahogany timber.

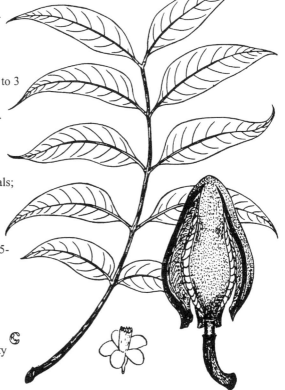

MENISPERMACEAE - MOONSEED FAMILY

DICOTYLEDONS; 65 GENERA AND ABOUT 350 SPECIES

GEOGRAPHY:	Predominantly tropical rain forest, but a few subtropical and temperate.
GROWTH HABIT:	Mostly woody vines, but with a few shrubs and rarely trees and herbs.
LEAVES:	Alternate, sometimes peltate, without stipules; venation distinctly palmate.
FLOWERS:	Small and inconspicuous, usually greenish-white; unisexual (plants dioecious); usually 3-merous or multiples; sepals in 2 sets of 3; petals in 2 or more sets of 3; stamens 3 to many and free or united; ovary superior, carpels 1 to numerous and free.
FRUIT:	Usually a horseshoe-shaped drupe.
ECONOMIC USES:	Only a few ornamentals but an important source of drugs (e.g., curare, a muscle relaxant, is obtained from *Chondrodendron tomentosum*).

ORNAMENTAL GENERA: *Cocculus, Menispermum.*

Cocculus laurifolius   LAUREL-LEAVED SNAILSEED

PRONUNCIATION - ˈkɑ kyə ləs   ˌlo rə ˈfō lē əs

TRANSLATION - [from Greek *kokkos* (= a berry), in reference to the fruit] [bay-leaved].

FORM - Dioecious, evergreen shrub, coarse-textured, weeping growth habit.

SIZE - Reaches a height of 20 feet with an equal spread. Growth rate is medium.

HARDINESS ZONE - Zone 8. Can be grown throughout Florida, but needs a protected location in north Florida.

NATIVE HABITAT - Himalayan foothills to southern Japan.

LEAVES - Simple, alternate, broadly lanceolate to 6 inches long, dark green, leathery, shiny, entire, with 3 prominent veins; more or less distichous (2-ranked).

STEM/BARK - The bark and the leaves contain a toxic alkaloid. Young stems green, strongly arching.

FLOWERS - Yellowish, tiny in many-flowered axillary panicles, 2 inches long, that appear in April or May. Not ornamental.

FRUIT - Drupes, black, subglobose, 0.25 inch wide, not normally produced in Florida. The seeds resemble coiled snail shells, hence the common name.

CULTURE - Grows in full sun or partial shade on a wide range of soils. It is not salt tolerant.

PROBLEMS - Scale insects.

PROPAGATION - Twig or leaf bud cuttings under mist in spring.

LANDSCAPE USES - Grown as a part of a shrubbery border, as a barrier, screen, tall hedge, foundation planting, or occasionally as a specimen.

COMMENTS - A related species, *C. carolinus*, the Carolina Snailseed, is native to north Florida. It is a twining, woody vine with ovate to hastate leaves and clusters of bright red fruit.

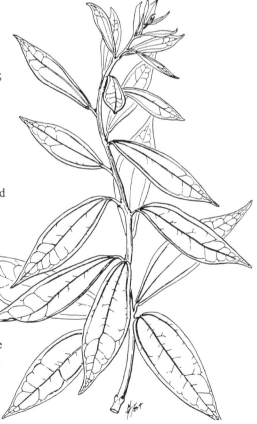

MORACEAE - FIG FAMILY

DICOTYLEDONS; 70-75 GENERA AND ABOUT 3,000 SPECIES

GEOGRAPHY: Tropics, subtropics, and some in temperate regions of Northern and Southern Hemispheres.

GROWTH HABIT: Trees and shrubs, and a few herbs, with milky latex.

LEAVES: Alternate (sometimes spiral) or opposite, entire or lobed and/or serrate; stipulate.

FLOWERS: Unisexual (plants monoecious or dioecious); 4-merous, in flattened heads (as in *Dorstenia*) or hallowed receptacles (as in *Ficus*), or occasionally in catkins (as in *Morus*); stamens 4 but sometimes reduced to 2 or 1; ovary superior to inferior.

FRUIT: Achenes, usually embedded in fleshy multiple structures.

ECONOMIC USES: In addition to ornamentals, members of this family are an important fruit source, timber, silkworm food, and minor source of rubber.

ORNAMENTAL GENERA: *Artocarpus, Brosimum, Broussonetia, Castilla, Cudrania, Dorstenia, Ficus, Maclura, Morus.*

COMMENTS: Species with 5-merous, bracteate flowers are currently included in Cannabidaceae (*Cannabis* and *Humulus*), but are sometimes included in Moraceae.

Ficus aurea

PRONUNCIATION - ˈfī kəs   ˈo rē ə

TRANSLATION - [Latin name for *F. carica*] [golden].

FORM - Evergreen tree; often starting as an epiphyte; vine-like while young, later strangling its host with heavy and arching aerial roots; eventually becomes a self-supporting, independent tree; irregular; coarse texture.

SIZE - Reaches a height of 60 feet with a 50 foot spread.

HARDINESS ZONE - Zones 10-11; grows outside only in south Florida.

NATIVE HABITAT - West Indies, hammocks of south Florida.

LEAVES - Simple; alternate; elliptic, to 4 inches long; narrowed at both ends; medium green.

STEM/BARK - Stems exude milky sap when injured.

FLOWERS - Minute, inside a syconium.

FRUIT - Syconium; sessile or nearly so; in pairs; to 0.75 inch in diameter.

CULTURE - Grows in partial shade to full sun on various soils; moderate salt tolerance.

PROBLEMS - Aphids and scales followed by sooty mold.

PROPAGATION - Seed or cuttings.

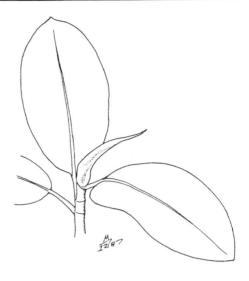

LANDSCAPE USES - Can be grown for the curiosity of its strangling habit. Not recommended for small sites.

COMMENTS - Although native, this species should be planted with caution, if at all. *Ficus citrifolia* (Shortleaf Fig) is also native to south Florida and is an epiphyte, at least initially.

Ficus benjamina

WEEPING FIG

PRONUNCIATION - 'fī kəs ˌben jə 'mī nə

TRANSLATION - [Latin name for *F. carica*] [from the Indian name *benjan*].

FORM - Evergreen tree; round; epiphytic when young; spreading; branches drooping, heavily foliated, dense symmetrical canopy, aerial roots; medium-fine texture.

SIZE - To 50 feet tall with an 80 foot spread; rapid growth rate.

HARDINESS ZONE - Zones 10-11; south Florida only.

NATIVE HABITAT - India, Southeast Asia.

LEAVES - Simple; alternate; ovate-elliptic to 4 inches long; acuminate tip; glossy-green, leathery; milky sap; entire margins; leaf habit differs somewhat in full sun vs. shade.

STEM/BARK - Gray; aerial roots brown; reddish tips when young; bleeds milky sap when injured.

FLOWERS - Minute; borne on interior of a hollow fleshy syconium or "fig."

FRUIT - Globose syconium, to 0.5 inch in diameter; borne in axillary pairs.

CULTURE - Grows in full sun to partial shade, on varied soils; moderate salt tolerance.

PROBLEMS - Scale, micronutrient deficiencies; surface roots.

PROPAGATION - Cuttings, layers.

LANDSCAPE USES - Use in parks, street plantings, or on large properties. Hedges well. Also used as an interior foliage plant; large specimens common in public interiorscapes such as shopping malls and hotels.

COMMENTS - Several varieties and cultivars are listed; there is considerable taxonomic confusion with this species. Some of the noteworthy varieties and cultivars include *F. benjamina* var. ***nuda** (= F.* var. *comosa), F. benjamina* var. ***nuda;*** **'Exotica'** and **'Schlechteri'**. **'Golden King', 'Golden Princess', 'Hawaii', 'Variegata'** (with variously yellowish-white markings) and others are also available.

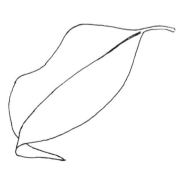

Ficus carica

FIG, COMMON FIG

PRONUNCIATION - ˈfī kəs   ˈka rə kə

TRANSLATION - [Latin name for the species] [named for Caria in Asia Minor].

FORM - Deciduous tree or large shrub, low-branching, spreading, branches leafless below, irregular canopy. Coarse texture.

SIZE - To 30 feet, commonly 10 to 15 feet, rapid growth.

HARDINESS ZONE - Zone 7. Grown throughout Florida. Cold tolerance varies with cultivar.

NATIVE HABITAT - Mediterranean region.

LEAVES - Simple, alternate, entire, usually deeply 3- to 5-lobed, rounded, to 8 inches across, cordate base, broadly toothed, scabrous above, pubescent below; petiole 1 to 4 inches long.

STEM/BARK - Dark brown, smooth at maturity. New growth gray-green, stout, with prominent leaf scars and stipular scars encircling stems at each node. Exudes milky sap when broken.

FLOWERS - Minute, borne on interior of hollow syconium.

FRUIT - Fleshy receptacle, (syconium), variable shape, usually round to pear-shaped, to 3 inches long, green turning brown or yellow at maturity, edible. Produced on new growth. Most plants begin bearing at 3 to 4 years of age. The fig of "Fig Newton" fame.

CULTURE - Full sun, various well-drained soils, slightly salt tolerant. Not adapted to wet sites or compacted soils. Moderately drought tolerant.

PROBLEMS - Caterpillars, scale, chewing insects, nematodes on sandy soils. Fruits can create a mess on pavement.

PROPAGATION - Cuttings, grafting of cultivars.

LANDSCAPE USES - Espalier, dooryard fruit tree, textural effect. Wildlife attracted by the fruit.

COMMENTS - Many cultivars; **'Celeste'** and **'Brown Turkey'**, popular in Florida, need no caprification (wasp pollination) to produce fruit.

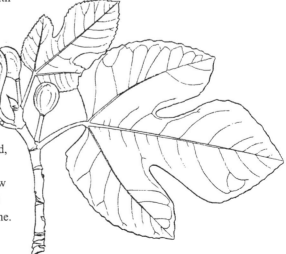

Ficus elastica   Indian Rubber Tree, Rubber Tree

PRONUNCIATION - 'fī kəs   ē 'las tə kə

TRANSLATION - [Latin name for *F. carica*] [producing latex].

FORM - Evergreen tree; multibranched; often suckering from the base to produce multiple trunks; spreading, irregular canopy; produces aerial roots; coarse texture.

SIZE - To 50 feet, commonly to 25 feet in Florida; rapid growth rate.

HARDINESS ZONE - Zones 10-11; south Florida only.

NATIVE HABITAT - Nepal and Burma.

LEAVES - Simple; spirally arranged; oblong or elliptic to 12 inches long; thick, glossy; entire margins; several color forms; green with a brownish-red cast, marbled with yellow.

STEM/BARK - New growth is green, becomes brown with age; stems exude milky sap when injured.

FLOWERS - Minute, inside a syconium.

FRUIT - Syconium; sessile; usually in pairs; to 0.75 inch in diameter; greenish-yellow turning brown.

CULTURE - Full sun to partial shade; various well-drained soils; moderate salt tolerance.

PROBLEMS - Scale. Aerial roots can become a problem.

PROPAGATION - Cuttings, layers.

LANDSCAPE USES - Use as a specimen for large properties, in street plantings, and parks. Commonly used as an interior plant.

COMMENTS - Many cultivars for leaf color and variegation: **'Decora'** (most popular cultivar horticulturally; leaves dark, glossy green above and reddish below) and **'Variegata'** (leaves light green with white or yellow margins). Other cultivars offered for sale include **'Abidjan' (= 'Burgundy'?)**, **'Asahi'**, **'Burgundy'**, **'Doescheri'**, and **'Rubra'**.

Ficus lyrata

FIDDLELEAF FIG

PRONUNCIATION - 'fī kəs   lī 'rā tə

TRANSLATION - [Latin name for *F. carica*] [fiddle-shaped, in reference to leaves].

FORM - Evergreen tree; upright; irregular growth; coarse texture.

SIZE - Can reach a height of 40 feet with an equal spread, but usually is smaller; medium growth rate.

HARDINESS ZONE - Zones 10-11; can be grown outdoors only in south Florida.

NATIVE HABITAT - Western tropical Africa.

LEAVES - Simple; alternate; fiddle-shaped in outline, to 14 inches long; apical half is largest; prominent venation; undulate margins; dark green.

STEM/BARK - Solitary trunks with rough, scaling bark; no aerial roots, surface roots, or buttresses.

FLOWERS - Minute; borne inside small, green receptacles; solitary or in pairs.

FRUIT - Syconiums; sessile; fleshy; 1.25 inches wide; greenish with white dots.

CULTURE - Grows in full sun or partial shade on a wide range of soils; no salt tolerance.

PROBLEMS - Scales. Large leaves are messy.

PROPAGATION - Air layers; cuttings will root, but are more difficult than other figs.

LANDSCAPE USES - A specimen or shade tree. Its smaller size and less aggressive growth make it more useful than other tree species of *Ficus*. Sometimes grown as a pot or tub plant for patios and interiors.

COMMENTS - *Ficus lyrata* 'Phyllis Craig' is sold in Florida.

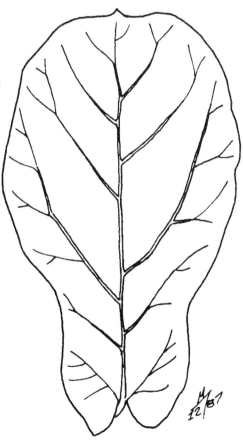

Ficus microcarpa

INDIAN LAUREL

PRONUNCIATION - 'fī kəs   ˌmī krō 'kɑr pə

TRANSLATION - [Latin name for *F. carica*] [*micro* (= small), *carpus* (= fruit)].

SYNONYM - *Ficus retusa.*

FORM - Monoecious, evergreen tree; round; spreading; densely foliated, symmetrical canopy; few aerial roots; medium texture.

SIZE - To 50 feet; rapid growth rate.

HARDINESS ZONE - Zones 10-11; south Florida only.

NATIVE HABITAT - Malay Peninsula to Borneo.

LEAVES - Simple; alternate; broad ovate or elliptic to 4 inches long; apex obtuse or barely elongated; leathery, stiff; entire margins; milky sap; medium green.

STEM/BARK - Gray; lenticels present.

FLOWERS - Minute; inside a syconium.

FRUIT - Syconium; sessile; axillary; borne in pairs; purplish; to 0.5 inch in diameter.

CULTURE - Grows in full sun to partial shade on various well-drained soils; moderate salt tolerance.

PROBLEMS - Scale, thrips, and surface roots.

PROPAGATION - Cuttings, layering.

LANDSCAPE USES - Use as a park or street tree, a large hedge, or a barrier.

COMMENTS - *Ficus nitida* (Cuban Laurel) is a misapplied name. *Ficus microcarpa* var. *hilii* has narrow leaves with cuneate base. Cultivar **'Variegata'** is a small plant, leaves with white variegation.

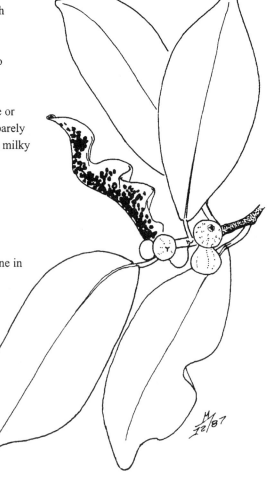

Ficus pumila

CREEPING FIG

PRONUNCIATION - ˈfī kəs   ˈpū mə lə

TRANSLATION - [Latin name for *F. carica*] [dwarf].

FORM - Monoecious, creeping or climbing woody, evergreen vine of fine (juvenile) and medium (adult) texture.

SIZE - Variable. Grows at a fast rate and will cover large areas rapidly if allowed.

HARDINESS ZONE - Zone 8. Can be grown in all areas of Florida.

NATIVE HABITAT - Eastern Asia.

LEAVES - Simple, alternate, both juvenile and adult types. The juvenile leaves are nearly sessile, oblique, cordate-ovate, to 1 inch long, pustulate (= blistered); adult leaves are oblong or elliptic, 2 to 4 inches long, not pustulate, with short petiole.

STEM/BARK - Juvenile twigs are creeping and vertical, climbing by numerous tenacious aerial roots. Mature twigs are short, stout and horizontal, lacking aerial roots. The twigs exude milky sap if injured.

FLOWERS - Minute, inside small green receptacles (syconiums). Found only on adult growth.

FRUIT - Fleshy syconiums or figs, pear-shaped and yellowish to 2 inches long. Not edible.

CULTURE - Will grow on almost any soil under any light conditions; good salt tolerance. Requires frequent pruning to keep size and shape under control. Roots adhere to wood and masonry when vine is removed.

PROBLEMS - Pest-free.

PROPAGATION - Cuttings root easily from juvenile plants.

LANDSCAPE USES - Grown mainly to cover sides of buildings and fences, which it does rapidly. Also used in topiaries or hanging baskets and interior scapes.

COMMENTS - Several cultivars are available: **'Minima'** - all juvenile leaves, 1/2 inch or less; **'Quercifolia'**- leaves pinnately lobed; **'Variegata'** - variegated with white; less cold tolerant than the typical species.

Adult foliage

Juvenile foliage

Ficus rubiginosa

PRONUNCIATION - ˈfī kəs   rū ˌbi jə ˈnō sə

TRANSLATION - [Latin name for *F. carica*] [rusty, in reference to the hairs on the underside of the leaves].

FORM - Monoecious, evergreen tree; dense; aerial roots may be present or absent; coarse texture.

SIZE - Grows to a height of 35 feet, but commonly 10 feet tall.

HARDINESS ZONE - Zones 10-11; south Florida only. This is one of the hardiest rubber trees.

NATIVE HABITAT - Australia.

LEAVES - Simple; alternate; ovate to elliptic-oblong, 3 to 6 inches long;lower blade surface and petiole rusty-pubescent to glabrescent; dark green.

STEM/BARK - Rusty pubescence is especially noticeable on young twigs; stems exude milky sap when injured.

FLOWERS - Minute, inside a syconium.

FRUIT - Syconium; axillary; paired; globose, warty; rusty-pubescent to glabrescent; to 0.5 inch in diameter.

CULTURE - Partial shade, will tolerate light intensities down to 150 foot-candles in interiors; various soils; slight salt tolerance.

PROBLEMS - Mites and scale; subject to root rot if overwatered.

PROPAGATION - Cuttings or air layers.

LANDSCAPE USES - Commonly used as an interior plant. Can be used as a specimen, street, or shade tree. Should be more widely used as a south Florida landscape ornamental because of its hardiness, dense habit of growth, and ability to withstand periods of drought.

COMMENTS - The cultivar **'Variegata'** has leaves variegated with cream-yellow. In addition to the *Ficus* species noted in this manual, more than 100 other species are grown in Florida. For a complete list, the reader should consult the *Checklist of the Woody Cultivated Plants of Florida* by D. Burch, D.B. Ward, and W.B. Hall (University of Florida Extension Publication SP-33, 1988). However, a few are noteworthy for their special growth habits or leaf characteristics: *F. benghalensis* (Banyan Fig), *F. citrifolia* (Short-leaved Fig), *F. macrophylla* (Moreton Bay Fig), *F. montana* (Oakleaf Fig), *F. natalensis* (Natal Fig), *F. americana* (= *F. perforata*) (West Indian Laurel), and *F. religiosa* (Bo Tree).

MYRICACEAE - BAYBERRY FAMILY

DICOTYLEDONS; 3 GENERA AND ABOUT 50 SPECIES

GEOGRAPHY:	Nearly cosmopolitan, absent only from Australia.
GROWTH HABIT:	Aromatic trees and shrubs.
LEAVES:	Alternate, simple or pinnately divided; stipules present or absent.
FLOWERS:	Unisexual (plants monoecious), on axillary catkin-like spikes; male flowers with 2 bracteoles and 4 stamens; female flowers with 2 to 4 bracteoles, superior ovary of 2 fused carpels.
FRUIT:	Small drupe, often covered with a waxy bloom.
ECONOMIC USES:	Ornamentals; fruit wax is used for candle making.

ORNAMENTAL GENERA: *Comptonia, Myrica*. The monotypic genus *Canacomyrica* is not reported from cultivation.

Myrica cerifera   SOUTHERN WAX MYRTLE

PRONUNCIATION - ˈmē rə kə   sə ˈri fə rə

TRANSLATION - [from the Greek name *myrike* for tamarisk] [wax-bearing].

FORM - Monoecious, large, evergreen shrub or small tree, clumping, irregular, rounded, densely foliated and medium-textured.

SIZE - Reaches a height and spread of 35 feet, but is usually seen in the 15 to 20 foot range. Growth rate is rapid.

HARDINESS ZONE - Zone 7. Can be grown throughout Florida.

NATIVE HABITAT - The coastal plain from Maryland to Texas; ubiquitous in Florida.

LEAVES - Simple, alternate, oblanceolate, to 4 inches long, often undulate. The thin, olive green leaves are often coarsely serrate along apical margins and dotted with tiny rusty glands on both sides. Aromatic.

STEM/BARK - Multiple, crooked trunks are covered with smooth, grayish-white bark. Young stems light green to gray, pubescent. Suckers frequently from trunk bases and roots.

FLOWERS - Plants dioecious; flowers inconspicuous, small axillary catkins appear in March.

FRUIT - Grayish-blue, 0.25 inch wide, in dense clusters along the twigs in fall. The fruit are heavily coated with wax, which can be made into candles if enough are collected. Birds eat the fruit in winter.

CULTURE - Grows in full sun or partial shade on almost any soil type. Withstands flooding but not excessive drought. Good salt tolerance. Withstands pruning well but makes a poor clipped hedge due to its rapid growth. Basal suckers need to be removed periodically.

PROBLEMS - Generally pest-free, but chewing insects can attack new growth and a canker disease occasionally kills trunks.

PROPAGATION - Seeds germinate easily and rapidly. Can be transplanted from the wild with care. Tip cuttings have also succeeded.

LANDSCAPE USES - As a screen or enclosure, also makes a good background shrub. Excellent for highway and park plantings. Lower branches may be removed to create a small tree. A very tough plant which is easy to grow, but may become weedy.

COMMENTS - A similar species, *M. pensylvanica*, is used in the northern states where temperatures are too cold for *M. cerifera*. Although native, *M. cerifera* may become a weed problem. A related species with edible fruit, *M. rubra*, is also in cultivation. There exists an unnamed cultivar of *M. cerifera* in the nursery trade which is useful for short hedges.

MYRSINACEAE - MYRSINE FAMILY

DICOTYLEDONS; 32 GENERA AND ABOUT 1000 SPECIES

GEOGRAPHY: Warm temperate, subtropical, and tropical regions of the Old
                    World and New World.

GROWTH HABIT: Trees and shrubs.

LEAVES: Alternate, simple, coriaceous, and conspicuously glandular dotted.

FLOWERS: Small, actinomorphic, bisexual or unisexual (plants dioecious), in
                    fascicles on axillary and/or terminal short shoots; 5-merous;
                    usually with 4 to 6 basally connate sepals and petals; stamens the
                    same number as the corolla and often adnate to them; ovary
                    superior or semi-inferior with usually one carpel.

FRUIT: A fleshy drupe.

ECONOMIC USES: Ornamentals, otherwise of little economic value.

ORNAMENTAL GENERA: *Ardisia, Maesa, Myrsine, Suttonia,* and probably others.

Ardisia crenata   CORAL ARDISIA

PRONUNCIATION - ar 'dē zhə   krə 'nā tə

TRANSLATION - [from Greek *ardis* (= pointed), referring to the pointed anthers] [crenate, scalloped, in reference to the leaf margins].

FORM - Monoecious, evergreen shrub, slender upright stems, often leafless at base, suckering, small oval canopy. Medium-fine texture.

SIZE - To 6 feet, commonly 2 to 4 feet, moderate growth rate.

HARDINESS ZONE - Zone 8b. Grows best in north and central Florida. Severely injured by temperatures in low twenties, but resprouts from the base.

NATIVE HABITAT - India to Japan.

LEAVES - Simple, spirally arranged, often clustered near stem tips, elliptic-lanceolate to 8 inches long, shiny dark green above, glabrous, leathery, small specks on surface, margin crenate and glandular.

STEM/BARK - Green, becoming woody with age. Stems not frequently branched.

FLOWERS - Axillary panicles, flower 5-petaled forming a united corolla, star-shaped, to 0.25 inch in diameter, white or pink, showy; flowers in late spring.

FRUIT - Drupe, red, globular to 0.25 inch in diameter, persistent, fall to winter, very showy.

CULTURE - Partial to deep shade, fertile, acid soils, not salt tolerant.

PROBLEMS - Scale, mites, sooty mold, nematodes. Tends to reseed itself and has become weedy in many areas.

PROPAGATION - Seeds, cuttings.

LANDSCAPE USES - Shaded shrubbery border, facer material, terrariums and dish gardens, interiorscapes.

COMMENTS - Frequently misidentified as *A. crispa*. *Ardisia crenata* '**Alba**' has white fruit. Related species in cultivation include *A. escallonioides* (Marlberry), *A. humilis, A. japonica* (an attractive ground cover), *A. polycephala, A. solanacea* (Night-shade Ardisia), and *A. wallichii.*

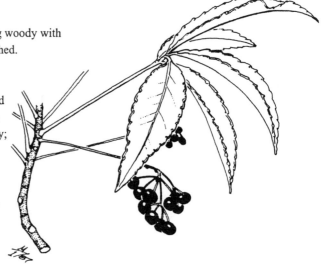

MYRTACEAE - MYRTLE FAMILY

DICOTYLEDONS; 100 GENERA AND 3000 OR MORE SPECIES

GEOGRAPHY:	Mostly tropical, especially in South America and Australia.
GROWTH HABIT:	Aromatic subshrubs, shrubs to very large trees.
LEAVES:	Evergreen, opposite or sometimes alternate, coriaceous, simple, entire, usually glandular dotted, and without stipules.
FLOWERS:	Actinomorphic, bisexual, on racemose or cymose inflorescences or rarely solitary; usually perigynous and 5-merous; sepals 4 to 5, usually free or sometimes reduced or absent; 4 to 5 petals, usually free but sometimes united; stamens numerous, free and often quite showy; ovary inferior and with one to many locules.
FRUIT:	Berry or capsule.
ECONOMIC USES:	Many ornamentals, but also an important source of timber (*Eucalyptus*), fruit (*Eugenea, Psidium, Feijoa, Myrciaria*, etc.), spices (*Eugenia, Pimenta, Syzygium*, etc.), and various medicinal oils.

ORNAMENTAL GENERA: *Agonis, Britoa, Callistemon, Calyptranthes, Campomanesia, Eucalyptus, Eugenia, Feijoa, Melaleuca, Myrciaria, Myrtus, Pimenta, Psidium, Rhodomyrtus, Syzygium, Tristania, Ugni,* and many others.

Acca sellowiana

PINEAPPLE GUAVA, FEIJOA

PRONUNCIATION - ˈa kə   sə ˌlō ē ˈā nə

TRANSLATION - [after the Roman goddess of the fields, Acca Larentia] [after its discoverer, Friedrich Sellow (1789-1831), a German botanist who collected in South America].

SYNONYM - *Feijoa sellowiana.*

FORM - Monoecious, evergreen shrub or small tree, low-branching, densely foliated, mound-shaped canopy. Medium texture.

SIZE - To 18 feet, medium growth rate.

HARDINESS ZONE - Zone 8b. Grown throughout Florida.

NATIVE HABITAT - Brazil, Paraguay, Argentina.

LEAVES - Simple, opposite, elliptic to elliptic-oblong to 3 inches long, green above, white-woolly pubescent below, margins entire.

STEM/BARK - New growth pubescent.

FLOWERS - Solitary, axillary, petals 4, white to pink, fleshy, to 1.5 inches across, red stamens protrude, flower in spring.

FRUIT - Berries, green tinged with red, to 3 inches long, edible.

CULTURE - Full sun to partial shade, various soils, slightly salt tolerant.

PROBLEMS - Scale.

PROPAGATION - Seed, vegetative propagation extremely difficult.

LANDSCAPE USES - Barrier, hedges, foundation planting for large buildings, dooryard fruit.

COMMENTS - Several cultivars selected for fruit, but most not readily available.

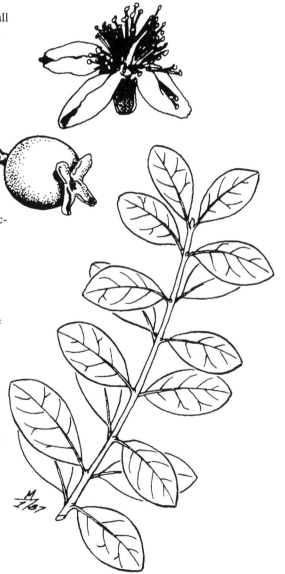

Callistemon citrinus

LEMON BOTTLEBRUSH

PRONUNCIATION - kə 'lis tə mən   sə 'trĭ nəs

TRANSLATION - [from Greek *kallos* (= beautiful) and *steman* (= a stamen)] [lemon-scented, in reference to the leaves].

FORM - Monoecious, evergreen shrub, upright, or small tree, fine-textured.

SIZE - Reaches a height of 20 feet and a spread of 10 feet. Grows at a rapid rate.

HARDINESS ZONE - Zone 8b. Can be grown everywhere in the state except the very coldest areas.

NATIVE HABITAT - Southeastern Australia.

LEAVES - Simple, alternate, broadly lanceolate, about 3 inches long. The stiff, pointed leaves have a prominent midrib, entire margins, and a citrus-like fragrance when crushed.

STEM/BARK - Branches are erect or droop only slightly.

FLOWERS - Red, cylindrical, sessile, dense spikes, composed mainly of numerous 1 inch stamens, resembling 4-inch-long brushes. Flowers appear at the base of each flush of new growth with the most bloom occurring in spring.

FRUIT - Capsules, depressed, globose, woody, sessile, persistent, to 0.5 inch wide, contain many tiny seeds.

CULTURE - Requires full sun but tolerates a wide range of soils. It has marginal salt tolerance.

PROBLEMS - Mites occasionally cause problems.

PROPAGATION - By mature cutting under mist. Seedling plants are too variable.

LANDSCAPE USES - Makes a good specimen or accent shrub. This is the most common and showiest species grown in Florida.

COMMENTS - Cultivar '**Burning Bush**' is a compact dwarf with carmine flowers; '**Splendens**' has linear-lanceolate leaves and dense flower spikes.

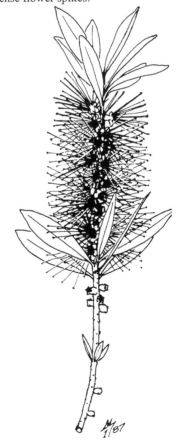

Callistemon rigidus   BOTTLEBRUSH

PRONUNCIATION - kə 'lis tə mən   'ri jə dəs

TRANSLATION - [from Greek *kallos* (= beautiful) and *steman* (= a stamen)] [rigid, in reference to the leaves].

FORM - Monoecious, evergreen shrub or small tree, erect, low-branching, many branched, dense, brittle. Fine texture.

SIZE - To 15 feet, rapid growth.

HARDINESS ZONE - Zone 8b. May be grown throughout Florida, but requires protection in the northern counties.

NATIVE HABITAT - Australia (New South Wales).

LEAVES - Simple, alternate or spiral, linear to 5 inches long, apex acuminate, stiff, leathery when mature, pubescent when young, aromatic, tiny translucent dots on leaf surface, margins entire.

STEM/BARK - Young twigs pubescent, bark brown and furrowed with age.

FLOWERS - Cylindrical spikes to 4 inches long, sessile flowers encircling stem; petals deciduous; stamens many, red, exserted, to 1 inch long; flowers in spring to summer.

FRUIT - Capsules, woody, brown, globular to 0.25 inch in diameter, in clusters around stem, persistent.

CULTURE - Full sun, lighter well-drained soils, moderately salt tolerant.

PROBLEMS - Mites, root rot, brittle.

PROPAGATION - Seeds, cuttings.

LANDSCAPE USES - Hedge, screen, specimen, accent.

COMMENTS - Several cultivars and many hybrids.

Callistemon viminalis   WEEPING BOTTLEBRUSH

PRONUNCIATION - kə 'lis tə mən   ˌvi mə 'næ ləs

TRANSLATION - [from Greek *kallos* (= beautiful) and *steman* (= a stamen)] [long slender shoot].

FORM - Monoecious, evergreen tree; weeping, pendulous habit; low-branching; often multiple trunked; dense; medium-fine texture.

SIZE - To 25 feet, commonly to 15 feet; rapid growth rate.

HARDINESS ZONE - Zone 9b; grown outside in central and south Florida.

NATIVE HABITAT - Australia (New South Wales).

LEAVES - Simple; alternate or spiral; lanceolate to 4 inches long; apex acuminate; heavy texture at maturity but are pliable; entire margins; medium green.

STEM/BARK - Older bark grayish-brown; branches weeping.

FLOWERS - Scarlet; borne in cylindrical spikes to 3 inches long and encircling the stem; sessile; deciduous petals, stamens many, exserted to 1 inch long. Blooms in spring.

FRUIT - Capsules; woody; globular to 0.25 inch in diameter; clustered around stem; persistent; ripen in summer.

CULTURE - Full sun on light, well-drained soils; moderate salt tolerance.

PROBLEMS - Mites, root rot, brittle wood.

PROPAGATION - Seeds, cuttings.

LANDSCAPE USES - Framing tree, street plantings, specimen, accent.

COMMENTS - No reported cultivars but many hybrids exist. Confusion in naming the bottlebrushes is a problem in Florida. However, in addition to the species noted here, a few others, such as *C. linearis, C. phoeniceus, C. salignus,* and *C. speciosus,* appear to be distinct species. Cultivar '**Red Cascade**' has weeping branches and rose-red flowers.

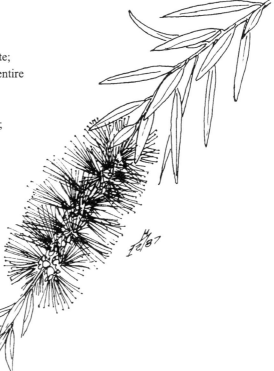

Eucalyptus cinerea   SILVER DOLLAR TREE

PRONUNCIATION - ˌyū kə ˈlip təs   sə ˈne rē ə

TRANSLATION - [from Greek *eu* (= well) and *kalipto* (= to cover), in reference to the calyx, which forms a lid over the flowers in bud] [ash colored, in reference to the canescent leaves].

FORM - Monoecious, evergreen tree, somewhat weeping habit, many-branched, irregular, open canopy. Medium texture.

SIZE - To 20 feet, commonly seen to 15 feet, very rapid growth.

HARDINESS ZONE - Zone 8b. Grown in south, central, and warmest areas of north Florida.

NATIVE HABITAT - Australia (New South Wales, Victoria).

LEAVES - Simple. Juvenile: perfoliate, clasping (but not connate), sessile, to 2 inches across. Adult: alternate, lanceolate to 6 inches long. Both juvenile and adult foliage are blue-green, glaucous, aromatic, thick, leathery, margins entire.

STEM/BARK - Reddish-brown, fibrous, exfoliating.

FLOWERS - Umbels, 3-flowered, small, cream colored, inconspicuous.

FRUIT - Globular woody capsule to 0.25 inch across, glaucous, many seeds.

CULTURE - Full sun, well-drained soils, slightly salt tolerant.

PROBLEMS - Few insects, brittle.

PROPAGATION - Seeds.

LANDSCAPE USES - Framing tree, specimen.

COMMENTS - Many related species. Leafy shoots are often used in floral arrangements. Of the more than 600 Eucalyptus species, relatively few are cultivated in Florida: *E. amplifolia* (Cabbage Gum), *E. camaldulensis* (Murray Red Gum), *E. cordata, E. crebra, E. ficifolia* (Red-flowering Gum), *E. megacornuta* (Warty Yate), *E. pulverulenta* (Silver-Dollar Eucalyptus), *E. robusta, E. rudis* (Desert Gum), *E. tereticornis* (Forest Red Gum), and *E. torelliana.*

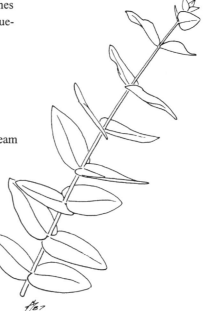

Eugenia uniflora   SURINAM CHERRY

PRONUNCIATION - yū ˈjē nē ə   ˌyū nə ˈflo rə

TRANSLATION - [after Prince Eugene of Savoy (1663-1736), presumably a patron of botany] [one-flowered].

FORM - Evergreen shrub or small tree; round; compact, dense; much-branched, slender branches; medium-fine texture.

SIZE - To 20 feet, commonly to 10 feet; rapid growth rate.

HARDINESS ZONE - Zones 8b-9; grown in central and south Florida.

NATIVE HABITAT - Tropical America.

LEAVES - Simple; opposite; ovate to 2.5 inches long; glossy-green above, pale beneath; young leaves reddish, aromatic; entire margins. Petioles short.

STEM/BARK - Tan, thin, peeling bark.

FLOWERS - White; to 0.5 inch across; solitary; axillary; with protruding stamens; fragrant.

FRUIT - Berry; red; globose, to 1 inch in diameter; with 8 longitudinal grooves. The edible fruits are used in jams, jellies, and preserves.

CULTURE - Grows in full sun on various soils; no salt tolerance.

PROBLEMS - Chewing insects, caterpillars, scale.

PROPAGATION - Seeds, cuttings.

LANDSCAPE USES - Use as a clipped or informal hedge, barrier, or dooryard fruit.

COMMENTS - Many other species are cultivated in south Florida: *E. aggregata* (Cherry of the Rio Grande), *E. anthera, E. atropunctata, E. axillaris* (White Stopper)*, E. brasiliensis* (Grumichama), *E. confusa* (Redberry Stopper)*, E. coronata, E. curranii, E. eucalyptoides, E. foetida* (Spanish Stopper, Anguila), *E. luschnathiana* (Pitomba), *E. pyriformis* (Pera de Campo)*, E. rhombea* (Red Stopper), *and E. uvalha* (Uvalha).

Melaleuca viridiflora   CAJEPUT TREE, PUNK TREE

PRONUNCIATION - ˌme lə lū kə   vi ˌri də ˈflo rə

TRANSLATION - [from Greek *melas* (= black) and *leukos* (= white), in reference to the black trunk and white shoots of many species] [five-nerved, in reference to the leaves].

SYNONYM - *Melaleuca quinquenervia.*

FORM- Evergreen tree; erect; often multi-trunked; many-branched, branches often pendulous; oval canopy; brittle; medium texture.

SIZE - To 40 feet, commonly to 25 feet; rapid growth rate.

HARDINESS ZONE - Zone 9b; grows outside in south and central Florida.

NATIVE HABITAT - Eastern Australia, New Guinea.

LEAVES - Simple; alternate or spiral; oblanceolate to 4 inches long, narrowed to a short petiole; 5 parallel veins; new growth pubescent, aromatic; entire margins. Medium green.

STEM/BARK - Papery, cream-colored bark; spongy; peeling in thin layers.

FLOWERS - White; borne in cylindrical spikes, to 3 inches long and encircling the stem; dense; petals deciduous, stamens many, exserted, to 0.75 inch long; fragrant. Blooms in spring.

FRUIT - Woody capsules in clusters surrounding stem; globular, to 0.25 inch in diameter; persistent.

CULTURE - Grow in full sun to partial shade; very tolerant of extreme soil and water conditions; high salt tolerance.

PROBLEMS - No major insect or disease problems. The tree has brittle wood and produces allergies in some humans. *Melaleuca* has escaped from cultivation and become a noxious weed in Florida.

PROPAGATION - Seed, cuttings.

LANDSCAPE USES - Use with extreme caution; can be a screen, hedge, specimen, or street tree. However, its use in Florida is forbidden by law.

COMMENTS - There are many related species cultivated in Florida: *M. armillaris, M. decora, M. halmaturorum, M. hesophylla, M. laxiflora, M. linariifolia, M. nodosa, M. styphelioides,* among others. In literature, *M. quinquenervia* is said to be a synonym of *M. viridiflora* var. *rubiflora*, which has red flowers.

Myrtus communis   MYRTLE

PRONUNCIATION - ˈmər təs   kə ˈmyū nəs

TRANSLATION - [ancient Greek and Latin name] [common].

FORM - Monoecious, evergreen shrub or small tree, freely branching, often multiple trunks, often leafless near soil line. Fine texture.

SIZE - To 15 feet, usually 5 to 10 feet, slow growth rate.

HARDINESS ZONE - Zone 8. Grows best in north and central Florida.

NATIVE HABITAT - Mediterranean region, Europe.

LEAVES - Simple, opposite, some whorled, closely arranged, ovate to lanceolate to 2 inches long, glossy-green, petioles reddish, margins entire, strongly aromatic.

STEM/BARK - Smooth, light brown.

FLOWERS - Axillary cymes, flowers, 5-petaled, white-pinkish to 0.75 inch across, prominent stamens, flowers in spring, fall.

FRUIT - Berries, blue-black, globose, drooping, to 0.5 inch long.

CULTURE - Full sun to partial shade, fertile organic soils, not salt tolerant.

PROBLEMS - Scale, root rot.

PROPAGATION - Seeds, cuttings.

LANDSCAPE USES - Screen, hedge, specimen, foundation plantings.

COMMENTS - Many cultivars, dwarf habit, white margins etc.: **'Compacta'** - dwarf form; dense, slow-growing; **'Flore Pleno'** - double flowered, white; **'Microphylla'** - Dwarf Myrtle - linear-lanceolate, overlapping leaves, less than 1 inch long; **'Variegata'** - white margin on leaves.

Psidium littorale

CATTLEY GUAVA,
STRAWBERRY GUAVA

PRONUNCIATION - ˈsi dē əm   ˌli tə ˈræ lē

TRANSLATION - [from *Psidion*, the Greek name for pomegranate] [seaside].

FORM - Monoecious, evergreen; large shrub, small tree, round; of medium texture.

SIZE - Can reach a height of 25 feet, commonly in the 10 to 15 foot range, with a nearly equal spread; moderate growth rate.

HARDINESS ZONE - Zone 9b; can be grown in central and south Florida.

NATIVE HABITAT - Brazil.

LEAVES - Simple; opposite; obovate, to 3 inches long; thick, leathery, dark green, smooth; glossy; entire margins.

STEM/BARK - Multiple trunks covered with smooth, gray-brown bark that peels off in thin sheets.

FLOWERS - White; solitary flowers with many prominent stamens; 1 inch wide. Main bloom is in April; may bloom sporadically at other times of the year.

FRUIT - Berry; pear-shaped; with persistent calyx, edible, to 1.5 inches wide; mainly ripens in July; red or yellow; red-fruited form better tasting.

CULTURE - Full sun or partial shade on a wide range of soils; best fruiting occurs in full sun on a fertile soil; no salt tolerance.

PROBLEMS - Pest-free except for ripe fruit, which is attacked by insects. Fallen fruits are messy.

PROPAGATION - Air layers. Seeds germinate easily and rapidly; seedlings take 7 or 8 years to bear fruit.

LANDSCAPE USES - As a specimen shrub or screen. Keep away from cars and sidewalks because of messy fruit.

COMMENTS - Variety *longipes*, the Strawbery Guava, has red fruit; var. *littorale* has yellow fruit and has become naturalized in some parts of Florida. Other available *Psidium* species and cultivars include: *P. friedrichsthalium*, *P. guajava* (Guava), and *P. guajava* 'Jose Jimenez'.

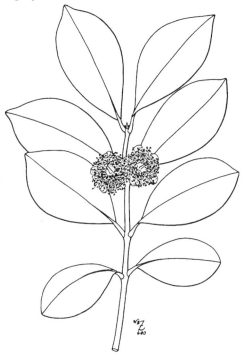

Syzygium paniculatum   AUSTRALIAN BUSH CHERRY

PRONUNCIATION - sə 'zi jē əm   pə ˌni kyə 'lā təm

TRANSLATION - [from Greek *suzugos* (= joined), in reference to the paired leaves and branches] [flowers in panicles].

FORM - Monoecious, evergreen tree; upright, columnar; densely foliated; medium texture.

SIZE - Reaches a height of 35 feet with a 15-foot spread; rapid growth rate.

HARDINESS ZONE - Zones 10-11; can be grown in south Florida and in protected locations in central Florida.

NATIVE HABITAT - Australia.

LEAVES - Simple; opposite; oblong-lanceolate, to 3 inches long; dark green, glossy; new growth reddish; entire margins.

FLOWER - White; 1 inch wide; with many prominent white stamens; borne in few-flowered axillary and terminal panicles. Blooms during warm months of the year.

FRUIT - Reddish-purple; fragrant; ovoid, to 0.75 inch long; ripen 2 months after flowering; used to make jelly.

CULTURE - Requires full sun; grows in a wide range of soils; moderate salt tolerance.

PROBLEMS - None of major consequence.

PROPAGATION - Seeds or cuttings.

LANDSCAPE USES - Although this plant grows into a tree, it is usually employed as a clipped specimen, hedge, or background shrubbery grouping. It withstands clipping well, retaining its ground-level branches.

COMMENTS - Several other *Syzygium* species are also available, including *S. aqueum* (Water Rose Apple), *S. cumini* (Jambolan), *S. grande* (Sea Apple), *S. jambos* (Rose Apple, Pomarrosa), *S. malaccense* (Malay Apple), *S. pycnanthemum*, and *S. samarangense* (Java Apple, Wax Jamby), as well as the cultivar, *S. paniculatum* 'Compactum'.

NANDINACEAE - NANDINA FAMILY

DICOTYLEDONS; MONOGENERIC AND MONOTYPIC

CHARACTERISTICS SAME AS THAT OF *NANDINA DOMESTICA.*

COMMENTS: Often included as a subfamily of Berberidaceae.

Nandina domestica   HEAVENLY BAMBOO, SACRED BAMBOO

PRONUNCIATION - næn 'dē nə   dō 'mes tə kə

TRANSLATION - [Latinized form of the Japanese name] [domesticated].

FORM - Monoecious, evergreen to semi-deciduous shrub, upright, clump-forming, leafless at base.

SIZE - To 8 feet, commonly 5 to 6 feet; rapid growth.

HARDINESS ZONE - Zone 7. Can be grown throughout Florida.

NATIVE HABITAT - India, eastern Asia.

LEAVES - Odd bi- and tripinnately compound, to 2 feet long, spirally arranged, clustered near stem tips, leaflets entire, elliptic to 4 inches long, bulbous swellings present along rachis, short petiole, leaves turning reddish in fall.

STEM/BARK - Leaf scars, young growth reddish. Stems cane-like.

FLOWERS - Small, white, 6-petaled, to 0.5 inch across, in panicles to 1 foot long, flowers late spring. Moderately showy.

FRUIT - Berry, red, ovate to 0.25 inch in diameter, in pendulous clusters, showy, toxic, late fall and winter.

CULTURE - Full sun (for best color) to partial shade, fertile, organic soils. Not salt tolerant. Although drought tolerant, it is not heat tolerant, therefore not a good candidate for parking lots, etc. A low-maintenance plant.

PROBLEMS - Scale, root rot, suckers. None serious.

PROPAGATION - Seed, division.

LANDSCAPE USES - Border, enclosure, accent, planter box.

COMMENTS - Several cultivars available: 'Alba' - dull-white fruit; 'Atropurpurea Nana' - dwarf form to 2 feet; foliage tinged reddish purple year round, leaves somewhat cupped; 'Compacta' - dwarf form to 3 feet; minimal fruiting; 'Harbor Dwarf' - dwarf form under 2 feet; pinkish-bronze spring color, red-bronze fall color; 'Nana' - dwarf to 2 feet; minimal fruiting. Several others.

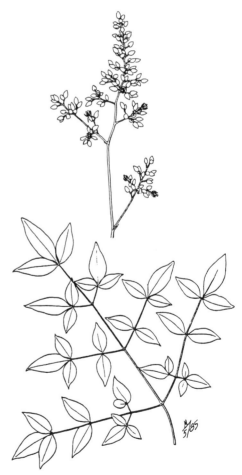

NYCTAGINACEAE - FOUR O'CLOCK FAMILY

DICOTYLEDONS; 30 GENERA AND ABOUT 300 SPECIES

GEOGRAPHY:	Tropical, especially the New World.
GROWTH HABIT:	Herbs, shrubs, and trees.
LEAVES:	Alternate or opposite, simple, and without stipules.
FLOWERS:	Bisexual or unisexual (plants monoecious), sometimes subtended by colorful involucral bracts; sepals usually petaloid and tubular; apetalous; stamens usually 5, but sometimes 1 to numerous; ovary superior, consisting of 1 carpel.
FRUIT:	An achene which is sometimes enclosed within the persistent calyx.
ECONOMIC USES:	Ornamentals, vegetables (*Pisonia*, cabbage and lettuce trees), and minor medicinal uses.

ORNAMENTAL GENERA: *Bougainvillea, Mirabilis, Pisonia.*

Bougainvillea spp.

PRONUNCIATION - ˌbō gən ˈvi lē ə

TRANSLATION - [after Louis Antonie de Bougainville (1729-1811), explorer and scientist].

FORM - Monoecious, evergreen; clambering woody vine, sprawling, rampant; occasionally trained as a shrub; medium texture.

SIZE - Variable; will cover large areas if allowed to grow; rapid growth rate.

HARDINESS ZONE - Zone 9; most species are limited to south Florida, but some hardier species can be grown in central Florida.

NATIVE HABITAT - South America.

LEAVES - Simple; alternate; elliptic to ovate, 2 to 4 inches long; entire margins.

STEM/BARK - Depending on the species, leaf axils may have a sharp, slender thorn up to 2 inches long. (The thorn in this case is a modified inflorescence.)

FLOWERS - White to yellow; tubular; small, not showy; solitary or in groups of 3; surrounded by 3 large, brightly colored bracts. The bracts, up to 2 inches long, form the colorful portion of the axillary bloom; colors vary from purple to white with many shades of red, pink, yellow, and orange in between.

FRUIT - Achenes; small, elongate; 5-ribbed; not commonly produced.

CULTURE - Requires full sun for best flowering and a sandy, well-drained soil; becomes chlorotic on alkaline soils; no salt tolerance. Frequent pruning is necessary to control size and shape, but bougainvilleas withstand clipping well.

PROBLEMS - Caterpillars can riddle new growth.

PROPAGATION - Mature wood cuttings root well.

LANDSCAPE USES - Very effective when allowed to grow over arbors, walls, fences, and carports, but must be given room to grow or will become a problem. Withstands hot, dry situations well.

COMMENTS - Several species, hybrids, and many named cultivars are available. Among these, *B. peruviana, B. glabra,* and *B. spectabilis* are well-known. Many cultivars are also available: **'Afterglow', 'Barbara Karst', 'Crimson Jewel', 'Jamaica White', 'May Palmer', 'Mrs. Butt' (= 'Crimson Lake'), and 'Texas Down'.**

NYSSACEAE - TUPELO FAMILY

DICOTYLEDONS; 3 GENERA AND 8 SPECIES

GEOGRAPHY: Eastern North America, China, and Tibet.

GROWTH HABIT: Trees and shrubs.

LEAVES: Alternate, entire or sometimes denticulate.

FLOWERS: Actinomorphic, bisexual or unisexual (plants polygamodioecious);
                    male flowers in heads or racemes; female and bisexual flowers
                    solitary in few-flowered heads; 5-merous; sepals minute or absent;
                    petals usually 5; stamens usually 10; ovary inferior consisting of 1
                    or 2 carpels.

FRUIT: Drupe- or samara-like.

ECONOMIC USES: Ornamentals, also edible fruit (from *Nyssa*).

ORNAMENTAL GENERA: *Camptotheca, Davidia,* and *Nyssa.*

Nyssa sylvatica

BLACK TUPELO, SOUR GUM,
BLACK GUM, PEPPERIDGE

PRONUNCIATION - 'ni sə   sil 'væ tə kə

TRANSLATION - [name of a water nymph, referring to swampy habitat of genus] [forest-loving].

FORM - Dioecious, deciduous, pyramidal tree with somewhat pendulous lower branches when young, becoming irregularly rounded with age, densely foliated. Medium texture.

SIZE - To 100 feet, commonly 30 to 50 feet with 20 to 30 foot spread. Slow to medium growth rate.

HARDINESS ZONE - Zone 4. Grown in north and central Florida only.

NATIVE HABITAT - Eastern North America from Ontario to Florida to Texas.

LEAVES - Alternate, simple, elliptic to ovate to obovate, to 5 inches long, margins wavy and entire or with a few irregularly spaced teeth near apex, apex acute or short-acuminate, dark green and glossy above, lighter green and pubescent on veins or glabrous below, often crowded at tips of branches, petioles 0.5 to 1 inch long and often reddish. Brilliant red fall color!

STEM/BARK - Young branches slender, reddish-brown, slightly pubescent at first, becoming glabrous, producing numerous short spurs. Main branches at right angle to trunk, lower branches drooping. Bark dark gray, almost black, with scaly ridges giving alligator-hide appearance.

FLOWERS - Small, greenish white, in axillary clusters, spring. Not showy, but excellent source of nectar for bees.

FRUIT - Oblong, berry-like drupe, blue-black, 0.5 inch long, ripening in fall. Hidden by foliage, therefore not showy.

CULTURE - Full sun or part shade, moist, well-drained soils, not tolerant of alkaline soils. Difficult to transplant from the wild due to deep taproot. While most *Nyssa* spp. are native to swampy areas, this species is native to drier, upland sites.

PROBLEMS - No serious insect or disease problems. Fruit can be messy on pavement.

PROPAGATION - Seed, which exhibits varying degrees of dormancy, or softwood cuttings.

LANDSCAPE USES - Shade tree, specimen tree, street tree in areas that are not heavily polluted. Fruit attracts birds and small mammals, bears.

COMMENTS - *N. sylvatica* var. *biflora*, Swamp Tupelo, considered by some authorities as a separate species, has 1 to 2 fruit per stalk, inhabits poorly drained areas. Black Tupelo typically has 3+ fruit per stalk and grows on well-drained sites. Other species sold in Florida include *N. aquatica* (Water Tupelo) and *N. ogeche* (Ogeechee Lime).

OLEACEAE - OLIVE FAMILY

DICOTYLEDONS; 29 GENERA AND ABOUT 600 SPECIES

GEOGRAPHY:	Nearly cosmopolitan, especially in Southeast Asia, with several endemic genera.
GROWTH HABIT:	Deciduous or evergreen trees, shrubs, and sometimes woody vines.
LEAVES:	Opposite, without stipules, simple, trifoliolate or pinnately compound, entire or lobed.
FLOWERS:	Bisexual or rarely unisexual (plants dioecious); 4-merous; sepals usually 4, free; petals usually 4, but may vary from 2 to 6, free or connate, or sometimes apetalous; stamens 2 or 4, epipetalous; ovary superior and of 2 fused carpels.
FRUIT:	Capsule, berry, nut, drupe, or single samara.
ECONOMIC USES:	Several common ornamentals, but olive fruit and oil (from *Olea europea*) are economically important, valuable timber (from *Fraxinus*), and perfumery (*Jasminum, Osmanthus,* etc.).

ORNAMENTAL GENERA: *Chionanthus, Forestiera, Forsythia, Fraxinus, Jasminum, Ligustrum, Noronhia, Olea, Osmanthus, Syringa,* and others.

Chionanthus retusus

CHINESE FRINGETREE

PRONUNCIATION - ˌkī ə ˈnæn thəs   rə ˈtū səs

TRANSLATION - [from Greek *chion* (= snow) and *anthos* (= flower), referring to the white flowers] [rounded but slightly notched, in reference to the leaf tip].

FORM - Dioecious, deciduous shrub or small tree, open, spreading, rounded. Sometimes multistemmed. Medium texture.

SIZE - To 20 feet. Slow growth rate.

HARDINESS ZONE - Zone 6. Use in north Florida.

NATIVE HABITAT - China.

LEAVES - Opposite, obovate to ovate, to 4 inches long, entire; apex acute or obtuse (sometimes emarginate); pubescent on veins beneath when young; lustrous; petioles pubescent. Leaves emerge several weeks ahead of *C. virginicus* in spring and are smaller and more leathery.

STEM/BARK - Gray bark; may be peeling or ridged and furrowed.

FLOWERS - Fragrant, with 4 white, ribbon-like petals, about 0.5 to 0.75 inch long, borne in 2 to 4-inch-long panicles on current season's growth, in April as leaves are expanding.

FRUIT - Drupe, blue-black, ellipsoidal, 0.5 inch long. Ripen late summer to early fall.

CULTURE - Full sun or partial shade in moist, fertile soils.

PROBLEMS - No serious pests.

PROPAGATION - Difficult to root from cuttings, although apparently less difficult than *C. virginicus*. Seeds have complex dormancy requirements, requiring 2 years to germinate.

LANDSCAPE USES - Specimen flowering tree.

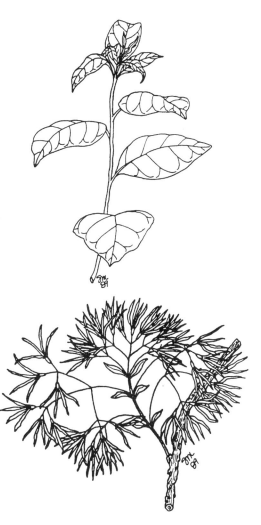

Chionanthus virginicus   FRINGE TREE, OLD MAN'S BEARD, GRAY BEARD

PRONUNCIATION - ˈkī ə ˈnæn thəs   vərˈji nə kəs

TRANSLATION - [from Greek *chion* (= snow) and *anthos* (= flower), referring to the white flowers] [from Virginia].

FORM - Dioecious, deciduous shrubby tree, spreading, open, rounded, of coarse texture.

SIZE - Can reach a height of 25 feet with an equal spread. Growth rate is slow.

HARDINESS ZONE - Zone 5. Grows in north and central Florida.

NATIVE HABITAT - An understory plant of moist woods in north and central Florida and the eastern United States.

LEAVES - Simple, opposite, elliptic, to 6 inches long, margins entire. The petioles and nodes are often maroon.

STEM/BARK - The 8-inch-thick trunks have brown, scaly bark; the twigs have prominent, warty lenticels.

FLOWERS - The male tree has larger flowers. Flowers are white, with four 1-inch-long ribbon-like petals, on 0.15-inch-long, loose, drooping axillary panicles in April, when leaves are almost fully expanded. The lacy, airy, copious fringe-like flower panicles give the tree its common name.

FRUIT - Drupes, blue-black, ovoid, to 0.75 inch long, ripening in August.

CULTURE - Plant in a full sun or partially shaded location with moist, fertile, sandy soils. It has no salt tolerance; however, it does tolerate wet sites and city conditions.

PROBLEMS - Scales and mites occasionally cause problems. None serious.

PROPAGATION - By air layers, grafting on ash seedlings, or seed which require cold-warm-cold stratification over 2 years to germinate. Removal of the seed coat in GA_3 soak results in quick germination.

LANDSCAPE USES - Grown as a specimen for its showy bloom, which occurs after the rest of the spring blooms have faded. Fruit attracts wildlife.

COMMENTS - *Chionanthus virginicus* is a valuable species with variation in its leaf morphology. The cultivar **'Angustifolius'** has narrow leaves; **'Latifolius'** has broad leaves. The closely related species *C. pygmaeus* is native to central Florida and is also cultivated.

Fraxinus americana   WHITE ASH

PRONUNCIATION - ˈfræk sə nəs   ə ˌme rə ˈkā nə

TRANSLATION - [ancient Latin name] [American].

FORM - Dioecious, deciduous, upright tree, oval when young, becoming open and rounded with age; medium texture.

SIZE - To 120 feet, usually 50 to 80 feet in both height and spread. Moderate growth rate.

HARDINESS ZONE - Zone 2. Should be grown only in north Florida.

NATIVE HABITAT - Eastern North America, from north Florida to Nova Scotia.

LEAVES - Opposite, odd-pinnately compound, 8 to 13 inches long, leaflets 5 to 9 (usually 7), ovate to ovate-lanceolate, 3 to 5 inches long, usually entire or denticulate toward apex; apex acute to acuminate; dark green above, glaucous beneath. Fall color yellow to maroon.

STEM/BARK - Twigs stout, glabrous, green to gray-brown with pale lenticels, brittle. Bark gray-brown, becoming deeply furrowed; ridges and furrows form diamond pattern.

FLOWERS - Small, inconspicuous, in dense panicles, appear in early spring before leaves.

FRUIT - Solitary samara, 1 to 2 inches long, oblong to spatulate, light brown, borne in loose panicles, not ornamental.

CULTURE - Full sun, fertile soils. Native to well-drained, upland woods, although will tolerate short periods of flooding. Not tolerant of compacted soils. Easily transplanted.

PROBLEMS - Ash borer, cankers, leaf spots, dieback; vigorous trees usually not affected by pests. Twigs break in heavy winds. Seeds germinate everywhere.

PROPAGATION - Seed or grafting (budding) of selected cultivars.

LANDSCAPE USES - Handsome native tree for parks and other large areas.

COMMENTS - Wood used in tool handles, baseball bats, furniture. Several cultivars, although none have been selected particularly for Florida: **'Autumn Applause'** - male (seedless); dark maroon fall color; **'Autumn Purple'** - male; reddish-purple fall color; **'Rosehill'** - male; bronze-red fall color, dark green summer color, tolerates alkaline soils; *Fraxinus pennsylvanica*, Red Ash, is somewhat similar in appearance, but has darker and somewhat larger leaflets. Other species available in Florida include *F. caroliniana* (Water Ash), *F. angustifolia* **'Raymond'** *(= F. oxycarpa)* (Claret Ash), *F. velutina* and var. *glabra* (Arizona Ash).

Jasminum mesnyi

PRIMROSE JASMINE

PRONUNCIATION - jæz 'mī nəm   'mez nē ī

TRANSLATION - [from Latinized Persian name *yasmin*] [after William Mesny (1842-1919), a major general in the Chinese National Army who collected plants].

FORM - Monoecious, evergreen shrub, rambling, vining habit, not climbing, densely foliated. Medium-fine texture.

SIZE - To 10 feet, commonly to 6 feet, rapid growth.

HARDINESS ZONE - Zone 8. Grows in north and central Florida.

NATIVE HABITAT - Western China.

LEAVES - Pinnately compound (trifoliolate), opposite; leaflets oblong to oblanceolate, to 3 inches long, entire.

STEM/BARK - Stems green, square, woody with age.

FLOWERS - Yellow; 6 united, lobed petals subtended by leaf-like bracts, to 3 inches across; often double; solitary, axillary, flowering in spring and sporadically throughout summer.

FRUIT - Berry, black, fleshy. Not showy.

CULTURE - Full sun, various soils, not salt tolerant.

PROBLEMS - Scale, root rot.

PROPAGATION - Cuttings.

LANDSCAPE USES - Hedge, border embankment, screen, foundation for large building, cascading over walls, and fences.

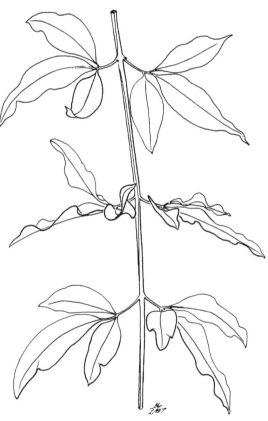

Jasminum multiflorum

PRONUNCIATION - jæz 'mī nəm ˌmul tə 'flo rə

TRANSLATION - [from Latinized Persian name *yasmin*] [many-flowered].

FORM - Evergreen climber, sprawling, low-growing; numerous slender stems; can be pruned into a shrub.

SIZE - Climbs to 12 feet or more with support, as a shrub to 2 feet, rapid growth.

HARDINESS ZONE - Zone 8b. Grown in south, central, and north Florida. May require protection in north Florida.

NATIVE HABITAT - India.

LEAVES - Simple, opposite, ovate, to 2 inches long; rounded or cordate base, acute tip, margins undulate; veins, petiole and leaf surface are pubescent.

STEM/BARK - Stems slender, pubescent young growth.

FLOWERS - White to 1 inch across with 6 to 10 united, lobed petals. Borne in terminal or axillary clusters. Blooms in summer and fall.

FRUIT - Capsules; small, rare in Florida.

CULTURE - Grow in full sun on various soils; not salt tolerant.

PROBLEMS - Scale.

PROPAGATION - Cuttings.

LANDSCAPE USES - Can be trained on a trellis; used in borders, planter boxes, and pruned as a foundation shrub.

COMMENTS - Often sold as *J. pubescens*. Other *Jasminum* species sold in Florida include *J. azoricum* (= *J. fluminense* - Pinwheel Jasmine), *J. dichotomum* (Gold Coast Jasmine), *J. floridum* (Showy Jasmine), *J. grassillimum* (Pinwheel Jasmine), *J. humele* (Italian Jasmine), *J. officinale* (Poet's Jasmine), *J. officinale* f. *grandiflorum* (= *J. grandiflorum* - Spanish Jasmine), *J. sambac* (Arabian Jasmine), including **'Grand Duke of Tuscany'** and **'Maid of Orleans'**, and *J. subhumile, J. volubile,* etc.

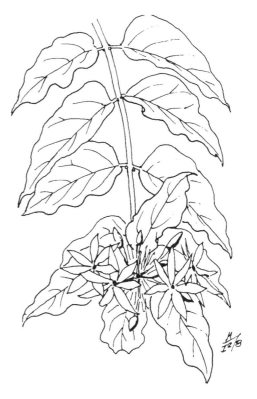

Jasminum nitidum

PINWHEEL JASMINE,
SHINING JASMINE

PRONUNCIATION - jæz ˈmī nəm   ˈni tə də

TRANSLATION - [from Latinized Persian name *yasmin*] [shining, in reference to the leaves].

FORM - Monoecious, evergreen vine, twining, sprawling, low-growing, can be pruned into a shrub.

SIZE - Climbs to 15 feet or more on support, as a shrub to 2 feet, rapid growth.

HARDINESS ZONE - Zone 9. Grown in south and central Florida. Can be grown with protection in warmest areas of north Florida.

NATIVE HABITAT - Admiralty Islands.

LEAVES - Simple, opposite, elliptic-lanceolate, to 3 inches long, acuminate apex, glossy-green, leathery; margins entire.

STEM/BARK - Glabrous, green; becomes woody with age.

FLOWERS - White, wavy, to 1 inch across, in cymes. Calyx and calyx teeth pinkish red, persistent. Blooms in summer.

FRUIT - Berry: 2-lobed, rare in Florida.

CULTURE - Grow in full sun to partial shade on various well-drained soils; slight salt tolerance.

PROBLEMS - Scale, root rot.

PROPAGATION - Cuttings.

LANDSCAPE USES - Train on a trellis or fence; as a shrub, use in foundation plantings or planter boxes.

Ligustrum japonicum

PRONUNCIATION - lə 'gus trəm   jə 'pɑ nə kəm

TRANSLATION - [Latin name] [Japanese].

FORM - Monoecious, evergreen shrub or small tree, upright, low-branching, dense, often irregular canopy.

SIZE - To 10 feet or more, rapid growth.

HARDINESS ZONE - Zone 7. Grown in all areas of Florida.

NATIVE HABITAT - Japan, Korea.

LEAVES - Simple, opposite, ovate to elliptic, to 4 inches long, glossy, dark green, leathery, margins entire and often undulate.

STEM/BARK - Raised lenticels on branches are more prominent than those on *L. lucidum*.

FLOWERS - Bisexual, in panicles, terminal, to 6 inches long, white, to 0.25 inch across, 4 united petals unpleasantly fragrant; flowers in summer through fall.

FRUIT - Berries; drupe-like, blue-black to 0.25 inch; maturing in fall.

CULTURE - Full sun to partial shade; various soils; moderately salt tolerant. Drought tolerant.

PROBLEMS - Scale, whitefly, sooty mold, nematodes, root rot; none serious.

PROPAGATION - Cuttings.

LANDSCAPE USES - Border, clipped or unclipped hedge, screen, urn.

COMMENTS - Several cultivars for leaf shape, growth habit, variegation, etc. Examples include **'Erecta'**, **'Fraseri'**, **'Gold Tip'**, **'Howardii'**, **'Nobile'**, **'Variegatum'**. Also, *L. japonicum* var. *rotundifolium*.

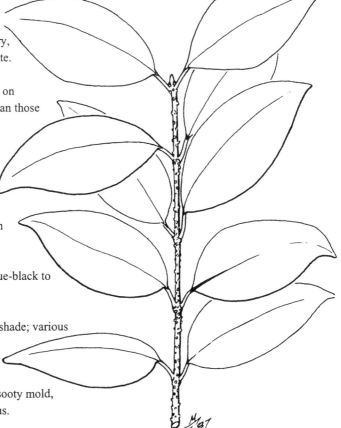

Ligustrum lucidum   GLOSSY PRIVET, TREE PRIVET

PRONUNCIATION - lə 'gus trəm   'lū sə dəm

TRANSLATION - [Latin name] [glossy, in reference to the leaves].

FORM - Monoecious, evergreen tree or large shrub, upright, often multitrunked, densely foliated, upper branches often drooping, compact globose canopy.

SIZE - To 30 feet, commonly 15 to 20 feet, rapid growth.

HARDINESS ZONE - Zone 7. Grown in all regions of Florida.

NATIVE HABITAT - China, Korea, naturalized in parts of Florida.

LEAVES - Simple, opposite, elliptic-lanceolate, to 6 inches long, acuminate tip, upper surface glossy; keeled along midrib; narrow, translucent, entire margins.

STEM/BARK - Light brown, lenticels not as apparent as *L. japonicum*.

FLOWERS - Bisexual, in terminal panicles, to 12 inches long, flowers white, to 0.25 inch across, very showy; flowers in spring. Some people find the fragrance offensive.

FRUIT - Berry, drupe-like, purple to 0.25 inch, in large clusters in fall. Showy.

CULTURE - Full sun to partial shade, various soils, moderately salt tolerant.

PROBLEMS - Scale, whitefly, sooty mold, nematodes, root rot; none serious.

PROPAGATION - Seed, cuttings, grafting of cultivars.

LANDSCAPE USES - Large shrub, framing tree, border.

COMMENTS - Many cultivars for leaf shape, size, variegation, and plant growth habit and shape.

Ligustrum sinense

PRONUNCIATION - lə 'gus trəm   sī 'nen sē

TRANSLATION - [Latin name] [from China].

FORM - Monoecious, deciduous or semi-evergreen shrub, rounded, densely foliated; fine texture.

SIZE - Reaches a height of 12 feet and a spread of 10 feet. Growth rate is rapid.

HARDINESS ZONE - Zone 7. Can be grown in all regions of Florida.

NATIVE HABITAT - China and Korea.

LEAVES - Simple, opposite, elliptic to oblong, 1.5 to 3 inches long, more or less 2-ranked. Midribs are pubescent and some cultivars have yellowish or pinkish marginal variegation.

STEM/BARK - Slender, spreading, unbranched shoots are downy when young.

FLOWERS - Bisexual, creamy white, 0.25 inch long, in loose, 4-inch-long terminal panicles in April; not showy.

FRUIT - Drupes; purple-black, ellipsoidal, to 0.33 inch long. Not showy.

CULTURE - Grows in full sun or partial shade on a wide range of soils. Not salt tolerant. Tolerates close clipping.

PROBLEMS - Bothered by nematodes, scales, and mites.

PROPAGATION - Softwood or hardwood cuttings root easily. Variegated cultivars are sports which must be propagated by cuttings; the species can be grown from seed, cleaned and sown immediately after harvest.

LANDSCAPE USES - Normally only the variegated forms are used as clipped hedges or as accent or contrast shrubs.

COMMENTS - Variegated cultivars, such as 'Variegatum', frequently revert to green. 'Multiflorum' is floriferous, 'Pendulum' has pendulous habit, 'Wimbei' is dwarf but columnar in habit.

Noronhia emarginata   MADAGASCAR OLIVE

PRONUNCIATION - no ˈrō nē ə   ē ˌmär jə ˈnā tə

TRANSLATION - [after Fernando de Noronha, traveler and naturalist (died 1787)] [shallow notch on apex, in reference to the leaves].

FORM - Monoecious, evergreen tree; oval; coarse texture.

SIZE - Reaches heights of 20 feet with a 10 foot spread; slow growth rate.

HARDINESS ZONE - Zone 9b; can be grown in south Florida and the warmer coastal areas of central Florida.

NATIVE HABITAT - Madagascar.

LEAVES - Simple; opposite; oval, to 6 inches long and 2 inches wide; leathery, olive green; emarginate apices; revolute margins.

FLOWERS - Yellowish; urceolate; to 0.25 inch long; corolla thick and fleshy, borne in short clusters.

FRUIT - Drupes; dark purple; globular, to 1 inch across; cream-colored, edible pulp.

CULTURE - Full sun to partial shade in a wide range of soils; resistant to wind; high salt tolerance; even more so than *Coccoloba uvifera.*

PROBLEMS - Pest-free.

PROPAGATION - Cuttings or seeds.

LANDSCAPE USES - A very tough tree for coastal and seaside locations.

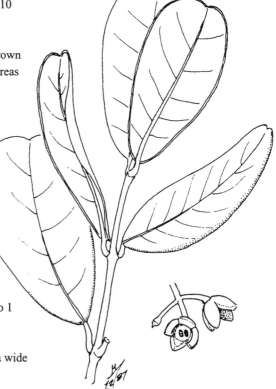

Osmanthus americanus

DEVILWOOD, AMERICAN OLIVE,
WILD OLIVE

PRONUNCIATION - ɑz ˈmæn thəs   ə ˌme rə ˈkā nəs

TRANSLATION - [from Greek *osme* (= fragrance) and *anthos* (= flower)] [American].

FORM - Monoecious, evergreen shrub or small tree, upright and open. Medium-coarse texture.

SIZE - To 45 feet, commonly 15 to 25 feet with 10 to 20 foot spread. Slow to medium growth rate.

HARDINESS ZONE - Zone 7. For use in north and central Florida only.

NATIVE HABITAT - Southeastern U.S. from North Carolina to central Florida to Mississippi, also Mexico.

LEAVES - Opposite, simple, elliptic to oblong-elliptic, to 9 inches (usually 4 to 5 inches) long, margins entire and revolute, apex usually acute but may be short-acuminate or obtuse, dark green and glossy above, light green and duller below, leathery, petioles 0.5 to 0.75 inch long.

STEM/BARK - Young branches light reddish-brown turning gray with age, slightly angled in cross-section, with numerous light-colored lenticels. Bark roughened, dark gray to reddish-brown, developing thin scales with age.

FLOWERS - Small white or cream-colored, bisexual or unisexual (plants usually monoecious) flowers in short, axillary panicles on previous season's growth; very fragrant. Not showy. Late winter to early spring. Immature flower clusters are apparent in late fall and early winter.

FRUIT - Drupe; ovoid, 0.5 inch long, dark blue (resemble small olives) in axillary clusters. Mature in the fall and may persist well into the next year.

CULTURE - Full sun or part shade; moist, well-drained soils; pH adaptable. Easily transplanted. Not salt tolerant.

PROBLEMS - No serious insect or disease problems.

PROPAGATION - Difficult to propagate by seed but cuttings may be propagated with IBA treatment in midsummer.

LANDSCAPE USES - Naturalized areas, hedges, borders; a tree for small lots. Fruit attracts birds and small mammals.

COMMENTS - Fine-textured wood is difficult to split and work, hence the common name Devilwood. A related species with larger fruit, *O. megacarpa*, a Florida endemic, is similar to *O. americana* but a smaller plant with wider, more or less ovate leaves.

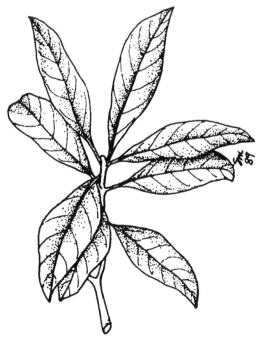

Osmanthus × *fortunei*

FORTUNE'S OSMANTHUS

PRONUNCIATION - ɑz ˈmæn thəs   for ˈtū nē ī

TRANSLATION - [from Greek *osme* (= fragrance) and *anthos* (= flower)] [after Robert Fortune, who introduced it in 1862].

FORM - Monoecious, evergreen shrub, compact, rounded form; medium texture.

SIZE - Can reach a height of 20 feet with a spread of 12 feet. Grows at a moderate pace.

HARDINESS ZONE - Zone 7b. Should be grown in north Florida only.

NATIVE HABITAT - A hybrid, originated in Japan, between *O. heterophyllus* and *O. fragrans*. Its characteristics are intermediate between the two parents.

LEAVES - Opposite, broadly elliptic, to 4 inches long, thick, dark green, leathery, with 10 to 12 sharp, 0.25-inch-long spines on each margin.

STEM/BARK - Multiple trunks.

FLOWERS - White, to 0.25 inch long, in axillary clusters that appear in midwinter; very fragrant but not showy.

FRUIT - Drupes black, rarely produced.

CULTURE - Grows in full sun or partial shade on any soil of reasonable drainage and fertility. It is not salt tolerant.

PROBLEMS - Scales, mushroom root rot when grown in wet soils.

PROPAGATION - Semi-hardwood cuttings.

LANDSCAPE USES - As a formal specimen, screen or clipped hedge, container specimen. Dense growth and spiny leaves make this a good barrier plant.

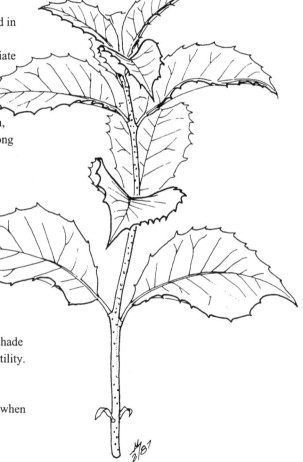

Osmanthus fragrans

PRONUNCIATION - ɑz ˈmæn thəs   ˈfrā grənz

TRANSLATION - [from Greek *osme* (= fragrance) and *anthos* (= flower)] [fragrant].

FORM - Monoecious, evergreen shrub, upright, rounded, of medium texture.

SIZE - Reaches a height of 25 feet with an almost equal spread. Growth rate is medium.

HARDINESS ZONE - Zone 8. Should be grown in north Florida only.

NATIVE HABITAT - Eastern Asia.

LEAVES - Simple, opposite, broadly elliptic, to 4 inches long, dark green; margins are either finely toothed or entire.

STEM/BARK - Multiple-trunked.

FLOWERS - White, 0.25 inch long, in axillary clusters appearing in late winter, extremely fragrant.

FRUIT - Drupes; bluish-black, ovoid to 0.5 inch long.

CULTURE - Grows in full sun or partial shade on soils of reasonable fertility and drainage. Salt tolerance is poor.

PROBLEMS - Scales, mushroom root rot when grown in wet soils.

PROPAGATION - Semi-hardwood cuttings, or by seed, which take 2 years to germinate.

LANDSCAPE USES - Planted as freestanding specimen or as a shrubbry grouping near patios or sidewalks for the fragrance of the flowers.

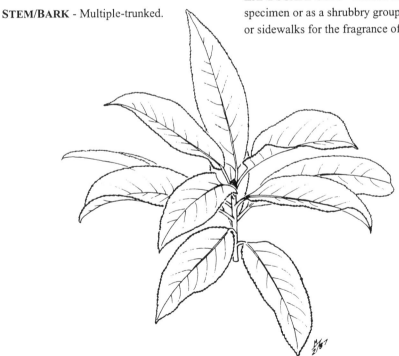

Osmanthus heterophyllus

PRONUNCIATION - ɑz 'mæn thəs   ˌhe tə rō 'fi ləs

TRANSLATION - [from Greek *osme* (= fragrance) and *anthos* (= flower)] [with variable leaves].

FORM - Monoecious, evergreen shrub, upright, medium-textured with densely foliated, irregular growth.

SIZE - Reaches a height of 15 feet and a spread of 10 feet. Growth rate is medium.

HARDINESS ZONE - Zone 7. Should be grown in north Florida only.

NATIVE HABITAT - Japan and Taiwan.

LEAVES - Simple, opposite, oblong, glossy, dark green, to 2.5 inches long. The thick, leathery leaves generally have 5 to 7 large spiny teeth, giving them a holly-like appearance. Petioles are short and stout.

FLOWERS - White, 1/4 inch long, in axillary clusters in late fall; very fragrant but not showy.

FRUIT - Drupes; purple, not usually seen.

CULTURE - Grows in full sun or partial shade in soil of fairly good fertility and drainage; pH adaptable. It is not salt tolerant.

PROBLEMS - Scales, mushroom root rot when grown in wet soils.

PROPAGATION - Semi-hardwood cuttings.

LANDSCAPE USES - Formal specimen, clipped hedge or background shrub, barrier plant.

COMMENTS - The variegated cultivars, include **'Aureo-marginatus'** (= **'Aureus'**) with green and yellow leaves; **'Goshiki'** is compact with pinkish young leaves; **'Golftide'** has very spiny leaves; **'Kembu'** is dwarf; **'Myrtifolius'** has entire leaves; **'Purpureus'** has dark purplish leaves.

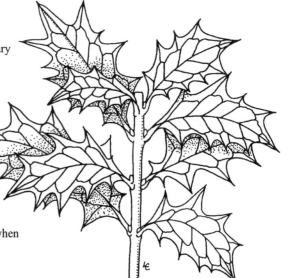

PITTOSPORACEAE - PITTOSPORUM FAMILY

DICOTYLEDONS; 9 GENERA AND ABOUT 240 SPECIES

GEOGRAPHY:	Old World tropics, especially Australia.
GROWTH HABIT:	Evergreen shrubs, small trees, and sometimes climbers.
LEAVES:	Coriaceous, simple, entire, and without stipules.
FLOWERS:	Usually bisexual, actinomorphic; 5-merous; sepals 5, free; petals 5, united at base; stamens 5, attached to the sepals; ovary superior consisting of 2 fused carpels.
FRUIT:	Loculicidal capsule or berry; seeds numerous and covered with resinous material.
ECONOMIC USES:	Ornamentals, edible berries, and local use of wood for inlay works.

ORNAMENTAL GENERA: *Billardiera, Hymenosporum, Pittosporum.*

Pittosporum tobira   PITTOSPORUM

PRONUNCIATION - ˌpi tə 'spo rəm   tō 'bī rə

TRANSLATION - [from Greek *pitta* (= pitch) and *sporum* (= a seed), referring to resinous coating of seeds] [the native Japanese name].

FORM - Monoecious, evergreen shrub or small tree, freely branching, dense, usually compact, rounded canopy. Medium texture.

SIZE - To 20 feet, usually 6 to 8 feet, moderate growth rate.

HARDINESS ZONE - Zone 8. Grown throughout Florida.

NATIVE HABITAT - China, Japan.

LEAVES - Simple, spirally arranged, entire, obovate, to 4 inches long, apex obtuse, margin revolute, glossy green above, lighter beneath, leathery, clustered at tips of branches, short-petioled.

STEM/BARK - Young stems green, turning light brown with age. Sympodial branching.

FLOWERS - White becoming lemon-yellow, 5-petaled to 0.5 inch long, in terminal umbels; flowers in late winter; fragrant.

FRUIT - Capsule; globose to 0.5 inch in diameter, green turning brown, tomentose; seeds red and covered with a sticky aril.

CULTURE - Full sun to partial shade, various soils, highly salt tolerant. Good heat and drought tolerance.

PROBLEMS - Leaf spot, micronutrient deficiencies, especially on high-pH soils.

PROPAGATION - Cuttings.

LANDSCAPE USES - Barrier, hedge, foundation, screen, specimen, planters.

COMMENTS - Several cultivars are available: **'Compactum'** - compact habit; **'Wheeleri'** (or **'Wheeler's Dwarf'**) - dwarf form, under 3 to 4 feet tall; smaller leaves; less cold-hardy than species and less tolerant of adverse conditions; **'Variegata'** - leaves variegated with white. Several related species, particularly *P. tenuifolium* and its cultivars, have been occasionally reported from Florida.

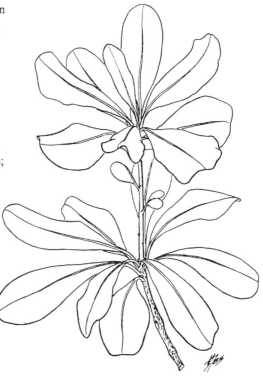

PLATANACEAE - PLANE TREE FAMILY

DICOTYLEDONS; MONOGENERIC WITH 10 SPECIES

GEOGRAPHY: Predominantly North America, but also one species each in the Himalayas and Indochina.

GROWTH HABIT: Deciduous large trees with flaking bark and generally covered with stellate hairs.

LEAVES: Simple, usually palmately lobed; petiole swollen and covers the lateral bud at the point of stem attachment; stipules large and early deciduous.

FLOWERS: Unisexual (plants monoecious), on long pedunculate globose heads; petals and sepals 3-8, small, free; male flowers with 3-8 stamens; female flowers with superior ovary which consists of 6-9 free carpels.

FRUIT: Globose head of achenes.

ECONOMIC USES: Ornamentals and minor use of wood.

ORNAMENTAL GENERA: *Platanus.*

Platanus occidentalis   SYCAMORE, AMERICAN PLANE TREE

PRONUNCIATION - ˈplæ tə nəs ˌɑk sə dən ˈtæ ləs

TRANSLATION - [from the Greek name for *P. orientalis*] [Western].

FORM - Monoecious, deciduous tree, many-branched, symmetrical, pyramidal when young, more globose with age, broad open canopy. Coarse texture.

SIZE - To 150 feet, commonly 50 to 60 feet, rapid growth.

HARDINESS ZONE - Zone 4. Grown in north and central Florida.

NATIVE HABITAT - Eastern United States.

LEAVES - Simple, alternate, shallowly 3 to 5 lobed, to 10 inches wide, lobes wider than long; coarsely toothed margin; tomentose beneath; petiole long with enlarged base enclosing the bud.

STEM/BARK - Whitish-brown, exfoliating in thin plates. On old trunks, bark rough and platy with dark brown to gray-brown scales.

FLOWERS - Axillary, in dense globose heads on long peduncles, staminate red, pistillate light green, not conspicuous.

FRUIT - Heads, globose, to 1.5 inches in diameter, usually solitary, smooth, many-seeded, persistent.

CULTURE - Full sun to partial shade, fertile organic soils, moderately salt tolerant. Not drought tolerant; will develop leaf scorch if irrigation is inadequate. Withstands some flooding. Also tolerant of smoke and dust typical of city conditions. Easily transplanted.

PROBLEMS - Mites, lace bugs, anthracnose.

PROPAGATION - Seeds.

LANDSCAPE USES - Shade tree, parks, large areas, naturalized areas. Sometimes used as street tree, but its peeling bark, large leaves, and fruit may be too messy for many such sites.

COMMENTS - One of the fastest-growing trees in cultivation.

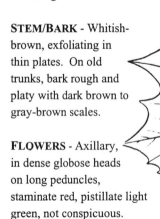

PLUMBAGINACEAE - LEADWORT FAMILY

DICOTYLEDONS; 22 GENERA AND ABOUT 450 SPECIES

GEOGRAPHY: Cosmopolitan, particularly common in coastal and saline areas.

GROWTH HABIT: Annual and perennial herbs, shrubs, and vines.

LEAVES: Basal rosettes or on aerial branches; simple, glandular, entire or lobed, and lack stipules.

FLOWERS: Bisexual, actinomorphic, in many-flowered, bracteate inflorescences; 5-merous; sepals fused, forming a 5-lobed tube which is sometimes colored and showy; petals are free, or connate only at base, or fused to form a tube; stamens 5, free or inserted at the base of the petals; ovary superior and consist of 5 fused carpels.

FRUIT: Drupe, usually enclosed within bracts.

ECONOMIC USES: Ornamentals and minor medicinal uses.

ORNAMENTAL GENERA: *Acantholimon, Armeria, Ceratostigma, Limonium, Plumbago*, and probably others.

Plumbago auriculata

PLUMBAGO

PRONUNCIATION - plum 'bā gō o ,ri kyū 'lā tə

TRANSLATION - [Latin name for *plumbum* (= lead)] [with ears, in reference to the leaves].

FORM - Evergreen, more or less vining shrub; irregular; heavily foliated, multibranched; can be trained as an upright shrub; medium texture.

SIZE - Variable, to 5 to 6 feet if supported, often seen 2 to 3 feet tall; rapid growth rate.

HARDINESS ZONE - Zone 8b; can be grown in south, central, and north Florida.

NATIVE HABITAT - South Africa.

LEAVES - Simple; alternate or spirally arranged; light green oblong-spatulate to 2 inches long; softly pubescent; entire margins; tapering to a short petiole.

STEM/BARK - Stems long and arching; new growth green, becoming woody with age.

FLOWERS - Azure blue; slender, funnelform corolla; 5-lobed, to 1.5 inches across; borne in short spikes. Blooms much of the year; very showy.

FRUIT - Capsule; bun-like; 1-seeded; dehiscent.

CULTURE - Full sun for best growth and flowering; various fertile soils; slight salt tolerance.

PROBLEMS - Cottony cushion scale, mites, and minor nutrient deficiencies on high-pH soils.

PROPAGATION - Seeds and cuttings.

LANDSCAPE USES - Use in foundation plantings, hedges, as a ground cover on embankments, or in planter boxes.

COMMENTS - Cultivar 'Alba' has white flowers.

POLYGONACEAE - BUCKWHEAT FAMILY

DICOTYLEDONS; ABOUT 30 GENERA AND 750 SPECIES

GEOGRAPHY: Cosmopolitan but predominantly in northern temperate region.

GROWTH HABIT: Mostly herbs, some shrubs and vines, and a few trees; often xerophytic or coastal.

LEAVES: Alternate, simple, and with the stipules united with each other by means of a sheath.

FLOWERS: Small, bisexual or sometimes unisexual (plants monoecious), white or greenish or pinkish, solitary or in a racemose group; sepals 3-6, large, membranous, and persistent; apetalous; stamens 6-9; ovary superior and consists of 2-4 carpels.

FRUIT: A triangular nut.

ECONOMIC USES: Ornamentals, especially for coastal areas; buckwheat (*Fagopyrum*); rhubarb (*Rheum*); and *Coccoloba* fresh fruit and jelly.

ORNAMENTAL GENERA: *Antigonon, Atraphaxis, Coccoloba, Eriogonum, Fagopyrum* (*F. esculentum* = buckwheat), *Homalocladium, Oxyria, Muehlenbeckia, Podopterus, Polygonum, Rheum* (rhubarb), *Ruprechtia, Triplaris*, and probably others.

Antigonon leptopus

CORAL VINE

PRONUNCIATION - æn ˈti gə ˌnɑn   ˈlep tə pəs

TRANSLATION - [from Greek *anti* (= like) and *polygonon* (= knotweed), referring to its relationship with **Polygonum**] [slender-stalked].

FORM - Vigorous, evergreen vine, climbing with tendrils, heavily foliated.

SIZE - Climbing to 40 feet or more, rapid growth rate.

HARDINESS ZONE - Zone 9. Can be grown in south, central, and north Florida. Will freeze back in north Florida but recovers rapidly.

NATIVE HABITAT - Mexico.

LEAVES - Simple, alternate, cordate-ovate to 4 inches long, light green, papery, bristly pubescence; margins entire to somewhat undulate.

STEM/BARK - New growth green, becoming woody with age, slender, jointed, terminating in tendrils.

FLOWERS - Bright pink in long axillary racemes. Blooms in the summer and fall.

FRUIT - Achenes, pointed, 3-angled.

CULTURE - Grow in full sun for best flowering on various soils. Not salt tolerant.

PROBLEMS - Chewing insects, caterpillars.

PROPAGATION - Seeds, cuttings.

LANDSCAPE USES - Use as a vine to cover fences, arbors, and trellises.

COMMENTS - The cultivar **'Album'** has white flowers.

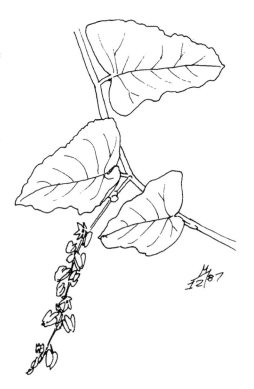

Coccoloba diversifolia   PIGEON PLUM

PRONUNCIATION - ˈkō kə ˈlō bə   də ˌvər sə ˈfō lē ə

TRANSLATION - [from Greek *kokkolobis*, ancient name for a kind of grape, in reference to arrangement of the fruit] [diversely leaved].

FORM - Evergreen tree, upright, columnar, densely foliated, and medium textured.

SIZE - Can reach a height of 70 feet but usually is smaller. Its spread is about 20 feet and growth rate is moderate.

HARDINESS ZONE - Zones 10-11, limited to south Florida.

NATIVE HABITAT - Coastal and interior hammocks of south Florida, the West Indies, and tropical America.

LEAVES - Simple, alternate, oblong to ovate, to 4 inches long with entire, revolute margins. Leaves have a rounded tip and the petiole base forms a sheath around the stem. New growth is bright red.

STEM/BARK - The 1-2 foot wide, straight, upright trunks have grayish-brown bark that falls off in plates to reveal dark purplish bark underneath.

FLOWERS - Whitish-green, small, numerous, on 2 to 3 inch axillary or terminal spikes borne in early summer.

FRUIT - Achene surrounded by the fleshy calyx; purple, pear-shaped, 1/3 inch long, somewhat edible. The single-seeded fruit ripen in late fall and winter.

CULTURE - Requires full sun or partial shade. Tolerates a wide range of soils, but does best in sandy soils with a high humus content. It has good salt tolerance. Fallen leaves and fruit may create a litter problem.

PROBLEMS - Chewing insects can riddle new growth.

PROPAGATION - Seed.

LANDSCAPE USES - Makes a superb specimen, shade, or street tree.

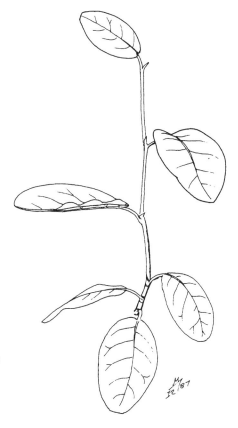

Coccoloba uvifera   SEA GRAPE

PRONUNCIATION - ˌkō kə ˈlō bə   yū ˈvi fə rə

TRANSLATION - [from Greek *kokkolobis*, ancient name for a kind of grape, in reference to arrangement of the fruit] [bearing grapes].

FORM - Evergreen tree, contorted, picturesque trunk, upright branching, often drooping at tip, rounded, spreading canopy, coarse textured.

SIZE - To 30 feet, commonly 15-20 feet, moderate growth rate.

HARDINESS ZONE - Zones 10-11. South Florida only.

NATIVE HABITAT - South Florida, to coastal South America.

LEAVES - Simple, spirally arranged, orbicular to 10 inches across, cordate base. The leathery, glossy green leaves have reddish primary veins, entire margins and are held on short pinkish, clasping petioles.

STEM/BARK - Cinnamon brown, seasonally exfoliating in thin plates; with sheathing stipules above the leaf bases on new growth.

FLOWERS - Whitish, small, not showy, borne in axillary and terminal racemes to 12 inches long.

FRUIT - Drupe-like achene, globular to 3/4 inch in diameter, in dense grape-like clusters, green ripening to purple, edible.

CULTURE - Requires full sun and sandy, well-drained soils. Highly salt tolerant.

PROBLEMS - Borers.

PROPAGATION - Seed, cuttings.

LANDSCAPE USES - Use as a border, windbreak, screen, or accent plant or in foundation plantings for large buildings. Sea grape is an excellent plant for seaside landscapes.

COMMENTS - A variegated cultivar is available.

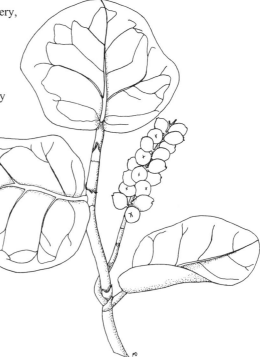

PORTULACACEAE - PURSLANE FAMILY

DICOTYLEDONS; 19 GENERA AND ABOUT 500 SPECIES

GEOGRAPHY:	Cosmopolitan but well represented in South Africa and America.
GROWTH HABIT:	Annual or perennial, somewhat succulent herbs or subshrubs.
LEAVES:	Somewhat fleshy, alternate or opposite, entire, and stipulate.
FLOWERS:	Mostly small, actinomorphic, bisexual; perianth of 2 green sepals and usually 5 free petals; stamens 5, free; ovary superior, usually consist of 5 fused carpels.
FRUIT:	Valvate or operculate capsule.
ECONOMIC USES:	Ornamentals, some sought after by succulent collectors, and the potherb (*Portulaca oleracea*).

ORNAMENTAL GENERA: *Anacampseros, Ceraria, Claytonia, Lewisia, Portulaca, Portulacaria, Talinum,* etc.

Portulaca grandiflora   PURSLANE, MOSS ROSE

PRONUNCIATION - ˈpor chū ˈlɑ kə ˌgræn də ˈflo rə

TRANSLATION - [Latin name for *P. oleracea*] [large-flowered].

FORM - Evergreen perennial used as an herbaceous annual; low growing, succulent, trailing, much-branched; fine texture.

SIZE - To 12 inches, usually 3 to 4 inches; rapid growth rate.

HARDINESS ZONE - Zone 9; can be grown as a perennial in central and south Florida. Common annual elsewhere.

NATIVE HABITAT - Brazil, Argentina, Uruguay.

LEAVES - Simple; alternate; cylindrical to 1 inch long; fleshy, light green, glabrous; entire margins.

STEM/BARK - Fleshy; often reddish in color.

FLOWERS - Various colors of red, yellow, orange, white, often striped; terminal, solitary; to 1 inch across; petals 4 to 5 or to 18, falling early; open only in sunshine; various forms with cultivars, i.e., double, etc. Blooms in warm weather.

FRUIT - Capsule; opening at the top.

CULTURE - Full sun, various well-drained soils; moderate salt tolerance.

PROBLEMS - Mealybugs, generally few pests; root rot in wet soils.

PROPAGATION - Seeds, cuttings.

LANDSCAPE USES - Used as a bedding plant, edging, ground cover, or in hanging baskets. It is commonly grown as a garden annual.

COMMENTS - Many cultivars for flower color and growth habit are available. Examples of these include **'Aztec Double'** - flowers double; **Calypso Hybrids** - flowers mostly double; **Cloudbeater Hybrids** - also double flowers; **Dwarf Double Minilacea Hybrids** - compact with large flowers; **Extra Double Hybrids** - spreading habit, double flowers; **Magic Carpet Hybrids** - double flowers of various colors; **'Peppermint Candy'** - flowers single, bicolored; **Sundance Hybrids** - spreading, flowers double; **Sunny Boy Hybrids** - dwarf spreading, flowers mostly double; **'Swanlake'** - flowers large, double; and **Wildfire Hybrids** - dwarf, spreading.

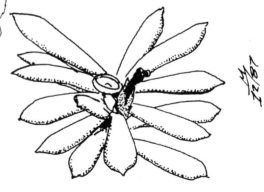

PROTEACEAE - PROTEA FAMILY

DICOTYLEDONS; 62 GENERA AND ABOUT 1200 SPECIES

GEOGRAPHY:	Usually in the seasonally dry regions of southern Africa, Asia, Australia, and Central and South America.
GROWTH HABIT:	Trees and shrubs.
LEAVES:	Alternate and sometimes spirally arranged, entire, divided, or sometimes acicular (in *Hackea*), coriaceous, and without stipules.
FLOWERS:	Bisexual or sometimes unisexual (plants dioecious), on showy dense inflorescences; zygomorphic; 4-merous; tepals 4, often recurved; stamens 4, often epipetalous and usually conspicuous; ovary superior and with a single carpel.
FRUIT:	Follicle, drupe, or nut, often with winged seeds.
ECONOMIC USES:	With some of the most unusual and showy flowers, this family is an important ornamental group; some such as *Gevuina avellana* and *Macadamia integrifolia* (macadamia nut) yield edible nuts, and some (e.g., *Grevillea*) provide timber.

ORNAMENTAL GENERA: *Banksia, Buckinghamia, Canospermum, Embothrium, Grevillea, Hackea, Leucodendron, Leucospermum, Macadamia, Protea, Stenocarpus, Telopea,* among others.

Grevillea robusta   SILK OAK

PRONUNCIATION - grə ˈvi lē ə   rō ˈbus tə

TRANSLATION - [after Charles Francis Greville (1749-1809), a founder of Horticultural Society of London and vice-president of the Royal Society] [stout, strong].

FORM - Evergreen tree; pyramidal when young, becoming irregular with age; medium-fine texture.

SIZE - Can reach a height of 150 feet, commonly 40 to 50 feet, with a 25 foot spread; rapid growth rate.

HARDINESS ZONE - Zone 9; grown widely in central and south Florida. Can be grown in protected locations in north Florida, but is damaged in severe winters.

NATIVE HABITAT - Australia, where it is a valuable timber tree.

LEAVES - Pinnately compound; alternate; to 1 foot long; fernlike appearance; lanceolate, pinnatifid leaflets; silvery undersides; revolute margins.

STEM/BARK - Grayish-brown, furrowed trunks; width to 3 feet.

FLOWERS - Orange-yellow; 4 inches; 1-sided; comb-like racemes of mainly stamens borne on short, leafless branches. Blooms in April or May.

FRUIT - Follicles; tan, leathery, dehiscent; mature in fall.

CULTURE - Full sun and well-drained, sandy soils; no salt tolerance.

PROBLEMS - Caterpillars, mushroom rot root on soggy soils. Tends to be a messy tree with lots of litter. Gets brittle and ragged with age.

PROPAGATION - Seed. Extract seed from mature but unopened follicles and plant immediately.

LANDSCAPE USES - A good specimen, street, or shade tree in areas with plenty of room. Seedlings occasionally used as pot plants indoors. Magnificent plant when in flower.

ROSACEAE - ROSE FAMILY

DICOTYLEDONS; 122 GENERA AND 3370 SPECIES

GEOGRAPHY: Cosmopolitan, but predominantly in north temperate regions.

GROWTH HABIT: Deciduous or evergreen trees, shrubs, subshrubs, woody vines, and herbaceous plants; thorns or prickles are present in many genera.

LEAVES: Alternate or rarely opposite, simple or pinnately compound, a pair of stipules present or absent.

FLOWERS: Usually showy, actinomorphic, bisexual; hypogynous, epigynous, or perigynous; an epicalyx is typical for all taxa; 5-merous; sepals and petals usually 5 but doubling as a result of petaloid stamens is not uncommon; stamens numerous and whorled; ovary inferior or partly inferior with usually numerous and free carpels in a receptacular cup (the hypanthium).

FRUIT: Variable: achene, drupe, follicle, pome, and accessory.

ECONOMIC USES: Analogous to Poaceae, which is the most significant group in terms of human nutrition, many members of the Rosaceae are extremely important sources of temperate fruits. Also, the family provides some of the most popular and commonly cultivated ornamentals.

CLASSIFICATION AND CHARACTERISTICS OF SUBFAMILIES:

SPIRAEOIDEAE. Carpels usually 2 to 5, whorled and not on a convex or conical gynophore, fruit usually dehiscent (follicles or capsules). Examples: *Holodiscus, Physocarpus, Sorbaria, Spiraea*, and others.

ROSOIDEAE. Carpels usually many, on a convex or conical gynophore, fruit usually fleshy (accessory - achene). Examples: *Cercocarpus, Filipendula, Fragaria* (strawberry), *Geum, Potentilla, Rosa, Rubus* (blackberry), *Sanguisorba,* etc.

PRUNOIDEAE. Fruit a drupe. Examples: *Prunus* (almond, apricot, peach, cherries, etc.), *Osmaronia* (oso berry), etc.

MALOIDEAE. Carpels 2 to 5, usually fused with the wall of the concave receptacle and together with the calyx enlarge to form the pome. Examples: *Amelanchier, Aronia, Chaenomeles, Cotoneaster, Crataegus, Cydonia* (quince), *Eriobotrya* (loquat), *Malus* (apple), *Mespilus, Photinia, Pyracantha, Pyrus* (pear), *Quillaja, Rhaphiolepis, Sorbus, Stranvaesia,* among others.

Aronia arbutifolia

RED CHOKEBERRY

PRONUNCIATION - ə ˈrō nē ə   ar ˌbyū tə ˈfō lē ə

TRANSLATION - [modified from *aria*, a Greek name for *Sorbus aria*] [*Arbutus*-like leaf)

SYNONYMS - *Sorbus arbutifolia; Pyrus arbutifolia.*

FORM - Deciduous, multistemmed shrub, upright to rounded, somewhat open, tends to become leggy with age. Medium texture.

SIZE - To 10 feet with 5 foot spread, tends to sucker and form a larger colony. Moderate growth rate.

HARDINESS ZONE - Zone 6. Grown in north Florida.

NATIVE HABITAT - Eastern North America from Nova Scotia to north Florida, west to Texas and Michigan.

LEAVES - Alternate, simple, elliptic to obovate, to 3.5 inches long, acute or short-acuminate, margin finely serrate, glabrous and dark green above, lighter green with gray tomentose beneath, pubescent petiole about 0.33 inch long. Red to orange fall color.

STEM/BARK - Stems slender, gray-brown to reddish-brown, young stems tomentose becoming glabrous. Bark smooth, exfoliating into tight curls.

FLOWERS - White, or may be red tinged, 0.5 inch across, in terminal, tomentose corymbs

consisting of 2 to 25 flowers, early spring as leaves are expanding. Somewhat showy.

FRUIT - Bright red pome, 0.25 inch across, slightly pear-shaped, borne in dense clusters, abundant, long persistent in fall and winter. Called chokeberry because of bitter taste; supposedly even birds do not like the fruit.

CULTURE - Full sun (for best fruiting) or partial shade, acid soils, tolerates flooding, moderately drought tolerant. Easily transplanted.

PROBLEMS - No serious insect or disease problems. Spreading due to suckering can be problem in confined areas.

PROPAGATION - Seed, softwood cuttings, division of clump.

LANDSCAPE USES - Border, accent planting, highway planting, naturalized areas, massing is an effective way to compensate for legginess, effective fruit display.

COMMENTS - Cultivar 'Brilliantissima' - lustrous dark green leaves turn brilliant red in autumn, more abundant flowers and glossier red fruit than the species; 'Erecta' - upright form, may be hybrid between *A. arbutifolia* and *A. elata.*

Crataegus spp.

HAWTHORN

PRONUNCIATION - krə 'tē gəs

TRANSLATION - [the Greek name for the tree, from *Kratas* (= strength), in allusion to the strength and hardness of the wood].

FORM - Deciduous shrubs or small trees of medium texture and irregular growth habit.

SIZE - Height ranges form 10 to 25 feet, spread from 5 to 10 feet. Growth rate is moderate.

HARDINESS ZONE - Florida native species are hardy to Zone 6; some other species can survive up to Zone 2. Hawthorns can be grown in north and central Florida.

NATIVE HABITAT - Temperate woods and fields of north and central Florida and the Northern Hemisphere.

LEAVES - Simple, alternate, ovate, to 2 inches long, with various degrees of lobing, margins serrate.

STEM/BARK - Stems have long, slender, sharp 1 to 3 inch thorns (a few are thornless).

FLOWERS - Small, white to pinkish, stamens roughly as long as petals, in corymbs that appear in March. Although individual flowers are small, they are borne in profusion and are very showy in mass.

FRUIT - Small pomes, green ripening red to orange-red or yellow, to 1 inch diameter, ripening in summer. Edible.

CULTURE - Hawthorns require full or partial sun. They tolerate a wide range of soils. Range of adaptability varies with species, from very dry to marshy conditions. Hawthorns are not salt tolerant.

PROBLEMS - Fire blight, cedar-apple rust, leaf spots, scale, mites, and bagworms can be problems.

PROPAGATION - Seed. Germination is variable and sporadic, taking from several months to several years, often requiring stratification. Can be transplanted from the wild, but this is difficult due to a long taproot.

LANDSCAPE USES - Makes a nice, small-scale specimens, hedges, barrier plants. Use with caution around children because of thorns.

COMMENTS - *Crataegus aestivalis*, the May Hawthorne, has fruits that make a fine jelly. *Crataegus marshallii*, the Parsley Hawthorn, has finely dissected leaves. There are 16 other species in Florida and roughly 200 species worldwide, though some estimate up to 1000 and others many fewer species.

Eriobotrya deflexa

BRONZE LOQUAT

PRONUNCIATION - ˌe rē ō ˈbō trē ə   dē ˈflek sə

TRANSLATION - [from Greek *erion* (= wool) and *botrys* (= hair), referring to the tomentose inflorescence] [bent downward].

FORM - Monoecious, small evergreen tree of coarse texture.

SIZE - Reaches a height of 15 feet with a 10 foot spread. Grows at a moderate pace.

HARDINESS ZONE - Zone 8b. Grows only in the warmer regions of Florida.

NATIVE HABITAT - Taiwan.

LEAVES - Simple, alternate, obovate to elliptic, coarsely serrate, to 8 inches long. New growth is reddish, bronze colored.

STEM/BARK - Young branches are tan or rusty tomentose.

FLOWERS - White, 0.75 inch across, in terminal panicles borne in March.

FRUIT - Subglobose, 0.75 inch pomes.

CULTURE - Requires full sun, but tolerates a wide range of soils, except poorly drained ones. It is not salt tolerant.

PROBLEMS - Fire blight, root rot on wet soils.

PROPAGATION - Seed.

LANDSCAPE USES - Used as a specimen or small tree.

COMMENTS - Good residential tree; should be used more. *Eriobotrya deflexa* **'Coppertone'** is gaining popularity.

Eriobotrya japonica   LOQUAT

PRONUNCIATION - ˌe rē ō ˈbō trē ə jə ˈpɑ nə kə

TRANSLATION - [from Greek *erion* (= wool) and *botrys* (= hair), referring to the tomentose inflorescence] [Japanese].

FORM - Monoecious, evergreen tree, freely branching, compact, heavily foliated, broad rounded canopy. Coarse texture.

SIZE - To 25 feet, medium to rapid growth rate.

HARDINESS ZONE - Zone 8. Grows throughout Florida. In north Florida, the flowers are frequently injured by frost.

NATIVE HABITAT - China, Japan.

LEAVES - Simple, spirally arranged, sharply serrate, elliptic-oblanceolate to 12 inches long, stiff, leathery, dark green, verrucate, dense woolly pubescence, rusty colored beneath, veins prominent, petiole short.

STEM/BARK - New growth rusty pubescent.

FLOWERS - Cream-colored, 5 petals to 1 inch across, in a terminal panicle to 6 inches long, brown pubescent, fragrant; flowers in fall.

FRUIT - A pome to 2 inches long, yellowish to orange, several-seeded, edible. Seldom matures in north Florida due to cold damage to the flowers.

CULTURE - Full sun, various soils; moderately salt tolerant.

PROBLEMS - Scale, fire blight,

caterpillars. To reduce fire blight problems, provide good air circulation and keep away from other fire blight hosts, such as *Pyracantha*, pears, etc.

PROPAGATION - Seeds, cuttings, graftage of cultivars.

LANDSCAPE USES - Specimen, terrace or patio shade, dooryard fruit.

COMMENTS - Many cultivars for fruit, most originating in Japan. The cultivar **'Variegata'**, which has leaves with white margins, is not known in Florida.

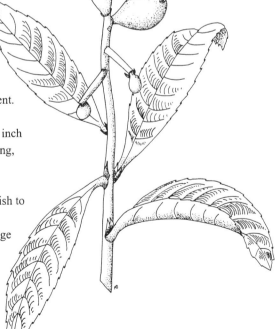

Photinia × *fraseri*   FRASER PHOTINIA, RED TIP

PRONUNCIATION - fō 'ti nē ə   'frā zər ī

TRANSLATION - [from Greek *photos* (= light), in reference to the shiny leaves] [after Fraser Nurseries in Alabama].

FORM - Evergreen large shrub or small tree, multistemmed, upright, oval, usually somewhat open. Medium texture.

SIZE - To 20 feet (usually 10 to 15 feet) with 8 to 10 foot spread. Moderate to fast growth rate.

HARDINESS ZONE - Zone 7. For use in North Florida only.

NATIVE HABITAT - Hybrid between *P. glabra* and *P. serrulata* (= *P. serratifolia*) introduced by Fraser Nurseries, Birmingham, Alabama, about 1940.

LEAVES - Alternate, simple, elliptic to elliptic-obovate, 3 to 4 inches long (intermediate in size between parents), serrations are coarser than *P. glabra* but finer than *P. serratifolia*, blade is softer and more pliable than *P. serratifolia*. New leaves brilliant red for several weeks, more or less remaining red throughout the year (hence the common name Red Tip). A second flush of summer growth renews the brilliant red color.

STEM/BARK - Young stems brilliant red initially, turning dark green, then gray-brown. Reddish terminal bud is similar to *P. glabra*, and smaller than *P. serratifolia*.

FLOWERS - Intermediate between parents, small (0.25 inch) whitish flowers in terminal panicles about 4 to 6 inches across, in early spring. Showy when present, but frequently removed by pruning. Objectionable odor (like both parents).

FRUIT - Berry-like pome, globose, to 0.25 inch diameter, red, usually removed by pruning.

CULTURE - Full sun, well-drained, fertile soils, pH adaptable, easily transplanted, does not tolerate extremely wet soils. Nitrogen deficiency shows up vividly as yellow foliage.

PROBLEMS - Scale, mites, fire blight, caterpillars.

PROPAGATION - Semi-hardwood cuttings.

LANDSCAPE USES - Large hedge or screen, small tree. Distinctive foliage color. Extremely popular, almost to the point of overuse in much of the South. **'Red Robin'** and **'Robusta'** are the common cultivars.

Photinia glabra   REDLEAF PHOTINIA, JAPANESE PHOTINIA

PRONUNCIATION - fō 'ti nē ə   'glā brə

TRANSLATION - [from Greek *photos* (= light), in reference to the shiny leaves] [glabrous, smooth].

FORM - Monoecious, evergreen shrub or small tree, upright, freely branching, often leafless on lower stems. Medium texture.

SIZE - To 20 feet, usually seen 4 to 6 feet, rapid growth.

HARDINESS ZONE - Zone 7. Grows well only in north Florida.

NATIVE HABITAT - Japan.

LEAVES - Simple, alternate, elliptic to oblong-obovate to 3 inches long, acuminate tip, glossy-green, leathery, pliable, margins finely serrate, petiole 0.5 inch long, glabrous at maturity.

STEM/BARK - New growth reddish, lenticels numerous.

FLOWERS - Flowers white to 0.25 inch across, 5-petaled; in short terminal panicles to 4 inches in diameter, flowers in winter, late spring.

FRUIT - A berry-like pome, globose to 0.25 inch in diameter, red turning to black.

CULTURE - Full sun, fertile organic soils, pH adaptable; not salt tolerant.

PROBLEMS - Scale, aphids, fire blight, caterpillars.

PROPAGATION - Cuttings.

LANDSCAPE USES - Clipped or unclipped hedge, border, screen, specimen, foundation.

COMMENTS - Several cultivars: **'Rosea Marginata'** - leaves variegated with pink and gray; **'Variegata'** - leaves with white margins.

Photinia serratifolia

CHINESE PHOTINIA

PRONUNCIATION - fō 'ti nē ə   sə 'ra tə 'fō lē ə

TRANSLATION - [from Greek *photos* (= light), in reference to the shiny leaves] [with small teeth, in reference to the leaf margins].

SYNONYM - *Photinia serrulata*.

FORM - Monoecious, evergreen shrub or tree, upright, free branching, lower portions often leafless, ovate canopy. Coarse texture.

SIZE - To 40 feet, commonly seen and maintained 6 to 10 feet, moderate growth rate.

HARDINESS ZONE - Zone 7. Grows well only in north Florida.

NATIVE HABITAT - China.

LEAVES - Simple, alternate, oblong to 6 inches long, sharp-pointed apex, dark green, lighter beneath, leathery, prominent midvein, margins serrate, abruptly acuminate.

STEM/BARK - New growth pinkish (not as much as *P. glabra*). Young twigs red to reddish-brown with brown vertical lenticels. Large reddish-green terminal bud, glabrous.

FLOWERS - Flowers white, to 0.25 inch across, 5 petals; in short terminal panicles to 8 inches across, flowers late spring to early summer. Showy.

FRUIT - A pome, globose to 0.25 inch in diameter, red.

CULTURE - Full sun, fertile organic soils, pH adaptable; not salt tolerant. Does not tolerate wet feet.

PROBLEMS - Scale, mites, fire blight, caterpillars, leaf spots, mildew.

PROPAGATION - Cuttings.

LANDSCAPE USES - Hedge, screen, foundation, specimen, small tree.

COMMENTS - Several cultivars, primarily with regard to leaf size and serration coarseness.

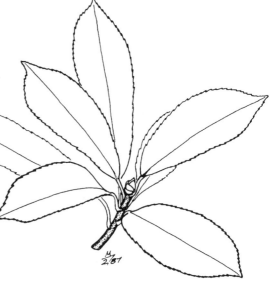

Prunus caroliniana   CHERRY LAUREL

PRONUNCIATION - ˈprū nəs   ˌkæ rə ˌli nē ˈā nə

TRANSLATION - [classical Latin name for plum tree] [from Carolina].

FORM - Monoecious, evergreen tree, much-branched, often multiple trunks, cylindrical to broadly rounded canopy. Medium texture.

SIZE - To 40 feet, often seen much smaller, rapid growth.

HARDINESS ZONE - Zone 8. Grown in north and central Florida.

NATIVE HABITAT - Eastern United States.

LEAVES - Simple, alternate to spirally arranged, lanceolate-oblong to 4 inches long, acuminate tip, glossy-green, conspicuous venation beneath, margin undulate, often serrate or with fine spines, 2 glands at base of leaf near petiole, petiole often red, leaf with maraschino cherry or bitter almond odor when crushed.

STEM/BARK - Grayish-brown.

FLOWERS - Flowers creamy-white to 0.25 inch across, in dense axillary racemes on previous season's growth to 1 inch long, fragrant.

FRUIT - Drupe, black pointed, to 0.5 inch long, shiny. Not showy but can be quite messy.

CULTURE - Full sun to partial shade, fertile organic soils, pH adaptable; not salt tolerant. Not adapted to wet sites.

PROBLEMS - Mites, leaf spot, fire blight, stem canker. Prolific seed production contributes to a "weedy" habit. Fruit can be messy on pavement.

PROPAGATION - Seeds, cuttings.

LANDSCAPE USES - Border, screen, hedge, specimen. Fruit attracts birds.

COMMENTS - Easily naturalizes, often weedy in moist sites.

Prunus umbellata   FLATWOODS PLUM

PRONUNCIATION - 'prū nəs   'um bə 'lā tə

TRANSLATION - [classical Latin name for plum tree] [with umbels, in reference to the inflorescence].

FORM - Monoecious, round-topped deciduous tree of medium texture.

SIZE - Reaches a height of 20 feet and a spread of 15 feet. Grows rapidly when young, growing much slower upon reaching maturity and bearing fruit.

HARDINESS ZONE - Zone 8, grown in north and central Florida.

NATIVE HABITAT - Woods of the southeastern United States.

LEAVES - Simple, alternate, elliptic to ovate, to 2 inches long, finely serrate, appear after flowering.

STEM/BARK - The short, crooked trunks have reddish-brown, thin, scaly bark.

FLOWERS - White, 0.5 inch wide, stamens exserted, in umbels of 2 to 5, appearing in late February. In full bloom, this tree takes on an attractive, misty "white cloud" effect.

FRUIT - Drupes, purple or rarely red, ovoid to 1 inch long, maturing in July. The fruits are edible, ranging from very tart to sweet in taste.

CULTURE - Does well in full sun or partial shade and tolerates a wide range of soils. It is not salt tolerant.

PROBLEMS - Tent caterpillars.

PROPAGATION - Seed, which must be stratified for several months to germinate.

LANDSCAPE USES - Grown as a specimen for its very attractive mass of flowers. Fruit quality can be improved with good fertilization and care, selecting seed from better-tasting parents.

COMMENTS - *Prunus angustifolia* is similar, but differs in usually having multiple trunks and forming thickets, thorny stems, and red or yellow fruits. These two plums are difficult to tell apart, and many native plums appear to have characteristics of both.

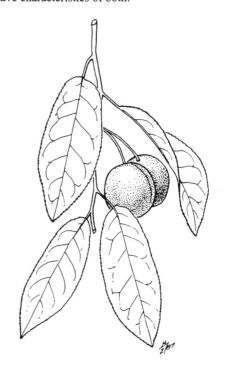

Pyracantha coccinea   FIRE THORN

PRONUNCIATION - ˈpī rə kæn thə   kɑk ˈsi nē ə

TRANSLATION - [from Greek *pyr* (= fire) and *akantha* (= a thorn), in reference to the red fruits and thorny stems] [scarlet, in reference to the fruit color].

FORM - Monoecious, evergreen, thorny shrub or small tree, pendulous, awkwardly sprawling, twiggy, much-branched, often multiple trunked, angular irregular canopy. Fine texture.

SIZE - To 15 feet, rapid growth.

HARDINESS ZONE - Zone 6. Grown throughout Florida.

NATIVE HABITAT - Southern Europe, Asia Minor.

LEAVES - Simple, alternate, closely arranged on short shoots (spurs), lanceolate to oblong-ovate, to 1.5 inches long, acute, finely crenulate-serrulate, dark green and glabrous above, lighter green and sometimes pubescent when young below.

STEM/BARK - Gray-brown, gray tomentose on new growth, axillary thorns.

FLOWERS - In corymbs to 1.5 inches wide, flowers white, to 0.25 inch across, showy; flowers in spring.

FRUIT - Pomes, green ripening to orange-red globose to 0.25 inch in diameter, colorful in fall, winter.

CULTURE - Full sun, various soils; slightly salt tolerant. Not adapted to wet sites. May need considerable pruning to keep it in bounds or otherwise trained.

PROBLEMS - Mites, scales, thrips, lace bugs, fire blight, scab.

PROPAGATION - Cuttings.

LANDSCAPE USES - Specimen, hedge, topiary, espalier, barrier plant.

COMMENTS - Many cultivars selected for habit, size, thornlessness. Also related species such as *P. koidzumii*, including its cultivars **'Low Dense'** and **'Victory'**, and many others not common in Florida. The cultivar **'Aurea'**, with yellow fruit, is a selection of *P. atatantoides.*

Pyrus calleryana   FLOWERING PEAR

PRONUNCIATION - ˈpī rəs   kə ˌlæ rē ˈā nə

TRANSLATION - [ancient Latin name for pear] [in honor of J. Callery, the French missionary who collected the type specimen in China].

FORM - A much-branched decurrent tree of medium texture, with initially pyramidal shape but becomes oval within a few years.

SIZE - To 30 or 40 feet tall and 25-30 feet wide, at maturity.

HARDINESS ZONE - Zone 5 (listed in Zone 4 but may be injured in severe years).

NATIVE HABITAT- China.

LEAVES - Simple, ovate-oblong, coriaceous, glossy-green, 2-4 inches long and nearly as wide, becoming bright red-purple in fall.

STEM/BARK - Smooth, reddish-brown, covered with distinct lenticels.

FLOWERS - White, showy but short-lived, with a characteristic offensive odor, about 1 inch across; appearing together with emerging foliage in spring.

FRUIT - A pome, less than 0.5 inch in diameter, often numerous.

CULTURE - Performs satisfactorily in well-drained, fertile soils, in sunny locations.

PROBLEMS - No major problems, except for occasional death of the grafted cultivar and growth of the original rootstalk.

PROPAGATION - Desirable cultivars are grafted onto callery seedlings.

LANDSCAPE USES - As a specimen flowering and street trees, especially suitable for smaller sites. May be used in large planters.

COMMENTS - 'Bradford', a USDA-introduced cultivar, is usually grafted onto *P. calleryana* and is commonly sold as the Bradford flowering pear. Often field grown and sold as large B & B trees.
     'Aristocrat', a recently introduced cultivar, has larger glossy-green leaves.

Rhaphiolepis indica

INDIAN HAWTHORN

PRONUNCIATION - ˌræ fē ō ˈle pəs   ˈin də kə

TRANSLATION - [from Greek *rhaphis* (= a needle) and *lepis* (= a scale), referring to bracteoles on inflorescence] [from India].

FORM - Monoecious, evergreen shrub, dwarf, rounded, of medium texture.

SIZE - Reaches a height of 5 feet with an equal spread. Grows at a slow rate.

HARDINESS ZONE - Zone 8, grows in all areas of Florida.

NATIVE HABITAT - Southern China.

LEAVES - Simple, alternate, clustered at twig tips, oblong, to 3 inches long, leathery, acute or acuminate, dark green above, light green and often brown pubescent on the veins on the underside; margins serrate, petioles burgundy-colored.

FLOWERS - Pinkish to white, 0.75 inch across, in loose terminal panicles, in spring.

FRUIT - Pome, purple to black, to 0.5 inch wide.

CULTURE - Tolerates full sun, but does better in partial shade. It needs fertile, well-drained soils and has fair salt tolerance. Moderately drought tolerant.

PROBLEMS - Nematodes, fire blight, scale, leaf spot.

PROPAGATION - Seed or semi-hardwood cuttings.

LANDSCAPE USES - Mainly used as a foundation shrub or informal hedge, planters.

COMMENTS - **'Rosea'** has deeper pink flowers, more compact; **'Compacta'** is a dwarf cultivar; **'Alba'** has white flowers. Other cultivars include **'Elizabeth'**, **'Clara'**, **'Peggy'**, **'Rosea Janice'**, **'Spring Rapture'**, among others. *R.* × *decourii* (*R. indica* × *R. umbellata*) and its cultivars are much larger plants and common in cultivation.

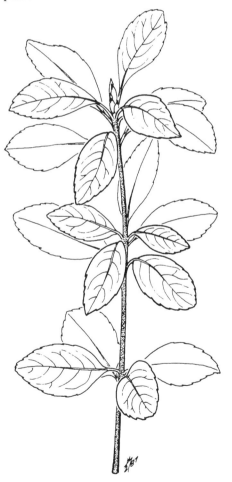

Rosa species and Hybrids ROSE

PRONUNCIATION - ˈrō zə

TRANSLATION - Latin name of rose.

FORM - Monoecious, fast-growing, deciduous, semi-evergreen, and evergreen upright shrubs and clambering or trailing vines of medium texture.

SIZE - From less than 10 inches (miniature roses) to more than 20 feet.

HARDINESS ZONE - Zones 4 to 10.

NATIVE HABITAT - Temperate Northern Hemisphere.

LEAVES - Alternate, usually odd-pinnate, with serrate-dentate leaflets and often spinose rachis; stipules adnate to the petiole; often aromatic and glandular.

STEM/BARK - Prickly.

FLOWERS - Solitary, corymbose or paniculate; 5-merous, with petals broad and rounded at the apex, the whorled stamens numerous and inserted on a disk at the rim of a hypanthium; carpels many and borne inside the hypanthium.

FRUIT - A fleshy "hip" (ripened hypanthium) containing numerous hairy achenes.

CULTURE - Should be planted bare-root when dormant in early spring or from containers at any time. Severe pruning is necessary in colder regions. With some exceptions, roses do not perform well in humid subtropical climates.

PROBLEMS - Best in open, sunny locations in well-drained, fertile soils where there is no competition from other plants. Leggy and vegetative in shady locations. Leaf spot may be a problem.

PROPAGATION - Most common cultivars are produced by budding on selected rootstocks. Roses may also are propagated by cuttings and grafting. Miniature roses, in particular, are produced by micropropagation.

LANDSCAPE USES - Hedges, background shrubbery, specimen and group plantings, wall and fence covering, and as garden and greenhouse commercial florist cut flowers. The climbing/clambering roses require support.

COMMENTS - According to *Hortus III*, some 20,000 cultivars of roses, 12,000 of which are recorded, are known as a result of hybridization and selection in the past 200 years. Although basic species groups are to a greater or lesser extent recognizable, taxonomy of roses is beset with considerable difficulty. The common garden roses include Hybrid Teas, Floribundas, Grandifloras, Miniatures, Climbers, and Shrubs. The most common parental rose species include *R. odorata, R. chinensis, R.×damascena,* and *R. multiflora* and *R. multiflora* var. *cathayensis*, among others. *Rosa banksiae* (Lady Banks Rose, a semi-evergreen vine with creamy white to yellow flowers), *R. laevigata* (Cherokee Rose, an evergreen clambering rose with white single flowers), and numerous new and old shrubby rose cultivars are frequent.

Spiraea cantoniensis   REEVE'S SPIRAEA

PRONUNCIATION - spī ˈrē ə   ˈkæn tō nē ˈen səs

TRANSLATION - [from Greek *speivaira* (a plant used for garlands and wreaths)] [from Canton, China].

FORM - Monoecious, semideciduous shrub, multibranched, of weeping growth habit and medium texture.

SIZE - Reaches a height of 6 feet with an equal spread. Growth rate is rapid.

HARDINESS ZONE - Zone 7, grown in north Florida.

NATIVE HABITAT - China.

LEAVES - Simple, alternate, rhombic-elliptic, to 2 inches long, occasionally 3-lobed. The leaves are medium green on the upper side, glaucous blue-green below, margins coarsely serrate.

STEM/BARK - The stems are long, arching, and rarely branching.

FLOWERS - White, 0.5 inch wide, in 2 inch hemisperical corymbs that appear in early April near the end of the azalea season. In full bloom, it forms an attractive mass of white.

FRUIT - Dehiscent follicles, often not present in Florida.

CULTURE - Full sun is best, but tolerates partial shade. *Spiraea* will grow in a wide range of soils, but are not salt tolerant. They should be pruned lightly immediately after bloom. Transplants easily.

PROBLEMS - Relatively pest-free.

PROPAGATION - Seeds, cuttings, division.

LANDSCAPE USES - Excellent as a specimen or in masses.

COMMENTS - Many cultivars, hybrids, ± 80 related species, though most not suitable for Florida's warmer regions. **'Flore Pleno'** (= **'Lanceolata'**?) has lanceolate leaves and double, pure white flowers.

RUBIACEAE - MADDER FAMILY

DICOTYLEDONS; 500 GENERA AND MORE THAN 7000 SPECIES

GEOGRAPHY: Cosmopolitan but predominantly tropical and subtropical, with a few, mostly herbaceous species in temperate regions, and one genus (*Galium*) with a few arctic species.

GROWTH HABIT: Trees, shrubs, vines, and herbs; sometimes epiphytic, caudiciform, and inhabited by ants (e.g., *Myrmecodia* and *Hydnophytum*).

LEAVES: Opposite or whorled, simple and usually entire; stipules conspicuous and often foliar and large and sometimes fused and intrapetiolar at nodes or interpetiolar. Stipules and leaves may sometimes be confused.

FLOWERS: In panicles, cyme, aggregate heads or rarely solitary; actinomorphic, bisexual; 5-merous; sepals 4-5, usually free and often one larger than others and colorful (e.g., *Mussaenda*); petals 4-5, fused or imbricate; stamens 4-5, epipetalous; ovary inferior or rarely superior, with 1 to many carpels.

FRUIT: Berry, drupe, capsule, or schizocarp.

ECONOMIC USES: Ornamental, but the most important product is coffee (*Coffea arabica*), quinine (*Cinchona* spp.) and other drugs, dyes, etc.

ORNAMENTAL GENERA: *Asperula, Bouvardia, Calycophyllum, Canthium, Casasia, Catesbaea, Cephalanthus, Chiococca, Coffea, Enterospermum, Galium, Gardenia, Genipa, Hamelia, Houstonia, Ixora, Manettia, Mitchella, Mussaenda, Nauclea, Pinckneya, Portlandia, Posoqueria, Psychotria, Randia, Rondeletia, Serissa, Vangueria, Warszewiczia,* and others.

Coffea arabica   COFFEE

PRONUNCIATION - ko ˈfē ə   ə ˈræ bə kə

TRANSLATION - [from the Latinized Arabic name *Kahwah*] [Arabian].

FORM - Monoecious, evergreen shrub; densely foliated; coarse texture.

SIZE - To 15 feet tall.

HARDINESS ZONE - Zones 10-11; south Florida only.

NATIVE HABITAT - Tropical Africa.

LEAVES - Simple; opposite; elliptic, to 6 inches long and 2 inches wide; glossy, dark green; wavy margins.

FLOWERS - White; salverform; corolla 5-lobed to 0.75 inch long; borne in axillary clusters; fragrant; showy when in flower. Blooms in spring.

FRUIT - A 2-seeded berry; red; to 0.5 inch long; becoming fleshy. The seeds are the coffee of commerce. Berries ripen in summer and are quite showy.

CULTURE - Partial shade; fertile, acid, organic soils; no salt tolerance.

PROBLEMS - Scale, mites, thrips, caterpillars, and mineral deficiencies.

PROPAGATION - Seed, cuttings.

LANDSCAPE USES - Can be grown for its attractive flowers and colorful fruit; specimen shrub or incorporated into shrubbery borders; sometimes seen as a conservatory specimen.

COMMENTS - *Coffea arabica* is the major source of quality coffee and is the principal species grown in Latin America. Several cultivars are listed.

Gardenia augusta   GARDENIA, CAPE JASMINE

PRONUNCIATION - gɑr ˈdē nyə   o ˈgus tə

TRANSLATION - [after Dr. Alexander Garden (1730-1791), a Scottish physician and botanist who lived in South Carolina] [name of female relatives of the Roman emperor].

SYNONYM - *Gardenia jasminoides.*

FORM - Monoecious, evergreen shrub, freely-branching, compact, densely foliated, globose crown. Medium texture.

SIZE - To 8 feet, commonly maintained 3 to 4 feet, moderate growth rate.

HARDINESS ZONE - Zone 8. Grown throughout Florida. Severely injured when temperatures drop to 0° F.

NATIVE HABITAT - China.

LEAVES - Simple, opposite or in whorls of 3, lanceolate to obovate to 4 inches long, acuminate tip, veins prominent, dark green, glabrous, margins entire.

STEM/BARK - Gray-brown, young growth green, glabrous, stipules present.

FLOWERS - Polypetalous, corolla white to 3 inches across, often double, waxy, calyx with 5 long teeth, extremely fragrant; flowers in spring and sporadically throughout summer.

FRUIT - Capsules, orange, ovate to 1.5 inches long, fleshy, ribbed. Not commonly seen.

CULTURE - Full sun to partial shade, fertile, acid soils; not salt tolerant. Requires a well-drained site. Develops minor element deficiencies on alkaline soils.

PROBLEMS - Scale, whiteflies, mealybugs, sooty mold, nematodes, aphids, requires a good deal of attention to keep it healthy; minor element deficiencies on high-pH soils.

PROPAGATION - Cuttings, graftage.

LANDSCAPE USES - Border, planter box, specimen, pot plant, foundation.

COMMENTS - Many cultivars selected for flower size, fragrance, color, plant habit, etc. Plants grown in Florida should be grafted on *G. thunbergia* rootstock for resistance to nematodes. The cultivar **'Radicans'** (= **'Prostrata'**) is a low-growing (less than 2 feet tall), spreading (to 4 feet wide) form with smaller leaves and flowers. Subject to the same insect and disease problems and not as cold hardy (injured when temperature drops to about 12° F) as the species; used as ground cover, edging, mass plantings; **'Radicans Variegata'** is also available.

Ixora coccinea

IXORA, FLAME OF THE WOODS

PRONUNCIATION - ik 'so rə kɑk 'si nē ə

TRANSLATION - [Portuguese version of the Sanskrit *Israra* (= lord), referring to the god Siva] [scarlet, in reference to flower color].

FORM - Monoecious, evergreen shrub; ascending; much-branched, densely foliated; medium texture.

SIZE - To 12 feet, commonly 4 to 6 feet; slow growth rate.

HARDINESS ZONE - Zone 9b; can be grown in south and central Florida.

NATIVE HABITAT - India.

LEAVES - Simple; opposite or whorled; oblong to 4 inches long; acuminate tip; leathery, pliable; prominent stipules; entire margins. Petioles short.

STEM/BARK - New growth reddish; bark dark brown.

FLOWERS - Reds, yellows, and pinks; corolla tubular, nearly 2 inches long; lobes spreading, 4 to 5; borne in large, dense, axillary corymbs. Blooms in summer.

FRUIT - Berries; globular to 0.5 inch in diameter; purplish-black.

CULTURE - Full sun for best form and flowering on fertile, acid soils; moderate salt tolerance.

PROBLEMS - Scales, root rot, sooty mold, nematodes, minor element deficiencies on high-pH soil.

PROPAGATION - Cuttings.

LANDSCAPE USES - Use as a hedge, barrier, in foundation plantings, or as a specimen shrub.

COMMENTS - This is a variable species with several flower color and size cultivars available, including *I. coccinea* f. *lutea*, **'Petite', 'Petite Dwarf', 'Petite Red', 'Petitit Yellow', 'Singapore', 'Sunset'**, among several other cultivars. Related species in cultivation include *I. acuminata* (Bola De Nieve), *I. chinensis, I. casei* (= *I. duffii*), *I. finlaysonia, I. javanica, I. pavetta* (= *I. parviflora*), *I.* × *westii*, and *I. williamsii.*

Psychotria nervosa

**WILD COFFEE,
SEMINOLE BALSAMO**

PRONUNCIATION - sī ˈkō trē ə   nər vō sə

TRANSLATION - [variant coined by Linnaeus of Greek *Psychotrophon*, in reference to betony but applied by Patrick Browne to Jamaican plants][with conspicuous veins].

FORM - Monoecious, evergreen large shrub or small tree.

SIZE - Reaches a maximum height of 18 feet, but usually smaller in cultivation.

HARDINESS ZONE - Zones 9b-11, warmer areas of central and south Florida.

NATIVE HABITAT - West Indies, the Bahamas, and south Florida.

LEAVES - Stipulate, opposite, ovate to elliptic-lanceolate, mostly to 6 inches long; glabrate, margins entire or slightly undulate, base cuneate; with prominent veins; petiolate.

STEM/BARK - Willowy branches.

FLOWERS - On terminal, initially flat-topped panicles; bisexual; small, to less than ˘ inch; calyx tube cup-shaped; corolla white, tubular; fragrant; in spring.

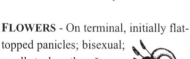

FRUIT - A berry, yellow to red, less than .5 inch, containing a pair of seeds.

CULTURE - May be grown in full sun or partial shade.

PROBLEMS - No major problems reported.

PROPAGATION - Usually by seed but also by cuttings under mist.

LANDSCAPE USES - As foundation or specimen plant.

COMMENTS - *Psychotria nervosa* is sometimes listed as a synonym of *P. undata*. However, the latter is a smaller species of less than 10 feet tall, with somewhat larger leaves and flowers, scarlet fruit, and it is native to Central America as well as Florida and the West Indies. A related species, *P. punctata* (= *P. bacteriophila*), has also been reported from cultivation in Florida.

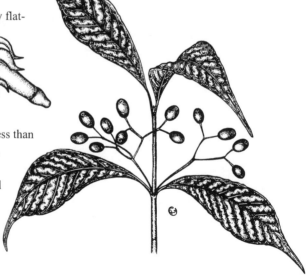

RUTACEAE - RUE FAMILY

DICOTYLEDONS; ABOUT 150 GENERA AND 900 SPECIES

GEOGRAPHY:
Nearly cosmopolitan, but predominantly in tropical and subtropical areas of South Africa and Australia.

GROWTH HABIT:
Strongly aromatic trees, shrubs, subshrubs, and a few perennial herbaceous plants, some xerophytic, most with long thorny stems.

LEAVES:
Alternate, trifoliolate (sometimes reduced to unifoliolate) or pinnately compound, often with a winged petiole, and without stipules.

FLOWERS:
In terminal corymbs or panicles, usually subtended by leafy bracts; white or greenish and very fragrant; 5-merous; sepals persistent; petals imbricate; 8-10 basal nectariferous glands; stamens 8-10; ovary superior and consists of 4-5 fused carpels.

FRUIT:
A berry or a hesperidium (septate berry with enlarged juice-filled hairs and a tough, leathery, oil-gland-filled skin).

ECONOMIC USES:
Ornamental, but economically important for production of citrus, as well as several medicinal and perfume products.

ORNAMENTAL GENERA: *Aegle, Atalantia, Calodendron, Casimiroa, Choisya,* × *Citrofortunella, Citrus, Clausena, Clymenia, Dictamnus, Eremocitrus, Evodia, Feroniella, Fortunella, Geijera, Glycosmis, Hesperethusa, Microcitrus, Murraya, Poncirus, Severinia, Swinglea, Triphasia, Zanthoxylum,* among many others.

Citrus spp.

CITRUS

PRONUNCIATION - ˈsi trəs

TRANSLATION - [Latin name for citron (*Citrus medica*), the fruit of which was substituted for cone of *Cedrus*].

FORM - Evergreen shrubs or small to medium-sized trees, low-branching, usually spiny, symmetrical, globular to oval canopy. Medium texture.

SIZE - To 50 feet, commonly seen 15 to 20 feet, rapid growth rate.

HARDINESS ZONE - Zone 9. South and central Florida, may be grown in protected areas in north Florida.

NATIVE HABITAT - Southeast Asia.

LEAVES - Simple, alternate, elliptic to ovate from 1 to 6 inches long, thick, leathery, glandular dots on surface, aromatic when crushed, petiole winged; margins have very fine serrations.

STEM/BARK - New growth green, not round (angular), axillary spines often present.

FLOWERS - White or purplish to 1 inch across, petals usually 5, calyx 4-5-lobed, numerous stamens, usually fragrant. Borne solitary or in axillary cymes. Blooms in spring.

FRUIT - Leathery skinned berry (hesperidium), aromatic, glandular dotted, edible.

CULTURE - Grow in full sun on fertile, well-drained soils; slightly salt tolerant.

PROBLEMS - Scale, mites, sooty mold, nematodes, viruses.

PROPAGATION - Grafting of cultivars, seeds which are grown primarily for rootstock.

LANDSCAPE USES - Use as a shade tree, patio tree or dooryard fruit tree. Some are grown indoors as pot plants.

COMMENTS - Several species are important citrus fruits of commerce. Many cultivars of each of the cultivated species are available. The most common are:
C. aurantiifolia - Lime, Key Lime, Limon
C. aurantium - Sour Orange
C. limon - Lemon
C. ✕ *paradisi* - Grapefruit
C. reticulata - Cleopatra Tangerine
C. sinensis - Sweet Orange
Each includes several cultivars, as well as less common citrus.

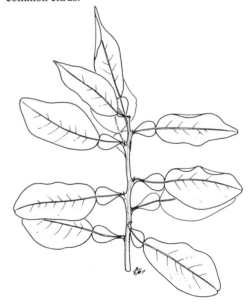

Murraya paniculata

ORANGE JASMINE, CAFE DE LA INDIA, STAINWOOD TREE

PRONUNCIATION - mə ˈrā ə   pə ˌni kyū ˈlā tə

TRANSLATION - [after Johann Andreas Murray (1740-1791), Swedish pupil of Linnaeus and professor of medicine and botany at Göttingen] [flowers in panicles].

FORM - Monoecious, evergreen; shrub or small tree; densely foliated, rounded; fine texture.

SIZE - Can reach a height of 20 feet, commonly to 10 to 12 feet with a spread of 8 feet; moderate growth rate.

HARDINESS ZONE - Zone 9b; grown in central and south Florida.

NATIVE HABITAT - Southeastern Asia and Polynesia.

LEAVES - Odd-pinnately compound; alternate; to 5 inches long; leaflets 3 to 9, ovate to obovate, to 2.75 inches long; glossy, dark green; gland-dotted.

FLOWERS - White; to 0.75 inch across; fragrant; borne in axillary cymes. Blooms periodically. Flowers very similar to orange blossoms in color, size, and fragrance.

FRUIT - Berries; ovoid, 0.75 inch long; green turning red when mature; fruit ripens periodically throughout the year.

CULTURE - Full sun or partial shade, in a fertile, well-drained, nematode-free soil; no salt tolerance.

PROBLEMS - Nematodes, scales, and whiteflies followed by sooty mold.

PROPAGATION - Seed, or cuttings for named clones.

LANDSCAPE USES - Makes an excellent small specimen tree, but most commonly used as a clipped hedge, screen, or foundation planting.

COMMENTS - The cultivar *M. paniculata* 'Lakeview' and a related species, *M. koenigii* (Curry-leaf), are also in cultivation.

Severinia buxifolia   BOXTHORN

PRONUNCIATION - ˈse və ˈri nē ə   ˈbuk sə ˈfō lē ə

TRANSLATION - [after Marco Aurelio Severino (1580-1656), professor of anatomy at Naples] [leaves like *Buxus*].

FORM - Monoecious, evergreen shrub or small tree often multiple trunked, low branching, dense, compact. Medium-fine texture.

SIZE - To 12 feet tall, commonly seen 2 to 6 feet tall, slow growth rate.

HARDINESS ZONE - Zone 8b. Can be grown in north, central, and south Florida, may need some protection in north Florida.

NATIVE HABITAT - South China, Taiwan.

LEAVES - Simple, alternate or spirally arranged, obovate to 1.5 inches long, retuse apex, leathery, dark green, aromatic when crushed; margins entire.

STEM/BARK - Young growth green, not round (angular), with sharp axillary thorns.

FLOWERS - White, 5 petals, inconspicuous, borne in small axillary cymes, fragrant. Blooms in spring and summer.

FRUIT - Berry, black, globular, to 0.25 inch in diameter, several seeded. Present much of the year.

CULTURE - Grown in full sun to partial shade on various well-drained soils; slightly salt tolerant.

PROBLEMS - Scale, whitefly, sooty mold.

PROPAGATION - Seeds, cuttings.

LANDSCAPE USES - Use as a sheared hedge, a barrier, or a foundation shrub.

COMMENTS - Should be planted only where there are no children or visually impaired pedestrians.

Triphasia trifolia   LIMEBERRY

PRONUNCIATION - trī 'fā zē ə   trī 'fō lē ə

TRANSLATION - [from Greek *triphasios* (= triple), in reference to the 3-merous flowers] [3-leaved].

FORM - Evergreen shrub; low-growing, dense; weeping habit; medium-fine texture.

SIZE - Can reach a height of 15 feet, commonly to 6 feet tall with an equal spread; moderate growth rate.

HARDINESS ZONE - Zone 9b; can be grown in south and central Florida.

NATIVE HABITAT - Southeastern Asia.

LEAVES - Trifoliolate; alternate; nearly sessile; to 2 inches long; leaflets dark green; the center one twice as large as the other two; emarginate apices; crenate margins.

STEM/BARK - Twigs zigzag; sharp stipular spines.

FLOWERS - White; 0.5 inch wide; fragrant; borne 1 to 3 in the leaf axils. Calyx 3-5, corolla 3-5, stamens 6-10, carpels 3-5. Blooms during warm months of the year.

FRUIT - Berries; dull red; 0.5 inch wide; thick-skinned; edible; sometimes made into preserves.

CULTURE - Full sun or partial shade on fertile, well-drained, nematode-free soil; no salt tolerance.

PROBLEMS - Nematodes, scales, and whiteflies followed by sooty mold.

PROPAGATION - Seeds or cuttings.

LANDSCAPE USES - Makes a very attractive, low, compact hedge or foundation planting. Can be trained as a sheared specimen. Occasionally grown for its fruit.

COMMENTS - Widely planted throughout the tropics.

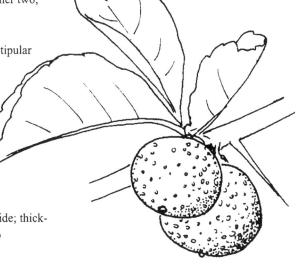

SAPINDACEAE - SOAPBERRY FAMILY

DICOTYLEDONS; 150 GENERA AND ABOUT 2,000 SPECIES

GEOGRAPHY: Throughout tropics and subtropics of the Old World and New
                  World.

GROWTH HABIT: Trees, shrubs, and woody vines; often with resinous or laticiferous
                  exudates.

LEAVES: Alternate, simple or pinnately or bipinnately compound, and
                  without stipules.

FLOWERS: Actinomorphic or zygomorphic, often unisexual (plants
                  monoecious), in cymose inflorescences; 5-merous: sepals 5, free
                  or connate; petals 5 or apetalous; stamens in 2 whorls of 5 or
                  occasionally 4; ovary superior and consists of 3 fused carpels.

FRUIT: Capsule, nut, berry, drupe, samara, or schizocarp, usually red and
                  with arilate seeds.

ECONOMIC USES: Several ornamentals, fruit trees (e.g., akee from *Blighia sapida*,
                  lychee from *Litchi chinensis*, rambutan from *Nephelium bijuga*,
                  etc.), the Brazilian drink "guarana" (from *Paullinia cupana*), and
                  other products.

ORNAMENTAL GENERA: *Alectryon, Blighia, Cardiospermum, Cupaniopsis, Dodonaea,
                   Euphoria, Exothea, Filicium, Harpullia, Hypelate, Koelreuteria,
                   Litchi, Melicoccus, Nephelium, Pometia, Sapindus, Schleichera,*
                   etc.

Koelreuteria elegans   GOLDENRAIN TREE

PRONUNCIATION - ˌkōl rə 'tē rē ə   'e lə gənz

TRANSLATION - [after Joseph Gottlieb Koelreuter (1733-1806), German professor of botany] [elegant].

FORM - Monoecious, deciduous, large tree, freely branching, heavily foliated, dense, mounded globose canopy.

SIZE - To 60 feet, rapid growth rate.

HARDINESS ZONE - Zone 8. Grown throughout Florida.

NATIVE HABITAT - Taiwan, Fiji.

LEAVES - Even-bipinnately compound to 18 inches long, 9 to 16 leaflets on the rachilla, usually narrowly ovate to 3.5 inches long, nearly entire to unevenly serrate margins, oblique base, pink tomentose rachis.

STEM/BARK - Lenticels on new growth.

FLOWERS - Flowers with 4-5 yellow petals, to 1 inch across; in large terminal panicles to 1.5 feet long, very showy, flowers in late summer.

FRUIT - Capsule to 2 inches long, 3-seeded, pinkish, ovate, papery segments, showy in the fall.

CULTURE - Full sun, various soils; not salt tolerant.

PROBLEMS - Scale, mites, brittle, many seeds which germinate easily create a weed problem.

PROPAGATION - Seeds.

LANDSCAPE USES - Shade, specimen, street plantings.

COMMENTS - Sometimes sold as *K. formosana*. Several related species exist. An attractive plant which is becoming much too widespread in Florida. Its use should be limited or avoided. Similar to *K. paniculata* which is represented in cultivation in cooler climates (Zone 6) by several cultivars.

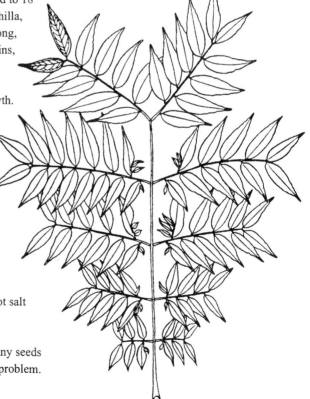

Litchi chinensis   LYCHEE

PRONUNCIATION - ˈlē chē   chī ˈnen səs

TRANSLATION - [Chinese name] [from China].

FORM - Monoecious, evergreen tree; upright, round-headed; densely foliated; medium texture.

SIZE - Reaches a height of 35 feet with a spread of 20 feet; medium growth rate.

HARDINESS ZONE - Zone 9b; can be grown in central and south Florida, but needs a protected location in central Florida. Young trees are more frost tender.

NATIVE HABITAT - Southern China.

LEAVES - Pinnately compound; alternate; to 8 inches long; 4 to 8 elliptic leaflets, leathery, glossy, 5 inches long; new growth copper-colored.

FLOWERS - Yellowish; small; borne in 12-inch-long terminal panicles. Blooms in February or March.

FRUIT - Drupes; red; ovate, to 1.5 inches long; leathery, pebbly skin containing delicious, white, translucent, gelatinous mesocarp surrounding a large shiny brown seed; resemble large strawberries; ripen in June and July.

CULTURE - Full sun on deep, fertile, moist, sandy soil; no salt tolerance. Young leaves easily wind-damaged; avoid windy locations.

PROBLEMS - Mushroom root rot on soils where oaks were grown.

PROPAGATION - Air layering is most successful; avoid seedlings.

LANDSCAPE USES - An excellent specimen or shade tree.

COMMENTS - Several dependable, high-quality fruit cultivars: **'Brewster,' 'Mauritius,'** and **'Sweet Cliff.'**

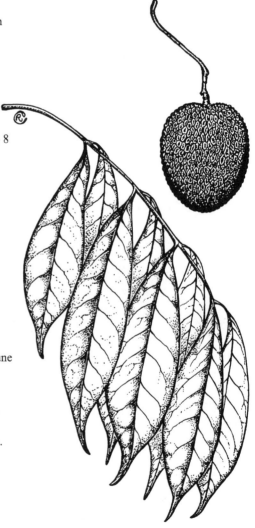

SAPOTACEAE - SAPODILLA FAMILY

DICOTYLEDONS; 35 TO 116 GENERA AND 800 TO 1,100 SPECIES

GEOGRAPHY: Pantropical, in lowlands and montane rain forest.

GROWTH HABIT: Evergreen trees with milky latex.

LEAVES: Simple, entire, spirally arranged but sometimes pseudowhorls at branch tips; stipules early deciduous.

FLOWERS: In fascicles, sometimes cauliflorus; bisexual; actinomorphic or zygomorphic; often white or cream-colored and fragrant at night; sepals in two whorls of 2, 3, 4, or one whorl of 5; petals usually equal in number to the sepals, fused at base; stamens equal in number to the corolla or more, but epipetalous; ovary superior and consists of several fused carpels.

FRUIT: Berry.

ECONOMIC USES: Ornamentals, but also an important source of timber, edible fruit (sapotilla plum from *Manilkara zapota*, star apple from *Chrysophyllum cainito*, sapote from *Calocarpum sapota* and other species), and guttapercha (from latex of *Palaquium* spp., *Mimusops balata*, etc.), chewing gum (from latex of *Manilkara zapota*), and edible oil (from *Butyrospermum paradoxa*), etc.

ORNAMENTAL GENERA: *Bumelia, Chrysophyllum, Dipholis, Malacantha, Manilkara* (= *Achras*), *Mastichodendron, Mimusops, Pouteria, Synsepalum,* among others.

COMMENTS: Generic limits in Sapotaceae are difficult to define, hence the number of genera and species vary according to the authority consulted.

Chrysophyllum oliviforme DAMSON PLUM, SATINLEAF

PRONUNCIATION - ˌkrī sə ˈfi ləm   ō ˌli və ˈfor mē

TRANSLATION - [from Greek *chrysos* (= golden) and *phyllon* (= a leaf), in allusion to golden color of leaves on the lower side] [olive-shaped, in reference to the fruit].

FORM - Monoecious, evergreen tree; outward-arching branches; coarse texture.

SIZE - Reaches a height of 40 feet with a spread of 20 feet; moderate growth rate.

HARDINESS ZONE - Zones 10-11; limited to south Florida.

NATIVE HABITAT - Coastal and inland hammocks of south Florida, the West Indies, and tropical America.

LEAVES - Simple; alternate; elliptic, 4 inches long; entire margins; dark green, glossy on the upper side; covered with shining, downy, golden-brown pubescence below. The satiny undersides flash attractively as the leaves flutter in the wind.

STEM/BARK - Young stems, new growth, and flower buds covered with shining golden-brown pubescence; trunks to 12 inches wide, covered with thin, light, reddish-brown, scaly bark in irregular plates.

FLOWERS - White; small; inconspicuous; borne in axillary clusters. 5-merous, sepals imbricate. Blooms all year.

FRUIT - Berries; purple; cylindrical to conical, 0.75 inch long; 1-seeded; sweet, edible, white flesh that is very gummy; ripen throughout the year.

CULTURE - Prefers full sun or partial shade on a well-drained, fertile soil; tolerates alkaline soils; marginal salt tolerance.

PROBLEMS - Pest-free.

PROPAGATION - Seed, or semi-hardwood cuttings under mist.

LANDSCAPE USES - Use as a specimen or street tree or incorporate in shrubbery borders.

COMMENTS - *Chrysophyllum cainito* (star-apple, caimito) is similar and is grown for its larger, more edible fruit.

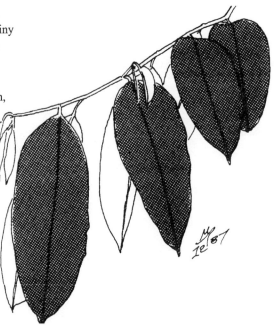

Manilkara zapota

CHICLE, SAPODILLA

PRONUNCIATION - mə ˈnil kə rə   zə ˈpō tə

TRANSLATION - [Indian vernacular name cited by von Rheede in 1683][Mexican name].

SYNONYM - *Acharas zapota.*

FORM - Monoecious, evergreen tree; upright, dense; coarse texture.

SIZE - Reaches a height of 45 feet with a spread of 25 feet; slow growth rate.

HARDINESS ZONE - Zones 10-11; south Florida only.

NATIVE HABITAT - Lowland tropics of Central America.

LEAVES - Simple; alternate; elliptic, to 6 inches long and 2.5 inches wide; clustered at the tips of twigs; stiff, glossy; entire margins.

STEM/BARK - Injured bark and branches bleed white latex, which is the source of chicle, the original base for chewing gum.

FLOWERS - Cream-colored with brown calyx; 0.5 inch wide; solitary; borne in the leaf axils. Sepals 6, in 2 series. Corolla 6-lobed, each lobe with 2 petaloid appendages; stamens the same number as corolla. Blooms appear all year with the main season in winter and spring.

FRUIT - Berries; oblate, to 4 inches wide; scurfy brown; main crop ripening in spring and summer; yellow-brown, juicy pulp, sweet and edible; esteemed by people in tropical countries.

CULTURE - Requires full sun for best form; almost any soil (alkaline to very poor), but grows better on well-drained soils; high salt tolerance.

PROBLEMS - Scales and fruit flies occasionally cause problems.

PROPAGATION - Usually by seed; superior varieties veneer grafted.

LANDSCAPE USES - A superb shade, street, or fruit tree; drought and wind resistant, withstanding hurricanes very well.

COMMENTS - **'Prolific,' 'Brown Sugar,' 'Modello,'** and **'Russell'** are superior fruit cultivars. *Manilkara bahamensis* (Wild Dilly) is native to the Florida Keys and has less desirable fruit. Also, *M. kauki* and *M. roxburghiana* are cultivated in Florida.

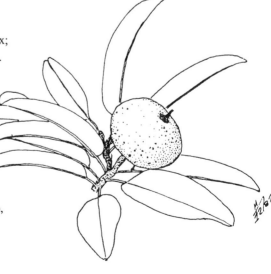

SAXIFRAGACEAE - SAXIFRAGE FAMILY

DICOTYLEDONS; 37 TO 80 GENERA AND 425 TO 1250 SPECIES

GEOGRAPHY: Nearly cosmopolitan but predominantly temperate, especially alpine and arctic regions.

GROWTH HABIT: Perennial or rarely annual herbs (and shrubs or small trees and vines if the families noted below are included - see *Comments*).

LEAVES: Alternate, simple (or opposite and compound if the families noted below are included - see *Comments*).

FLOWERS: Actinomorphic, 4- or 5-merous; sepals and petals free, imbricate; stamens twice as many as the petals or numerous. Ovary superior consisting of 2 fused carpels in a receptacular cup (ovary may be inferior and consists of 4 carpels if other families are included - see *Comments*).

FRUIT: A capsule (and also berry if other families are included - see *Comments*).

ECONOMIC USES: Ornamentals, but such fruits as gooseberry and currants (*Ribes* spp.) may be included if Grossulariaceae is included.

ORNAMENTAL GENERA: *Brexia, Deutzia, Escallonia, Philadelphus, Saxifraga*, etc.

COMMENTS: In some classifications, Saxifragaceae may include such distinct families as Escalloniaceae, Grossulariaceae, Hydrangeaceae, Parnassiaceae, and Philadelphaceae, all of which are then treated as subfamilies.

Escallonia spp.

ESCALLONIA

PRONUNCIATION - ˌes kə ˈlō nē ə

TRANSLATION - [after Señor Escallon, a Spanish traveler in South America].

FORM - Monoecious, rounded, dense evergreen shrubs of medium texture.

SIZE - To 25 feet tall, depending on species, generally seen in the 6 to 10 foot range with an equal spread. Growth rate is fairly rapid.

HARDINESS ZONE - Zone 8, can be grown in all areas of Florida.

NATIVE HABITAT - Brazil, Chile, Argentina.

LEAVES - Simple, alternate or whorled, narrowly oblong, elliptic, or lanceolate, finely serrated, to 3 inches long. The petioles, new growth, and serrations are burgundy colored.

FLOWERS - White to rose or pinkish, about 1/3 inch wide, flowers borne in short, dense, broad, terminal clusters, 5-merous, sometimes fragrant, in May.

FRUIT - 2 or 3-valved capsules, many-seeded, not usually produced in Florida.

CULTURE - Will grow in partial shade, but flowers better in full sun. *Escallonia* spp. prefer fertile, well-drained soil and have no salt tolerance.

PROBLEMS - Relatively pest-free.

PROPAGATION - Softwood cuttings, which root easily.

LANDSCAPE USES - As a specimen shrub, hedge, or as a screen.

COMMENTS - Several species of *Escallonia* are good ornamental shrubs. There is considerable taxonomic confusion because cultivated plants hybridize readily. Many hybrids and cultivars exist. Common examples include: *E. bifida* and *E. laevis*. *Escallonia* is variously placed in Escalloniaceae, Grossulariaceae, or Saxifragaceae.

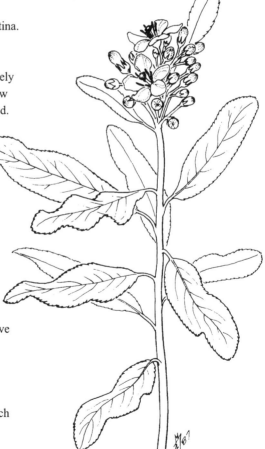

SCROPHULARIACEAE - FIGWORT FAMILY

DICOTYLEDONS; ABOUT 230 GENERA AND 3,000 SPECIES

GEOGRAPHY: Cosmopolitan, but predominantly north temperate.

GROWTH HABIT: Annual and perennial herbs, a few shrubs and subshrubs, and only one tree genus (*Pawlonia*); a few are parasitic.

LEAVES: Alternate or opposite, simple or pinnately lobed, and lack stipules.

FLOWERS: Usually zygomorphic, bisexual; 5-merous; sepals 5; petals 5, bilabiate; stamens 4, two longer than others, but all epipetalous; ovary superior and consists or 2 fused carpels.

FRUIT: Capsules containing numerous seeds.

ECONOMIC USES: Mostly as ornamentals and a few for pharmaceuticals (e.g., *Digitalis*).

ORNAMENTAL GENERA: *Antirrhinum, Calceolaria, Collinsia, Digitalis, Hebe, Leucophyllum, Mimulus, Paulownia, Penstemon, Russelia, Torenia, Veronica,* and *Wulfenia,* among others.

Antirrhinum majus   SNAPDRAGON

PRONUNCIATION - ˈæn tə ˈrī nəm   ˈmā jəs

TRANSLATION - [from Greek *anti* (= like) and *rhis* (= a snout), in reference to the flower shape] [larger].

FORM - Herbaceous annual or perennial, erect, stiff stems. Fine texture.

SIZE - Highly variable with cultivar, range from 6 inches to 6 feet, rapid growth.

HARDINESS ZONE - Zone 7. Grown throughout Florida as an annual bedding plant and sometimes for cut flowers.

NATIVE HABITAT - Mediterranean region.

LEAVES - Simple, alternate, lanceolate to oblong-lanceolate to 3 inches long, sometimes bluntly-lobed, pubescent, margins entire.

STEM/BARK - Sometimes covered with short, sticky hairs.

FLOWERS - Red, pink, orange, yellow, purple, all shades and combinations, corolla tubular to 2 inches long, pouched, forming a mouth, upper 2-lobed, lower 3-lobed, turning outward, in terminal racemes, flowers growing from the axil of a small leafy bract, fragrant.

FRUIT - Dry, 2-celled, capsule, many-seeded. Not ornamental.

CULTURE - Full sun, various well-drained soils.

PROBLEMS - Aphids, mites, thrips, rust, nematodes, fungus diseases.

PROPAGATION - Seed.

LANDSCAPE USES - Cut flowers, bedding plants, planter box.

COMMENTS - Many named cultivars, hybrids: Liberty Series (long-blooming spikes); Longshot Series (upright, various colors); Rocket Series (tall, vigorous); Sonnet Series (early, free flowering); Tahiti Series (dwarf, rust-resistant); also **'Bells'**, **'Madame Butterfly'**, **'Black Prince'**, etc. are specific cultivars.

Leucophyllum frutescens   TEXAS SAGE

PRONUNCIATION - ˌlū kə ˈfi ləm   frū ˈte sənz

TRANSLATION - [from Greek *leukos* (= white) and *phylon* (= a leaf), in reference to the canescent leaves] [shrubby, bushy].

FORM - Monoecious, evergreen shrub, compact, of medium texture.

SIZE - Can reach a height of 8 feet with an equal spread. Grows at a moderate pace.

HARDINESS ZONE - Zone 8b, can be grown in all areas of Florida, but does not do well because of high humidity.

NATIVE HABITAT - Desert areas of Texas and Mexico.

LEAVES - Simple, alternate, obovate, nearly sessile, to 1 inch long. The leaves are spirally arranged, and are covered with silvery-white tomentum, margins entire.

STEM/BARK - The stems are also silvery-white, downy when young.

FLOWERS - Mauve, bell-shaped to 1 inch across, axillary and solitary. The main season of bloom is in spring to early summer, but high humidity adversely affects bloom, especially in south Florida.

FRUIT - 2-valved capsules, with many seeds. Not showy.

CULTURE - Prefers full sun (for best flowering) and sandy, dry, well-drained soil. It has good salt and drought tolerance, but will not tolerate wet sites or poor soil aeration.

PROBLEMS - Sooty mold from sucking insect secretions and mushroom root rot.

PROPAGATION - Cuttings.

LANDSCAPE USES - Can be used as a low hedge or as a specimen shrub. Likes hot, dry situations like those found in parking lots. Tends to be short-lived.

SIMAROUBACEAE - QUASSIA FAMILY

DICOTYLEDONS; ABOUT 20 GENERA AND 120 SPECIES

GEOGRAPHY: Widely distributed in the tropical and subtropical regions of both hemispheres.

GROWTH HABIT: Trees and shrubs.

LEAVES: Alternate, pinnately compound or rarely simple; without stipules.

FLOWERS: Small, numerous, actinomorphic, bisexual or unisexual (plants usually dioecious); petals and sepals 3 to 7, connate or free, or rarely apetalous; stamens the same or twice the number of petals; there is a cup-shaped disk between the petals and the stamens; ovary superior and consists of 2-5 connate or free carpels.

FRUIT: Samara, schizocarp, or capsule.

ECONOMIC USES: Ornamentals and a few for their medicinal value or wood (e.g., *Quassia amara, Picrasma,* etc.).

ORNAMENTAL GENERA: *Ailanthus, Alvaradoa, Kirkia, Quassia, Simarouba,* and others.

Simarouba glauca   PARADISE TREE

PRONUNCIATION - ˌsi mə ˈrū bə ˈglau kə

TRANSLATION - [Carib Indian name] [glaucous].

FORM - Dioecious, evergreen tree; upright, with a rounded crown; medium texture.

SIZE - Grows to 50 feet tall with a 30 foot spread; slow growth rate.

HARDINESS ZONE - Zones 10-11; grown in south Florida only. It should be planted in protected locations as it is badly damaged by freezes.

NATIVE HABITAT - Hammocks of south Florida, the West Indies, and Central America.

LEAVES - Usually even-pinnately compound; alternate; to 16 inches long; 6 to 19 leathery, shining leaflets, oblong to obovate, 3 inches long; new growth reddish-colored.

STEM/BARK - Trunks straight, upright, 1.5 feet wide; covered with thick, smooth, grayish bark.

FLOWERS - Yellowish; small; borne in large, many-branched terminal panicles; 5-merous: sepals and petals 5, stamens 10. Blooms in April.

FRUIT - Drupes; dark purple; ellipsoidal, 1 inch long; ripening in June; edible when fully ripe, but not very tasty. Seeds yield a useful oil; trees are grown for seed oil extraction in El Salvador.

CULTURE - Full sun or partial shade; almost any well-drained soil; marginal salt tolerance.

PROBLEMS - No major pest problems. Surface roots preclude use near sidewalks and driveways.

PROPAGATION - Seeds, which germinate easily and rapidly.

LANDSCAPE USES - A superb specimen or shade tree.

SOLANACEAE - NIGHTSHADE FAMILY

DICOTYLEDONS; ABOUT 90 GENERA AND 2,000-3,000 SPECIES

GEOGRAPHY:	Cosmopolitan but best represented in Australia and Central and South America.
GROWTH HABIT:	Predominantly erect annual or perennial herbs or climbers, but also a few shrubs and trees.
LEAVES:	Extremely variable, ranging from simple and entire to variously dissected; usually alternate; stipules absent.
FLOWERS:	Solitary or in cymes; usually actinomorphic but rarely zygomorphic; bisexual; 5-merous; sepals usually 5, partly fused and often persistent, enlarging and remaining around the fruit; petals usually 5, variously fused to form rotate, salverform, tubular, or trumpet-shaped flowers; stamens usually 5, epipetalous; ovary superior and consists of 2 fused carpels.
FRUIT:	Commonly a berry but sometimes a capsule; seeds numerous.
ECONOMIC USES:	In addition to ornamentals, members of this family provide some of the most important vegetables for human consumption (e.g., potato from *Solanum tuberosum*, tomato from *Lycopersicum esculentum*, various green or red peppers from *Capsicum* spp., eggplant from S. melongena, to mention a few), *Nicotiana tabacum* provides the tobacco leaves and other species of the genus contain nicotines used as insecticides. Species of many genera are deadly poisons and/or have medicinal value (e.g., *Atropa, Cestrum, Nicandra, Physalis, Datura, Mandragora, Hyoscyamus,* etc.).

ORNAMENTAL GENERA: *Acnistus, Browallia, Brugmansia, Brunfelsia, Capsicum, Cestrum, Cyphomandra, Datura, Lycianthes, Nicotiana, Nierembergia, Parmentiera, Petunia, Salpichroa, Salpiglossis, Schizanthus, Solandra, Solanum,* and many others.

Cestrum nocturnum

NIGHTBLOOMING JESSAMINE,
NIGHT CESTRUM

PRONUNCIATION - 'ses trəm   nɑk 'tər nəm

TRANSLATION - [Greek name] [night-blooming].

FORM - Monoecious, evergreen shrub, sprawling, spreading, medium-textured.

SIZE - Can reach a height of 12 feet with an equal spread; growth is rapid.

HARDINESS ZONE - Zone 9, can be grown in south and central Florida.

NATIVE HABITAT - West Indies.

LEAVES - Simple, alternate, narrowly ovate, to 6 inches long, glabrous, margins entire, yellowish-green in color.

STEM/BARK - Long, slender, drooping, greenish branches.

FLOWERS - Greenish-white, salverform, 1 inch long, in dense axillary clusters, extremely fragrant at night, 5-merous, stamens epipetalous. Blooms periodically throughout the year.

FRUIT - Berries, white, 0.5 inch long, ripening throughout the year, poisonous.

CULTURE - Requires full sun for best flowering and growth habit but can be grown in light shade. Tolerates a wide range of soils but has no salt tolerance. Requires frequent pruning to shape and control rampant sprawling growth.

PROBLEMS - Chewing insects can riddle leaves, aphids, mealybugs, sooty mold.

PROPAGATION - Semi-hardwood cuttings root very easily.

LANDSCAPE USES - Primarily grown for the nighttime fragrance of the flowers, this plant has little visual appeal. Plant it where the fragrance may be enjoyed, perhaps near a patio, but not where the fragrance becomes overpowering, such as under a bedroom window. Do not use in places where children may eat the fruit.

COMMENTS - Several other species, such as *C. diurnum* (Day Cestrum), a pubescent shrub or small tree which is fragrant during the day, *C. aurantiacum* (Orange Cestrum), *C. elegans* (Purple Cestrum), *C. fasciculatum*, and *C. parqui*, are also in cultivation.

Petunia × hybrida

PRONUNCIATION - pə ˈtū nyə   ˈhī brə də

TRANSLATION - [from *petun*, the Brazilian name for tobacco] [hybrid].

FORM - Herbaceous perennial, weak, low growing, trailing branches, dense foliage.

SIZE - Variable with cultivar, range 6 to 12 inches, rapid growth rate.

HARDINESS ZONE - Zones 10-11 if grown as a perennial in south Florida although this is not recommended. The most popular annual bedding plant in the United States, petunias can be grown in the cool months throughout Florida.

NATIVE HABITAT - A complex hybrid involving three species, the species are native to tropical America.

LEAVES - Simple, alternate or the upper sometimes opposite, entire, shape variable, linear-oblong to spatulate, to 5 inches long, viscid, pubescent, soft.

STEM/BARK - Green, pubescent, viscid.

FLOWERS - Many colors and combinations, whites, yellows, reds, blues, may be variously striped, barred, or with starlike markings, corolla funnelform, to 5 inches across, often deeply fringed or fully double. The solitary, axillary flowers are often fragrant especially at night. Blooms best in spring and fall.

FRUIT - 2-celled capsule, many seeded. Not ornamental.

CULTURE - Grow in full sun to light shade on fertile soils; not salt tolerant.

PROBLEMS - Mealybugs, downy mildew, caterpillars.

PROPAGATION - Seed, cuttings.

LANDSCAPE USES - A common annual used as edging, bedding plants, in planter boxes and hanging baskets.

COMMENTS - Many cultivars selected for flower form, size, and color are available. These are usually produced as line or line hybrids.

STERCULIACEAE - STERCULIA FAMILY

DICOTYLEDONS; 60 GENERA AND ABOUT 600 SPECIES

GEOGRAPHY: Pantropical, extending into subtropics.

GROWTH HABIT: Trees, shrubs, vines, and a few herbaceous species. Nearly all
                      have stellate hairs.

LEAVES: Alternate, simple and partly divided or lobed; stipulate.

FLOWERS: Actinomorphic, bisexual or unisexual (plants monoecious); sepals
                      3-5, partly fused; petals 5, free or fused by the staminal tube,
                      sometimes quite small and occasionally absent; stamens often
                      reduced to staminodia or lacking; ovary superior and consist of 2
                      to numerous carpels.

FRUIT: A dry capsule or follicle and often dehiscent or berry-like.

ECONOMIC USES: Ornamentals, but economically important crops are cola (*Cola
                      nitida* and *C. acuminata*) and cacao (*Theobroma cacao*).

ORNAMENTAL GENERA: *Abroma, Brachychiton, Dombeya, Firmiana, Fremontodendron,
                    Guazuma, Heritiera, Pterospermum, Reevesia, Sterculia,* etc.

Dombeya wallichii PINKBALL

PRONUNCIATION - dɑm ˈbā ə   wə ˈli kē ī

TRANSLATION - [after Joseph Dombey (1742-1794), French botanist who collected in South America] [after Nathaniel Wallichi (1786-1854), Danish botanist, who was the superintendent of the Calcata Botanic Garden from 1814 to 1841].

FORM - Monoecious, shrub or small tree; large, dense, bushy; rounded, mound-forming; coarse texture.

SIZE - To 30 feet tall with an equal spread; rapid growth rate.

HARDINESS ZONE - Zone 8b; can be grown in south, central, and very protected locations in north Florida.

NATIVE HABITAT - Madagascar and eastern Africa.

LEAVES - Simple; alternate; broadly cordate-ovate; usually with 3 large, pointed lobes, to 12 inches long; soft, fuzzy; palmately veined and lobed; serrate margins. Petioles long and stalked.

STEM/BARK - Vigorous, multiple trunks with minor lateral branches.

FLOWERS - Pink; fragrant; 1 inch wide; borne in dense, pendant, axillary umbels; flowers dangle on 12-inch peduncles, turn brown, and wither with age; persist in unsightly clusters. Blooms in winter.

FRUIT - Capsules; ovoid; 5-celled; dehiscent; rarely produced.

CULTURE - Full sun or partial shade on a wide range of soils; no salt tolerance.

PROBLEMS - Aphids, soft scale, nematodes, sooty molds.

PROPAGATION - Softwood cuttings root quickly and easily.

LANDSCAPE USES - An attractive specimen when in full bloom, but use carefully due to huge size and ratty appearance when not in bloom. It is frost sensitive and tends to get killed back by cold just as it reaches full bloom.

COMMENTS - There are hybrids available with similar characteristics. *Dombeya* × *cayeuxii* (Pink Ball) is *D. burgessiae* × *D. wallichii.* Cultivars of hybrid origin include **'Perrine', 'Pink Clouds', 'Pinwheel', 'Rosemound',** and **'Seminole'.** Cultivated related species include *D. burgessiae (= D. calantha* and *D. masterii)* and others.

THEACEAE - TEA FAMILY

DICOTYLEDONS; ABOUT 29 GENERA AND 1,100 SPECIES

GEOGRAPHY: Restricted to tropical and subtropical regions of Asia and North
                    America.

GROWTH HABIT: Evergreen trees, shrubs, and rarely scrambling vines.

LEAVES: Alternate or rarely opposite, coriaceous, stipules usually absent.

FLOWERS: Very showy, actinomorphic, unisexual, usually solitary but
                    occasionally in few-branched inflorescences; sepals and petals 4-
                    7, free, persistent, and remaining at the fruit base; stamens usually
                    numerous and free or in tubular or irregular bunches; ovary
                    superior or rarely inferior and consists of 3-5 or rarely numerous
                    fused carpels.

FRUIT: Capsule, berry, or achene.

ECONOMIC USES: Important ornamentals, tea (from *Camellia sinensis*), and
                    specialized red woods.

ORNAMENTAL GENERA: *Camellia, Cleyera, Eurya, Franklinia, Gordonia, Ternstroemia*,
                    among others (excluding genera in the families listed below).

COMMENTS: Several segregate families have been recognized, including
                    Pelicieraceae, Pentaphyllaceae, Tetrameristicaceae,
                    Medusagynaceae, Stachyuraceae, Caryocaraceae, and
                    Symplocaceae.

Camellia japonica

PRONUNCIATION - kə 'mēl yə   jə 'pɑ nə kə

TRANSLATION - [after George Joseph Kamel (1661-1706), pharmacist who studied flora of the Philippines] [from Japan].

FORM - Monoecious, evergreen shrub or small tree, often with a central leader, densely foliated, compact, oval canopy.

SIZE - To 45 feet, commonly seen 6 to 15 feet, slow growth rate.

HARDINESS ZONE - Zone 7. Grown in north and central Florida.

NATIVE HABITAT - Japan, South Korea.

LEAVES - Simple, alternate to spiral arrangement, broadly elliptic, to 4 inches long, acuminate apex, shallowly serrate margins.

STEM/BARK - Smooth, new growth brown.

FLOWERS - Many colors, corolla varies, petals 5 to 18, stamens many; to 5 inches across, solitary or clustered, terminal, flowers in winter and spring.

FRUIT - Capsule, greenish-red, woody, dehiscent, globose to 1.5 inches in diameter.

CULTURE - partial shade; fertile, well-drained, acidic soils; not salt tolerant.

PROBLEMS - Scale, aphids, chewing insects, fungus.

PROPAGATION - Cuttings, layers.

LANDSCAPE USES - Hedge, screen, specimen.

COMMENTS - More than 2,000 cultivars for flowers, growth habit, etc., have been listed as seven Groups: Single, Semi-double, Anemone Form, Peony Form, Rose Form Double, Formal Double, and Higo Japonicas.

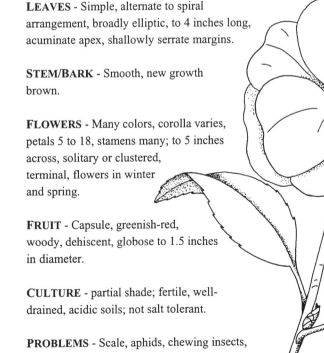

Camellia sasanqua   SASANQUA CAMELLIA

PRONUNCIATION - kə 'mēl yə   sə 'sæŋ kwə

TRANSLATION - [after George Joseph Kamel (1661-1706), pharmacist who studied flora of the Philippines] [Japanese name for *Camellia*].

FORM - Monoecious, evergreen shrub or small tree; erect, compact, densely foliated, oval canopy.

SIZE - To 15 feet, slow growth rate.

HARDINESS ZONE - Zone 7; grows well only in north Florida.

NATIVE HABITAT - Japan.

LEAVES - Simple, alternate to spirally arranged, elliptic, to 3 inches long, acute apex, glossy deep green, leathery; margins serrate; petiole and midrib pubescent. Generally smaller and shinier than leaves of *C. japonica.*

STEM/BARK - Branchlets pubescent.

FLOWERS - Many colors, petals 6 to 8; to 3 inches across; stamens numerous, solitary or clustered; flowers in fall and winter.

FRUIT - Capsule, globose, to 0.75 inch in diameter, woody, dehiscent.

CULTURE - Full sun or partial shade; fertile, acid soils; not salt tolerant.

PROBLEMS - Scale, mites, aphids, chewing insects.

PROPAGATION - Cuttings, layers.

LANDSCAPE USES - Hedge, screen, specimen.

COMMENTS - Many cultivars, and hybrids with *C. japonica* and other species. More than 300 cultivars have been recorded, including double and single flowers.

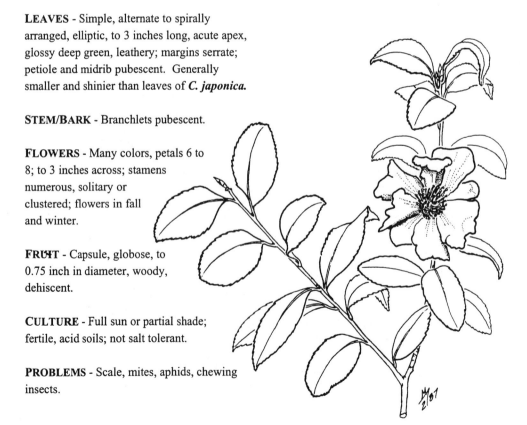

Gordonia lasianthus   LOBLOLLY BAY

PRONUNCIATION - gor ˈdō nē ə ˌlā sē ˈæn thəs

TRANSLATION - [after James Gordon (died 1781), a nurseryman who introduced *Ginkgo biloba*] [from Greek *lasio* (= wooly) and *anthos* (= flower)].

FORM - Monoecious, evergreen tree, pyramidal, coarse texture.

SIZE - Mature trees obtain a height of 70 feet and a spread of 25 feet;growth rate is rapid.

HARDINESS ZONE - Zone 7b, can be grown throughout Florida.

NATIVE HABITAT - Swamps, bayheads, and other low areas of the southeastern United States.

LEAVES - Simple, alternate, to 6 inches long, elliptic, leathery, dark green and shiny; margins finely serrate; individual leaves often turn bright red in the fall.

STEM/BARK - Bark thick, dark gray, furrowed; young twigs are red.

FLOWERS - White, 3 inches wide; 5 large petals and numerous golden stamens, solitary on long axillary stalks on new growth; flowers from May to September.

FRUIT - Capsules, woody, ovoid, 5-parted, 0.75 inch long, ripening in fall and early winter, 0.5 inch long, winged.

CULTURE - Partially shaded location with fertile, moist soil; sensitive to lack of water

and will die if not watered during times of drought; not salt tolerant.

PROBLEMS - Borers in weakened trees, caterpillars, aphids.

PROPAGATION - Seeds, which germinate well after stratification, softwood cuttings under mist or transplanting from wild.

LANDSCAPE USES - A superb specimen if cultural requirements are met.

COMMENTS - Two related species, *G. axillaris* and *G. chrysandra,* are also grown in Florida.

Ternstroemia gymnanthera   CLEYERA

PRONUNCIATION - tərn 'strō mē ə   jim 'næn thə rə

TRANSLATION - [after Christopher Tärnström (1703-1746), Swedish student of Linneus, who attempted to investigate natural history of China] [from Greek *gymnos* (= naked) and *antherus* (= anther)].

SYNONYM - *Cleyera gymnanthera.*

FORM - Monoecious, evergreen tree, upright, small, normally maintained as a dense shrub; medium-textured.

SIZE - If allowed to grow, will obtain a height of 25 feet, but is normally seen as an 8 to 10 foot shrub with a 6 foot spread; growth rate is slow to moderate.

HARDINESS ZONE - Zone 7, can be grown in all areas of Florida.

NATIVE HABITAT - India and eastern Asia.

LEAVES - Alternate, elliptic to obovate, to 3.5 inches long, thick and leathery, dark green on the upper side, light green underneath; short, burgundy petioles; clustered at the ends of twigs.

STEM/BARK - Slender, gray twigs become leggy if not pruned back.

FLOWERS - Pale yellow, to 0.75 inch wide, solitary, not showy, on short, hanging peduncles in leaf axils of new growth; perianth of 5 petals and 5 sepals, stamens numerous; in the spring.

FRUIT - Berry, red, to 0.75 inch long, globose with several large seeds; ripening in fall.

CULTURE - Partial to full shade and well-drained, fertile soils; not salt tolerant.

PROBLEMS - Scales are the only pest problem.

PROPAGATION - Seeds germinate readily, or mature wood cuttings with rooting hormone treatment under mist.

LANDSCAPE USES - Hedges, shrubbery borders, corner plantings, or as a screen. A very useful plant for deeply shaded areas.

TILIACEAE - BASSWOOD FAMILY

DICOTYLEDONS; 41 GENERA AND 400 SPECIES

GEOGRAPHY:
Predominantly in the Old and New World tropics, with a few representatives in temperate regions.

GROWTH HABIT:
Usually deciduous trees and shrubs, often with fibrous or mucilaginous bark.

LEAVES:
Alternate, distichous, simple, with oblique base, and branched hairs; stipulate.

FLOWERS:
Small, whitish-green, actinomorphic, usually bisexual, in axillary cymose inflorescences; sepals 5, free or connate; petals 5, free and with glandular hairs at or near their bases, or occasionally apetalous; stamens numerous; ovary superior and consists of 2 to 10 carpels.

FRUIT:
Nut-like drupe or capsule which are collectively often subtended by a large conspicuous bract.

ECONOMIC USES:
Ornamentals, valuable wood (basswood from *Tilia* spp.), economically important fiber (jute from *Corchorus capsularis* and *C. olitorius*), leaves of *C. olitorius* are used as vegetable, and bark of several species is used for rope making (e.g., *Grewia, Triumfetta, Clappertonia,* etc.).

ORNAMENTAL GENERA: *Berrya, Carpodiptera, Clappertonia, Grewia, Sparmannia, Tilia.*

Tilia americana

AMERICAN LINDEN, BASSWOOD

PRONUNCIATION - ˈti lē ə   ə ˌme rə ˈkā nə

TRANSLATION - [classical Latin name, probably from the Greek *ptilon* (= wing), referring to the wing-like bract of the flower cluster] [American].

FORM - Monoecious, deciduous tree, pyramidal when young, becoming dense and ovate to rounded with age, lower branches often pendulous. Coarse texture.

SIZE - To 120 feet, usually 60 to 80 feet with 30 to 40 foot spread. Moderate to fast growth rate.

HARDINESS ZONE - Zone 3. Grown in central and north Florida.

NATIVE HABITAT - Eastern North America, from north Florida to New Brunswick.

LEAVES - Alternate, 2-ranked, simple, broadly ovate, 4 to 8 inches long, obliquely cordate or truncate at base, abruptly acuminate at apex, coarsely serrate, dark green above, light green lower surface glabrous or with varying degrees of pubescence; long petiolate.

STEM/BARK - Young stems moderately stout, glabrous, often reddish at first, zigzag. Bark gray to brown with long, narrow scaly ridges.

FLOWERS - Pale yellow, about 0.5 inch across, borne in 5- to 10-flowered pendulous cymes about 3 inches wide. Inflorescence subtended by a wing-like bract, 2 to 6 inches long and 0.25 to 1 inch wide. Late spring. Fragrant flowers attract many bees; basswood honey is considered one of the finest.

FRUIT - Nut-like, about 0.5 inch across, woody, covered with gray tomentose, not ornamental.

CULTURE - Full sun or partial shade. Prefers moist, fertile soils, tolerates somewhat drier sites (although not drought tolerant). Transplants readily, pH adaptable.

PROBLEMS - Generally no serious pests; borers may attack weak trees and several leaf feeding insects (caterpillars, sawfly, etc.) may strip trees of foliage. Leaf scorch when grown under drought conditions. Sprouts from roots when cut down.

PROPAGATION - Seed, grafting (budding) of selected cultivars.

LANDSCAPE USES - Handsome shade tree for parks and other large sites, naturalized areas.

COMMENTS - Several cultivars exist, but are not widely available: **'Fastigiata'** - narrow, pyramidal form, could be used on smaller sites; **'Redmond'** - densely pyramidal with large leaves, appears to be intermediate between *T. americana* and *T. × euchlora*. Other taxa reported in cultivation in Florida include *T. caroliniana, T. heterophylla,* and *T. × vulgaris (T. cordata × T. platyphylla).*

ULMACEAE - ELM FAMILY

DICOTYLEDONS; 16 GENERA AND ABOUT 140 SPECIES

GEOGRAPHY: Predominantly north temperate.

GROWTH HABIT: Primarily trees, with a few shrubs.

LEAVES: Alternate, simple, often oblique bases, pinnately or palmately veined, and fugacious stipules.

FLOWERS: Small, green, and inconspicuous, usually in dense clusters, bi- or unisexual (plants monoecious); sepals 4-8, imbricate; apetalous; stamens equal in number and attached opposite the base of each sepal; ovary superior and consists of 2 fused carpels.

FRUIT: Nut, samara, or drupe.

ECONOMIC USES: Ornamentals and choice timber from several genera.

ORNAMENTAL GENERA: *Aphananthe, Celtis, Holoptelea, Planera, Trema, Ulmus, Zelkova,* and others.

Celtis laevigata   Sugarberry, Sugar Hackberry

PRONUNCIATION - ˈsel təs   ˈlē və ˈgā tə

TRANSLATION - [a Greek vernacular name for another tree] [smooth].

FORM - Monoecious, deciduous large tree, broad, rounded with spreading, pendulous branches. Fine to medium texture.

SIZE - To 100 feet, commonly 60 to 80 feet. Medium-fast growth rate.

HARDINESS ZONE - Zone 6. Grown in north and north-central Florida only.

NATIVE HABITAT - Eastern U.S, from southern Indiana, to north Florida to Texas, northeastern Mexico.

LEAVES - Alternate, simple, often 2-ranked, oblong-lanceolate to ovate, falcate, unequally rounded at base, acuminate apex, usually entire or may have a few teeth near apex, glabrous above; 2 to 4 inches long. Medium green above, pale green below. Leaves on mature trees or older branches tend to be long and narrow with entire margins, while those on young branches, saplings, and sprouts are usually shorter, wider, and more serrate. Turn yellow in fall, but not showy.

STEM/BARK - Slender, young stems somewhat zigzag, initially green turning reddish-brown, glabrous. Bark gray-brown to silvery. Large stems and trunk with warty projections or corky ridges.

FLOWERS - Small, greenish, inconspicuous.

FRUIT - Round, thin-fleshed, berry-like drupe, 0.25 to 0.33 inch across, orange to reddish-brown when mature in fall. Born singly on long pedicels. Not showy. Common name is derived from sweet taste of fruit.

CULTURE - Full sun, moist, fertile soils, pH adaptable. Tolerates temporary inundation. Moderately drought tolerant.

PROBLEMS - No serious insect or disease problems. Seedlings pop up everywhere. Limb breakage due to high winds and heavy snows.

PROPAGATION - Seed.

LANDSCAPE USES - Shade tree for parks and other large areas. Good for naturalized areas. Sometimes used as street tree in the South, but not a recommended use due to limb breakage. Fruit attracts birds.

COMMENTS - In the North and Midwest, the native *C. occidentalis* is used in place of *C. laevigata*. Somewhat similar in overall appearance, it is a smaller tree (to 60 feet) with a more warty bark and sandpapery leaves.

Ulmus alata   Winged Elm

PRONUNCIATION - ˈūl məs   ə ˈlā tə

TRANSLATION - [ancient Latin name; Romans used pollarded elms in vineyards on which to grow their vines] [*alatus* (= wings), in reference to winged branches].

FORM - Monoecious, deciduous tree, pyramidal when young but becoming vase-shaped with maturity. Texture is medium.

SIZE - Can reach a height of 60 feet with a 30 foot spread, but usually smaller. Growth rate is fast.

HARDINESS ZONE - Zone 5, can be grown in north and central Florida.

NATIVE HABITAT - Dry woodlands and riverbanks of north and central Florida and the southeastern United States.

LEAVES - Alternate, elliptic, stiff, with only a slightly asymmetric base, to 2 inches long. They have doubly serrate margins, scabrous upper surfaces, and pubescent underside.

STEM/BARK - Bark is grayish brown, in interlacing, flat-topped ridges. The slender twigs frequently have thin, corky, lateral winglike outgrowths on each side.

FLOWERS - Greenish, inconspicuous, small, in clusters on slender, drooping stalks; flowers in February.

FRUIT - Samaras, elliptically beaked, ripening before or as the leaves appear in March.

CULTURE - Grows in full sun or partial shade on almost any drained soil; no salt tolerance.

PROBLEMS - Relatively pest-free.

PROPAGATION - Seeds sown immediately after harvest germinate promptly and easily.

LANDSCAPE USES - A tough, sturdy shade or street tree. Other native species of *Ulmus* in cultivation are *U. americana* (American Elm), *U. americana* var. *floridana*, *U. crassifolia* (Cedar Elm), and *U. rubra* (Slippery Elm).

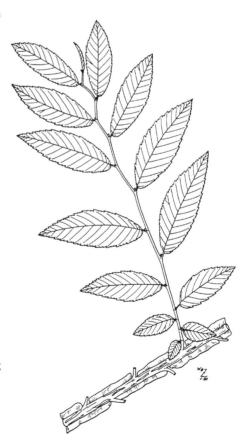

Ulmus parvifolia

CHINESE ELM

PRONUNCIATION - ˈūl məs ˌpɑr və ˈfō lē ə

TRANSLATION - [ancient Latin name; Romans used pollarded elms in vineyards on which to grow their vines] [with small leaves].

FORM - Monoecious, deciduous tree, symmetrical, freely branching at acute angles, spreading, open canopy, slightly weeping.

SIZE - To 80 feet, often much less, rapid growth rate.

HARDINESS ZONE - Zone 5. Grown in north and central Florida.

NATIVE HABITAT - China, Japan.

LEAVES - Simple, alternate, elliptic-ovate to 3 inches long, shiny dark green, leathery, margins serrate.

STEM/BARK - Branchlets sparingly pubescent, exfoliating bark showy.

FLOWERS - Bisexual, greenish-white, in axillary racemes, inconspicuous; blooms in fall.

FRUIT - Winged samara to 0.25 inch long.

CULTURE - Full sun, various soils; not salt tolerant.

PROBLEMS - Borers, chewing insects.

PROPAGATION - Seeds.

LANDSCAPE USES - Shade, patio, terrace, street plantings, specimen.

COMMENTS - Several cultivars for form, upright habit, etc. *Ulmus parvifolia* 'Sempervirens' has an upright growth habit.

Ulmus pumila

DWARF ELM, SIBERIAN ELM

PRONUNCIATION - 'ūl məs   'pū mə lə

TRANSLATION - [ancient Latin name; Romans used pollarded elms in vineyards on which to grow their vines] [dwarf].

FORM - Small, deciduous tree or large shrub, many-branched, branches slender, often drooping.

SIZE - To 25 feet, rapid growth rate.

HARDINESS ZONE - Zone 5, grows in northern Florida only.

NATIVE HABITAT - East Siberia, North China.

LEAVES - Simple, alternate to spiral arrangement, doubly serrate margin, oblique base, acuminate tip, elliptic-oblong, to 3 inches long, pubescence in vein axils beneath, papery texture.

STEM/BARK - Gray, furrowed with age.

FLOWERS - Axillary racemes, inconspicuous, green; flowers in spring.

FRUIT - Small, winged samara to 0.25 inch long.

CULTURE - Full sun, various soils; moderately salt tolerant.

PROBLEM - Mites, brittle, generally short-lived.

PROPAGATION - Seeds.

LANDSCAPE USES - Shade, specimen.

COMMENTS - Several cultivars, though practically none commonly used in Florida.

URTICACEAE - NETTLE FAMILY

DICOTYLEDONS; ABOUT 50 GENERA AND MORE THAN 1000 SPECIES

GEOGRAPHY: Cosmopolitan.

GROWTH HABIT: Herbs, shrubs, and a few small trees; herbaceous taxa often with stinging hairs.

LEAVES: Alternate or opposite, simple, stipulate, and often with stimulose hairs and superficially visible crystals (cystoliths).

FLOWERS: Small, greenish, actinomorphic, unisexual (plants monoecious) or rarely bisexual, usually in clusters; perianth of 4-5 segments, sepal-like; stamens 4-5, usually explosive when releasing pollen; ovary superior and consists of a single carpel.

FRUIT: Nutlet or berry-like drupe.

ECONOMIC USES: A few ornamentals (usually indoor foliage plants) and the notable "ramie fiber" source (*Boehmeria nivea*).

ORNAMENTAL GENERA: *Cecropia, Elatostema, Pellionia, Pilea,* and probably others.

Pilea microphylla

ARTILLERY PLANT

PRONUNCIATION - pī 'lē ə   ˌmī krə 'fi lə

TRANSLATION - [from Latin *pileus* (= a cap), in reference to the shape of the female flowers] [from Greek *mikros* (= small) and *phylos* (= a leaf)].

FORM - Monoecious, succulent, annual or short-lived perennial; ground cover; ferny appearance;fine texture.

SIZE - To 1 foot tall, spread varies; rapid growth rate.

HARDINESS ZONE - Zone 9; can be grown in south Florida and warmer parts of central Florida.

NATIVE HABITAT - American tropics.

LEAVES - Simple; opposite; obovate, to 0.25 inch long; subsessile; light green, fleshy; entire margins.

STEM/BARK - Weak, reclining, succulent, with green stems.

FLOWERS - Greenish-white and red; minute; borne in sessile, axillary cymes. Mature anthers eject pollen forcefully when jostled, giving this plant its common name.

FRUIT - Achene.

CULTURE - Tolerates a wide range of both light and soil types, but does best in shady, moist locations; no salt tolerance.

PROBLEMS - Generally pest-free; occasionally bothered by chewing insects.

PROPAGATION - Cuttings and fragments of plants root easily. Once established in a favorable environment, this plant spreads by itself.

LANDSCAPE USES - A popular ground cover for moist, shady locations. Becomes a pestiferous weed in greenhouses and containerized woody ornamentals.

COMMENTS - Two species of *Pilea* with much larger leaves, *P. cadierei* (Aluminum Plant) and its cultivar 'Nana', with silvery foliage, and *P. involucrata* (Friendship Plant), with its copper-colored leaves, are commonly sold as foliage plants.

VERBENACEAE - VERBENA FAMILY

DICOTYLEDONS; ABOUT 75 GENERA AND 3,000 SPECIES

GEOGRAPHY: Predominantly tropical and subtropical, with only a few temperate species.

GROWTH HABIT: Perennial herbs, subshrubs, shrubs, trees, and woody vines.

LEAVES: Usually opposite or rarely whorled or alternate, entire or divided, and without stipules.

FLOWERS: Usually zygomorphic, bisexual, arranged in various inflorescence types; perianth 4-5 lobed; corolla tubular and often bilabiate; stamens usually 4, alternating with the petals; ovary superior, usually consisting of 2 fused carpels.

FRUIT: Drupe or sometimes a capsule or schizocarp.

ECONOMIC USES: Several ornamentals, but also the source of the famous teak wood (from *Tectona grandis*) and other valuable timber, edible fruits, gum, oil, and tannins, and for medicinal purposes.

ORNAMENTAL GENERA: *Aloysia, Callicarpa, Caryopteris, Citharexylum, Clerodendrum, Congea, Cornutia, Duranta, Gmelina, Holmskioldia, Lantana, Lippia, Petrea, Stachytarpheta, Tectona, Verbena, Vitex,* among others.

Callicarpa americana

AMERICAN BEAUTYBERRY,
FRENCH MULBERRY

PRONUNCIATION - ˌkæ lə ˈkɑr pə   ə ˌme rə ˈkā nə

TRANSLATION - [from Greek *kallos* (= beautiful) and *karpos* (= fruit), hence the common name] [American].

FORM - Monoecious, deciduous woody shrub, rounded, rather open, medium-coarse texture.

SIZE - To 8 feet with equal spread. Rapid growth rate.

HARDINESS ZONE - Zone 7. Grown in north and central Florida only.

NATIVE HABITAT - Southeastern U.S. from Virginia to Texas to central Florida, and West Indies.

LEAVES - Opposite, elliptic to ovate-lanceolate, 2.5 to 5 inches long, serrate, acuminate, pubescent beneath, relatively long, pubescent petioles, prominent veins, light green color.

STEM/BARK - New growth very pubescent, older growth gray-brown with prominent white lenticels, branches somewhat flattened at nodes.

FLOWERS - Small pale lavender-pink flowers in axillary cymes, in late spring, produced on new growth. Somewhat showy.

FRUIT - Berry-like drupe, about 0.33 inch across, magenta colored but also various shades of red, showy from August to November, persisting after leaves drop.

CULTURE - Full sun (heavier fruit set) or light shade, tolerates most well-drained soils. Not salt tolerant. Low-maintenance plant. Easily transplanted. Prune in fall after fruiting.

PROBLEMS - Relatively short-lived, reseeds readily. Few insect or disease problems.

PROPAGATION - Seed or softwood cuttings.

LANDSCAPE USES - Mass plantings, naturalized areas, attracts birds which feed on fruit. Cut fruiting branches are attractive in flower arrangements.

COMMENTS - Not readily available in the trade, but common in wooded areas. Variety *lactea* (syn. var. *alba*) has white fruit.

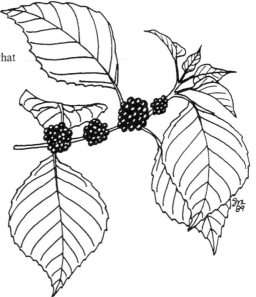

Clerodendrum thomsoniae

**BLEEDING HEART,
GLORYBOWER**

PRONUNCIATION - ˌkle rə ˈden drəm   tɑm ˈsō nē ē

TRANSLATION - [from Greek *kleros* (= chance) and *dendron* (= a tree), apparently in reference to the various medicinal properties of the plants] [after the wife of Rev. W. C. Thomson, who was in Africa 1849-1865].

FORM - Monoecious, evergreen; vine or semi-shrub; twining; coarse texture.

SIZE - Variable, up to 15 feet, height and spread determined by the size of support it grows on; rapid growth rate.

HARDINESS ZONE - Zones 9-11; persists year-round outdoors only in south Florida; can be grown in north and central Florida, but is killed to the ground by freezing temperatures.

NATIVE HABITAT - Tropical West Africa.

LEAVES - Simple; opposite; ovate, to 6 inches long; dark green; prominent veins, acuminate tips; entire margins.

STEM/BARK - Stems climb by twining around supports.

FLOWERS - Blood-red; salverform, to 0.5 inch wide; exserted styles and stamens; contained in greenish-white; 0.5 inch long; bag-like calyces; borne in cymes in the axils of terminal leaves. Blooms May to September.

FRUIT - Drupe; subtended by the persistent calyx.

CULTURE - Partial shade on fertile, well-drained, nematode-free soil; no salt tolerance.

PROBLEMS - Nematodes and mites.

PROPAGATION - Cuttings or seed.

LANDSCAPE USES - Grown as a vine or houseplant for the curiosity of its flowers.

Duranta erecta

GOLDEN DEWDROP

PRONUNCIATION - dū ˈræn tə ē ˈrek tə

TRANSLATION - [after Castore Durante (ca. 1529-1590), papal physician and botanist in Rome] [erect].

SYNONYM - *Duranta repens.*

FORM - Monoecious, evergreen; shrub or small tree; freely branching, irregular; pendulous growth, sprawling; medium-fine texture.

SIZE - To 18 feet, commonly 4 to 6 feet; moderate growth rate.

HARDINESS ZONE - Zone 9; can be grown in central and south Florida.

NATIVE HABITAT - Florida to Brazil.

LEAVES - Simple; opposite; ovate to obovate, to 4 inches long; papery texture; often clustered in leaf axils; serrate margins, especially at the apex. Petioles short.

STEM/BARK - Green, becoming woody with age; axillary thorns often present.

FLOWERS - Lilac; to 0.5 inch across; borne in pendulous terminal or axillary racemes, to 12 inches long; fragrant. Blooms in summer and fall.

FRUIT - Drupe; globular; yellow; to 0.5 inch in diameter; calyx lobes persist with fruit.

CULTURE - Full sun for best flowering, tolerates partial shade, various soils; no salt tolerance.

PROBLEMS - Scale, nematodes, chewing insects; sap may irritate; thorns a hazard.

PROPAGATION - Seeds, cuttings.

LANDSCAPE USES - Use as a border, hedge, or specimen plant or in foundation plantings for large buildings.

COMMENTS - A white-flowered cultivar, 'Alba', is available. Also, the related species *D. stenostachya* is grown in Florida.

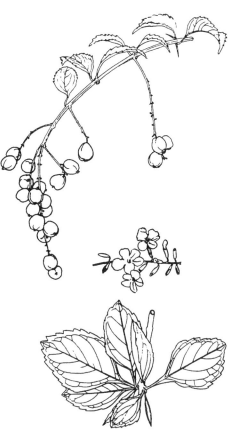

Lantana camara   LANTANA, YELLOW SAGE

PRONUNCIATION - læn ˈtæ nə   kə ˈmɑ rə

TRANSLATION - [Latin name for *Viburnum*, transferred on the basis of their inflorescence similarity] [South American name].

FORM - Evergreen shrub, erect, many-branched, spreading, rambling habit.

SIZE - To 5 feet, rapid growth rate.

HARDINESS ZONE - Zone 8. Can be grown in north, central, and south Florida. In north Florida it freezes back in winter but regrowth is rapid.

NATIVE HABITAT - Tropical America, naturalized in Florida, Australia, south Africa, India, and many other regions.

LEAVES - Simple, opposite, oblong-ovate, to 5 inches long, puckered interveinal regions; rough, rugose surface; aromatic when crushed; margins bluntly toothed.

STEM/BARK - Young growth square, stems hairy, prickly.

FLOWERS - Orange, yellow, reds, pinks; petals 4- to 5-lobed, united; to 0.25 inch across; in terminal or axillary heads to 2 inches across; flowers in summer and fall.

FRUIT - Drupe-like berry, clustered, fleshy, black, to 0.5 inch in diameter, toxic.

CULTURE - For best form and flowering: full sun on various, well-drained soils; highly salt tolerant.

PROBLEMS - Chewing insects, irritant sap, poisonous.

PROPAGATION - Seeds, cuttings.

LANDSCAPE USES - Borders or in planters. Heavily fruiting cultivars should be avoided.

COMMENTS - Many cultivars for flower color: combinations of orange, red, yellow, white, and purple are available. Several cultivars of various characteristics and flower colors are commonly offered for sale, including **'Banana Yellow', 'Confetti', 'Creme', 'Dallas Red', 'Denholm White', 'Flame', 'Gold Mound', 'Irene Red', 'New Gold', 'Orange', 'Patriot Rainbow', 'Pink Caprice', 'Pink Petite', 'Raspberry', 'Salmon', 'Samantha', 'Silver Mound', 'Sunburst Orange', 'Tangerine', 'Yellow Sage',** and **'Zeke Red'.** Also, other species and cultivars offered for sale include **L. depressa** (Pineland Trailing Lantana) and **L. involucrata 'Native White', 'Lavendar Swirl',** and **'Lavendar Weeping'.**

Lantana montevidensis   TRAILING LANTANA

PRONUNCIATION - læn ˈtæ nə   ˌmɑn tə və ˈden səs

TRANSLATION - [Latin name for *Viburnum*, transferred on the basis of their inflorescence similarity] [from Montevideo].

FORM - Monoecious, evergreen shrub or ground cover, low-growing, sprawling, fine-textured.

SIZE - Obtains a maximum height of 2 feet with a wide, variable spread; growth rate is rapid.

HARDINESS ZONE - Zone 9, grows in central and south Florida.

NATIVE HABITAT - South America, naturalized in lower southeastern United States.

LEAVES - Simple, opposite, rugose, ovate, to 1 inch long, with dentate margins and a pungent odor.

STEM/BARK - Unarmed, square, to 3 feet long.

FLOWERS - Lavender to purple, 1 to 2 inch wide dense heads on long, axillary peduncles; flowers during frost-free months of the year.

FRUIT - Drupe, small, black in blackberry-like clusters; normally not produced in Florida.

CULTURE - For compact growth and best flowering, full sun and well-drained soil; good salt tolerance. Needs topping twice a year; will not stand mowing or foot traffic.

PROBLEMS - Mites, caterpillars chew the leaves.

PROPAGATION - Softwood cuttings or ground layers.

LANDSCAPE USES - Ground cover in dry, rocky places or as a weeping planter specimen--very attractive spilling over a wall.

COMMENTS - Several cultivars are offered for sale, including **'Arlene Purple'** and **'Alba'**.

Petrea volubilis   QUEEN'S WREATH, SANDPAPER VINE

PRONUNCIATION - pə 'trē ə   vɑl 'yū bə ləs

TRANSLATION - [after Lord Robert James Petre (1713-1743), botanical and horticultural patron] [twining].

FORM - Monoecious, evergreen; woody vine; medium-coarse texture.

SIZE - Can climb to 35 feet; height and spread depend on plant age and size of the support; medium growth rate.

HARDINESS ZONE - Zones 10-11; can be grown in south Florida only.

NATIVE HABITAT - West Indies and Central America.

LEAVES - Simple; opposite or whorled; elliptic, to 6 inches long; very scabrous (like sandpaper) cuneate base, acuminate tip.

STEM/BARK - Stems climb by twining.

FLOWERS - Purple; 0.5 inch wide; subtended by 2-inch-wide, persistent lavender calyces, which are the main showy portion of the bloom; borne in 12-inch-long, hanging, axillary racemes, giving a wisteria-like effect. Blooms several times a year in spring and summer, with the best bloom in spring.

FRUIT - Drupe; enclosed by the withered calyx.

CULTURE - Full sun in any reasonably good soil; no salt tolerance.

PROBLEMS - No major pests.

PROPAGATION - Cuttings, air layers, or division of root suckers.

LANDSCAPE USES - Employed to cover arbors, fences, and other small structures.

Verbena × hybrida

GARDEN VERBENA

PRONUNCIATION - vər 'bē nə   'hī brə də

TRANSLATION - [Latin name for the foliage of ceremonial and medicinal plants] [hybrid].

FORM - Monoecious, evergreen; herbaceous perennial; usually grown as an annual; freely branching; stems creeping or decumbent.

SIZE - Varies with cultivar, to 1.5 feet; rapid growth rate.

HARDINESS ZONE - Zone 9; can be grown throughout Florida, mostly used as an annual. Killed to the ground by freezing temperatures, the plant will grow back from the rootstock.

NATIVE HABITAT - A selection from interspecific hybrid, the parents of which are native to North and South America.

LEAVES - Simple; opposite; ovate to ovate-oblong, to 4 inches long; truncate or broadly cuneate at base; margins toothed and cut or 3-cleft.

STEM/BARK - Green; 4-angled.

FLOWERS - Pink, red, white, yellowish, blue, purple, often with variegated, contrasting centers; corolla salverform, 5-lobed to 0.75 inch across; borne in terminal corymbs or broad panicles; fragrant.

FRUIT - Dry; enclosed in the persistent calyx; separating into 4 nutlets at maturity.

CULTURE - Full sun on various soils; no salt tolerance.

PROBLEMS - Scale, mealybugs, and chewing insects.

PROPAGATION - Seeds, cuttings.

LANDSCAPE USES - Use as an edging or bedding plant, or in window boxes, planters, and hanging baskets.

COMMENTS - Many cultivars for flower color and habit are available.

Vitex trifolia   VITEX

PRONUNCIATION - ˈvī teks   trī ˈfō lē ə

TRANSLATION - [Latin name for *Vitex agnus-castus*] [3-leaved].

FORM - Monoecious, evergreen shrub; irregular; fine texture.

SIZE - Reaches a height of 15 feet with a spread of 12 feet; rapid growth rate.

HARDINESS ZONE - Zone 9; can be planted in central and south Florida, but needs a protected location in central Florida.

NATIVE HABITAT - Asian tropics and Australia.

LEAVES - Trifoliolate; opposite; leaflets oblong-elliptic to obovate, to 3 inches long; white tomentose on undersides; pungent odor when crushed; middle leaflet largest.

STEM/BARK - New growth square.

FLOWERS - Blue to lilac; tiny, inconspicuous; borne in panicles of many-flowered cymes to 9 inches long. Blooms in summer.

FRUIT - Drupes; small.

CULTURE - Full sun or partial shade on a wide range of soils; does very well on sandy soils; marginal salt tolerance.

PROBLEMS - Scale and mushroom root rot can be problems.

PROPAGATION - Softwood cuttings.

LANDSCAPE USES - Employed as a hedge or screen, but requires much pruning to keep rampant weedy growth in check. Should not be used unless rapid growth is a major consideration.

COMMENTS - Cultivar **'Variegata'** has leaves with white marginal variegation and is most commonly planted. Other species of *Vitex* cultivated in Florida include *V. agnus-castus* (Chaste Tree), *V. cymosa* (Taruma Guazu), and *V. quinata*.

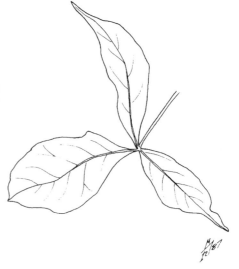

VITIDACEAE (= VITACEAE) - GRAPE FAMILY

DICOTYLEDONS; 12 GENERA AND ABOUT 700 SPECIES

GEOGRAPHY:	Mostly tropical and subtropical with a few representatives in the temperate regions.
GROWTH HABIT:	Tendril-bearing (usually modified inflorescences or shoots often with discoid suckers) climbers or sometimes erect caudiciform or succulent shrubs, often with swollen nodes.
LEAVES:	Alternate, simple or pinnately or palmately compound, usually distichous, often stipulate, frequently with pellucid dots on the lamina and sometimes succulent or leathery.
FLOWERS:	Inflorescences cymose, commonly opposite the leaves, bracteate; flowers small, unisexual or bisexual (plants usually monoecious but sometimes dioecious); sepals 4-5, small, and cup-shaped; petals 4-5, valvate, often united at the tips and falling off as a hood upon opening of the bud; stamens 4-5, epipetalous; carpels usually 2 but sometimes 3-6 and multilocular.
FRUIT:	A berry.
ECONOMIC USES:	*Vitis* (grapes) is economically very important as fruit and for wine making. Indeed, an entire field of agriculture (viticulture) is based on this genus. Several genera are important as ornamentals and succulent (especially caudiciform) species of *Cissus* (the largest genus) are much sought after.
ORNAMENTAL GENERA:	*Ampelopsis, Cissus, Parthenocissus, Rhoicissus, Tetrastigma, Vitis,* and perhaps others.
COMMENTS:	In earlier classifications the genera currently included in Leeaceae were recognized as members of Vitidaceae. Leeaceae is now generally accepted as a distinct family.

Cissus rhombifolia   GRAPE IVY

PRONUNCIATION - ˈsi səs ˌrɑm bə ˈfō lē ə

TRANSLATION - [from Greek *kissos* (= ivy)] [diamond-shaped leaves].

FORM - Monoecious, evergreen; herbaceous vine; trailing, or cascading; climbing by tendrils; medium texture.

SIZE - Variable, depends on support.

HARDINESS ZONE - Zones 10-11; south Florida only.

NATIVE HABITAT - Central and South America.

LEAVES - Trifoliolate; alternate; leaflets rhombic-ovate to 4 inches long; dark green; waxy above, pubescent beneath; coarsely serrate margins. Petioles and young stems covered with soft, shaggy, reddish-brown hairs.

STEM/BARK - Stems weak, hairy; with forked tendrils.

FLOWERS - Greenish; inconspicuous; 4 petals; borne in cymes.

FRUIT - Berry; small; inedible and may contain calcium oxalate crystals; rarely produced.

CULTURE - Outdoors in partial shade; tolerates light from 75 to 5000 foot-candles indoors; various well-drained soils; no salt tolerance.

PROBLEMS - Aphids, scale, mites, mealybugs, and nematodes.

PROPAGATION - Cuttings or layering.

LANDSCAPE USES - As an interior plant, used in hanging baskets or on pedestals where the cascading stems with long internodes can trail. Outdoors used as a ground cover or lattice covering.

COMMENTS - Several other species of *Cissus* are cultivated in Florida, including *Cissus amazonica, C. antarctica* (Kangaroo Vine), *C. discolor* (Rex-begonia Vine), *C. trifoliata (= C. incisa),* and *C. quadrangularis* (Four-Angled Vine). Several caudiciform succulent species are grown by collectors.

Glossary of the Common Terms Used in Plant Identification

A

A - A Greek prefix meaning 'without'.

Ab - A Latin prefix meaning 'away from'.

Abaxial. On the side away from the axis. For example, the lower side of a leaf is its abaxial side. (*syn.* **Dorsal**, *opp.* **Ventral** or **Adaxial**).

Abscission. Falling off, as in leaves or flowers.

Acaulescent. Without a stem; or with very short, scarcely evident stem, as in *Gerbera jamesonii* (Asteraceae).

Accessory fruit. A fruit in which a major portion consists of tissue derived from other parts of the flower, as in apple, pear, strawberry, etc.

Accessory organ. Any organ additional to the normal number; sometimes specifically in reference to the calyx and/or corolla which have no direct function in reproduction.

Achene. A small, dry, one-chambered, one-seeded indehiscent fruit. For example, fruit of the family Asteraceae.

Acicular. Needle-shaped.

Acorn. Fruit of *Quercus* spp. (oaks), consisting of a nut embedded in a cup (*cf.* **Cupule**).

Acrid. Sharp, bitter, or irritating acid taste.

Actinomorphic. Flowers with radial symmetry (*cf.* **Regular**). A line drawn through the center of such flower, in any direction, will divide the flower into two equal halves, for example, in *Petunia*.

Aculeate. Armed with a thorn or prickle, as the stem of a rose.

Acuminate. Narrowly tapering to a sharp point, as in a leaf apex.

Acute. Tapering more broadly than acuminate to a sharp point.

Ad -. A Latin prefix meaning 'at' or 'toward'.

Adaxial. Facing toward the primary axis. For example, the upper side of a leaf. (*syn.* **Ventral**, *opp.* **Dorsal** or **Abaxial**).

Adnate, adnation. United, referring to the union of dissimilar organs, such as ovary with receptacle, or stamen with corolla. (*cf.* **Connate**).

Adpressed, appressed. Pressed closely to an axis upward with a narrow angle of divergence, such as subulate leaves of *Juniperus*.

Adventitious. Appearing in other than the usual place, as roots from the stem or stems from roots (suckers).

Aerating roots. Knee roots; horizontal or vertical above ground roots (also see **Pneumatophore**).

Aerial. Living above the surface of the ground.

Aestivation, estivation. The mode of folding of flower parts in the bud before expansion.

Aggregate fruit. Fruit formed by the coherence of the carpels that were distinct in the flower, as in raspberry.

Air plants. See **Epiphyte**.

Air roots. See **Adventitious, Pneumatophore, Knee**.

Ala (*pl.* **Alae**). One of the lateral petals (wings) of papilionaceous flower.

Alate. Winged, as in stem of *Ulmus alatus* (winged elm); having a winglike extension, as in petiole of *Citrus* spp., rachis of *Rhus capolina*, and samara of *Acer* and other plants.

586

Alba, albus. A Latin word meaning 'white'.

Ament. See **Catkin**.

Amentiferous. Bearing aments or catkins, as in Salicaceae and Betulaceae.

Amplexicaul. Said of a sessile leaf whose base clasps the stem. (*syn.* **Clasping**)

Analytical key. An orderly arrangement of contrasting or comparable statements about plants or plant structures, leading to identification.

Andro -. A Greek prefix meaning 'male'.

Androecium. Collective term for the stamens of a flower.

Angiosperm. Any flowering plant; plants that produce seeds enclosed within a carpel. (*syn.* **Anthophyta**)

Annual. A plant that completes its life cycle in one growing season. In horticulture this term sometimes used in reference to perennial plants which are used as bedding plants but are replaced seasonally (*Antirrhinum, Petunia, Impatiens*, etc.).

Ante -. A Latin prefix meaning 'before'.

Anterior. Position of the flower when it is turned away from the axis and toward the bracts.

Anther. The pollen-bearing segment of the stamen.

Anthesis. Time when a flower begins to expand. (This term has been defined by various authors as the beginning of the opening of a flower; a fully expanded flower; when a flower is ready to be pollinated; or the period from flowering to fruit set).

Anthophyta. Flowering plants. (*syn.* **Angiospermae**)

Apetalous. A flower lacking petals. (*cf.* **Petaliferous, Polypetalous**).

Apex (*pl.* **Apices**). Summit; the tip; the growing point of roots and shoots (apical meristem).

Apical. Belonging to or situated at the apex.

Apocarpous, apocarpy. Composed of distinct or separate carpels. (*cf.* **Syncarpous**).

Apogeotropic. Negatively geotropic, such as the specialized roots of cycads that grow upward above the soil surface.

Apomictic. Plants that produce seed without fertilization.

Apomixis. The ability of certain plants to produce seeds without fertilization.

Apopetalous. Having many free petals. (*syn.* **Polypetalous**)

Aquatic. Plants that are adapted to growing in water.

Arbor. A Latin word meaning 'tree'.

Arborescent. Tree-like; attaining the size or character of a tree.

Arboretum (*pl.* **arboreta**). A place where trees, shrubs, and other primarily woody plants are grown for research, education, and introduction purposes.

Aril. An outgrowth or covering of a seed originating from the helium or funiculus (*cf.* aril in Taxaceae and Podocarpaceae).

Arillate. Seed with an aril, such as that of Taxaceae, Podocarpaceae, etc.

Arista. An awn; a bristle-like appendage on the glums of grasses.

Aristate. Awned; bearing a stiff, bristly appendage, as in Poaceae.

Armature. Bristles, barbs, hooks, prickles, spines, or thorns.

Armed. Any structure with stiff, sharp bristles, spines, or thorns.

Armor. A covering of old leaf bases on cycads, palms, and some ferns.

Aromatic. Having an aroma, as when some leaves are crushed; a group of organic compounds, as essential oils of plants.

Arrangement. Disposition of organs or parts with respect to one another.

Asepalous. Without sepals.

Asymmetric. Without symmetry; irregular in shape and outline. (*syn.* **Zygomorphic**)

Attenuate. Narrowed; terminating in a long, slender point, as in the apex of a leaf.

Atypical. Not typical; unusual; abnormal.

Aureus. A Latin word meaning 'golden'.

Auto -. A Greek prefix meaning 'self'.

Autogamy. Self-pollination. (*opp.* **outcrossing, xenogamy**)

Awl-shaped. Narrow and gradually tapering to a sharp point, as in juvenile leaves of *Juniperus*. (*syn.* **Subulate**)

Awn. A stiff, bristle-like appendage. A beard, as on the tip of the glumes and lemmas of most grasses.

Axial. Belonging to the main axis.

Axil. The angle formed by a leaf with the stem to which it is attached.

Axillary. Situated in the axil of a leaf.

Axis. The line running lengthwise through the center of an organ, as in a flower or a stem. The term is also applied to the stem itself or to the receptacle of a flower.

B

Banner. The large, broad, upper petal in the flower of Fabaceae (*syn.* **Standard**).

Barb. A hooked or doubly hooked trichome.

Barbate. Bearded, usually with a tuft of long, stiff hairs.

Barbed. Having barbs.

Bark. Protective suberized tissue on the stem of woody plants.

Basal. Situated at the base.

Base. The end or the lower portion of a plant organ nearest to the point of attachment to another organ.

Beaked. A prominent stiff projection on certain carpels, fruit, or seeds.

Beard. An awn, as in the grasses. A cluster of hairs in some corollas, as in some species of *Iris*.

Bedding plants. A common term used in horticulture to designate annual or perennial flowering plants used in the garden for temporary color, usually replaced seasonally.

Berry. A fleshy indehiscent fruit, from one or more carpels and with one to many seeds, for example, *Persea* (avocado), *Lycopersicum* (tomato), etc.

Bi -. From the Latin word Bis, meaning 'two', 'twice', or 'having two'.

Biennial. A plant that lives through two growing seasons, flowering and fruiting the second year, then dying, for example, *Dacus carrota* (carrot).

Bifid. Two-cleft; forked into two limbs to near the middle, for example, stigmata of the Euphorbiaceae.

Bifoliate. A plant with two leaves, as *Welwitschia mirabilis*.

Bifoliolate. A compound leaf with two leaflets.

Bifurcate. Branched, as a Y-shaped stigmata or trichome, or **Dichotomous** venation.

Bigeminate. In two pairs; with two orders of leaflets. (*syn*. **Bijugate**)

Bijugate. See Bigeminate.

Bilabiate. Two-lipped, referring especially to the corolla, as in Scrophulariaceae or Lamiaceae (Labiatae).

Bilocular. Two-celled, as applied to an ovary or a fruit with two locules.

Binomial nomenclature. According to the code of botanical nomenclature, which is also fully accepted by horticultural taxonomists, the name of each plant species consists of two parts: a generic name and a specific epithet, both in Latin or Latinized form.

Biogeography. The geographical distribution of living organisms. (*cf.* **Phytogeography**)

Bipinnate. Twice-pinnate, referring to compound leaves.

Bipinnatifid. Twice-pinnatifid, for example, *Nandina domestica* and certain ferns.

Bisexual. Having both stamens and carpels (a "perfect" flower).

Blade. The expanded portion of a leaf, which is usually broad, flat, thin, and green. (*syn*. **Lamina**)

Bloom. The white waxy covering on many leaves and fruits; in vernacular sense synonymous with blossom or flower.

Blotched. The color disposed in broad, irregular spots, on leaves or petals.

Bole. The main trunk of a tree; a caudex.

Bonsai. The exaggerated dwarfing of plants by means of root and shoot pruning; a plant so created.

Bordered. One color surrounded by a narrow margin of another, often characteristic of cultivars, as in *Euonymous*.

Bract. A much reduced leaf, usually subtending a flower or an inflorescence, for example, red bracts of *Euphorbia pulcherima* (poinsettia), colored bracts of *Bougainvillea*, petal-like bracts of *Cornus florida* (dogwood). (*cf.* **Involucre**; **Phyllary**).

Bracteate. Furnished with bracts.

Bracteole. A small bract, usually on the pedicel.

Bramble. Any prickly, sprawling shrub or vine, as blackberry.

Brevi -. A Latin prefix meaning 'short'.

Breviloba, brevilobus. With short lobes.

Bristle. Stiff hairs.

Bristly. Covered with stiff hairs; like a bristle.

Bud. A resting structure that may develop into an inflorescence or stem.

Bud scales. Specialized protective leaves that cover the buds during winter months to prevent desiccation and injury.

Bud scale scars. Scars left on the branch by the abscission of the bud scales from the terminal buds of the previous year.

Bulb. A short, thick, modified stem, the leaves of which are thickened and store reserved food, as in Amaryllidaceae (*Eucharis*, *Hippeastrum*, etc.) and Alliaceae (*Allium*, *Tulbaghia*, etc.). (*cf.* **Tunicate, Nontunicate,** or **Scaly bulb**).

Bulbel. A bulblet that arises from the mother bulb.

Bulbiferous. A bulbous plant.

Bulblet. A small bulb.

Bulbil. Bulblets borne singly or in clusters in the leaf axil (as in some Liliaceae) or in the inflorescences (as in some Amaryllidaceae).

Bulbous. Having the characteristic of a bulb; producing bulb.

Bush. A vernacular word referring to small shrubs or subshrubs. In plant geography it denotes scrubby vegetation.

Buttress. Tree trunk with a widening base, caused by the extension of the roots on the soil surface, as in *Taxodium distichum* (swamp cypress) or *Ficus* (figs) in the tropics.

C

Caespitose, cespitose. In tufts; in cushions, often characteristic of plants at higher elevations or some members of the Cactaceae, Crassulaceae, etc.

Callus. A thickened, raised area, which is usually hard; specifically in reference to the hard and often waxy projections on lips of orchid flowers, such as that of *Phalaenopsis*.

Calybium. A hard unilocular, dry fruit derived from an inferior ovary, as in *Quercus* (Fagaceae).

Calyx (*pl*. **Calyces**). The outer set of the perianth segment of a flower; collective term for sepals. It may be distinct or connate, and in some plants it may resemble the petals (*cf.* **Tepal**).

Calyx lobe. The free portion of a gamopetalous calyx.

Calyx tube. The tube of a gamopetalous calyx. Sometimes used for the hypanthium or receptacle of perigynous and epigynous flowers.

Campanulate. Bell-shaped, usually in reference to form of flowers, as in Campanulaceae.

Canescence, canescent. Bearing a hoary, grayish pubescence.

Capitulum. A dense inflorescence consisting of an aggregation of sessile or subsessile flowers.

Capsule. A dry dehiscent fruit (pod); with two or more carpels (compound ovary), usually with several to many seeds.

Carpel. The ovuliferous organ of the flower; a simple pistil or one of the segments of a compound pistil. It is a modified seed-bearing leaf, consisting of three segments: the swollen basal portion (ovary), the elongated portion (style), and a receptive head (stigma). (*cf.* **Gynoecium**).

Carpellate. Possessing carpel(s), in reference to pistillate (female) flowers.

Caryopsis. The one-seeded, indehiscent grain (fruit) of grasses.

Cataphyll. Small scale leaves of the rhizome in angiosperms; protective winter bud scales of trees and shrubs; scale leaves of cycads. They function in storage and protection.

Catkin. An ament; an elongate, pendulous, cluster (spike) of unisexual, apetalous, and often bracteate flowers, as in Salicaceae, Betulaceae, Fagaceae, etc.

Caudex. The short thickened stem of some xerophytic plants. It may be above or below ground; it functions as water storage and occurs in several angiosperm families, for example, Agavaceae (*Beaucarnia*), Apocynaceae (*Pachypodium*, *Adenium*), Passifloraceae (*Adenia*), etc. The word is also used for the trunk of cycads.

Caul -. A Latin prefix meaning 'stem'.

Caulescent. With a leafy stem. Usually in reference to a flower stalk with leaves. (*cf.* **Acaulescent**).

Cauliflory. Bearing flowers on old stems, as in *Cercis* (Redbud, Fabaceae), *Crecetia cujete* (Cannonball tree, Bignoniaceae).

Cauline. Growing on a stem; belonging to a stem or branch.

Chaff. Small, more or less dry, membranous bract; especially the small bracts at the base of disk flowers of some Asteraceae. Flower parts of the cereal grains removed during milling.

Chambered pith. In stems, where a solid core is replaced by a partitioned pith.

Channeled. With one or more longitudinal grooves. Hollowed like a gutter, as in the petiole of some monocotolydons.

Character. Taxonomically, any well-defined feature that distinguishes one taxon from another. Genetically, any feature that is transmitted from parents to offspring, or may result from gene-environment interaction.

Chimera. A plant composed of two genetically distinct tissues adjacent to one another, for example, by spontaneous mutation, as in branches with variegated leaves in otherwise normally green plants, or may be artificially induced by grafting (Periclinal chimera) or colchicine treatment.

Ciliate. Fringed with hairs along the margins.

Circinate. Said of a leaf that is coiled or rolled from the tip toward the base with the lower surface outermost and the tip near the center, for example, circinate vernation of ferns.

Circumscissile. Dehiscing or separating by a circular zone, as the valve of a capsule coming off as a lid.

Cirrhous, cirrhus, cirrus. A coiled apex; a curl, tendril-like climbing organ, as in leaf tips of *Gloriosa* (Liliaceae), or the antennae on the lips of some orchids, such as *Phalaenopsis amabilis*.

Cladode, cladophyll. A branch modified so as to resemble a leaf; a flattened photosynthetic stem as in certain species of *Asparagus* (Liliaceae) and *Epiphyllum* (Cactaceae), *Ruscus* (Ruscaceae), etc.

Clambering. Sprawling across objects but not climbing, as *Wisteria* spp. and other vines.

Clasping. A sessile leaf that partly or wholly surrounds the stem, as in most monocots. (*syn.* **Amplexicaul**)

Class. A group of plants ranking above an order and below a division.

Classification. The orderly (systematic) arrangement of plants into groups, or their assignment to a hierarchy, based on common characteristics. For example, a group of species make up a genus, and a group of genera constitute a family, etc.

Claw. The narrow stalk (base) of some petals, resembling a petiole, as in some members of Brassicaceae (mustard family). Also **Tendril.**

Cleft. Divided to the middle, as in palmately lobed leaves in which the sinus is only about halfway to the midrib.

Climber, climbing. A plant that grows upward and uses other plants or objects as support. Various specialized organs may be used for this purpose, such as roots, claws, or growing tip of the plant..

Clone. From the Greek word *clon* (a branch), a group of genetically identical individuals resulting from vegetative propagation (cuttings, grafting, tissue culture, or division). In horticulture this is considered one of the categories of cultivar.

Clustered. A general term used to describe a closely crowded, many-branched inflorescence of small flowers.

Coalescence. Union of like parts; coming together. (*cf.* **Connate**)

Column. The part of the flower of an orchid which is formed by the fusion of the style and the filaments, and which supports the anthers and the stigma (*syn.* **Gynostemium**); the basal twisted portion of an awn in grasses; the fused staminal tube in Malvaceae; the structure that supports the hood of a pitcher plant leaf.

Columnar. Trees that have an erect main trunk but missing or self-pruning lateral branches, as pines and arborescent single trunk palms.

Coma. The trichomes attached to the testa of some seeds; the leafy crown of such plants as palms and cycads.

Comose. Having tufted hairs.

Companulate. Bell-shaped, as in flowers of Companulaceae.

Complete flower. A flower with all parts present: sepals, petals, stamens, and carpels.

Complete leaf. Leaf with blade, petiole, and stipules.

Compound. Composed of a number of similar united parts, as carpels in a syncarpus gynoecium; divided into a number of similar parts or divisions, as leaflets of a compound leaf.

Compound cyme. A branched cyme.

Compound fruit. See **Aggregate fruit**.

Compound inflorescence. An inflorescence with secondary branches (coflorescences), as in some Euphorbiaceae (e.g., *Jatropha*).

Compound leaf. A leaf with two or more leaflets; in some cases the lateral leaflet may have been lost (e.g., *Citrus*) and only the terminal leaflet remains. Ternately compound, when the leaflets are in threes. Palmately compound, when all leaflets arise from a common point at the end of the petiole, as in *Schefflera*. Pinnately compound, when leaflets are arranged along a rachis, as in species of Anacardiaceae (e.g., *Pistacia*). Odd-pinnate, when the total number of leaflets is an odd number and a single leaflet terminates the leaf (e.g., *Carya*, *Juglans*; Juglandaceae). Even-pinnate, when the total number of leaflets is an even

number and there is no terminal leaflet (e.g., *Koelreuteria*, goldenrain tree).

Compound umbel. A raceme consisting of a large number of heads rising close together at the end of a main branch, as in *Fatsia* (Araliaceae).

Condensed. An inflorescence the flowers of which are crowded together, and are nearly or completely sessile.

Cone. See **Strobilus**.

Congested. Crowded.

Conical. Cone-shaped.

Conifer. A general term referring to the Coniferales, one of the four groups of gymnosperms, as *Juniperus*, *Cupressus*, *Taxodium*, *Podocarpus*, *Pinus*, etc.

Coniferous. Cone-bearing, as in conifers.

Connate. Union or fusion of similar structures, as in petals, sepals, or leaves.

Connate-perfoliate. When the bases of two opposite, sessile leaves appear to have fused around the stem, as in the juvenile form of some *Eucalyptus* species, or the pair of leaves immediately below the inflorescence in *Lonicera sempervirens*.

Coralloid roots. The dichotomously branched, nodulated roots of cycads which occur on or near the soil surface (*cf.* **Apogeotropic**) and are associated with nitrogen-fixing blue-green algae (*Nostoc*, *Anabaena*).

Cordate, cordiform. Heart-shaped, in reference to the base or shape of a leaf.

Coriaceous. Thick and leathery, often in reference to leaf texture.

Corm. A short, erect, thick, solid, subterranean stem, with distinct nodes and internodes, enclosed within dry scale-like leaves, and functioning in food storage.

Cormel. A corm arising vegetatively along a node from a mother corm.

Corolla. A collective term referring to petals of a flower; the inner perianth segments. If the petals are separate the corolla is said to be polypetalous, but if the corolla is fused (connate) then it is gamopetalous or sympetalous.

Corolla tube. A tube-like structure resulting from fusion of the petals along their edges, as in tubular flowers of some Amaryllidaceae and Rubiaceae.

Corona. A collar-like or tubular appendage of the corolla and the stamens, as in *Narcissus* (not to be confused with staminal cup of such genera as *Eucharis*). The outgrowth of the staminal part of the flowers in milkweeds (Asclepiadaceae).

Coronate. Having a corona.

Corrugate. Irregularly folded or wrinkled.

Corymb. A flat-topped racemose inflorescence, the main axis of which is elongated, but the pedicels of the older flowers longer than those of the younger flowers (the outer flowers open first).

Corymbose. Arranged in corymbs.

Cosmopolitan. An organism that is worldwide in distribution.

Costa (*pl.* **costae**). The midvein of a single leaf in angiosperms or the pinna or pinnule of ferns, or the rachis of a pinnately compound leaf.

Costapalmate. A petiole that extends into the palmately compound leaf of certain palms, as in *Sabal palmetto*.

Cotyledon. Seed leaf; embryonic leaves which often appear upon germination of seeds.

Creeper. A plant with trailing shoots that root along the length of the stem as it grows. Such plants are often used as ground covers in the landscape.

Crenate. Shallowly round-toothed; scalloped.

Crenulate. Minutely or finely crenate.

Crest, crested. An irregular ridge or an outgrowth on a structure, as in the hornlike projection from the hood of the corona in milkweed (Asclepiadaceae) flowers or lips of orchids. In some plants such as cacti or cactoid euphorbs the term refers to a grotesque form of flattened stems with irregular ridges.

Cross-pollination. The transfer of pollen from the anther of one plant to the stigma of another. (*syn.* **Xenogamy**; *opp.* **Self-pollination** or **Autogamy**)

Crownshaft. A green pillar-like extension of the trunk in certain palms, formed by the overlapping petiole bases of new leaves, as in *Roystonia* (Arecaceae).

Crozier. The curled end of the developing frond of a fern.

Culm. The stem of grasses or bamboos.

Cultigen. Plants or group of plants originating in cultivation and known only from cultivation, for example, maize and cabbage. (*cf.* **Indigen**).

Cultivar. Cultivated variety. Plants selected from the wild or individuals cultivated because of a particularly desirable morphological, physiological, chemical, or other feature. Most cultivated food, fiber, and ornamental plants are actually cultivars.

Cuneate. Wedge-shaped; triangular, with the narrow end at the point of attachment, as the bases of some leaves or petals.

Cuneiform. See **Cuneate**.

Cup. A hollow floral receptacle.

Cupped. In reference to cup-shaped floral segments.

Cupule. Cuplike structure at the base of some fruits, formed by the fusion of involucral bracts at their bases, as in some palms and oaks.

Cuspidate. Having a rigid, sharp point.

Cuticle. A layer of waxy or fatty material on the outer walls of epidermal cells, as in leaf surfaces.

Cutting. A method of vegetative propagation, using pieces of leaves, stems, or roots.

Cyathium. A reduced inflorescence resembling a single flower, as in the subfamily Euphorbioidae, family Euphorbiaceae (*Euphorbia*, *Pedilanthus*, etc.). A cyathium includes one pistillate and several staminate flowers, as well as one or more large nectariferous glands.

Cyclic. Having floral parts in whorls.

Cymba. Boat-shaped.

Cyme. A broad, more or less flat-topped determinate inflorescence, with the central flowers opening first.

Cypsela. An achene derived from a unilocular, inferior ovary, as in the indehiscent fruits of Asteraceae (Compositae).

D

Deciduous. The falling of leaves at the end of a growing season by trees and shrubs, usually in the fall. The term may also refer to early shedding of petals, sepals, or stipules.

Decompound. More than once compound.

Decumbent. Declining or lying on the ground, but with branch tips ascending and without formation of adventitious roots. (*cf.* **Procumbent, Repens**).

Decurrent. Said of trees without a central leader and many lateral branches (*cf.* **Deliquescent, Excurrent**). A leaf base that extends down the stem, resembling two wings, as in many Asteraceae.

Decussate. Opposite leaves alternating at right angles with those above and below.

A four-ranked leaf arrangement. (*cf.* **Distichous**).

Definite. When parts are always the same number in a given species, as in stamens.

Dehiscence. The method or process of opening of a fruit (seed pod) or anther; **Loculicidal** when the split opens into a cavity or locule, **Septicidal** when opening at the point of union of septum (partition) to the side, **Circumscissile** when the top valve comes off as a lid, and **Poricidal** when opening by means of pores.

Deliquescent. Trees having many lateral branches but lacking a central leader, as in maple (*Acer*), elm (*Ulmus*), etc. (*cf.* **Decurrent, Excurrent**).

Deltoid. Triangular.

Dendron. A Greek word meaning *tree*.

Dentate. A leaf or petal margin with teeth.

Denticulate. Of a leaf margin having small teeth.

Depressed. Pressed downward close to the axis; more or less flattened endwise or from above.

Descending. Growing or hanging downward, as in the branches of certain trees.

Desert. A region of scant rainfall and with poor or more or less xerophytic vegetation.

Determinate growth. Growth of limited duration, characteristic of leaves and inflorescences. (*opp.* **Indeterminate growth**).

Determinate inflorescence. An inflorescence in which the terminal flower develops first, thereby arresting further elongation of the axis. (*opp.* **Indeterminate inflorescence**).

Diagnosis. A brief description of a taxon (often in Latin), with special reference to the characteristics that distinguish it from related, morphologically similar taxa.

Diagnostic characteristics. Clearly defined characteristics that separate one plant from another.

Dichasium. A determinate cymose inflorescence with a central female and lateral male flowers, the female developing first.

Dichotomous, dichotomy. Forked branching, produced by division of the apical meristem into two branches and may be repeated several times. This feature is primarily characteristic of such primitive plants as *Psilotum*, but also occurs in advanced plants such as *Adenium* (Apocynaceae).

Dichotomous key. An identification tool in which each division is divided into a pair of contrasting statements.

Diclesium. An achene or nut enclosed within a free but persistent calyx, as in *Mirabilis* (Nyctaginaceae).

Dicot. An abbreviated term for dicotyledons.

Dicotyledon, dicotyledonous. One of the two divisions of angiosperms, which is characterized by two cotyledons, netted (*cf.* **Reticulate**) leaves, well-organized vascular bundles, a tap root, and flower parts in fours, fives, or rarely in twos (or multiples thereof). (*cf.* **Monocotyledon**)

Digitate. Diverging from a central point as in the fingers of a hand. Usually in reference to palmately compound leaves, such as *Shefflera*.

Dimorphic, dimorphous. Having two distinct forms.

Dioecious. Having pistillate and staminate flowers on different plants, as in *Ilex* spp., Cycadales, etc.

Disc. A fleshy outgrowth from the receptacle of a flower beneath carpels or stamens; the receptacle in the head of

Asteraceae (in this case the word is spelled **Disk**).

Discolor. Not the same color throughout.

Disk floret. The tubular flowers in central portion of the capitulum of Asteraceae. (*cf.* **Ray floret**)

Dissected. Divided into many slender segments.

Distichous. In two rows, on opposite sides of the stem; leaves that are arranged in two vertical rows, as in two-ranked leaves. (*cf.* **Decussate**).

Distinct. Separate, not united with parts in the same series, as in petals of a polypetalous flower. (*cf.* **Free**).

Distribution. Geographical area inhabited by a given taxonomic unit (**Taxon**).

Diurnal. Opening only during daylight hours.

Divided. Cut or separated nearly to the base or to the midrib, as in a leaf.

Division. The largest unit in classification hierarchy of plants and animals.

Dormancy. A period of inactivity. The term applies to plants or the seeds after maturation but before germination.

Dorsal. Back, referring to the back or outer surface of an organ, as the lower side of a leaf. (*syn.* **Abaxial**; *opp.* **Ventral**).

Double flower. A flower with more than the usual number of petals.

Double-serrate. With coarse serrations bearing minute teeth in their margins, or alternating fine and coarse teeth.

Downy. Covered with a dense but fine coat of short soft hairs.

Drupaceous. Of the nature or texture of a drupe, but not necessarily with the structure of one.

Drupe. A fleshy one-seeded indehiscent fruit with a single seed enclosed within a stony endocarp, as in *Prunus* spp. (peach, cherry, etc.) (*syn*. **Stone Fruit**).

Druplet. A single fruit of an aggregate drupe, as in raspberry or blackberry.

Dry fruit. Any fruit which at maturity has dry ovary walls.

Dwarf. Very small, as selected cultivars of fruit trees or landscape plants.

E

E - or ex -. A Latin prefix meaning *without*; missing parts, as in estipulate or exstipulate (without stipules).

Ebracteate. Without bracts.

Ecotype. An ecological variant of a species which is adapted to a particular environment. For example, *Acer rubrum* (red maple) is found from south Florida to Canada, from subtropical to cool temperate climate. Although infrequently used in horticulture, this term is most useful in plant selection for climatic adaptability.

Elliptic (elliptical). Like an ellipse, broadest at the middle, tapering broadly and evenly toward each end.

Elongate. Stretched out, lengthened.

Emarginate. With a shallow notch at the apex.

Embryo. A young plant developing from an egg cell (zygote) within a seed; the juvenile sporophyte in the seed which consists of cotyledons, the radicle, and the plumule.

Enation. An epidermal outgrowth.

Endemic. Native and geographically restricted to a given area. (*cf*. **Indigenous**).

Endo -. A Greek prefix meaning 'within'.

Endocarp. The inner layer of a fruit wall, usually woody, as in the stony part of a drupe.

Entire. Without indentation or lobes on the margins, as in leaves of *Magnolia*.

Epetiolate. Without a petiole. (*cf*. **Sessile**)

Epetiolulate. Without a petiolule. (*cf*. **Sessile**)

Epi -. A Greek prefix meaning 'upon' or 'above'.

Epicalyx. A series of bracts below and alternating with sepals but resembling a true calyx.

Epicarp. The outer layer of the pericarp (syn. **Exocarp**).

Epigynous, epigyny. Flowers with an inferior ovary are said to be epigynous because all floral parts arise on top of the ovary or gynoecium, as in the family Onagraceae (for example, *Fuchsia*).

Epipetalous. Borne on or attached to the petals, often in reference to the stamens.

Epiphyte, epiphytic. Plants that grow on branches of trees (or on other objects) but are not parasitic, as in most orchids, ferns, bromeliads, etc.

Epithet, epecific epithet. The specific name applied to a species binomial. For example the word 'virginiana' is the specific epithet for *Magnolia virginiana*.

Equitant. Two ranked leaves with overlapping bases, as in *Iris*.

Eramous. Having unbranched stems, as in *Nandina domestica*.

Erect. Upright. straight up from the ground.

Erose. A leaf margin that appears eroded and jagged, but not toothed or fringed.

Espalier. Plants that are trained to grow in a geometric design against walls or

Estipulate. Without stipules.

Ethnobotany. Study of plants with respect to their use by various cultures.

Even-pinnate. See **Compound leaf**.

Evergreen. A plant that remains green during the dormant season. Although this term is properly applied to plants rather than leaves, the reference is made to the green leaves that remain on the plant for more than one growing season. (*cf.* **Deciduous**).

Excurrent. Extending beyond the apex, as in a vein that runs out beyond the lamina to form a mucronate apex; a tree with a central leader and self-pruning or relatively short lateral branches, for example, most conifers, many palms, and many dicotyledonous trees (e.g., *Liquidambar styraciflua, Liriodendron tulipifera*).

Exfoliate. The falling away in flakes, layers, or scales, usually in reference to tree bark.

Exindusiate. Without an indusium, as in the Polypodiaceae ferns.

Exo -. A Greek prefix meaning 'without' or 'outside of'.

Exocarp. The outermost layer of a fruit. (*syn.* **Epicarp**)

Exotic. Not native, introduced from a distant area.

Exstipulate. Without stipules.

Extant. Currently living (*opp.* **Extinct**).

Extinct. No longer living (*opp.* **Extant**).

Eye. A vegetative bud, as in potato.

F

F1. The first generation of a cross between two individuals.

F2, F3, F4, etc. The second, third, fourth, etc. generations of a cross resulting from self-fertilization of the F1.

Falcate. Sickle-shaped.
Falls. The drooping portion of the perianth of an *Iris* flower. (*cf.* **Standard**).

False indusium. A covering formed by the inrolling of the leaf margin of some ferns, as in *Adiantum*.

Family. A taxonomic category between an order and a genus. A group of related genera constitute a family. Familial names of plants terminate with the suffix -aceae. Eight family names have been conserved and terminate with the suffix -ea, although their use is optional (e.g., Palmae = Arecaceae).

Fascicle, fasciculate. A tuft of leaves or flowers arising from the same location, as in needles of pines, or tuberous roots, as in *Dahlia*.

Fastigiate. With erect branches that are more or less appressed to form an exaggerated form of excurrent growth habit, for example, *Cupressus sempervirens* 'Italica Stricta' (Italian cypress) or *Cephalotaxus harringtonia* 'Fastigiata'.

Fibrous. Having fibers or structures that resemble fibers, as in the leaves or trunk of some palms.

Fibrous root. A mass of fine adventitious roots of more or less equal thickness. These are primarily characteristic of monocotyledons.

Filament. The stalk of a stamen that supports the anther.

Filiferous. With thread-like appendages, often used in reference to leaf margins. (*syn.* **Filamentous**)

Filiform. Thread-like.

Fimbriate. Fringed along the margins, as in flower of *Brassavola digbyana*.

Fissured. Split or cracked, as in some tree barks.

Flabellate, flabelliform. Fan-shaped, as in the leaves of *Ginkgo biloba*

(Ginkgoaceae) and *Caryota mitis* (Arecaceae), pinnae of *Adiantum*, etc.

Flaccid. Lax, weak, or limp.

Fleshy root. A thick, succulent root. (*cf.* **Tuberous root**)

Flora. The plants of a particular area; a descriptive treatment of plants of a particular area which includes a key for identification.

Floral tube. A tubular flower formed by the fusion of sepals, petals, and stamens, usually characteristic of perigynous or epigynous flowers.

Floret. A small flower, as in the spikelet of grasses or the ray and disk florets of Asteraceae.

Floriculture. The growing of flowers under controlled conditions, including cut flowers and potted flowering plants.

Floriferous. Flowering freely; producing a profusion of flowers.

Flower. The reproductive structure of angiosperms, typically made up of a calyx (the sepals), corolla (the petals), androecium (the stamens), and gynoecium (the carpels). The axis upon which these organs are attached is the **Receptacle**.

Foliaceous. Leafy, leaflike.

Foliage. A collective term for leaves of a plant. In horticulture leafy plants specifically grown for indoor use.

Foliar. Pertaining to leaves or leaf-like parts.

Foliate. Having leaves.

Foliolate. Having leaflets, as in compound leaves.

Follicetum. An aggregate of follicles, the product of multiple carpels, as in Magnoliaceae.

Follicle. A dry fruit formed from a single carpel, usually dehiscing along the ventral suture and often with many seeds.

Foot. The projection at the base of the column in Orchidaceae flowers.

Forked. Separating into two distinct and more or less equal divisions. (*syn.* **Dichotomous**)

Free. Distinct, not united, as in floral organs.

Fringe. Margins with hairlike appendages. (*syn.* **Fimbriate**)

Frond. The leaf of a fern. Although used to designate leaves of palms, the term should be reserved for ferns and cycads.

Fruit. The ripened ovary of angiosperms.

Funnelform. Funnel-shaped, gradually widening upward.

Furrowed. With longitudinal channels or grooves. (*syn.* **Sulcate**)

Fusiform. Spindle-shaped; elongated and tapering toward each end.

G

Genus (*pl.* **Genera**). A taxonomic rank between family and species. Related species are grouped into a genus and related genera into a family.

Germination. The emergence of the juvenile plant from the seed coat.

Glabrous. Without pubescence or glands, not hairy or glandular.

Gland. A uni- or multicellular secretory structure often found on various plant organs.

Glandular, glanduliferous. Having glands.

Glandular hair. A trichome with a uni- or multicellular gland.

Glandular-pubescent. Having glands and hairs intermixed.

Glaucous. Covered with a whitish or bluish "waxy bloom" that rubs off.

Globose, globular. Spherical or rounded.

Glochid. Barbed bristles, often occurring in tufts, as in the cacti (Cactaceae).

Glochidiate. Having glochids.

Glume. Rigid, chaff-like or scale-like bracts, referring especially to the two empty bracts at the base of the spikelet in grasses.

Glutinous. Sticky or mucilaginous; with a waxy exudate.

Graft, grafting. The union of a small piece of meristematic tissue (usually a bud) or actively growing stem (the **Scion**) with another plant (the **Rootstock**). Successful grafts usually indicate a close taxonomic relationship.

Grain. The fruit or seed of Poaceae (grasses). (*syn*. **Caryopsis**)

Granular. Covered with fine mealy granules.

Growth form. Habit or shape of plants in the landscape, such as trees, shrubs, etc.

Gymno -. A Greek prefix meaning 'naked'.

Gymnospermae. A class of vascular plants the seeds of which are not enclosed within a **carpel** (fruit) but are borne on **sporophylls** (seed leaves), a group of which are organized into a cone. The extant members of the group include **Cycadales, Coniferales, Gingkoales,** and **Gnetales** (when considered as a single order).

Gynoecium. A carpel or an aggregation of carpels, whether free or united.

Gynostemium. A compound structure in orchid flowers formed by the adnation of stamens and carpels. (*syn*. **Column**)

H

Habit. The general appearance of a plant in terms of its characteristic form, as in erect, prostrate, climbing, etc.

Hastate. Shaped like an arrowhead, but with the basal lobes pointed or narrow and at right angles.

Hastiform. Triangular with two basal lobes; the condition of being hastate.

Hastula. Terminal part of the petiole on surface(s) of leaf blade in palmately lobed leaves of palms, as in *Chamaerops humilis* (Arecaceae).

Head. The inflorescence of Asteraceae; a compact inflorescence. (*syn*. **Capitulum**)

Helicoid. Coiled like a spring; curved.

Helicoid cyme. A sympodial inflorescence in which all branches develop on the same side of the main axis, although not in the same plane.

Herb. An annual, biennial, or perennial plant without woody parts above the ground. In vernacular sense it is used to designate a plant with medicinal properties.

Herbaceous. A plant that is soft and green and has little or no woody tissue.

Herbals. Botanical writings of the fifteenth, sixteenth, and seventeenth centuries in which specific plants were recommended for medicinal purposes.

Herbarium. A collection of preserved or dried and pressed plant specimens kept for identification and taxonomic studies.

Hermaphrodite. Bisexual; having both the

androecium and gynoecium present in the same flower; a perfect flower.

Hesperidium. The fruit of the orange and other citrus plants.

Hetero -. A Greek prefix meaning 'different'.

Heteromorphic. Existing in more than one form; having more than one kind of flower on the same plant.

Heterophylly, Heterophyllous. With leaves of different forms or sizes.

Hip. Fruit of the genus *Rosa*.

Hirsute. With stiff hairs.

Hispid. With bristly hair.

Hood. The lid that hangs over the pitcher of the pitcher plant trap; the concave segment of the corona in *Asclepias* (Asclepiadaceae) flower.

Horn. A projection that is part of the corona of milkweed flower (Asclepiadaceae).

Horticulture. Literally culture of gardens, in reference to vegetable, fruit (including viticulture), and ornamental crops, as opposed to field crops such as agronomy.

Hortus. Garden. Originally intended as a private place with flowers and trees and surrounded by walls.

Hyaline. Thin and translucent, as in some leaf margins.

Hybrid. The offspring of a cross between two taxa, at the generic, specific, or lower rank.

Hydric. Growing in water (*cf.* **Aquatic, Mesic, Xeric**).

Hypanthium. The tube of the receptacle upon which the calyx, corolla, and stamens are born; "calyx tube".

Hypo -. A Latin prefix meaning 'under', 'below'.

Hypogyny, hypogenous. Borne below the gynoecium or the ovary, in reference to calyx, corolla, and stamens. Flowers with this arrangement have a superior ovary.

I

Illegitimate. In botanical nomenclature, a name improperly used.

Imbricate. Overlapping like tiles of a roof, referring to sepals and petals in the bud. (*cf.* **Valvate**).

Imparipinnate. An odd-pinnately compound leaf with a terminal leaflet.

Imperfect flower. A flower that lacks either or both stamens or carpels, without regard to condition of the perianth; a unisexual flower. (*cf.* **Perfect flower**).

Inbred line. Homozygous plants produced by repeated selfing (inbreeding) or backcrossing between closely related individuals, as in most bedding plants which are uniform in habit and flower color. It is designated "In" by the code of nomenclature.

Incised. Margins that are deeply cut, irregular, or have jagged teeth.

Incomplete flower. A flower that is lacking one or more of the four regular sets of parts; absence of sepals, petals, stamens, or carpels.

Inconspicuous. Not easily seen because of small size or lack of color.

Indefinite. Inconstant with numbers; applied also to the continuous (indeterminate) growth of a racemose inflorescence.

Indehiscent. Not splitting open; remaining closed, as a drupe or an achene.

Indeterminate growth. Of indefinite growth, as a racemose inflorescence whose terminal flower opens last so that there is no restriction to continued growth. (*cf.* **Determinate growth**)

Indeterminate inflorescence. An inflorescence in which the basal flower develops and opens first, thereby allowing development of additional flowers at the apex. (*opp.* **Determinate inflorescence**)

Indigen, indigenous. Native to a region, not introduced.

Indument, indumentum. Pubescence or other coverings on plant surfaces.

Induplicate. Folded inward, as in leaflets of some palms where a V-shaped groove is formed by the margins.

Indusium (*pl.* **indusia**). The cover growing over the sporangia of some ferns.

Inferior. Below, usually referring to the position of the ovary in an epigynous flower.

Inflorescence. A flower cluster, such as a panicle, spike, raceme, etc. An inflorescence may consist of only one (solitary) or many flowers.

Innocuous. Unarmed, spineless.

Inrolled. Said of floral segments in which the margins on rolled inward, as in the lip of *Cypripedium* (Orchidaceae).

Insectivorous. In reference to insect-trapping plants such as *Dionaea*, *Sarracenia*, etc.

Inserted. Growing on or attached to another organ, as in stamens growing on the corolla.

Inter -. A Latin prefix meaning *between*.

Intergeneric hybrid. A hybrid between species of two genera of the same family, for example, X *Fatshedera* which is a hybrid between *Fatsia* and *Hedera* in Araliaceae.

Intermittent. Discontinuous; irregular, usually in reference to periodicity of growth.

Internode. Part of the stem lying between two successive nodes.

Interspecific. The relationship between two populations or two species.

Interspecific hybrid. A hybrid between two related species of the same genus, for example, *Osmanthus* × *fortunei*, which is a hybrid of *O. fragrance* and *O. heterophyllus*.

Introduced. A plant not native to an area but brought from another region. (*syn.* **Exotic**)

Involucral. Belonging to an involucre.

Involucrate. Bearing an involucre.

Involucre. Cluster of bracts subtending an inflorescence, as in the heads of Asteraceae or umbels of Apiaceae.

Involute. A leaf in which the margins are rolled upward toward the midrib. (*cf.* **Revolute**).

Irregular. Differing in size and shape; asymmetrical, referring to flowers that are not divisible into halves by an indefinite number of longitudinal planes (*syn.* **Zygomorphic**).

J

Joint. A node, as in a grass culm.

Jointed. Said of stems with prominent nodes.

Juvenile form. A young plant with features different from the adult form of the same plant, as in *Eucalyptus*, *Hedera*, etc. which differ in their leaf characteristics.

K

Keel. A prominent dorsal rib or ridge, as in some carpels or in glumes of grasses, the lower petals of the flowers of legumes (Fabaceae).

Keeled. Ridged like the bottom of a boat.

Key. See **Dichotomous key.**

Kingdom. The highest taxonomic rank in living organisms, including plants.

Knee. An aboveground outgrowth of roots in certain plants when grown in wet habitats, as in Bald Cypress (*Taxodium distichum*). (*cf.* **Pneumatophore**); a swelling on the leaf sheath at the base of the petiole present in most rattan palms.

L

Labellum. Lip; the modified, often enlarged lowermost petal of an orchid flower.

Labiate. Lipped; when the corolla forms an upper and a lower lip, as in flowers of Lamiaceae (Labiatae).

Lacerate. Cut irregularly; appearing torn or cut, as in certain leaves.

Laciniate. Cut into narrow deep lobes.

Lamina. Leaf blade.

Laminar. Thin and flattened, as in a leaf blade.

Lanceolate. Lance-shaped, broadest below the middle and tapering gradually to the apex.

Lateral. Arising from or attached to the side of an axis, as a lateral bud. (*syn.* **Axillary**)

Latex. A viscous fluid contained in special structures (**Laticifer**) of certain groups of plants. For example, in the Euphorbiaceae, the latex may be milky (*Euphorbia*) or may be red, yellow, cloudy, or clear (*Jatropha*).

Lax. Arranged loosely (*opp.* **Congested**).

Layering. A method of propagation whereby a small section of the stem is buried shallowly below the soil surface to promote formation of adventitious roots.

Leader. The main stem or trunk of trees.

Leaf. The usually green-colored, expanded, flattened portion of plants. It consists of a **Lamina** or **Blade**, the **Petiole**, and when present, the stipules.

Leaf axil. The angle between the leaf petiole and the stem from which it arose.

Leaf bud. A **Vegetative bud**.

Leaflet. A segment of a compound leaf (*syn.* **Pinna/pinnae**).

Leaf scar. A scar on the stem left after the leaf falls.

Leaf sheath. The expanded base of the leaf which covers the stem in most monocots and some dicots.

Legume. The pod of members of the family Fabaceae (Leguminosae), a pod dehiscent on two sides; any member of the Fabaceae.

Lemma. The outer (lower) bract of the floret of grasses.

Lenticels. Porous spots in the periderm of woody plants, giving the appearance of a rough surface on the stem or other plant parts.

Lepidote. Covered with small scurfy scales.

Liana. Woody vines found in tropical forests.

Ligulate. Strap-shaped or tongue-shaped, as in a petal or a leaf; having a ligule.

Ligule. The strap-shaped part of the corolla in Asteraceae; the annular collar-like projection at the junction of the leaf blade and the sheath in grasses.

Limb. The expanded flat part of a gamopetalous corolla; a large tree branch.

Line. In horticulture, homozygous plants with uniform characteristic(s), resulting from repeated selfing, as in most bedding plants; a measure of length, 1/12th of an inch.

Linear. Long and narrow with nearly parallel sides.

Lobate. Having lobes.

Lobe. Any segment of an organ, particularly when rounded, as in leaves or perianth.

Lobed. Margin cut less than halfway to the center, incurved or angular segments.

Location. The approximate position of an organ in relation to other organs.

Locule. Compartment or cell of an ovary or an anther.

Loculicidal. See **Dehiscence**.

Loment. A leguminous fruit (pod) that is constricted between the seeds, as in *Parkinsonia aculeata*.

Long shoot. The normal branches of woody plants, with considerable distance between the nodes. (*cf*. **Short shoot**)

Lyrate. Lyre-shaped; a leaf that is pinnately lobed and has a terminal lobe much larger than the lateral lobes.

M

Macro -. A prefix meaning 'long' or 'large'. (*syn*. **Mega-**; *opp*. **Micro-**)

Margin. The edge or boundary line of a body.

Marginal. Placed upon or attached to the margin.

Marginate. Having a distinct margin or border, often differing in color from the rest of the member.

Mealy. Covered with a scurfy powder.

Mega -. A Greek prefix meaning 'very large'.

Megaspore. Ovules of angiosperms and gymnosperms; the larger of the two spores (female) in pteridophytes.

Megasporophyll. The leaflike structure of cycads which bear the megasporangia or seeds; a carpel in angiosperms.

Megastrobilus. The female strobilus (cone) of gymnosperms.

Mericarp. One of the halves of Apiaceae fruit.

Merosity. The absolute number of parts within a whorl, as the number of parts in a flower.

- Merous. A Latin suffix which indicates the number of flower parts. For example, 3-merous, 4-merous, or 5- merous.

Mesic. A term that denotes moist habitats. (*cf*. **Aquatic**, **Xeric**, **Hydric**).

Mesocarp. The middle layer of the Pericarp in fruit, as in *Prunus* (peach, apricot, etc.). (*cf*. **Endocarp**, **Exocarp**).

Mesomorphic. Having the structure of a mesophyte.

Mesophyte. A plant that occurs in moist (but not wet) habitats.

Micro -. A prefix meaning 'small'.

Micropyle. The canal into the nucellus; a minute pore through which water enters the seed before germination.

Microspore. The pollen grain in angiosperms or the smaller of the two spores (male) in pteridophytes. (*cf*. **Megaspore**)

Microsporophyll. Usually said of the leaflike structure of gymnosperm male cones but also in reference to the anther in angiosperms. (*cf.* **Megasporophyll**)

Microstrobilus. Male cone of gymnosperms. (*cf.* **Megastrobilus**)

Midrib. The largest vein of a leaf, longitudinally running through the blade. (*cf.* **Midvein**)

Midvein. The central, primary vein of a leaflet. (*cf.* **Midrib**)

Mono -. A Latin prefix meaning 'one'.

Monocarpic. A perennial plant that may live for many years but dies soon after flowering, as in *Agave americana*, Bromeliaceae, etc.

Monocotyledon. One of the subdivisions of the angiosperms, which is characterized by one cotyledon, parallel venation, scattered vascular bundles, a fibrous root system, and flower parts in threes or multiples thereof. (*cf.* **Dicotyledon**)

Monoculture. Uniform planting of a single species, such as turf, orchards, citrus groves, etc.

Monoecious. Having the androecium (stamens) and the gynoecium (carpels) in separate flowers but on the same plant; a plant with unisexual flowers.

Monogeneric. Referring to a family with a single genus, such as Cycadaceae, which includes only *Cycas*.

Monomorphic. Having uniform shape (*cf.* **Polymorphic, Dimorphic, Heteromorphic**).

Monopodial. Branching with a main axis and reduced or missing laterals, as in pines, palms, etc.

Monotypic. A genus that consists of only one species. (*cf.* **Monogeneric**)

Morphology. The study of form and structure of plants.

Mucronate. Said of a leaf terminating in a sharp point.

Multiple fruit. A fruit formed from several flowers into a single structure, as in mulberry (*Morus*).

Muricate. A rough surface caused by short, sharp points.

N

Naked. Lacking a perianth; not enclosed within a pericarp, as in seeds of gymnosperms.

Nana, nanus. A Latin word meaning 'dwarf'.

Native. Said of plants that naturally occur only in a given geographical area, such as *Zamia floridana* (Florida coontie), *Eschscholtzia californica* (California poppy), etc. (*cf.* **Naturalized, Indigenous**)

Naturalized. A plant that was originally introduced from another region but now grows wild, such as *Casuarina* in Florida or *Eucalyptus* in California, both native to Australia. (*cf.* **Indigenous**)

Nectar. A glandular secretion, containing sugars and amino acids, produced by insect-pollinated flowers or extrafloral nectaries.

Nectar guides. Markings of flowers that are often invisible to the human eye but function as orientation cues to insects.

Nectariferous. Nectar-producing; having a nectary.

Nectary. Glands of flowers (floral) or other parts of the plant (extrafloral) that secrete nectar.

Needle. The long and narrow leaves of pines and some species of *Hakea* (Proteaceae). (*syn.* **Acicular**)

Netted. See **Reticulate**.

Nocturnal. Said of flowers that open at night and close during the day. (*opp.* **Diurnal**)

Node. A joint, as in a stem where buds and leaves occur.

Nodules. Enlargements or swellings on roots of nitrogen-fixing plants, as in legumes, *Alnus*, *Ceonothus*, *Myrica*, etc.

Nomenclature. The naming of plants and other organisms.

Nontunicate. See **Scaly bulb**.

Nut. A dry, indehiscent, one-seeded fruit, derived from a single or a compound ovary.

Nutlet. A small nut.

O

Ob -. A Latin prefix meaning 'reversed' or 'inverted'.

Obconic, obconical. Inverse of conical, but attached at the narrow point.

Obcordate, obcordiform. Inversely cordate; wide at the apex but narrow at the base.

Oblanceolate. Inverse of lanceolate; wide at the apex, tapering toward the base.

Oblique. With the two sides unequal, especially at the base of leaf blades, as in some species of Betulaceae.

Oblong. With nearly parallel sides and two to four times longer than broad.

Obovate. Inversely ovate, the apical half broader than the basal.

Obovoid. Egg-shaped and attached at the narrow end.

Obscure. Not visible to the naked eye; not distinct.

Obsolete, obsolescent. Vestigial; rudimentary; not evident, such as stipules of certain species.

Obtuse. Blunt; rounded, such as a leaf apex.

Odd-pinnate. See **Compound leaf**.

Open dichotomous venation. Dichotomous venation with free vein endings, as in *Ginkgo biloba*, *Stangeria eriopus*, etc.

Operculate. Possessing a lid; opening by means of a lid.

Operculum. A lid, as in capsule-type fruit of certain angiosperms.

Opposite. Occurrence of organs on facing sides of an axis, as in opposite leaves that arise from the same node.

Orbicular, orbiculate. Nearly circular in outline.

Orchidology. The study of orchids.

Order. The taxonomic unit below class which includes one or more closely related families. The suffix for an ordinal name is -ales; said of sequence of events or developments, such as branching or venation.

Ornamental horticulture. The science and art of growing plants for environmental, psychological, and aesthetic purposes. As a field of study, it is also referred to as Environmental Horticulture, Urban Horticulture, or Urban Forestry.

Outcrossing. See **Xenogamy.**

Oval. Broadly elliptical, two times longer than wide.

Ovary. Part of the carpel or gynoecium containing the ovule.

Ovate. Egg-shaped, much broader below the middle.

Ovoid. A solid oval organ that is attached by the broader end.

Ovule. The megasporangium; the egg, which upon fertilization develops into a seed.

Ovuliferous. Bearing ovules.

Ovuliferous scale. The scale-like structure in the cones of gymnosperms which bear the ovule and later the seed; the megasporophyll.

P

Pachycauly. Having a short, thick, often succulent stem, as in the majority of Cactaceae, *Pachypodium* (Apocynaceae), etc.

Palea (*cf*. **Palet**). The upper or inner of the two bracts of the floret in grasses, often partly enclosed by the lemma.

Paleaceous. Chaffy; furnished with a palea; chaff-like in texture.

Paleobotany. The study of fossil plants.

Palet. See **Palea**.

Palmate. Palm-like; applied to venation of a simple leaf when the major veins radiate from a common point at the base of the blade (palmately veined). (*syn*. **Digitate**)

Palmately compound. See **Compound leaf**.

Palmatifid. A leaf blade cut halfway down, so that a number of lobes are formed.

Palmatisect. A leaf blade cut nearly to the base, so that a number of distinct lobes are formed.

Palynology. The study of pollen grains and spores.

Pandurrate, Panduriform. Fiddle-shaped; obovate but with distinct shallow lobes near the base, as in certain leaves.

Panicle. A compound racemose inflorescence, as in oat.

Paniculate. Of the character of a panicle; bearing panicles.

Papilionaceous. Butterfly-shaped, referring to the corolla of subfamily Paplionoideae of Fabaceae (Leguminosae).

Papilla (*pl*. **Papillae**). A small nipple-shaped protuberance or trichome.

Papillate. Bearing papillae.

Papillose. Bearing nipple-like projections.

Pappose. Having a pappus.

Pappus. The modified bristly or scale-like corolla of Asteraceae, which persists on the fruit and aids in dispersal.

Parasite. A plant that lives on other plants and derives subsistence from it, as some members of Scrophulariaceae, Orabanchaceae, etc.

Parted. Margin cut nearly to the base or the midrib, as in some leaves.

Pedate. A palmately lobed or divided leaf with lateral lobes divided or cleft.

Pedicel. The stalk of a flower or a fruit. (*cf*. **Peduncle**)

Pedicellate. Said of a flower or a fruit that is borne on a pedicel.

Peduncle. The stalk of an inflorescence or a solitary flower, when reduced.

Peltate, peltiform. Shield-shape, as leaves that have the petiole attached at or near the center of the blade (peltate leaf).

Pendent, pendulous. Drooping, hanging downward, as in branches of *Ilex vomitoria* 'Pendula'.

Penninerved. Pinnately veined.

Pepo. The fruit of Cucurbitaceae; a berry

with a hard rind derived from an inferior ovary.

Perennial. A plant that lives for more than two years and flowers more than once (**Polycarpic**), or a plant that lives for several years but dies after the first flowering (**Monocarpic**).

Perfect flower. Having both androecium (stamens) and gynoecium (carpels) in the same flower; bisexual; hermaphroditic.

Perfoliate. Said of a sessile leaf that surrounds a stem completely so that the stem appears to pass through it.

Peri -. A Greek prefix meaning 'around'.

Perianth. A collective term for the floral envelope, including calyx or corolla, but usually both.

Pericarp. The wall of the ovary (ripened fruit), which consists of three distinct layers: exocarp, mesocarp, and endocarp.

Periclinal chimera. Graft hybrid.

Perigynous, perigyny. A condition in which floral parts are borne around the gynoecium, as when the calyx, corolla, and stamens arise from the edge of a cup-shaped hypanthium (e.g., Rosaceae). (*cf.* **Epigynous, Hypogenous**)

Persistent. Remaining attached, not falling off.

Petal. The usually colored inner perianth (*cf.* **Corolla**) segments.

Petaliferous. Flowers with petals.

Petaloid. Petal-like, resembling a petal, in reference to sepals (e.g. *Hydrangea*) or bracts (e.g. *Cornus florida*).

Petiolar. Referring to a petiole.

Petiolate. Having a petiole. (*cf.* **Sessile**)

Petiole. The leaf stalk; the stem with which a leaf attaches to the stem.

Petiolulate. Having a petiolule.

Petiolule. The leaflet stalk in a compound leaf.

Phyllary. One of the bracts of the involucre, as in Asteraceae.

Phyllotaxy. The arrangement of leaves on the stem, such as alternate, opposite, or whorled.

Phylum (*pl.* **phyla**). A major division of the plant or animal kingdom, whose members are presumed to have common ancestry.

Phyto -, - phyte. A Latin prefix or suffix meaning 'plant'.

Phytogeography. The study of the distribution of plants.

Pilose. Covered with soft, slender hairs.

Pinna (*pl.* **pinnae**). The primary division of a compound leaf; a leaflet. The term is primarily used for fern fronds. (*cf.* **Pinnule**)

Pinnate. Feather-like; applied to veation of a simple leaf when the principal veins are extended from the midrib toward the margin (pinnately veined), or arrangement of leaflets of a compound leaf when they are on opposite side of a rachis (pinnately compound).

Pinnatifid. Said of a leaf blade which is cut halfway toward the midrib into a number of pinnately arranged lobes.

Pinnatisect. Pinnatifid, but with the cuts reaching nearly to the midrib.

Pinninerved. Pinnately veined.

Pinnule. One of the segments when the pinna (leaflet) is itself divided, as in a bipinnate leaf. The term is most often used for segments of fern fronds.

Pistil. The ovuliferous or seed-bearing organ of a flower; carpel; gynoecium (collective term), consisting of ovary, style, and stigma.

Pistillate. Bearing the pistil or pistils only; carpellate; a unisexual (female) flower.

Pitcher plants. Plants of the genus *Sarracenia,* which trap insects in pitcher-like, inflated appendages at their leaf apex.

Pith. The soft, spongy central tissue in the stem of most angiosperms.

Plantlet. A small plant, such as those formed by propagation of *Begonia* leaves.

Pleated. Used in reference to folded, crinkled, or creased leaves.

Plicate. Said of a leaf in which the blade is folded back and forth along the main veins like pleats in an accordion.

Plumule. The terminal bud of an embryo in seed plants.

Pneumatophore. A specialized root that grows vertically upward, often referred to as "breathing roots," occur in plants of wet habitats, such as *Taxodium distichum* (swamp cyprus). (*syn.* **Knee**)

Pod. A dry fruit formed from a single carpel, containing one to many seeds, and opening along two sutures. The term, however, is most often used in reference to any dry, dehiscent fruit.

Pollarding. A method of pruning where branches are severely cut in order to promote growth of a thick mass of lateral branches, thus creating an umbrella-shaped tree.

Pollen. The grains or male spores of angiosperms and gymnosperms. (*syn.* **Microspore**)

Pollination. The transfer of pollen from anthers to a stigma in angiosperms or from male to female cones in gymnosperms.

Pollinium (*pl.* **pollinia**). A mass of pollen held together by a sticky substance and transported as a unit by pollinating agents, as in Asclepiadaceae and Orchidaceae.

Poly -. A Greek prefix meaning 'many'.

Polycarpic. A perennial plant that lives for many years and flowers many times.

Polypetalous, polypetaly. Having separate petals.

Pome. A fruit, like an apple or pear, in which most of the edible part is the enlarged axis of the flower, rather than the ovary.

Poricidal. See **Dehiscence**.

Posterior. The upper side; the side toward the axis. (*cf.* **Adaxial**, *opp.* **Anterior**)

Pouch. A saclike structure, as the spur in many orchids.

Prickle. A small and hard spine appearing on the bark or epidermis.

Primary axis. The main stem.

Primary root. The main root developed from the radicle.

Primary shoot. The main stem developed from the **Plumule**.

Primitive. Most similar to the ancestral condition; not highly evolved.

Procumbent. Trailing or lying flat on the ground, but not rooting. (*cf.* **Decumbent**)

Propagation. The reproduction of plants by sexual (seed) or asexual (vegetative) means.

Propagule. Any structure that becomes detached from the mother plant and grows into a new plant.

Prophyll. The first bract of an inflorescence.

Prop roots. The adventitious roots that are formed on the trunk of certain plants, as in *Ficus*, *Pandanus*, etc. (*syn.* **Stilt roots, Aerial roots**)

Prostrate. A general term for plants whose branches lie flat on the ground. (*cf.* **Procumbent, Decumbent**)

Protective stipules. Sheathing stipules that protect a bud or a flower, as in members of Magnoliaceae.

Prune, pruning. The selective removal of branches or stems of plants to improve their health, vigor, and appearance.

Pseud -, pseudo -. A Latin prefix meaning 'false', 'untrue', 'atypical'.

Pseudanthium. An inflorescence that resembles a flower because the individual flowers are reduced to single stamens or carpels, as in the genus *Euphorbia* (Euphorbiaceae) and its related genera.

Pseudobulb. The thickened lateral, or bulb-like basal portion of sympodial orchids.

Pseudoverticillate. See **Pseudowhorled**.

Pubescence, pubescent. A general term used to indicate presence of hairs on various surfaces.

Pulvinate. Shaped like a cushion.

Pulvinule. The small pulvinus at the base of a petiolule.

Pulvinus. A swelling at the base of a petiole, which is responsible for movement of leaves in the presence of a stimulus, as in *Mimosa* (sensitive plant).

Punctate. Dotted or marked with small dots; speckled.

Punctiform. Dot-like.

Pungens. A Latin word meaning 'ending in a sharp point'.

Pungent. Ending in a rigid and sharp point, as in leaves of *Ilex opaca* (American holly).

Pure line. The descendant of a homozygous plant obtained by repeated self-fertilization; inbred homozygous individuals, as in most annual bedding plants which have uniform growth habit and flower color.

Pyramidal. Shaped like a pyramid.

Pyrene. The nutlet or seed of a drupe; a seed surrounded by a bony endocarp, as in a cherry or peach pit.

R

Raceme. A simple, elongated, indeterminate inflorescence with pedicellate (stalked) flowers.

Racemose. Having flowers in a raceme or raceme-like inflorescence.

Rachilla. A small raceme; in grasses and sedges the spikelet that bears the florets; in decompound leaves, secondary division attached to rachis.

Rachis. The axis of a compound leaf, above the petiole to which the leaflets are attached; the main axis of an inflorescence.

Radial symmetry. When a flower can be dissected into two similar halves in any direction, it is radially symmetrical. (*syn.* **Actinomorphic**)

Ray floret. One of the zygomorphic flowers radiating from the margin of the capitulum in Asteraceae. (*cf.* **Disk floret**)

Receptacle, receptaculum. The enlarged part of the floral axis that bears the floral organs; the hypanthium of epigynous and perigynous flowers; the common axis of the flowers in the inflorescence of Asteraceae. (*syn.* **Torus**)

Recurved. Bent or curved backward, as in revolute leaf margins.

Reduplicate. Said of inverted V-shaped leaflets.

Reflexed. Turned backward or downward abruptly.

Regular. See **Actinomorphic**.

Reniform. Kidney-shaped.

Repens, repent, reptans. Prostrate plants whose stems produce adventitious roots at the nodes when in contact with moist soil.

Reticulate. Having a network, as in venation of some leaves. (*syn.* **Netted**)

Retuse. Slightly notched at a usually rounded apex.

Revolute. A leaf in which margins are rolled backward and usually downward, as in *Quercus virginiana* (Fagaceae), *Cycas revoluta* (Cycadaceae). (*cf.* **Involute**)

Ridged. In reference to plant parts having distinctly raised lines, such as pseudobulb of *Gongora* (Orchidaceae) or leaves of *Begonia* (Begoniaceae).

Rhizomatous. Producing or bearing rhizomes.

Rhizome. An elongated subterranean, usually horizontal stem of rootlike appearance.

Rhomboid, rhomboidal. An oblique-angled parallelogram with only the opposite sides equal; shaped like a rhomboid.

Rib. The primary or any of the larger veins of a leaf.

Rind. The outer layer of the bark of a tree; the outer layers of a fruit.

Robust. Large; healthy.

Root. The descending axis of vascular plants, growing in the opposite direction from the stem, and functioning in absorption of water and nutrients.

Rootlet. A very small root; the branch of a root.

Rootstock. Subterranean stem; rhizome; in horticulture, the seedling onto which the desired cultivar is grafted.

Rosette. A cluster of closely crowded leaves radiating from a very short stem near the surface of the ground, as in *Lactuca* (lettuce), most Crassulaceae, etc.

Rostellum. A beaklike outgrowth; a gland; in Orchidaceae, the pointed apex of the column that separates the pollinia from the stigmatic surface; flowers of Orchidaceae.

Rostrate, rostrum. Any beaklike projection.

Rotate. Wheel-shaped, referring to a sympetalous corolla with a short tube, as in that of Solanaceae.

Rotund. Round or nearly circular in outline.

Rough. Scabrous; covered with stiff hairs.

Rugose. Having a wrinkled surface.

Runner. A prostrate shoot with roots at the end, giving rise to new plants, as in *Fragaria* (strawberry), *Chlorophytum* (spider plant), etc. (*syn.* **Stolon**)

Rupestral. Plants that grow on walls or rocks.

S

Sagittate. Arrow-shaped, with the basal lobes enlarged and directed downward.

Salverform. Trumpet-shaped; said of a corolla that is long and tubular and the upper part spreads horizontally, as in *Phlox*.

Samara. An indehiscent, dry, one- or two-seeded, winged fruit, as in *Acer*, *Fraxinus*, *Ulmus*, etc.

Samaracetum. An aggregation of samaras, as in *Liriodendron*.

Sarcotesta. The outer fleshy seed coat, such as that of cycads. (*cf.* **Sclerotesta**)

Savanna (savannah). Grassland with scattered trees or patches of forest.

Scabrid, scabrous. Rough; rough pubescent; having a surface covered with wartlike projections. (*syn.* **Scurfy**)

Scale. Any small, usually dry, appressed leaf or bract, as in scale leaves of pines; in common usage it refers to peltate hairs.

Scale leaf. A reduced leaf, such as that of adult leaves of conifers. (*cf.* **Microphyll**)

Scaly bulb. Bulbs that have several segments (leaves) arising from a common base, such as that of garlic, Easter lily (*Lilium longiflorum*), etc. (*syn.* **Non-tunicate**)

Scape. A leafless flowering stalk (peduncle) of an acaulescent plant, such as that of Amaryllidaceae, some Asteraceae, etc.

Scapigerous, scapose. A plant that has one or more scapes.

Schizocarp. A dry fruit formed from a syncarpous ovary that splits at maturity into its constituent one-seeded carpels. (*cf.* **Mericarps**)

Scion. The portion of a stem that is grafted onto a rootstock.

Sclerotesta. The stony layer of the seed coat, as in cycads. (*cf.* **Sarcotesta**)

Scorpoid, scorpoidal. Resembling a scorpion; coiled (circinate) like the tail of a scorpion.

Scorpoid cyme. When the main axis of an inflorescence is coiled so that the flowers occur alternately on opposite sides, as in Boraginaceae.

Scrumbler. A plant with long, weak shoots which grows over other plants.

Scurfy. Covered with small, bran-like scales.

Seed. The ripened ovule of seed plants, which develops after fertilization, containing the embryo and endosperm or female gametophyte tissue.

Seed coat. The outer protective covering of seeds, consisting of one or more layers, such as Sarcotesta and Sclerotesta. (*syn.* **Testa**)

Seed leaf. See **Cotyledon**.

Seedling. The young plant developing from a germinating seed.

Seed plant. A plant that produces seeds, as in gymnosperms and angiosperms. (*syn.* **Spermatophyta**)

Segment. A portion of the lamina of a leaf which is deeply lobed but not divided into leaflets; one of a series, as one petal of a polypetalous flower.

Selection. In horticulture, the deliberate (nonrandom) process of favoring a particular genotype for a specific purpose, such as food, fiber, or ornamental. (*cf.* **Cultivar**)

Sepal. A segment of the calyx, usually green and **foliaceous** but sometimes **petaliferous**.

Septate. Divided by a partition.

Septicidal. Dehiscence along the septa, rather than directly into the locules.

Septum. Partitions or segments of a compound ovary; a wall.

Serrate. With sharp marginal teeth that point forward.

Sessile. Without a stalk, as in a leaf without a petiole or a flower without a pedicel.

Sexual propagation. Reproduction of plants by seed.

Shape. An outline of specific form that is plain or two-dimensional; a specific three-dimensional figure.

Sheath. The tubular leaf base that forms a casing around the stem.

Sheathing. Enclosing; covering; surrounding.

Shining. A clear and polished surface; lucid.

Shoot. Aerial portions of the plant to which leaves, buds, flowers, and other organs are attached. (*cf.* **Stem**)

Short shoot. A small shoot with short internodes and numerous leaves, as in Pinus. (*syn.* **Spur**)

Shrub. A woody plant with multiple trunks, not exceeding 5 meters in height. (*cf.* **Subshrub, Tree**)

Silicle. A short, dry, dehiscent fruit formed from a superior ovary of two united carpels, and united by a septum between the two loculi, as in many Brassicaceae.

Silique. The same as silicle, but long.

Simple. Not branched or divided into segments, as in gynoecia, inflorescences, leaves, or venation.

Sinus. The cleft or indentation between the lobes of a leaf blade.

Solitary. Single or alone, as when the flowers are borne one per axil.

Spadix. A succulent axis supporting an inflorescence, which is subtended by a **spathe**, as in Araceae (e.g., *Anthurium*); in palms the term is used to refer to the entire inflorescence.

Spathe. The leaflike, often showy bract or

prophyll (in palms) which encloses or subtends a spadix, as in Araceae. (*cf.* **Cymba** in palms)

Spathe valves. The herbaceous or scarious bract(s) that subtend or enclose a flower or an inflorescence in the bud, as in some monocotyledons.

Spathulate, spatulate. Spoon-shaped; broad and rounded in the middle and tapering gradually to a narrow base.

Species. An interbreeding group of individuals which are morphologically similar but not necessarily identical. The word is abbreviated as sp. when singular, and spp. when plural.

Specific. Of or pertaining to a species.

Specific epithet. Second designation of a binomial, analogous to the first name of a person; often erroneously referred to as species name.

Specimen. An individual plant representing a population of a species; a dried or preserved sample of a plant, such as a herbarium sheet.

Spermatophyta. A seed plant; any angiosperm or gymnosperm.

Spherical. Relating to a sphere; with multidimensional radial symmetry. (*syn.* **Orbicular**)

Spheroid. Perfectly rounded, with a 1:1 ratio.

Spike. An elongated, usually unbranched, inflorescence bearing sessile flowers.

Spikelet. A small spike; the unit of inflorescence of grasses (Poaceae) and sedges (Cyperaceae).

Spine. A hard, sharp-pointed, modified tip of a branch, leaf, or stipule; an enation arising directly from the epidermis. (*cf.* **Thorn**)

Spinescent. Having spines; terminating in a spine.

Spinose. Spiny; spine-like.

Spinulose. With small spines over the surface.

Spiral. Arranged in a coiled series around an axis, as in leaves around a stem.

Sporangium (*pl.* **sporangia**). The saclike structure that contains the spores; a spore case.

Spore. A haploid uni- or multicellular reproductive unit of ferns and lower plants. The term is also used in reference to pollen of spermatophyta.

Sporophyll. A modified leaf that bears sporangia, as in stamens and carpels of angiosperm flowers, mega- or microsporophyll of gymnosperm cones, or fronds of ferns.

Sporophyte. The foliaceous vegetative plants in ferns and seed plants.

Sport. A plant or portion of a plant that arises by spontaneous mutation, and differs from the mother plant by one or more significant features, such as leaf coloration, growth habit, etc. Sports are important sources of new plants in horticulture and are often propagated vegetatively.

Spreading. Growing outward or horizontally, as in some ground cover plants.

Sprig. A small shoot or twig; in horticulture it refers to small pieces of lawn grass rhizomes used for turf planting (sprigging).

Sprout. The newly emerging shoots of plants; the beginning of growth in bulbs. The term is sometimes used incorrectly for seed germination.

Spur. The tubular projection of corolla in certain plants, such as *Impatiens* (Balsaminaceae). (*syn.* **Short shoot**)

Stalk. The stem or main supporting axis of an organ.

Stamen. The pollen-bearing organ of a flower, consisting of an anther and a filament. (*cf.* **Androecium**)

Staminal disc. A fleshy cushion of tissue found at the base of an ovary, formed by the coalesced staminodia or nectaries.

Staminal nectary. Said of nectaries that occur at the base of the filaments.

Staminate. Having stamens but no carpels; a male flower.

Staminodium. An abortive or sterile stamen.

Standard. The broad upper petal of Papilionaceous (Fabaceae) corolla (*syn.* **Banner**); the narrow erect or ascending portion of the *Iris* (Iridaceae) perianth. (*syn.* **Falls**)

Stellate. Star-shaped, in reference to trichomes that have radiating branches.

Stem. The above- or below-ground (bulb, corm, rhizome, and tuber) axis of a plant. (*cf.* **Shoot**)

Sterile. Not productive; not capable of producing seeds or spores.

Stigma. That part of the style which is modified for the reception and germination of the pollen.

Stilt roots. See **Prop roots**.

Stimulose. Bearing stinging hairs.

Stinging hair. The stiff hairs of certain plants at the tip of which irritating compounds are stored so that upon contact they are released, causing a stinging sensation, for example, *Cnidoscolus*, *Tragia*, *Dalechampia*, etc. in the Euphorbiaceae and most members of the Urticaceae.

Stipe. The stalk (petiole) of a fern frond.

Stipel. The stipule-like structure at the base of the petiolule of a leaflet.

Stipellate. Having stipels.

Stipulate. Having stipules.

Stipule. Appendages at the base of some leaves. Stipules may be foliar, glandular, or spinose.

Stolon. A slender modified stem growing along the surface of the ground and rooting at the nodes, as in *Saxifraga sarmentosa* (Saxifragaceae), *Chlorophytum* spp. (Liliaceae), etc.

Stoloniferous. Producing or bearing stolons.

Stoma (*pl*. **stomata**). Minute pore on the epidermis of leaves, stems , etc., through which gaseous exchange takes place.

Stone fruit. The drupe or drupelet of such fruits as peach, plum, olive, avocado, etc.

Stool. A plant that produces several stems together, or from which off-sets may be taken.

Strap. The ligule of the ray floret in Asteraceae.

Strap-shaped. Long and narrow, as in leaves of Amaryllidaceae or ligules of the Asteraceae flowers.

Striate. Marked with parallel, longitudinal lines, furrows, ridges, or streaks of color.

Strict. Straight and upright; rigid and stiff.

Strobilus (*pl*. **strobili**). A cone, made up of sporophylls which are tightly arranged around an axis.

Style. The contracted upper part of a carpel or gynoecium that supports the stigma, often considerably elongated, sometimes lacking.

Sub-. A Latin prefix meaning under, below, or almost.

Subfamily. A taxonomic category below the rank of family.

Subgenus. A taxonomic category below the rank of genus.

Subopposite. Nearly opposite, as in closely spaced alternately arranged or **pseudoverticillate** leaves, such as *Pittosporum tobira* (Pittosporaceae).

Subshrub. A woody plant with several branches from the ground and not exceeding 1 meter in height.

Subspecies. A taxonomic category below the rank of species, usually based on latitudinal or altitudinal disjunction.

Subtend. Occurring immediately below or close to, as a bract below a flower.

Subterranean. Growing below the soil surface.

Subtropical. Nearly tropical, but somewhat seasonal, as in central and southern Florida. In such areas freezing temperatures are rare.

Subulate. Awl-shaped, tapering from base to apex.

Succulent. Juicy; fleshy, soft, and thickened; generally refers to plants that store water in their leaves, stem, or root and are most often characteristic of dry habitats, as in Cactaceae, Euphorbiaceae, Apocynaceae, Asclepiadaceae, etc.

Sucker. A shoot that originates from the older part of an existing shoot below ground.

Suffrutescent, suffruticose. Perennial plants with persistent woody base but herbaceous flowering shoots.

Sulcate. Marked by distinct longitudinal parallel grooves or furrows. (*syn.* **Furrowed**)

Summer annual. In horticulture, plants that are grown as bedding plants only for duration of the summer, although they may be perennials, such as *Impatiens*,

Petunia, etc.; true annuals that germinate in spring and grow and flower during summer months. (*cf.* **Winter annual**)

Super -. A Latin prefix meaning 'above'.

Superficial. On or near the surface; shallow.

Superior ovary. See **Hypogynous**.

Superposed. One placed above another, as in superposed bud, where a lateral bud is positioned above an axillary bud.

Suspensor. A structure that develops with the embryo and pushes it into the endosperm or the female gametophyte tissue, as in cycads.

Suture. The line of dehiscence of dry fruits; the line of junction or cleavage of two united organs.

Syconium. The fleshy fruit of *Ficus* (fig), which consists of achenes embedded in an enlarged receptacle.

Symmetrical, symmetry. In reference to flowers that are regular in shape, size, and number of parts. (*syn.* **Actinomorphic**)

Sympodial, sympodium. Growth pattern of a plant in which the central leader produces successive superposed branches, so that in time a main axis does not appear to exist; in orchids the term is used to refers to plants whose primary stem grows horizontally and has determinate lateral branches, flowers may be terminal or axillary. (*cf.* **Monopodial**)

Sympodial inflorescence. A determinate inflorescence that simulates a sympodial growth pattern, thus appears indeterminate. (*cf.* **Scorpioid cyme**)

Syncarp. A multiple fleshy fruit.

Syncarpous, syncarpy. Having united carpels. (*cf.* **Apocarpous**)

Synonym. An untenable taxonomic name, rejected in favor of another based on the

International Rules of Botanical Nomenclature.

Systematics. The scientific study of evolutionary relationships of organisms. This term has been used interchangeably with **Taxonomy** and variously defined by different authors.

T

Taiga. Coniferous forest belt of the Northern Hemisphere.

Tapering. Gradually becoming narrower toward one end.

Taproot. A permanent, more or less thickened, often fleshy, primary root.

Tassel. The staminate inflorescence of corn.

Taxon (*pl.* **Taxa**). Any taxonomic unit irrespective of rank, such as family, genus, species, etc.

Taxonomy. The principles and procedures of classification, including nomenclature.

Tendril. A slender, coiling, branched or unbranched, modified leaf or stem, used by many vines for attachment, often by adhesive terminal disks (as in *Ficus pumila*), claws (as in *Macfadyena unguis-cati*), or simply twining (as in *Clytostoma callistegioides* or *Vitis vinifera*).

Tepal. A perianth segment, not differentiated into calyx and corolla, as in most members of Amaryllidaceae.

Terminal, terminus. Situated at the tip, such as the apical bud.

Ternate. Arranged in threes, such as a compound leaf with three leaflets.

Terrestrial. Living in soil. (*cf.* **Epiphyte**)

Testa. The outer coat of a seed. (*cf.* **Sclerotesta**)

Texture. Consistency or feel (to the touch) of an organ. In horticulture this term is used to designate visual appearance of plants in the landscape: fine, plants with many small leaves; medium, plants with relatively large leaves; coarse, plants with few but very large leaves.

Thorn. A hard, sharp-pointed modified shoot. (*cf.* **Spine**)

Thyrse, thyrsus. A compact inflorescence in which lateral branches are determinate but the main branch indeterminate, as in *Syringa*, *Ligustrum* (Oleaceae), etc.

Tiller. A grass shoot growing from the base of the plant.

Tomentose. Covered with dense, short, fine hairs.

Tomentum. A covering of short, woolly hairs.

Topiary. The pruning of dense trees or shrubs to make sculptured forms, such as animal figures.

Torus (*pl.* **Tori**). The receptacle of a flower.

Trailing. Prostrate, but not rooting when the stem touches moist soil.

Translator. The structure that connects the pollinia in Asclepiadaceae.

Translucent. Semitransparent, as in the leaf margin of *Ligustrum lucidum* (Oleaceae), *Ilex rotunda* (Aquifoliaceae), etc.

Transverse. Broader than long; perpendicular to the long axis.

Tree. A woody perennial plant with a single trunk and a height that exceeds 5 meters (15 feet). In horticulture trees are divided into small (5-10 meters), medium (10-20 meters), and large (greater than 20 meters).

Trichome. A hair.

Trifoliate. Having three leaves.

Trifoliolate. A compound leaf with three leaflets.

Trifurcate. Having three forks or branches.

Trilobate. With three lobes.

Trilocular. A fruit consisting of three locules.

Trimerous. Having parts in threes or multiples thereof.

Truncate. An apex or base that ends bluntly, as if cut off abruptly.

Trunk. The primary axis of a tree.

Tryma (*pl.* **trymata**). A nut with two or four locules and surrounded by a dehiscent involucre, as in *Juglans* or *Carya* (Juglandaceae).

Tube. The cylindrical part of the perianth.

Tuber. A much thickened, usually short, subterranean, modified stem, as in *Solanum tuberosum* (potato).

Tubercle. A rounded protuberance, as in the finger-like tubercles of some Cactaceae; short, stout, persistent floral stalk, appearing as small bumps in Coryphoid palms; small tubers.

Tubercule. A small swelling (nodule) on the root of leguminous plants.

Tuberculate. Having tubercles.

Tuberous. Having tubers or resembling one.

Tuberous root. Fleshy roots resembling stem tubers but lacking buds or other stem characteristics.

Tubular. Cylindrical and hollow.

Tufted. Having many short branches; occurring in clumps; clustered. (*syn.* **Caespitose**)

Tunic. The membranous outer skin of some bulbs or corms.

Tunicate, tunicated. Having a layer or layers of membranous outer skin.

Turgid. Swollen or inflated, filled with water.

Turion. A young shoot or sucker arising from underground, such as the vegetative bud of a rhizome in the spring.

Tussock. A tuft of grass or grass-like plant.

Twig. A young woody stem; current season's shoot.

Twining. Climbing by means of a spirally coiling stem.

Two-lipped. See **Bilabiate**.

U

Umbel. An umbrella-shaped inflorescence, in which the pedicels radiate from a common point at the summit of the peduncle.

Umbellate. Of the form of an umbel.

Unarmed. Lacking spines, thorns, prickles, or any other type of armature.

Undershrub. See **Subshrub**.

Understory. Small trees and shrubs under the main tree canopy of a forest.

Undulate. Wavy at the margin.

Ungulate, unguicular, unguiculate. Furnished with a claw.

Uni -. A Latin prefix meaning 'one'; 'single'.

Unifoliate. Having a single leaf, as in *Cattleya* (Orchidaceae).

Unifoliolate. Said of a compound leaf that has been reduced to a single terminal leaflet, as in some *Citrus* spp.

Unigeneric. See **Monogeneric**.

Unilateral. One-sided, as in a raceme with all flowers borne on one side.

Unilocular. Having a single locule, as in an ovary.

Unisexual. Said of a flower that has either stamens or pistils, but not both, although male and female flowers may occur in the same inflorescence.

Unit cup fruit. A fruit derived from a flower with inferior ovary and united carpels. The fruit wall consists of an ovary wall (pericarp) and accessory parts.

Urceolate. Urn-shaped, as in flowers of certain Ericaceae; in pollen, bearing urnlike enations.

Urticating hairs. Said of stinging hairs of Urticaceae (nettles), Loasaceae, and such genera as *Cnidoscolus* (Euphorbiaceae).

Urticle. An inflated, bladder-like envelope; a one-seeded, dry, indehiscent fruit, as in some Amaranthaceae.

V

Valvate. Dehiscing by valves or equal sections; in aestivation, when the segments of the perianth are so placed that they touch but do not overlap. (*cf.* **Imbricate**)

Variant. Individual that differs in some respect from the norm.

Variation. The occurrence of differences in individuals of a population.

Variegated. Said of leaves or flowers that lack uniform pigmentation, appearing blotched, yellowish, or white.

Variety. A subdivision of species, differing in certain genetically fixed characteristic(s) from the rest of the population. (*cf.* **Cultivar**)

Vascular. Pertaining to the presence of vessels or conducting tissue (xylem and phloem).

Vascular plant. A plant having a vascular system, as in Pteridophyta and Spermatophyta.

Vegetative. Pertaining to all but reproductive organs, such as leaves, stems, roots, etc.

Vegetative bud. A stem or leaf bud.

Vegetative propagation. Reproduction of plants by means of stem, leaves, roots, or any meristematic tissue. Plants reproduced by cuttings, division, tissue culture, layering, or grafting are genetically uniform and identical to the mother plant. These are often referred to as clones.

Vein. Vascular strand of leaves.

Veinlet. A small vein.

Velamen. The multiple epidermis of the aerial roots of epiphytic Orchidaceae and Araceae, functioning in water absorption.

Venation. The arrangement of veins in a leaf blade.

Vernalization. The process of dormancy break in buds, requiring low temperature.

Vernation. The arrangement or mode of folding of leaves in the bud. (*cf.* **Aestivation**)

Verrucate. Warty.

Verrucose. With minute warts or blunt projections.

Verticilliate. See **Whorl.**

Viable. Capable of survival and development or germination.

Viability. A measure of seed germination capability.

Villose, villous. Covered with long, shaggy trichomes.

Vine. A plant of weak structure, often with climbing, clambering, or twining stem.

Viscid, viscous. Sticky. (*syn.* **Glutinous**)

Viviparous, vivipary. Germination of seeds while still attached to the plant, as in some Amaryllidaceae and *Avecinia* or other mangrove species.

W

Weed. A plant growing where it is not wanted.

Weeping. See **Pendant, pendulus.**

Whorl. A circle or ring of organs inserted around an axis, as floral segments or leaves on a stem.

Winged bark. An outgrowth on the stem of certain species, as in *Liquidambar styraciflua*, *Ulmus alata*, etc. (*cf.* **Alate**)

Winter annual. An annual that usually germinates in the fall, flowers in the winter, sets fruit in early spring, and dies. In horticulture, winter annuals used as bedding plants are not necessarily true annuals, such as *Viola* spp.

Woody. In reference to stems or branches that have secondary growth. The term is also used in a vernacular sense for very hard fruits.

Woolly. See **Tomentose.**

X

Xenogamy. Cross-pollination between flowers of separate individuals of the same species. (*syn.* **Outcrossing**; *opp.* **Autogamy**)

Xeric. Dry habitat; plants of dry habitats. (*cf.* **Mesic**, **Aquatic**)

Xeromorphic. Having the characteristics of plants adapted to xeric habitats, such as thick cuticle, succulent habit, etc.

Xerophyte. A plant of dry habitat, such as a desert.

Z

Zygomorphic. Said of a flower having bilateral symmetry; divisible in half by one longitudinal plane only, as in flowers of *Antirrhinum* (Scrophulariaceae), *Orchidaceae*, etc. (*syn.* **Irregular**; *opp.* **Actinomorphic**)

SELECTED REFERENCES

Bechtel, H., P. Cribb, and E. Launert. 1980. *The Manual of Cultivated Orchid Species*. English Language Edition, 1981. MIT Press. Cambridge, Massachusetts.

Brickell, C. and J.D. Zuk (Eds.). 1996. *The American Horticultural Society A-Z Encyclopedia of Garden Plants*. DK Publishing, Inc. New York.

Broschat, T. K., and A. W. Meerow. 1991. *Betrock's Reference Guide to Florida Landscape Plants*. Betrock Information Systems, Inc. Cooper City, Florida.

Brown, C. L. and L. K. Kirkman. 1990. *Trees of Georgia and Adjacent States*. Timber Press. Portland, Oregon.

Burch, D., B. D. Ward, and D. W. Hall. 1988. *Checklist of Woody Cultivated Plants of Florida*. Extension Sale Publication SP-33. Institute of Food and Agricultural Sciences, University of Florida, Gainesville.

Coombs, A. J. 1985. *Dictionary of Plant Names*. Timber Press. Portland, Oregon.

Duncan, W. H. and M. B. Duncan. *Trees of the Southern United States*. University of Georgia Press. Athens, Georgia.

Elias, T. S. 1980. *The Complete Trees of North America: Field Guide and Natural History*. Outdoor Life/Nature Books, Van Nostrand Reinhold Co. New York.

Godfrey, R. K. 1988. *Trees, Shrubs, and Woody Vines of Northern Florida and Adjacent Georgia and Alabama*. University of Georgia Press. Athens.

Griffiths, M. 1994. *The New Royal Horticultural Society Dictionary: Index of Garden Plants*. Macmillan Press, Ltd. London.

Harris, G. H. and M. W. Harris. 1994. *Plant Identification Terminology*. Spring Lake, Utah.

Heywood, V. H., consulting editor. 1978. *Flowering Plants of the World*. Mayflower Books. New York.

Jones, D. L. 1987. *Encyclopedia of Ferns: An Introduction to Ferns, Their Structure, Biology, Economic Importance, Cultivation, and Propagation*. Timber Press. Portland, Oregon.

Jones, D. L. 1993. *Cycads of the World: Ancient Plants in Today's Landscape*. Smithsonian Institution Press. Washington, D. C.

Krussmann, G. 1977. *Manual of Cultivated Broad-Leaved Trees & Shrubs*. Volumes I-III. English Translation by M. E. Epp. 1985. Timber Press. Portland, Oregon.

Krussmann, G. 1983. *Manual of Cultivated Conifers*. English translation by M. E. Epp, 1985. Timber Press. Portland, Oregon.

Little, J. R., and C. E. Jones. 1980. *A Dictionary of Botany*. Van Nostrand Reinhold Co. New York.

Meerow, A. W. 1992. *Betrock's Guide to Landscape Palms*. Betrock Information Systems, Inc. Cooper City, Florida.

Miller, H. 1990. *Top Plants for Tropical Gardens*. Australian Government Publishing Service. Canberra.

Motron, J. F. 1991. *500 Plants of South Florida*. 2nd ed. Fairchild Tropical Garden. Miami, Florida.

Neal, M. C. 1965. *In Gardens of Hawaii*. Bernice P. Bishop Museum Special Publication 50, Bishop Museum Press. Honolulu, Hawaii.

Nelson, G. 1994. *The Trees of Florida: A Reference and Field Guide*. Pineapple Press, Inc. Sarasota, Florida.

Odenwals, N. and J. Turner. 1987. *Identification, Selection, and Use of Southern Plants for Landscape Design*. Claitor's Publishing Division. Baton Rouge, Louisiana.

Rogers, D. J. and C. Rogers. 1991. *Woody Ornamentals for Deep South Gardens*. University of West Florida Press. Pensacola.

Sheehan, J. T. and M. R. Sheehan. 1994. *An Illustrated Survey of Orchid Genera*. Timber Press. Portland, Oregon.

Smith, A. W. (Revised by W. T. Stearn). 1972. *A Gardener's Dictionary of Plant Names: A Handbook of the Origin and Meaning of Some Plant Names*. St. Martin Press. New York.

Staff of the L. H. Bailey Hortorium. 1976. *Hortus Third: A Concise Dictionary of Plants Cultivated in the United States and Canada*. Macmillan Publishing Co., Inc. New York.

Stearn, W. T. 1983. *Botanical Latin: History, Grammar, Syntax, Terminology and Vocabulary*. Third Edition. David and Charles. London.

Tomlinson, P. B. 1980. *The Biology of Trees Native to Tropical Florida*. Harvard University Printing Office. Allston, Massachusetts.

Uhl, N. W. and J. Dransfield. 1987. *Genera Palmarum: A Classification of Palms Based on the Work of Harold E. Moore, Jr.* The L. H. Bailey Hortorium and the International Palm Society. Allen Press. Lawrence, Kansas.

Zomlefer, W.B. 1994. *Guide to Flowering Plant Families*. University of North Carolina Press. Chapel Hill.

Index of Families

Index of Common and Scientific Names

S